The Best Of
FRENCH & ITALIAN
Cooking

The Best Of
FRENCH & ITALIAN
Cooking

CAXTON

This edition © Macdonald & Co (Publishers) Ltd, 1989

French section © Edition No. 1, 1982
Italian section © Editoriale Del Drago, 1983

Some of the material in this book previously appeared in
La Cucina and La Cuisine

This edition specially produced for CEEPI Ltd/Dealerfield Ltd
in 1989

ISBN 0-907305-34-2

Printed and bound in Italy by G. Canale & Co, Turin

Contents

Symbols

The symbols will enable you to see at a glance how easy a recipe is, and the preparation and cooking times

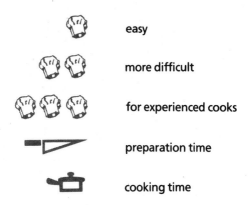

easy

more difficult

for experienced cooks

preparation time

cooking time

When using the recipes in this book, remember the following points:

All quantities are for six people, unless otherwise stated.

Use only one set of measurements for the recipes, since American, imperial and metric measurements are not exact equivalents.

In the text of the recipes, American quantities and ingredients are listed first, with the British equivalents in square brackets.

The Best Of
French Cooking

Sauces

Sauces

This is not a definitive collection of recipes for sauces, but it includes those that are most often found in French cooking.

For ease of reference the sauces are divided into four broad categories.

1. Composite butters
2. Sauce stocks and thickenings
3. Cold sauces
4. Hot sauces

Some special sauces and stuffings will be explained in greater detail in individual recipes.

Composite butters

Beurre d'anchois
Anchovy Butter

	00:20 plus soaking		00:00

American	Ingredients	Metric/Imperial
½ lb	Salted anchovies	250 g / 8 oz
1	Garlic clove	1
1 cup	Butter, at room temperature	250 g / 8 oz
	Pepper	

1. Put the anchovies into a mixing bowl, cover with water and leave to soak for 2 hours, changing the water several times. Drain.
2. Fillet the anchovies, discarding all skin and bones. Rinse and pat dry with paper towels.
3. Place the anchovies in a mortar. Peel the garlic and add to the mortar. Pound with the pestle to make a fine cream. Gradually add the butter and mix until very smooth. Season lightly with pepper.
4. This anchovy butter, which may be kept at least 3 weeks in the refrigerator, gains in flavour if you make it about 1 hour before using.
5. To serve anchovy butter warm, melt it in a bowl standing in a pan of hot water, whisking it as you do so. To make it finer, you may put it through a very fine strainer to remove fragments of anchovy.

Beurre d'escargot
Snail Butter

	00:20 plus standing		00:00

American	Ingredients	Metric/Imperial
5	Shallots	5
4	Garlic cloves	4
1 cup	Butter, at room temperature	250 g / 8 oz
½	Lemon	½
	Ground fennel	
	Salt and pepper	
3 tbsp	Chopped fresh parsley	3 tbsp

1. Peel and finely chop the shallots. Peel and crush the garlic.
2. Mix together the butter, juice of the ½ lemon, a pinch of fennel, and salt and pepper to taste. Work the butter, adding the garlic, shallots and parsley gradually.
3. Leave to stand for 30 minutes before stuffing the snail shells (see page 192).
4. Will keep for 10 days in the refrigerator.

Beurre d'ail
Garlic Butter

	00:10		00:00

American	Ingredients	Metric/Imperial
3	Garlic cloves	3
½ cup	Butter, at room temperature	125 g / 4 oz
	Salt and pepper	

1. Peel the garlic cloves. Crush them as finely as possible using a mortar and pestle.
2. Blend the garlic with the butter, working with the pestle to obtain an even paste. Add salt and pepper to taste.
3. Shape the garlic butter into a roll and wrap in foil. Chill until firm.
4. The butter will keep, in the refrigerator, for a few days. Cut it into equal slices to serve.

Cook's tip: if you don't like the aftertaste of garlic, chew some fresh parsley at the end of the meal.

Crush garlic to extract the maximum flavor

Beurre fondu

Drawn or Clarified Butter

American	Ingredients	Metric/Imperial
½ cup	Butter	125 g / 4 oz
½	Lemon (optional)	½
	Salt and pepper	

1. Warm the butter in a bowl placed over a saucepan of boiling water. As soon as the butter has melted, leave it to cool until it is lukewarm. After a moment or two, you will see a whitish deposit forming at the bottom of the bowl: this is the whey.
2. Pour the melted butter very gently into a container so that the whey is left behind. Add the juice of the ½ lemon, if liked, and season to taste.

Beurre maître d'hôtel

Parsley Butter

American	Ingredients	Metric/Imperial
⅔ cup	Butter, at room temperature	150 g / 5 oz
1 tbsp	Chopped fresh parsley	1 tbsp
½	Lemon	½
	Salt and pepper	

1. Put the butter on a plate. Mash it with a fork, then add the chopped parsley and juice of the ½ lemon. Add salt and pepper to taste. Work the mixture with the fork so as to make it very smooth.
2. Shape the butter into a roll and wrap in foil. Place in the refrigerator, where it will keep for a few days, and chill until firm.
3. When required, cut into equal slices and place on broiled [grilled] meat or fish.

Beurre de roquefort

Roquefort Butter

American	Ingredients	Metric/Imperial
½ cup	Butter, at room temperature	125 g / 4 oz
2 oz	Roquefort cheese	50 g / 2 oz
1 tsp	Cognac	1 tsp
1 tbsp	Prepared mustard	1 tbsp
	Pepper	

1. Mix the butter and roquefort with a fork, then add the cognac, mustard and pepper to taste. Continue to work the butter with the other ingredients to form a cream.
2. Shape into a roll, wrap in foil and chill until set.
3. You may serve roquefort butter, cut into thin slices, on canapés topped with tomatoes, gherkins or sausage.

Anchovy butter and snail butter

Beurre manié

Kneaded Butter

American	Ingredients	Metric/Imperial
1 tbsp	Butter, at room temperature	15 g / ½ oz
1 tbsp	Flour	1 tbsp

1. Mix the butter with the flour, using a fork, to make a paste.
2. Add the kneaded butter in one lump to a boiling sauce, and cook for a further 3-4 minutes, stirring constantly.
3. This quantity will thicken 2 cups [500 ml / ¾ pint].

Beurre noir

Black Butter

Black butter is the traditional accompaniment for skate.

American	Ingredients	Metric/Imperial
1 cup	Butter	250 g / 8 oz
5 tbsp	Vinegar	5 tbsp
3 tbsp	Capers	3 tbsp
	Salt and pepper	

1. Heat the butter in a frying pan over a brisk heat until it is a beautiful brown color. Remove from the heat.
2. Gently add the vinegar and capers. Add salt and pepper to taste. Stir to mix.

Sauce stocks and thickenings

Courts-bouillons and concentrates

Courts-bouillons and concentrates form the basis of a large number of fish soups and preparations for fish and shellfish. These are sometimes obtainable ready made, but their flavor does not compare at all with those you can make yourself. The recipe given here for a court-bouillon with vinegar, is extremely good for poaching fat fish (mackerel, tuna, salmon, etc), and that for a fish stock with white wine for lean white fish (sole, bream, etc).

Concentrate (fumet) is prepared from the bones and heads of fish, and is normally used for poaching. Courts-bouillons and concentrates may be kept in the freezer for several months.

Stocks

Stocks made from meat, poultry, fish or just vegetables form the basis for many soups, sauces and stews, and are also used for braising.

White stock, made from white meats (veal or poultry) and flavorings, is used for all dishes based on velouté sauce. Brown stock is made from beef, veal or poultry and flavorings first browned in butter. It is used for making soups, brown sauces, and for moistening stews and braises made with dark meats.

Stocks will keep perfectly for several months in the freezer.

Brown stock is used in the making of sauces as well as soups

Court-bouillon au vin blanc
Court-Bouillon with White Wine

00:15		00:40
American	**Ingredients**	**Metric/Imperial**
4	Carrots	4
4	Large onions	4
2	Celery stalks	2
2 quarts	Dry white wine	2 l / 3½ pints
2 quarts	Water	2 l / 3½ pints
1	Fresh thyme sprig	1
1	Bunch of fresh parsley	1
4	Cloves	4
8	Black peppercorns	8
	Salt	

1. Peel the carrots and cut into slices. Peel and thinly slice the onions. Cut the celery into pieces about ¾ in / 2 cm long.
2. Pour the wine into a large saucepan and add the water, carrots, onions, celery, thyme, parsley, cloves, peppercorns and salt to taste. Bring to a boil and simmer for 40 minutes.
3. Leave to cool before straining.

Fonds brun
Brown Stock

This is made from beef, veal, poultry and vegetables, browned in butter before simmering in water with herbs and flavorings. It serves as a base for a large number of sauces.

00:15		05:00
American	**Ingredients**	**Metric/Imperial**
3 tbsp	Butter or oil	3 tbsp
4	Carrots	4
4	Onions	4
1	Garlic clove	1
2 lb	Meaty bones (beef and veal), cut into pieces by the butcher	1 kg / 2 lb
1 lb	Beef for stew	500 g / 1 lb
2 quarts	Water	2 l / 3½ pints
1	Fresh thyme sprig	1
1	Bay leaf	1
2	Fresh parsley sprigs	2
	Salt and pepper	

1. Put the butter or oil into a large roasting pan.
2. Peel the carrots, onions and garlic and cut into large pieces. Place in the roasting pan with the bones and pieces of beef. Brown over a vigorous heat.
3. Add one-quarter of the water and scrape the bottom of the pan with a wooden spatula to detach the sediment.
4. Pour into a stewing pot and add the remaining water, the thyme, bay leaf, parsley, and salt and pepper to taste. Bring to a boil and simmer for 5 hours, skimming the scum from the surface occasionally.
5. Strain the stock through a dampened cloth placed over a large bowl. Twist the corners of the cloth to squeeze out all the liquid. Leave to cool.
6. Store the stock in the freezer if you are not going to use it during the following week.

Fonds blanc
White Stock

⏱ 00:30		04:00 🍲
Makes about 3 quarts [3 l / 5 pints]		
American	**Ingredients**	**Metric/Imperial**
	Giblets from 3 chickens or 3 carcasses	
1½ lb	Shoulder of veal	750 g / 1½ lb
2 lb	Shin [knuckle] of veal	1 kg / 2 lb
4 quarts	Cold water	4 l / 7 pints
5	Carrots	5
4	Onions	4
2	Leeks	2
1	Celery stalk	1
1	Fresh thyme sprig	1
1	Bay leaf	1
2	Fresh parsley sprigs	2
	Salt and pepper	

1. Put the giblets into a cooking pot together with the shoulder of veal and the veal shin [knuckle]. Add the cold water. Place the pot over a medium heat and bring to a boil.
2. Meanwhile, peel and slice the carrots and onions. Slice the leeks and celery lengthwise. Skim the stock, then add the vegetables, thyme, bay leaf, parsley, and salt and pepper.
3. Simmer steadily for 3½ hours.
4. Leave the stock to cool until it is lukewarm, then remove any fat from the surface.
5. Strain the stock through a dampened cloth placed over a large bowl. Twist the corners of the cloth so as to squeeze out all the liquid. Cool completely.
6. Remove any remaining fat from the surface of the liquid.

Court-bouillon au vinaigre
Court-Bouillon with Vinegar

⏱ 00:15		00:40 🍲
American	**Ingredients**	**Metric/Imperial**
4	Carrots	4
4	Large onions	4
2	Celery stalks	2
2	Garlic cloves	2
1¼ - 2 cups	Wine vinegar	300 - 450 ml / ½ - ¾ pint
2 quarts	Water	2 l / 3½ pints
2	Fresh thyme sprigs	2
2	Bay leaves	2
6	Cloves	6
12	Black peppercorns	12
	Salt	

1. Peel and slice the carrots. Peel and thinly slice the onions. Cut the celery into pieces about ¾ in / 2 cm long. Peel and crush the garlic.
2. Pour the vinegar into a large saucepan and add the water, carrots, onions, celery, thyme, bay leaves, garlic and cloves. Bring to a boil, then add the peppercorns and salt to taste. Simmer for 40 minutes.
3. Leave to cool, then strain.

Fumet de poisson
Fish Stock

Fish stock forms the basis for a large number of sauces.

⏱ 00:15		01:00 🍲
Makes 2 cups [500 ml / ¾ pint]		
American	**Ingredients**	**Metric/Imperial**
2	Large onions	2
2	Shallots	2
2	Large carrots	2
1½ lb	Fish trimmings (heads and bones)	750 g / 1½ lb
1	Bouquet garni	1
½	Lemon	½
1 cup	White wine	250 ml / 8 fl oz
1 quart	Water	1 l / 1¾ pints
	Salt and pepper	

1. Peel and finely chop the onions, shallots and carrots. Roughly crush the fish trimmings.
2. Place the vegetables and fish trimmings in a large saucepan and add the bouquet garni and the ½ lemon cut in two. Pour in the wine and water. Add salt and pepper to taste.
3. Bring to a boil, then reduce the heat and simmer for 1 hour.
4. Strain the stock. It will keep several months in the freezer.

Sauce espagnole (simplifiée)
Rich Brown Sauce
simplified

⏱ 00:20		04:00 🍲
Makes 2 cups [500 ml / ¾ pint]		
American	**Ingredients**	**Metric/Imperial**
1 lb	Meaty veal bones, cut into pieces by the butcher	500 g / 1 lb
	Giblets from 2 chickens	
2	Carrots	2
2	Onions	2
1	Leek	1
3	Tomatoes	3
6 tbsp	Lard	75 g / 3 oz
1½ tbsp	Flour	1½ tbsp
1 tbsp	Tomato paste [purée]	1 tbsp
1 quart	Water	1 l / 1¾ pints
2 cups	White wine	500 ml / ¾ pint
	Salt and pepper	
1	Bouquet garni	1

1. Place the bones and giblets in a frying pan and brown.
2. Meanwhile, peel and chop the carrots and onions. Chop the leek. Peel the tomatoes (first plunging them in boiling water for 10 seconds) and cut into large pieces.
3. Melt the lard in a stewpan and add the onions, leek, carrots and tomatoes. Sprinkle with the flour. Mix well, then add the tomato paste diluted in the water, the wine, and salt and pepper to taste. Add the browned bones and giblets and bouquet garni. Bring to a boil. Leave to cook, uncovered, over a gentle heat for about 4 hours. Skim off the scum from the surface from time to time.
4. Strain the sauce. Leave it to cool, then remove any fat from the surface. Keep in the refrigerator until ready to use.

Aspic

This is a clear meat or fish stock which, once it has cooled, solidifies because of the gelatinous substances it contains. Aspics may be obtained naturally or by adding gelatin.

To color aspic
In order to obtain a beautiful amber tint, use caramel or food coloring which you add just before putting the aspic to cool. If you want to amuse your guests, tint it red, or why not green! Use the same colors as for confectionery or cocktails.

To flavor aspic
You may use different wines, spirits or liqueurs which you add, to taste, when the aspic has cooled but not set.

To chop aspic
Turn the firmly-set aspic onto a damp cloth, so that it does not stick, and chop it with a large knife.

To glaze food with aspic
Melt the set aspic without boiling. As soon as it is liquid, remove from the heat and leave to cool, stirring it with a wooden spoon in order to avoid air bubbles. As soon as the aspic begins to take on the consistency of a syrup, ladle it over the very cold food once or twice, putting the food in the refrigerator between the applications.

Gelée de viande

Aspic

This is a recipe for aspic made without gelatin, prepared from naturally gelatinous meat and bones.

⏲ 00:35 — Makes 2½ quarts [2.5 l / 4½ pints] — 05:00 🍲

American	Ingredients	Metric/Imperial
¼ cup	Butter	50 g / 2 oz
2 lb	Beef for stew (from the leg)	1 kg / 2 lb
1 lb	Shin [knuckle] of veal	500 g / 1 lb
1 lb	Crushed veal and beef bones	500 g / 1 lb
4	Carrots	4
2	Onions	2
1	Large leek	1
1	Celery stalk	1
4 quarts	Water	4 l / 7 pints
2	Boned calf's feet and the crushed bones	2
½ lb	Fresh bacon rind	250 g / 8 oz
1	Bouquet garni	1
	Salt and pepper	
½ lb	Chopped lean beef	250 g / 8 oz
3	Egg whites	3
1 tbsp	Chopped fresh tarragon	1 tbsp
1 tbsp	Chopped fresh chervil or parsley	1 tbsp

1. Heat the butter in a roasting pan and add the leg of beef, shin of veal, cut into pieces, and the crushed bones. Cook until well browned.
2. Meanwhile, peel and chop the carrots and onions. Chop the leek and celery.

3. Place the chopped vegetables in the bottom of a large stewpot together with the meat and place the bones on top. Pour on the water and add the sediment from the roasting pan. Bring to a boil, skimming off the scum that forms on the surface.
4. Add the calf's feet together with the crushed bones, the bacon rind and bouquet garni. Season with salt and pepper and simmer for about 4 hours.
5. Strain the stock. Leave to cool until lukewarm, then skim off the fat from the surface.
6. To clarify the stock, place it in a large saucepan with the chopped beef, egg whites, tarragon and chervil. Blend the whole thoroughly with a wooden spoon. Cook just at simmering point for 35 minutes.
7. Strain the stock through a dampened cloth, squeezing the cloth to extract all the liquid. Leave to cool, then place in the refrigerator to chill for 1-2 hours.
8. You may flavor the aspic before it has cooled using fortified wines such as port, sherry, madeira, etc, ⅔ cup [150 ml / ¼ pint] to each quart [1 l / 1¾ pints] aspic, or with dry white wine, 1¼ cups [300 ml / ½ pint] to each 1 quart [1 l / 1¾ pints] aspic.
9. The aspic will keep well in the freezer.

Gelée de poisson

Fish Aspic

This is a fish stock concentrate to which gelatin is added.

⏲ 00:30 — Makes 2 quarts [2 l / 3½ pints] — 00:55 🍲

American	Ingredients	Metric/Imperial
2	Large carrots	2
2	Onions	2
2	Shallots	2
1 lb	Fish bones and trimmings	500 g / 1 lb
2	Fresh parsley sprigs	2
2	Fresh thyme sprigs	2
2	Bay leaves	2
⅔ cup	White wine	150 ml / ¼ pint
2 quarts	Water	2 l / 3½ pints
	Salt and pepper	
¾ lb	Whiting fillets	350 g / 12 oz
1	Bunch of fresh tarragon	1
2	Egg whites	2
2 envelopes	Unflavored gelatin	4 sachets

1. Peel and finely chop the carrots, onions and shallots. Crush the fish bones and trimmings. Place in a large saucepan and add the parsley, thyme, bay leaves, wine, water, and salt and pepper to taste. Cook for 30 minutes over a gentle heat, skimming off any froth that rises to the surface.
2. Meanwhile, chop the whiting fillets and tarragon. Place in a large bowl together with the egg whites and 1 cup [250 ml / 8 fl oz] water. Blend using a whisk.
3. Remove the fish stock from the heat and leave to cool. Strain the stock and add to the whiting mixture.
4. Pour the mixture back into the stewpot and bring to a boil over a gentle heat, stirring constantly with a wooden spoon. Simmer for 25 minutes.
5. Dissolve the gelatin in the remaining water. Stir into the fish stock.
6. Strain the fish stock through a dampened cloth, squeezing the cloth to extract all the liquid. Leave to cool, then place in the refrigerator to chill for 30 minutes before use.

Cold sauces

Tartare Sauce
Sauce tartare

	00:25		00:00
	Makes 2 cups [500 ml / ¾ pint]		
American	**Ingredients**	**Metric/Imperial**	
2 cups	Mayonnaise (see page 119)	500 ml / ¾ pint	
2 tsp	Vinegar	2 tsp	
8	Gherkins	8	
1 tsp	Capers	1 tsp	
2 tbsp	Chopped mixed fresh chives, tarragon and chervil	2 tbsp	
	Salt and pepper		

1. If the mayonnaise is too thick, thin it with a little more vinegar, mixing vigorously.
2. Cut the gherkins into very small cubes. Chop the capers. Add to the mayonnaise with the herbs, and salt and pepper to taste. Mix well.
3. Keep in a cool place.

Garlic Mayonnaise
Aïoli

	00:15		00:00
	Makes 1 cup [250 ml / 8 fl oz]		
American	**Ingredients**	**Metric/Imperial**	
7	Garlic cloves	7	
1 cup	Olive oil	250 ml / 8 fl oz	
1 - 2	Egg yolks, at room temperature	1 - 2	
2 tbsp	Lemon juice	2 tbsp	
	Salt and pepper		

1. Peel the garlic and crush in a mortar. Reduce to a cream by adding 1 or 2 tablespoons oil.
2. Add the egg yolks, then the remainder of the oil in a trickle, stirring the sauce continuously to thicken it like a mayonnaise. Add the lemon juice, and salt and pepper to taste.
3. Keep in a cool place.

Cook's tip: garlic mayonnaise is served as a dip with raw and cooked young vegetables, and with cold fish and boiled chicken.

Mayonnaise
Mayonnaise

	00:20		00:00
	Makes 2 cups [500 ml / ¾ pint]		
American	**Ingredients**	**Metric/Imperial**	
2	Egg yolks, at room temperature	2	
2 cups	Peanut [groundnut] oil	500 ml / ¾ pint	
1 tbsp	Strong prepared mustard	1 tbsp	
2 tbsp	Lemon juice or vinegar	2 tbsp	
	Salt and pepper		

1. For the mayonnaise to be a success, the egg yolks and oil must be at the same temperature. Place the egg yolks and mustard in a large bowl. Add a very small quantity of oil and whisk it in with a balloon whisk or electric beater.
2. Add the remaining oil, very slowly at first. As soon as the sauce is thickening, the oil may be added more rapidly. While adding the oil, whisk or beat constantly. (The mayonnaise may also be made in a blender or food processor.)
3. Add the lemon juice or vinegar, a large pinch of salt, and pepper to taste. Mix well.

Cook's tip: if your mayonnaise separates or curdles, you can save it as follows: put 1 tablespoon of ice water in a clean bowl and gradually whisk or beat in the curdled mayonnaise.

Vinaigrette Dressing
Sauce vinaigrette

	00:07		00:00
	Makes 4 tablespoons		
American	**Ingredients**	**Metric/Imperial**	
	Salt and pepper		
1 tbsp	Vinegar	1 tbsp	
1 tsp	Prepared mustard	1 tsp	
3 tbsp	Oil	3 tbsp	
	Chopped mixed fresh herbs (parsley, tarragon, chervil chives) to taste		

1. Dissolve a pinch of salt in the vinegar. Mix in the mustard. Add pepper to taste.
2. Add the oil and chopped herbs. Mix thoroughly.

Garlic mayonnaise

Sauce raifort
Horseradish Sauce

	00:15		00:00

American	Ingredients	Metric/Imperial
2 - 3 tbsp	Grated horseradish	2 - 3 tbsp
2 tbsp	White wine vinegar	2 tbsp
2 tsp	Sugar	2 tsp
½ tsp	Mustard powder	½ tsp
½ tsp	Salt	½ tsp
½ tsp	White pepper	½ tsp
1 cup	Chilled crème fraîche	250 ml / 8 fl oz

1. Drain the horseradish, if necessary. Mix the horseradish with the vinegar, sugar, mustard powder, salt and white pepper.
2. Put the crème fraîche into another mixing bowl and whip until thick. Fold in the horseradish mixture. Taste and adjust the seasoning, if necessary.
3. Serve with red meats and broiled [grilled] and smoked fish, especially trout.

Crème fraîche
Crème Fraîche

	00:05		00:00
	plus maturing and chilling		

American	Ingredients	Metric/Imperial
1 cup	Heavy [double] cream	300 ml / ½ pint
1 cup	Sour cream	300 ml / ½ pint

1. Combine the creams in a mixing bowl and whisk lightly together.
2. Cover the bowl loosely with plastic wrap and leave in a warm place (at warm room temperature is sufficient) overnight for the culture to develop. (In cold weather, this may take up to 24 hours). At the end of the maturing time, the cream mixture will be thick and subtly tart.
3. Transfer the bowl to the refrigerator and chill for at least 4 hours.
4. Crème fraîche will keep in the refrigerator for 2-3 weeks, and will continue to develop its delicate tartness as it matures.

Cook's tip: crème fraîche can be purchased, or made at home if time permits. If you have no crème fraîche, heavy [double] cream may be used instead for cooked dishes, and sour cream for cold dishes.

Sauce vinaigrette au lard
Vinaigrette with Bacon

	00:00		00:05

American	Ingredients	Metric/Imperial
6 tbsp	Diced bacon	6 tbsp
2 tbsp	Vinegar	2 tbsp
	Salt and pepper	

1. Cook the diced bacon in a frying pan until crisp and brown and rendered of fat.
2. Pour the bacon and fat over a salad such as dandelion leaves, corn salad [lamb's lettuce] or red cabbage.
3. Pour the vinegar into the still-warm frying pan and stir to mix in the sediment on the bottom and sides of the pan. Pour over the salad. Add salt and pepper to taste and toss.

Artichokes can be served with melted clarified butter or hollandaise sauce

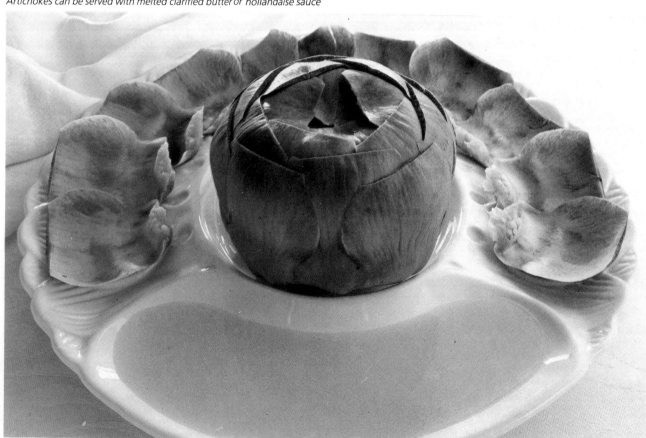

Hot sauces

Beurre blanc
White Butter Sauce

White butter sauce is a hot emulsified sauce which is often served with fish. It is rather tricky to make, because it is an unstable emulsion which tends to curdle. To make it successfully, add the cold butter cut into small pieces all at once to the boiling wine and shallots, whisking quickly to emulsify it.

◢ 00:20   00:15 🍲

American	Ingredients	Metric/Imperial
12	Shallots	12
⅔ cup	Dry white wine	150 ml / ¼ pint
1 cup	Very cold butter	250 g / 8 oz
1 tbsp	Crème fraîche	1 tbsp
	Salt and pepper	

1. Peel and finely chop the shallots. Place in a saucepan with the wine. Bring to a boil and boil over a moderate heat until the mixture is reduced to one-third.
2. Meanwhile, cut the butter into pieces the size of a walnut.
3. Add the butter all at once to the shallots and cook over a gentle heat, whisking continuously to blend in the butter. Whisk in the crème fraîche.
4. As soon as the sauce has turned white (hence the name of the sauce), add salt and pepper to taste and pour it into a sauceboat.
5. If the sauce has curdled, put 1-2 tablespoons of cold water and 2 teaspoons very cold butter in a saucepan. Place over a gentle heat and gradually incorporate the curdled sauce, whisking vigorously.

Coulis de tomates
Thick Tomato Sauce

◢ 00:20   00:45 🍲

American	Ingredients	Metric/Imperial
3 lb	Tomatoes	1.5 kg / 3 lb
2	Garlic clove	2
2	Small onions	2
⅔ cup	Olive oil	150 ml / ¼ pint
1	Bouquet garni	1
5	Fresh basil leaves or	5
1	Fresh tarragon sprig	1
	Salt and pepper	
1 tbsp	Butter	1 tbsp
1 tbsp	Flour	1 tbsp

1. Peel the tomatoes (first plunging them into boiling water for 10 seconds), remove the seeds and chop into large pieces.
2. Peel and chop the garlic and onions. Place in a saucepan with the oil, bouquet garni, basil (or tarragon) and tomatoes. Add salt and pepper to taste. Cover and cook over a gentle heat for 25 minutes.
3. Uncover and cook for a further 10 minutes.
4. Remove the bouquet garni, squeezing it to extract the liquid. Strain the sauce into a clean saucepan. Return to the heat and bring back to a boil.

5. Mix the butter and flour to a smooth paste. Add this kneaded butter (beurre manié) to the boiling sauce and cook for 3-4 minutes, stirring continuously, until thickened.

Sauce aurore
Tomato Cream Sauce

◢ 00:05   00:25 🍲

American	Ingredients	Metric/Imperial
1	Onion	1
2 tbsp	Butter	25 g / 1 oz
2 tbsp	Flour	2 tbsp
2 cups	Milk	500 ml / ¾ pint
1	Small bouquet garni	1
2 tbsp	Tomato paste [purée]	2 tbsp
2 tbsp	Crème fraîche	2 tbsp
	Grated nutmeg	
	Salt and pepper	

1. Peel and coarsely chop the onion. Melt the butter in a saucepan, add the onion and cook for 5 minutes without browning. Add the flour and cook for 2 minutes, stirring continuously.
2. Remove from the heat and add the cold milk. Bring to a boil, stirring continuously. Add the bouquet garni and leave to simmer for 20 minutes.
3. Strain the sauce and return it to the saucepan. Add the tomato paste and crème fraîche. Add nutmeg, and salt and pepper to taste. Mix well.

Sauce barbecue
Barbecue Sauce

◢ 00:10   00:25 🍲

American	Ingredients	Metric/Imperial
3	Onions	3
5 tbsp	Olive oil	5 tbsp
1 cup	Tomato paste [purée]	250 ml / 8 fl oz
¼ cup	Vinegar (preferably cider vinegar)	4 tbsp
⅔ cup	White wine or stock	150 ml / ¼ pint
⅔ cup	Worcestershire sauce	150 ml / ¼ pint
3	Fresh thyme sprigs	3
1	Bay leaf	1
2	Garlic cloves	2
¼ cup	Honey	4 tbsp
1 tsp	Prepared mustard	1 tsp
	Salt and pepper	
	Tabasco sauce	

1. Peel and finely chop the onions. Heat the oil in a heavy saucepan, add the onions and soften over a moderate heat.
2. When the onions begin to brown, add the tomato paste mixed with the vinegar. Bring to a boil.
3. Add the wine, worcestershire sauce, thyme, bay leaf, peeled and crushed garlic, honey and mustard. Leave to simmer uncovered for 12 minutes.
4. Add salt and pepper and 2 or 3 drops of tabasco sauce.

Sauce béchamel

Béchamel Sauce

00:05   00:45

American	Ingredients	Metric/Imperial
5 tbsp	Butter	5 tbsp
5 tbsp	Flour	50 g / 2 oz
1 quart	Milk	1 l / 1¾ pints
	Grated nutmeg	
	Salt and pepper	
1	Medium-size onion (optional)	1
1	Clove	1
1	Small bouquet garni (optional)	1

1. Melt the butter in a heavy saucepan. Add the flour and stir vigorously with a wooden spoon until the butter completely absorbs the flour. Cook, stirring, for 2-3 minutes.
2. Remove from the heat and gradually pour in the milk, stirring continuously. Return the saucepan to the heat and bring slowly to a boil, stirring. Cook over a gentle heat for 10 minutes. Add nutmeg, salt and pepper to taste. The sauce is now ready to serve.
3. If liked, peel and halve the onion and stud with the clove. Add to the sauce with the bouquet garni and leave to simmer for a further 25-30 minutes, stirring frequently. Strain through a fine sieve.
4. This sauce keeps very well in the refrigerator. Cover it with a sheet of plastic wrap to prevent a skin forming.

Sauce tomate

Tomato Sauce

00:10   00:45

American	Ingredients	Metric/Imperial
3 lb	Tomatoes	1.5 kg / 3 lb
2	Small onions	2
2	Garlic cloves (optional)	2
⅔ cup	Olive oil	150 ml / ¼ pint
1	Bay leaf	1
1	Fresh thyme sprig	1
1	Bunch of fresh parsley	1
5	Fresh basil leaves or	5
1	Fresh tarragon sprig	1
	Salt and pepper	
1 - 2	Sugar cubes	1 - 2

1. Peel the tomatoes (first plunging them into boiling water for 10 seconds), remove the seeds and chop roughly. Peel and chop the onions and garlic.
2. Place the tomatoes, onions and garlic in a saucepan and add the oil, bay leaf, thyme, parsley and basil or tarragon. Add salt and pepper to taste. Cook over a high heat until excess liquid has completely evaporated. This will take about 40 minutes.
3. Taste and if you find the sauce too sharp, add the sugar cubes. Pass the sauce through a food mill or sieve.
4. You will obtain a more or less liquid sauce depending on the season and quality of the tomatoes. If after straining you find it rather thin, reduce it quickly over a brisk heat until it is of the desired consistency.
5. This sauce will keep for a week in the refrigerator.

another large saucepan. Twist the corners of the cloth to squeeze out all the liquid. Boil to reduce over a low heat until only 1 quart [1 l / 1¾ pints] remains.
5. Beat the egg yolks with the crème fraîche in a cold bowl. Gradually add the stock, whisking continuously. Finally add the butter, cut into small pieces, stirring well. Taste and adjust the seasoning.
6. Place the food to be coated on a rack over a tray. Spoon over the sauce several times. Leave to cool completely before serving.

Sauce bourguignonne

Burgundy Sauce

00:00   00:30

American	Ingredients	Metric/Imperial
¼ lb	Mushrooms	125 g / 4 oz
3 - 4	Shallots	3 - 4
¼ lb	Fresh pork sides [belly pork]	125 g / 4 oz
6 tbsp	Butter	75 g / 3 oz
1 quart	Red wine	1 l / 1¾ pints
1	Bouquet garni	1
	Salt and pepper	
2 tbsp	Flour	25 g / 1 oz

1. Chop the mushrooms. Peel and chop the shallots. Dice the pork very finely.
2. Melt 2 tablespoons [25 g / 1 oz] butter in a saucepan, add the mushrooms and pork and cook until lightly browned.
3. Add the red wine, shallots, bouquet garni, and salt and pepper to taste. Bring to a boil and reduce by half.
4. Remove the bouquet garni. Blend the flour and 2 tablespoons [25 g / 1 oz] butter to a paste (beurre-manié) and add to the sauce, stirring it with a whisk. Boil for 3-4 minutes until thickened, then add the remainder of the butter and whisk it in.

Burgundy sauce

Sauce blanche
White Sauce

White sauce is prepared like béchamel (see page 124), but the milk is replaced by the same quantity of water or stock.

Sauce choron
Tomato Béarnaise Sauce

	00:20		00:30

American	Ingredients	Metric/Imperial
2 lb	Tomatoes	1 kg / 2 lb
1 quantity	Béarnaise sauce	1 quantity

1. Cut the tomatoes into large pieces and place in a heavy saucepan. Cook over a medium heat until thick and well reduced.
2. Strain through a food mill or conical strainer: you should obtain a very thick purée.
3. Mix the tomato purée with the béarnaise sauce.

Sauce béarnaise
Béarnaise Sauce

This sauce can be difficult to make. The secret of success is to stir it continuously during preparation. Also, the butter must be fresh and of excellent quality.

	00:10		00:20

American	Ingredients	Metric/Imperial
2	Shallots	2
2 - 3	Fresh tarragon sprigs	2 - 3
2	Fresh chervil or parsley sprigs	2
¾ cup	Butter	175 g / 6 oz
1 tbsp	Oil	1 tbsp
⅔ cup	Vinegar	150 ml / ¼ pint
	Salt and pepper	
3	Egg yolks, at room temperature	3
2 tbsp	Cold water	2 tbsp

1. Peel and finely chop the shallots. Chop the tarragon and chervil.
2. Heat 1 tablespoon [15 g / ½ oz] butter and the oil in a saucepan and add the shallots, half the chopped tarragon and chervil and the vinegar. Add pepper to taste. Place over a gentle heat and leave to reduce for 20 minutes until only 1 tablespoon of the vinegar remains.
3. Meanwhile, heat the remaining butter in a bowl standing over a pan of hot water. When the butter has melted, leave it to cool until it is lukewarm. After a moment or two, a whitish deposit will appear and fall to the bottom of the pan. Pour the melted butter into a bowl, leaving the sediment behind.
4. Place the egg yolks in a bowl over the pan of hot water, add the vinegar reduction and whisk well. Gradually incorporate the water, and salt and pepper to taste. Continue to whisk vigorously until the mixture becomes creamy. Remove from the

heat and, continuing to whisk, add the melted butter in a thin trickle. When all the butter has been incorporated, you will have a very smooth sauce.
5. Strain the sauce, if liked, then add the remaining tarragon and chervil.
6. If you do not use the sauce immediately, place the bowl over a pan of hot, but not boiling, water.

Cook's tip: Béarnaise sauce is taditionally served with all broiled [grilled] red meats, especially steak.

Sauce hollandaise
Hollandaise Sauce

	00:05		00:15

American	Ingredients	Metric/Imperial
1½ cups	Butter	350 g / 12 oz
4	Egg yolks, at room temperature	4
2 tsp	Cold water	2 tsp
½ tsp	Salt	½ tsp

1. Work the butter on a plate with a fork to soften it.
2. Place a saucepan half filled with water over the heat (choose a saucepan large enough for a large bowl to fit over it) and bring to a boil.
3. Put into a large bowl the egg yolks, cold water and salt. Place the bowl on the saucepan of boiling water and stir vigorously with a whisk.
4. As soon as the eggs begin to thicken, remove the bowl from the heat and add the softened butter in small pieces, whisking continuously (this is very important). You will then have a very smooth, pale yellow sauce. If you do not want to serve it immediately, place the bowl of hollandaise sauce back over the pan of hot but not boiling water, off the heat, to keep warm.

Cook's tip: when you incorporate the butter, if the sauce becomes too thick, immediately add a few more drops of cold water to thin it out.

Béarnaise sauce and Hollandaise sauce

Sauce bordelaise

Bordelaise Sauce

This sauce usually accompanies steak. The traditional recipe is a very complicated brown sauce enriched with poached beef marrow, but the one given here is a simplified version which is quicker and less expensive.

00:10 00:15 to 00:20

American	Ingredients	Metric/Imperial
5	Shallots	5
1 ¼ cups	Red wine	30 ml / ½ pint
1	Fresh thyme sprig	1
1	Bay leaf	1
	Salt and pepper	
¼ cup	Butter	50 g / 2 oz
1 tbsp	Flour	1 tbsp
1 ¼ cups	Beef stock	300 ml / ½ pint
2 oz	Beef marrow	50 g / 2 oz
2 - 3 tbsp	Meat juice	2 - 3 tbsp
1	Small bunch of fresh parsley	1

1. Peel and chop the shallots and place in a saucepan. Add the red wine, thyme, bay leaf and a pinch of salt. Bring to a boil and reduce by half.
2. Meanwhile, melt 1 tablespoon [15 g / ½ oz] butter in another saucepan. Add the flour and cook, stirring, until the roux has browned. Add the stock and salt and pepper to taste, stirring well. Cook over a low heat for 15 minutes, stirring frequently.
3. Dice the marrow. Poach for 5 minutes in boiling water, then drain.
4. Remove the thyme and bay leaf from the wine reduction. Add the wine to the other saucepan. Add the marrow cubes, adjust the seasoning and leave to simmer for 2-3 minutes.
5. Add the meat juice. Remove from the heat and add the remainder of the butter and the chopped parsley, stirring continuously.
6. If you do not use the sauce immediately, keep it warm in a bowl standing over a pan of hot water.

Sauce brune

Brown Sauce

00:15 00:35

American	Ingredients	Metric/Imperial
3	Onions	3
5 oz	Bacon	150 g / 5 oz
6 tbsp	Butter	75 g / 3 oz
6 tbsp	Flour	75 g / 3 oz
1 quart	Beef stock	1 l / 1¾ pints
	Salt and pepper	
1	Bouquet garni	1

1. Peel and thinly slice the onions. Cut the bacon into small cubes. Melt the butter in a saucepan, add the onions and bacon and cook over a very gentle heat until lightly browned.
2. Add the flour and stir to mix. Cook, stirring, until the mixture becomes light brown.
3. Add the stock and bring to a boil, stirring well. Add salt and pepper to taste. Add the bouquet garni. Cook for 20 minutes over a very gentle heat.
4. Taste and adjust the seasoning, then boil the sauce to reduce it for a further 10 minutes.
5. Before serving skim off any fat or scum from the surface and discard the bouquet garni.

Béchamel sauce

Sauce diable

Devil Sauce

00:15 00:45

American	Ingredients	Metric/Imperial
4	Shallots	4
2 cups	White wine	450 ml / ¾ pint
5 tbsp	Vinegar	5 tbsp
1	Fresh thyme sprig	1
1	Bay leaf	1
	Salt and pepper	
¼ cup	Butter	50 g / 2 oz
3 tbsp	Flour	25 g / 1 oz
2 cups	Beef stock	500 ml / ¾ pint
1	Bunch of fresh parsley	1

1. Peel and chop the shallots. Place them in a saucepan with the wine, vinegar, thyme sprig, bay leaf, and salt and pepper to taste. Boil until reduced to ½ cup [125 ml / 4 fl oz] liquid.
2. Meanwhile, melt 2 tablespoons [25 g / 1 oz] butter in a heavy saucepan over a medium heat. Add the flour and stir with a wooden spoon until the roux turns light brown in color. Add pepper to taste and pour on the stock, stirring constantly. Cook gently for 15 minutes, stirring from time to time.
3. Add the reduced wine mixture to the sauce and stir. Leave to cook over a low heat for about 5 minutes longer.
4. Chop the parsley. Remove the saucepan from the heat. Discard the thyme sprig and bay leaf. Swirl in the rest of the butter and the chopped parsley. Serve hot.

Sauce veloutée
Velouté Sauce

	00:15	00:03
	Makes 2 cups [500 ml / ¾ pint]	

American	Ingredients	Metric/Imperial
2 tbsp	Butter	25 g / 1 oz
1 tbsp	Flour	1 tbsp
⅔ cup	Cooking liquid from the dish to be accompanied	150 ml / ¼ pint
2	Egg yolks	2
½ cup	Crème fraîche	125 ml / 4 fl oz
	Lemon juice	
	Salt and pepper	

1. Melt the butter in a saucepan, add the flour and cook for 2 minutes, stirring.

2. Pour in the cooking liquid, stirring well. Bring to a boil and simmer for 1 minute over a gentle heat.

3. Leave to cool a little, then add the egg yolks mixed with the crème fraîche. Add a few drops of lemon juice, and salt and pepper to taste. Cook, stirring, until thick and smooth. Do not allow to boil.

Sauce riche
Rich Sauce

This is a variation of mushroom and chicken cream sauce (see page 131). To the diced mushrooms, add ⅔ cup [150 ml / ¼ pint] cognac, 1-2 tablespoons truffle peelings and, to be completely traditional, 1 tablespoon lobster butter.

Sauce zingara
Brown Julienne Sauce

This sauce is served with all roast meats.

	00:30	00:25 to 00:30

American	Ingredients	Metric/Imperial
3	Shallots	3
2	Carrots	2
1	Onion	1
1	Leek, white part only	1
7 tbsp	Butter	90 g / 3½ oz
2 cups	Beef stock	500 ml / ¾ pint
1	Bouquet garni	1
	Cayenne pepper	
¼ lb	Large mushrooms	125 g / 4 oz
½	Lemon	½
2 oz	Cooked tongue	50 g / 2 oz
2 oz	Cooked ham	50 g / 2 oz
¼ cup	Port wine	4 tbsp
1 - 2 tbsp	Truffle peelings	1 - 2 tbsp
	Salt and pepper	

1. Peel and chop the shallots, carrots and onions. Chop the leek. Melt 3 tablespoons [40 g / 1½ oz] butter in a saucepan and add the chopped vegetables, stock, bouquet garni and a pinch of cayenne pepper. Bring to a boil and leave to reduce for 15 minutes.

2. Meanwhile, dice the mushrooms. Place them in a bowl of water to which the juice of ½ lemon has been added to prevent them from discoloring. Cut the tongue and ham into small cubes. Place the drained mushrooms, tongue and ham in a heavy saucepan and add the port, 2 tablespoons [25 g / 1 oz] butter and the truffle peelings. Cook over a low heat until the port has reduced by half.

3. Strain the brown sauce into the saucepan containing the tongue, mushrooms and truffles and cook for 2-3 minutes, stirring well. Add salt and pepper to taste.

4. Swirl in the remainder of the butter.

Robert sauce

Sauce Robert
Robert Sauce

	00:05	00:25

American	Ingredients	Metric/Imperial
6	Onions	6
¼	Butter	50 g / 2 oz
3 tbsp	Flour	25 g / 1 oz
1 tbsp	Tomato paste [purée]	1 tbsp
⅔ cup	White wine	150 ml / ¼ pint
1 cup	Beef broth or stock	250 ml / 8 fl oz
	Salt and pepper	
2 tbsp	Prepared mustard	2 tbsp

1. Peel and thinly slice the onions. Heat the butter in a saucepan, add the onions and cook over a gentle heat, stirring frequently, until soft and golden. Add the flour and cook for a few minutes, continuing to stir.

2. Add the tomato paste. Stir in the white wine and broth. Add salt and pepper to taste. Leave to simmer for 20 minutes.

3. Add the mustard and mix thoroughly.

Sauce miroton
Brown Onion Sauce

⏱ 00:15 00:40 🍲

American	Ingredients	Metric/Imperial
4	Large onions	4
¼ cup	Lard	50 g / 2 oz
2 tbsp	Flour	25 g / 1 oz
2 tbsp	Tomato paste [purée]	2 tbsp
2½ cups	Beef stock	600 ml / 1 pint
	Salt and pepper	
2 tsp	Vinegar	2 tsp

1. Peel and finely chop the onions. Melt the lard in a saucepan, add the onions and brown slightly. Add the flour and stir vigorously until it browns.
2. Mix the tomato paste with the stock and add to the pan, stirring well. Add salt and pepper to taste. Leave to cook for a further 10 minutes, stirring frequently.
3. Stir in the vinegar and serve hot.

Sauce mornay
Cheese Sauce

⏱ 00:05 00:15 🍲

American	Ingredients	Metric/Imperial
6 tbsp	Butter	75 g / 3 oz
6 tbsp	Flour	75 g / 3 oz
1 quart	Milk	900 ml / 1 ½ pints
	Grated nutmeg	
	Salt and pepper	
1¼ cups	Grated gruyère cheese	150 g / 5 oz

1. Melt the butter in a heavy saucepan. Add the flour and cook, stirring with a wooden spoon, for 2-3 minutes. Remove from the heat and add the milk, stirring well. Return to the heat and cook, stirring, until the sauce has thickened. Leave to cook for about 10 minutes. Add nutmeg, salt and pepper to taste.
2. Add the cheese gradually, continuing to stir the sauce so that the cheese will melt evenly as it blends in.

Sauce mousseline
Whipped Cream Sauce

⏱ 00:00 00:10 🍲

American	Ingredients	Metric/Imperial
6 tbsp	Very fresh butter	75 g / 3 oz
½ cup	Crème fraîche	125 ml / 4 fl oz
⅔ cup	Vinegar	150 ml / ¼ pint
6	Black peppercorns	6
2	Egg yolks	2

1. Work the butter on a plate with a fork to soften it.
2. Pour the crème fraîche into an ice cold bowl. Whip until thick. Set aside.
3. Place the vinegar and peppercorns in a saucepan and cook over a low heat until only 1 tablespoon of liquid remains.

4. Remove from heat. Remove the peppercorns and beat in the egg yolks. As soon as the eggs begin to thicken, add the softened butter in small pieces, beating continuously.
5. Add the whipped cream and beat well. Serve the sauce with baked fish, or with lightly cooked young vegetables.

Sauce Nantua
Crayfish Sauce

⏱ 01:00 00:45 🍲

American	Ingredients	Metric/Imperial
2	Small onions	2
1	Shallot	1
10 tbsp	Butter	150 g / 5 oz
3 tbsp	Flour	3 tbsp
3 cups	Milk	750 ml / 1 ¼ pints
5	Fresh parsley sprigs	5
1	Fresh thyme sprig	1
	Grated nutmeg	
	Salt and pepper	
1	Small carrot	1
1	Small garlic clove	1
1	Small bouquet garni	1
8 - 10	Crayfish	8 - 10
1 tbsp	Vinegar	1 tbsp
1 cup	Crème fraîche	250 ml / 8 fl oz

1. Peel and finely chop one onion and the shallot. Melt 2 tablespoons [25 g / 1 oz] butter in a saucepan, add the onion and shallot and cook over a very moderate heat without browning. Sprinkle with the flour, stirring, and leave to cook for 2 minutes.
2. Pour on the milk, stirring well. Bring to a boil, stirring, then add the parsley, thyme and a pinch of nutmeg. Add salt and pepper to taste. Simmer over a very low heat until the sauce has reduced by about one-third.
3. Strain the sauce, pressing down on the solids to extract all liquid. Cover the surface with wax [greaseproof] paper to prevent a skin from forming and set aside.
4. Peel and thinly slice the remaining onion. Peel and grate the carrot. Peel and crush the garlic. Heat 2 tablespoons [25 g / 1 oz] butter in a frying pan, add the carrot, sliced onion, garlic and bouquet garni. Add pepper to taste and cook over a gentle heat until lightly browned.
5. Meanwhile, prepare the crayfish. Take them with one hand by the head, lowering the pincers forwards. With the other hand, grasp the central tail fin between the thumb and index finger. Twist and pull: a small black intestine will come out with the fin. Remove it. Pat the crayfish dry with paper towels.
6. Add the vinegar to the frying pan. Toss the crayfish into the pan and cook briskly until they turn red. Reduce the heat, cover and leave to cook for 8-10 minutes.
7. Remove from the heat. Leave to cool slightly, then peel the crayfish tails. Set aside. Crush the shells, heads and pincers in a mortar. Add the remainder of the butter and the vegetable mixture in the frying pan and knead it in with the pestle. Press the butter through a sieve with the pestle.
8. Uncover the white sauce and warm over a gentle heat. Add the crème fraîche and cook for 2-3 minutes, stirring.
9. Put the pan over another pan containing hot water. Incorporate the crayfish butter in small pieces. Add the crayfish tails.
10. Serve with eggs, fish and shellfish.

Crayfish sauce

Soups

Guidelines

Vegetable stocks and broths

Soak dried legumes and pulses in water for several hours, then put them in fresh cold water to cook. Lentils are an exception to this rule, since they are not normally soaked.

Thicken soup when necessary with a spoonful of instant mashed potato flakes.

Beef or poultry stocks and broths

Try to make your stock the day before it is needed so the fat will have time to rise to the surface and solidify. You will be able to remove it in this form easily by drawing a skimming ladle or spoon over the surface.

Bouillon or stock cubes are often very salt, so keep this in mind when you are seasoning your soup.

Making a bouquet garni

Used to flavor soups and broths, a traditional bouquet garni consists of a fresh or dried bay leaf, several sprigs of fresh parsley or parsley stalks (with stems and roots) and a sprig of fresh or dried thyme, all tied together with kitchen thread. Try a selection of different herbs and flavorings for variety – tarragon, marjoram, basil, sage, fennel, oregano, rosemary or dried lemon and orange rind for example – or even a little celery or the green part of a leek.

Puréed vegetable soups

Wash the vegetables carefully to remove any dirt, but do not leave them to soak or they will lose most of their vitamins and mineral salts.

Raw vegetables will cook more quickly if you first mince them in a food processor. Remember that the flavor of garlic, shallots, onions and leeks is intensified by mincing so reduce the proportion of these foods accordingly. Process the vegetables once again after they have been cooked.

Croûtons

For best results, use stale rather than fresh bread. Toast croûtons instead of frying them for a healthy result. If you must fry croûtons, use only a little butter or oil and brown them over a gentle heat.

Leftovers

Save vegetable peelings (making sure you have scrubbed the vegetables first) and the water in which they have been cooked to make an economical basis for soups.

Bouillon de poule
Chicken Broth

American	Ingredients	Metric/Imperial
	Giblets of 3 chickens	
2 quarts	Water	2 l / 3½ pints
1	Bouquet garni	1
3	Carrots	3
1	Turnip	1
1	Celery stalk	1
1	Large onion	1
2	Garlic cloves	2
3	Leeks	3
	Salt and pepper	

1. Place the giblets in a large saucepan and add the water and bouquet garni. Bring to a boil. Cover and simmer over a medium heat for 45 minutes.
2. Meanwhile, peel and dice the carrots and turnip. Chop the celery. Peel and quarter the onion. Peel the garlic and split the cloves in half. Trim the leeks, cut in half lengthwise and wash well in cold water, separating the leaves. Drain and chop coarsely.
3. Place all the vegetables in the pan. Add salt and pepper to taste. Return to a boil and simmer, covered, for a further 45 minutes.
4. Strain the broth into a warmed soup tureen. If liked, serve the giblets on a plate with a sauceboat of vinaigrette dressing.

Soupe de poissons
Fish Soup

American	Ingredients	Metric/Imperial
1	Porgy or scup [sea bream]	1
3	Small ocean perch [gurnards]	3
2	Whiting	2
6	Small red snappers or mullet	6
3	Slices of eel	3
6	Small sea bass	6
1	Onion	1
1	Leek, white part only	1
5 tbsp	Olive oil	5 tbsp
6	Garlic cloves	6
1	Fresh fennel sprig	1
1	Fresh thyme sprig	1
	Pared rind of 1 orange	
	Salt and pepper	
2 quarts	Water	2 l / 3½ pints
½ tsp	Saffron powder	½ tsp
1	Sliced french loaf	1
1 cup	Grated gruyère cheese	125 g / 4 oz

1. Ask your fish merchant to clean and scale all the fish. Cut the porgy, perch and whiting into slices. Peel and thinly slice the onion. Trim and thinly slice the leek.

2. Heat the olive oil in a large saucepan. Add the onion, leek, heads and tails from the larger fish, 4 garlic cloves (unpeeled but crushed), fennel, thyme and orange rind. Add salt and pepper to taste. Cook for 3-4 minutes, then cover with the water. Bring to a boil and leave to cook for 20 minutes.
3. Preheat the oven to 350°F / 180°C / Gas Mark 4.
4. Strain the soup. Return the strained soup to the pan and add the saffron, eel, perch and porgy. Bring to a boil over a brisk heat, then simmer for 5 minutes. Add the rest of the fish and leave to simmer for a further 5 minutes.
5. Meanwhile, rub the bread slices with the remaining garlic, peeled and halved. Discard the garlic. Sprinkle the bread with the cheese and arrange the slices on a baking sheet. Bake for 3-4 minutes or until the cheese has melted.
6. Arrange the fish on a warmed serving dish. Serve the fish with the soup and slices of french bread.

Fish soup

Bouillon gras
Beef Broth

American	Ingredients	Metric/Imperial
2 lb	Beef for stew with bones	1 kg / 2 lb
2 tsp	Salt	2 tsp
6	Black peppercorns	6
3 quarts	Water	3 l / 5 pints
3	Carrots	3
3	Turnips	3
2	Leeks	2
1	Celery stalk	1
	Slices of bread for serving	

00:25 / 03:30

1. Put the beef and bones, salt and peppercorns into a large pan and cover with the cold water. Bring to a boil, skimming off the scum that rises to the surface.
2. Meanwhile, peel the carrots and turnips. Trim the leeks and celery.
3. Add the vegetables to the pan. Bring back to a boil, then lower the heat and leave to simmer for 3 hours.
4. A few minutes before serving, toast a few slices of bread and place them in a warmed soup tureen.
5. Skim off any fat from the surface of the broth and strain the broth into the tureen.

Cook's tip: if you leave the broth to cool, so much the better. The fat will set on the surface and can therefore be removed easily.

Crème aux champignons
Cream of Mushroom Soup

00:15 / 00:35

American	Ingredients	Metric/Imperial
1½ lb	Mushrooms	750 g / 1½ lb
¼ cup	Lemon juice	4 tbsp
3	Shallots	3
6 tbsp	Butter	75 g / 3 oz
6 tbsp	Flour	75 g / 3 oz
1½ quarts	Chicken broth	1.5 l / 2½ pints
	Salt and pepper	
1¼ cups	Crème fraîche	300 ml / ½ pint

1. Set 6 mushrooms aside for the garnish and chop the remainder. Sprinkle with 3 tablespoons of lemon juice. Peel and chop the shallots.
2. Melt the butter in a saucepan, add the chopped shallots and mushrooms and cook until all the vegetable water has evaporated. Sprinkle with the flour and stir thoroughly.
3. Add the broth and bring to a boil, stirring continuously with a wooden spoon. Season with salt and pepper, if necessary. Leave to cook over a gentle heat for 15 minutes.
4. Put the soup into a food processor or blender and purée until smooth. Return to the saucepan and add the crème fraîche, beating with a whisk. Simmer over a medium heat for 10 minutes.
5. Meanwhile, chop the reserved mushrooms and sprinkle with the remaining lemon juice. Add to the soup and serve hot.

Consommé Belle-Hélène
Consommé with Eggs and Milk

00:05 / 00:15

American	Ingredients	Metric/Imperial
3 cups	Cold broth (see left)	750 ml / 1¼ pints
1	Egg, separated	1
¼ cup	Ground rice	4 tbsp
3 cups	Milk	750 ml / 1¼ pints
1	Egg yolk	1
½ cup	Grated gruyère cheese	50 g / 2 oz

1. Remove the layer of fat from the broth using a skimming spoon. Heat the broth in a saucepan.
2. Beat the egg white in a bowl. Pour it in a trickle into the hot (but not boiling) broth. Stir gently until the egg white has solidified. Pour the whole through a strainer into a clean saucepan. You have now made what is referred to in culinary terms as a 'clarification.'
3. Return the consommé to the heat. Mix the ground rice with the cold milk, and when the consommé begins to boil, add the rice mixture, stirring thoroughly. When it boils for a second time, lower the heat and leave to simmer for 10 minutes.
4. Mix the egg yolks with 1 tablespoon cold milk in a soup tureen. Pour in the consommé, stirring continuously. Serve the consommé with the cheese.

Consommé madrilène

Consommé with Tomatoes and Sherry

	00:10		00:45

American	Ingredients	Metric/Imperial
2 quarts	Cold chicken broth (see page 136)	2 l / 3½ pints
1	Egg white	1
6	Tomatoes	6
2 tbsp	Oil	2 tbsp
1	Fresh thyme sprig	1
½	Bay leaf	½
	Salt and pepper	
⅔ cup	Sherry	150 ml / ¼ pint

1. Remove the layer of fat from the broth.
2. Heat the broth in a saucepan. Beat the egg white in a bowl. Pour it in a trickle into the hot (but not boiling) broth. Stir gently until the egg white has solidified. Pour the whole through a strainer into a clean saucepan. You have now made what is referred to in culinary terms as a 'clarification.'
3. Return the consommé to the heat. Simmer uncovered to reduce by one-third (about 45 minutes).
4. Meanwhile, peel the tomatoes (first plunging them in boiling water for 10 seconds), then cut them into quarters and remove the seeds. Dice the flesh.
5. Heat the oil in a small frying pan. Add the tomatoes, thyme, bay leaf and salt and pepper to taste and leave to cook until the tomatoes have melted. Sieve the tomato mixture to make a purée, or blend it in a blender or food processor.
6. When the consommé is reduced, add the tomato purée together with the sherry. Mix and pour into cups.

Bisque de crevettes

Creamed Shrimp [Prawn] Soup

	00:25		00:30

American	Ingredients	Metric/Imperial
2 lb	Large raw shrimp [prawns]	1 kg / 2 lb
1	Large onion	1
2	Medium-size carrots	2
2 tbsp	Oil	2 tbsp
6 tbsp	Butter	75 g / 3 oz
2 tbsp	Cognac	2 tbsp
1	Bay leaf	1
1	Fresh thyme sprig	1
1	Fresh parsley sprig	1
	Salt and pepper	
	Cayenne pepper	
2 cups	Dry white wine	450 ml ¾ pint
2 tbsp	Tomato paste [purée]	2 tbsp
1 quart	Fish stock	1 l / 1¾ pints
3	Egg yolks	3
1¼ cups	Crème fraîche	300 ml / ½ pint

1. Rinse the shrimp and drain. Peel the onion and carrots and chop finely.
2. Heat the oil and butter in a wide saucepan over a brisk heat. Add the shrimp. As soon as the shells become red, pour on the heated cognac and set it alight immediately. Add the onion, carrots, bay leaf, thyme and parsley. Add salt and pepper to taste and a touch of cayenne pepper. Leave to cook for 5 minutes, stirring frequently.
3. Remove the shrimp and set aside. Add the wine to the pan, cover and cook over a gentle heat for 15 minutes.
4. Add the tomato paste and stir well. Cook for a further 10 minutes over a gentle heat.
5. Remove the thyme, bay leaf and parsley and discard. Add the fish stock to the pan and bring to a boil. Simmer for 5 minutes.
6. Meanwhile, peel the shrimp.
7. Purée the soup and shrimp in a blender or food processor until smooth. Taste and adjust the seasoning.
8. Place the egg yolks in a soup tureen with the crème fraîche and mix thoroughly with a sauce whisk. Gradually whisk in the puréed soup.
9. Serve immediately.

Bourride

Fish Stew with Garlic Mayonnaise

	00:30		00:40

American	Ingredients	Metric/Imperial
2	Onions	2
4	Garlic cloves	4
½ lb	Tomatoes	250 g / 8 oz
1	Orange	1
12	Fennel seeds	12
	Saffron powder	
1	Bouquet garni	1
⅔ cup	Olive oil	150 ml / ¼ pint
1¼ pints	Dry white wine	300 ml / ½ pint
2 quarts	Boiling water	2 l / 3½ pints
	Salt and pepper	
5 lb	Mixed fish (monkfish, red snapper or mullet, bream or porgy, gurnard or small ocean perch, John Dory, a piece of conger eel, etc.) cleaned and scaled if necessary	2.5 kg / 5 lb
1	Egg yolk	1
6	Slices of stale bread	6
	For the garlic mayonnaise:	
6 - 8	Garlic cloves	6 - 8
1 cup	Olive oil	250 ml / 8 fl oz
2	Egg yolks	2
2 tbsp	Lemon juice	2 tbsp
	Salt and pepper	

1. Peel and chop the onions and garlic. Peel the tomatoes (first plunging them in boiling water for 10 seconds) and chop them. Thinly pare ¼ of the rind from the orange.
2. Place the onions, garlic, tomatoes, orange rind, fennel seeds, a pinch of saffron and the bouquet garni in a large

saucepan. Pour on the oil and stir, then add the wine, boiling water and salt and pepper to taste. Bring to a boil and leave to simmer for 20 minutes.

3. Meanwhile, prepare the mayonnaise. Peel the garlic cloves and crush in a mortar, with a pestle, adding 1 or 2 tablespoons of the olive oil to obtain a paste. Add the egg yolks, then drizzle in the remaining oil in a trickle, blending with a whisk, as for mayonnaise. Add the lemon juice, and salt and pepper to taste.

4. Place all the fish in the pan and simmer for 15 minutes.

5. Drain the fish, place it on a warmed serving dish and keep hot. Put the vegetables into a blender or food processor with a little of the broth and blend to a purée. Pour this back into the remaining broth and reheat.

6. Mix the egg yolk with 2 tablespoons of the mayonnaise. Whisk in 1 ladle of the broth. Pour this mixture into the pan of broth, off the heat, and stir. Discard the bouquet garni.

7. Arrange the slices of bread on the bottom of a warmed soup tureen and pour over the thickened soup. Serve the fish with the soup and the remaining mayonnaise.

Crème d'asperges
Cream of Asparagus Soup

	00:45	00:30 to 00:40	

American	Ingredients	Metric/Imperial
1 quart	Milk	1 l / 1¾ pints
1	Medium-size onion	1
1	Clove	1
6	Black peppercorns	6
1	Bouquet garni	1
5 tbsp	Ground rice	5 tbsp
1 lb	Fresh asparagus	500 g / 1 lb
	Salt and pepper	
¼ cup	Butter	50 g / 2 oz
½ cup	Crème fraîche	125 ml / 4 fl oz

1. Put the milk into a saucepan, and add the peeled onion studded with the clove, the peppercorns and bouquet garni. Bring to a boil.

2. Dissolve the ground rice in a little cold water and pour this mixture into the boiling milk, stirring constantly. Lower the heat and leave to simmer for 20 minutes.

3. Meanwhile, trim the woody ends from the asparagus, and scrape the stalks if necessary.

4. Put just enough salted water into an asparagus steamer or tall saucepan to cover the stalks of the asparagus. Bring to a boil. Add the asparagus (the tips should be above the water), cover and steam until crisp-tender. This will take 8-20 minutes, depending on the age and size of the asparagus.

5. Remove the asparagus from the water, reserving the water, and drain on paper towels. Cut off the tips and keep them to garnish the soup. Chop the asparagus stalks.

6. Melt the butter in a saucepan. Add the chopped asparagus stalks and cook until very soft. Add to the flavored milk with 1 tablespoon of the reserved asparagus cooking water. Simmer until the asparagus breaks down.

7. Strain through a fine sieve, squeezing all liquid from the solids with the back of a spoon. Measure the strained milk, and add enough asparagus cooking water to make 1½ quarts [1.5 l / 2½ pints].

8. Add the crème fraîche and reserved asparagus tips. Taste and adjust the seasoning. Reheat gently and serve.

Cream of asparagus soup

Consommé Colbert
Consommé with Poached Eggs and Port Wine

	00:10	00:15	

American	Ingredients	Metric/Imperial
1½ quarts	Cold beef broth	1.5 l / 2½ pints
1	Egg white	1
1	Large carrot	1
1	Turnip	1
½ cup	Fresh shelled peas	50 g / 2 oz
6	Eggs	6
3 tbsp	Vinegar	3 tbsp
⅔ cup	Port wine	150 ml / ¼ pint

1. Remove the layer of fat from the broth using a skimming spoon.

2. Heat the broth in a saucepan. Beat the egg white in a bowl. Pour it in a trickle into the hot (but not boiling) broth. Stir gently until the egg white has solidified. Pour the whole through a conical strainer into a clean saucepan. You have now made what is referred to in culinary terms as a 'clarification.'

3. Return the consommé to the heat and bring back to a boil.

4. Meanwhile, peel the carrot and turnip and cut into small cubes.

5. Add the carrot to the boiling consommé and leave to cook for 5 minutes, then add the turnip and peas. Simmer for 7-10 minutes.

6. Meanwhile, poach the eggs: heat water in a wide saucepan or frying pan and add the vinegar. When the water is simmering, break one egg into a ladle. Slide the egg down the side of the pan and when it is in the water, quickly fold over the white around the yolk. Cook until the egg white has just set. Remove the egg with a slotted spoon and drain on paper towels. Poach the remaining eggs in the same way.

7. Trim the poached eggs to neaten the edges. Place an egg in each of 6 warmed soup plates.

8. Put the port into a soup tureen and strain the consommé into the tureen. Ladle the consommé over the poached eggs.

Potage Saint-Germain
Cream of Split Pea Soup

⏱ 00:10   01:15

American	Ingredients	Metric/Imperial
5	Leeks	5
1	Celery stalk	1
3	Onions	3
¼ cup	Butter	50 g / 2 oz
2 cups	Split green peas	500 g / 1 lb
2 quarts	Water	2 l / 3½ pints
1 cup	Crème fraîche	250 ml / 8 fl oz
	Salt and pepper	
	Croûtons for serving	

1. Trim the leeks and celery. Peel the onions. Chop all the vegetables roughly. Melt the butter in a large saucepan and add the leeks, onions and celery. Cook over a low heat until golden brown.
2. Add the split peas and water. Bring to a boil and leave to cook for 1 hour.
3. Purée the soup in a blender or food processor until smooth. Return to the saucepan.
4. Add the crème fraîche. Bring to a boil and simmer for 15 minutes. Add salt and pepper to taste. Serve hot, sprinkled with croûtons.

Potage printanier
Spring Vegetable Soup

⏱ 00:25   01:00

American	Ingredients	Metric/Imperial
2	Turnips	2
1	Carrot	1
2	Potatoes	2
2	Leeks, white part only	2
1	Celery stalk	1
1 quart	Chicken broth	1 l / 1¾ pints
1	Cucumber	1
½ lb	Sorrel or spinach	250 g / 8 oz
3 tbsp	Butter	40 g / 1½ oz
	Salt and pepper	
1	Egg yolk	1
¼ cup	Crème fraîche	4 tbsp
	Chopped fresh parsley	

1. Peel and chop the turnips, carrot and potatoes. Trim and chop the leeks and celery.
2. Pour the chicken broth into a saucepan and bring to a boil, then add the prepared vegetables. Cook for 30 minutes.
3. Meanwhile, peel the cucumber, remove the seeds and cut into cubes. Set aside.
4. Clean and chop the sorrel. Melt the butter in a saucepan, add the sorrel and cook over a low heat until wilted.
5. Purée the soup in a blender or food processor until smooth and return to the pan. Place over a gentle heat and add the

sorrel and salt and pepper to taste. When the soup boils, stir in the cucumber and leave to cook over a low heat for 8 minutes.
6. Mix the egg yolk and crème fraîche with a ladle of soup in a small bowl. Add the mixture to the remainder of the soup in the pan and cook, stirring, until thickened. Do not boil.
7. Serve hot, sprinkled with chopped parsley.

Soupe à l'oignon
Onion Soup

⏱ 00:20   00:30

American	Ingredients	Metric/Imperial
¾ lb	Onions	350 g / 12 oz
¼ cup	Butter	50 g / 2 oz
1 tbsp	Flour	1 tbsp
1½ quarts	Beef broth	1.5 l / 2½ pints
	Salt and pepper	
¼ cup	Crème fraîche	4 tbsp
6	Slices of bread	6
1¼ cups	Grated emmental or gruyère cheese	150 g / 5 oz

1. Peel the onions and cut into fine strips. Heat the butter in a saucepan, add the onions and cook very gently until very soft and almost melted. Do not allow to burn.
2. When the onions are light brown, sprinkle with the flour and leave to cook for 2-3 minutes, stirring continuously, until the flour turns light brown.
3. Add the broth, stirring to avoid lumps. Add salt and pepper to taste and leave to cook for 30 minutes over a low heat.
4. Preheat the oven to 475°F / 240°C / Gas Mark 9.
5. Add the crème fraîche to the soup and pour into an ovenproof serving dish. Place the bread slices on the soup and sprinkle with the cheese.
6. Place in the oven and bake until the cheese has browned.

Soupe au cantal
Cheese and Potato Soup

⏱ 00:10   00:35

American	Ingredients	Metric/Imperial
8	Potatoes	8
	Salt and pepper	
2 quarts	Milk	2 l / 3½ pints
2	Garlic cloves	2
2 cups	Grated cantal	250 g / 8 oz
6 tbsp	Crème fraîche	6 tbsp

1. Peel the potatoes and cut into small cubes.
2. Add salt and pepper to the milk and bring to a boil in a large saucepan. Add the potato cubes and leave to cook over a very gentle heat for 25 minutes.
3. Rub a soup tureen with the halved garlic cloves and discard the garlic. Scatter the cheese on the bottom. Pour the soup into the tureen, add the crème fraîche and stir well to mix.

Soupe au pistou

Vegetable Soup with Basil Paste

▱▱▷ 00:30   01:00 to 01:30 ▭

American	Ingredients	Metric/Imperial
1½ lb	Fresh broad beans	750 g / 1½ lb
3	Potatoes	3
2	Carrots	2
¾ lb	Green beans	350 g / 12 oz
¾ lb	Lightly salted lean bacon	350 g / 12 oz
3 quarts	Water	3 l / 5 pints
¼ lb	Noodles	125 g / 4 oz
2	Garlic cloves	2
15	Large fresh basil leaves	15
2	Tomatoes	2
1 cup	Grated gruyère cheese	125 g / 4 oz
5 tbsp	Olive oil	5 tbsp

1. Shell the broad beans. Peel the potatoes and carrots. Trim the green beans. Dice the potatoes, carrots and green beans.
2. Place the bacon in a saucepan with the water. Bring to a boil, then add the broad beans and carrots. Cover and leave to cook for 45 minutes.
3. Add the green beans and potatoes. Leave to cook for a further 30 minutes.
4. Add the noodles and leave to cook uncovered for 10 minutes.
5. Meanwhile, peel the garlic and place in a mortar with the basil. Crush to a paste with a pestle.
6. Peel the tomatoes (first plunging them in boiling water for 10 seconds) and remove the seeds. Add to the mortar and continue working with the pestle, adding the cheese and olive oil alternately, to make a paste.
7. Pour the paste into a soup tureen and gradually stir in the boiling soup. Leave to infuse for 5 minutes before serving.

Cook's tip: the basil paste can also be served as a delicious sauce for fresh pasta.

Soupe Parmentière

Thick Potato Soup

▱▱▷ 00:10   00:15 ▭

American	Ingredients	Metric/Imperial
6	Potatoes	6
1½ quarts	Water	1.5 l / 2½ pints
	Salt and pepper	
1 cup	Crème fraîche	250 ml / 8 fl oz
2 cups	Grated gruyère cheese	250 g / 8 oz

1. Peel and grate the potatoes.
2. Pour the water into a saucepan, add a pinch of salt and bring to a boil. Add the grated potatoes and leave to cook over a gentle heat for 15 minutes.
3. In a soup tureen, mix together the crème fraîche and grated gruyère. Pour in the soup and stir well. Add pepper to taste.

Mussel soup

Soupe de moules

Mussel Soup

▱▱▷ 00:25   00:45 ▭

American	Ingredients	Metric/Imperial
1	Fish head	1
	Few fish bones	
4	Onions	4
1	Bouquet garni	1
2 quarts	Water	2 l / 3½ pints
2	Carrots	2
2	Shallots	2
1 oz	Celeriac	25 g / 1 oz
2 tbsp	Olive oil	2 tbsp
3	Tomatoes	3
1¼ cups	Dry white wine	300 ml / ½ pint
	Saffron powder	
3 quarts	Fresh mussels	3 l / 5 pints
1 cup	Light [single] cream	250 ml / 8 fl oz
1½ cups	Grated edam cheese	175 g / 6 oz

1. Place the fish head, bones, 2 peeled onions and bouquet garni in a saucepan. Add the water and bring to a boil. Simmer for 20 minutes. Strain this stock.
2. Peel and dice the remaining onions, the carrots, shallots and celeriac. Heat the olive oil in a clean saucepan, add the vegetables and cook gently until softened.
3. Peel the tomatoes (first plunging them in boiling water for 10 seconds), then remove the seeds and chop the flesh. Add the tomatoes to the pan with half the wine, a pinch of saffron and the strained fish stock. Leave to cook for 20 minutes.
4. Scrub the mussels under running water. Place them in a saucepan with the remaining wine and cook until they open (discard any that remain closed). Remove the mussels from their shells and strain the liquor.
5. Add the strained cooking liquor, the mussels and cream to the soup and stir well.
6. Serve hot with the cheese.

Soupe de crabes
Crab Soup

American	Ingredients	Metric/Imperial
2	Carrots	2
2	Leeks	2
1	Celery stalk	1
3	Onions	3
4	Cloves	4
1	Garlic clove	1
3	Tomatoes	3
¼ cup	Olive oil	4 tbsp
2 lb	Small hard-shell crabs, cooked	1 kg / 2 lb
2 quarts	Water	2 l / 3½ pints
1	Fresh thyme sprig	1
1	Bay leaf	1
1	Fresh fennel sprig	1
2 - 3	Fresh parsley sprigs	2 - 3
	Saffron powder	
	Salt and pepper	
½ lb	Vermicelli	250 g / 8 oz

1. Peel and chop the carrots. Trim and chop the leeks and celery. Peel and thinly slice 2 onions. Stud the third peeled onion with the cloves. Peel and crush the garlic. Chop the tomatoes.
2. Heat the oil in a large saucepan. Add the carrots, leeks, celery, sliced onions and garlic. Cook until softened, then add the clove-studded onion, crabs, tomatoes, water, herbs, a pinch of saffron, and salt and pepper to taste. Simmer over a low heat for 45 minutes (the longer the soup cooks, the more accentuated will be its taste of crab).
3. Remove the crabs from the saucepan and set aside. Strain the soup and return it to the pan. Bring back to a boil, then add the vermicelli and simmer for 10 minutes or until just tender.
4. Meanwhile, crack open the crabs and remove the edible meaty parts.
5. Add the crabmeat to the soup. Taste and adjust the seasoning, and serve hot with croûtons.

Soupe aux poireaux
Leek Soup

American	Ingredients	Metric/Imperial
4	Large leeks	4
6	Potatoes	6
3 cups	Water	750 ml / 1 ¼ pints
1 quart	Milk	1 l / 1¾ pints
	Salt and pepper	
¼ cup	Butter	50 g / 2 oz

1. Clean the leeks, remove the roots and the green part of the leaves, and quarter the whites. Clean them under cold water, separating the leaves, then drain and cut into thin shreds crosswise. Peel the potatoes and cut into cubes.
2. Place the leeks and potatoes in a large saucepan together

with the water and milk. Add salt and pepper to taste and bring to a boil. Cover and simmer gently for 1 hour.
3. Purée the soup in a blender or food processor until smooth.
4. Put the butter in a soup tureen and pour the soup over it. Stir and serve very hot.

Chilled leek and potato soup

Soupe aux pois cassés
Split Pea Soup

American	Ingredients	Metric/Imperial
2 quarts	Water	2 l / 3½ pints
1 cup	Split peas	250 g / 8 oz
½	Pig's foot [trotter]	½
1	Celery stalk	1
1	Onion	1
1	Bouquet garni	1
	Salt and pepper	
¼ cup	Crème fraîche	4 tbsp
	Croûtons for serving	

1. Pour the cold water into a saucepan. Add the split peas, pig's foot, celery, peeled onion, bouquet garni and salt and pepper to taste. Bring to a boil and leave to cook for 1 hour 10 minutes.

2. Remove the pig's foot and put to one side. Remove and discard the onion and bouquet garni. Purée the soup in a blender or food processor until smooth and return it to the pan. If the soup is too thick, add a little water. Reheat the soup.
3. Cut the pig's foot into small pieces.
4. Add the crème fraîche to the soup and stir to mix. Serve hot with the pig's foot and croûtons.

Soupe au potiron
Pumpkin Soup

	00:10		00:50

American	Ingredients	Metric/Imperial
4 lb	Pumpkin	2 kg / 4 lb
⅔ cup	Water	150 ml / ¼ pint
1 quart	Milk	1 l / 1¾ pints
2 tbsp	Sugar	2 tbsp
	Salt	
2 tbsp	Butter	25 g / 1 oz
1 tbsp	Chopped fresh parsley	1 tbsp

1. Peel the pumpkin, remove the seeds and cut into cubes. Place in a saucepan, add the water and cook over a moderate heat for about 20 minutes. At the end of the cooking time, if there is too much liquid, evaporate it quickly over a brisk heat.
2. Purée the pumpkin in a blender or food processor until smooth.
3. Bring the milk to a boil in the saucepan. Add the pumpkin, sugar and a pinch of salt. Cook over a low heat for 25 minutes, stirring occasionally.
4. Stir in the butter and parsley and serve hot.

Vichyssoise
Chilled Leek and Potato Soup

	00:30 plus chilling		00:30

American	Ingredients	Metric/Imperial
4	Leeks, white part only	4
4	Onions	4
3 tbsp	Butter	40 g / 1½ oz
5	Potatoes	5
1½ quarts	Chicken stock	1.5 l / 2½ pints
⅔ cup	Crème fraîche	150 ml / ¼ pint
	Salt and pepper	

1. Clean the leeks and chop finely. Peel the onions and cut into thin strips. Melt the butter in a saucepan, add the leeks and onions and cook for about 15 minutes over a gentle heat. Do not allow the vegetables to brown.
2. Peel and thinly slice the potatoes. Add to the pan and cook for 3-4 minutes, stirring continuously.
3. Bring the chicken stock to a boil. Add the vegetables and leave to cook for about 15 minutes or until the potatoes are tender.
4. Purée the soup in a blender or food processor until smooth,

then strain through a fine sieve. Leave to cool.
5. Add the crème fraîche and whisk vigorously, then add salt and pepper to taste. Chill until ready to serve.

Pumpkin soup

Velouté à la tomate
Tomato Cream Soup

	00:15		00:30

American	Ingredients	Metric/Imperial
2	Onions	2
2 tbsp	Butter	25 g / 1 oz
2 lb	Tomatoes	1 kg / 2 lb
1	Garlic clove	1
1	Fresh thyme sprig	1
1 quart	Water	1 l / 1¾ pints
3 tbsp	Cornstarch [cornflour]	3 tbsp
1 tsp	Sugar	1 tsp
¼ cup	Thick crème fraîche	4 tbsp
	Salt and pepper	
1	Egg yolk	1
2 tbsp	Chopped fresh parsley	2 tbsp
	Croûtons for serving	

1. Peel and thinly slice the onions. Melt half of the butter in a saucepan over a gentle heat and add the onions. Cook until softened.
2. Meanwhile, peel the tomatoes (first plunging them in boiling water for 10 seconds) and cut into small pieces. Add to the onions with the remaining butter and cook until the tomatoes are pulpy.
3. Add the peeled garlic clove, thyme and water. Bring to a boil and leave to cook for 25 minutes.
4. Remove and discard the thyme, then purée the soup in a blender until smooth. Return to the saucepan.
5. Mix the cornstarch with a little cold water and the sugar. Add to the soup and cook, stirring, until thickened. Remove from the heat and stir in the crème fraîche and salt and pepper to taste.
6. Mix the egg yolk and chopped parsley in a soup tureen. Gradually add the soup, stirring well. Serve with croûtons.

Onion soup (see page 32)

First Courses

Cold hors d'oeuvres

Preparing raw vegetables

Asparagus
Hold the asparagus spear with its tip toward you. Using a swivel-bladed vegetable peeler and working towards the base of the spear, carefully peel away the outer skin.

Cabbage
With a large pointed knife, slice the cabbage in two and cut away the woody core of each half.

Endive [chicory] heart
Insert a small sharp knife at the base of the head to a depth of ¾ in / 2 cm, and cut out the cone formed by the center leaves.

Fennel and celery
Remove the leafy green part of the celery stalk or fennel bulb, then pull off any tough fibers or strings with a paring knife.

Garlic clove
Place the clove under the flat surface of a kitchen knife and press down firmly. This will flatten the garlic and burst the outer skin, which will then come away easily. Remove the outer skin and crush the garlic in a garlic press, or using a mortar and pestle.

Globe artichoke hearts
Cut off the stalk with a stainless steel knife. Pull the thick outside leaves away. Remove the choke with a grapefruit knife or a teaspoon and rub the cut surface of the heart with a slice of lemon to prevent discoloration.

Green beans
Make a cut across one end of the bean without severing it completely. Catching the string with the blade of your knife, pull it away along the bean's length. Repeat at the other end to remove the string from the other side.

Leeks
Remove any roots, cut off the damaged ends of the green leaves and slice the leek lengthwise into quarters. Holding the leaves open, wash each section thoroughly under cold running water.

Pumpkin
Cut the pumpkin into quarters and peel away its skin with a small sharp knife. Remove and discard the seeds and the coarse stringy material inside.

Shallots
Cut a thin slice from each end of the shallot, then remove and discard the papery skin and the first fleshy layer.

Spinach and sorrel leaves
Fold the leaf in two along the central stalk. Hold the folded leaf in one hand, and with the other tear the stalk away working from the base to the tip.

Sweet pepper [capsicum]
Cut the pepper in half lengthwise and remove the core, seeds and whitish membrane.

Céleri rémoulade

Celeriac in Mayonnaise

00:20 plus marinating   00:00

American	Ingredients	Metric/Imperial
1 (1 lb)	Head of celeriac	1 (500 g / 1 lb)
1	Lemon	1
	Salt and pepper	
1	Egg yolk	1
2 tbsp	Strong prepared mustard	2 tbsp
1 tbsp	Vinegar	1 tbsp
1 cup	Oil	250 ml / 8 fl oz
2 tbsp	Chopped fresh parsley	2 tbsp

1. Peel the celeriac and sprinkle it with the juice of half the lemon so that it does not discolor. Grate it coarsely.
2. Place the celeriac in a bowl and sprinkle with the remaining lemon juice in which you have dissolved ½ teaspoon of salt. Leave to blanch for 30 minutes to 1 hour, stirring occasionally.
3. Meanwhile, place the egg yolk in a bowl and add the mustard, vinegar, and salt and pepper to taste. Mix well. Gradually add the oil, whisking vigorously. The mayonnaise must be quite thick and adhere to the whisk. If it is too thick, add a little more vinegar.
4. Drain the celeriac, squeezing it in your hand, and place in a salad bowl. Add the mayonnaise gradually, stirring to combine the ingredients thoroughly.
5. Leave to stand for 30 minutes before serving, sprinkled with chopped parsley.

Chou rouge en salade

Red Cabbage Salad

00:20 plus soaking   00:03

American	Ingredients	Metric/Imperial
1	Head of red cabbage	1
	Salt and pepper	
1¼ cups	Wine vinegar	300 ml / ½ pint
6	Eggs	6
1 cup	Crème fraîche	250 ml / 8 fl oz
1	Lemon	1
1 tbsp	Chopped fresh chervil or parsley	1 tbsp
1 tbsp	Chopped fresh chives	1 tbsp
1 tbsp	Chopped fresh fennel	1 tbsp

1. Remove the coarse and discolored outer leaves from the cabbage. Quarter the cabbage and remove the core. Cut the cabbage into thin strips (julienne).
2. Boil a large quantity of salted water in a saucepan. Add the cabbage. Return to a boil and continue boiling for 2 minutes. Drain the cabbage in a colander, run it under cold water and drain again. Put the cabbage into a mixing bowl and pour over the wine vinegar. Add salt and pepper to taste and leave to marinate for 1 hour, stirring frequently.
3. Hard-cook the eggs for 10 minutes in boiling water. Drain. Remove the shells and crush the eggs with a fork.
4. Mix the eggs with the crème fraîche, the juice of the lemon, the chervil, chives and fennel. Add salt and pepper to taste.
5. Drain the cabbage, discarding the marinade, and place in a salad bowl. Pour the cream sauce over and stir carefully.

Asperges sauce mousseline

Asparagus with Mousseline Sauce

American	Ingredients	Metric/Imperial
3 lb	Asparagus	1.5 kg / 3 lb
⅔ cup	Vinegar	150 ml / ¼ pint
6	Black peppercorns	6
	Salt	
2	Egg yolks	2
6 tbsp	Butter	75 g / 3 oz
⅔ cup	Heavy [double] cream	150 ml / ¼ pint

1. Trim the woody ends from the asparagus, then scrape the stalks. Tie the asparagus spears in 4 equal bunches, and set aside.
2. Place the vinegar and peppercorns in a small saucepan and bring to a boil. Boil until reduced to 1 tablespoon.
3. Meanwhile, put salted water on to boil in a large saucepan. When the water is boiling, add the bunches of asparagus. As soon as boiling resumes, reduce the heat to keep the water simmering. Leave to cook for 5-20 minutes (depending on the age and size of the asparagus) or until tender.
4. When the asparagus is cooked, remove it from the water and drain well. Arrange on a folded napkin on a warmed serving dish and keep hot.
5. Strain the peppercorns from the reduced vinegar. Remove the pan from the heat and add the egg yolks, whisking vigorously. Gradually incorporate the butter, cut into small pieces, continuing to whisk until thickened. Add salt to taste.
6. Whip the cream until thick and fold into the sauce.
7. Serve the mousseline sauce in a sauceboat with the asparagus.

Artichauts vinaigrette

Artichokes Vinaigrette

00:10   00:25 to 00:30

American	Ingredients	Metric/Imperial
6	Globe artichokes	6
	Salt and pepper	
1 tbsp	Vinegar	1 tbsp
1 tbsp	Prepared mustard, preferably Dijon	1 tbsp
3 tbsp	Oil	3 tbsp
1	Fresh parsley sprig	1

1. Break off the stalks of the artichokes, pulling them to remove the strings also. Remove any damaged or discolored leaves.
2. Bring a large saucepan of salted water to a boil. Add the artichokes and leave to cook for about 30 minutes. To test if they are done, pull out one of the large leaves near the base. If it comes out easily, the artichokes are ready.
3. Remove the artichokes from the water, and drain upside-down in a colander.
4. For the dressing, dissolve a pinch of salt in the vinegar. Stir in the mustard. Season with pepper to taste. Add the oil and chopped parsley and mix thoroughly.
5. Serve the vinaigrette with the warm or cold artichokes.

Caviar d'aubergines

Eggplant [Aubergine] Caviar

00:20   plus chilling   00:35

American	Ingredients	Metric/Imperial
2	Eggplant [aubergines]	2
1	Large, very firm tomato	1
1	Shallot	1
1	Garlic clove (optional)	1
	Salt and pepper	
⅔ cup	Olive oil	150 ml / ¼ pint
1 tbsp	Chopped fresh dill or parsley	1 tbsp

1. Preheat the oven to 350°F / 180°C / Gas Mark 4.
2. Place the whole eggplant in the oven and bake until the skin becomes cracked and the eggplant are soft to the touch. Remove them from the oven and peel.
3. Peel the tomato (first plunging it in boiling water for 10 seconds), remove the seeds and cut into pieces.
4. Mince the eggplant and tomato purée in a blender or food processor until smooth.
5. Peel the shallot and garlic. Crush them in a mortar or blend to a purée.
6. Put all the puréed ingredients into a salad bowl and add salt and pepper to taste. Stir with a wooden spoon, gradually adding the olive oil in a trickle as for mayonnaise. You should obtain a thick paste. Chill lightly.
7. Add the chopped dill or parsley just before serving.

Cook's tip: choose firm glossy eggplant, as dull soft ones will be stale.

Aspics de foies de volaille

Chicken Livers in Aspic

00:20   plus chilling   00:08

American	Ingredients	Metric/Imperial
1	Shallot	1
3 tbsp	Butter	40 g / 1½ oz
1 lb	Chicken livers	500 g / 1 lb
	Salt and pepper	
	Dried thyme	
1 tbsp	Cognac	1 tbsp
1 quart	Liquid aspic	1 l / 1¾ pints
	Lettuce or other salad greens	
2 - 3	Tomatoes	2 - 3

1. Peel the shallot and chop finely. Melt the butter in a saucepan over a moderate heat, add the shallot and cook until softened.
2. Halve the livers and add to the pan. Cook over a brisk heat until they are firm and browned but still pink inside.
3. Add salt and pepper to taste. Add a pinch of thyme and the cognac. Remove from the heat and allow to cool completely.
4. Divide the livers between six individual molds and cover with warm aspic. Chill for at least 6 hours or until set.
5. Unmold the livers in aspic onto serving dishes garnished with salad greens and tomato quarters.

Assiette de crudités

Raw Vegetable Platter

| | 00:40 to 00:50 plus infusing | 00:10 |

American	Ingredients	Metric/Imperial
2 tbsp	Cider vinegar	2 tbsp
½ cup	Oil	125 ml / 4 fl oz
2	Canned anchovy fillets	2
1 tbsp	Chopped fresh chives	1 tbsp
1 tbsp	Chopped fresh tarragon	1 tbsp
1	Small cauliflower	1
1	Head of red cabbage	1
6	Carrots	6
1	Head of celery	1
2	Cooked beets [beetroot]	2
1	Bunch of radishes	1
¾ lb	Mushrooms	350 g / 12 oz
1	Lemon	1
6	Eggs	6
	Salt and pepper	

1. About 2 hours before serving, prepare the vinaigrette. Mix the cider vinegar and oil in a bowl. Pound the anchovy fillets to a cream in a mortar with a pestle. Add to the oil and vinegar with the chives and tarragon. Leave to infuse for 2 hours, stirring occasionally. Do not add salt and pepper until you are ready to serve.
2. Break the cauliflower into florets. Core the red cabbage, and cut it into thin strips. Peel the carrots and grate them finely. Trim the celery and cut into small cubes. Peel the beets and dice them. Trim the radishes, leaving some of the leaves on them. Thinly slice the mushrooms, then sprinkle them with the juice of the lemon to keep them white.
3. Arrange all the vegetables on a large serving dish.
4. Hard-cook the eggs for 10 minutes in boiling water. Run them under cold water to cool, and remove the shells.
5. Cut the pointed tip off each egg. Remove the yolk from the cut-off pieces and crush it finely with a fork. Add the crushed yolk to the vinaigrette and season with salt and pepper. Decorate the serving dish with the rest of the eggs.
6. Serve the vegetables accompanied by the vinaigrette in a sauceboat.

Raw vegetable platter

Cervelle de canut

Herb-flavored Cream Cheese

| | 00:15 plus chilling | 00:00 |

American	Ingredients	Metric/Imperial
2	Shallots	2
1 cup	Crème fraîche	250 ml / 8 fl oz
1 lb (2 cups)	Firm cream cheese	500 g / 1 lb
2 tsp	Chopped fresh parsley	2 tsp
1 tbsp	Chopped fresh chives	1 tbsp
3 tbsp	Chopped fresh chervil	3 tbsp
	Salt and pepper	
3 tbsp	Olive oil	3 tbsp
1 tsp	Vinegar	1 tsp

1. Peel and finely chop the shallots.
2. Whisk together the crème fraîche, cream cheese, chopped herbs and shallots. Add salt and pepper to taste. Continuing to stir, incorporate the olive oil and vinegar.
3. Line a round bowl with cheesecloth or muslin. Pour in the cheese mixture, heaping it up well. Fold over the cheesecloth or muslin. Chill for 4 hours.
4. To serve, unwrap the cheese and unmold it onto a serving dish. Serve with raw vegetables or on its own before dessert. The French name for this cheese, which originated in Lyons, means 'silk weaver's brain.'

Citrons farcis au thon

Lemons Stuffed with Tuna

| | 00:30 plus chilling | 00:00 |

American	Ingredients	Metric/Imperial
6	Large, thick-skinned lemons	6
1 (7 oz)	Can of tuna	1 (200 g / 7 oz)
1	Egg yolk	1
1 tsp	Prepared mustard	1 tsp
1 cup	Oil	250 ml / 8 fl oz
1 tbsp	Vinegar	1 tbsp
	Salt and pepper	
	Tabasco sauce (optional)	
6	Black olives	6

1. Cut off the pointed ends of the lemons and scrape out the pulp using a small spoon. Do not pierce the lemon skins. Set aside the lemon shells and cut-off ends.
2. Cut the lemon pulp into cubes and place these in a mixing bowl. Drain and flake the tuna and add to the diced lemon pulp.
3. Place the egg yolk in another bowl with the mustard and add the oil gradually in a trickle, blending with a whisk. When the mayonnaise is quite firm, incorporate the vinegar and season with salt, pepper and a few drops of tabasco sauce.
4. Add the mayonnaise to the tuna mixture and stir well. Stuff the lemon shells with the tuna mayonnaise. Garnish with olives and cover with the cut-off ends of the lemons. Chill until ready to serve.

Coeurs d'artichaut à la provençale
Artichoke Hearts Provençal Style

	00:15		01:00

American	Ingredients	Metric/Imperial
36	Small purple globe artichokes	36
1	Lemon	1
4	Tomatoes	4
12	Pearl [button] onions	12
½ lb	Lightly salted bacon	250 g / 8 oz
6 tbsp	Olive oil	6 tbsp
1 tsp	Chopped fresh thyme	1 tsp
2	Bay leaves	2
	Salt and pepper	
1 tbsp	Chopped fresh basil	1 tbsp

1. Break off the artichoke stalks. Cut away the small outside leaves. Sprinkle the juice of half the lemon over the outside of the artichoke hearts so that they do not turn black. Continue cutting away all the side leaves, leaving only the center ones. Cut off the center leaves at their base. Completely remove the hairy choke, leaving the heart clean. Sprinkle with the remaining lemon juice.
2. Quarter and core the tomatoes. Peel the onions. Dice the bacon.
3. Place the bacon in a heavy saucepan and heat until it renders its fat. Drain the bacon on paper towels. Pour off the fat from the pan.
4. Heat the olive oil in a saucepan. Add the artichoke hearts, thyme and bay leaves cut into thin strips and cook until the artichoke hearts are lightly browned. Add the onions and brown lightly, turning them to cook evenly.
5. Return the bacon to the pan with the tomatoes, and salt and pepper to taste. Cover and leave to cook over a low heat for about 1 hour.
6. About 15 minutes before cooking is finished, add the basil. Serve hot or cold.

Concombres à la crème
Cucumbers in Cream

	00:20 plus draining and chilling		00:00

American	Ingredients	Metric/Imperial
2	Cucumbers	2
	Salt and pepper	
10	Fresh tarragon sprigs	10
2	Lemons	2
1 cup	Crème fraîche	250 ml / 8 fl oz

1. Wipe the cucumbers and cut into thin slices. Place the slices in a colander and sprinkle with salt. Stir and leave to drain for 30 minutes.
2. Rinse the cucumber slices in cold water and drain again. Pat the slices dry with paper towels.
3. Chop the leaves from the tarragon sprigs and put in a salad bowl with the juice from the 2 lemons. Add pepper to taste. Gradually stir in the crème fraîche.
4. Add the cucumber slices and fold together gently. Chill well.
5. Serve very cold, garnished with a few leaves of tarragon.

Shrimp and rice vinaigrette

Coquilles aux crevettes
Shrimp [Prawns] and Rice Vinaigrette

	00:20 plus marinating		00:18

American	Ingredients	Metric/Imperial
1 ½ cups	Water	350 ml / 12 fl oz
	Salt and pepper	
1 cup	Long grain rice	200 g / 7 oz
2	Red apples	2
2	Lemons	2
6	Celery stalks	6
1	Green pepper	1
2	Tomatoes	2
¾ cup	Peeled cooked shrimp [prawns]	150 g / 5 oz
1 tbsp	Vinegar	1 tbsp
1 tsp	Prepared mustard	1 tsp
3 tbsp	Oil	3 tbsp
1 tbsp	Chopped fresh parsley	1 tbsp
	Cooked shrimp [prawns] in shell for garnish	

1. Bring the water to a boil with salt to taste. Add the rice and simmer for 15-18 minutes or until tender. Drain in a colander and dry the rice by spreading it out on a cloth.
2. Dice the apples and sprinkle with the juice of the lemons so that they do not discolor.
3. Trim the celery. Core and seed the green pepper. Peel the tomatoes (first plunging them in boiling water for 10 seconds). Dice all these vegetables.
4. Put the rice, apples, celery, tomatoes and green pepper into a mixing bowl and add the shrimp.
5. Dissolve a pinch of salt in the vinegar. Stir in the mustard. Add the oil, parsley and pepper to taste.
6. Add this dressing to the shrimp mixture and fold together. Cover and leave to marinate for 30 minutes.
7. To serve, divide the mixture between 6 scallop shells or other individual dishes and garnish with a few shrimp in shell.

Trois viandes en salade

Three Meats Salad

	00:20 plus chilling	00:00

American	Ingredients	Metric/Imperial
4	Boiled potatoes	4
4	Cooked carrots	4
1	Medium-size onion	1
1 cup	Diced cooked chicken meat	250 g / 8 oz
¾ cup	Diced cooked tongue	150 g / 5 oz
¾ cup	Diced garlic sausage	150 g / 5 oz
½ lb	Cooked green beans	250 g / 8 oz
3 cups	Cooked peas	350 g / 12 oz
1 cup	Mayonnaise	250 ml / 8 fl oz
1	Hard-cooked egg	1

1. Peel the potatoes and carrots and dice them. Peel the onion and cut into rings. Place these ingredients in a salad bowl and add the chicken, tongue, sausage, beans and peas.
2. Add the mayonnaise and incorporate into the salad. Garnish with slices of hard-cooked egg. Chill for 20 minutes before serving.

Tomatoes fourrées au thon

Tomatoes Stuffed with Tuna

	00:30 plus chilling	00:10

American	Ingredients	Metric/Imperial
6	Medium-size tomatoes	6
	Salt and pepper	
1 lb	Fresh peas in their shells	500 g / 1 lb
1 (3½ oz)	Can of tuna in brine	1 (75 g / 3 oz)
7	Garlic cloves	7
1 cup	Olive oil	250 ml / 8 fl oz
2	Egg yolks	2
2½ - 3 tbsp	Lemon juice	2½ - 3 tbsp
1 tbsp	Chopped fresh parsley	1 tbsp

1. Wipe the tomatoes. Cut off the tops and put to one side. Empty out the insides using a small spoon. Remove and discard the seeds from the flesh which you have taken out. Chop the flesh, add salt and pepper to taste and put to one side.
2. Shell the peas. Toss them into a saucepan of boiling salted water, bring back to a boil, and leave to cook for 2 minutes. Drain in a colander and run under cold water to chill.
3. Drain the tuna in a strainer and flake it.
4. Peel and crush the garlic in a mortar. Add 1-2 tablespoons of the olive oil and reduce to a paste. Add the egg yolks and mix well. Tip into a mixing bowl and add the rest of the oil in a trickle, whisking constantly until thickened to a mayonnaise. Add the lemon juice, salt and pepper to taste and mix well.
5. Mix the tuna, peas and tomato flesh. Fold in the garlic mayonnaise.
6. Fill the tomatoes with the tuna mixture and sprinkle each with chopped parsley. Replace the tops and serve the tomatoes lightly chilled.

Cook's tip: you can replace the tuna with flaked poached white fish.

Tapenade

Olive, Anchovy and Caper Spread

	00:25	00:00

American	Ingredients	Metric/Imperial
1½ cups	Large black olives	250 g / 8 oz
4 oz	Canned anchovy fillets	125 g / 4 oz
1½ tbsp	Capers	1½ tbsp
1¼ cups	Olive oil	300 ml / ½ pint
1	Lemon	1
	Salt and pepper	

1. Pit [stone] the olives, then put them into a food processor or blender with the anchovies and capers. Blend to a smooth cream.
2. Pour and scrape the mixture into a bowl. Gradually beat in the olive oil as if making mayonnaise, adding a few drops of lemon juice from time to time. Season with salt and pepper to taste.
3. Cover and keep in a cool place, in a tight-sealed container, until ready to serve.
4. Serve as a dip, or spread on small savory crackers [biscuits] or slices of french bread and sprinkle with a few more drops of lemon juice.

Poivrons grillés en salade

Broiled [Grilled] Pepper Salad

	00:30 plus marinating	00:15

American	Ingredients	Metric/Imperial
2 lb	Sweet red peppers	1 kg / 2 lb
1	Garlic clove	1
1¼ cups	Olive oil	300 ml / ½ pint
	Salt and pepper	

1. Preheat the broiler [grill].
2. Halve the peppers and place them cut sides down under the broiler. Cook until the skins are charred and blistered.
3. Wrap the peppers in paper and allow to cool for 10 minutes. Remove them from the paper and peel off the skins.
4. Remove the core and seeds from the peppers and cut them into strips. Peel and finely chop the garlic and sprinkle over the peppers. Cover with oil. Add salt and pepper to taste. Leave to marinate for at least 24 hours.
5. Serve as an hors d'oeuvre or condiment.

Vegetables make a colorful and appetizing hors d'oeuvre

Salads

The sauce or dressing which binds the ingredients of a salad usually has an oil and vinegar base. According to a Roman saying, four people are needed to make a good salad dressing: a miser to pour the vinegar, a squanderer to add the oil, a wise man for the salt and a madman to stir it.

Salade alsacienne

Cheese and Egg Salad

■━━▷ 00:30   00:10 🍲

American	Ingredients	Metric/Imperial
¾ lb	Emmental cheese	350 g / 12 oz
5	Celery stalks	5
½ lb	Fribourg or other cheese	250 g / 8 oz
1 cup	Walnuts (optional)	125 g / 4 oz
2 tsp	Prepared mustard	2 tsp
2½ - 3 tbsp	Cider vinegar	2½ - 3 tbsp
⅔ cup	Crème fraîche	150 ml / ¼ pint
	Salt and pepper	
3	Eggs	3
1	Bunch of radishes	1

1. Cut the emmental and celery into thin sticks. Dice the fribourg. Put all these ingredients into a salad bowl and mix.
2. In a mixing bowl, mix the mustard with the cider vinegar. Add the crème fraîche gradually, stirring constantly for the ingredients to blend properly. Add salt and pepper to taste.
3. Hard-cook the eggs for 10 minutes in boiling water. Drain. Remove the shells and cut the eggs in half.
4. Trim and slice the radishes.
5. Put a few spoonfuls of the sauce into the salad bowl and toss well. Garnish with the egg halves and the radishes. Serve the remainder of the sauce separately.

Cheese and egg salad

Salade de boeuf 🍞

Beef Salad

■━━▷ 00:10
plus marinating   00:10 🍲

American	Ingredients	Metric/Imperial
¾ lb	Cooked beef	350 g / 12 oz
2	Eggs	2
2	Shallots	2
	Salt and pepper	
1 tbsp	Vinegar	1 tbsp
1 tbsp	Strong prepared mustard	1 tbsp
3 tbsp	Oil	3 tbsp
1 tbsp	Chopped fresh parsley	1 tbsp

1. Remove the fat from the beef. Cut the meat into large cubes.
2. Hard-cook the eggs for 10 minutes in boiling water. Run them under cold water and remove the shells. Quarter the eggs and set aside.
3. Peel and chop the shallots.
4. Dissolve a pinch of salt in the vinegar. Mix with the mustard. Add the oil, shallots, parsley and pepper to taste. Mix together.
5. Pour the dressing over the meat and leave to marinate for 1 hour.
6. Stir and serve garnished with the egg quarters.

Salade camarguaise 🍞🍞

Tuna, Anchovy and Rice Salad

■━━▷ 00:45   00:20 🍲

American	Ingredients	Metric/Imperial
3 cups	Water	750 ml / 1 ¼ pints
	Salt and pepper	
2 cups	Long-grain rice	400 g / 14 oz
1	Cucumber	1
6	Very firm tomatoes	6
1	Green pepper	1
1	Onion	1
1	Garlic clove	1
1 (2 oz)	Can of anchovies in oil	1 (50 g / 2 oz)
3 tbsp	Capers	3 tbsp
¼ cup	Diced canned pimiento	4 tbsp
¾ cup	Black olives	125 g / 4 oz
2 tbsp	Vinegar	2 tbsp
2 tbsp	Prepared mustard	2 tbsp
1 cup + 3 tbsp	Oil	250 ml / 8 fl oz + 3 tbsp
2 tsp	Chopped fresh parsley	2 tsp
1	Egg yolk	1
	Lettuce leaves	
1 (7½ oz)	Can of tuna in oil	1 (200 g / 7 oz)

1. Place the water and salt to taste in a saucepan and bring to a boil. Add the rice and cover. Leave to cook for 15-20 minutes or until the rice is tender.
2. Drain the rice if necessary. Rinse in cold running water and drain again. Set aside to cool.
3. Wash the cucumber. Cut 10 very thin slices for the garnish,

and cut the rest into small cubes. Wash 4 of the tomatoes and cut into small cubes. Core and seed the green pepper, then dice it. Peel and finely chop the onion. Peel and crush the garlic. Finely chop the drained anchovies.

4. Mix the cucumber and tomato cubes, green pepper, onion, garlic, capers, pimiento, half the olives and anchovies with the rice.

5. Dissolve a pinch of salt in 1 tablespoon of the vinegar. Mix in 1 tablespoon mustard. Add 3 tablespoons of the oil, the chopped parsley and pepper to taste. Mix thoroughly. Pour this dressing over the rice salad, toss and leave to soak for 30 minutes.

6. Put the egg yolk into a bowl and add the remaining mustard, 1 teaspoon of the vinegar, and salt and pepper to taste. Stir vigorously with a whisk. Then add the remaining oil gradually in a thin trickle, stirring vigorously. When all the oil has been added, the mayonnaise should be thick. If it is too thick, thin it out with the remaining vinegar. Add the mayonnaise to the rice salad and toss well.

7. Put the salad into a serving dish lined with lettuce leaves. Garnish with the cucumber slices, the rest of the olives, and a few extra pieces of pimiento. Surround with the remaining tomatoes, cut into quarters, alternating with chunks of drained tuna.

Salade blanche
White Salad

	00:30		00:50
	plus chilling		

American	Ingredients	Metric/Imperial
4	Potatoes	4
2	Apples	2
1	Head of celery	1
1	Fennel bulb	1
2/3 cup	Dry white wine	150 ml / 1/4 pint
1 tbsp	Strong prepared mustard	1 tbsp
1 1/2 tbsp	Vinegar	1 1/2 tbsp
4 1/2 tbsp	Oil	4 1/2 tbsp
3 tbsp	Chopped fresh chives or parsley	3 tbsp
	Salt and pepper	
1/2 cup	Long-grain rice	90 g / 3 1/2 oz
1 quart	Court-bouillon	1 l / 1 3/4 pints
3/4 lb	Cod or other white fish fillet	350 g / 12 oz
1	Head of Romaine [cos] lettuce	1
1 cup	Mayonnaise	250 ml / 8 fl oz
1/2 cup	Walnuts	50 g / 2 oz
1 cup	Black olives	150 g / 5 oz

1. Place the potatoes in a saucepan and cover with cold water. Bring to a boil and cook for about 20 minutes or until tender. Drain and leave until cool enough to handle.

2. Meanwhile, peel, core and dice the apples. Trim and dice the celery. Cut the fennel into thin strips.

3. Peel and dice the potatoes. Place in a mixing bowl together with the apples, celery and fennel. Add the white wine.

4. Combine the mustard, vinegar, oil and chopped herbs. Season to taste with salt and pepper. Add this dressing to the potato mixture. Toss and chill for 1 hour.

5. Meanwhile, cook the rice in boiling salted water for about 15 minutes or until tender. Drain the rice and add to the potato.

6. Bring the court-bouillon to a simmer in a saucepan. Add the cod and poach for 5 minutes. Remove from the heat and allow the fish to cool in the liquid. Drain the fish and flake into small pieces. Add to the potato mixture.

7. Remove any damaged leaves from the lettuce. Wash in several changes of water and drain. Cut the leaves into strips and use them to line the bottom of a salad bowl.

8. Add half the mayonnaise to the fish salad and fold together gently. Pile on top of the lettuce. Garnish with the walnuts and olives. Serve accompanied by the remainder of the mayonnaise.

Salade de carottes
Carrot Salad

	00:20		00:00

American	Ingredients	Metric/Imperial
1 1/2 lb	Carrots	750 g / 1 1/2 lb
	Salt and pepper	
1 tbsp	Vinegar	1 tbsp
1 tbsp	Prepared mustard	1 tbsp
3 tbsp	Oil	3 tbsp
1 tbsp	Chopped fresh chervil or chives	1 tbsp

1. Peel the carrots and grate them.
2. Dissolve a pinch of salt in the vinegar. Mix in the mustard. Add the oil and pepper to taste and mix well.
3. A few minutes before serving, sprinkle the carrots with the dressing and toss well. Sprinkle with the chervil or chives.

Cook's tip: you may replace the vinaigrette dressing with a mixture of crème fraîche (see page 122) and lemon juice.

Salade composée
Mixed Salad

	00:15		00:00

American	Ingredients	Metric/Imperial
1	Head of chicory [curly endive]	1
2	Apples	2
	Lemon juice	
10	Radishes	10
3	Tomatoes	3
1	Head of celery	1
1 cup	Chopped walnuts	125 g / 4 oz
1 tbsp	Prepared mustard with green peppercorns	1 tbsp
3/4 cup	Crème fraîche	175 ml / 6 fl oz
2 tbsp	Cider vinegar	2 tbsp
	Salt and pepper	

1. Rinse and drain the chicory. Cut into crosswise shreds with a pair of scissors. Peel and core the apples. Cut into thin slices, sprinkling them with lemon juice as you go to prevent them from discoloring. Trim and slice the radishes. Dice the tomatoes and celery. Place all these ingredients in a salad bowl and scatter over the walnuts.

2. In a mixing bowl, combine the mustard, crème fraîche, vinegar and salt and pepper to taste. Mix well. Serve with the salad.

Salade de crabes à la languedocienne

Languedoc Crab Salad

	00:20 plus chilling	01:10

American	Ingredients	Metric/Imperial
4	Carrots	4
2	Garlic cloves	2
4	Onions	4
1	Fresh thyme sprig	1
1	Bay leaf	1
2 quarts	Water	2 l / 3 ½ pints
1 ¼ cups + 3 tbsp	Vinegar	300 ml / ½ pint + 3 tbsp
	Salt and pepper	
2 (1 lb)	Crabs	2 (500 g / 1 lb)
2	Eggs	2
1 tsp	Prepared mustard	1 tsp
5 tbsp	Oil	5 tbsp

1. Peel and slice the carrots, garlic and onions. Place in a large saucepan together with the thyme, bay leaf, water, 1¼ cups [300 ml / ½ pint] vinegar, and salt and pepper to taste. Bring to a boil and simmer for 40 minutes.
2. Place the crabs in the simmering court-bouillon. Cook for 15 minutes.
3. Meanwhile, hard-cook the eggs for 10 minutes in boiling water. Drain and cool.
4. When the crabs are cooked, drain them. Detach the claws and legs, remove the flesh and cut into small pieces. Open the shell. Discard all inedible parts, then remove the creamy parts and the flesh and cut into small cubes.
5. Shell the eggs and cut in half. Cut the whites into thin strips and crush the yolks with a fork.
6. In a mixing bowl, mix the creamy parts of the crabs with the egg yolks until smooth. Add salt and pepper to taste, the mustard, the remaining vinegar and the oil, stirring well. Add the crabmeat to this dressing and toss to coat.
7. Place in a salad bowl. Scatter over the strips of egg white and chill for 1 hour before serving.

Salade Carmen

Chicken, Rice and Tarragon Salad

	00:20 plus cooling	00:40

American	Ingredients	Metric/Imperial
3 quarts	Water	3 l / 5 pints
	Salt and pepper	
1 ½ cups	Long-grain rice	300 g / 11 oz
2	Chicken wings	2
2	Sweet red peppers	2
2 ¾ cups	Peas	300 g / 11 oz
1	Sugar cube	1
1 tbsp	Vinegar	1 tbsp
1 tsp	Strong prepared mustard	1 tsp
3 tbsp	Oil	3 tbsp
2 tbsp	Chopped fresh tarragon	2 tbsp

1. Bring the water to a boil and add salt to taste. Add the rice and cook for approximately 15 minutes after boiling has

recommenced. Drain the rice, reserving the cooking water, and rinse in cold water. Leave to cool.
2. Skin the chicken wings, place them in a saucepan and cover with the rice water. Bring to a boil and simmer for about 30 minutes. Drain and leave to cool. Remove the meat from the bones and dice it. Set aside.
3. Preheat the oven to 450°F / 230°C / Gas Mark 8.
4. Place the peppers in the oven and bake until the skins blister. Take them out of the oven, wrap in a damp cloth and set aside for 5 minutes. The skin will then come off without any difficulty. When you have peeled the peppers, remove the core and seeds, and cut into cubes. Set aside.
5. Bring a saucepan of water to a boil and add the peas, sugar and salt to taste. Bring back to a boil and leave to cook for 10 minutes.
6. Meanwhile, dissolve a pinch of salt in the vinegar. Mix in the mustard. Add the oil, chopped tarragon and pepper to taste. Mix.
7. Drain the peas and put them in a salad bowl. Add the rice, chicken and diced peppers. Mix and add the vinaigrette dressing. Toss again. Serve cool.
8. If liked, garnish the salad with anchovy fillets and hard-cooked eggs.

Spinach salad

Salade d'épinards au lard

Spinach Salad with Bacon

	00:20	00:05

American	Ingredients	Metric/Imperial
½ lb	Smoked bacon	250 g / 8 oz
2	Eggs	2
1 tsp	Strong prepared mustard	1 tsp
1	Lemon	1
	Salt and pepper	
1 ¼ cups	Olive oil	300 ml / ½ pint
1 lb	Tender young spinach	500 g / 1 lb
1 tbsp	Vegetable oil	1 tbsp
2 tbsp	Wine vinegar	2 tbsp

1. Plunge the bacon into a pan of boiling water and leave to blanch for 5 minutes. Drain, cool and pat dry.
2. Remove any rind and cut the bacon into small pieces.
3. Hard-cook the eggs for 10 minutes in boiling water. Run

them under cold water and remove the shells. Separate the yolks from the whites and cut the whites into small cubes. Set the whites aside.

4. Crush the yolks with the mustard and the juice of the lemon until smooth. Add salt and pepper to taste. Incorporate the oil gradually, beating constantly with a wire whisk. Set this mayonnaise aside.

5. Remove the stalks from the spinach and rinse in several changes of water. Drain and pat or shake dry. Place in a salad bowl or on individual plates. Garnish the spinach with the diced egg white.

6. Heat the vegetable oil in a frying pan and add the bacon. Fry until brown and crisp. Drain the bacon on paper towels, then scatter over the spinach.

7. Pour away the oil from the frying pan. Add the vinegar to the pan and stir to mix with the sediment. Boil for a few seconds, then pour over the spinach.

8. Serve accompanied by the mayonnaise.

Mâche, Céleri, Betterave

Corn Salad with Beets and Celery

American	00:10	00:00

American	Ingredients	Metric/Imperial
1	Head of celery	1
2	Cooked beets [beetroot]	2
¾ lb	Corn salad or lamb's lettuce	350 g / 12 oz
	Salt and pepper	
1 tbsp	Vinegar	1 tbsp
1 tbsp	Strong prepared mustard	1 tbsp
3 tbsp	Oil	3 tbsp

1. Cut the celery into small cubes. Peel the beets and cut into small pieces. Remove any damaged leaves from the corn salad. Rinse carefully and drain in a salad basket. Combine these vegetables in a salad bowl.

2. Dissolve a pinch of salt in the vinegar. Mix in the mustard. Add the oil and pepper to taste and blend.

3. Pour the dressing over the vegetables, toss and serve.

Chou en salade

Cabbage Salad

	00:20	00:00
	plus marinating	

American	Ingredients	Metric/Imperial
1	Head of white cabbage	1
2	Large lemons	2
5 tbsp	Olive oil	5 tbsp
	Salt and pepper	

1. Cut the cabbage into quarters and cut out the core. Cut the cabbage into very thin strips, removing the large ribs.

2. Place the cabbage in a salad bowl and add the juice of the lemons, the oil, and salt and pepper to taste.

3. Leave to marinate in a cool place for 1½-2 hours, stirring from time to time.

4. When you are about to serve, taste and adjust the seasoning if necessary. The salad should be quite well seasoned.

Salade au lard ardennaise

Bacon and Potato Salad

	00:10	00:35

American	Ingredients	Metric/Imperial
6	Large potatoes	6
	Salt and pepper	
¾ lb	Dandelion leaves	350 g / 12 oz
1	Shallot	1
1	Garlic clove	1
3 tbsp	Oil	3 tbsp
¾ lb	Bacon	350 g / 12 oz
¼ cup	Vinegar	4 tbsp

1. Peel the potatoes. Cook in boiling salted water for 30 minutes or until tender.

2. Meanwhile, rinse the dandelion leaves in cold water, removing any withered leaves. Drain. Peel and chop the shallot.

3. Rub the salad bowl with the cut sides of the halved garlic clove. Discard the garlic. Add the oil, chopped shallot, and salt and pepper to taste to the bowl. Cover with the dandelion leaves.

4. Drain the potatoes and cut into slices while they are still warm. Place in the salad bowl.

5. Dice the bacon and cook in a frying pan without fat until crisp. Pour the bacon and its fat over the salad. Pour the vinegar into the frying pan and boil for 4 minutes, stirring to mix in the sediment in the pan. Pour over the salad, toss and serve.

Chicorée frisée aux croûtons aillés

Chicory [Endive] with Garlic-Flavored Croûtons

	00:15	00:05

American	Ingredients	Metric/Imperial
1	Head of chicory [curly endive]	1
4	Slices of bread	4
7 tbsp	Oil	7 tbsp
2	Garlic cloves	2
	Salt and pepper	
1 tbsp	Vinegar	1 tbsp
1 tbsp	Strong prepared mustard	1 tbsp

1. Remove any damaged leaves from the chicory, rinse carefully and drain in a salad basket.

2. Remove the crust from the slices of bread and dice the bread. Heat 2 tablespoons of the oil in a frying pan and fry the bread dice until golden brown all over. Drain.

3. Peel the garlic, crush finely and mix with 1 tablespoon oil. Add the croûtons to this mixture and stir so that they become saturated.

4. Mix a pinch of salt with the vinegar. Add the mustard and stir thoroughly. Add the remaining oil, pepper to taste and the garlic-flavoured croûtons. Blend. Pour over the chicory [endive] when you are about to serve.

Salade Sylvie

Citrus, Ham and Cheese Salad

⏱ 00:30   00:00 🍳

American	Ingredients	Metric/Imperial
1	Lettuce heart	1
3	Oranges	3
2	Grapefruit	2
¼ lb	Gruyère cheese	125 g / 4 oz
1	Hard-cooked egg	1
5 oz	Cooked ham	150 g / 5 oz
¼ lb	Button mushrooms	125 g / 4 oz
1	Lemon	1
½ cup	Cream cheese	125 g / 4 oz
	Chopped fresh herbs (chives, tarragon, parsley, etc)	
	Salt and pepper	

1. Rinse and drain the lettuce. Tear into small pieces. Peel the oranges and grapefruit. Separate into sections, removing the seeds and membrane.
2. Cut the gruyère, egg, ham, mushrooms, oranges and grapefruit into small pieces.
3. Place all the prepared ingredients in a salad bowl.
4. Mix the juice of the lemon with the cream cheese. Add the chopped herbs, and salt and pepper to taste.
5. Pour the dressing over the salad, toss and serve.

Salade à la tapenade

Piquant Olive Salad

⏱ 00:25   00:20 🍳

American	Ingredients	Metric/Imperial
1 lb	Small potatoes	500 g / 1 lb
1 lb	Small tomatoes	500 g / 1 lb
½ lb	Small onions	250 g / 8 oz
1	Garlic clove	1
2 tbsp	Olive, anchovy and caper spread	2 tbsp
6 tbsp	Olive oil	6 tbsp
1 tbsp	Vinegar	1 tbsp
2 tbsp	Chopped fresh parsley	2 tbsp
	Salt and pepper	
1 cup	Black olives	150 g / 5 oz

1. Put the unpeeled potatoes in a saucepan of cold water. Bring to a boil and cook for 20 minutes. Drain and leave to cool, then peel and quarter.
2. Quarter the tomatoes.
3. Peel and thinly slice the onions. Peel and crush the garlic.
4. Mix the olive, anchovy and caper spread in a bowl with the olive oil, garlic, vinegar and chopped parsley. Taste, then add salt and pepper.
5. Put the potatoes, tomatoes and onions in a salad bowl. Add the dressing and olives, toss and serve. You may also present this delicious salad with the dressing served separately in a sauceboat.

Saucisson en salade

Sausage Salad

⏱ 00:30   00:20 🍳

American	Ingredients	Metric/Imperial
1	Uncooked sausage with pistachios	1
½ lb	Smoked bacon	250 g / 8 oz
	Salt and pepper	
1 tbsp	Vinegar	1 tbsp
1 tbsp	Prepared mustard	1 tbsp
3 tbsp	Oil	3 tbsp
1	Head of chicory [curly endive]	1
	Toast for serving	

1. Prick the sausage. Place in a pan of boiling water and simmer for 20 minutes. Drain. Leave to cool, then slice.
2. Toss the bacon into a saucepan of boiling water and blanch for 5 minutes after boiling has resumed. Drain and pat dry, then cut into pieces. Brown the pieces in a frying pan without fat. Drain on paper towels, reserving the bacon fat in the pan.
3. Dissolve a pinch of salt in the vinegar. Mix in the mustard. Add the oil and bacon fat and blend.
4. Rinse the chicory, remove any damaged leaves and drain in a salad basket. Put the lettuce into a salad bowl together with the sausage and bacon. Sprinkle with the dressing and toss together.
5. Serve with slices of toast.

Corn salad

Hot hors d'oeuvres

Artichauts Barigoule

Stuffed Artichokes, Provençal Style

01:00   00:40

American	Ingredients	Metric/Imperial
6	Globe artichokes or	6
12	Small purple artichokes	12
	Lemon juice	
	Salt and pepper	
½ lb	Button mushrooms	250 g / 8 oz
¼ lb	Unsmoked bacon	125 g / 4 oz
3	Shallots	3
2 tbsp	Olive oil	2 tbsp
1 tbsp	Chopped fresh parsley	1 tbsp
2	Onions	2
2	Carrots	2
6	Thin slices of smoked bacon	6
⅔ cup	White wine	150 ml / ¼ pint
1	Bouquet garni	1

1. Trim the stalks from the artichokes and remove all the leaves. Dip the peeled hearts immediately in lemon juice to prevent them from turning black.
2. Put some salted water and a little lemon juice into a saucepan, add the artichoke hearts and bring to a boil. Leave to cook for 15-30 minutes or until tender but still firm. Drain and remove the hairy chokes.
3. Preheat the oven to 425°F / 220°C / Gas Mark 7.
4. Finely chop the mushrooms. Chop the unsmoked bacon. Peel and chop the shallots.
5. Heat 1 tablespoon of the oil in a frying pan, add the bacon, mushrooms, shallots, parsley, and salt and pepper to taste and cook, stirring, until lightly browned. Drain off excess fat.
6. Peel and chop the onions and carrots and brown them in the remaining olive oil in another pan.
7. Wrap each artichoke heart in a slice of smoked bacon. Top with the mushroom mixture and then with the carrot mixture. Arrange the hearts in a casserole.
8. Add the wine and bouquet garni and cover the casserole. Put the casserole into the oven and braise for 30-40 minutes. Remove the lid 10 minutes before cooking finishes for the sauce to reduce.
9. Remove the bouquet garni and serve.

Bananes au bacon

Bananas with Bacon

00:05   00:05

American	Ingredients	Metric/Imperial
6	Bananas	6
12	Small, thin slices of bacon	12
	Pepper	

1. Preheat the broiler [grill] to high.
2. Peel the bananas and cut in half crosswise. Wrap each banana half in a slice of bacon and push a wooden toothpick through the banana to hold the bacon securely in place.
3. Place the bananas in a flameproof baking dish. Add pepper to taste. (Do not add salt, because the bacon is already salty.)
4. Place the dish under the broiler and cook for about 5 minutes or until the bacon is crisp and browned. Turn the banana pieces to cook evenly. Serve hot.

Amuse-gueule saucisse

Sausage Cocktail Snacks

00:20   00:10 to 00:15

plus thawing or making pastry   Makes 32

American	Ingredients	Metric/Imperial
14 oz	Puff pastry	400 g / 14 oz
8	Cocktail sausages [chipolatas]	8
	Cayenne pepper	
1	Egg	1

1. If you are using frozen pastry, leave to thaw for 3 hours at room temperature.
2. Preheat the oven to 450°F / 230°C / Gas Mark 8.
3. Roll out the pastry ⅛ in / 3 mm thick, and cut out pieces which will *just* wrap around each sausage.
4. Lightly sprinkle the sausages with cayenne pepper and wrap each of them in a piece of pastry. Dampen the longest edge with water and press to seal. Coat the rolls with beaten egg. Cut each pastry-wrapped sausage into 4.
5. Arrange on a baking sheet and bake for 15 minutes. Pile them in a dish and pierce each of them with a toothpick. Serve hot.

Beignets d'avocats

Avocado Fritters

00:15   00:20

plus standing time

American	Ingredients	Metric/Imperial
2	Eggs	2
1 tsp	Salt	1 tsp
1¼ cups + 3 tbsp	Flour	150 g / 5 oz + 3 tbsp
	Pepper	
1 - 1½ cups	Beer	150 ml / ¼ pint
4	Avocados	4
	Oil for deep frying	
1	Egg white	1
	Lemon wedges	

1. Prepare the batter: whisk the whole eggs and salt in a mixing bowl and add 1¼ cups [150 g / 5 oz] of the flour and pepper to taste. Mix thoroughly. Gradually stir in the beer. Leave to stand for 2 hours.
2. Peel the avocados. Cut in half lengthwise, remove the seed and cut the flesh into ¾ in / 2 cm cubes. Coat in the remaining flour.
3. Heat oil for deep frying to 345°F / 175°C.
4. Beat the egg white into a firm snow and fold into the batter.
5. Dip the avocado cubes into the batter, then plunge into the oil. Cook until puffed and brown, then drain on paper towels. Serve hot, surrounded by lemon wedges.

Bouchées au roquefort
Roquefort Puffs

⏱ 00:40   00:15 to 00:18 🍲

American	Ingredients	Metric/Imperial
1 cup	Water	250 ml / 8 fl oz
¾ cup	Butter	175 g / 6 oz
	Salt	
1 cup	Flour	125 g / 4 oz
4	Eggs	4
½ lb	Roquefort cheese	250 g / 8 oz
1 tbsp	Crème fraîche	1 tbsp

1. Preheat the oven to 400°F / 200°C / Gas Mark 6.
2. Place the water, 5 tbsp [65 g / 2½ oz] of the butter and a pinch of salt in a saucepan. Bring to a boil. Add the flour all at once and stir until the dough comes away from the sides of the pan. Remove from the heat. Add one egg and mix thoroughly, then add another egg and mix. Continue adding the eggs, incorporating each thoroughly before adding the next.
3. Using a pastry bag fitted with a small tube, pipe the pastry onto a greased baking sheet. You should obtain 36 small heaps. Put into the oven and bake for 15-18 minutes or until risen and golden brown.
4. Turn off the oven and open the door. Leave the choux puffs inside for 2-3 minutes, then remove them.
5. Mix together the roquefort, remaining butter and crème fraîche, using a wooden spoon to obtain a very smooth mixture.
6. Split open the choux puffs with a knife and fill with the cheese mixture. Serve warm or cold.

Courgettes farcies
Stuffed Zucchini [Courgettes]

⏱ 00:20   00:30 🍲

American	Ingredients	Metric/Imperial
6	Zucchini [courgettes]	6
	Salt and pepper	
¾ lb	Cooked meat (pork, veal or beef)	350 g / 12 oz
4	Onions	4
2	Garlic cloves	2
1	Bunch of fresh parsley	1
2	Eggs	2
	Grated nutmeg	
½ cup	Grated gruyère cheese	50 g / 2 oz
¼ cup	Butter	50 g / 2 oz

1. Preheat the oven to 350°F / 180°C / Gas Mark 4.
2. Wipe the zucchini and cut them in half lengthwise. Remove most of the flesh with a small spoon and keep it in reserve.
3. Toss the zucchini shells into a saucepan of boiling salted water and cook for 2 minutes. Drain and run under cold water, then drain in a colander.
4. Grind [mince] together the cooked meat, peeled onions, peeled garlic cloves, parsley and the flesh from the zucchini. Add the eggs, a pinch of nutmeg, and salt and pepper to taste, mixing thoroughly with a fork.

5. Fill the zucchini shells with the stuffing and place them in a buttered baking dish. Sprinkle with the cheese and dot with small pieces of butter.
6. Place in the oven and bake for about 20 minutes. While they are cooking, baste the zucchini halves occasionally with the cooking juice.

Chavignols grillés
Baked Goat's Cheese Toasts

⏱ 00:15   00:12 to 00:13 🍲

American	Ingredients	Metric/Imperial
	Salt and pepper	
1 tbsp	Vinegar	1 tbsp
3 tbsp	Walnut oil	3 tbsp
15	Walnuts	15
1	Head of chicory [curly endive]	1
6	Crottin de Chavignol or similar small, soft goat's cheese	6
6	Slices of bread	6

1. Preheat the oven to 425°F / 220°C / Gas Mark 7.
2. Dissolve a pinch of salt in the vinegar. Add the oil, walnuts and pepper to taste. Place in the bottom of a salad bowl and set aside.
3. Rinse and drain the chicory. Separate the leaves. Add to the salad bowl but do not toss.
4. Cut a ½ in / 1 cm slice from the base of each cheese. Reserve these slices for another recipe. Cut the cheeses in half.
5. Trim the slices of bread so they are just slightly larger than the cheeses. Place a halved cheese on each slice of bread.
6. Arrange the toasts on a baking sheet and bake for 8 minutes. Then preheat the broiler [grill] and broil the cheese toasts for 4-5 minutes, watching them carefully.
7. Toss the chicory with the dressing. Serve with the hot cheese toasts.

Crêpes à la florentine
Spinach Crêpes

⏱ 00:20
plus standing time   00:30 🍲

American	Ingredients	Metric/Imperial
2	Eggs	2
1¼ cups	Flour	150 g / 5 oz
1¼ cups	Milk	250 ml / 8 fl oz
1 cup	Beer	150 ml / ¼ pint
	Salt and pepper	
6 tbsp	Butter	75 g / 3 oz
2 lb	Fresh spinach	1 kg / 2 lb
1¼ cups	Thick crème fraîche	300 ml / ½ pint
1 cup	Grated gruyère cheese	125 g / 4 oz

1. Prepare the crêpe batter: break the eggs into a mixing bowl, beat them together and add the flour. Stir with a wooden spoon to obtain a smooth batter and thin it out gradually with the milk. Blend thoroughly. Add the beer and a pinch of salt. Gently melt half of the butter in a saucepan. Incorporate it into the batter and leave to stand for 2 hours.

2. Preheat the oven to 450°F / 230°C / Gas Mark 8.
3. Carefully clean the spinach and remove the stalks. Add to a saucepan of boiling salted water and cook for 10 minutes. Drain, run under cold water and squeeze in your hands to extract all the water. Coarsely chop the spinach.
4. Put half the crème fraîche and half the gruyère into a small frying pan. Add the spinach and pepper to taste, and blend thoroughly. Leave to warm, with the lid on, over a gentle heat.
5. Melt a small piece of butter in a crêpe or frying pan. Add a ladleful of the batter and tilt the pan in all directions to spread the batter evenly over the bottom. Cook over a medium heat for 1½-2 minutes, then turn the crêpe over and cook the other side. Continue making crepes in this way until all the batter has been used up.
6. Fill the crêpes with the spinach mixture and roll them up. Arrange in a buttered baking dish. Heat the remainder of the crème fraîche in a small saucepan and use to coat the crêpes. Sprinkle with the remainder of the grated cheese.
7. Place in the oven and bake until the top is golden brown and the crêpes are piping hot.

Spinach crêpes

Crêpes au roquefort
Roquefort Crêpes

American	Ingredients	Metric/Imperial
2	Eggs	2
1¼ cups	Flour	150 g / 5 oz
1¼ cups	Milk	250 ml / 8 fl oz
1 cup	Beer	150 ml / ¼ pint
	Salt and pepper	
½ cup	Butter	125 g / 4 oz
2 oz	Roquefort cheese	50 g / 2 oz
	Melted butter for serving	

00:15 plus standing time   00:30

1. Prepare the crêpe batter: break the eggs into a mixing bowl, beat them together and add the flour. Stir with a wooden spoon to obtain a smooth batter and thin it out gradually with the milk. Blend thoroughly. Add the beer and a pinch of salt. Gently melt 3 tbsp [40 g / 1½ oz] of the butter in a saucepan. Incorporate it into the batter and leave to stand for 2 hours.

2. Finely crush the roquefort using a fork to obtain a smooth cream. Heat ¼ cup [50 g / 2 oz] of the butter and incorporate it into the roquefort cream. Add this mixture to the crêpe batter and whisk until very smooth. If the batter is too thick, add a little more beer.
3. Melt a small piece of butter in a crêpe or frying pan. Add a ladleful of the batter and tilt the pan in all directions to spread the batter evenly over the bottom. Cook over a medium heat for 1½-2 minutes, then turn the crêpe over and cook the other side. Continue making crepes in this way until all the batter has been used up.
4. As each crêpe is cooked, coat it with a little melted butter before rolling it up. Keep warm between 2 plates placed over a saucepan of boiling water.

Crêpes aux champignons
Mushroom Crêpes

00:30 plus standing time   00:45

American	Ingredients	Metric/Imperial
2	Eggs	2
1¼ cups + 3 tbsp	Flour	190 g / 6½ oz
3¼ cups	Milk	750 ml / 1¼ pints
1 cup	Beer	150 ml / ¼ pint
	Salt and pepper	
¾ cup	Butter	175 g / 6 oz
	Grated nutmeg	
14 oz	Button mushrooms	400 g / 14 oz
2	Shallots	2
1	Garlic clove	1
1 cup	Grated gruyère cheese	125 g / 4 oz

1. Prepare the crêpe batter: break the eggs into a mixing bowl, beat them together and add 1¼ cups [150 g / 5 oz] of the flour. Stir with a wooden spoon to obtain a smooth batter and thin it out gradually with 1¼ cups [250 ml / 8 fl oz] of the milk. Blend thoroughly. Add the beer and a pinch of salt. Gently melt 3 tablespoons [40 g / 1½ oz] of the butter in a saucepan. Incorporate it into the batter and leave to stand for 2 hours.
2. Meanwhile, melt 3 tablespoons [40 g / 1½ oz] of the butter in a saucepan, stir in the remaining flour and cook for 1 minute. Gradually stir in the remaining milk and then, continuing to stir, leave to thicken over a gentle heat for about 8-10 minutes. Season with salt, pepper and nutmeg to taste.
3. Finely chop the mushrooms. Peel and chop the shallots and garlic. Heat 3 tablespoons [40 g / 1½ oz] butter in a small frying pan, add the mushrooms, shallots and garlic and leave to cook over a gentle heat, stirring frequently, until all the liquid has evaporated. Add salt and pepper to taste.
4. Add half the sauce and mix thoroughly. Set aside.
5. Preheat the oven to 475°F / 240°C / Gas Mark 9.
6. Melt a small piece of butter in a crêpe or frying pan. Add a ladleful of batter and tilt the frying pan in all directions to spread the batter evenly over the bottom. Cook over a medium heat for 1½-2 minutes, then turn the crêpe over and cook the other side. Continue making crepes in this way until all the batter has been used up.
7. Fill the crêpes with the mushroom mixture and roll them up. Arrange very tightly in a buttered baking dish. Cover them with the remainder of the sauce and dot with small pieces of butter. Sprinkle with gruyère.
8. Bake for 5-10 minutes and serve hot.

Croque-monsieur
Fried Ham and Cheese Sandwiches

	00:25		00:05
			per sandwich

American	Ingredients	Metric/Imperial
3	Slices of cooked ham	3
12	Slices of bread	12
12	Thin slices of emmental cheese	12
¾ cup	Butter	175 g / 6 oz

1. Preheat the oven to 425°F / 220°C / Gas Mark 7.
2. Cut each slice of ham in half. On one slice of bread, place a slice of cheese, a piece of ham and another slice of cheese. Cover with a second slice of bread. Trim the edges of the ham and cheese so they don't hang out. Make 5 more sandwiches in the same way.
3. Melt half of the butter in a frying pan and add 3 of the sandwiches. Brown one side over a very moderate heat. Using a spatula and a fork, turn the sandwiches over and brown the other side, adding more butter, if necessary. (This first cooking must be done slowly so that the butter does not burn and so that the cheese will stick to the bread as it begins to melt.)
4. Transfer the sandwiches to a baking sheet and place them in the oven to keep hot while you cook the remaining sandwiches.
5. Serve the crusty, hot sandwiches as an entrée or a light lunch, accompanied by a green salad.

Endives au jambon
Endives [Chicory] with Ham

	00:10		01:10

American	Ingredients	Metric/Imperial
12	Medium-sized heads of endive [chicory]	12
½ cup	Butter	125 g / 4 oz
2 tsp	Sugar	2 tsp
	Salt and pepper	
1 tbsp	Flour	2 tbsp
⅔ cup	Milk	150 ml / ¼ pint
1 cup	Crème fraîche	250 ml / 8 fl oz
½ cup	Grated gruyère cheese	50 g / 2 oz
	Grated nutmeg	
12	Thin slices of cooked ham	12
12	Thin slices of gruyère cheese	12

1. Remove the damaged leaves from the endives [chicory]. Using a pointed knife, remove the hard part from the base of the leaves by hollowing out the center. Wash and drain.
2. Melt 2 tablespoons [25 g / 1 oz] butter in a thick-bottomed saucepan. When it froths, add the endives, sugar and salt and pepper to taste. Leave to cook over a gentle heat for approximately 40 minutes. The endives are done when they are slightly browned and the point of a knife can pass through them easily.

3. Meanwhile, melt 1 tablespoon butter in another thick-bottomed saucepan. Add the flour and cook, stirring, for 1 minute. Remove the saucepan from the heat and gradually add the milk, continuing to stir. Return to the heat and cook, stirring, until thickened. Add the crème fraîche, half of the grated gruyère, a pinch of nutmeg, and salt and pepper to taste. Leave to cook for 5 minutes over a gentle heat, stirring continuously.
4. Preheat the oven to 425°F / 220°C / Gas Mark 7.
5. On each slice of ham, place a slice of gruyère and then a braised endive. Roll up the ham which should go right around the endive. Arrange the rolls in a buttered ovenproof dish. Cover them with the sauce and sprinkle with the remaining grated gruyère.
6. Bake for about 30 minutes. Serve in the cooking dish.

Ficelles picardes
Ham and Mushroom Crêpes

	00:20		00:30
	plus making crêpes		

American	Ingredients	Metric/Imperial
1 lb	Button mushrooms	500 g / 1 lb
2 tbsp	Butter	25 g / 1 oz
1 cup	Crème fraîche	250 ml / 8 fl oz
1 cup	Grated gruyère cheese	125 g / 4 oz
	Salt and pepper	
6	Sliced of cooked ham	6
6	Crêpes	6

1. Preheat the oven to 400°F / 200°C / Gas Mark 6.
2. Chop the mushrooms. Heat the butter in a frying pan, add the mushrooms and cook until all their moisture has evaporated. Remove from the heat and add 1 tablespoon of the crème fraîche and 1-2 tablespoons of the gruyère. Add salt and pepper to taste.
3. Place a slice of ham on each crêpe. Cover with the mushroom mixture and roll up. Place the crêpes very close together in a buttered ovenproof dish. Pour over the remaining crème fraîche, which has been lightly seasoned with salt and pepper, and sprinkle with the remaining gruyère cheese. Place in the oven and bake for 30 minutes.

Escargots de Bourgogne
Snails with Garlic Butter

	01:00		00:30
	plus standing time		

American	Ingredients	Metric/Imperial
2 oz	Shallots	50 g / 2 oz
2	Garlic cloves	2
1 lb (2 cups)	Butter, at room temperature	500 g / 1 lb
2 tbsp	Chopped fresh parsley	2 tbsp
	Salt and pepper	
72	Canned snails with shells	72

1. Prepare the snail butter: peel and finely chop the shallots and garlic. Mix with the butter. Add the parsley and mash the mixture with a fork to blend thoroughly. Season to taste with salt and pepper.

2. Drain the snails. Drop them into a pan of simmering water and cook for 5 minutes. Drain, cool with cold water and drain again.

3. Put a pat of snail butter in each snail shell. Put the snails in the shells and fill with the rest of the snail butter.

4. Leave the snails in a cool place for 24 hours so that they absorb the flavor of the garlic butter.

5. Preheat the oven to 325°F / 160°C / Gas Mark 3.

6. Arrange the snails on snail dishes and put in the oven. Bake until the butter has melted and the snails are piping hot.

Crêpes farcies
Stuffed Crêpes

00:25 plus standing time   **00:20 to 00:25**

American	Ingredients	Metric/Imperial
2	Eggs	2
1¼ cups	Flour	150 g / 5 oz
1¼ cups	Milk	250 ml / 8 fl oz
1 cup	Beer	150 ml / ¼ pint
	Salt and pepper	
10 tbsp	Butter	150 g / 5 oz
¼ lb	Cooked ham or	125 g / 4 oz
3	Eggs	3
1 lb	Spinach or beet tops	150 g / 5 oz
	Grated nutmeg	
1¼ cups	Grated gruyère cheese	150 g / 5 oz
½ cup	Crème fraîche	125 ml / 4 fl oz

1. Prepare the crêpe batter: break the 2 eggs into a mixing bowl, beat them together and add the flour. Stir with a wooden spoon to obtain a smooth batter and thin it out gradually with the milk. Blend thoroughly. Add the beer and a pinch of salt. Gently melt 3 tablespoons [40 g / 1½ oz] of the butter in a saucepan. Incorporate it into the batter and leave to stand for 2 hours.

2. Melt a small piece of butter in a crêpe or frying pan. Add a ladleful of batter and tilt the frying pan in all directions to spread the batter evenly over the bottom. Cook over medium heat for 1½-2 minutes, then turn the crêpe over and cook the other side. Continue making crêpes in this way until all the batter has been used up.

3. If preparing the crêpes the day before, wrap them in foil, interleaving each one with wax [greaseproof] paper and store in the refrigerator.

4. Preheat the oven to 400°F / 200°C / Gas Mark 6.

5. Chop the ham, or hard-cook the eggs in boiling water for 10 minutes. Drain, run under cold water and remove the shells. Chop the eggs.

6. Remove any damaged leaves and large ribs from the spinach or beet tops, rinse and toss into a saucepan of boiling salted water. Leave to cook for 5 minutes after boiling has resumed, then drain. Squeeze out excess moisture, then chop coarsely.

7. Melt 2 tablespoons [25 g / 1 oz] butter in a saucepan, add the spinach and leave to cook until all the vegetable water has evaporated. Add a pinch of nutmeg, ½ cup [50 g / 2 oz] of the gruyère, the chopped eggs or ham, and salt and pepper to taste. Mix thoroughly.

8. Fill the crêpes with the spinach mixture and roll them up. Arrange very tightly in a buttered ovenproof dish. Coat them with the crème fraîche, scatter over the remaining cheese and a few small pieces of butter. Bake for about 25 minutes.

Stuffed crêpes

Croûtes du skieur
Ham, Bread and Cheese Pudding

01:00   **00:15**

American	Ingredients	Metric/Imperial
¼ cup	Butter	50 g / 2 oz
1 tbsp	Oil	1 tbsp
6	Slices of bread, ½ in / 1 cm thick	6
6 tbsp	Dry white wine	6 tbsp
6	Thin slices of cooked ham	6
1 tbsp	Vinegar	1 tbsp
7	Eggs	7
2 cups	Grated comté or similar cheese	250 g / 8 oz
2 tbsp	Crème fraîche	2 tbsp
	Grated nutmeg	
	Pepper	

1. Heat the butter with the oil in a frying pan. Add the bread slices and brown on both sides.

2. Place the bread in one layer in an ovenproof dish and moisten each with 1 tablespoon of the wine. Cover each with a slice of ham cut to the same size.

3. Heat 2 in / 5 cm of water in a saucepan and add the vinegar. Break 6 of the eggs, one at a time, into a ladle and plunge the ladle into the boiling water. When all the eggs are in the water, remove the saucepan from the heat, cover and leave to poach for 3 minutes. Remove the eggs and place them in a bowl of warm water. (Alternatively, use an egg poacher.)

4. Preheat the broiler [grill] to high.

5. Take the eggs out of the water and drain on a cloth. Cut off the excess white so as to give them a regular shape. Place an egg on each slice of ham.

6. Mix together the cheese, remaining egg and crème fraîche. Add a pinch of nutmeg and pepper to taste. Pour this mixture over the eggs in the dish.

7. Place under the broiler and cook for 5 minutes.

Tourte aux morilles
Morel Pie

	00:20	00:40
	plus thawing or making pastry	

American	Ingredients	Metric/Imperial
2 oz	Dried morels or other mushrooms	50 g / 2 oz
1¼ lb	Puff pastry	625 g / 1¼ lb
1	Egg	1
1	Onion	1
¼ cup	Butter	50 g / 2 oz
1 cup	Crème fraîche	250 ml / 8 fl oz
	Salt and pepper	

1. Put the dried morels into warm water to soak for 2 hours.
2. Thaw the pastry if using frozen. Preheat the oven to 425°F / 220°C / Gas Mark 7.
3. Roll out half the pastry to about ⅛ in / 3 mm. Use to line a buttered 10 in / 25 cm quiche or flan dish or pan. Line the pastry with a sheet of wax [greaseproof] paper and fill the dish with dried beans. Roll out the rest of the pastry and lay over the beans, making a pastry lid. Moisten the edge, twist it up and make oblique cuts in it. Draw lozenges on the top with a pointed knife, and glaze with beaten egg.
4. Bake for 40 minutes.
5. Meanwhile, peel and chop the onion. Heat the butter in a saucepan, add the onion and cook gently until softened. Do not allow it to turn brown.
6. Drain the morels and cut into pieces if large. Add to the onion and cook until the moisture has completely evaporated.
7. Add the crème fraîche, and simmer until it thickens. Season to taste with salt and pepper.
8. To serve, carefully remove the hot pastry lid with a knife and take out the paper and beans. Pour in the morel mixture and replace the pastry lid. Serve hot.

Tourte au jambon
Ham Pie

	00:30	01:00 to 01:15
	plus thawing or making pastry	

American	Ingredients	Metric/Imperial
1¼ lb	Puff pastry	625 g / 1¼ lb
6	Thin slices of cooked ham	6
14 oz	Emmental cheese	400 g / 14 oz
1	Egg	1

1. Preheat the oven to 450°F / 230°C / Gas Mark 8. Thaw the pastry if using frozen.
2. Roll out half the pastry to a thickness of about ⅛ in / 3 mm. Cut out a 10 in / 25 cm round and place it on a lightly oiled and floured baking sheet.
3. Arrange 3 slices of ham (with the fat cut off) on the pastry base. Cover with half of the emmental cheese, cut into thin slices, then place another 3 slices of ham on top of the cheese. Finally add a layer of the remaining cheese cut into thin slices. Leave a clear border of ½ in / 1 cm around the edge of the pastry round.
4. Roll out the other half of the pastry and cut out a round as before. Moisten the edge with beaten egg and place this round on top of the first one. Press down the edge to seal the pastry rounds together, and crimp or flute the edge.

5. Glaze the top with beaten egg. Prick in 3 or 4 places with a fork, and draw a pattern with the tip of a knife.
6. Bake for 30 minutes, then reduce the heat to 425°F / 220°C / Gas Mark 7, and bake for a further 30-45 minutes. Serve warm.

Ham pie

Vol-au-vent
Sweetbread Vol-au-Vent

	00:30	00:50

American	Ingredients	Metric/Imperial
1½ lb	Veal sweetbreads	750 g / 1½ lb
	Salt and pepper	
1	Calf's brain	1
1 tbsp	Vinegar	1 tbsp
14 oz	Button mushrooms	400 g / 14 oz
10 tbsp	Butter	150 g / 5 oz
1	Carrot	1
2	Shallots	2
3 tbsp	Flour	3 tbsp
1 tbsp	Tomato paste [purée]	1 tbsp
2 cups	Chicken stock	500 ml / ¾ pint
1¼ cups	Madeira wine	300 ml / ½ pint
2 tbsp	Oil	2 tbsp
5 tbsp	Brandy	5 tbsp
1	Large patty shell (vol-au-vent case)	1
1	Slice of cooked ham	1
1	Egg yolk	1
½ cup	Crème fraîche	125 ml / 4 fl oz

1. Put the sweetbreads in a saucepan of cold, salted water, bring to a boil, and simmer for 5 minutes. Drain and cool in cold water, then trim off any tough portions and outer membranes. Cut into large dice.
2. Wash the brain, and soak for 15 minutes in cold water to

which the vinegar has been added. Drain and remove all fiberlike membranes and surrounding threads. Rinse well and cut into dice.

3. Thinly slice the mushrooms. Melt 2 tablespoons [25 g / 1 oz] of the butter in a saucepan, add the mushrooms and cook until all the moisture has evaporated. Set aside.

4. Peel and dice the carrot. Peel and thinly slice the shallots. Melt 2 tablespoons [25 g / 1 oz] butter in another saucepan and add the carrot and shallots. Fry gently until softened, then sprinkle on 2 tablespoons of the flour and cook for a few moments, stirring.

5. Add the tomato paste, chicken stock and madeira. Season to taste with salt and pepper. Bring to a boil, then reduce the heat and leave to simmer gently for 20 minutes.

6. Leave the sauce to cool, then remove any fat which has risen to the surface. Strain the sauce.

7. Preheat the oven to 300°F / 150°C / Gas Mark 2.

8. Coat the diced sweetbreads with the remaining flour. Heat the oil and 2 tablespoons [25 g / 1 oz] butter in a frying pan, add the sweetbreads and brown on all sides for 10 minutes. Season with salt and pepper. Add the brandy and set it alight, then add the mushrooms and madeira sauce. Cover and leave to cook for 15 minutes over a gentle heat.

9. Meanwhile, heat the pastry case in the oven.

10. Melt the remaining butter in a frying pan, add the diced brain and cook until browned, for 5 minutes. Dice the ham. Add the brain and ham to the sweetbread mixture.

11. Mix the egg yolk in a bowl with the crème fraîche. Add to the sweetbread mixture, off the heat, then use to fill the hot pastry case. Serve immediately.

Tarte aux bettes

Swiss Chard Tart

	00:45		00:45
	plus thawing or making pastry		

American	Ingredients	Metric/Imperial
¾ lb	Puff pastry	350 g / 12 oz
2 lb	Swiss chard or beet tops [spinach beet]	1 kg / 2 lb
6 tbsp	Butter	75 g / 3 oz
	Grated nutmeg	
	Salt and pepper	
¾ lb	Onions	350 g / 12 oz
¾ lb	Tomatoes	350 g / 12 oz
2	Garlic cloves	2
1 tsp	Dried thyme	1 tsp
¾ cup	Grated gruyère cheese	75 g / 3 oz

1. Thaw the pastry if using frozen. Preheat the oven to 450°F / 230°C / Gas Mark 8.

2. Roll out the pastry and use to line a buttered and floured 10 in / 25 cm quiche or flan dish or pan. Prick the bottom with a fork and keep cool.

3. Remove the ribs from the chard, wash and cut them into thin strips. Melt 2 tablespoons [25 g / 1 oz] of the butter in a saucepan, add the chard and cook until all the moisture has evaporated. Add a pinch of grated nutmeg, and salt and pepper to taste.

4. Peel and slice the onions. Melt 2 tablespoons [25 g / 1 oz] of the butter in a frying pan, add the onions and cook until softened, without letting them turn brown.

5. Peel the tomatoes (first plunging them into boiling water for 10 seconds), then remove the seeds. Cut the flesh into pieces. Melt the remaining butter in a saucepan, add the tomatoes and cook until reduced to a pulp.

6. Peel and crush the garlic. Add to the tomatoes with the onions and thyme. Season to taste with salt and pepper.

7. Cover the bottom of the pastry case with half the tomato mixture. Sprinkle with half of the grated gruyère cheese and arrange the chard in an even layer on top. Cover with the remaining tomato mixture, and sprinkle with the rest of the cheese.

8. Bake for 20 minutes, then lower the heat to 350°F / 180°C / Gas Mark 4 and bake for 25 minutes longer. Serve warm or cold.

Tarte aux oignons

Onion Tart

	00:45		00:50
	plus chilling		

American	Ingredients	Metric/Imperial
½ cup + 2 tbsp	Butter	150 g / 5 oz
	Salt and pepper	
2 cups + 2 tbsp	Flour	250 g / 8 oz + 2 tbsp
4	Egg yolks	4
1 lb	Onions	500 g / 1 lb
2 cups	Milk	500 ml / ¾ pint
	Grated nutmeg	

1. Cut ½ cup [125 g / 4 oz] of the butter into small pieces, and leave to soften at room temperature. Mix a pinch of salt, 2 cups [250 g / 8 oz] of the flour and 1 egg yolk in a bowl. Add the softened butter and mix to a dough. Roll the dough into a ball, and chill for 1 hour.

2. Preheat the oven to 425°F / 220°C / Gas Mark 7.

3. Roll out the dough thinly and use to line a buttered 10 in / 25 cm quiche or flan dish or pan. Prick the bottom with a fork.

4. Peel and slice the onions. Melt the remaining butter in a saucepan, add the onions and fry over a low heat, so that they will be softened before they start to brown.

5. Sprinkle the onions with the remaining flour and stir well to mix. Add three-quarters of the milk, and bring to a boil, stirring continuously. Add the rest of the milk. Remove from the heat and beat in the remaining egg yolks, one at a time. Season with salt and pepper to taste and a pinch of nutmeg.

6. Pour the onion mixture into the pastry case. Bake for 35-40 minutes. Serve warm.

Onion tart

Terrines, Pâtés and Galantines

Do you know the difference between a pâté and a terrine? The word pâté is used for all sorts of preparations based on meat or fish, covered with pastry and baked in the oven.

On the other hand, terrines are cooked in fireproof earthenware or china, stoneware, enameled iron, or glass containers. In everyday speech, terrines and pâtés are often confused. Many 'pâtés' are cooked in terrines.

Galantines, however, consist of chopped meat or fish rolled up in the animal's skin, then cooked in bouillon in a saucepan. The word 'galantine' is said to come from the words *geline* or *galine*, the Old French for 'chicken,' since this dish was at first made of poultry, and then later, at the end of the seventeenth century, of game and meat.

There are many varieties of pâté. Each region of France has its own recipe for pâtés, terrines and galantines. We have only selected a few simple ones for this chapter.

Guidelines

The ingredients
The ingredients used to make the filling can be many and varied: pork, mixtures of pork and veal, poultry and game (hare, duck, young wild boar, pheasant, quail, etc), foie gras, usually covered with a thin caul of pork and placed whole in the middle of the filling, panadas (a mixture of bread soaked in milk, flour, water, butter and egg, which is for binding light fillings such as fish or shellfish fillings), truffles, which give the filling their very characteristic flavor and note of refinement, and alcohols such as brandy, armagnac or calvados and white wine, madeira, port and sherry.

Lastly, the seasoning: only if none of the ingredients of the filling has been already salted, add salt.

Equipment
A meat grinder [mincer] or food processor is essential to grind the ingredients quickly and cleanly. It replaces our grandmothers' heavy mortar and pestle.

Cooking terrines and pâtés
The inside of a terrine must be lined with fat for the cooking process. The filling should also be covered with fat. A bay leaf and some sprigs of thyme are placed on top, and flavor the terrine by being concentrated under the lid during the cooking process. The terrine is next placed in a shallow baking pan, and surrounded by hot (but not boiling) water up to one-third of its height. Using a water bath or prevents the filling from drying out.

Checking the cooking process
You can usually expect the cooking to take about 1½ hours, but the time actually depends on the composition of the terrine or pâté. Check the fat surrounding the terrine. As soon as it becomes very clear, the terrine is cooked.

After cooking
The terrine must cool for 1 hour. The filling is then compressed by putting a board on it, on top of which is placed a weight, and the terrine is kept overnight in the refrigerator. It will keep for a week.

Cooking galantines
These are cooked slowly for about 1½ hours. The water or broth must be just barely simmering. The best way to check the temperature is to put a cooking thermometer in the liquid. To ensure that the galantine keeps its cylindrical shape during cooking, wrap it in cheesecloth or muslin.

Galantine

Galantine

	01:00 plus cooking and chilling	01:30 Serves 8
American	**Ingredients**	**Metric/Imperial**
1 (3½ lb)	Chicken	1 (1.5 kg / 3½ lb)
	Salt and pepper	
½ lb	Boneless pork shoulder	250 g / 8 oz
½ lb	Boneless veal shoulder	250 g / 8 oz
¼ lb	Veal kidney fat	125 g / 4 oz
¾ cup	Soft bread crumbs	40 g / 1½ oz
⅔ cup	Milk	150 ml / ¼ pint
3	Shallots	3
2	Onions	2
2 tbsp	Chopped fresh herbs (tarragon, parsley and chives)	2 tbsp
2	Eggs	2
2	Fresh thyme sprigs	2
	Grated nutmeg	
2	Chicken livers	2
2 quarts	Water	2 l / 3½ pints
1	Chicken bouillon [stock] cube	1
1 envelope	Unflavored gelatin	1 tbsp

1. Have the butcher or poulterer prepare the chicken if possible: remove the skin from the chicken, with the meat adhering to it, cut the wing and thigh joints, and remove and discard the carcass.
2. Spread out the skin. Cut away the area in front of the thighs, and sew up the tail opening with kitchen string. Season with salt and pepper to taste.
3. Finely grind [mince] all the chicken meat, including the breast fillets. Also grind the pork, veal and kidney fat. Mix these together in a bowl.
4. Moisten the breadcrumbs with the milk and squeeze out the excess. Peel and chop the shallots and onions. Add the breadcrumbs, shallots and onions to the meat mixture. Add the chopped herbs, eggs, crumbled thyme, a pinch of grated nutmeg and salt and pepper to taste. Mix the filling thoroughly.
5. Arrange half the filling on the chicken skin. Place the chicken livers on top, and cover with the rest of the filling. Fold over the edges of the skin and sew it up with kitchen string. Wrap the whole thing in cheesecloth or muslin and tie it up with string.
6. Bring the water to a boil in a saucepan and dissolve the bouillon cube in it. Put the galantine in the saucepan and bring back to a boil over a high heat. Reduce the heat and leave to simmer gently for 1½ hours. Leave to cool in the stock.
7. Take the galantine out of the stock, unwrap it, and leave to become completely cold. Boil the stock until reduced to 2 cups [500 ml / ¾ pint].
8. Dissolve the gelatin according to package directions, then add to the stock. Allow this aspic to cool until lukewarm.
9. Coat the galantine with the warm, jellying aspic and chill until set.

Pâté de foies de volaille
Chicken Liver Pâté

	00:30		00:35	
	plus chilling			

American	Ingredients	Metric/Imperial
¾ lb	Onions	350 g / 12 oz
¼ cup	Goose fat or butter	4 tbsp
1¼ lb	Chicken livers	625 g / 1¼ lb
2 tsp	Dried thyme	2 tsp
	Salt and pepper	

1. Peel and chop the onions. Heat 2 tablespoons of the goose fat or butter in a frying pan, add the onions and cook until softened. Remove the onions with a slotted spoon and put to one side.
2. Put the rest of the goose fat or butter in the frying pan. Add the livers and cook for 5-7 minutes, stirring frequently. Add the thyme, mix together and allow to cool.
3. Put the livers and onions in a blender or food processor, or through a food mill, to obtain a very smooth purée. If necessary, put the mixture through twice. Season to taste with salt and pepper and mix thoroughly. Spoon the mixture into a 1½ quart [1.5 l / 2½ pint] terrine. Chill for several hours.
4. This pâté will keep perfectly for 8-10 days in the refrigerator. Ensure that the terrine is covered, so that it does not dry out.

Pâté de foie de porc
Pork Liver Pâté

	00:50		03:00	
	plus cooling			

American	Ingredients	Metric/Imperial
3	Carrots	3
3	Turnips	3
4	Onions	4
3	Cloves	3
3	Leeks	3
2 lb	Pork bones	1 kg / 2 lb
1	Piece of bacon rind	1
1	Bouquet garni	1
	Salt and pepper	
3 quarts	Water	3 l / 5 pints
¼ lb	Fatty bacon	125 g / 4 oz
1 lb	Fresh pork sides [belly pork]	500 g / 1 lb
1	Bunch of fresh parsley	1
1	Large piece of pork caul	1
1 lb	Pork liver	500 g / 1 lb
2 tbsp	Brandy	2 tbsp
	Cayenne pepper	
	Grated nutmeg	
1	Bay leaf	1

1. Peel the carrots and turnips. Peel 1 onion and stud it with 2 of the cloves. Put these vegetables in a saucepan, together with the leeks, bones, bacon rind, bouquet garni, and salt and pepper to taste. Cover with the water, bring to a boil and simmer gently for 1½ hours.
2. Meanwhile, peel and chop the remaining onions. Grind the

remaining clove to a powder. Finely grind [mince] the bacon and pork sides. Chop the parsley. Put the caul to soak in cold water.
3. Preheat the oven to 400°F / 200°C / Gas Mark 6.
4. After the stock has simmered for 1½ hours, add the pork liver and continue to simmer for 8-10 minutes. Drain the liver and leave it to cool, then grind it finely.
5. In a bowl, mix together the liver, bacon, pork, parsley and onions. Add the brandy, and season to taste with salt, pepper, cayenne and a pinch of grated nutmeg. Add the ground clove, and mix all these ingredients together thoroughly.
6. Carefully drain the caul and lay it out on a cloth. Pat it dry. Arrange it in a 1½ quart [1.5 l / 2½ pint] terrine, leaving it hanging over the sides. Put the bay leaf on the bottom, and fill the terrine with the liver mixture, heaping it up well. Fold the caul over the top.
7. Put the lid on the terrine and put it in a baking pan containing 2 in / 5 cm water. Put both in the oven and cook for 1¼ hours. The water must just simmer.
8. Remove the terrine from the oven. Take off the lid, put a board and then a weight on top of the pâté and leave to cool. Then place in the refrigerator and chill for several hours or overnight before serving.

Pâté chaud paysan
Hot Country Pâté

	00:20		01:00	
	plus marinating, and thawing or making pastry			

American	Ingredients	Metric/Imperial
1 lb	Boneless pork shoulder	500 g / 1 lb
1 lb	Boneless veal shoulder	500 g / 1 lb
⅔ cup	Riesling or other white wine	150 ml / ¼ pint
1	Bay leaf	1
1	Fresh thyme sprig	1
1	Clove	1
	Chopped fresh parsley	
	Grated nutmeg	
	Salt and pepper	
2 tbsp	Oil	2 tbsp
¼ lb	Puff pastry	125 g / 4 oz
½ quantity	Basic short pastry	½ quantity
1	Egg yolk	1

1. Cut the pork and veal into thin slices. Put into a mixing bowl with the wine, crumbled bay leaf and thyme, crushed clove, chopped parsley, a pinch of grated nutmeg, and salt and pepper to taste. Add the oil and stir to mix. Leave to marinate in a cool place for 12 hours.
2. The next day, preheat to 425°F / 220°C / Gas Mark 7. Thaw the puff pastry if using frozen.
3. Roll out the basic short pastry on a lightly floured surface and cut into an 8×6 in / 20×15 cm strip. Use to line the bottom and sides of a terrine or loaf pan.
4. Pour the marinated meat mixture into the terrine.
5. Roll out the puff pastry and use to cover the meat filling. Press the edges of the pastries together to seal. Brush the surface with egg yolk. Make a small hole in the center and insert a piece of rolled-up cardboard as a 'chimney' or use a pie funnel.
6. Bake for 15 minutes, then reduce the temperature to 350°F / 180°C / Gas Mark 4 and bake for 45 minutes longer. Serve hot.

Gâteau de foies de volaille

Chicken Liver Cake

	00:20	00:30

American	Ingredients	Metric/Imperial
¼ lb	Pork fat	125 g / 4 oz
¾ lb	Chicken livers	350 g / 12 oz
4	Shallots	4
5 oz	Stale crustless bread	150 g / 5 oz
5 tbsp	Milk	5 tbsp
3 tbsp	Chopped fresh parsley	3 tbsp
2	Egg yolks	2
2½ tsp	Dried thyme	2½ tsp
	Salt and pepper	
	Grated nutmeg	
2 lb	Tomatoes	1 kg / 2 lb
2	Large garlic cloves	2
1	Large onion	1
2 tbsp	Olive oil	2 tbsp
	Cayenne pepper	

1. Preheat the oven to 425°F / 220°C / Gas Mark 7.
2. Cut the pork fat into dice, put in a frying pan over a medium heat and leave to soften and render some fat. Remove the cubes of fat with a slotted spoon and put to one side.
3. Add the chicken livers to the frying pan and stir for 1 minute over a high heat. Remove with the slotted spoon.
4. Peel and slice 2 of the shallots. Add to the frying pan and cook until translucent. Drain.
5. Put the stale bread into a bowl, moisten with the milk and, when soft, squeeze out excess milk with your hands.

Terrines and pâtés can be smooth- or coarse-textured

6. Combine the chicken livers, parsley, bread, pork fat cubes and cooked shallots in a blender or food processor and blend until smooth. Add the egg yolks and 2 teaspoons of the thyme. Season with salt and pepper and a pinch of grated nutmeg.
7. Put the mixture into a buttered 6 in / 15 cm soufflé dish and place it in a baking pan containing 2 in / 5 cm water. Bake for 30 minutes, keeping the water at a gentle simmer. Once the pâté pulls away from the side of the dish it is cooked.
8. Meanwhile, make the tomato sauce. Peel the tomatoes (first plunging them into boiling water for 10 seconds), cut them in half and remove the seeds. Cut the flesh into large dice. Peel and chop the garlic. Peel and chop the onion and remaining shallots. Heat the oil in a saucepan, add the onion and shallots and cook until softened. Add the tomatoes, remaining thyme, and salt, pepper and cayenne pepper to taste. Cook over a low heat for about 30 minutes or until all the moisture from the tomatoes has evaporated. Strain the sauce and keep hot.
9. Unmold the chicken liver cake onto a warmed serving dish. Coat with the tomato sauce, and serve immediately.

Terrine de faisan

Pheasant Terrine

	00:40	01:30

American	Ingredients	Metric/Imperial
1	Small pheasant, with giblets	1
½ lb	Boneless pork shoulder	250 g / 8 oz
½ lb	Boneless fatty veal shoulder	250 g / 8 oz
¾ lb	Lightly salted bacon	350 g / 12 oz
6	Dried sage leaves	6
1	Bay leaf	1
3	Fresh thyme sprigs	3
	Salt and pepper	
⅔ cup	Dry white wine	150 ml / ¼ pint
2 tbsp	Brandy	2 tbsp
2 - 4	Very thin strips of fatty bacon	2 - 4
1 tbsp	Flour	1 tbsp
2 tbsp	Water	2 tbsp

1. Preheat the oven to 400°F / 200°C / Gas Mark 6.
2. Bone the pheasant and remove the skin, trying not to tear it. Put the skin to one side. Also put aside the breast. Grind [mince] the rest of the pheasant meat, with the giblets, pork, veal, bacon, sage, bay leaf and thyme. Season with salt and a lot of pepper. Add the white wine, and carefully mix together all these ingredients.
3. Cut the pheasant breast into thin slices. Season to taste with salt and pepper. Line the bottom and sides of a terrine with the pheasant skin. Fill one third of the terrine with the ground meat, cover with half the pheasant breast slices, and repeat until the terrine is completely full, finishing with a layer of ground meat.
4. Prick here and there with a skewer, and pour over the brandy. Cover with the strips of bacon and put the lid on the terrine. Mix the flour and water to make a very soft paste and put this in a strip all around the lid to seal the terrine.
5. Place the terrine in a baking pan containing 2 in / 5 cm of water. Bake for 1½ hours.
6. Take the terrine out of the oven and let it cool slightly (10 minutes), then take off the lid. Put a board with a weight on top. Leave in a cool place for 12 hours before serving.

Preserves are a delicious accompaniment to pâtés, terrines and galantines

Eggs

Oeufs en brioche
Eggs in Brioche

	00:30		01:15

American	Ingredients	Metric/Imperial
1	Onion	1
1	Carrot	1
¼ cup	Butter	50 g / 2 oz
	Dried thyme	
½	Bay leaf	½
¼ cup	Tomato paste [purée]	4 tbsp
⅔ cup	White wine	150 ml / ¼ pint
⅔ cup	Water	150 ml / ¼ pint
	Salt and pepper	
	Cayenne pepper or tabasco sauce	
6	Small brioches	6
6	Eggs	6
⅔ cup	Crème fraîche	150 ml / ¼ pint
1	Egg yolk	1

1. Peel and finely chop the onion. Peel and grate the carrot. Heat the butter in a saucepan, add the onion, carrot, a pinch of thyme and the bay leaf and cook until softened but not browned. Add the tomato paste, wine and water. Stir well. Cook over a low heat for 1 hour.
2. Preheat the oven to 400°F / 200°C / Gas Mark 6.
3. Strain the sauce and season with salt and pepper. Add a small pinch of cayenne pepper or a few drops of tabasco sauce. This sauce must be quite highly seasoned. Keep hot.
4. Take the tops off the brioches and hollow out the insides with a small pointed knife. Put the brioches in the oven, without their tops, for a few minutes to heat through.
5. Break an egg into each brioche. Season lightly with salt and pepper. Put back in the oven and bake for 12-15 minutes, just enough to cook the eggs. Heat the brioche tops as well.
6. Mix the crème fraîche with the egg yolk. Add to the sauce and heat through, stirring. Do not allow to boil. Serve the sauce with the eggs in brioche.

Oeufs en cocotte
Baked Eggs with Sorrel Cream

	00:15		00:06 to 00:08

American	Ingredients	Metric/Imperial
1	Loaf of french bread	1
6 tbsp	Butter	75 g / 3 oz
	Chopped fresh chives	
	Chopped fresh parsley	
½ lb	Sorrel (or spinach)	250 g / 8 oz
	Salt and pepper	
1 cup	Crème fraîche	250 ml / 8 fl oz
12	Eggs	12

1. Preheat the oven to 400°F / 200°C / Gas Mark 6.
2. Cut the french loaf into 3 pieces, each 5 in / 12 cm long, and split each piece open. Butter the cut surfaces lightly.

Sprinkle with chopped chives and parsley. Cut each piece in half crosswise to make 6 pieces. Set aside.
3. Clean the sorrel, removing the stalks and keeping only the green part of the leaves. Rinse and drain. Put it in a saucepan with 2 tablespoons [25 g / 1 oz] of the butter, and salt and pepper to taste. Cover and cook for 1 minute, then remove the lid and continue cooking until the moisture has evaporated.
4. Bring the crème fraîche to a boil in a small saucepan. Season with salt and pepper, add the cooked sorrel and stir gently. Remove from the heat and keep hot.
5. Generously butter 6 ramekins. Sprinkle the bottoms with salt and pepper. Break 2 eggs into each ramekin without breaking the yolks. Place the ramekins in an ovenproof dish and add water to the dish to come halfway up the sides of the ramekins. Cover with foil and bake for 6-8 minutes, or until the whites become opaque and the yolks are still liquid. (This is a matter of taste: some people prefer both white and yolk well done.)
6. Take the ramekins out of the oven, cover with the sorrel sauce and serve very hot with the herbed bread.

Brioche

Oeufs aux fines herbes
Eggs with Herbs

	00:05		00:15

American	Ingredients	Metric/Imperial
6 tbsp	Butter	75 g / 3 oz
6	Eggs	6
1 ½ cups	Crème fraîche	350 ml / 12 fl oz
⅛ tsp	Cornstarch [cornflour]	⅛ tsp
1	Bunch of fresh chervil or parsley	1
1	Bunch of fresh chives	1
	Salt and pepper	

1. Melt the butter and divide between 6 small ramekins. Break an egg into each dish. Heat about 1 in / 2.5 cm water in a pan large enough to hold the ramekins. When the water is almost simmering put the ramekins in the pan. Cook gently until the eggs are just set.
2. Meanwhile, place the crème fraîche in a saucepan and boil to reduce by half. Add the cornstarch, dissolved in a tiny amount of water. The sauce should just coat the back of a spoon.
3. Add the chopped chervil and chives, and season with salt and pepper.
4. Pour the sauce onto the eggs and serve immediately.

Oeufs au gratin
Baked Eggs with Mushrooms

	00:10	00:25 to 00:30
		including egg boiling

American	Ingredients	Metric/Imperial
8	Hard cooked eggs	8
¼ lb	Mushrooms	100 g / 4 oz
1	Shallot	1
	Chopped fresh parsley	
⅓ cup	Tomato sauce	6 tbsp
	Salt and pepper	
3 tbsp	Butter	40 g / 1½ oz
2 tbsp	Dry bread crumbs	2 tbsp

1. Preheat the oven to 400°F / 200°C / Gas Mark 6.
2. Peel the eggs and cut them in half lengthwise. Remove the yolks and mash them. Chop the mushrooms. Peel and chop the shallot. Add the mushrooms, shallot and parsley to the egg yolks and mix well.
3. Add the tomato sauce and season with salt and pepper. Melt 1 tablespoon [15 g / ½ oz] butter in a small heavy pan and cook the mixture for a few minutes.
4. Arrange the egg whites in a buttered gratin dish. Stuff the centers with the mixture. Sprinkle with the bread crumbs. Melt the remaining butter and pour over. Bake for 10-12 minutes or until the eggs are golden on top. Serve hot.

Oeufs en matelote
Eggs with Red Wine Sauce

	00:15	00:45

American	Ingredients	Metric/Imperial
1	Large onion	1
2	Garlic cloves	2
1	Bouquet garni	1
2 cups	Water	500 ml / ¾ pint
2 cups	Red wine	500 ml / ¾ pint
	Salt and pepper	
6	Eggs	6
¼ cup	Butter	50 g / 2 oz
2 tbsp	Flour	2 tbsp
6	Slices of toast	6

1. Peel the onion and 1 clove of garlic and put in a saucepan with the bouquet garni. Add the water and red wine, then season to taste with salt and pepper. Bring to a boil and cook for 20 minutes.
2. Strain the liquid and return it to the pan. Put over a low heat. Break the eggs one by one into a ladle and put into the simmering liquid. Take the pan off the heat, cover and leave the eggs to poach for 3 minutes.
3. When the eggs are cooked, use a slotted spoon to transfer them to a bowl of warm water to keep hot. Strain the egg cooking liquid again.
4. Melt the butter in a saucepan, add the flour and cook, stirring, until the flour becomes golden. Add the strained liquid and stir until the sauce thickens.
5. Cut the remaining garlic clove in half and rub the cut surfaces over the toast. Discard the garlic.
6. Drain the eggs on paper towels and cut them into neat shapes, discarding any excess white.
7. Put one egg on each slice of toast and top with the hot sauce.

Oeufs en meurette
Eggs Poached in Wine

	00:00	01:00

American	Ingredients	Metric/Imperial
2	Onions	2
2	Garlic cloves	2
6 tbsp	Butter	75 g / 3 oz
1	Bottle of red Burgundy wine	1
	Salt and pepper	
1	Bouquet garni	1
2	Cloves	2
2 tbsp	Oil	2 tbsp
6	Slices of bread	6
1	Sugar cube (optional)	1
6	Eggs	6

1. Peel and chop the onions. Peel and crush 1 garlic clove. Heat ¼ cup [50 g / 2 oz] of the butter in a saucepan, add the onions and cook until golden brown. Add the wine, and season with salt and pepper. Add the bouquet garni, cloves and crushed garlic. Cover the saucepan and leave to cook for approximately 45 minutes.
2. Meanwhile, heat the oil in a frying pan, add the bread slices and fry until golden brown on both sides. Drain on paper towels. Halve the remaining garlic clove and rub the cut surfaces over the fried bread. Discard the garlic and keep the bread hot.
3. Taste the sauce: if you find it too acid, sweeten with the sugar.
4. Break the eggs one by one into a ladle, and put into the sauce. Take the saucepan off the heat, cover and leave the eggs to poach for 3 minutes. Take the eggs out of the sauce with a skimmer, and drain them on paper towels. Cut the eggs into neat shapes, discarding any excess white. Put the eggs on the fried bread and keep warm.
5. Strain the sauce and add the remaining butter. Leave to reduce and thicken over a low heat. Taste and adjust the seasoning.
6. Pour the hot sauce onto the eggs and serve immediately.

Oeufs aux crevettes
Eggs with Shrimp [Prawns]

00:20   00:20 to 00:25

American	Ingredients	Metric/Imperial
⅔ cup	Dry white wine	150 ml / ¼ pint
5 oz	Peeled cooked shrimp [prawns]	150 g / 5 oz
1 tbsp	Potato flour or cornstarch [cornflour]	1 tbsp
1 cup	Crème fraîche	250 ml / 8 fl oz
1 tbsp	Tomato paste [purée]	1 tbsp
	Salt and pepper	
½ cup	Butter	125 g / 4 oz
12	Medium eggs	12
12	Round slices of bread	12
2 tbsp	Oil	2 tbsp

1. Pour the wine into a saucepan and bring to a boil. Boil until reduced by half. Add the shrimp.
2. Mix the potato flour with a little cold water. Add this to the wine mixture, with the crème fraîche and tomato paste. Cook, stirring, until thickened and heated through. Season with salt and pepper to taste. Keep warm.
3. Generously butter 6 large ramekins. Break 2 eggs into each one.
4. Heat about 1 in / 2.5 cm water in a pan large enough to hold the ramekins. When the water begins to simmer, put the ramekins into the pan. Cover and cook for 6-7 minutes. The water must never boil. When cooked, the white of the egg should be firm, but the yolk still liquid.
5. Meanwhile, cut the crusts off the slices of bread. Heat the remaining butter with the oil in a frying pan, add the bread slices and fry until golden brown on both sides. Drain on paper.
6. Unmold the eggs onto the fried bread, cover with the shrimp sauce, and serve very hot.

Oeufs durs au fromage
Hard-cooked Eggs with Goat's Cheese

00:20   00:12
plus chilling

American	Ingredients	Metric/Imperial
6	Eggs	6
5 oz	Fresh goat's milk cheese	150 g / 5 oz
	Chopped fresh chives	
	Chopped fresh parsley	
	Chopped fresh chervil	
	Chopped fresh tarragon	
3	Shallots	3
12	Green peppercorns	12
	Salt and pepper	
2 tbsp	Olive oil	2 tbsp
	Lettuce leaves	

1. Hard-cook the eggs for 10 minutes in boiling water, then put them in cold water. Peel them, and leave to cool. Cut them in half lengthwise.

2. Put the goat's milk cheese in a blender or food processor. Add the herbs. Peel and chop the shallots. Add to the cheese mixture with the peppercorns.
3. Remove the yolks from the eggs with a small spoon, keeping the whites intact, and put into the blender with the cheese mixture. Season with salt and pepper to taste. Mix everything together, adding the olive oil a little at a time in order to make a smooth paste.
4. Fill the egg white halves with the cheese mixture and arrange them on a dish lined with lettuce leaves. If liked, sprinkle with a little more chopped parsley. Chill until ready to serve.

Oeufs en gelée
Eggs in Aspic

00:15   00:45
plus chilling

American	Ingredients	Metric/Imperial
1	Bunch of fresh tarragon	1
2 cups	Liquid aspic	500 ml / ¾ pint
2	Thin slices of cooked ham	2
1 tbsp	Vinegar, preferably white wine vinegar	1 tbsp
12	Eggs	12
2 tbsp	Coarsely chopped fresh chives	2 tbsp
	Lettuce leaves	

1. Arrange tarragon leaves on the bottoms of 12 small molds or ramekins. Carefully pour ½ in / 1 cm warm aspic into the bottom of each. Chill until set.
2. Cut the slices of ham into 12 diamond shapes.
3. Put 1 in / 2.5 cm of water and the vinegar in a large saucepan. Bring to a boil, then lower the heat to keep the water at a gentle simmer.
4. Break the eggs into the water one by one, using a ladle to put them into the liquid. Cover and poach for 3 minutes. Take the eggs out with a skimmer and drain on paper towels. Leave to cool, then trim the eggs into a neat shape, discarding any excess white.
5. Take the molds out of the refrigerator and put a poached egg into each. Add a few chives to each egg, and a diamond of ham, then cover with the remaining liquid aspic. Chill for 3-4 hours.
6. Unmold the eggs onto a dish lined with lettuce leaves.

Oeufs miroir
Baked Eggs with Cream

00:05   00:05

American	Ingredients	Metric/Imperial
6 tbsp	Butter	6 tbsp
12	Eggs	12
	Salt and pepper	
1 cup	Crème fraîche	250 ml / 8 fl oz

1. Preheat the oven to 350°F / 180°C / Gas Mark 4.
2. Put 1 tablespoon butter in each of 6 ramekins. Put into the oven to melt the butter.

3. Break 2 eggs into each dish. Season to taste with salt and pepper. Spoon over the crème fraîche.
4. Place in the oven and bake for 4-5 minutes or until the whites become opaque. Serve in the ramekins.

Cook's tip: before putting the eggs in the oven, you could sprinkle them with grated gruyère cheese.

Oeufs mimosa

Stuffed Eggs with Herbs and Tomatoes

⊳ 00:30   00:12 🍲

American	Ingredients	Metric/Imperial
6	Eggs	6
2	Tomatoes	2
	Salt and pepper	
3 tbsp	Chopped fresh chives or parsley	3 tbsp
1 cup	Mayonnaise	250 ml / 8 fl oz
1	Lettuce heart	1

1. Hard-cook the eggs for 10 minutes in boiling water. Drain, put them in cold water and allow them to cool.
2. Cut the tomatoes into 3 slices each, and season with salt.
3. Peel and halve the hard-cooked eggs. Remove the yolks and put to one side. Reserve 6 egg white halves, and mash the other whites with a fork. Mix with the chopped herbs and add the mayonnaise spoonful by spoonful, to obtain an elastic but not soft consistency.
4. Fill the reserved egg white halves with the herb mixture and arrange each on a slice of tomato on top of a lettuce leaf. Sieve the egg yolks and sprinkle over the stuffed whites.

Oeufs mollets sauce verte

Soft-cooked Eggs in Green Sauce

⊳ 00:30   00:05 to 00:06 🍲

American	Ingredients	Metric/Imperial
12	Eggs	12
¼	Bunch of watercress	¼
1	Bunch of fresh chervil	1
4	Fresh parsley sprigs	4
1 cup	Mayonnaise	250 ml / 8 fl oz
6 tbsp	Crème fraîche	6 tbsp
	Salt and pepper	

1. Cook the eggs in boiling water for 5-6 minutes. Drain and put them under cold water immediately. Peel and wipe them dry. Cut a small slice off the flat end so the eggs will stand upright. Arrange them in a serving dish and set aside.
2. Carefully wash the watercress and chop it very finely. Chop the chervil and parsley.
3. Mix the mayonnaise with the crème fraîche and chopped herbs. Taste and adjust the seasoning.
4. Cover the eggs with some of the herb sauce and serve the rest in a sauceboat.

Oeufs au parmesan

Eggs with Parmesan Cheese

⊳ 00:10   00:05 🍲

American	Ingredients	Metric/Imperial
6	Eggs	6
1 cup	Grated parmesan cheese	125 g / 4 oz
5 tbsp	Butter	65 g / 2½ oz
⅔ cup	Crème fraîche	150 ml / ¼ pint
	Salt and pepper	

1. Preheat the oven to 350°F / 180°C / Gas Mark 4.
2. Separate the eggs, being careful not to break the yolks. Put the egg whites into a bowl and beat into stiff peaks. Spoon the egg white into 6 buttered ramekins.
3. Sprinkle the egg white with half the parmesan cheese, then gently rest a whole yolk on the white in each ramekin. Cover with the parmesan. Put a pat of butter on top of each.
4. Bake for 5 minutes.
5. Spoon over the crème fraîche, season to taste with salt and pepper and serve hot.

Oeufs pochés Bénédictine

Poached Eggs Benedict

⊳ 00:10   00:20 🍲

American	Ingredients	Metric/Imperial
6	Slices of bread	6
2	Slices of cooked ham	2
1¾ cups	Butter	400 g / 14 oz
6	Egg yolks	6
6 tbsp	Crème fraîche	6 tbsp
	Salt and pepper	
½	Lemon	½
1 tbsp	White wine vinegar	1 tbsp
6	Eggs	6

1. Cut the crusts off the bread and toast lightly. Set aside.
2. Cut the slices of ham into 6 pieces the same size as the bread slices. Place the ham on the toast and set aside. Melt the butter and skim off the foam.
3. Half fill a large saucepan with water and bring to a boil. Lower the heat to keep the water at a simmer.
4. Put the egg yolks in a bowl and add the crème fraîche. Put the bowl over the pan of water and heat gently, beating with a whisk. When the mixture thickens, beat in the melted butter little by little. Season to taste with salt and pepper and add the juice of the ½ lemon. Leave the bowl standing in the pan of water to keep the sauce hot.
5. Put 2 in / 5 cm of water and the vinegar in a saucepan. Bring to a boil, then lower the heat to keep the liquid at a simmer. One by one, break the whole eggs into a ladle and slide them into the simmering liquid. Take the saucepan off the heat, cover and leave to poach for 3 minutes. Remove the eggs with a skimmer and drain on paper towels. Trim the eggs into neat shapes, discarding any excess white.
6. Arrange each egg on a piece of ham-topped toast. Cover with the hot sauce and serve.

Omelette

Plain Omelette

| 00:05 | 00:08 |

American	Ingredients	Metric/Imperial
12	Eggs	12
	Salt and pepper	
2 tbsp	Water, milk or crème fraîche	2 tbsp
¼ cup	Butter	50 g / 2 oz

1. Break the eggs into a bowl. Add salt and pepper to taste and the water, milk or crème fraîche, if desired. Beat well with a fork for a few seconds to obtain a uniform mixture.
2. Heat the butter in an 11 in / 28 cm frying pan. As soon as it foams (it must not be allowed to brown), pour in the beaten egg all at once. Cook over a low heat, constantly pushing the cooked part of the eggs at the edge towards the center with a wooden spatula. Shake the pan regularly to prevent the omelette from sticking.
3. Slide the omelette onto a dish and fold it over. Serve immediately.
4. You can also cook the omelette on both sides, in which case put a plate over the pan, turn it over quickly and tip out the omelette and slide the omelette back into the pan, cooked side upwards. This is a 'flat omelette'.

Omelette au fromage

Cheese Omelette

| 00:06 | 00:05 to 00:08 |

American	Ingredients	Metric/Imperial
12	Eggs	12
2 tbsp	Milk	2 tbsp
1 cup	Grated gruyère cheese	125 g / 4 oz
	Salt and pepper	
¼ cup	Butter	50 g / 2 oz

1. Break the eggs into a bowl and add the milk, cheese and salt and pepper to taste. Beat well with a fork for a few seconds.
2. Melt the butter in a large frying pan, pour in the egg mixture and cook over a gentle heat, constantly pushing the cooked edges towards the center with a wooden spatula. When the omelette is cooked to your taste, slide it onto a warmed serving dish. Fold it over and serve immediately.

Omelette au four

Baked Omelette

| 00:10 plus cooling | 00:55 |

American	Ingredients	Metric/Imperial
1½ lb	Potatoes	750 g / 1½ lb
½ cup	Butter	125 g / 4 oz
1 tbsp	Oil	1 tbsp
1	Garlic clove	1
	Salt and pepper	
12	Eggs	12

1. Put the potatoes in a saucepan of cold water. Bring to a boil and cook for 20 minutes. Drain and allow to cool.
2. Preheat the oven to 475°F / 250°C / Gas Mark 9.
3. Peel the potatoes and cut them into slices. Heat 2 tablespoons [25 g / 1 oz] of the butter and the oil in a frying pan, add the potato slices and fry until golden. At the last minute, add the garlic clove, peeled and crushed.
4. Turn the potatoes into a buttered ovenproof dish and season to taste with salt and pepper.
5. Break the eggs into a bowl and season lightly with salt and pepper. Beat well with a fork for a few seconds, then pour the eggs onto the potatoes. Put the dish in the oven and bake for 15 minutes.
6. As soon as the top sets, dot it with the remaining butter and lower the oven heat to 350°F / 180°C / Gas Mark 4. Continue baking until the omelette comes away from the sides of the dish, about 15-20 minutes.
7. This omelette can be made with all the standard omelette fillings: mushrooms, bacon, herbs, etc. While it is difficult to make omelettes with more than 6 eggs in a frying pan, this omelette can have as many eggs as the dish can hold. It is an ideal recipe for improvised dinners.

Omelette au plat à la tomate

Baked Tomato Omelette

| 00:10 | 00:15 |

American	Ingredients	Metric/Imperial
12	Eggs	12
	Salt and pepper	
½ cup	Grated gruyère cheese	50 g / 2 oz
1 tbsp	Chopped fresh chives or parsley	1 tbsp
3	Medium-size tomatoes	3
3 tbsp	Butter	40 g / 1½ oz

1. Preheat the oven to 425°F / 220°C / Gas Mark 7.
2. Break the eggs into a bowl and add salt and pepper to taste. Add the cheese and herbs. Beat well with a fork for a few seconds.
3. Peel the tomatoes (first plunging them into boiling water for 10 seconds) and slice them.
4. Heat the butter in an ovenproof dish. Arrange the tomato slices over the bottom of the dish and cover with the beaten eggs.
5. Bake for 15 minutes. Serve hot.

Omelette au haddock

Smoked Haddock Omelette

| 00:10 | 00:25 |

American	Ingredients	Metric/Imperial
½ cup	Peas	50 g / 2 oz
½ lb	Smoked haddock fillets (finnan haddie)	250 g / 8 oz
6 tbsp	Butter	75 g / 3 oz
8	Eggs	8
	Salt and pepper	

1. Cook the peas in boiling water for 10 minutes (less time if using frozen peas), then drain them.
2. Put the haddock in a large saucepan of water, bring to a boil and simmer for 5 minutes. Take the saucepan off the heat and leave the fish to cool in the cooking water. Drain and cut into small pieces.
3. Heat 2 tablespoons [25 g / 1 oz] butter in a saucepan. Add the haddock and drained peas, cover and leave to cook over a very low heat.
4. Meanwhile, break the eggs into a bowl and add salt and pepper to taste. Beat well with a fork for a few seconds.
5. Melt the rest of the butter in a frying pan over a low heat and add the eggs. Cook the omelette, pushing the cooked edges towards the center, until done to your taste. Add the haddock and peas and fold the omelette over. Serve hot.

Omelette aux herbes

Herb Omelette

00:15 00:30

American	Ingredients	Metric/Imperial
3	*Onions*	3
1	*Garlic clove*	1
1	*Bunch of fresh chives*	1
2	*Fresh basil sprigs*	2
1	*Handful of spinach*	1
3 tbsp	*Olive oil*	3 tbsp
12	*Eggs*	12
	Salt and pepper	

1. Peel and slice the onions and garlic. Chop the chives and basil. Cut the stalks off the spinach. Rinse in plenty of water, drain and chop.
2. Heat 1 tablespoon oil in a frying pan and add the onions and garlic. Cook gently until translucent. Add the chives, spinach and basil. Cover and cook over a low heat until the mixture is reduced to a purée (about 15 minutes).
3. Break the eggs into a bowl and add salt and pepper to taste. Add the herb mixture. Beat well together with a fork for a few seconds.
4. Heat the remaining oil in a frying pan and add the egg mixture. Cook the omelette, constantly pushing the cooked edges towards the center until it is done to your taste. Slide onto a dish and fold over. Serve immediately.

Omelette paysanne

Peasant Omelette

00:10 00:06 to 00:08

American	Ingredients	Metric/Imperial
4	*Scallions [spring onions]*	4
1	*Bunch of fresh parsley*	1
	A handful of sorrel leaves	
12	*Eggs*	12
	Salt and pepper	
3-4 tbsp	*Butter or bacon fat*	40-60 g / 1½-2 oz

1. Chop the scallions, parsley and the sorrel leaves and mix together.
2. Break the eggs into a bowl, add salt and pepper and the vegetables and beat well together.
3. Melt the butter or bacon fat in a large omelette pan, pour in the mixture and cook over low heat. Keep moving the egg from the sides to the center as it cooks.
4. When the omelette is cooked to your liking slide it out onto a serving dish and fold it over. Serve at once.

Omelette aux oignons

Onion Omelette

00:10 00:35 to 00:40

American	Ingredients	Metric/Imperial
6	*Medium-size onions*	6
3 tbsp	*Olive oil*	3 tbsp
	Salt and pepper	
8	*Eggs*	8

1. Peel and slice the onions. Heat 2 tablespoons of the oil in a frying pan, add the onions and cook over a moderate heat until softened without browning. Season to taste with salt and pepper.
2. Break the eggs into a bowl and season lightly with pepper. Beat the eggs well for a few seconds.
3. Add the remaining oil to the onions, then pour over the eggs. Cook the omelette on both sides, using a plate to turn it over, until golden but still runny in the center.

Pipérade

Scrambled Eggs with Tomatoes and Peppers

00:20 00:30

American	Ingredients	Metric/Imperial
3	*Onions*	3
3	*Garlic cloves*	3
5 tbsp	*Olive oil*	5 tbsp
2 lb	*Tomatoes*	1 kg / 2 lb
2	*Green peppers*	2
6	*Slices of bayonne ham or prosciutto*	6
6	*Eggs*	6
	Salt and pepper	

1. Peel and chop the onions and garlic. Heat 2 tablespoons of the oil in a frying pan, add the onions and garlic and cook for about 10 minutes over a low heat.
2. Peel the tomatoes (first plunging them in boiling water for 10 seconds). Cut the peppers in half. Remove the core, seeds and white ribs, then cut the flesh into small pieces. Add the tomatoes and peppers to the frying pan and continue cooking for 30 minutes.
3. Heat the remaining oil in another frying pan, add the ham and cover. Brown over a low heat.
4. Break the eggs into a bowl. Season to taste with salt and pepper and beat well for a few moments. Add to the tomato mixture. Stir vigorously, then leave to cook over a low heat until the eggs are creamy.
5. Pour the pipérade into a serving dish, put the slices of ham on top and serve immediately.

Shellfish and Fish

pepper to taste. Bring to a boil, stirring frequently to obtain a velvety sauce. Add the scallops and the reserved whole corals.
5. Mix the egg yolks with 4 tablespoons of the sauce. Add this mixture to the remaining sauce and stir over a low heat, without boiling, until lightly thickened. Serve immediately.

Coquilles Saint-Jacques à la bretonne

Breton Style Scallops

00:40		00:40

American	Ingredients	Metric/Imperial
6	Soft-shell crabs	6
1 tbsp	Oil	1 tbsp
1 tbsp	Butter	1 tbsp
3 tbsp	Brandy	3 tbsp
3	Shallots	3
1	Garlic clove	1
1	Fresh parsley sprig	1
1 lb	Cleaned squid	500 g / 1 lb
¼ cup	Tomato paste [purée]	4 tbsp
1¼ cups	Dry white wine	300 ml / ½ pint
	Salt and pepper	
6	Sea scallops	6

1. Rinse and drain the crabs. Heat the oil and butter in a saucepan, add the crabs and cook, stirring occasionally, until red (about 10 minutes). Add the brandy and set it alight. When the flames die down, remove the crabs with a slotted spoon.
2. Peel and chop the shallots and garlic. Chop the parsley. Add the shallots, garlic and parsley to the saucepan and cook until softened.
3. Cut the squid into small pieces and add to the saucepan. Mix the tomato paste with the wine. Add to the squid with salt and pepper to taste. Leave to cook gently for 20 minutes.
4. Add the scallops and crabs to the saucepan and continue cooking for 10 minutes. Serve hot.

Beignets de crevettes

Shrimp [Prawn] Fritters

00:20 plus resting time		00:06 to 00:07

American	Ingredients	Metric/Imperial
1¼ cups	Flour	150 g / 5 oz
1 tbsp	Oil plus oil for deep frying	1 tbsp
½ cup	Water	4 tbsp
	Salt	
1	Egg white	1
1½ lb	Raw peeled shrimp [prawns]	750 g / 1½ lb

1. Sift the flour into a mixing bowl and make a well in the center. Add the tablespoon of oil, the water and a pinch of salt. Mix well. Leave to rest for 2 hours.
2. Beat the egg white into stiff peaks. Fold into the batter.
3. Heat oil for deep frying to 350°F / 180°C.
4. Dip the shrimp into the batter, then drop them into the oil. Cook for a few minutes until golden brown. Drain and serve hot, sprinkled with salt.

Scallops Newburg (see page 233)

Coquilles Saint-Jacques au safran

Scallops with Saffron

00:20 plus marinating		00:30

American	Ingredients	Metric/Imperial
24	Sea scallops	24
3 tbsp	Brandy	3 tbsp
	Salt and pepper	
¼ cup	Butter	50 g / 2 oz
1 cup	Crème fraîche	250 ml / 8 fl oz
¼ tsp	Saffron powder	¼ tsp
	Cayenne pepper	
2	Egg yolks	2

1. Place the scallops in a mixing bowl, with their corals if available. Add the brandy, season to taste with salt and pepper and stir well. Leave to marinate for 30-40 minutes.
2. Put the 6 best corals to one side. Drain the others and mash them with a fork to make a purée. Put this purée through a food mill or sieve to make it smooth. Drain the scallops, reserving the marinade.
3. Melt the butter in a frying pan, add the scallops and cook until firm but not browned. Add the reserved marinade. Remove from the heat, cover the pan and leave to infuse for 5 minutes.
4. Remove the scallops with a slotted spoon and put to one side. Heat the butter-brandy mixture and add the crème fraîche, the puréed corals, saffron, and cayenne, salt and

Araignées de mer à la bretonne
Spider Crabs Breton Style

 00:45 00:15

American	Ingredients	Metric/Imperial
	Sea salt	
1	Bouquet garni	1
6	Medium-size spider crabs	6
5	Shallots	5
5	Gherkins	5
5	Hard-cooked eggs	5
1 tbsp	Prepared mustard	1 tbsp
1¼ cups	Oil	300 ml / ½ pint
	Salt and pepper	
1	Lemon	1

1. Bring a saucepan of water to a boil and add a handful of sea salt and the bouquet garni. Add the spider crabs and cook for 15 minutes at a simmer. Remove from the heat and leave the crabs to cool in the cooking water.
2. Peel and chop the shallots. Chop the gherkins. Cut 3 of the eggs in half and remove the yolks. (Discard the whites or keep them for another dish.) Mash the yolks in a bowl with the mustard and shallots. Add the oil in a thin stream, whisking vigorously as for mayonnaise. Add the chopped gherkins and season to taste with salt and pepper.
3. Drain the spider crabs. Break off the legs and remove the meat. Open the shells, and remove the creamy parts and the coral, as well as all the meat in the cells. Clean the shells thoroughly and put to one side.
4. Mash the coral and creamy parts and add the mayonnaise to them. Mix well. Stir in the meat and juice of the lemon. Fill the shells with this mixture.
5. Put the remaining 2 eggs through a food mill or sieve and sprinkle them over the filled shells. Serve cold.

Coquilles Saint-Jacques à l'ancienne
Old-Fashioned Style Scallops

 00:40 00:30

American	Ingredients	Metric/Imperial
2	Shallots	2
1 cup	Dry white wine	250 ml / 8 fl oz
	Salt and pepper	
12 - 18	Sea scallops	12 - 18
2 tbsp	Butter	25 g / 1 oz
1 tbsp	Flour	1 tbsp
1 cup	Crème fraîche	250 ml / 8 fl oz
½	Lemon	½
2	Egg yolks	2
	Bread crumbs	

1. Preheat the oven to 475°F / 240°C / Gas Mark 9. Peel the shallots and cut them into thin slices.
2. Pour the wine into a saucepan, season with salt and pepper and add the scallops. Bring to a boil and simmer for 2 minutes.

Remove from the heat and allow to cool, then remove the scallops with a slotted spoon. Set aside.
3. Add the shallots to the wine and boil until reduced to 3 tablespoons of liquid.
4. Melt the butter in a saucepan, sprinkle with the flour and brown lightly, stirring with a wooden spoon. Add the reduced wine and crème fraîche and bring to a boil, stirring. Remove from the heat. Add the juice of the ½ lemon and salt and pepper to taste. Add the egg yolks, one at a time, whisking vigorously.
5. Fill 6 scallop shells with the scallops and coat with the sauce. Sprinkle with bread crumbs and brown quickly in the hot oven.

Calmars sautés
Fried Squid

 00:30 00:30

American	Ingredients	Metric/Imperial
1½ lb	Cleaned squid	750 g / 1½ lb
2	Large onions	2
3	Garlic cloves	3
1¼ lb	Tomatoes	625 g / 1¼ lb
5 tbsp	Oil	5 tbsp
1	Bouquet garni	1
	Salt and pepper	

1. Cut the tentacles off the squid. Cut the bodies into strips and the tentacles into pieces.
2. Peel and chop the onions and garlic. Peel the tomatoes (first plunging them into boiling water for 10 seconds). Cut them into quarters, remove the seeds and coarsely chop the flesh.
3. Heat the oil in a frying pan, add the squid and cook for 3-4 minutes, stirring. Add the onions, tomatoes, garlic and bouquet garni. Season to taste with salt and pepper. Leave to cook for 30 minutes, stirring from time to time.
4. Discard the bouquet garni before serving.

Coques en salade
Cockle or Clam Salad

 00:20 00:10

American	Ingredients	Metric/Imperial
3 quarts	Cockles or small clams	3 l / 5½ pints
2 tbsp	Water	2 tbsp
1 cup	Mayonnaise	250 ml / 8 fl oz
1 tbsp	Chopped fresh chervil	1 tbsp
1 tbsp	Chopped fresh parsley	1 tbsp
3	Hard-cooked eggs	3

1. Put the cockles or clams into a saucepan with the water. Place over a high heat and cook, shaking the pan from time to time, until the shells open (discard any that remain closed).
2. Remove the cockles or clams from the shells, reserving any liquor. Rinse the cockles or clams to remove any sand.
3. Strain the liquor from the shells and the cooking liquid from the pan into a bowl. Add the cockles or clams and leave them in the liquid until ready to serve.
4. Drain the cockles or clams. Add the mayonnaise and stir. Sprinkle with the chervil and parsley. Quarter the eggs and arrange around the salad. Serve cold.

Encornets sétoise
Squid in Chili Sauce

◢▷   00:30   01:00 to 01:30 🍲

American	Ingredients	Metric/Imperial
2½ lb	Small squid	1.25 kg / 2½ lb
3	Tomatoes	3
2	Garlic cloves	2
2	Onions	2
⅔ cup	Olive oil	150 ml / ¼ pint
2 in	Piece of orange peel	5 cm / 2 in
2 tbsp	Brandy	2 tbsp
1 tbsp	Tomato paste [purée]	1 tbsp
1 cup	Dry white wine	250 ml / 8 fl oz
1	Bouquet garni	1
2	Hot red peppers [chillies]	2
	Salt and pepper	
1	Egg yolk	1

1. Clean the squid (see recipe for stuffed squid), discarding everything except the bodies. Rinse the bodies under cold running water. Pat dry with paper towels and cut into thin strips.
2. Peel the tomatoes (first plunging them in boiling water for 10 seconds) and chop the flesh coarsely. Peel and chop the garlic and onions.
3. Heat 2 tablespoons of olive oil in a frying pan. Add the strips of squid and cook over a high heat until all the moisture has evaporated. Add the onions, garlic and orange peel and stir for 3 minutes over a high heat. Add the brandy and mix well, then remove from heat and cover the frying pan. Leave to infuse for 5 minutes.
4. Put the frying pan back over the heat and add the tomatoes, tomato paste, wine, bouquet garni, hot peppers, crushed, and salt and pepper to taste. Leave to cool, covered, over a low heat for 1-1½ hours, adding a little water from time to time if necessary.
5. A few moments before serving, put the egg yolk in a mixing bowl and gradually whisk in the remaining olive oil. Add 4 tablespoons of the sauce and stir well. Take the frying pan off the heat, add the egg yolk mixture and stir well to bind the sauce. Discard the bouqet garni and serve immediately.

Crevettes grises
Boiled or Fried Shrimp

◢▷   00:05   00:04 to 00:05 🍲

American	Ingredients	Metric/Imperial
2 quarts	Water	2 l / 3½ pints
6	Fresh thyme sprigs	6
4	Bay leaves	4
	Sea salt	
1 lb	Small raw shrimp	500 g / 1 lb
	Oil for deep frying	
	Bread	
	Lightly salted butter	

1. *Cooking in water:* Pour the water into a saucepan and add the thyme sprigs, bay leaves and a large handful of sea salt. Bring to a boil. Rinse the shrimp, put them into the stock and,

without waiting for it to come back to a boil, count 5 minutes cooking time. Remove from the heat and let cool for 2 minutes. Drain the shrimp and serve hot, warm or cold.
2. *Cooking in oil:* Rinse the shrimp in a strainer under cold running water and drain them on a cloth. Remove the shells. Heat oil for deep frying to 350°F / 180°C. Put in the shrimp and cook for 30 seconds. Remove the shrimp with a slotted spoon and arrange them on a dish lined with paper towels. Sprinkle with salt, and serve immediately with bread and butter.

Cooked crayfish

Écrevisses à la nage
Poached Crayfish

◢▷   00:30   00:40 to 00:50 🍲

American	Ingredients	Metric/Imperial
1½ quarts	Water	1.5 l / 2½ pints
1	Bottle of dry white wine	1
12	Coriander seeds	12
1	Clove	1
1	Small bay leaf	1
½ tsp	Crushed black peppercorns	½ tsp
1	Hot red pepper [chilli]	1
12	Fennel seeds	12
	Pinch of dried savory	
1	Small fresh thyme sprig	1
	Salt	
2	Onions	2
2	Carrots	2
1	Celery stalk	1
1	Garlic clove	1
40 - 50	Crayfish	40 - 50

1. Pour the water into a large saucepan and add the wine, coriander seeds, clove, bay leaf, peppercorns, hot pepper, fennel seeds, savory, thyme sprig and salt to taste. Heat over a low heat.
2. Meanwhile, peel the onions and carrots and slice them. Chop the celery. Peel the garlic and cut it into quarters. Add these ingredients to the saucepan. Bring to a boil over a high

heat, then simmer over a medium heat for 20 minutes.

3. Rinse the crayfish and clean them by pulling out the central fin of the tail, to remove the small black vein or bowel. Pat dry with paper towels.

4. Add the crayfish to the stock. Bring back to a boil and simmer for 15 minutes. Remove the crayfish with a slotted spoon. Set aside.

5. Strain the stock into another saucepan and boil to reduce it over a high heat until about 3 cups [750 ml / 1¼ pints] remain.

6. Serve the crayfish hot or cold in the reduced stock, or with the hot stock served separately in cups.

Crayfish in tomato wine sauce

Écrevisses cardinalisées

Crayfish in Piquant Wine Sauce

◧ 00:15   01:40 ◧

American	Ingredients	Metric/Imperial
1	Carrot	1
2	Onions	2
5	Shallots	5
2	Garlic cloves	2
1 oz	Fresh pork back fat	25 g / 1 oz
⅔ cup	Dry white wine	150 ml / ¼ pint
⅔ cup	White wine vinegar	150 ml / ¼ pint
⅓ cup	Meat gravy	5 tbsp
2½ tbsp	Brandy	2½ tbsp
2	Fresh thyme sprigs	2
½	Bay leaf	½
	Grated rind of ¼ orange	
1 tbsp	Sea salt	1 tbsp
1 tbsp	Black peppercorns	1 tbsp
	Ground white pepper	
	Cayenne pepper	
36	Crayfish	36

1. Peel the carrot, onions, shallots and garlic and chop them into dice. Cut the pork fat into small dice. Put the diced vegetables and pork fat into a stewpan and add the wine, wine vinegar, gravy, brandy, thyme sprigs, bay leaf, orange rind, sea salt, peppercorns, 2 pinches of ground white pepper and a pinch of cayenne pepper.

2. Bring to a boil and cook very gently until the sauce has reduced by half (about 1½ hours).

3. Meanwhile, rinse the crayfish and clean them by pulling out the central fin of the tail, to remove the small black vein or bowel. Pat dry with paper towels.

4. When the sauce has reduced, put in the crayfish and leave to cook for about 10 minutes.

5. Remove the crayfish with a slotted spoon and pile up in a serving dish. Strain the sauce and serve with the crayfish.

Écrevisses bordelaise

Crayfish in Tomato Wine Sauce

◧ 00:20   00:40 ◧

American	Ingredients	Metric/Imperial
2	Carrots	2
1	Onion	1
2	Shallots	2
1	Fresh thyme sprig	1
½ cup	Butter	125 g / 4 oz
2	Tomatoes	2
36	Crayfish	36
2 tbsp	Olive oil	2 tbsp
3 tbsp	Brandy	3 tbsp
1 tbsp	Chopped fresh parsley	1 tbsp
1 cup	Dry white wine	250 ml / 8 fl oz
	Cayenne pepper	
	Salt and pepper	

1. Peel the carrots and cut them into small dice. Peel and chop the onion and shallots. Take the leaves off the sprig of thyme. Heat 2 tablespoons [25 g / 1 oz] of the butter in a saucepan and add the carrots, onion, shallots and thyme leaves. Cover and cook over a low heat for 20 minutes.

2. Meanwhile, peel the tomatoes (plunge them in boiling water for 10 seconds first), remove the seeds and coarsely chop the flesh. Set aside. Rinse the crayfish and clean them by pulling out the central fin of the tail, to remove the small black vein or bowel. Pat dry with paper towels.

3. Heat the olive oil and 1 tablespoon of butter in a saucepan. Add the crayfish and cook, stirring, until they turn red. Add the brandy and set it alight.

4. Add the cooked vegetables, the tomatoes, half of the chopped parsley, the wine, a pinch of cayenne, and salt and pepper to taste. Bring to a boil over a high heat, then cover and cook over a low heat for 6-8 minutes, according to the size of the crayfish.

5. Remove the crayfish with a slotted spoon and keep hot. Leave the sauce to simmer, uncovered, for 10 minutes.

6. Remove the pan from the heat. Add the rest of the butter, cut into small pieces, then put the pan back over a very low heat. Stir in to bind the sauce. Taste and adjust the seasoning, adding more cayenne if liked.

7. Put the crayfish back in the sauce and reheat briefly. Pour into a warmed dish, sprinkle with the rest of the chopped parsley and serve immediately.

Homards à l'américaine
Lobsters in Rich Tomato Sauce

	00:40	00:25

American	Ingredients	Metric/Imperial
2	Carrots	2
3	Onions	3
2	Shallots	2
1	Garlic clove	1
3	Tomatoes	3
1 cup	Butter	250 g / 8 oz
1 tbsp	Oil	1 tbsp
3 (1½ lb)	Live lobsters	3 (750 g / 1½ lb)
⅓ cup	Brandy	5 tbsp
1 tbsp	Tomato paste [purée]	1 tbsp
2 cups	Dry white wine	500 ml / ¾ pint
1	Bouquet garni	1
	Cayenne pepper	
	Salt and pepper	
1 tbsp	Chopped fresh parsley	1 tbsp

1. Peel the carrots and grate them. Peel and chop the onions and shallots. Peel and crush the garlic. Peel the tomatoes (first plunging them in boiling water for 10 seconds) and chop the flesh roughly.
2. Heat 1 tablespoon of butter and the oil in a large saucepan. Add the carrots, onions and shallots. Cook over a low heat until all the ingredients have softened.
3. Meanwhile, cut up the lobsters. First sever the spinal cord by plunging a knife into the crack on top of the back between the body and tail sections. This will kill the lobster. Cut off the claws and cut the tail section from the body. Cut the tail into sections. Remove the greenish liver, or tomalley, and coral if any and put them in a mixing bowl.
4. Add the claws and tail sections to the saucepan and stir well until the shell turns red. Add the brandy and set it alight. Shake the pan gently until the flame goes out.
5. Mix the tomato paste with the wine and tomatoes. Add to the pan with the bouquet garni, garlic, a pinch of cayenne pepper, and salt and pepper to taste. Cover and cook over a medium heat for 20 minutes.
6. Remove the lobster pieces with a slotted spoon and put them on a dish. Add 2 tablespoons [25 g / 1 oz] of the butter to the lobster liver and mix well. Add this mixture to the sauce with the chopped parsley. Boil for 3 minutes over a high heat, stirring, then taste and adjust the seasoning.
7. Take the saucepan off the heat and add the rest of the butter, cut into small pieces. Whisk vigorously until the sauce is well bound. Discard the bouquet garni. Put the lobster pieces back into the sauce, reheat gently and serve immediately.

Homards grillés
Broiled [Grilled] Lobster

	00:05	00:15

American	Ingredients	Metric/Imperial
3 (1¼ lb)	Live lobsters	3 (625 g / 1¼ lb)
½ cup	Butter	125 g / 4 oz
	Lemon wedges	

1. Have the fish merchant kill the lobsters by severing the spinal cord, then split open the lobsters lengthwise.
2. Melt the butter in a bowl placed over a pan of hot water. Once the butter has melted, leave it to cool. After a moment you will see a whitish sediment form at the bottom of the bowl. Pour the melted butter very carefully into a container, leaving the sediment behind.
3. Preheat the broiler [grill].
4. Arrange the lobsters, cut sides up, in a shallow baking dish and brush them with the clarified butter. Broil for 15 minutes, brushing with more butter from time to time.
5. Serve with lemon wedges, and provide nutcrackers to break the claws.

Langoustines frites
Fried Breaded Scampi

	00:25 plus resting time	00:02 to 00:03

American	Ingredients	Metric/Imperial
24	Scampi or Dublin Bay prawns	24
	Salt and pepper	
1	Egg	1
1½ tsp	Oil	1½ tsp
3 tbsp	Flour	3 tbsp
3 tbsp	Bread crumbs	3 tbsp
½ cup	Butter	125 g / 4 oz

1. If using frozen scampi, allow them to thaw completely. Remove the head and legs. Carefully shell the tails and take out the meat. Thread the scampi onto 6 skewers. Season with salt and pepper and leave to rest for 10 minutes.
2. Break the egg into a bowl and beat it lightly, then add the oil and mix thoroughly. Put the flour and bread crumbs into separate dishes.
3. Heat the butter in a large saucepan. (Alternatively, the scampi may be deep-fried in hot oil.)
4. Dip each skewer first into the flour, then into the beaten egg, and lastly into the bread crumbs. Fry in the butter for about 3 minutes, turning to brown evenly. Serve very hot with tartare sauce or mayonnaise.

Huîtres chaudes au champagne
Hot Oysters with Champagne

	00:30	00:30

American	Ingredients	Metric/Imperial
36	Oysters	36
2	Shallots	2
1 tbsp	Butter	1 tbsp
¼ cup	Crème fraîche	4 tbsp
⅔ cup	Champagne	150 ml / ¼ pint
1 quantity	Hollandaise sauce	1 quantity

1. Open the oysters (see page 229), reserving the liquor, and set them aside on the half shell. Pour the liquor into a saucepan.

2. Peel and chop the shallots. Add them to the saucepan with the butter. Cook gently until the shallots become translucent. Add 2 tablespoons of the crème fraîche and the champagne. Leave to reduce over a low heat, stirring occasionally.
3. Meanwhile, whip the remaining crème until stiff.
4. Preheat the oven to 500°F / 250°C / Gas Mark 9.
5. Add the reduced champagne mixture to the hollandaise sauce, whisking vigorously. Fold in the whipped crème.
6. Coat each oyster with the sauce and put them on a baking sheet in the oven. Bake for a few minutes to brown. Serve hot.

Langoustines en beignets

Scampi Fritters

	00:30 plus resting time		00:20

American	Ingredients	Metric/Imperial
1¾ cups	Flour	200 g / 7 oz
⅔ cup	Beer	5 tbsp
⅔ cup	Warm water	150 ml / ¼ pint
	Salt	
2 tbsp	Oil plus oil for deep frying	2 tbsp
	Sea salt	
24	Scampi or Dublin Bay prawns	24
2	Egg whites	2

1. Put 1¼ cups [150 g / 5 oz] of the flour in a mixing bowl. Add the beer and warm water and mix well, then add a pinch of salt and the 2 tablespoons of oil. Leave to rest for 2 hours.
2. If using raw scampi, pour 4 quarts [4 l / 7 pints] of water into a saucepan and add 2 handfuls of sea salt. Put in the scampi, bring to a boil and cook for 3-4 minutes over a high heat. Drain the scampi. (Allow frozen scampi to thaw completely.) Remove the head and legs. Carefully shell the tails, take out the meat and pat it dry on paper towels.

3. Heat oil for deep frying to 350°F / 180°C. Beat the egg whites until stiff and fold into the batter.
4. Coat the scampi lightly in the remaining flour, then dip them into the batter. Put them in the oil and fry for about 5 minutes or until golden. Remove them with a slotted spoon and arrange them on a dish lined with paper towels. Serve hot with a well-seasoned mayonnaise or with tartare sauce.

Langoustes rôties

Baked Spiny Lobsters

	00:10	00:20 to 00:25	

American	Ingredients	Metric/Imperial
3 (1½ lb)	Live spiny or rock lobsters	3 (750 g / 1½ lb)
¼ cup	Olive oil	4 tbsp
1	Bunch of dried thyme	1
1 tbsp	Crumbled dried thyme	1 tbsp
3 tbsp	Pernod or Ricard	3 tbsp

1. Preheat the oven to 475°F / 240°C / Gas Mark 9.
2. Skewer each lobster under the tail and all the way along the body to keep it flat during cooking. Arrange the lobsters in an ovenproof dish and brush them with 2 tablespoons of the olive oil. Bake for 20-25 minutes.
3. Remove the skewers. Split the lobsters in half lengthwise and arrange them on a broiler [grill] rack, meat side upwards.
4. Put the leaves from the bunch of thyme in the broiler pan, add the rest of the oil and heat on top of the stove. Mix together the crumbled thyme and Pernod.
5. Put the rack holding the lobsters over the broiler pan and pour the Pernod mixture over them. Immediately set it alight, lifting up the lobsters so that everything is flamed. Serve as soon as the flames go out, together with some melted butter or lemon-flavored drawn or clarified butter.

Shellfish

Homards hollandaise

Lobsters with Hollandaise Sauce

| 00:30 | | 00:20 |

American	Ingredients	Metric/Imperial
3 (1½ lb)	Live lobsters	3 (750 g / 1½ lb)
4 quarts	Water	4 l / 7 pints
	Sea salt	
½ cup	Butter	125 g / 4 oz
1 tbsp	Fresh thyme leaves	1 tbsp
1 tbsp	Chopped fresh rosemary	1 tbsp
	Salt and pepper	
	Cayenne pepper	
1 tsp	Lemon juice	1 tsp
1 quantity	Hollandaise sauce	1 quantity

1. Have the fish merchant tie the lobster claws together. Put the water in a large saucepan with 2 large handfuls of sea salt. Put the lobsters into the water, bring to a boil and leave to simmer for 5 minutes. Take the pan off the heat and leave the lobsters in the cooking water for another 5 minutes. Drain and let cool a little.
2. Preheat the oven to 400°F / 200°C / Gas Mark 6.
3. Use scissors to detach the soft, transparent membrane under the lobster tail from both sides. Break the claws with a nutcracker or hammer, without detaching them from the body. Remove the greenish liver, or tomalley, and coral if any from the body and place them in a mixing bowl.
4. Put 2 tablespoons [25 g / 1 oz] of the butter, the thyme leaves and rosemary in a small frying pan. Melt over a low heat, without allowing the butter to foam. Season with salt, pepper and a pinch of cayenne pepper.
5. Lift the lobster tail meat and pour a little of this seasoned butter into the shells. Brush the meat with seasoned butter and put it back in the shells.
6. Add the rest of the butter to the liver and coral with the lemon juice. Heat over a very low heat, stirring, then pour this mixture into the lobster bodies.
7. Arrange the lobsters in a baking dish and bake for 12 minutes.
8. Coat with a little of the hollandaise sauce and brown quickly under the broiler [grill]. Serve immediately with the rest of the hollandaise sauce.

Langoustines nature

Scampi with Mayonnaise

| 00:10 | | 00:10 |
| plus cooling | | |

American	Ingredients	Metric/Imperial
24 - 30	Scampi or Dublin Bay prawns	24 - 30
4 quarts	Water	4 l / 7 pints
	Sea salt	
1 cup	Mayonnaise	250 ml / 8 fl oz
	Tabasco sauce	

1. If using frozen scampi, allow them to thaw completely.
2. Put the water in a saucepan with a handful of sea salt. Put in the scampi, bring to a boil and cook for 2 minutes. Remove

the saucepan from the heat and leave the scampi in the water for 5 minutes.
3. Meanwhile, spice the mayonnaise with tabasco sauce to taste.
4. Drain the scampi in a strainer and cool them under cold running water. Serve cold with the mayonnaise.

Mussels in wine and cream

Mouclade

Mussels in Wine and Cream

| 00:10 | | 00:20 |

American	Ingredients	Metric/Imperial
3 quarts	Fresh mussels	2 kg / 4 lb
2	Onions	2
1	Fresh thyme sprig	1
1	Bay leaf	1
1¼ cups	Dry white wine	300 ml / ½ pint
½	Lemon	½
	Curry powder	
	Salt and pepper	
2 tbsp	Crème fraîche	2 tbsp

1. Scrub the mussels thoroughly and rinse in cold water. Peel and chop the onions.
2. Place the mussels in a large pan with the onions, thyme sprig, bay leaf and wine. Cover and cook until all the mussels open. (Discard any that remain closed.)
3. Take the mussels out of the pan, discarding the empty half-shells. Keep the mussels on the half-shell hot in a dish.
4. Heat up the cooking juices and add the juice of the ½ lemon, a pinch of curry powder and salt and pepper to taste. At the last minute, stir in the crème fraîche. Pour the sauce over the mussels and serve immediately.

Macaronade de moules

Mussels in Tomato Sauce with Macaroni

⊳ 00:40   00:30 🍲

American	Ingredients	Metric/Imperial
30	Large fresh mussels	30
3	Garlic cloves	3
3	Fresh parsley sprigs	3
2	Eggs	2
1½ lb	Pork sausage meat	750 g / 1½ lb
1 tbsp	Soft bread crumbs	1 tbsp
	Salt and pepper	
1 (5 oz)	Slice of salt pork [belly]	1 (150 g / 5 oz)
1	Onion	1
6 tbsp	Tomato paste [purée]	6 tbsp
3 cups	Water	750 ml / 1¼ pints
¾ lb	Macaroni	350 g / 12 oz
1 cup	Grated gruyère cheese	125 g / 4 oz

1. Scrub the mussels thoroughly and rinse with cold water. Place in a saucepan and heat until they open. (Discard any mussels that remain closed.) Drain upside-down.
2. Peel and chop the garlic. Chop the parsley. Mix together the eggs, sausage meat, garlic, parsley, bread crumbs and salt and pepper to taste in a bowl.
3. Put this filling into the mussel shells and close them up. Tie them with string so that they cannot open while cooking. Set aside.
4. Put the slice of salt pork into a pan of cold water. Bring to a boil and blanch for 3-4 minutes, then drain and rinse under cold water. Pat dry. Chop the salt pork. Peel and chop the onion.
5. Place the pork and onion in a saucepan and cook until lightly browned. Add the tomato paste and water and stir well. Add the mussels and cook for 30 minutes.
6. Meanwhile, cook the macaroni in boiling salted water for about 10 minutes or until tender but still firm.
7. Drain the macaroni and put it in a serving dish. Cover with the gruyère cheese and pour the mussels and sauce over the top. Serve immediately.

Moules Daniel

Mussels with Thyme

⊳ 00:50   00:05 🍲

American	Ingredients	Metric/Imperial
50 - 60	Large fresh mussels	50 - 60
	Pepper	
3 tbsp	Crumbled thyme	3 tbsp
	Olive oil	

1. Scrub the mussels thoroughly and rinse with cold water. Open them with a knife and, as you do so, arrange them on their half-shells on a large flameproof dish.
2. Season the mussels with pepper and sprinkle with the thyme. Sprinkle a few drops of olive oil over each mussel.
3. Put the dish over a high heat and cook for about 5 minutes. When the mussels are cooked, sprinkle a little more olive oil over them and serve immediately.

Cook's tip: oil flavored with Provençal herbs is available in the shops and is ideal for this dish. It is also very useful for broiled [grilled], poached or baked fish.

Moules au fromage

Mussels with Cheese

⊳ 00:30   00:20 🍲

American	Ingredients	Metric/Imperial
1½ quarts	Fresh mussels	1.5 kg / 3 lb
3	Celery stalks	3
1	Bay leaf	1
1	Fresh thyme sprig	1
1	Bunch of fresh parsley	1
⅔ cup	Water	150 ml / ¼ pint
	Salt and pepper	
½ lb	Tomatoes	250 g / 8 oz
1	Onion	1
1 cup	Grated cheddar cheese	125 g / 4 oz

1. Scrub the mussels thoroughly and rinse with cold water. Put them in a saucepan. Cut the celery into small dice. Add to the mussels with the bay leaf, thyme sprig, parsley, water and salt and pepper to taste.
2. Cover the pan and cook over a high heat for about 3 minutes, shaking the pan, until the mussels open. (Discard any mussels that remain closed.) Drain them and remove the empty half-shells. Arrange the mussels in an ovenproof dish.
3. Peel the tomatoes (first plunging them into boiling water for 10 seconds). Cut them into quarters, remove the seeds and finely chop the flesh. Peel and very finely chop the onion. Mix the cheese with the chopped tomatoes and onion. Season with salt and pepper to taste and cover each mussel with this mixture.
4. Preheat the broiler [grill]. Put the dish of mussels under the broiler and cook for about 15 minutes or until golden brown. Serve very hot.

Moules en brochettes

Mussel Kebabs

⊳ 00:25   00:06 🍲

American	Ingredients	Metric/Imperial
1 quart	Fresh mussels	1 kg / 2 lb
	Salt and pepper	
5 oz	Thin smoked bacon slices	150 g / 5 oz
	Oil	

1. Scrub the mussels thoroughly and rinse with cold water. Put them in a saucepan, cover and cook over a high heat, shaking the pan from time to time, until the mussels open. (Discard any that remain closed.) Take the mussels out of their shells and season with salt and pepper.
2. Wrap the mussels, 2 at a time, in the slices of bacon and thread them onto 12 skewers.
3. Preheat the broiler [grill].
4. Baste the kebabs with oil, then arrange them under the broiler. Broil them for about 3 minutes, then turn them over and cook the other side.
5. Serve plain or with tartare sauce.

Riz pilaf aux fruits de mer

Seafood Pilaf

	00:30	00:30

American	Ingredients	Metric/Imperial
2	Onions	2
¼ cup	Olive oil	4 tbsp
1¾ cups	Long-grain rice	350 g / 12 oz
2⅔ cups	Boiling water	600 ml / 1 pint
	Salt and pepper	
	Saffron powder	
1 pint	Clams or cockles	500 g / 1 lb
1 quart	Mussels	1 kg / 2 lb
12	Scampi or Dublin Bay prawns	12
6	Scallops	6
4	Small cleaned squid	4
3 tbsp	Flour	3 tbsp
3 tbsp	Butter	40 g / 1½ oz

1. Peel and chop the onions. Heat 2 tablespoons olive oil in a saucepan, add the chopped onions and cook until softened. Add the rice and stir for 3 minutes.
2. Remove from the heat and pour the boiling water carefully into the pan. Season to taste with salt and pepper and add a pinch of saffron. Cover the pan and leave the rice to cook for 15 minutes over a medium heat.
3. Meanwhile, scrub the clams or cockles and mussels thoroughly. Put them in a saucepan, cover and cook over a high heat, shaking the pan occasionally until they open. (Discard any that remain closed.) Drain them, take them out of their shells and rinse them under cold water to remove any sand.
4. Peel the scampi. Wipe the scallops. Cut the squid into rings.
5. Cook the squid for 15 minutes in boiling salted water. Drain and dry on paper towels.
6. Put the flour in a dish. Dip the mussels, clams or cockles, scampi, scallops and squid rings into the flour to coat on all sides. Shake to remove excess flour.
7. Heat the remaining olive oil and the butter in a frying pan. Fry all the floured ingredients in it one after the other until golden brown. When they have all been fried, put them together, season to taste with salt and pepper and add the rice. Mix well and serve immediately.

Pain aux moules

Mussel Loaf

	00:35	00:10

American	Ingredients	Metric/Imperial
1 (8 in)	Round loaf of bread	1 (20 cm / 8 in)
1	Large bunch of fresh parsley	1
3	Garlic cloves	3
4 quarts	Fresh mussels	2.5 kg / 5 lb
3 tbsp	Oil	3 tbsp
	Pepper	
1 cup	Crème fraîche	250 ml / 8 fl oz

1. Preheat the oven to 350°F / 180°C / Gas Mark 4.
2. With a pointed knife, cut a lid off the top of the loaf, then

scoop out the soft inside. Wrap the bread in foil and put it in the oven to heat.
3. Chop the scooped-out bread. Chop the parsley. Peel and chop the garlic.
4. Scrub the mussels thoroughly and rinse in cold water. Place the mussels in a pan, cover and cook over a high heat until they open. Remove the mussels from their shells. (Discard any mussels that remain closed.)
5. Heat the oil in a frying pan. Add the mussels, the chopped bread, parsley and garlic and stir to mix with a wooden spoon. Season lightly with pepper and cook for 2 minutes. Remove from the heat and stir in the crème fraîche.
6. Take the bread out of the oven and fill with the mussels and sauce. Put the lid back on and return to the oven to heat for 5 minutes longer.

Crêpes aux fruits de mer

Seafood Crêpes

	01:00	00:12 to 00:15

American	Ingredients	Metric/Imperial
1 quart	Fresh mussels	1 kg / 2 lb
1 quart	Clams or cockles	1 kg / 2 lb
12	Medium-sized scampi or Dublin Bay prawns	12
	Salt and pepper	
1	Shallot	1
½ cup	Butter	125 g / 4 oz
¼ lb	Cooked peeled shrimp [prawns]	125 g / 4 oz
6 tbsp	Madeira wine	6 tbsp
6 tbsp	Crème fraîche	6 tbsp
1	Egg yolk	1
12 (6 in)	Crêpes	12 (15 cm / 6 in)
1 tbsp	Flour	1 tbsp
½ cup	Grated gruyère cheese	50 g / 2 oz

1. Scrub the mussels and clams or cockles well and rinse in cold water. Put in 2 separate pans, cover and cook over a high heat until they open. (Discard any that remain closed.)
2. Strain the clam liquor (from the shells) and put to one side. Take the clams or cockles out of their shells and rinse quickly to remove any sand. Set aside. Take the mussels out of their shells and set aside.
3. Cook the scampi for 8 minutes in boiling salted water. Drain and leave to cool. Peel and cut them in half lengthwise.
4. Peel and finely chop the shallot. Heat 1 tablespoon butter in a saucepan, add the shallot and cook until softened. Add the shrimp [prawns] and 2 tablespoons of madeira. Remove from the heat, cover and leave to infuse for 10 minutes.
5. Return to the heat, uncovered, and add the clams or cockles, mussels, scampi and 1 tablespoon of crème fraîche. Season to taste with salt and pepper. Mix well. Taste and, if liked, add another tablespoon of madeira. Bring to a boil.
6. Remove from the heat. Add the egg yolk and mix carefully with a whisk. Leave to cool.
7. Preheat the oven to 475°F / 250°C / Gas Mark 9.
8. Fill each crêpe with the seafood mixture. Fold over into triangles and arrange them in an ovenproof dish.
9. Melt 2 tablespoons of butter in a heavy saucepan and add the flour. Stir in ½ cup [125 ml / 4 fl oz] of the clam liquor and the remaining madeira and crème fraîche. Season to taste with salt and pepper. Leave to cook for 10 minutes over a low heat, stirring frequently.

10. Cover the crêpes with the sauce and sprinkle them with the gruyère cheese. Place a pat of butter on each crêpe. Brown for 12-15 minutes in the oven.

Cassolettes aux fruits de mer
Seafood Ramekins

▸▱ 00:30		00:30 🍲
American	**Ingredients**	**Metric/Imperial**
1 quart	Clams or cockles	1 kg / 2 lb
6	Scampi or Dublin Bay prawns	6
¾ lb	Cooked shrimp [prawns]	350 g / 12 oz
1 tbsp	Flour	1 tbsp
½ cup	Butter	125 g / 4 oz
5 tbsp	Crème fraîche	5 tbsp
	Salt and pepper	
10	Eggs	10

1. Wash the clams or cockles in cold water, then put them in a saucepan. Cover and cook over a high heat until the shells open. (Discard any that remain closed).
2. Remove the clams or cockles from their shells and rinse them to remove any sand. Set aside.
3. Peel the scampi and shrimp [prawns].
4. Put the flour in a dish and dip the scampi in it. Heat ¼ cup [50 g / 2 oz] of the butter in a frying pan. Add the scampi and cook until firm. Add the shrimp and stir for 3-4 minutes over a low heat. Add 2 tablespoons of the crème fraîche and salt and pepper to taste. Mix together, then add the clams or cockles. Cook, stirring, until the sauce is thick enough to coat the ingredients. Keep warm.
5. Break the eggs into a bowl, season with salt and pepper and mix the eggs without beating them. Heat the remaining butter in a thick-bottomed saucepan, pour in the eggs and stir over a very low heat until the mixture thickens. Add the remaining crème fraîche and continue to stir over a low heat until the mixture is amalgamated.
6. Add the seafood mixture to the scrambled eggs and fold together. Divide the mixture between 6 ramekins or other small dishes and serve immediately.

Moules marinière
Steamed Mussels in White Wine

▸▱ 00:15		00:10 🍲
plus cooling		
American	**Ingredients**	**Metric/Imperial**
2	Onions	2
½ cup	Butter	125 g / 4 oz
1 tbsp	Chopped fresh parsley	1 tbsp
2 cups	Dry white wine	500 ml / ¾ pint
3 quarts	Fresh mussels	2 kg / 4 lb
	Lemon juice	
	Salt and pepper	

1. Peel and chop the onions. Heat the butter in a saucepan, add the onions and cook over a low heat until softened but not browned. Add the chopped parsley and white wine. Bring to a boil. Remove from the heat, cover and leave to cool.
2. Meanwhile, scrub the mussels thoroughly and rinse in cold water. Add them to the saucepan. Add a few drops of lemon juice and salt and pepper to taste.
3. Place the covered pan over a high heat and cook, shaking the pan to cook the mussels evenly, until they open. (Discard any that remain closed.)
4. Serve very hot.

Cook's tip: accompany this dish with french or italian bread.

Timbale de fruits de mer
Seafood Mold

▸▱ 00:30		00:40 🍲
American	**Ingredients**	**Metric/Imperial**
1	Lobster tail	1
12	Scampi or Dublin Bay prawns	12
½ lb	Sole fillets	250 g / 8 oz
2	Onions	2
1	Garlic clove	1
2	Tomatoes	2
¼ cup	Olive oil	4 tbsp
12	Scallops	12
2 cups	Dry white wine	500 ml / ¾ pint
1	Fresh thyme sprig	1
1	Bay leaf	1
5	Rosemary leaves	5
2	Lemon slices	2
⅔ cup	Water	150 ml / ¼ pint
1 tsp	Cornstarch [cornflour]	1 tsp
	Salt and pepper	
	Cayenne pepper	
1 tsp	Tomato paste [purée]	1 tsp

1. Remove the lobster meat from the shell and reserve the shell. Cut the meat into round slices. Pull the heads off the scampi and keep the heads. Peel the scampi and set aside. Chop the fillets of sole.
2. Peel the onions and cut them into thin slices. Peel and crush the garlic. Peel the tomatoes (plunge them into boiling water for 10 seconds first), then cut them in half, remove the seeds and coarsely chop the flesh.
3. Heat 3 tablespoons olive oil in a saucepan, add the scallops and the pieces of lobster meat and stir for 2 minutes over a high heat. Remove the scallops and lobster with a slotted spoon. Put the scampi in the saucepan and stir for 4 minutes over a high heat. Remove. Put the sole in the saucepan, stir until firm and remove.
4. Add the remaining oil to the saucepan and heat it, then add the scampi heads, lobster shell, onions and garlic. Stir for 3 minutes over a medium heat. Add the wine, chopped tomatoes, thyme sprig, bay leaf, rosemary leaves, lemon slices and water. Cover and simmer over a low heat for 20 minutes.
5. Mix the cornstarch with 1 tablespoon of water.
6. When the sauce is cooked, put it through a strainer over another saucepan. Press all the solids with a wooden spoon to extract as much liquid as possible. Season to taste with salt and pepper and a pinch of cayenne. Add the tomato paste and dissolved cornstarch. Stir over a low heat until the sauce is thickened and well mixed.
7. Add the scallops, lobster, scampi and sole to the sauce. Heat through gently, stirring, and serve hot.

Alose au beurre blanc

Shad with White Butter Sauce

| 00:20 | | 00:40 |

American	Ingredients	Metric/Imperial
1 (3 lb)	Shad, scaled and cleaned	1 (1.5 kg / 3 lb)
2 tbsp	Marc or brandy	2 tbsp
3	Lemons	3
	Court-bouillon	
1¼ cups	Dry white wine	300 ml / ½ pint
1	Bouquet garni	1
9	Shallots	9
	Salt and pepper	
1 cup	Butter	250 g / 8 oz
1 tbsp	Crème fraîche	1 tbsp

1. Preheat the oven to 425°F / 220°C / Gas Mark 7.
2. Carefully rinse the shad in cold water, then wipe dry with paper towels. Pour the marc inside the fish. Thinly slice 1 lemon.
3. Place the fish in an ovenproof dish. Add enough court-bouillon to come halfway up the fish. Add half of the white wine and the bouquet garni, and put the lemon slices on the fish. Cover with foil and bake for about 40 minutes.
4. Meanwhile, make the sauce. Peel and chop the shallots. Put them in a saucepan with the remaining wine and salt and pepper to taste. Boil to reduce the liquid by two-thirds.
5. Cut the butter into small pieces. When the sauce has reduced, add the butter all at once, whisking vigorously, then add the crème fraîche, continuing to whisk. This will prevent the sauce from curdling. Pour the sauce into a warmed sauceboat.
6. Drain the fish and place on a warmed serving dish. Garnish with the remaining lemons, cut into quarters, and serve immediately with the white butter sauce.

Anguilles en matelote

Eels in Red Wine Stew

| 00:40 | | 00:15 |

American	Ingredients	Metric/Imperial
2 lb	Fresh eels	1 kg / 2 lb
1	Medium-size onion	1
10 tbsp	Butter	150 g / 5 oz
1 tbsp	Oil	1 tbsp
1½ tsp	Flour	1½ tsp
1 quart	Red wine	1 l / 1¾ pints
2 tbsp	Brandy or marc	2 tbsp
2	Garlic cloves	2
1	Small ripe tomato	1
	Salt and pepper	
10	Pearl [button] onions	10
5 oz	Smoked bacon	150 g / 5 oz
½ lb	Mushrooms	250 g / 8 oz
	Lemon juice	

1. Clean and skin the eels, then cut them into segments.
2. Peel and chop the medium-size onion. Heat 2 tablespoons

[25 g / 1 oz] butter and the oil in a saucepan, add the chopped onion and cook until softened. Sprinkle in the flour and stir well. Add the pieces of eel and brown them all over.
3. Bring the wine to a boil in another saucepan. Heat the brandy or marc and pour over the eels. Set alight and shake the pan until the flames go out. Add the boiling red wine. Stir well.
4. Peel and chop the garlic. Peel the tomato (first plunging it into boiling water for 10 seconds), remove the seeds and crush the flesh. Add the garlic and tomato to the saucepan. Season to taste with salt and pepper and mix together. Cook for 15 minutes over a medium heat.
5. Peel the small onions. Heat ¼ cup [50 g / 2 oz] butter in a frying pan, add the onions and brown lightly on all sides. Add them to the saucepan.
6. Cut the bacon into dice and blanch for 5 minutes in boiling water. Drain and add to the saucepan.
7. Slice the mushrooms. Heat ¼ cup [50 g / 2 oz] butter in the frying pan, add the mushrooms and brown lightly. Add them to the saucepan.
8. Take the pieces of eel out of the saucepan and keep them hot in a serving dish.
9. Reduce the cooking liquid by half over a high heat. Remove from the heat and add the rest of the butter, whisking well. Add a few drops of lemon juice.
10. Coat the eel pieces with the sauce and serve.

Bar au cidre

Bass with Cider

| 00:20 | | 00:50 |

American	Ingredients	Metric/Imperial
1 (4 lb)	Bass	1 (2 kg / 4 lb)
1	Carrot	1
2	Onions	2
1	Celery stalk	1
1	Bouquet garni	1
2 lb	White fish bones and trimmings	1 kg / 2 lb
	Salt and pepper	
2 quarts	Water	2 l / 3 pints
1 cup	Hard [dry] cider	250 ml / 8 fl oz
2 tsp	Butter	2 tsp
1 tsp	Cornstarch [cornflour]	1 tsp
⅔ cup	Crème fraîche	150 ml / ¼ pint
½	Lemon	½

1. Clean and scale the bass, reserving the head and trimmings. Cut the fish into 6 thick slices. Set aside.
2. Peel and thinly slice the carrot and onions. Thinly slice the celery. Put the vegetables in a large saucepan with the bouquet garni, fish bones and trimmings (including the bass head and trimmings) and ½ teaspoon salt. Add the water. Bring to a boil and cook over a high heat for 20-25 minutes. Strain the fish stock and leave to cool.
3. Preheat the oven to 400°F / 200°C / Gas Mark 6.
4. Arrange the 6 fish slices in a buttered ovenproof dish. Add the cider and 1 ladle of the stock. Season to taste with pepper.
5. Put the dish in the oven. When the liquid starts to simmer, cook for 15-20 minutes. Do not allow to boil.
6. Meanwhile, mash the butter and cornstarch to a paste.
7. Remove the fish pieces with a slotted spoon and arrange them on a hot serving dish. Keep warm. Strain the cooking juices into a saucepan and boil them to reduce.
8. Add the crème fraîche, whisk and add the juice of the

½ lemon. Taste and adjust the seasoning, adding a little more salt and pepper if necessary. Take the saucepan off the heat and add the butter and cornstarch mixture. Whisk well, then put back over the heat to thicken, still whisking. Coat the fish with the sauce and serve immediately.

Barbue farcie à l'oseille

Brill or Flounder with Sorrel Stuffing

⊏▽   00:30   00:40 ⊂⊐

American	Ingredients	Metric/Imperial
1 (4 lb)	Brill or flounder	1 (2 kg / 4 lb)
5	Shallots	5
1½ lb	Sorrel or spinach	750 g / 1½ lb
6 tbsp	Butter	75 g / 3 oz
2 cups	Dry white wine	500 ml / ¾ pint
	Salt and pepper	
1 tbsp	Flour	1 tbsp
1 cup	Crème fraîche	250 ml / 8 fl oz
2	Egg yolks	2

1. Preheat the oven to 350°F / 180°C / Gas Mark 4.
2. Have the fish filleted and keep the head and backbone.
3. Peel and chop the shallots. Rinse, drain and trim the sorrel. Heat 2 tablespoons [25 g / 1 oz] butter in a flameproof dish, add the chopped shallots and soften without browning. Add the fish backbone and head as well as the fillets (flattened with a spatula). Add the white wine and enough water so that the ingredients are just covered with liquid. Season to taste with salt and pepper. Bring to a boil over a low heat, then remove from the heat, cover the dish and poach the fillets for 10 minutes.
4. Meanwhile, heat the rest of the butter in a frying pan, add the sorrel leaves and soften them over a low heat, stirring. Sprinkle with the flour and mix together, then add 4 tablespoons of the crème fraîche and salt and pepper to taste. Cook, stirring, until thickened.
5. Remove the fillets with a slotted spoon and cut them into 12 pieces. Reserve the cooking liquid.
6. Put aside 2 tablespoons of the sorrel mixture, and spread the fish pieces with the rest. Arrange them in an ovenproof dish. Mix the rest of the crème fraîche with the egg yolks.
7. Strain the fish cooking liquid and return to the saucepan. Boil to reduce over a high heat until only about 1 cup [250 ml / 8 fl oz] remains. Add the reserved sorrel and crème and egg yolk mixture. Stir over a low heat, without allowing to boil, until thickened. Coat the fish with this sauce.
8. Bake for about 10 minutes until the top is lightly browned. Serve immediately.

Baked bass

Bar rôti

Baked Bass with Lemon

◤▭▷ 00:10   00:30 🥘

American	Ingredients	Metric/Imperial
1 (3 lb)	Bass, cleaned and scaled	1 (1.5 kg / 3 lb)
	Salt and pepper	
6	Shallots	6
½ lb	Mushrooms	250 g / 8 oz
2	Lemons	2
1	Bouquet garni	1
2 cups	Dry white wine	500 ml / ¾ pint
¼ cup	Oil	4 tbsp

1. Preheat the oven to 450°F / 230°C / Gas Mark 8.
2. Wipe the bass. Make some slashes on the back of the fish and season with pepper. Place the fish in a buttered ovenproof dish.
3. Peel and chop the shallots. Thinly slice the mushrooms. Cut one lemon into slices. Surround the fish with the shallots and mushrooms and put the lemon slices on top. Add the bouquet garni. Pour over the wine, the juice of the second lemon and the oil.
4. Put the dish in the oven and cook for 30 minutes, basting the fish frequently with the juices and only adding salt after the first 15 minutes. Cover the fish with foil if it seems to be drying out too much.

Bar à la Duglére

Bass with Tomato Sauce and Mushrooms

◤▭▷ 00:30   00:30 🥘

American	Ingredients	Metric/Imperial
6	Medium-size tomatoes	6
2	Onions	2
2	Shallots	2
2	Garlic cloves	2
¾ lb	Mushrooms	350 g / 12 oz
1 (3 lb)	Bass	1 (1.5 kg / 3 lb)
3 tbsp	Chopped fresh parsley	3 tbsp
1	Bouquet garni	1
	Salt and pepper	
½ cup	Butter	125 g / 4 oz
2 cups	Dry white wine	500 ml / ¾ pint
2 tbsp	Oil	2 tbsp
1 tbsp	Flour	1 tbsp
	Cayenne pepper	

1. Preheat the oven to 400°F / 200°C / Gas Mark 6.
2. Peel the tomatoes (first plunging them in boiling water for 10 seconds) and chop them coarsely. Peel and chop the onions, shallots and garlic. Slice the mushrooms.
3. Clean and scale the bass and cut into 6 thick slices.
4. Generously butter an ovenproof dish and cover the bottom with half the tomatoes, onions and shallots. Add the garlic and parsley, and arrange the fish pieces over this layer. Cover with the rest of the tomatoes, onions and shallots. Add the bouquet garni and salt and pepper to taste. Dot ¼ cup [50 g / 2 oz]

butter, cut into pieces, over the top, then add the white wine. Put the dish in the oven and cook for 30 minutes.
5. Meanwhile, heat the oil in a frying pan and add the mushrooms. Stir thoroughly and season with salt and pepper, then leave to cook until all the moisture has evaporated. Keep hot. Mash 1 tablespoon of butter with the flour to make a paste. Set aside.
6. When the fish pieces are cooked, remove them with a slotted spoon and arrange them on a serving dish. Keep hot. Pour the cooking juices into a saucepan. Remove the bouquet garni and evaporate half the liquid by boiling over a high heat.
7. Whisk in the butter and flour mixture and adjust the seasoning, adding a pinch of cayenne pepper. Remove from the heat and add the rest of the butter, cut into small pieces, still whisking.
8. Coat the fish with the sauce. Surround with the mushrooms and serve immediately.

Fried anchovies

Anchois frits

Fried Anchovies

◤▭▷ 00:40   00:05 to 00:06 🥘
                 per batch

American	Ingredients	Metric/Imperial
2¾ lb	Fresh anchovies or other very small oily fish	1.25 kg / 2¾ lb
	Oil for deep frying	
	Flour	
	Salt and pepper	

1. Clean the anchovies by removing the heads. Rinse, then pat dry with paper towels.
2. Heat the oil to 345°F / 175°C.
3. Season some flour with salt and pepper. Coat the anchovies in it and shake them so that they retain only a thin film of flour. Arrange a batch of anchovies in a frying basket in one layer. (They must not stick together.)
4. Put into the oil and cook until the fish are just firm and golden brown, about 6 minutes. Drain on paper towels. Keep hot until all the anchovies have been fried.

5. Small fried fish soften quickly, so do not cook them too far in advance. Serve with bread, butter and lemon wedges.

Anguilles au vert

Eels in Green Sauce

⏱ 00:30   00:20 to 00:30 🍲

American	Ingredients	Metric/Imperial
4 lb	Fresh medium-size eels	2 kg / 4 lb
½ lb	Sorrel or spinach	250 g / 8 oz
½ lb	Watercress	250 g / 8 oz
2	Onions	2
3	Celery stalks	3
¼ cup	Butter	50 g / 2 oz
1	Bottle of white wine	1
¾ cup	Chopped fresh parsley	25 g / 1 oz
¾ cup	Chopped fresh chervil	25 g / 1 oz
1 tsp	Chopped fresh sage	1 tsp
1 tsp	Chopped fresh mint	1 tsp
1 tsp	Chopped fresh savory	1 tsp
	Salt and pepper	
6	Egg yolks	6
1 cup	Crème fraîche	250 ml / 8 fl oz
	Lemon juice	

1. Clean and skin the eels (or have this done for you), then cut them into segments.
2. Trim the sorrel, removing the stalks and keeping only the green part of the leaves. Rinse it, drain well and cut it into thin strips. Remove the stalks from the watercress, rinse it and dry well.
3. Peel and finely chop the onions and celery. Heat the butter in a saucepan, add the onions and celery and soften over a medium heat.
4. Add the eel pieces and cook until they are just firm.
5. Add the wine, sorrel, watercress and herbs. Season to taste with salt and pepper. Cover and simmer for 15 minutes.
6. Remove from the heat. Add the egg yolks mixed with the crème fraîche, whisking vigorously. Add a few drops of lemon juice. Heat without boiling, stirring constantly, and serve hot or cold.

Bonite au four

Baked Bonito with Fennel

⏱ 00:40   00:45 🍲

American	Ingredients	Metric/Imperial
1 (3 lb)	Bonito or tuna	1 (1.5 kg / 3 lb)
3	Garlic cloves	3
1	Small sweet red or green pepper	1
3	Fresh fennel sprigs	3
⅔ cup	Olive oil	150 ml / ¼ pint
	Salt and pepper	
1	Bunch of fresh thyme	1
1	Fresh rosemary sprig	1

1. Clean the fish, wipe it and put it in an ovenproof dish. Make 3 or 4 slashes on the top of the fish.
2. Peel and thinly slice one clove of garlic. Remove the core and seeds from the pepper and cut it into strips. Insert the garlic slices and pepper strips in the cuts in the fish. Stuff the fish with fennel sprigs.
3. Pour the olive oil into a bowl and season to taste with salt and pepper. Add the remaining garlic, peeled and crushed. Make a brush with the bunch of thyme and sprig of rosemary. Dip it into the flavored oil and brush the fish several times. Leave to marinate for at least 30 minutes.
4. Preheat the oven to 425°F / 220°C / Gas Mark 7.
5. Place the fish in the oven and bake for 45 minutes, basting it several times with the flavored oil.

Quenelles de brochet

Pike Dumplings

⏱ 01:30   01:00 🍲

American	Ingredients	Metric/Imperial
1¼ cups	Water	300 ml / ½ pint
1¼ cups + 2 tbsp	Butter	300 g / 11 oz
	Salt and pepper	
1¼ cups	Flour	200 g / 8 oz
6	Eggs	6
1 (2 lb)	Pike, filleted	1 (1 kg / 2 lb)
	Cayenne pepper	
1 quart	Milk	1 l / 1¾ pints
	Grated nutmeg	
⅔ cup	Crème fraîche	150 ml / ¼ pint

1. Place the water and 2 tablespoons [25 g / 1 oz] of the butter in a saucepan. Add a pinch of salt. Bring to a boil, then remove from the heat and add ¾ cup [100 g / 4 oz] flour all at once, stirring vigorously. Stir over the heat to dry this paste. Remove from the heat again and add one egg, stirring quickly and carefully. Leave to cool completely, then place the panada in the refrigerator to chill.
2. Meanwhile, take the skin off the pike fillets. Put the flesh through a grinder [mincer] or food processor. Chill for 1 hour.
3. Put the bowl containing the puréed pike in a bowl of crushed ice. Season with salt, pepper and a pinch of cayenne and mix with a wooden spatula. Add the panada and stir over the ice until amalgamated. Add the remaining eggs, one at a time, stirring well.
4. Soften ¾ cup [175 g / 6 oz] butter with a wooden spatula and add it to the mixture. Work all the ingredients thoroughly together to obtain a fine homogeneous paste.
5. Flour your hands. Divide the paste into balls and roll them on a floured worktop to obtain cylinders 2½ in / 6 cm long and 1 in / 2.5 cm in diameter.
6. Heat a saucepan of water to 175°F / 90°C and poach the dumplings in it for 15 minutes, without allowing the water to boil. Remove the dumplings with a slotted spoon, put in cold water to cool and then drain.
7. Preheat the oven to 400°F / 200°C / Gas Mark 6.
8. Melt the remaining ½ cup [100 g / 4 oz] butter in a saucepan, add the remaining ½ cup [100 g / 4 oz] flour and mix well. Add the milk. Leave to thicken over a medium heat, stirring constantly, then season with salt, pepper and a pinch of grated nutmeg. Stir in the crème fraîche.
9. Butter a gratin dish and arrange the dumplings in it. Coat with the white sauce. Bake for 15 minutes. Serve at once.

Colin poché au court-bouillon
Poached Hake with Lemon Butter

	00:10	00:45

American	Ingredients	Metric/Imperial
2 quarts	Cold water	2 l / 3½ pints
⅓ cup	Vinegar	5 tbsp
2	Onions	2
2	Cloves	2
2	Carrots	2
1	Bouquet garni	1
	Salt and pepper	
1 (2 - 3 lb)	Hake, cleaned	1 (1-1.5 kg / 2-3 lb)
1 cup	Butter	250 g / 8 oz
1	Lemon	1

1. Put the water, vinegar, peeled onions studded with the cloves, peeled and sliced carrots, bouquet garni and salt and pepper to taste into a saucepan. Bring to a boil, then cover and leave to simmer gently for 30 minutes. Leave the stock to cool.
2. Add the hake to the stock, put back over a very low heat and simmer for about 15 minutes.
3. Meanwhile, melt the butter without allowing it to brown. Cool, then carefully pour the liquid, yellow butter into a bowl, without disturbing the white sediment at the bottom. Season with salt and pepper and add the juice of the lemon.
4. Drain the hake and serve with the lemon butter.

Cook's tip: you can replace the lemon butter with white butter sauce or hollandaise sauce.

Carpe farcie au Sancerre

Stuffed Carp

	00:30	01:00

American	Ingredients	Metric/Imperial
2	Slices of bread	2
⅔ cup	Milk	150 ml / ¼ pint
3	Hard-cooked eggs	3
1	Onion	1
3	Garlic cloves	3
¾ lb	Pork sausage meat	350 g / 12 oz
1 (4 lb)	Carp, cleaned and scaled, with its roe (or other soft roe)	1 (2 kg / 4 lb)
	Salt and pepper	
2 tbsp	Butter	25 g / 1 oz
1 tbsp	Flour	1 tbsp
½	Bottle of dry white wine	½

1. Preheat the oven to 350°F / 180°C / Gas Mark 4.
2. Soak the bread in the milk. Chop the eggs. Peel and chop the onion and garlic. Mix together the eggs, onion, garlic, sausage meat, soaked bread and carp roe in a bowl. Season with salt and pepper.
3. Fill the fish with the stuffing and sew up with a trussing needle and fine string.
4. Melt the butter in a flameproof dish. Add the flour and

brown lightly, stirring. Stir in the wine. Put the fish in the dish.
5. Bake for about 1 hour, basting the fish with the liquid from time to time. Cut into fairly thick slices and serve hot with the sauce.

Cabillaud mornay
Cod in Cheese Sauce

	00:10	01:00

American	Ingredients	Metric/Imperial
1 (2¾ lb)	Cod, cleaned	1 (1.25 kg / 2¾ lb)
	Court-bouillon	
6	Fresh mussels	6
1 tbsp	Butter	1 tbsp
1 tbsp	Flour	1 tbsp
⅔ cup	Milk	150 ml / ¼ pint
⅔ cup	Crème fraîche	150 ml / ¼ pint
½ cup	Grated gruyère cheese	50 g / 2 oz
	Salt and pepper	

1. Put the cod into a large saucepan and cover with court-bouillon. Bring to a boil, then lower the heat and cook for 10 minutes. Turn off the heat, cover the saucepan and leave the fish to poach for a further 5 minutes. Drain the fish, reserving 1¼ cups [300 ml / ½ pint] of the cooking liquid. Remove all the skin and bones and break the flesh into pieces the size of an egg. Set aside.
2. Thoroughly scrub the mussels. Rinse and drain them.
3. Preheat the oven to 400°F / 200°C / Gas Mark 6.
4. Melt the butter in a saucepan, sprinkle with the flour and stir for 1 minute over a medium heat. Add the milk, reserved cooking liquid and crème fraîche. Leave to thicken over a low heat, stirring constantly. Add 2 tablespoons of the cheese and salt and pepper to taste.
5. Arrange the fish in an ovenproof dish with the mussels. Coat with the sauce. Sprinkle with the remaining cheese and dot with a little extra butter. Bake for 20 minutes.

Darnes de colin meunière

Sautéed Hake Steaks

	00:10	00:20 to 00:25

American	Ingredients	Metric/Imperial
⅔ cup	Milk	150 ml / ¼ pint
	Salt and pepper	
3 tbsp	Flour	3 tbsp
6	Hake steaks, 1 in / 2.5 cm thick	6
½ cup	Butter	125 g / 4 oz
⅓ cup	Oil	5 tbsp

1. Pour the milk into a dish and add ½ teaspoon salt. Put the flour in another dish. Dip the fish steaks first in the milk and then in the flour. Shake to remove the excess flour.
2. Preheat the oven to 425°F / 220°C / Gas Mark 7.
3. Heat the butter and oil in a large frying pan. Fry the fish steaks on one side until golden, then turn them over and fry the other side over a low heat.

4. Arrange the steaks on a serving dish, season lightly with salt and pepper and put the dish into the oven with the door open. Leave to crisp, about 3 minutes.
5. Serve with melted butter mixed with lemon juice.

Eglefins à la mode de Porto
Haddock with Tomato Rice

00:15   00:45

American	Ingredients	Metric/Imperial
2 lb	Tomatoes	1 kg / 2 lb
3	Onions	3
2	Shallots	2
3	Garlic cloves	3
¼ cup	Oil	4 tbsp
1	Bouquet garni	1
	Salt and pepper	
1 cup	Long-grain rice	250 g / 8 oz
1½ quarts	Water	1.5 l / 2½ pints
6	Haddock steaks	6
1 quart	Dry white wine	1 l / 1¾ pints

1. Peel the tomatoes (first plunging them in boiling water for 10 seconds), remove the seeds and chop the flesh coarsely. Peel the onions, shallots and garlic and chop them.
2. Heat the oil in a saucepan, add the onions, garlic and shallots and brown them lightly. Add the tomatoes, bouquet garni, and salt and pepper to taste. Leave to cook over a low heat for 20 minutes, stirring occasionally.
3. Meanwhile, put the rice in a saucepan with the water. Bring to a boil and boil for 5-6 minutes.
4. Add the rice to the tomato sauce and stir to mix. Put the fish steaks on the top. Add the wine (which must cover the rice). Cover and cook over a low heat for 20 minutes. Serve very hot.

Porgy with white wine

Daurade au vin blanc
Porgy [Sea Bream] with White Wine

00:10   00:30 to 00:40

American	Ingredients	Metric/Imperial
1 (3 lb)	Porgy [sea bream], cleaned and scaled	1 (1.5 kg / 3 lb)
	Salt and pepper	
2 tbsp	Olive oil	2 tbsp
1	Large onion	1
4	Medium-size tomatoes	4
1 cup	Dry white wine	250 ml / 8 fl oz
¼ cup	Butter	50 g / 2 oz
1 tbsp	Chopped fresh parsley	1 tbsp
1	Lemon	1

1. Preheat the oven to 425°F / 220°C / Gas Mark 7.
2. Season the inside of the fish with salt and pepper, and coat the outside with the olive oil. Put the fish in an ovenproof dish.
3. Peel and slice the onion. Break the slices into rings. Cut the tomatoes into quarters. Surround the fish with the tomatoes and cover it with the onion rings. Season with salt and pepper and add the wine.
4. Put the dish in the oven. When the liquid boils, cook for 30-40 minutes, basting with the juices from time to time.
5. Turn off the oven. Add the butter, cut into small pieces, to the dish with the parsley and the juice of the lemon. Leave in the oven for 5 minutes longer before serving.

Daurade au fenouil
Porgy [Sea Bream] with Fennel

00:10   00:20 to 00:30

American	Ingredients	Metric/Imperial
2 (1½ lb)	Porgy [sea bream], cleaned and scaled	2 (750 g / 1½ lb)
	Salt and pepper	
2 tbsp	Fennel seeds	2 tbsp
⅔ cup	Olive oil	150 ml / ¼ pint
10	Fresh fennel sprigs	10
3	Lemons	3

1. Preheat the oven to 350°F / 180°C / Gas Mark 4.
2. Season the inside of the fish with salt and pepper, and put 1 teaspoon of fennel seeds in each fish. Season the outside with salt. Slash both fish twice and brush with a little olive oil.
3. Put the sprigs of fennel side by side in an ovenproof dish and place the fish on top. Cut one lemon into slices and arrange these over the fish. Put the dish in the oven and bake for 20-30 minutes without turning the fish over.
4. Meanwhile, put the remaining olive oil in a saucepan or bowl with the juice of a second lemon and the remaining fennel seeds. Season with salt and pepper to taste. Put the saucepan or bowl over another saucepan containing hot water and heat.
5. When the fish are cooked, arrange them on a serving dish and garnish with the remaining lemon, quartered. Serve with the lemon and fennel oil.

Lotte au poivre vert

Monkfish with Green Peppercorns

▸ 00:10   00:30 to 00:40 🍲

American	Ingredients	Metric/Imperial
¼ cup	Butter	50 g / 2 oz
2¾ lb	Thin slices of monkfish (scaloppine or escalopes)	1.25 kg / 2¾ lb
	Salt	
2 tbsp	Bottled green peppercorns, drained	2 tbsp
1¼ cups	White wine	300 ml / ½ pint
1 cup	Crème fraîche	250 ml / 8 fl oz
2	Egg yolks	2

1. Heat the butter in a large frying pan, add the fish slices and cook until firm without browning (do not overlap them). Season with salt and cook gently for about 10 minutes. Remove the fish with a slotted spatula and keep hot.
2. Roughly crush the green peppercorns. Add them to the pan with the wine and boil over a medium heat to reduce to about half the quantity.
3. Return the fish to the pan. Add 6 tablespoons of the crème fraîche and bring to simmering point. Adjust the seasoning if necessary and leave to cook for a further 15-20 minutes.
4. Arrange the fish slices on a warmed serving dish and keep hot. Mix the egg yolks with remaining crème fraîche and 1 tablespoon of the sauce. Add this mixture to the rest of the sauce, whisking, then cook without boiling, stirring, until the mixture will coat the back of a spoon.
5. Pour the sauce over the fish and serve immediately.

Lotte en blanquette

Monkfish in White Sauce

▸ 00:20   00:45 🍲

American	Ingredients	Metric/Imperial
24	Pearl [button] onions	24
¾ cup	Butter	175 g / 6 oz
1 tbsp	Sugar	1 tbsp
	Salt and pepper	
2 lb	Monkfish fillet	1 kg / 2 lb
1½ cups	Dry white wine	350 ml / 12 fl oz
	Court-bouillon	
½ lb	Mushrooms	250 g / 8 oz
1	Lemon	1
2 tbsp	Flour	2 tbsp
1	Egg yolk	1
⅔ cup	Crème fraîche	150 ml / ¼ pint

1. Peel the onions. Put them in a saucepan with 3 tablespoons [40 g / 1½ oz] of the butter, the sugar, a pinch of salt and some pepper, and add just enough water to cover the onions. Cover and cook over a low heat until the onions are tender and the liquid has formed a clear caramel.

2. Meanwhile, cut the fish into large cubes. Melt 3 tablespoons [40 g / 1½ oz] butter in a saucepan, add the pieces of fish and cook until firm without browning. Add the wine and enough court-bouillon to cover the fish. Bring to a boil, then simmer for about 20 minutes.
3. While the fish is cooking, heat 3 tablespoons [40 g / 1½ oz] of the butter in a saucepan and add the mushrooms, the juice of the lemon, and salt and pepper to taste. Cover and cook for 10 minutes over a medium heat.
4. Melt the rest of the butter in a saucepan, add the flour and stir for 2 minutes over a low heat. Add the fish cooking liquid and cook, stirring, for 10 minutes over a medium heat until thickened. Add the mushrooms.
5. Mix the egg yolk in a bowl with crème fraîche. Add a few spoonfuls of the sauce, whisking vigorously, then stir this into the remaining sauce. Put the fish pieces in the sauce and heat without boiling.
6. Arrange the fish stew in a serving dish, surround with the onions and serve immediately.

Lotte en matelote

Monkfish Stew in Red Wine

▸ 00:30   01:00 🍲

American	Ingredients	Metric/Imperial
½ lb	Bacon, in a piece	250 g / 8 oz
½ lb	Pearl [button] onions	250 g / 8 oz
3 lb	Monkfish fillet	1.5 kg / 3 lb
¼ cup	Brandy	4 tbsp
2 cups	Red wine	500 ml / ¾ pint
1	Bouquet garni	1
	Salt and pepper	
5 tbsp	Butter	65 g / 2½ oz
½ lb	Mushrooms	250 g / 8 oz
2 tbsp	Flour	40 g / 1½ oz

1. Put the bacon in a saucepan of cold water, bring to a boil and blanch for 5 minutes. Drain and cut into dice. Peel the onions. Set aside.
2. Put the bacon dice in a sauce and brown over a low heat. Remove with a slotted spoon and put to one side.
3. Cut the fish into equal-size pieces. Add to the bacon fat in the pan and cook over a high heat, turning the pieces, until firm. Remove from the heat. Add the brandy and stir, then cover the saucepan and leave on one side for 10 minutes.
4. Put the saucepan back over the heat. Add the red wine and enough water to cover the fish. Add the bouquet garni and bacon. Season with salt and pepper. Cover and bring to a boil over a high heat, then leave to cook over a low heat for 20 minutes.
5. Meanwhile, melt 3 tablespoons [40 g / 1½ oz] butter in a saucepan, add the onions and fry them, with the lid on, over a medium heat until golden brown on all sides. Remove the onions with a slotted spoon and add to the fish. Put the mushrooms in the saucepan with the onion cooking butter, and cook until all their moisture has evaporated. Add to the fish and cook for a further 15-18 minutes.
6. Remove the bouquet garni. Mix the remaining butter with the flour to make a paste. Add to the fish stew, off the heat, stirring well. Put the pan back over the heat and boil for 2 minutes, stirring constantly, to thicken the sauce. Serve immediately.

Limandes à la provençale
Provençal Style Dabs

	00:15 plus soaking		00:40

American	Ingredients	Metric/Imperial
6	Dabs (portion-sized)	6
2	Lemons	2
1	Fennel bulb	1
4	Onions	4
1	Sweet red or green pepper	1
6	Tomatoes	6
3	Garlic cloves	3
5 tbsp	Oil	5 tbsp
1	Bouquet garni	1
	Salt and pepper	
1 cup	Rosé wine	250 ml / 8 fl oz
20	Olives	20

1. Cut all around the backbone of the dabs with scissors. Slash the flesh in 2 or 3 places with a sharp knife, and sprinkle the fish with the juice of the lemons. Leave to soak for 2 hours.
2. Trim and thinly slice the fennel. Peel and thinly slice the onions. Cut the pepper in half, remove the core and seeds and cut the flesh into strips. Peel the tomatoes (first plunging them in boiling water for 10 seconds) and coarsely chop the flesh. Peel and crush the garlic.
3. Heat the oil in a frying pan, add the fennel, onions and pepper strips and cook until softened. Add the tomatoes, garlic, bouquet garni and salt and pepper to taste. Leave to cook for about 15 minutes or until thickened, stirring occasionally.
4. Arrange the dabs on the tomato sauce. Add the wine. Cover and cook for 10 minutes over a medium heat.
5. Meanwhile, pit [stone] the olives. Add them to the frying pan and continue cooking for 10 minutes. Serve very hot.

Cook's tip: You can prepare sole or other flat fish in the same way as the dabs.

Lotte à l'américaine
Monkfish in Tomato Sauce

	00:15		00:25

American	Ingredients	Metric/Imperial
½ lb	Onions	250 g / 8 oz
2	Shallots	2
2	Garlic cloves	2
5	Tomatoes	5
3 lb	Monkfish fillet	1.5 kg / 3 lb
	Flour	
¼ cup	Olive oil	4 tbsp
2 tbsp	Brandy	2 tbsp
½	Bottle of dry white wine	½
1	Bouquet garni	1
2	Sugar cubes	2
1 tbsp	Tomato paste [purée]	1 tbsp
	Salt and pepper	
	Cayenne pepper	

1. Peel and chop the onions, shallots and garlic. Peel the tomatoes (first plunging them in boiling water for 10 seconds), remove the seeds and coarsely chop the flesh. Cut the fish into pieces and coat them in flour.
2. Heat 1 tablespoon of oil in a saucepan, add the onions, shallots and garlic and soften over a low heat, stirring frequently.
3. Heat the rest of the oil in a frying pan, add the pieces of fish and cook until the fish is golden brown on all sides.
4. Add the brandy to the fish and set it alight. When the flames die down, add the fish and its juices to the vegetables in the saucepan. Add the wine, bouquet garni, tomatoes, sugar and tomato paste. Season to taste with salt, pepper and cayenne.
5. Bring to a boil, then cover and cook over a low heat for 20-25 minutes. Serve hot.

Lamproie bordelaise

Bordeaux Lamprey

	00:25		02:40

American	Ingredients	Metric/Imperial
1 (3 lb)	Lamprey	1 (1.5 kg / 3 lb)
3	Leeks (white part only)	3
2	Celery stalks	2
1	Carrot	1
1	Large onion	1
½ lb	Mushrooms	250 g / 8 oz
6	Tomatoes	6
4	Shallots	4
4	Garlic cloves	4
¼ cup	Oil	4 tbsp
3 tbsp	Flour	3 tbsp
1	Bouquet garni	1
1 tbsp	Sugar	1 tbsp
1	Bottle of red wine	1
	Salt and pepper	
1 (5 oz)	Slice of cooked ham	1 (150 g / 5 oz)
6 tbsp	Butter	75 g / 3 oz
3 tbsp	Brandy	3 tbsp

1. Plunge the lamprey into a saucepan of boiling water. Bring back to a boil and simmer for 3 minutes. Drain the lamprey, skin it and cut it into 2 in / 5 cm pieces. Set aside.
2. Thinly slice the leeks and celery. Peel and thinly slice the carrot and onion. Remove the stems from the mushrooms and set aside. Dice the mushroom caps. Peel the tomatoes (first plunging them in boiling water for 10 seconds), remove the seeds and coarsely chop the flesh. Peel and chop the shallots and garlic.
3. Heat 3 tablespoons of oil in a saucepan, add the celery, leeks, carrot, shallots, onion, mushroom stems and cook over a low heat, stirring, until lightly browned. Sprinkle with the flour. Cook stirring, for 4 minutes. Add the bouquet garni, garlic, tomatoes, sugar, wine and salt and pepper to taste. Cover and simmer over a low heat for 2 hours.
4. In the meantime, cut the ham into dice. Heat the rest of the oil and the butter in a saucepan, add the ham and diced mushroom caps and cook until golden. Add the pieces of lamprey. Add the brandy and set alight.
5. Strain the wine sauce and add to the eel mixture. Cover and leave to cook over a low heat for 30 minutes.
6. Spoon the pieces of lamprey onto a serving dish and surround with the mushrooms and ham. Serve with the sauce.

Maquereaux marinés

Marinated Mackerel

	00:45	00:35
	plus marinating	

American	Ingredients	Metric/Imperial
3	Onions	3
4	Shallots	4
2	Medium-size carrots	2
5 tbsp	Oil	5 tbsp
2 cups	Tarragon wine vinegar	500 ml / ¾ pint
1 quart	Water	1 l / 1¾ pints
1	Bunch of fresh parsley	1
10	Black peppercorns	10
2	Cloves	2
4	Bay leaves	4
	Salt	
6	Small mackerel, cleaned	6

1. Peel the onions, shallots and carrots and cut them into thin slices. Heat the oil in a saucepan, add the onions and shallots and soften without browning. Add the vinegar and water. Add the carrot slices, bunch of parsley, peppercorns, cloves, bay leaves and salt to taste. Cover and cook over a low heat for 30 minutes. Allow to cool. Remove the bunch of parsley.
2. Preheat the oven to 450°F / 230°C / Gas Mark 8.
3. Arrange the mackerel in an ovenproof dish, in one layer. Add the cold marinade and put the dish in the oven. When the liquid boils, open the oven door and with it ajar, simmer for 5 minutes.
4. Take the fish out of the oven and leave to cool completely. Cover and keep in the refrigerator for 4 days before serving. The mackerel will keep very well for about 2 weeks in the refrigerator, provided that they are always well covered with marinade.

Marinated mackerel

Maquereaux à la moutarde

Mackerel with Mustard

	00:05	00:25 to 00:30

American	Ingredients	Metric/Imperial
6 (6-8 oz)	Mackerel, cleaned	6 (175-250 g / 6-8 oz)
1 cup	Crème fraîche	250 ml / 8 fl oz
3 tbsp	Prepared mustard	3 tbsp
1	Lemon	1
2 tbsp	Chopped fresh parsley	2 tbsp
	Salt and pepper	
¼ cup	Butter	50 g / 2 oz

1. Preheat the oven to 400°F / 200°C / Gas Mark 6.
2. Arrange the fish in an ovenproof dish. Mix the cream with the mustard, the juice of the lemon, chopped parsley and salt and pepper to taste. Coat the fish with this sauce and dot with the butter.
3. Put the dish in the oven and bake for 25-30 minutes or until the sauce has slightly reduced and browned. Serve at once.

Morue en acras

Salt Cod Fritters

	00:30	00:20
	plus soaking and resting	

American	Ingredients	Metric/Imperial
¾ lb	Salt cod fillets	350 g / 12 oz
2	Eggs	2
	Salt and pepper	
2 tbsp	Oil plus oil for deep frying	2 tbsp
1¼ cups	Flour	150 g / 5 oz
1 cup	Beer	150 ml / ¼ pint
1	Garlic clove	1
1	Onion	1
1	Small sweet red pepper	1
1	Small bunch of fresh parsley	1
1	Small bunch of fresh chives	1
1	Egg white	1

1. Soak the cod fillets in cold water for at least 12 hours, changing the water from time to time.
2. Beat the whole eggs in a bowl. Add salt and pepper to taste and then the oil and flour. Stir well and gradually incorporate the beer. Leave to rest for 2 hours.
3. Peel the garlic and onion. Core and seed the red pepper.
4. Drain the fish and rinse it under cold running water. Put it in a heavy saucepan. Cover the fish with fresh cold water and bring to a boil over a low heat. Simmer for 2 minutes, then drain. Cut the fish into small pieces.
5. Put the fish in a blender or food processor with garlic, red pepper, onion, parsley, chives and pepper to taste. Stir the cod mixture into the batter. Beat the egg white into stiff peaks and fold into the cod batter.
6. Heat the oil for deep frying. Drop tablespoonfuls of the batter into the hot oil. Fry until the fritters are golden and puffed up. Drain on paper towels and serve hot with a salad, with raw vegetables as an hors d'oeuvre, or as canapés with cocktails.

Poached Skate with Anchovy Sauce

Raie pochée sauce anchois

00:25   00:50

American	Ingredients	Metric/Imperial
2	Onions	2
2	Carrots	2
4	Cloves	4
1	Garlic clove	1
2 quarts	Water	2 l / 3½ pints
⅔ cup	Wine vinegar	150 ml / ¼ pint
1	Bouquet garni	1
	Salt and pepper	
	Black peppercorns	
3 lb	Skate wing	1.5 kg / 3 lb
3 tbsp	Butter	40 g / 1½ oz
½ cup	Flour	50 g / 2 oz
3 cups	Milk	750 ml / 1¼ pints
6 tbsp	Crème fraîche	6 tbsp
3 tbsp	Anchovy paste	3 tbsp
½	Lemon	½
1	Egg yolk	1

1. Peel the onions and carrots. Slice the carrots. Leave the onions whole and stick 2 cloves into each onion. Peel the garlic.
2. Pour the water and wine vinegar into a large stewpan and add the carrots, onions, garlic and bouquet garni. Season with salt and add a few peppercorns. Bring to a boil and simmer on a low heat for 30 minutes.
3. Cut the skate into sections if the wings are large. Add to the pan and simmer very gently for 10 minutes or until cooked.
4. Meanwhile, melt the butter in a heavy saucepan on a low heat. Add the flour and stir until the butter has absorbed the flour. Add the milk, season to taste with salt and pepper and cook, stirring, on a low heat until the sauce thickens (10 minutes).
5. Add crème fraîche, anchovy paste, the juice of the ½ lemon and the egg yolk and stir thoroughly.
6. To serve, drain the skate, remove the skin and bones and pour the anchovy sauce over the fish.

Red Mullet or Goatfish Baked in Paper

Rougets en papillotes

00:30   00:15 to 00:18

American	Ingredients	Metric/Imperial
3	Medium-sized onions	3
6	Red mullet or goatfish, cleaned	6
	Olive oil	
	Fennel seeds	
	Salt and pepper	

1. Preheat the oven to 350°F / 180°C / Gas Mark 4.
2. Using parchment [greaseproof] paper, cut out 6 heart shapes, each sufficiently large to wrap a fish. Peel and chop the onions.
3. Coat the fish with olive oil. Put a pinch of chopped onion, a few fennel seeds and a pinch of salt on one half of each paper heart. Put the fish on the paper hearts, season again with onions, fennel seeds, salt and pepper and fold over the other half of each heart. Roll the edges of the hearts, twisting the paper from the head down to the tail so that the fish is completely enclosed.
4. Arrange the wrapped fish on a rack in a roasting pan and bake for 15-18 minutes.
5. Serve the fish in the paper wrapping. When cooked in this way, they can be removed from the oven and kept hot for a few minutes without becoming dry.

Broiled [Grilled] Sardines

Sardines grillées

00:05 plus salting   00:04 to 00:06

American	Ingredients	Metric/Imperial
30	Fresh sardines or other small oily fish	30
2 tbsp	Sea salt	2 tbsp

1. Fresh sardines cooked in this way are not cleaned, scaled or washed. About 30-50 minutes before cooking, sprinkle the fish with the salt.
2. Preheat the broiler [grill].
3. Shake the sardines, holding them by the tail, so that the excess salt falls off. Arrange them on the broiler rack. Broil them for 2-3 minutes on each side, turning them over carefully. Do not overcook them as they will become dry. Cooked in this way, the skin comes off easily and the flesh underneath is moist and tender.
4. Serve with lemon wedges and garlic butter.

Marinated Sardines

Sardines à l'escabèche

00:15 plus marinating   00:15

American	Ingredients	Metric/Imperial
18	Medium-sized fresh sardines or other small oily fish, cleaned	18
3 tbsp	Flour	3 tbsp
⅔ cup	Olive oil	150 ml / ¼ pint
½	Garlic clove	½
4	Fresh mint leaves	4
	Salt and pepper	
1 tbsp	Vinegar	1 tbsp

1. Cut the heads off the fish. Coat the fish in flour.
2. Heat the olive oil in a frying pan, add the sardines and fry for about 1 minute on each side. The sardines are cooked when they are gold and firm. As soon as they are cooked, drain them and leave to cool. Reserve the oil.
3. Peel and crush the garlic. Chop the mint. Dissolve a pinch of salt in the vinegar. Season with pepper to taste. Add the reserved, cooled oil, garlic and chopped mint. Mix well.
4. Serve the sardines cold in the mint dressing.

Saumon au champagne
Salmon with Champagne

	00:30	01:15
	Serves 8–10	

American	Ingredients	Metric/Imperial
1 (4½-5 lb)	Salmon, cleaned	1 (2-2.4 kg / 4½-5 lb)
	Salt and pepper	
3	Shallots	3
¼ lb	Mushrooms	125 g / 4 oz
½ cup	Butter	125 g / 4 oz
½	Bottle of dry champagne or other sparkling white wine	½
½ cup	Crème fraîche	125 ml / 4 fl oz
2 - 3	Egg yolks	2 - 3

1. Preheat the oven to 400°F / 200°C / Gas Mark 6.
2. Season the inside of the salmon with salt and pepper. Wrap the head and tail in foil. Line the bottom of a roasting pan with foil so that you can remove the fish without breaking it.
3. Peel and finely chop the shallots. Finely chop the mushrooms. Spread the vegetables over the bottom of the roasting pan (on the foil). Put the fish on top and dot with pieces of butter. Season with salt and pepper and pour half the champagne over the top. Cover closely with foil and bake for about 1¼ hours. Baste frequently with the liquid in the pan, and gradually add the rest of the champagne, heated but not boiling. The liquid in the pan should not boil.
4. Check whether the salmon is done by cutting along the bone line with a knife: the flesh should separate from the bone. If not, continue cooking. Do not overcook or the fish will be dry.
5. Take the fish out with the aid of the foil. Skin it immediately on both sides, slide onto a serving dish and keep hot.
6. Pour the cooking liquid into a saucepan. Bring to a boil, remove from the heat and add the crème fraîche blended with the egg yolks, beating vigorously. Adjust the seasoning. Thicken without boiling, beating continuously with a whisk.
7. Pour some sauce over the fish and serve the rest in a sauceboat. In season, garnish the dish with cooked crayfish.

Saumon poché, sauce sabayon
Poached Salmon with Sabayon Sauce

	00:10	01:20
	plus cooling	

American	Ingredients	Metric/Imperial
3	Carrots	3
1	Onion	1
2	Cloves	2
1	Leek	1
1	Bouquet garni	1
2 cups	Dry white wine	500 ml / ¾ pint
2 cups	Water	500 ml / ¾ pint
1 (3 lb)	Piece of salmon, cleaned and scaled	1 (1.5 kg / 3 lb)
2½ cups	Crème fraîche (see page 122)	600 ml / 1 pint
4	Egg yolks	4
	Salt and pepper	

1. Peel and slice the carrots. Peel the onion and stud it with the cloves. Cut the leek in half. Put all the vegetables in a saucepan and add the bouquet garni, wine and water. Bring to a boil and simmer for 40 minutes.
2. Strain the stock and allow it to cool.
3. Put the salmon in a fish kettle (or a large saucepan) and add the stock. Poach for 40 minutes over a low heat.
4. About 10 minutes before the end of the cooking time, make the sauce. Put the cream in a bowl or saucepan and add the egg yolks, 4 tablespoons of the stock from the salmon, and salt and pepper to taste. Put the bowl or saucepan over another saucepan containing hot water and heat, stirring gently with a whisk. As soon as the mixture thickens, pour it into a sauceboat.
5. Drain the salmon and serve with the sauce.

Fried strips of sole

Soles en goujonnettes
Fried Strips of Sole

	00:20	00:06

American	Ingredients	Metric/Imperial
2 (1½ lb)	Soles, filleted	2 (750 g / 1½ lb)
4	Garlic cloves	4
1	Egg yolk	1
	Cayenne pepper	
	Paprika	
	Saffron powder	
	Salt and pepper	
1 cup	Olive oil plus oil for deep frying	250 ml / 8 fl oz
1¼ cups	Flour	150 g /5 oz
	Bread crumbs	
2	Eggs	2
2 tbsp	Water	2 tbsp

1. Cut the sole fillets into pieces ½ in / 1 cm wide and 3 in / 7.5 cm long. Set aside.
2. Peel the garlic, put it in a mortar and pound to a fine paste. Add the egg yolk, a pinch each of cayenne pepper, paprika and saffron, and salt and pepper to taste. Mix together. Add all but 2 tablespoons of the olive oil in a thin stream, beating with a whisk, as for mayonnaise. (If preferred, the spicy garlic mayonnaise may be made in a blender or food processor.) Set aside.

3. Spread out the flour and bread crumbs on 2 plates. Beat the eggs with the water and remaining oil in a shallow dish. Heat the oil for deep frying.

4. Dip the pieces of fish in flour, then in the beaten egg mixture and finally in the bread crumbs. Drop the pieces into the oil, which should be hot but not smoking, and fry for about 6 minutes or until golden.

5. Drain the pieces of fish on paper towels and serve immediately with the spicy garlic mayonnaise.

Filets de sole normande

Normandy Style Sole

| | 00:20 | | 00:40 |

American	Ingredients	Metric/Imperial
4 (¾ lb)	Soles, filleted (bones reserved)	4 (350 g / 12 oz)
	Court-bouillon	
	Hard [dry] cider	
⅔ cup	Water	150 ml / ¼ pint
1 pint	Fresh mussels	500 g / 1 lb
1 tbsp	Butter	1 tbsp
1 tbsp	Flour	1 tbsp
¼ cup	Crème fraîche	4 tbsp
	Grated nutmeg	
	Salt and pepper	

1. Roll up each sole fillet and secure with a wooden toothpick. Arrange all the fish rolls in a frying pan or flameproof casserole. Pour over half court-bouillon and half cider, enough liquid to cover the fish. Heat until the liquid simmers. Turn the fish rolls and cook for a further 5 minutes.

2. Remove the fish rolls with a slotted spatula and keep hot.

3. Add the fish bones to the pan with the water and simmer gently for 15 minutes.

4. Meanwhile, scrub the mussels thoroughly. Put them in a saucepan, cover and heat briskly, shaking the pan, until they open (discard any that remain closed). Remove the mussels from their shells, reserving all the liquid from the shells, and keep hot. Strain the liquid. Also strain the cider mixture.

5. Heat the butter in a saucepan, add the flour and stir for 2 minutes. Add crème fraîche and bring to a boil, stirring. Gradually blend in the strained mussel liquid and cider to obtain a thick cream sauce. Add a pinch of nutmeg and season to taste with salt and pepper. Stir in the mussels.

Sole with lemon butter

6. Remove the toothpicks from the fish rolls. Pour over the sauce and serve immediately.

Soles au Pouilly

Sole in White Wine Sauce

| | 00:15 | | 00:25 |

American	Ingredients	Metric/Imperial
12	Sole fillets	12
2	Shallots	2
¼ cup	Butter.	50 g / 2 oz
½	Bottle of dry white wine	½
	Salt and pepper	
1 tbsp	Flour	1 tbsp
1 cup	Crème fraîche	250 ml / 8 fl oz
1 tsp	Tomato paste [purée]	1 tsp

1. Pound the sole fillets lightly with a wooden spatula so that they do not roll up during cooking. Peel and chop the shallots.

2. Heat 1 tablespoon of butter in a frying pan, add the shallots and cook until soft and translucent. Pour in the wine and season with salt and pepper. Bring to a simmer. Add 4 sole fillets and cook for 8 minutes. Remove the fish with a slotted spatula and keep hot. Cook the remaining 8 fillets in this way, remove and keep hot.

3. Reduce the cooking liquid by half, then strain it. Heat the rest of the butter in a saucepan, add the flour and stir for 1 minute. Add crème fraîche and bring to a boil, stirring. Add the reduced cooking liquid a little at a time and the tomato paste, just enough to color the sauce. Stir over a low heat to obtain a thick cream sauce. Adjust the seasoning if necessary.

4. Pour the sauce over the sole fillets and serve immediately.

Sole meunière

Sole with Lemon Butter

| | 00:10 | | 00:45 |

American	Ingredients	Metric/Imperial
3 tbsp	Flour	3 tbsp
	Salt and pepper	
6 (6 oz)	Soles, cleaned and skinned	6 (175 g / 6 oz)
1¼ cups	Oil	300 ml / ½ pint
1 cup	Butter	250 g / 8 oz
3	Lemons	3
2 tbsp	Chopped fresh parsley	2 tbsp

1. Season the flour with salt and pepper. Coat the soles with the flour.

2. Heat the oil in a frying pan and fry the soles, 2 or 3 at a time, for 8 minutes on each side. Drain the soles as they are cooked and keep hot on a serving dish.

3. When all the soles are cooked, pour the oil out of the frying pan and wipe the pan clean with paper towels. Cut the butter into small pieces and heat it in the frying pan until it bubbles. Add the juice of 1 lemon, stir well and pour over the soles. Sprinkle with the parsley.

4. Cut the remaining lemons into quarters or slices and arrange them around the fish. Serve immediately.

Thon grillé
Broiled [Grilled] Tuna

⬛▭▷ 00:10   00:10 to 00:12 🍲

American	Ingredients	Metric/Imperial
¾ cup	Butter	175 g / 6 oz
2 tbsp	Chopped fresh parsley	2 tbsp
1	Lemon	1
	Salt and pepper	
6 (½ lb)	Tuna steaks	6 (250 g / 8 oz)
¼ cup	Oil	4 tbsp
	Parsley sprigs for garnish	
	Lemon wedges for serving	

1. Cream the butter with a wooden spoon. Add the chopped parsley and juice from the lemon. Blend well and season with salt and pepper. Put in the refrigerator to chill.
2. Preheat the broiler [grill].
3. Brush the tuna steaks with the oil. Put them on the broiler rack and broil for 10-12 minutes, turning them over halfway through the process.
4. When the tuna steaks are cooked, arrange them on a hot serving dish. Season with salt and pepper to taste and garnish with parsley sprigs and lemon wedges. Serve with the parsley butter.

Truites au bleu
Blue Trout

⬛▭▷ 00:15   00:45 🍲
This recipe can only be made with freshly caught trout

American	Ingredients	Metric/Imperial
3	Carrots	3
2	Onions	2
3	Shallots	3
2 quarts	Water	2 l / 3½ pints
1	Bouquet garni	1
	Few fresh parsley sprigs	
	Salt and pepper	
6 (½ lb)	Trout, cleaned	6 (250 g / 8 oz)
3 cups	Wine vinegar	750 ml / 1¼ pints
	Chopped fresh parsley for garnish	
	Lemon wedges	

1. Peel the carrots, onions and shallots and cut them into thin strips. Put the vegetables into a saucepan with the water, bouquet garni, parsley sprigs, and salt and pepper to taste. Bring to a boil. Cover and simmer over a low heat for 30 minutes. Strain into a fish kettle or large pan and leave to cool.
2. Put the trout in a shallow dish. Boil the wine vinegar and pour it over the trout (this gives them their color). Leave to cool slightly, then plunge the fish into the stock in the fish kettle. Heat slowly until the liquid begins to simmer and simmer gently for 8-10 minutes.
3. Drain the trout carefully and arrange them on a serving dish. Sprinkle with chopped parsley and surround with lemon wedges. Serve with melted butter.

Truites à la parisienne
Parisian Style Trout

⬛▭▷ 01:30   00:10 🍲

American	Ingredients	Metric/Imperial
1 envelope	Unflavored gelatin	1 sachet
1⅓ cups	Water	450 ml / ¾ pint
⅔ cup	Port wine	150 ml / ¼ pint
1 quart	Dry white wine	1 l / 1¾ pints
	Salt and pepper	
6 (½ lb)	Trout, cleaned	6 (250 g / 8 oz)
4	Tomatoes	4
4	Hard-cooked eggs	4
1 tbsp	Chopped fresh chives	1 tbsp

1. Dissolve the gelatin in the water, according to package directions, and stir in the port. Chill until this aspic is syrupy.
2. Meanwhile, bring the white wine to a boil. Season the inside and outside of the trout with salt and pepper and poach them in the wine for 10 minutes. Drain. Leave to cool, then remove the skin with a knife.
3. Put the trout on a grid placed over a dish. Pour a layer of the port aspic over them and put them in the refrigerator to set.
4. Meanwhile, peel the tomatoes (first plunging them for 10 seconds in boiling water), remove the seeds and slice them. Slice the eggs.
5. Garnish the trout with the tomato and egg slices and chopped chives. Pour a second layer of port aspic over the top. Chill until set.
6. Chill the rest of the port aspic until set. Before serving, dice it and arrange it around the trout.

Truite aux amandes
Trout with Almonds

⬛▭▷ 00:20   00:15 🍲

American	Ingredients	Metric/Imperial
1¼ cups	Milk	300 ml / ½ pint
	Salt and pepper	
6 tbsp	Flour	6 tbsp
6 (6 oz)	Trout, cleaned	6 (175 g / 6 oz)
10 tbsp	Butter	150 g / 5 oz
3 tbsp	Oil	3 tbsp
1 cup	Flaked or sliced almonds	125 g / 4 oz
	Chopped fresh parsley for garnish	
	Lemon wedges for serving	

1. Pour the milk into a shallow dish and season with salt and pepper. Put the flour into another dish. Dip the trout in the milk, then roll them in the flour.
2. Heat ¼ cup [50 g / 2 oz] butter and oil in a large frying pan, add the trout and fry for 7 minutes on each side, turning them with a metal spatula.
3. Meanwhile, heat the remaining butter in a small saucepan. Add the almonds, stir well and brown lightly, shaking the pan from time to time.
4. When the trout are cooked, transfer them to a warmed serving dish. Pour over the almond butter mixture. Serve the trout sprinkled with the chopped parsley and surrounded with lemon wedges.

Trout with almonds

Truites aux pruneaux
Trout with Prunes

▭▷ 00:15   00:15 🍲

American	Ingredients	Metric/Imperial
¼ cup	Potato starch or flour	50 g / 2 oz
6 (½ lb)	Trout, cleaned	6 (250 g / 8 oz)
6 tbsp	Butter	75 g / 3 oz
3 tbsp	Oil	3 tbsp
1 quart	Dry red wine	1 l / 1¾ pints
	Lemon juice	
	Salt and pepper	
1	Fresh thyme sprig	1
1	Bay leaf	1
	Grated nutmeg	
30	Prunes, soaked	30
2	Onions	2

1. Preheat the oven to 350°F / 180°C / Gas Mark 4.
2. Put the potato starch or flour on a plate and roll the trout in it one by one. Heat the butter and oil in a frying pan, add the trout and cook for 7 minutes on each side, turning them with a metal spatula.
3. Put the trout in an ovenproof dish. Pour in the red wine and add a few drops of lemon juice. Season with salt and pepper to taste. Add the thyme sprig, bay leaf, a pinch of grated nutmeg and the prunes. Peel and quarter the onions and add to the dish.
4. Bake for 15 minutes.

Truites en papillotes
Trout Baked in Foil

▭▷ 00:20   00:20 🍲
     plus marinating

American	Ingredients	Metric/Imperial
6 (6 oz)	Trout, cleaned	6 (175 g / 6 oz)
	Salt and pepper	
1 tbsp	Fennel seeds	1 tbsp
6	Coriander seeds	6
2	Fresh thyme sprigs	2
2	Bay leaves	2
¼ cup	Olive oil	4 tbsp
	Lemon wedges	

1. Season the inside and outside of the fish with salt and pepper. Put the fennel and coriander seeds in a mortar and grind them to a powder. Crumble the thyme and bay leaves. Arrange the trout in a deep dish. Sprinkle with thyme, bay, and the fennel and coriander mixture. Pour the oil over the top and leave to marinate for 1 hour in a cool place, but not in the refrigerator.
2. Preheat the oven to 425°F / 220°C / Gas Mark 7.
3. Cut out 6 large rectangles of foil. Without wiping the trout, place each one in the center of a foil rectangle. Fold the foil over so that each trout is completely enclosed and twist the edges to seal. Arrange on a baking sheet.
4. Bake for 20 minutes.
5. When the trout are cooked, set them on a serving dish without opening the foil, surround them with lemon wedges and serve immediately.

Thon basquaise
Basque Style Tuna

▭▷ 00:40   01:00 🍲

American	Ingredients	Metric/Imperial
1	Garlic clove	1
1	Onion	1
	Oil	
1 lb	Tomatoes	500 g / 1 lb
1	Sweet red or green pepper	1
2 tbsp	Flour	2 tbsp
1 (3 lb)	Piece of tuna	1 (1.5 kg / 3 lb)
	Salt and pepper	
1¼ cups	Dry white wine	300 ml / ½ pint

1. Peel and finely chop the garlic and onion. Heat 1 tablespoon of oil in a frying pan, add the garlic and onion and fry until soft.
2. Peel the tomatoes (first plunging them in boiling water for 10 seconds), cut into quarters and remove the seeds. Remove the core and the seeds from the pepper and cut the flesh into thin strips. Put the tomatoes and pepper in the frying pan and cook over a low heat for 30 minutes, stirring occasionally.
3. Preheat the oven to 350°F / 180°C / Gas Mark 4.
4. Flour the piece of tuna lightly, season with the salt and pepper and put it in an ovenproof dish. Pour in the white wine. Add the tomato sauce. Bake for about 10 minutes. Serve hot.

Turbot à la normande
Normandy Style Turbot

▭▷ 00:15   00:40 🍲

American	Ingredients	Metric/Imperial
1	Turbot, cleaned	1
½ lb	Onions	250 g / 8 oz
2	Carrots	2
1	Bouquet garni	1
	Salt and pepper	
2½ cups	Hard [dry] cider	600 ml / 1 pint
36	Fresh mussels	36
12	Scampi or Dublin Bay prawns	12
1 tbsp	Butter	1 tbsp
1 tbsp	Flour	1 tbsp
2	Egg yolks	2
½ cup	Crème fraîche	125 ml / 4 fl oz
½ lemon	Lemon	½

1. Cut the turbot into 6 pieces. Peel and slice the onions and carrots. Put the pieces of fish in a large pan with the onions and carrots. Add the bouquet garni and season with salt and pepper. Pour in the cider and add sufficient water to cover the pieces of fish. Bring to boil over a moderate heat, then turn down the heat and cook gently for 15-18 minutes.
2. Meanwhile, scrub the mussels thoroughly. Put them in a large saucepan and heat briskly, shaking the saucepan from time to time, until they open (discard any that remain closed). Remove the mussels from the shells and set aside. Reserve the liquid from the shells. Strain the liquid.
3. Cook the scampi in simmering water for 8 minutes. Drain and peel them.

4. Drain the pieces of fish, reserving the cooking liquid, and remove the skin. Arrange the fish on serving dish and keep hot. Strain the liquid into a saucepan and boil to reduce it by half. Add the liquid from the mussels.
5. Blend the butter with the flour to make a paste (beurre manié). Beat the egg yolks with the crème fraîche and the juice of ½ lemon. Add the beurre manié to the cooking liquid and simmer, stirring, until thickened. Remove from the heat. Add 1 tablespoon of this liquid to the egg yolk and crème fraîche mixture, mix well and pour back into the pan. Heat, whisking, and add salt and pepper to taste. Do not boil.
6. Surround the fish with the mussels and scampi and coat with the sauce. Serve immediately.

Turbot hollandaise

Turbot with Hollandaise Sauce

◄▱	00:30		00:32 ◖
American	**Ingredients**		**Metric/Imperial**
1	Turbot, cleaned and skinned		1
	Court-bouillon		
3	Egg yolks, at room temperature		3
2 tbsp	Cider vinegar		2 tbsp
	Pepper		
1 cup	Lightly salted butter		250 g / 8 oz
1	Lemon		1

1. Cut the turbot into 6 pieces and arrange in a large pan so that they do not overlap. Cover with court-bouillon. Bring to a boil, then cover and simmer for 15 minutes over a very low heat so that the liquid barely trembles. Remove from the heat, remove the lid and leave to cool slightly.
2. Meanwhile, put the egg yolks in a bowl or saucepan, add the vinegar and season with pepper. Stir and put the saucepan over another saucepan half filled with hot but not boiling water. Whisk until the mixture thickens, then gradually blend in the butter cut into small pieces. Continue to whisk until the sauce is smooth and thick. Gradually add the juice of the lemon and continue to whisk.
3. Drain the pieces of fish and place on a dish lined with a folded napkin. Serve the sauce separately.

Turbotin frit

Fried Turbot Steaks

◄▱	00:15	00:10 to 00:15 ◖
American	**Ingredients**	**Metric/Imperial**
6	Turbot steaks, 1 in / 2.5 cm thick	6
	Salt and pepper	
1 cup	White bread crumbs	50 g / 2 oz
⅔ cup	Oil	150 ml / ¼ pint
1 cup	Butter	250 g / 8 oz
2	Lemons	2
	Tomato slices	
	Lemon slices	

1. Season the turbot steaks on both sides with salt and pepper. Coat with the bread crumbs, pressing them on well with a spatula so that they adhere firmly.
2. Heat the oil in a frying pan, add the fish and cook over a moderate heat for 10-15 minutes, turning them halfway through the process.
3. Meanwhile, melt the butter in a small bowl placed over a saucepan half filled with hot water. Season with salt, pepper and the juice of the lemons.
4. Arrange the fish steaks on a serving dish and garnish with the tomato and lemon slices. Serve the lemon butter separately in a sauceboat.

Thon braisé aux petits oignons

Braised Tuna with Onions

◄▱	00:30		01:20 ◖
American	**Ingredients**		**Metric/Imperial**
2	Carrots		2
2	Medium-size onions		2
1	Shallot		1
1	Garlic clove		1
¼ lb	Fresh pork sides [belly pork]		125 g / 4 oz
6 tbsp	Butter		75 g / 3 oz
1 (2¾ lb)	Piece of tuna		1 (1.25 kg / 2¾ lb)
1 tbsp	Flour		1 tbsp
⅔ cup	Fish stock		150 ml / ¼ pint
⅔ cup	Dry white wine		150 ml / ¼ pint
1	Bouquet garni		1
	Salt and pepper		
24	Tiny onions		24
1 tbsp	Sugar		1 tbsp
	Chopped fresh parsley		

1. Peel the carrots, onions, shallot and garlic. Chop the carrots, onions and shallot and crush the garlic. Remove any rind from the pork and cut the pork into strips.
2. Heat half of the butter in a flameproof casserole, add the strips of pork and brown slightly. Remove with a slotted spoon. Put the piece of tuna into the casserole. Brown it lightly on both sides and remove it. Put the carrots, chopped onion and shallot in the casserole, stir well and leave the vegetables to brown over a moderate heat.
3. Put the tuna and strips of pork back into the casserole. Sprinkle with the flour and brown, stirring constantly. Pour in the fish stock and white wine. Add the garlic and bouquet garni and season with salt and pepper. Cook, covered, for 1 hour over a low heat.
4. Meanwhile, peel the tiny onions. Put them in a heavy saucepan with the sugar and the remaining butter. Season to taste with salt and pepper. Cover with water and cook with the lid on over a low heat until the onions are tender and the sugar, butter and water have formed a caramel syrup. Roll the onions in the caramel so that they are coated all over and keep warm over a very low heat.
5. When the tuna is cooked, transfer it to a serving dish, using a slotted spatula. Strain the sauce onto the fish, sprinkle with chopped parsley and surround with the caramelized onions. Serve immediately.

Cook's tip: although tuna is more usually bought canned, it has an excellent flavor when used fresh.

Preparing shellfish

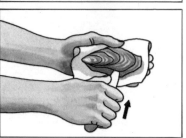

Opening deep-shelled oysters
1. Insert the blade of a knife between the shells at the point where the muscle is located.

2. Push the blade in toward the center.

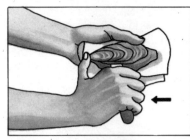

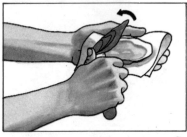

3. Pull the blade toward you, cutting through the muscle.

4. Lift the lid.

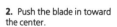

Opening flat oysters
1. Holding the oyster in the palm of your hand, place the blade of a knife against its tip.

2. Apply repeated pressure in a squeezing movement with your fingers until the blade has been forced into the oyster.

3. Pull the blade toward you, cutting through the muscle.

4. Lift the lid.

Cleaning mussels
1. Soak the mussels in fresh water.

2. Scrape them with a small, pointed knife.

3. Cut away the byssus (a fibrous attachment at the hinge of the valves).

4. Rinse the mussels quickly in a colander without leaving them to soak. (Although usually sold cleaned, mussels will need to be washed again before cooking.)

Meat

Cooking times for poultry

To cook	Cooking time	Average weight per portion
Capon, roasted	20 min per pound	12 oz / 350 g
Chicken, boiled	1 hr 30-3 hr	10 oz / 300 g
Chicken, casseroled	45-50 min	10 oz / 300 g
Chicken, roasted	25-30 min per pound	10 oz / 300 g
Cornish game hen [pullet or poussin], roasted	20-40 min	1 or 2 per person
Duck breast fillets (scaloppine), fried	10 min (7-8 min on the skin side) 2 min on the flesh side	5 oz / 150 g
Duck breast fillets (scaloppine), roasted	15 min	5 oz / 150 g
Duck (cut up), sautéed	45 min	12 oz / 350 g
Duck or duckling, roasted	50 min to 1 hr 50 min	12 oz / 350 g
Goose	15-25 min per pound (according to age)	10 oz / 300 g
Pigeon, casseroled	40-45 min	1 or 2 per person
Guinea fowl, casseroled	55 min to 1 hr	8 oz / 250g
Guinea fowl, roasted	about 45 min	8 oz / 250 g
Guinea fowl, salmis	1 hr 10 min to 1 hr 15 min	7 oz / 200 g
Quail (cut up), casseroled	25-30 min	2 per person
Quail, roasted	about 15 min	2 per person
Rabbit, casseroled	1 hr to 1 hr 15 min	8 oz / 250 g
Rooster, (3 lb / 1.5 kg), casseroled	1 hr 30-2 hr (according to weight)	10 oz / 300 g
Turkey (whole), roasted	20 min per pound (including stuffing)	8 oz / 250 g
Young pigeon (squab), casseroled	25-30 min	1 per person
Young rabbit, casseroled, roasted or sautéed	50-55 min	8 oz / 250 g

Cailles rôties sur canapés

Roast Quails on Canapés

00:10   00:20

American	Ingredients	Metric/Imperial
12	Slices of bread, ½ in / 1 cm thick	12
⅔ cup	Butter	150 g / 5 oz
12	Small quails with livers	12
24	Juniper berries	24
	Salt and pepper	
12	Thin bacon slices	12

1. Preheat the oven to 450°F / 230°C / Gas Mark 8.
2. Cut the crust off the slices of bread. Butter the bread sparingly and arrange in a greased ovenproof dish.
3. Put 1 liver and 2 juniper berries inside each quail. Season with salt and pepper and wrap a slice of bacon around each bird. Tie with string.
4. Arrange the quails on the buttered bread and roast for 10 minutes.
5. Remove the bacon and roast for a further 5-10 minutes, according to taste.

Duck with orange sauce

Cailles aux raisins

Quails with Grapes

| | 00:20 | | 00:30 |

American	Ingredients	Metric/Imperial
12	Thin bacon slices	12
6 (5 oz) or 12 small	Quails	6 (150 g / 5 oz) or 12 small
2 tbsp	Butter	25 g / 1 oz
¼ cup	Brandy	4 tbsp
1 lb	White grapes	500 g / 1 lb
1 tsp	Potato starch or flour	1 tsp
	Grated nutmeg	
	Salt and pepper	
3 tbsp	Oil	3 tbsp
6	Slices of bread, ½ in / 1 cm thick	6

1. Wrap a slice of bacon around each quail and tie with string. Brown the quails rapidly in a large frying pan without any fat, then remove. Throw away any fat and wipe the pan with paper towels.

2. Put half the butter in the pan. Return the quails to the pan and heat until the butter sizzles without turning brown. Add the brandy, then remove from the heat, cover the pan and set aside to infuse for 5 minutes so that the alcohol flavors the quails.

3. Meanwhile, squeeze the juice from one-third of the grapes (use a juicer, or liquidize briefly or press and strain). Mix the juice with the potato starch. Add this mixture to the quails in the saucepan. Season with a pinch of nutmeg and salt and pepper to taste. Leave to simmer for 15-20 minutes over a very low heat.

4. Meanwhile, cut the remaining grapes in half and remove the seeds. Heat them in a saucepan with the rest of the butter until the skins start to wrinkle.

5. Heat the oil in another frying pan. Remove the crusts from the bread and fry until golden on both sides.

6. Serve the quails on the fried bread surrounded by the grapes and topped with the sauce.

Canard à l'orange

Duck with Orange Sauce

| | 00:45 | | 01:15 |

American	Ingredients	Metric/Imperial
1	Carrot	1
1	Onion	1
½ cup	Butter	125 g / 4 oz
1 (5 lb)	Duck, trussed	1 (2.5 kg / 5 lb)
1	Bouquet garni	1
3 tbsp	Boiling water	3 tbsp
	Salt and pepper	
6	Oranges	6
¼ cup	Orange liqueur	4 tbsp
2 tbsp	Brandy	2 tbsp
1 tbsp	Vinegar	1 tbsp
2 tsp	Potato starch or flour	2 tsp

1. Peel the carrot and onion and cut into thin strips.

2. Melt 6 tablespoons [75 g / 3 oz] of the butter in a flame-proof casserole, add the duck and brown on all sides over a moderate heat. Add the carrot, onion and bouquet garni. Moisten with 1 tablespoon of boiling water and season to taste with salt and pepper. Cover and simmer very gently for 1 hour.

3. Meanwhile, peel 2 of the oranges with a vegetable peeler and cut the rind into thin strips. Blanch the strips of rind in boiling water for 5 minutes. Drain and set aside.

4. Squeeze the juice from the 2 peeled oranges and one other orange. With a sharp knife, peel the remaining oranges without leaving any white pith. Separate into sections, discarding the membrane and seeds. Collect any further juice by holding the oranges over a bowl as they are prepared. Set the sections and juice aside.

5. Sprinkle the duck with the orange liqueur and brandy. Remove from the heat and leave to infuse for 10 minutes. Remove the duck from the casserole and wrap it in foil and keep hot.

6. Add the vinegar and orange juice to the casserole. Simmer over a very low heat, skimming off the fat until the sauce is clear. Strain the sauce into a saucepan. Leave to cool, then remove any more fat which has floated to the surface.

7. Return the sauce to the heat. Dissolve the potato starch in the remaining water and add to the sauce. Bring to a boil, stirring constantly. Adjust the seasoning, if necessary.

8. Melt the rest of the butter in another pan. Add the orange sections and strips of rind, then add the sauce. As soon as the sauce begins to boil, remove from the heat.

9. Carve the duck into portions. Arrange on a serving platter, surround with the orange sections and pour the sauce over the top of the duck.

Canard aux cerises

Duck with Cherries

| | 00:25 | | 00:50 |

American	Ingredients	Metric/Imperial
3 tbsp	Butter	40 g / 1½ oz
2 (2¾ lb)	Ducklings, trussed	2 (1.25 kg / 2¾ lb)
1	Orange	1
1¼ cups	Port wine	300 ml / ½ pint
5	Cloves	5
	Ground cinnamon	
	Salt and pepper	
1 cup	Red currant jelly	350 g / 12 oz
1 (12 oz)	Can of pitted [stoned] cherries in natural juice	1 (350 g / 12 oz)

1. Heat the butter in a flameproof casserole, add the ducks and brown on all sides. Cover and cook over a moderate heat for 40 minutes. The ducks should be underdone.

2. Drain the ducks over the casserole so that the meat juices run into it, then keep them hot.

3. Finely grate the rind from the orange, then squeeze out the juice. Put in a large saucepan with the port, crushed cloves, a pinch of cinnamon and salt and pepper to taste. Simmer over a low heat until the mixture reduces by one-third.

4. Add the red currant jelly. Remove from the heat and stir until the jelly melts. Strain the sauce and add the drained cherries, reserving a few for decoration.

5. Carve the ducks, collecting the juice, then return the duck portions and the juice to the casserole. Add the sauce and cook for a further 10-12 minutes over a very low heat.

6. Arrange the portions of duck on a warmed platter. Garnish with the reserved cherries and a little of the sauce and serve the rest of the sauce separately.

6. Put the bacon, mushrooms and liver through a grinder [mincer] or food processor to obtain a smooth mixture. Add the olives, and salt and pepper to taste.
7. Stuff each duck with half of the olive mixture. Truss and coat each bird with 2 tablespoons [25 g / 1 oz] of butter seasoned with salt and pepper.
8. Put the ducks on a rack in a roasting pan and roast for 40 minutes, turning the ducks 4 times so that they brown evenly on all sides. When the fat in the roasting pan starts to burn, add the water.
9. Meanwhile, peel the turnips. Cook in boiling salted water for 10 minutes and drain. Melt the remaining butter in a frying pan over a low heat, add the turnips and cook gently until they begin to brown. Sprinkle them with the sugar and continue to cook over a moderate heat for 10-15 minutes.
10. Carve the ducks into portions and serve with the stuffing and glazed turnips. Serve the roasting juices separately.

Roast duck with turnips

Canard rôti aux navets

Roast Duck with Turnips

⊳ 00:30   01:00 🍲

American	Ingredients	Metric/Imperial
¼ lb	Smoked bacon	125 g / 4 oz
2	Chicken livers	2
2 (2¾ lb)	Ducks, with their livers	2 (1.25 kg / 2¾ lb)
¼ lb	Button mushrooms	125 g / 4 oz
1 cup	Green olives	125 g / 4 oz
	Salt and pepper	
½ cup	Butter	125 g / 4 oz
⅔ cup	Water	150 ml / ¼ pint
3 lb	Small, young turnips	1.5 kg / 3 lb
3 tbsp	Sugar	3 tbsp

1. Preheat the oven to 450°F / 230°C / Gas Mark 8.
2. Cut the bacon into thin strips. Cook in a frying pan until lightly browned. Remove the bacon and set aside.
3. Cut the chicken and duck livers into quarters and add to the bacon fat in the pan. Cook over a medium heat until browned on all sides. Remove the livers and set aside.
4. Thinly slice the mushrooms. Add to the pan and cook, stirring occasionally, until the liquid has evaporated.
5. Meanwhile, remove the pits [stones] from the olives. Blanch the olives in boiling water for 2 minutes, drain and pat dry.

Canetons aux pêches

Ducklings with Peaches

⊳ 00:15   01:00 🍲

American	Ingredients	Metric/Imperial
2 (2 lb)	Ducklings, with the livers	2 (1 kg / 2 lb)
½ cup	Butter	125 g / 4 oz
2 tbsp	Flour	2 tbsp
	Salt and pepper	
2	Carrots	2
2	Onions	2
2	Celery stalks	2
1	Bouquet garni	1
1 (1 lb 12 oz)	Can of yellow peaches in syrup	1 (800 g / 1 lb 12 oz)
2 tbsp	Brandy	2 tbsp
1 tbsp	Potato starch or flour	1 tbsp
2 tbsp	Sugar	2 tbsp
1 tbsp	Vinegar	1 tbsp

1. Preheat the oven to 400°F / 200°C / Gas Mark 6.
2. Truss the ducklings.
3. Work 2 tablespoons [25 g / 1 oz] butter with the flour to a smooth paste. Season the ducklings with salt and pepper and coat them with this beurre manié.
4. Peel and slice the carrots and onions. Slice the celery. Put the vegetables in a roasting pan with the bouquet garni and duck liver and place the metal rack for the ducklings on top. Put the ducklings on the rack and roast for 45 minutes.
5. Remove the ducklings from the pan and keep hot.
6. Leave the vegetables and liver to cook for a further 10 minutes, then strain the liquid into a frying pan. Skim as much fat as possible from the surface of the liquid, then add the peaches and 6 tablespoons of the peach syrup. Cook for 5-6 minutes, turning the peaches halfway through.
7. Carve the ducklings into quarters and arrange on a warmed serving platter. Reserve the carving juices. Arrange the drained peaches around the duckling pieces. Keep hot.
8. Pour the carving juices into the frying pan. Mix the brandy with the potato starch and add to the pan. Bring to a boil, stirring, and adjust seasoning to taste.
9. Meanwhile, dissolve the sugar in the vinegar in a small heavy saucepan over a moderate heat. As soon as you obtain a brown caramel, beat it into the sauce. Finally, whisk in the remaining butter. Serve the sauce with the duck.

Aiguillettes de canard

Duck Scaloppine [Escalopes]

	00:10		00:15

American	Ingredients	Metric/Imperial
6 (5 oz)	Duck breast fillets	6 (150 g / 5 oz)
3 tbsp	Butter	40 g / 1½ oz
2 tbsp	Honey	2 tbsp
1½	Lemons	1½
⅔ cup	Raisins	125 g / 4 oz
	Salt and pepper	
3 tbsp	White rum	3 tbsp

1. Cut the breast fillets into thin scaloppine, each weighing about 50 g / 2 oz.
2. Heat the butter in a frying pan, add the duck slices and cook gently for 10-15 minutes, turning frequently until the duck is lightly colored or cooked according to taste. Remove from the pan, arrange on a platter and keep hot.
3. Return the pan to a medium heat and add the honey. When it bubbles, add the juice of the lemons and the raisins. Season to taste with salt and pepper and cook gently for 3-4 minutes. Finally, add the white rum and heat through.
4. Pour the hot sauce over the scaloppine and serve immediately.

Canard rôti aux pommes

Roast Duck with Apples

	00:20 plus soaking		00:35

American	Ingredients	Metric/Imperial
12	Prunes	12
⅔ cup	Port wine	150 ml / ¼ pint
3	Apples	3
1	Large onion	1
1 (3 lb)	Duck	1 (1.5 kg / 3 lb)
	Salt and pepper	
6 tbsp	Butter	75 g / 3 oz
⅔ cup	Chicken stock	150 ml / ¼ pint

1. The day before, put the prunes in a bowl, cover with the port and leave to soak for 12 hours.
2. Preheat the oven to 450°F / 230°C / Gas Mark 8.
3. Drain the prunes, reserving any remaining port. Remove the pits [stones] from the prunes. Peel the apples, remove the core and seeds and cut into quarters. Peel and finely chop the onion. Mix together the prunes, apples and onion.
4. Sprinkle the duck with salt and pepper inside and out. Stuff with half of the prune mixture. Truss.
5. Coat the duck with 3 tablespoons [40 g / 1½ oz] butter and put it in a roasting pan. Roast for about 40 minutes, basting frequently with the melted butter so that the duck browns well.
6. Meanwhile, melt the rest of the butter in a small heavy saucepan. Add the remaining prune mixture and cook over a low heat for about 15 minutes.
7. As soon as the duck is cooked, drain and keep hot.
8. Skim the fat from the juices in the roasting pan, then add any remaining port and the chicken stock. Heat briskly, stirring to loosen the solids at the bottom of the pan.
9. Pour the prune mixture into the sauce and simmer until the liquid reduces by half.
10. Carve the duck and arrange on a platter with the stuffing and prune mixture from the sauce. Serve the sauce separately.

Chapon au champagne

Capon with Champagne

	00:15		02:00

American	Ingredients	Metric/Imperial
7 tbsp	Butter	90 g / 3½ oz
1 (6 lb)	Capon, trussed	1 (3 kg / 6 lb)
1	Onion	1
3	Shallots	3
3 tbsp	Brandy	3 tbsp
	Salt and pepper	
½	Bottle of champagne or other sparkling white wine	½
12	Small blood sausages [black and white puddings]	12
1 tbsp	Cornstarch [cornflour]	1 tbsp
1 tbsp	Cold water	1 tbsp
1 tbsp	Sugar	1 tbsp
1 tbsp	White vinegar	1 tbsp

1. Heat 3 tbsp [40 g / 1½ oz] of the butter in a flameproof casserole, add the capon and brown on all sides for 25 minutes, without allowing the butter to burn. Meanwhile, peel the onion and shallots. Thinly slice the shallots.
2. Sprinkle the capon with the warmed brandy. Set it alight and shake the casserole gently, until the flames die out.
3. Season to taste with salt and pepper. Add the whole onion and 5 tablespoons of the champagne and cook gently for 1½ hours.
4. About 20 minutes before the capon has finished cooking, preheat the broiler [grill]. Prick the skins of the blood sausages with a fork so that the fat runs out when they are being cooked. Put them under the broiler and cook for 12-15 minutes, turning them several times. Keep hot.
5. Remove the capon from the casserole and keep it hot. Allow the cooking liquid to cool slightly, then skim off the fat which floats to the surface.
6. Heat 1 tablespoon [15 g / 1½ oz] butter in a saucepan, add the shallots and soften. Add the remaining champagne. Bring to a boil and add the skimmed cooking liquid from the capon.
7. Remove from the heat. Dissolve the cornstarch in the cold water. Add to the saucepan and thicken over a low heat, stirring continuously. Strain the sauce.
8. Put the sugar and vinegar in a small heavy saucepan and cook until you obtain a dark brown caramel. Thin it with a few drops of boiling water, then add the caramel to the strained sauce and heat for a few minutes. Taste, and adjust the seasoning if necessary.
9. Remove the saucepan from the heat and vigorously beat in the rest of the butter, a little at a time.
10. Carve the capon and arrange on a hot serving platter. Surround with the blood sausages and coat with a little of the sauce. Serve the rest of the sauce separately.

Cook's tip: this dish should not be reheated.

Canard aux olives

Duck with Olives

00:25   01:00

American	Ingredients	Metric/Imperial
2½ cups	Green olives	300 g / 10 oz
2 (2¾ lb)	Ducks, with livers	2 (1.25 kg / 2¾ lb)
¼ lb	Bayonne ham or prosciutto	125 g / 4 oz
6	Garlic cloves	6
3 tbsp	Olive oil	3 tbsp
5 oz	Button mushrooms	150 g / 5 oz
	Salt and pepper	
⅔ cup	Dry white wine	150 ml / ¼ pint
2	Tiny onions	2
3 tbsp	Butter	40 g / 1½ oz

1. Remove the pits [stones] from the olives. Blanch the olives in boiling water for 5 minutes. Drain and set aside.
2. Dice the duck livers. Cut the ham into thin strips. Peel the garlic cloves.
3. Heat 1 tablespoon of olive oil in a frying pan, add the ham and cook for 1 minute. Add the diced livers and cook for a further minute. Remove the meat, then add the garlic. Brown lightly and remove from the pan. Finally add the mushrooms and cook until they begin to brown. Remove.
4. Put all these ingredients in a bowl and mix well. Season to taste with salt and pepper and add half the olives.
5. Stuff each duck with half the olive mixture and truss. Heat the remaining oil in a flameproof casserole, add the ducks and brown on all sides. Remove them and wipe the inside of the casserole with paper towels.
6. Return the ducks to the casserole, season to taste with salt and pepper and add the wine and peeled onions. Cover and simmer for 30 minutes over a very low heat, turning the ducks halfway through the cooking time. Add the rest of the olives and cook for a further 15 minutes.
7. Remove the ducks from the casserole, carve them and arrange the pieces on a warmed serving platter with the stuffing. Keep hot.
8. Add the butter to the cooking liquid a little at a time, beating with a whisk until thick and creamy. Pour a little sauce over the duck and serve the rest separately.

Coq au cidre

Chicken with Cider

00:20   01:15

American	Ingredients	Metric/Imperial
2 (2¾ lb)	Chickens	2 (1.25 kg / 2¾ lb)
	Salt and pepper	
6	Apples	6
½ cup	Butter	125 g / 4 oz
6	Shallots	6
2½ cups	Dry cider	600 ml / 1 pint
1	Bouquet garni	1
1 cup	Crème fraîche	250 m / 8 fl oz

1. Preheat the oven to 450°F / 230°C / Gas Mark 8.
2. Season the insides of the chickens with salt and pepper. Peel the apples, cut them into quarters and remove the cores and seeds. Put the apple quarters inside the birds and sew up the

openings with kitchen string.
3. Put the birds in a large buttered flameproof casserole and coat them with 6 tablespoons [75 g / 3 oz] of the butter. Bake for about 20 minutes, turning the chickens several times so that they are brown on all sides.
4. Meanwhile, peel and chop the shallots. Heat the remaining butter in a small pan, add the shallots and cook until translucent. Heat the cider in a saucepan over a very low heat.
5. Remove the casserole from the oven. Reduce the oven temperature to 375°F / 190°C / Gas Mark 5.
6. Add the shallots, hot cider and bouquet garni to the casserole. Salt lightly and season generously with pepper. Cover and return to the oven. Cook for 45 minutes.
7. Remove the birds (return the apple quarters to the casserole) and keep them hot. Remove the bouquet garni from the casserole and add the crème fraîche. Reduce the sauce over a brisk heat, stirring constantly. When thickened, put the sauce through a strainer, pressing the ingredients with a spoon.
8. Carve the birds. Arrange the pieces on a serving platter and pour the sauce over the top.

Dinde roulée du pot

Boiled Rolled Turkey with Vegetables

00:25   01:15

American	Ingredients	Metric/Imperial
4	Leeks	4
1	Celery stalk	1
2	Onions	2
4	Cloves	4
6	Carrots	6
2	Turnips	2
2 lb	Brussels sprouts	1 kg / 2 lb
5 quarts	Water	5 l / 9 pints
	Salt and peper	
1	Bouquet garni	1
1 (2 lb)	Rolled boneless turkey roast	1 (1 kg / 2 lb)
6	Slices of marrow bone	6

1. Quarter the leeks and clean them, ruffling back the layers. Tie the celery with the leeks to form a bundle. Peel the onions and stud each one with 2 cloves. Peel the carrots and turnips. Remove the outer leaves of the brussels sprouts.
2. Pour the cold water into a large saucepan and add a pinch of salt. Put in the carrots and bring to a boil. Simmer for 20 minutes, then add the leeks and celery tied together, the onions studded with cloves, the turnips and the bouquet garni. Cook for about 20 minutes over a moderate heat.
3. Remove the vegetables and put them aside.
4. Pour half the vegetable stock into another saucepan. Add the turkey roast, bring to a boil and simmer for about 40 minutes.
5. Meanwhile, pour the other half of the stock into another pan and add the brussels sprouts. Cook for about 10-15 minutes or until tender. Drain.
6. About 5 minutes before the end of the cooking time, take a small panful of stock from the turkey, put in the pieces of marrow bone and cook for 5 minutes over a moderate heat.
7. Shortly before the end of the turkey's cooking time, add all the vegetables to reheat them. Season with salt and pepper.
8. Serve the turkey surrounded with the drained vegetables and marrow bones. The stock will make a delicious clear soup.

Escalopes de dinde normande
Normandy Style Turkey Scaloppine [Escalopes]

⏱ 00:15   00:30 🍲

American	Ingredients	Metric/Imperial
5 oz	Button mushrooms	150 g / 5 oz
	Lemon juice	
3 tbsp	Butter	40 g / 1½ oz
6	Turkey scaloppine [escalopes]	6
⅔ cup	Dry white wine	150 ml / ¼ pint
2 tsp	Tarragon mustard	2 tsp
½ cup	Crème fraîche	125 ml / 4 fl oz
	Salt and pepper	
2	Egg yolks	2

1. Sprinkle the mushrooms with lemon juice.
2. Melt the butter in a large frying pan. As soon as it bubbles, add the turkey scaloppine and seal on both sides for a few seconds without allowing them to color. Remove them from the frying pan and set aside.
3. Pour the wine into the pan and bring to a boil, then add the tarragon mustard. Stir to mix. Return the scaloppine to the frying pan. Add the mushrooms and crème fraîche. Season to taste with salt and pepper and cook for about 15 minutes over a moderate heat.
4. Arrange the turkey on a hot serving dish and keep warm.
5. Take 2 tablespoons of sauce and blend in a bowl with the egg yolks. Remove the frying pan from the heat and add this mixture to the remaining sauce, stirring thoroughly. If necessary, reheat the sauce but do not allow it to boil. Pour it over the turkey and serve immediately.

Rôti de dindonneau aux pommes
Roast Turkey with Apples

⏱ 00:25   01:15 🍲

American	Ingredients	Metric/Imperial
1 (3 lb)	Young turkey	1 (1.5 kg / 3 lb)
6 tbsp	Butter	75 g / 3 oz
	Salt and pepper	
6	Sweet apples	6
1	Lemon	1
	Ground cinnamon	

1. Preheat the oven to 450°F / 230°C / Gas Mark 8.
2. Lightly butter an ovenproof dish. Spread the turkey with butter, season with salt and pepper and put it in the dish. Roast for about 1¼ hours, turning it 4 times. Baste at regular intervals with the roasting juices and add 6 tablespoons of water during the last 30 minutes of the cooking time.
3. Meanwhile, peel the apples leaving them whole. Remove the cores with an apple corer and sprinkle them with the juice of the lemon so that they do not turn brown. About 15 minutes before the end of the roasting time, put the apples in the baking dish around the turkey. Put a pat of butter in the center of each apple and sprinkle with pepper to taste and a little cinnamon. Finish roasting.

4. Arrange the turkey on a platter surrounded by the apples and serve the roasting juices separately.

Coq au vin
Chicken in Red Wine

⏱ 00:30   01:30 🍲

American	Ingredients	Metric/Imperial
1 (3 lb)	Chicken	1 (1.5 kg / 3 lb)
6 tbsp	Butter	75 g / 3 oz
	Salt and pepper	
5 oz	Lighty salted lean bacon	150 g / 5 oz
15	Tiny onions	15
2 tbsp	Brandy	2 tbsp
1	Bottle of full-bodied red wine	1
1	Garlic clove	1
1	Bouquet garni	1
1 tbsp	Flour	1 tbsp
	Chopped fresh parsley for garnish	

1. Cut the chicken into pieces.
2. Heat ¼ cup [50 g / 2 oz] of the butter in a flameproof casserole and add the chicken pieces. Season with salt and pepper and brown the chicken on all sides over a medium heat.
3. Meanwhile, finely dice the bacon and put it in a saucepan of cold water. Bring to a boil and blanch for 5 minutes. Drain. Peel the onions.
4. Remove the pieces of chicken and keep them hot. Put the onions and bacon in the casserole and fry for about 10 minutes, stirring frequently.
5. Return the chicken to the casserole and add the brandy. Heat and set alight, then, when the flames have died out, add the red wine so that all the chicken is well covered. Season to taste with salt and pepper. Add the peeled garlic and bouquet garni. Cover and simmer for 1 hour.
6. About 15 minutes before the end of the cooking time, work the rest of the butter with the flour to form a soft paste. Beat in 2 tablespoons of hot sauce, then return this mixture to the casserole and stir well.
7. Serve garnished with a little chopped parsley.

Roast quails on canapés (see page 98)

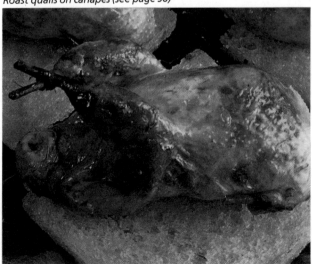

Lapin chasseur

Rabbit in Mushroom and Wine Sauce

	00:15		00:55

American	Ingredients	Metric/Imperial
1 (2¾ lb)	Rabbit	1 (1.25 kg / 2¾ lb)
¼ lb	Bacon	125 g / 4 oz
2	Onions	2
3	Shallots	3
1	Garlic clove	1
1¼ cups	Dry white wine	300 ml / ½ pint
⅔ cup	Water	150 ml / ¼ pint
1	Bouquet garni	1
	Grated nutmeg	
	Salt and pepper	
½ lb	Button mushrooms	250 g / 8 oz
1 tbsp	Butter	1 tbsp
1 tbsp	Flour	1 tbsp
	Chopped fresh parsley for garnish	

1. Cut the rabbit into portions.
2. Put the bacon in a saucepan. Cover it with water, bring to a boil and blanch for 5 minutes. Drain and cut it into strips. Peel and chop the onions, shallots and garlic.
3. Put the strips of bacon in a flameproof casserole over a moderate heat and cook to render the fat. Add the rabbit pieces and brown gently for about 10 minutes so that the fat does not burn.
4. Add the onions, shallots and garlic. As soon as they start to cook, add the wine and water. Add the bouquet garni, a pinch of nutmeg, and salt and pepper to taste. Bring to a boil, then reduce the heat, cover and simmer for 30 minutes.
5. Thinly slice the mushrooms. Add them to the casserole and cook for a further 15 minutes.
6. Remove the pieces of rabbit from the casserole, place them on a serving dish and keep hot.
7. Mix the butter with the flour to a smooth paste. Add 3 tablespoons of the cooking liquid. Stir well, then return this mixture to the casserole. Bring to a boil and cook, stirring, until the sauce is thick and creamy.
8. Pour the sauce over the rabbit and serve sprinkled with chopped parsley.

Lapin aux pruneaux

Rabbit with Prunes

	00:30		01:00

American	Ingredients	Metric/Imperial
20	Large prunes	20
1¼ cups	Madeira wine	300 ml / ½ pint
1 (2¾ lb)	Young rabbit	1 (1.25 kg / 2¾ lb)
1 tbsp	Oil	1 tbsp
¼ cup	Butter	50 g / 2 oz
1 (5 oz)	Slice of cooked ham	1 (150 g / 5 oz)
	Salt and pepper	

1. Remove the pits [stones] from the prunes with a small pointed knife. Soak the prunes in the madeira for 1 hour.

2. Cut the rabbit into pieces. Heat the oil and 2 tablespoons [25 g / 1 oz] butter in a flameproof casserole. As soon as the butter bubbles, add the pieces of rabbit and brown lightly over a moderate heat.
3. Cut the ham into strips, add to the casserole and fry for 5 minutes. Season to taste with salt and pepper. Add the madeira and prunes. Cover and cook over a very low heat for 45 minutes to 1 hour, until tender.
4. Put the pieces of rabbit in a warmed serving dish with the prunes and ham. Bring the sauce back to a boil, then remove from the heat and beat in the remaining butter, a little at a time. Adjust the seasoning and pour the sauce over the rabbit.

Rabbit with cream and brandy sauce

Lapin en civet

Jugged Rabbit

	00:15		02:00

American	Ingredients	Metric/Imperial
1 (3 lb)	Rabbit	1 (1.5 kg / 3 lb)
½ lb	Bacon	250 g / 8 oz
4	Carrots	4
4	Shallots	4
3 tbsp	Flour	3 tbsp
	Salt and pepper	
1	Bottle of red wine	1
1	Bouquet garni	1
20	Tiny onions	20
	Grated nutmeg	

1. Cut the rabbit into pieces.
2. Put the bacon in a saucepan, cover with cold water and bring to a boil. Blanch for 5 minutes. Drain and cut into small strips. Peel and finely chop the carrots and shallots.
3. Put the flour on a plate. Roll the pieces of rabbit in the flour to coat all over, then shake to remove excess flour.
4. Brown the strips of bacon in a flameproof casserole over a moderate heat without adding any fat. Remove them from the casserole and set aside.
5. Add the pieces of rabbit to the casserole. Season to taste with salt and pepper. Lightly brown the rabbit over a brisk heat. Add the carrots and shallots. When the vegetables are browned, pour in the red wine. Add a little water if necessary so that the pieces of rabbit are just covered with liquid. Add the strips of bacon and the bouquet garni. Cover the casserole and simmer gently for 1 hour.
6. Meanwhile, peel the onions.
7. Taste the cooking liquid and adjust the seasoning. Add a

pinch of nutmeg and the onions. Leave the casserole uncovered and simmer gently for another hour, stirring from time to time, until the rabbit is tender.

8. Discard the bouquet garni before serving.

Lapin sauce poulette
Rabbit with Rich Mushroom Sauce

	00:25	01:00	

American	Ingredients	Metric/Imperial
1 (2¾ lb)	Rabbit	1 (1.25 kg / 2¾ lb)
3	Onions	3
2	Carrots	2
6 tbsp	Butter	75 g / 3 oz
2 tbsp	Flour	2 tbsp
1 cup	Dry white wine	250 ml / 8 fl oz
	Salt and pepper	
1	Bouquet garni	1
5 oz	Button mushrooms	150 g / 5 oz
½	Lemon	½
2	Egg yolks	2
1 cup	Crème fraîche	250 ml / 8 fl oz

1. Cut the rabbit into pieces. Peel and slice the onions and carrots. Melt the butter in a flameproof casserole. As soon as it bubbles, add the rabbit pieces, onions and carrots and fry over a moderate heat until light brown.

2. Sprinkle with the flour. Stir so that all the pieces are coated, and lightly brown the flour. Pour in the wine and add enough water so that the liquid covers the rabbit and vegetables. Season to taste with salt and pepper and add the bouquet garni. Cover and simmer for 45 minutes to 1 hour or until the rabbit is tender.

3. Sprinkle the mushrooms with the juice of the ½ lemon. About 15 minutes before the end of the cooking time, remove the bouquet garni from the casserole and add the mushrooms.

4. Mix the egg yolks with the crème fraîche.

5. Just before serving, remove the casserole from the heat and add the egg mixture. Stir thoroughly and adjust the seasoning, if necessary.

Lapin à la fine
Rabbit with Cream and Brandy Sauce

	00:10	00:30 to 00:40	

American	Ingredients	Metric/Imperial
2 (1½ lb)	Rabbits	2 (750 g / 1½ lb)
¾ lb	Tiny onions	350 g / 12 oz
2 tbsp	Butter	25 g / 1 oz
1 tbsp	Oil	1 tbsp
	Salt and pepper	
½ cup	Cognac	125 ml / 4 fl oz
¼ cup	Crème fraîche	4 tbsp
1 tbsp	Flour	1 tbsp

1. Cut the rabbits into pieces. Peel the onions. Heat 1 tablespoon [15 g / ½ oz] butter with the oil in a flameproof casserole, add the pieces of rabbit and brown gently for about 7 minutes. Add the onions and cook for a further 10 minutes or until golden brown.

2. Season to taste with salt and pepper. Add the cognac, cover and cook over a very low heat for 30-40 minutes.

3. Remove the rabbit and onions from the casserole and keep hot. Skim the fat from the cooking liquid. Add the crème fraîche and boil for a few seconds. Remove from the heat.

4. Blend the rest of the butter with the flour to a smooth paste. Add a tablespoon of the cooking liquid and stir well, then add to the casserole, whisking. Return to the heat and bring to a boil. The sauce should be creamy without being thick. Taste and adjust the seasoning.

5. Serve the rabbit and onions coated with the hot sauce.

Cook's tip: this recipe is best if young rabbits are used.

Lapin farci
Stuffed Rabbit

	00:25	01:00 to 01:30	

American	Ingredients	Metric/Imperial
15	Green olives, pitted [stoned]	15
½ lb	Smoked bacon	250 g / 8 oz
1 (2¾ lb)	Young rabbit	1 (1.25 kg / 2¾ lb)
2	Chicken livers	2
2	Small pork link sausages [chipolatas]	2
6	Tiny onions	6
6	Garlic cloves	6
5 oz	Button mushrooms	150 g / 5 oz
	Thyme leaves	
1	Bay leaf	1
	Salt and pepper	
2 tbsp	Olive oil	2 tbsp
1	Bouquet garni	1
⅔ cup	Dry white wine	150 ml / ¼ pint
¼ cup	Butter	50 g / 2 oz

1. Blanch the olives in boiling water for 5 minutes, then drain. Cut the bacon into small strips, put them in a frying pan and cook over a moderate heat until brown. Remove them from the frying pan and set aside.

2. Cut the rabbit liver, chicken livers and sausages into dice and brown in the bacon fat. Remove from the frying pan.

3. Peel the onions and garlic. Add to the pan and cook for 10 minutes. Remove and set aside.

4. Cut the mushrooms into quarters and add to the frying pan. Cook until the liquid escapes from the mushrooms, then return the bacon, sausages, livers, onions and garlic to the pan. Add the olives, a pinch of thyme leaves and the bay leaf, crushed. Mix well, adding salt and pepper to taste.

5. Stuff the rabbit with the liver mixture and tie securely.

6. Heat the olive oil in a flameproof casserole. Add the rabbit, season with salt and pepper and brown on all sides. Add the bouquet garni and wine. Cover and cook over a low heat for about 1½ hours.

7. Carve the rabbit and arrange it on a serving dish surrounded by the stuffing. Remove the casserole from the heat and add the butter to the sauce a little at a time, beating well. Serve the sauce separately.

Lapin à la moutarde
Rabbit with Mustard

⏱ 00:10   01:15 🍲

American	Ingredients	Metric/Imperial
1	Large piece of caul fat	1
1 (3 lb)	Rabbit	1 (1.5 kg / 3 lb)
5 tbsp	Strong prepared mustard	5 tbsp
	Salt and pepper	
1¼ cups	Crème fraîche	300 ml / ½ pint

1. Soak the caul fat in cold water. Preheat the oven to 450°F / 230°C / Gas Mark 8.
2. Coat the rabbit with the mustard and season lightly with salt and pepper. Drain the caul fat, spread it out on a cloth and pat it dry. Wrap the rabbit in it.
3. Put the rabbit in a buttered roasting pan. Roast for 50 minutes, turning and basting frequently. When the rabbit is cooked, remove it from the pan and keep it hot.
4. Pour the crème fraîche into the roasting pan and cook on top of the stove, scraping the bottom of the pan with a wooden spatula to dissolve the sediment. Simmer until the sauce thickens.
5. Cut the rabbit into portions (the caul will have dissolved) and serve very hot with the sauce.

Lapin au pineau
Rabbit with Pineau des Charentes

Pineau des Charentes is an aperitif made from fresh grape juice and cognac.

⏱ 01:00
plus marinating
00:40 🍲

American	Ingredients	Metric/Imperial
2	Onions	2
2	Shallots	2
3	Carrots	3
1	Bouquet garni	1
½	Bottle of Pineau des Charentes or sherry	½
	Salt and pepper	
1 (6 lb)	Rabbit	1 (3 kg / 6 lb)
½ cup	Butter	125 g / 4 oz
⅔ cup	Beef stock or broth	150 ml / ¼ pint
1 tbsp	Flour	1 tbsp
½ lb	Prunes	250 g / 8 oz

1. The day before cooking, prepare the marinade. Peel and slice the onions, shallots and carrots. Put them in a bowl with the bouquet garni and pour in the Pineau des Charentes. Season with salt and pepper.
2. Cut the rabbit into pieces. Place in the bowl and marinate for 12 hours. Turn the pieces of rabbit 2 or 3 times.
3. Drain the pieces of rabbit, reserving the marinade. Melt ¼ cup [50 g / 2 oz] butter in a flameproof casserole, add the pieces of rabbit and cook until they are well browned.
4. Strain the marinade and add it to the casserole with the stock or broth. Simmer for about 40 minutes.
5. Remove the pieces of rabbit and keep them hot. Mix the

remaining butter and the flour to a paste. Add to the cooking liquid a little at a time, stirring well, and cook until thickened. Add the prunes to this sauce and heat through.
6. Arrange the pieces of rabbit on a serving platter. Surround with the prunes and serve the sauce separately.

Lapin coquibus
Rabbit Casseroled with Onions and Bacon

⏱ 00:20   01:15 🍲

American	Ingredients	Metric/Imperial
1 (3 lb)	Rabbit	1 (1.5 kg / 3 lb)
¼ cup	Butter	50 g / 2 oz
3 tbsp	Olive oil	3 tbsp
½ lb	Smoked bacon	250 g / 8 oz
24	Tiny onions	24
1 tbsp	Flour	1 tbsp
2 cups	Chicken stock	500 ml / ¾ pint
1¼ cups	White wine	300 ml / ½ pint
	Salt and pepper	
1	Bouquet garni	1

1. Cut the rabbit into 9 pieces. Heat the butter and oil in a flameproof casserole, add the pieces of rabbit and brown on all sides over a medium heat.
2. Meanwhile, cut the bacon into strips. Peel the onions.
3. Remove the pieces of rabbit from the casserole and set aside. Add the strips of bacon and onions to the casserole and brown them lightly. Return the pieces of rabbit to the casserole. Sprinkle with the flour and cook, stirring, until browned.
4. Pour in the stock and wine. Season with salt and plenty of pepper and add the bouquet garni. Cover and cook over a low heat for about 50 minutes.
5. Discard the bouquet garni. Put the pieces of rabbit in a warmed serving dish and pour the sauce over the top. Serve.

Pigeons aux herbes
Pigeons with Herbs

⏱ 00:20   00:25 to 00:35 🍲
plus standing time

American	Ingredients	Metric/Imperial
1 cup	Cream cheese	250 g / 8 oz
2 tbsp	Dried herbs of Provence	2 tbsp
1 tsp	Brandy	1 tsp
6 tbsp	Butter	75 g / 3 oz
	Salt and pepper	
3	Large pigeons	3
9	Bacon slices	9
⅔ cup	Boiling water	150 ml / ¼ pint
2 tbsp	Oil	2 tbsp
6	Slices of bread, ½ in / 1 cm thick	6

1. About 2 hours before cooking the pigeons, mix the cream cheese with the herbs, brandy and 2 tablespoons [25 g / 1 oz] of butter. Season with salt and pepper. Divide this mixture in 3 and stuff the pigeons with it. Wrap 3 slices of bacon around each bird. Leave them to stand in a roasting pan for 2 hours at room temperature.

2. Preheat the oven to 425°F / 220°C / Gas Mark 7.

3. Roast the pigeons for about 30 minutes without adding any liquid. Turn several times to brown evenly.

4. Remove the pigeons from the pan and keep warm. Put the pan over a low heat on top of the stove and add the boiling water. Heat, stirring to dissolve the solids in the bottom of the pan. Leave the sauce to reduce for 5 minutes.

5. Meanwhile, heat 1 tablespoon butter and the oil in a frying pan and fry the bread over a brisk heat until golden brown on both sides.

6. Beat the remaining butter into the sauce. Season to taste with salt and pepper and pour into a hot sauceboat. Cut each pigeon in half and place a half on each slice of fried bread. Serve immediately.

Pigeons with herbs

Guinea Fowl with Cabbage

Pintade au chou

American	Ingredients	Metric/Imperial
1	Large head of white cabbage	1
¾ lb	Smoked bacon	350 g / 12 oz
	Salt and pepper	
1	Large guinea fowl	1
4	Bacon slices	4

00:30   01:30 to 02:00

1. Cut the cabbage into quarters and remove the core. Put the quarters in a saucepan of boiling salted water. Bring back to a boil and cook for 10 minutes. Drain well.

2. Preheat the oven to 450°F / 230°C / Gas Mark 8.

3. Cut the smoked bacon into large strips. Put them into a flameproof casserole and cook gently so that the fat is rendered without the bacon browning. Remove the bacon from the casserole with a slotted spoon and set aside.

4. Add the cabbage to the casserole and cook in the bacon fat until it softens. Return the strips of bacon to the casserole.

Season to taste with salt and pepper. Cover and cook over a low heat for 30 minutes.

5. Meanwhile, season the guinea fowl with salt and pepper and cover with the slices of bacon. Truss the bird and roast for about 30 minutes or until well browned.

6. Put the guinea fowl in the casserole with the cabbage and finish cooking gently until the cabbage is very soft (about 1 hour).

7. Just before serving, if there is too much liquid, reduce it rapidly over a brisk heat. Serve the guinea fowl carved into portions, on a bed of cabbage and bacon.

Cook's tip: this recipe can be made in large quantities as it is very good when reheated.

Stuffed Guinea Fowl

Pintades farcies

American	Ingredients	Metric/Imperial
⅔ cup	Milk	150 ml / ¼ pint
2 cups	Fresh bread crumbs	125 g / 4 oz
5 oz	Lightly salted bacon	150 g / 5 oz
1	Shallot	1
2 (2 lb)	Guinea fowl, with livers	2 (1 kg / 2 lb)
½	Chicken livers	250 g / 8 oz
1	Egg	1
3½ oz	Pâté de foie gras	100 g / 3½ oz
1	Fresh thyme sprig	1
	Salt and pepper	
	Grated nutmeg	
	Oil	
⅔ cup	Boiling water	150 ml / ¼ pint
¼ cup	Butter	50 g / 2 oz

00:30   00:40

1. Pour the milk over the bread crumbs and set aside to soak. Cut the bacon into strips, put them in a saucepan of cold water and bring to a boil. Blanch for 5 minutes. Drain.

2. Peel and thinly slice the shallot. Put the shallot and bacon in a frying pan and fry over a medium heat until the shallot becomes translucent. Add the guinea fowl livers and the whole chicken livers. Fry them lightly so that they are not completely cooked.

3. Preheat the oven to 425°F / 220°C / Gas Mark 7.

4. Squeeze the liquid from the bread crumbs and put them in a bowl. Add the egg, foie gras, the ingredients in the frying pan and the thyme leaves. Work all these ingredients with a fork, mashing the livers. Season to taste with salt and pepper and add a pinch of nutmeg.

5. Divide this mixture in half and use to stuff the guinea fowl. Truss them and brush the skin with a little oil. Place on a metal rack in a roasting pan and roast for about 40 minutes. Turn them while roasting so that they brown on all sides, and pour half the boiling water into the dish halfway through the process. When the birds are cooked, turn off the oven and leave them inside for 5 minutes.

6. Carve the guinea fowl into portions, keeping the juices, and arrange the pieces on a serving dish. Garnish the dish with the stuffing and keep warm.

7. Pour the remaining boiling water into the roasting pan and heat briskly on top of the stove for a few minutes, scraping the bottom well to loosen all the solids. Beat in the carving juices and the butter. Taste and adjust the seasoning if necessary. Serve this sauce with the guinea fowl.

Pintadeaux rôtis sur canapés

Roast Guinea Fowl with Foie Gras

◢▱ 00:10   00:40 🍲

American	Ingredients	Metric/Imperial
3 (1 lb)	Young guinea fowl (with the livers)	3 (500 g / 1 lb)
	Salt and pepper	
3 tbsp	Butter	40 g / 1½ oz
6	Bacon slices	6
3 tbsp	Water	3 tbsp
2 tbsp	Oil	2 tbsp
6	Slices of bread	6
1	Small can of pâté de foie gras	1
¼ cup	Brandy	4 tbsp

1. Preheat the oven to 425°F / 220°C / Gas Mark 7.
2. Season the inside of each guinea fowl with salt and pepper and put 1 tablespoon of butter inside each. Cover the birds with bacon and tie it on with string. Place the birds on a rack in a roasting pan. Roast for 10-15 minutes.
3. Pour the juices from the guinea fowl into the roasting pan. Add the water. Continue roasting for 30 minutes.
4. Meanwhile, heat the oil and brown the slices of bread in a frying pan on both sides. Mash the livers of the guinea fowl in a bowl using a fork. Season to taste with salt and pepper and add the pâté de foie gras. Mix well.
5. When the guinea fowl are cooked, pour the juice which remains inside them into the roasting pan. Add the brandy and scrape well to loosen all the sediment at the bottom of the pan. Add the liver mixture and bring to a boil.
6. Cut the guinea fowl in half and serve each piece on a slice of fried bread topped with some of the sauce. Serve the rest of the sauce in a sauceboat.

Pintade en cocotte aux cerises fraîches

Casserole of Guinea Fowl with Fresh Cherries

◢▱ 00:40   01:15 🍲

American	Ingredients	Metric/Imperial
2	Young guinea fowl	2
¼ cup	Brandy	4 tbsp
	Salt and pepper	
4	Thin bacon slices	4
½ cup	Butter	125 g / 4 oz
5	Shallots	5
½ lb	Button mushrooms	250 g / 8 oz
½	Lemon	½
1	Small fresh thyme sprig	1
2 lb	Cherries	1 kg / 2 lb
⅔ cup	Water	150 ml / ¼ pint
6 tbsp	Sugar	6 tbsp
1¼ cups	Crème fraîche	300 ml / ½ pint

1. Preheat the oven to 450°F / 230°C / Gas Mark 8.
2. Rub the insides of the guinea fowl with a few drops of

brandy, then season them with salt and pepper. Cover the back and breast of the guinea fowl with the bacon and tie with kitchen string. Heat ¼ cup [50 g / 2 oz] of the butter in a flameproof casserole, add the guinea fowl and brown on all sides over a medium heat.
3. Meanwhile, peel and chop the shallots. Thinly slice the mushrooms and sprinkle with the juice of the ½ lemon. Melt the rest of the butter in a frying pan, add the shallots and cook until softened. Add the mushrooms and cook until all the liquid has evaporated.
4. Add the mushrooms and shallots to the casserole. Pour the remaining brandy over the birds and set alight, lifting the guinea fowl so that their whole surface absorbs the flavor. Add the thyme. Cover the casserole, put it in the oven and cook for 30 minutes.
5. While the guinea fowl are cooking, wash the cherries and remove the pits [stones]. Put them in a saucepan with the water and sugar. Cover and cook over a low heat for 15 minutes.
6. Remove the guinea fowl from the casserole and discard the bacon. Return them to the casserole and cook, uncovered, for 10 minutes longer. Add the cherries and cook for a further 10 minutes.
7. Drain the birds, carve them into portions and arrange them on a serving dish. Keep hot. Pour the crème fraîche into the casserole and boil briskly to thicken, stirring constantly. Adjust the seasoning, if necessary.
8. Pour the sauce into a sauceboat and serve, very hot, with the guinea fowl.

Salmis de pintade

Salmis of Guinea Fowl

◢▱ 00:20   01:15 🍲

American	Ingredients	Metric/Imperial
5 tbsp	Butter	65 g / 2½ oz
2 (2¾ lb)	Guinea fowl, with giblets	2 (1.25 kg / 2¾ lb)
	Salt and pepper	
2	Onions	2
2	Shallots	2
2	Carrots	2
1	Garlic clove	1
¼ lb	Lightly salted bacon	125 g / 4 oz
¼ cup	Brandy	4 tbsp
1	Bottle of dry red wine	1
	Grated nutmeg	
1	Bouquet garni	1
2 tbsp	Flour	2 tbsp
3	Slices of bread, ½ in / 1 cm thick	3
2 tbsp	Oil	2 tbsp

1. Heat ¼ cup [50 g / 2 oz] butter in a flameproof casserole, add the guinea fowl and brown lightly on all sides over a low heat. Do not let them get too dark. Season to taste with salt and pepper. Cover and cook over a low heat for 30 minutes.
2. Meanwhile, peel and dice the onions, shallots, carrots and garlic.
3. Cut up the guinea fowl for serving and put the pieces aside. Chop the giblets.
4. Chop the bacon and put the pieces in a saucepan of cold water. Bring to a boil and blanch for 5 minutes, then drain. Put the bacon in the casserole with the diced vegetables and cook until golden. Add the giblets and brown over a brisk heat.
5. Add the brandy and set alight, then pour over the red wine.

The liquid should cover the contents of the casserole, so add a little water if necessary. Season with pepper and a pinch of nutmeg and add the bouquet garni. Cover and simmer for 45 minutes.

6. Strain the contents of the casserole into a bowl, pressing with the back of a spoon to extract as much liquid as possible from the solids.

7. Wipe the casserole and put in the remaining butter. Heat it, then add the flour, mixing well. Brown this roux. Add the strained liquid, stirring, and cook until the sauce thickens.

8. Put the pieces of guinea fowl in the sauce and simmer for 10 minutes.

9. Meanwhile, remove the crusts from the slices of bread and cut diagonally into quarters. Heat the oil in a large frying pan and fry the bread until golden brown on both sides.

10. Put the pieces of guinea fowl in a serving dish together with the sauce and garnish with the croûtons.

Roast guinea fowl with foie gras

Poularde en chaud-froid

Cold Chicken in Aspic Cream

	01:00	03:00
	plus cooling and chilling	

American	Ingredients	Metric/Imperial
1 lb	Carrots	500 g / 1 lb
2	Turnips	2
3	Onions	3
1	Garlic clove	1
3	Cloves	3
4	Leeks	4
1	Celery stalk	1
1	Bouquet garni	1
	Salt and pepper	
3 quarts	Water	3 l / 5 pints
1 (4 lb)	Chicken	1 (2 kg / 4 lb)
2	Calf's feet, halved	2
2 cups	Crème fraîche	450 ml / ¾ pint
½ oz	Truffle slices	15 g / ½ oz

1. Peel the carrots, turnips, onions and garlic. Stud each onion with a clove. Put all these vegetables in a large pan, and add the leeks, celery and bouquet garni. Season to taste and cover with the water. Bring to a boil and simmer for 30 minutes.

2. Remove from the heat and add the chicken. Wait

5 minutes, then return the pan to a medium heat. Bring slowly back to a boil and simmer gently for 1 hour. Allow the chicken to cool in the stock.

3. Take the chicken out of the pan. Carve into equal pieces and remove all the skin. Set aside. Strain the stock and put 1 quart [1 l / 1¾ pints] aside.

4. Put the remaining stock back into the pan. Add the halved calf's feet and simmer for 45 minutes.

5. Reduce the reserved stock by one-third over a brisk heat, then add 3 cups [750 ml / 1¼ pints] of the stock from the calf's feet. Again boil to reduce by one-third. Gradually add ⅔ cup [150 ml / ¼ pint] crème fraîche, stirring constantly.

6. Pour the reduced sauce into a bowl and gradually stir in the rest of the crème. Beat vigorously until the sauce becomes silky.

7. Dip the pieces of chicken in the sauce to coat them. Arrange them on a sheet of foil and garnish them with thin slices of truffle. Using a pastry brush, coat them with the rest of the sauce which should be still slightly liquid but on the point of setting. Chill thoroughly in the refrigerator before serving.

Pigeons en compote

Braised Pigeons

	00:15	01:00

American	Ingredients	Metric/Imperial
5 oz	Bacon	150 g / 5 oz
3	Large pigeons	3
¼ cup	Butter	50 g / 2 oz
3	Onions	3
1	Garlic clove	1
1 tbsp	Flour	1 tbsp
1 tbsp	Tomato paste [purée]	1 tbsp
⅔ cup	Chicken stock	150 ml / ¼ pint
⅔ cup	Dry white wine	150 ml / ¼ pint
	Salt and pepper	
1	Bouquet garni	1
½ lb	Button mushrooms	250 g / 8 oz
½	Lemon	½
1¼ cups	Crème fraîche	300 ml / ½ pint

1. Cut the bacon into small strips, plunge them into boiling water and blanch for 5 minutes. Drain and set aside.

2. Cut the pigeons in half. Heat half the butter in a flameproof casserole, add the pigeons and brown on all sides. Meanwhile, peel and thinly slice the onions. Peel and crush the garlic.

3. Drain the pigeon halves and set aside. Put the onions and strips of bacon into the casserole to brown. Sprinkle with the flour and stir to brown well.

4. Return the pigeon halves to the casserole. Mix the tomato paste with the stock and white wine and pour this mixture over the pigeons. Season to taste with salt and pepper. Add the garlic and bouquet garni. Cover the casserole and cook over a low heat for 45 minutes.

5. Meanwhile, thinly slice the mushrooms and sprinkle with the juice of the lemon. Heat the rest of the butter in a frying pan, add the mushrooms and cook until all the liquid has evaporated. Add the mushrooms to the casserole 5 minutes before the end of the cooking time.

6. Discard the bouquet garni. Drain the pigeon halves, put them in a deep serving dish and keep hot.

7. Add the crème fraîche to the casserole and stir for a few minutes over a moderate heat until the sauce thickens. Pour it over the pigeon halves. Serve immediately.

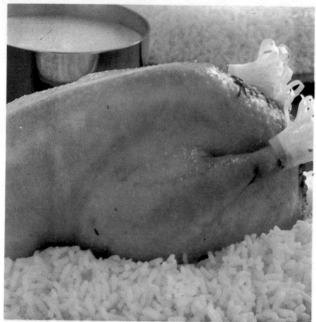

Stuffed chicken with rice

Poule au riz

Stuffed Chicken with Rice

▱▷ 00:30   02:30 🍲

American	Ingredients	Metric/Imperial
6 tbsp	Butter	75 g / 3 oz
½ lb	Chicken livers	250 g / 8 oz
1 (½ lb)	Slice of cooked ham	1 (250 g / 8 oz)
1	Shallot	1
2	Garlic cloves	2
1	Bunch of fresh parsley	1
3	Slices of bread	3
1¼ cups	Milk	300 ml / ½ pint
1	Egg	1
1	Grated nutmeg	1
	Salt and pepper	
1 (4 lb)	Chicken	1 (2 kg / 4 lb)
	Chicken stock	
3 cups	Water	750 ml / 1¼ pints
2 cups	Long-grain rice	400 g / 14 oz
2 tbsp	Flour	25 g / 1 oz
3	Egg yolks	3
⅔ cup	Crème fraîche	150 ml / ¼ pint
1	Lemon	1

1. Heat 2 tablespoons [25 g / 1 oz] butter in a frying pan, add the chicken livers and brown for a few minutes. Purée the livers in a blender or food processor with the ham, peeled shallot and garlic, and parsley. Put into a mixing bowl.
2. Remove the crusts from the bread and soak the slices in the milk. When they are saturated, squeeze out the excess milk and add the bread to the bowl. Add the whole egg and a pinch of grated nutmeg. Season with pepper and mix well.
3. Stuff the chicken with the liver mixture. Put the chicken in a large cooking pot and cover with chicken stock. Bring to a boil

over a medium heat, then turn down the heat and simmer gently for about 2½ hours.
4. When the chicken is cooked, remove 1½ quarts [1.5 l / 2½ pints] of the stock. Allow it to stand for a few minutes so that the fat floats to the surface, then skim off the fat carefully. Pour the stock into a saucepan and boil it briskly until it is reduced by half.
5. Meanwhile, bring the water to a boil in a saucepan. Add salt to taste and the rice and cook for 15-18 minutes or until tender and the water has been absorbed. Remove from the heat and keep hot.
6. Melt the rest of the butter in another saucepan, add the flour and cook, stirring, for a few minutes. Remove from the heat and add the reduced stock, beating vigorously with a whisk. Return to the heat and cook for 5 minutes, stirring continuously, until thickened.
7. Mix together the egg yolks, crème fraîche and juice of the lemon in a bowl. Pour the mixture into the sauce and heat, stirring, without allowing it to boil.
8. Carve the chicken into portions. Put the stuffing in the center of a serving platter, arrange the pieces of chicken all around and serve the sauce in a sauceboat. Serve with rice.

Poulet au blanc

Chicken in White Sauce

▱▷ 00:10   01:30 🍲

American	Ingredients	Metric/Imperial
1 (3 lb)	Chicken	1 (1.5 kg / 3 lb)
3	Lemons	3
10	Tiny onions	10
2	Carrots	2
2 tbsp	Butter	25 g / 1 oz
2 tbsp	Flour	2 tbsp
1¼ cups	Water	300 ml / ½ pint
	Grated nutmeg	
	Salt and pepper	
2 cups	Dry white wine	500 ml / ¾ pint
1	Bouquet garni	1
½ lb	Button mushrooms	250 g / 8 oz
2	Egg yolks	2
⅔ cup	Crème fraîche	150 ml / ¼ pint

1. Truss the chicken. Squeeze 2½ lemons to extract the juice and rub about half the juice all over the chicken. Peel and slice the onions and carrots.
2. Heat the butter in a flameproof casserole. Add the flour and cook, stirring, for 2 minutes. Add the cold water a little at a time. Bring to a boil, stirring, then add a pinch of nutmeg and season to taste with salt and pepper.
3. Put the chicken in the casserole and add sufficient wine just to cover the bird. Add the onions, carrots and bouquet garni. Simmer over a low heat for 1¼ hours.
4. Sprinkle the mushrooms with lemon juice. Add them to the casserole 30 minutes before the end of the cooking time.
5. Remove the chicken from the casserole and keep it hot. Remove the bouquet garni from the sauce and discard. Blend the egg yolks with the crème fraîche and the remaining lemon juice and stir into the sauce. Taste and adjust the seasoning, if necessary. Reheat the sauce over a low heat. Do not allow to boil.
6. Carve the chicken into portions, arrange on a platter and pour a little sauce over the top. Serve the rest of the sauce separately.

Poulet au citron
Lemon Chicken

	00:20		01:30

American	Ingredients	Metric/Imperial
1 (4 lb)	Chicken	1 (1.8 kg / 4 lb)
2	Lemons	2
30	Tiny onions	30
20	Green olives	20
3 tbsp	Olive oil	3 tbsp
	Salt and pepper	
¾ lb	Button mushrooms	350 g / 12 oz

1. Cut the chicken into pieces. Halve 1 of the lemons and rub the chicken pieces with the juice.
2. Peel the onions. Remove the pits [stones] from the olives.
3. Heat the oil in a flameproof casserole over a brisk heat. Add the pieces of chicken and brown them on all sides for about 15 minutes. Season to taste with salt and pepper.
4. Add the juice of the remaining lemon, cover the casserole and cook over a very low heat for 45 minutes.
5. Add the olives, mushrooms and onions and cook for 30 minutes longer. Serve hot.

Poule en daube
Braised Chicken

	00:25		02:00

American	Ingredients	Metric/Imperial
1	Calf's foot	1
¼ lb	Bacon	125 g / 4 oz
6	Carrots	6
2	Onions	2
2	Shallots	2
1 (4 lb)	Chicken	1 (2 kg / 4 lb)
1	Bouquet garni	1
2 cups	Dry white wine	450 ml / ¾ pint
⅔ cup	Water	150 ml / ¼ pint
	Salt and pepper	

1. Split the calf's foot in half lengthwise so that the gelatin will run out easily during cooking. Cut the bacon into 2 in / 5 cm squares. Put the calf's foot and bacon in a saucepan of water. Bring to boil and blanch for 5 minutes. Drain and cool with fresh water.
2. Peel and dice the carrots, onions and shallots.
3. Line the bottom of a casserole with a few pieces of bacon and the calf's foot. Cut the chicken into pieces and put into the casserole with the carrots, onions, shallots and pieces of bacon in successive layers. Finish with a layer of vegetables and bacon. Add the bouquet garni.
4. Pour over the wine and water. Add salt and pepper to taste. Bring to a boil and simmer gently for 2 hours over a very low heat.
5. Remove the pieces of chicken from the casserole, drain them and set them on a serving dish. Discard the bouquet garni. Pour the cooking juices over the chicken and serve surrounded by the vegetable mixture.

Cook's tip: the chicken can be served hot immediately after cooking or chilled overnight in the refrigerator. The cooking juices will set and can be served cold, with the chicken.

Poulet à la crème
Chicken with Cream and Mushroom Sauce

	00:25		00:45

American	Ingredients	Metric/Imperial
1 (3 lb)	Chicken	1 (1.5 kg / 3 lb)
	Salt and pepper	
3 tbsp + 1 tsp	Butter	40g / 1 ½ oz + 1 tsp
3 tbsp	Oil	3 tbsp
1	Thin bacon slice	1
1 lb	Button mushrooms	500 g / 1 lb
½	Lemon	½
4	Shallots	4
1 ¼ cups	White wine	300 ml / ½ pint
1 tsp	Flour	1 tsp
1 ¼ cups	Crème fraîche	300 ml / ½ pint

1. Cut the chicken into 6 pieces and season with salt and pepper. Heat 3 tablespoons [40 g / 1½ oz] butter with 2 tablespoons of the oil in a flameproof casserole. Add the pieces of chicken and brown on all sides over a medium heat.
2. Meanwhile, cut the bacon into small strips. Dice the mushrooms and sprinkle them with the juice of the ½ lemon. Peel and chop the shallots. Gently fry the strips of bacon in a frying pan without any fat, then drain them and set aside.
3. Heat the remaining oil in the frying pan. Add the mushrooms and shallots and cook until all the liquid has evaporated. Season to taste with salt and pepper.
4. Add the bacon, mushrooms and shallots to the casserole. Pour in the white wine. Cover and cook over a medium heat for 40 minutes.
5. Blend the flour with a teaspoon of butter to a paste.
6. Drain the pieces of chicken and put them on a warm serving platter. Add the crème fraîche to the casserole, then add the butter and flour paste and thicken over a brisk heat, stirring. Adjust the seasoning.
7. Pour this sauce over the chicken and serve immediately.

Poulet Vallée d'Auge
Auge Valley Chicken

	00:15		01:15

American	Ingredients	Metric/Imperial
1 (4 lb)	Chicken	1 (2 kg / 4 lb)
⅔ cup	Butter	150 g / 5 oz
	Salt and pepper	
¼ cup	Calvados or applejack	4 tbsp
1 ¼ cups	Thick crème fraîche	300 ml / ½ pint

1. Cut the chicken into pieces.
2. Heat the butter in a flameproof casserole, add the chicken and brown for about 10 minutes. Season with salt and pepper. Cover and cook over a very low heat for 1 hour.
3. Pour the calvados into the casserole, heat and set alight. When the flames have died out, remove the pieces of chicken, arrange them on a warmed serving platter and keep hot.
4. Add the crème fraîche to the liquid, stir and bring to a boil. Simmer for 5-6 minutes or until the sauce has thickened. Pour the sauce over the chicken and serve immediately.

Chicken with whiskey sauce

Poulet au whisky

Chicken with Whiskey Sauce

	00:15	00:50

American	Ingredients	Metric/Imperial
1 (4 lb)	Chicken	1 (1.8 kg / 4 lb)
6 tbsp	Butter	75 g / 3 oz
⅔ cup	Whiskey	150 ml / ¼ pint
5 oz	Button mushrooms	150 g / 5 oz
	Lemon juice	
1	Shallot	1
½ cup	Crème fraîche	125 ml / 4 fl oz
	Salt and pepper	
1 tsp	Cornstarch [cornflour]	1 tsp

1. Cut the chicken into quarters. Heat 2 tablespoons [25 g / 1 oz] butter in a flameproof casserole, add the chicken pieces and cook over a medium heat for about 10 minutes or until golden on all sides.
2. Pour the whiskey over the chicken. Remove from the heat, cover and leave to steep for 10 minutes.
3. Meanwhile, quarter the mushrooms and sprinkle with a few drops of lemon juice. Peel and chop the shallot. Melt the rest of the butter in a frying pan, add the mushrooms and cook, stirring occasionally, until all the liquid has evaporated. Add the chopped shallot and cook for a few minutes longer.
4. Put the mushrooms and shallot in the casserole with the chicken, add half the crème fraîche and season with salt and pepper. Cover and cook over a medium heat for about 30 minutes or until the chicken pieces are tender.
5. Arrange the pieces of chicken on a serving platter and keep hot. Return the casserole to the heat and bring back to a boil.

Mix together the remaining crème fraîche and cornstarch and add to the sauce, whisking well. Cook, stirring, until thickened. Add a few drops of lemon juice. Adjust the seasoning and pour the sauce over the pieces of chicken.

Aspic de volaille

Chicken in Aspic

	01:00 plus chilling	01:00

American	Ingredients	Metric/Imperial
3 quarts	Water	3 l / 5 pints
3	Carrots	3
3	Leeks	3
3	Onions	3
2	Cloves	2
2	Celery stalks	2
	Salt and pepper	
1	Bouquet garni	1
1 (3 lb)	Chicken	1 (1.5 kg / 3 lb)
2 envelopes	Unflavored gelatin	2 sachets
1 (½ lb)	Slice of cooked ham	1 (250 g / 8 oz)
1	Truffle (optional)	1
½ lb	Pâté de foie gras	250 g / 8 oz

1. Bring the water to a boil in a large pan. Meanwhile, peel the carrots. Cut the leeks into quarters. Peel the onions and stud one with 2 cloves. Add the carrots, leeks, onions and celery to the boiling water. Season with salt and pepper, add the bouquet garni and simmer gently for 30 minutes.
2. Add the chicken and cook for 1 hour.
3. Remove the chicken and set aside. Strain the cooking liquid through a strainer into a bowl, then through a fine strainer into a saucepan. Bring to a boil and simmmer until the liquid is reduced to 1 quart [1 l / 1¾ pints].
4. Dissolve the gelatin following the instructions on the package. Stir into the reduced cooking liquid and allow to cool until syrupy.
5. Pour a ½ in / 1 cm layer of the cooking liquid onto the bottom of an oiled 1½ quart [1.5 l / 2½ pint] charlotte mold. Chill until set.
6. Meanwhile, cut a ½ in / 1 cm wide strip from the slice of ham and dice it. Remove the chicken meat from the carcass, discarding all skin, and thinly slice the meat. Slice the truffle.
7. Arrange the truffle slices, diced ham and a few slices of chicken on the set aspic at the bottom of the mold. Cover with another layer of still liquid aspic and leave to set in the refrigerator.
8. Cut the rest of the ham into thin strips. Fold into the pâté. Remove the mold from the refrigerator and add a layer of the ham-pâté mixture. Cover with slices of chicken, then alternate the chicken and ham-pâté mixture until all the ingredients are used up.
9. Pour most of the remaining cold, but still liquid, aspic into the mold (warm the aspic again before pouring, if necessary), making sure that the aspic fills all the gaps between the mold and the filling.
10. Cover with a board, place a weight on top and chill for 6 hours.
11. To remove the chicken in aspic from the mold, carefully slide the blade of a knife between the aspic and the edge of the mold or plunge the mold into hot water for a few moments only. Put an inverted serving dish on top of the mold and turn them both over. Cut the rest of the aspic into small dice and arrange it around the chicken in aspic. Serve well chilled.

Poulet printanier

Chicken with Spring Vegetables

00:25   01:00

American	Ingredients	Metric/Imperial
¼ cup	Butter	50 g / 2 oz
1 (3 lb)	Chicken, trussed	1 (1.5 kg / 3 lb)
	Salt and pepper	
2 lb	Carrots	1 kg / 2 lb
1	Small lettuce heart	1
6	Small onions	6
3 lb	Garden peas	1.5 kg / 3 lb
2	Sugar cubes	2
1	Bouquet garni	1

1. Heat 1 tablespoon [15 g / ½ oz] butter in a flameproof casserole. Season the chicken inside and out with salt and pepper and add to the casserole. Brown it on all sides for about 10 minutes.

2. Peel and dice the carrots (or leave them whole if they are small). Rinse the lettuce heart and cut it in half. Peel the onions. Shell the peas. Add all these vegetables to the casserole with the sugar cubes and bouquet garni. Season to taste with salt and pepper. Add just enough cold water to cover the vegetables. Cover the casserole and bring to a boil, then reduce the heat and simmer for 1 hour. Do not stir during this time. At the end of the cooking time, take out and discard the bouquet garni.

3. To serve, remove the chicken from the casserole and carve it into portions. Remove the vegetables with a slotted spoon and arrange them on a serving platter with the pieces of chicken. Keep hot.

4. Reduce the cooking juices by half over a brisk heat. Add the rest of the butter a little at a time, beating with a whisk. Pour the hot sauce over the chicken.

Chicken with spring vegetables

Partridge Pies

Friands à la perdrix

00:40   00:12 to 00:15

American	Ingredients	Metric/Imperial
1	Cooked partridge	1
¼ lb	Cooked, cold meat (pork, veal, poultry)	125 g / 4 oz
	Salt and pepper	
1 lb	Puff pastry	500 g / 1 lb
1	Egg, separated	1

1. Preheat the oven to 450°F / 230°C / Gas Mark 8.
2. Remove the meat from the partridge carcass, discarding all skin. Grind [mince] it finely or use a food processor. Grind the cold meat and mix the two meats together. Season with salt and pepper.
3. Roll out the puff pastry to a thickness of ⅛ in / 3 mm. Using a cutter or saucer with a diameter of about 3 in / 7.5 cm, cut the pastry into 24 rounds. Put 1 tablespoon of meat on 12 of the rounds, leaving ½ in / 1 cm edge all around.
4. Using a pastry brush dipped in egg white, moisten the edge of each filled round of dough. Cover them with the 12 remaining rounds and pinch the edges together to stick them firmly.
5. Brush the surfaces of the pies with beaten egg yolk. Make a pattern on the dough with the point of a knife and put the pies on a lightly oiled baking sheet.
6. Bake for 12-15 minutes, then turn off the oven and leave the pies inside with the door ajar for 5 minutes. Serve hot.

Casseroled Pheasant

Faisans rôtis en cocotte

00:25   00:35

American	Ingredients	Metric/Imperial
2	Young pheasants, with the livers	2
4	Chicken livers	4
½ cup	Butter	125 g / 4 oz
2	Fresh thyme sprigs	2
3	Fresh sage leaves	3
	Salt and pepper	
5 tbsp	Brandy	5 tbsp
6	Slices of bread, ½ in / 1 cm thick	6

1. Chop the pheasant livers finely with the chicken livers. Add ¼ cup [50 g / 2 oz] of the butter, the leaves of one of the thyme sprigs and the sage leaves and season to taste with salt and pepper. Work the mixture together thoroughly. Stuff the pheasants with it. Truss them with kitchen string.
2. Heat 1 tablespoon [15 g / ½ oz] of butter in a flameproof casserole, add the pheasants and brown them on all sides over a moderate heat. Pour over the brandy, cover the casserole and remove from the heat. Leave to steep for 10 minutes.
3. Return the casserole to a low heat and cook, covered, for 35 minutes, turning the pheasants halfway through the cooking time.
4. Meanwhile, melt the remaining butter in a frying pan over a low heat and fry the slices of bread until golden brown on both sides. Drain and keep them hot.

5. Carve the pheasants into portions. Add their juices to the cooking liquid, and spread the slices of fried bread with the stuffing. Arrange the pieces of pheasant on the slices of fried bread and garnish with the rest of the fresh thyme. Serve immediately with the cooking liquid in a sauceboat.

Casseroled pheasant

Venison Steaks Braised in Red Wine

Filet de chevreuil chasseur

00:45 plus marinating   01:00

American	Ingredients	Metric/Imperial
2 lb	Venison steaks	1 kg / 2 lb
3	Onions	3
2	Shallots	2
1	Garlic clove	1
4	Cloves	4
2	Bay leaves	2
	Salt and pepper	
2½ cups	Wine vinegar	600 ml / 1 pint
¼ cup	Oil	4 tbsp
3 oz	Bacon	75 g / 3 oz
1 cup	Red wine	250 ml / 8 fl oz
1 cup	Vegetable or beef stock	250 ml / 8 fl oz

1. If the meat is likely to be a little tough, marinate it before cooking. Put it in a dish or bowl in which it fits comfortably. Peel and slice the onions, shallots and garlic. Scatter these vegetables over the meat with the cloves, bay leaves and salt and pepper to taste. Pour the vinegar and oil over the top. Leave to marinate for 3-4 days, turning the meat over every day.
2. On the day of cooking, cut the bacon into strips. Cook them in a flameproof casserole until browned and rendered of fat.
3. Drain the venison, reserving the marinade, and add to the casserole. Brown it on all sides over a medium heat. Add the red wine, stock and 1 cup [250 ml / 8 fl oz] of the strained marinade.
4. Cover the casserole and simmer over a very low heat for 1 hour. Serve hot.

Perdreaux à la broche
Spit-Roasted Partridge

01:00	00:30

American	Ingredients	Metric/Imperial
3	Partridges, with their livers	3
5 tbsp	Brandy	5 tbsp
	Salt and pepper	
9	Large grape or vine leaves	9
3	Bacon slices	3
3 tbsp	Goose fat or lard	3 tbsp
6	Chicken livers	6
6	Slices of bread, ½ in / 1 cm thick	6
6 tbsp	Butter	75 g / 3 oz

1. Brush the inside of each partridge with a few drops of brandy and season with salt and pepper. Wrap each bird in 3 grape leaves and cover with a piece of bacon. Tie on with kitchen string. Put the partridges on a rotisserie spit and cook them above a dripping pan for about 18 minutes, basting them frequently with the juices that drip from them.
2. Meanwhile, heat the goose fat or lard in a frying pan, add the partridge livers and chicken livers and cook over a brisk heat until browned all over. Season with salt and pepper. Purée the livers in a blender or food processor. Add the rest of the brandy and mix well.
3. Remove the crusts from the slices of bread. Heat the butter in a large frying pan and fry the bread until golden brown on both sides. Spread these canapés with the liver mixture.
4. Remove the bacon and grape leaves from the partridges and cook the birds for a few more minutes to brown. Put the canapés in the oven and heat them until the liver mixture begins to bubble.
5. Cut each partridge in half. Sprinkle the canapés with the juices, arrange them on the serving dish and put the halved partridges on top. Serve immediately.

Faisan au chou
Pheasant with Cabbage

00:25	01:15

American	Ingredients	Metric/Imperial
1	Large pheasant	1
	Salt and pepper	
1	Large head of green cabbage	1
½ lb	Bacon	250 g / 8 oz
1	Garlic clove	1
2 tbsp	Butter	25 g / 1 oz
1	Bouquet garni	1
1	Clove	1

1. Season the inside and outside of the pheasant with salt and pepper.
2. Wash the cabbage, remove the damaged outer leaves and core and cut the rest into strips. Cook the cabbage in boiling salted water for 10 minutes, then drain it thoroughly.
3. Cut the bacon into small strips. Peel and crush the garlic. Heat the butter in a flameproof casserole, add the pheasant

and half the bacon and cook until the pheasant is well browned on all sides (about 10 minutes). Reduce the heat, cover and cook for a further 35 minutes.
4. Cook the rest of the bacon strips in another flameproof casserole until browned and rendered of fat. Add the cabbage, bouquet garni, garlic and clove, and season to taste. Cover and cook over a low heat for 30 minutes, stirring frequently.
5. Spoon the cabbage and bacon mixture onto a warmed serving dish and put the pheasant, carved into portions, on top. Serve the cooking juices separately in a sauceboat.

Roast haunch of venison

Gigue de chevreuil
Roast Haunch of Venison

00:10 plus marinating	01:15 to 01:30 Serves 8–10

American	Ingredients	Metric/Imperial
½	Bay leaf	½
2 tbsp	Olive oil	2 tbsp
1 tsp	Fresh thyme leaves	1 tsp
	Grated nutmeg	
	Salt and pepper	
1 (5 lb)	Haunch of venison	1 (2.5 kg / 5 lb)
6 tbsp	Water	6 tbsp
3	Shallots	3
3	Celery stalks	3
6 tbsp	Butter	75 g / 3 oz
1	Bouquet garni	1
½ lb	Crushed venison bones	250 g / 8 oz
1	Bottle of red wine	1
1 tsp	Potato starch or flour	1 tsp
3 tbsp	Brandy	3 tbsp
2 tbsp	Red currant jelly	2 tbsp

1. Finely crush the bay leaf. Mix the olive oil with the crushed bay leaf, thyme, a pinch of nutmeg, and salt and pepper to taste in a bowl. Add the venison haunch and turn to coat with the oil. Leave to marinate for 2 hours.
2. Preheat the oven to 450°F / 230°C / Gas Mark 8.
3. Put the venison on a rack in a roasting pan and place it in the oven. Roast for 1¼ / 1½ hours. Turn the meat halfway

through the cooking process and add 5 tablespoons of the water to the pan. Do not baste the meat.

4. While the meat is roasting, peel and chop the shallots. Chop the celery. Melt 1 tablespoon [15 g / ½ oz] butter in a saucepan and add the shallots, celery, bouquet garni and crushed venison bones. Pour in the red wine. Cook over a low heat until the wine has reduced by half.

5. Strain this sauce into a clean saucepan, pressing all the solids well with a wooden spoon. Season with a pinch of nutmeg, and salt and pepper to taste. Return to the heat.

6. Dissolve the potato starch in the remaining water and add to the pan. Stir with a whisk over a very low heat until the sauce thickens. Add the brandy and red currant jelly, and continue stirring until the sauce is smooth. Remove from the heat. Add the remaining butter cut into small pieces, beating with a whisk. Pour the sauce into a sauceboat.

7. Serve the venison with the sauce.

Cook's tip: do not overcook the meat; usually venison is eaten underdone.

Sanglier sauce moscovite

Wild Boar with Muscovite Sauce

| | 00:40 | 03:15 |
| | plus marinating | |

American	Ingredients	Metric/Imperial
3	Carrots	3
3	Shallots	3
1	Onion	1
1	Garlic clove	1
1¼ cups	Oil	300 ml / ½ pint
2	Fresh thyme sprigs	2
1	Bay leaf	1
3	Cloves	3
2 cups	Vinegar	450 ml / ¾ pint
1½ quarts	White wine	1.5 l / 2½ pints
1 (5 lb)	Haunch of wild boar or peccary	1 (2.5 kg / 5 lb)
	Salt and pepper	
½ lb	Lightly salted bacon	250 g / 8 oz
⅓ cup	Currants	50 g / 2 oz
1½ tsp	Potato starch or flour	1½ tsp
2 tbsp	Water	2 tbsp
2 tbsp	Butter	25 g / 1 oz
⅔ cup	Madeira wine	150 ml / ¼ pint
½ cup	Toasted pine nuts	50 g / 2 oz

1. Peel and thinly slice the carrots, shallots, onion and garlic. Heat 3 tablespoons of oil in a frying pan, add the carrots, shallots, onion and garlic and cook until softened. Add the thyme, bay leaf, cloves, vinegar and wine. Cover the pan and cook gently for 30 minutes. Allow to cool, then add the rest of the oil to this marinade.

2. Rub the haunch of wild boar with 1 tablespoon of salt. Put it in bowl and pour over the marinade. Marinate in a cool place for 4-5 days, turning the meat frequently.

3. Preheat the oven to 400°F / 200°C / Gas Mark 6.

4. Drain the haunch, reserving the marinade. Strain the marinade keeping all the flavorings. Cut the bacon into strips.

5. Brown the haunch in a flameproof casserole with the strips of bacon until it is well colored on all sides. Pour in enough

strained marinade to come halfway up the haunch. Place in the oven and braise for 2 hours, turning the meat frequently. Cover with foil halfway through the process.

6. When the haunch is cooked, pour the cooking juices into a saucepan and keep the meat hot. Add the rest of the strained marinade to the saucepan as well as the reserved flavorings and boil to reduce over a brisk heat until only half the liquid remains.

7. Meanwhile, soak the currants in warm water so that they swell. Mix the potato starch with the water. Cut the butter into small pieces. Warm the madeira.

8. When the marinade has reduced sufficiently, strain it into another saucepan, pressing all the flavorings well with a wooden spoon. Add the warm madeira, the drained currants, toasted pine nuts, dissolved potato starch and pepper to taste. Stir over a brisk heat until the sauce thickens, then remove from the heat and add the pieces of butter, beating rapidly. Serve immediately with the boar.

Wild boar with muscovite sauce

Faisans aux raisins

Pheasant with Grapes

| | 01:00 | 00:45 |

American	Ingredients	Metric/Imperial
4	Bacon slices	4
2	Young pheasants	2
4 lb	White grapes	2 kg / 4 lb
5 tbsp	Cognac or armagnac	5 tbsp
6 tbsp	Butter	75 g / 3 oz
	Salt and pepper	

1. Wrap the slices of bacon around the pheasants and truss them.

2. Extract the juice from one-third of the grapes (use a juice extractor, or liquidize briefly or press and strain). Peel the remaining grapes and leave to steep in the cognac.

3. Heat the butter in a large flameproof casserole, add the pheasants and brown on all sides over a medium heat. Sprinkle them with the grape juice and season to taste with salt and pepper. Cook, covered, over a medium heat for 30 minutes.

4. Remove the bacon from the pheasants, then add the peeled grapes to the casserole. Continue cooking for 15 minutes longer.

5. Carve the pheasants into portions and arrange the pieces on a warmed serving dish. Surround them with the grapes and pour the cooking liquid over the top. Serve very hot.

Faisans bohémienne
Bohemian Style Pheasant

	00:30 plus standing time	00:40

American	Ingredients	Metric/Imperial
½ lb	Fresh foie gras	250 g / 8 oz
	Paprika	
½ cup	Butter	125 g / 4 oz
	Salt and pepper	
2	Young pheasants	2
6	Slices of bread ½ in / 1 cm thick	6
¼ cup	Brandy	4 tbsp
½ cup	Crème fraîche	125 ml / 4 fl oz

1. Cut the foie gras into dice and roll it lightly in paprika. Leave for 1 hour to absorb the flavor.
2. Preheat the oven to 425°F / 220°C / Gas Mark 7.
3. Melt 1 teaspoon of butter in a frying pan, add the diced foie gras and brown lightly. Season with salt, then remove from the pan with a slotted spoon and allow to cool. Put aside the frying pan containing the butter.
4. Stuff the pheasants with the foie gras and sew up the openings with kitchen string. Put the pheasants in a roasting pan and roast for 40 minutes, turning them over carefully after 20 minutes.
5. Just before the pheasants have finished cooking, cut the crusts from the bread and cut each slice in half, diagonally. Heat the rest of the butter in the frying pan used earlier and fry the slices of bread until golden brown on both sides.
6. Heat the brandy in a saucepan. Pour it over the pheasants and set alight. When the flames have died away, remove the string from the pheasants and catch the juices which run out in the pan. Add the crème fraîche and a pinch of paprika to the juices. Heat, stirring to loosen all the sediment at the bottom.
7. Spread the pieces of fried bread with the melted foie gras. Put the pheasants on a serving platter, pour the sauce over them and surround with the garnished fried bread. Serve.

Lièvre à la crème
Hare with Cream Sauce

	00:15	01:30 to 02:00

American	Ingredients	Metric/Imperial
¼ cup	Butter	50 g / 2 oz
1 (4 lb)	Young hare	1 (2 kg / 4 lb)
4	Shallots	4
1 (½ lb)	Slice of cooked ham	1 (250 g / 8 oz)
⅓ cup	Vinegar	5 tbsp
⅔ cup	Dry white wine	150 ml / ¼ pint
	Salt and pepper	
1 cup	Crème fraîche	250 ml / 8 fl oz
1 tbsp	Cornstarch [cornflour]	1 tbsp

1. Melt the butter in a flameproof casserole, add the hare and brown on all sides.
2. Peel and finely chop the shallots. Add them to the casserole with the slice of ham. Cook for 2-3 minutes, then pour in the vinegar and one-third of the wine. Season to taste.

3. Cover and cook over a very low heat for 1 hour, adding the rest of the wine during this time.
4. Add the crème fraîche and cook for a further 30 minutes to 1 hour or until the hare is very tender.
5. Remove the ham, shallots and hare to a deep serving dish. Mix the cornstarch with 2 tablespoons of the cooking liquid and add to the casserole. Cook over a low heat until the sauce thickens. Pour over the hare and serve immediately.

Civet de lièvre
Jugged Hare

	00:30 plus marinating	02:30 to 03:00

American	Ingredients	Metric/Imperial
1 (4 lb)	Ready-to-cook hare, with the liver	1 (2 kg / 4 lb)
1 tbsp	Vinegar	1 tbsp
2	Onions	2
5 tbsp	Brandy	5 tbsp
2 tbsp	Olive oil	2 tbsp
	Salt and pepper	
1	Garlic clove	1
½ cup	Butter	125 g / 4 oz
2 tbsp	Flour	2 tbsp
1	Bottle of full-bodied red wine	1
1	Bouquet garni	1
½ lb	Slightly salted bacon	250 g / 8 oz
20	Tiny onions	20
1 tsp	Sugar	1 tsp
⅔ cup	Water	150 ml / ¼ pint
½ lb	Button mushrooms	250 g / 8 oz

1. Ask your butcher to skin the hare and collect the blood. Add to it the vinegar to prevent coagulation. Cut the hare into portions and put the liver aside.
2. Peel 1 onion and slice it thinly. Put the pieces of hare in a mixing bowl, add the onion slices, brandy and olive oil and season with salt and pepper. Stir and leave to marinate in a cool place for 6 hours.
3. Peel the remaining onion and the garlic clove and chop them finely. Melt 2 tablespoons [25 g / 1 oz] of butter in a flameproof casserole, add the flour and stir for 2 minutes over a medium heat. Add the pieces of hare. Stir, then pour in the marinade and red wine. Add the bouquet garni, garlic and onion and cook, covered, over a low heat for 2½-3 hours.
4. Meanwhile, cut the bacon into strips. Blanch the bacon in boiling water for 3 minutes and drain. Put the bacon in a frying pan and cook until browned and rendered of fat. Remove with a slotted spoon.
5. Peel the tiny onions. Drop into a pan of boiling water and boil for 2 minutes, then drain. Add 1 tablespoon [15 g / ½ oz] of butter to the frying pan containing the bacon fat, add the onions and sprinkle with sugar. Pour in the water and cook, uncovered, over a low heat until the water has evaporated.
6. Heat 1 tablespoon [15 g / ½ oz] of butter in another frying pan, add the mushrooms and cook until all the liquid has evaporated. Season with salt and pepper.
7. When the hare is tender, take the pieces from the casserole and carefully remove and discard all the bones. Set the meat aside. Mash the hare's liver with a fork and blend in the blood and vinegar mixture. Add this to the sauce together with the bacon, tiny onions and mushrooms.
8. Return all the meat to the casserole, mix well and heat through. Serve immediately.

Perdreaux aux morilles

Partridge with Morels

00:40   00:30

American	Ingredients	Metric/Imperial
1 oz	Dried morels or other wild mushrooms	25 g / 1 oz
3	Partridges, with their livers	3
	Salt and pepper	
½ lb	Bacon slices	250 g / 8 oz
½ cup	Butter	125 g / 4 oz
4	Chicken livers	4
2	Fresh parsley sprigs	2
2	Fresh thyme sprigs	2
6 tbsp	Brandy	6 tbsp
	Grated nutmeg	
1 tbsp	Oil	1 tbsp
6	Slices of bread, ½ in / 1 cm thick	6

1. Carefully wash the dried morels in a colander under the cold tap, then put them in a bowl, cover them with lukewarm water and leave to soak for 2-3 hours. Drain them and dry well on paper towels.

2. Season the insides of the partridge with salt and pepper, then cover with some of the bacon and tie on with string.

3. Preheat the oven to 450°F / 230°C / Gas Mark 8.

4. Heat 2 tablespoons of butter in a frying pan, add the partridge livers and chicken livers and brown on all sides. Remove them from the pan with a slotted spoon and purée in a blender or food processor. Also purée the morels, the remaining bacon, the parsley and thyme. Combine all the puréed ingredients, add a few drops of brandy and season with salt, pepper and a pinch of nutmeg.

5. Stuff the inside of each partridge with a large piece of butter and the morel mixture. Put the partridges on a rack in a roasting pan and roast for 30 minutes. Turn the partridges twice during this time and, after 15 minutes, add a few tablespoons of cold water to the roasting pan.

6. Melt the oil and remaining butter in a frying pan and fry the slices of bread until golden brown on both sides. Drain.

7. Pour the rest of the brandy into the roasting pan and set it alight. When the flames die away, cut the partridges in half, and put each on a slice of fried bread. Serve with cooking liquid.

Jugged hare

Boeuf bourgeoise

Beef Pot Roast with Vegetables

	00:30		03:00

American	Ingredients	Metric/Imperial
3 tbsp	Oil	3 tbsp
1 (3 lb)	Boneless chuck eye [blade or brisket] roast	1 (1.5 kg / 3 lb)
1	Calf's foot	1
2	Onions	2
1 tbsp	Butter	1 tbsp
1 quart	Red wine	1 l / 1¾ pint
1 cup	Tomato paste [purée]	250 g / 8 oz
2 cups	Water	500 ml / ¾ pint
1	Bouquet garni	1
	Salt and pepper	
14 oz	Carrots	400 g / 14 oz
14 oz	Turnips	400 g / 14 oz
14 oz	Potatoes	400 g / 14 oz
14 oz	Green beans	400 g / 14 oz

1. Preheat the oven to 425°F / 220°C / Gas Mark 7.
2. Heat the oil in a frying pan. Add the beef and calf's foot and brown on all sides over a high heat.
3. Peel and chop the onions. Melt the butter in a flameproof casserole, add the onions and cook until lightly browned.
4. Add the beef and calf's foot to the casserole. Moisten with the wine, tomato paste and water. Add the bouquet garni, and salt and pepper to taste. Bring to a boil, then cover the casserole and transfer to the oven. Cook for 2½-3 hours.
5. Meanwhile, peel the carrots, turnips and potatoes. Trim the green beans. Cut all the vegetables into thin strips. Cook them separately in boiling water until tender. Drain and keep hot.
6. Remove the meat to a warmed serving platter and keep hot. Bring the cooking liquid to a boil again and reduce to about half. Discard the bouquet garni.
7. Chop the calf's foot into small pieces and mix with the vegetables. Arrange around the meat. Serve sauce separately.

Boeuf en daube

Rich Beef Casserole

	00:10 plus marinating		04:00

American	Ingredients	Metric/Imperial
2 lb	Boneless beef shank [shin] or chuck steak	1 kg / 2 lb
2	Carrots	2
2	Onions	2
4	Garlic cloves	4
4	Juniper berries	4
1	Bouquet garni	1
1	Clove	1
6	Black peppercorns	6
	Salt	
2 cups	Red wine	500 ml / ¾ pint
1	Calf's foot	1
1	Piece of orange rind	1

1. Carefully remove all fat from the beef, and cut it into 12 pieces. Place the meat in a casserole.
2. Peel and slice the carrots. Peel the onions. Peel and crush the garlic. Crush the juniper berries. Add all these ingredients to the casserole with the clove, peppercorns, and salt to taste. Cover with the wine and marinate for 12 hours in a cool place.
3. Preheat the oven to 400°F / 200°C / Gas Mark 6.
4. Add the calf's foot cut in half and the orange rind to the casserole. Cover and cook in the oven for 3¾ hours. Uncover and cook for a final 15 minutes to reduce the liquid.

Cook's tip: any vegetable in season can be served with this dish: Belgian endive [chicory], tomatoes, cauliflower, turnips, salsify or potatoes.

Aloyau aux cèpes

Sirloin of Beef with Cèpes

	00:15 plus marinating		01:20

American	Ingredients	Metric/Imperial
2	Carrots	2
4	Shallots	4
1	Garlic clove	1
1 (3 lb)	Tenderloin [fillet] or boneless sirloin roast	1 (1.5 kg / 3 lb)
1	Bouquet garni	1
1 tbsp	Olive oil	1 tbsp
½	Bottle of good red wine	½
5 oz	Bayonne ham or prosciutto	150 g / 5 oz
½ lb	Fresh cèpes or other mushrooms	25. g / 8 oz
¼ cup	Butter	50 g / 2 oz
¼ cup	Brandy	4 tbsp
	Salt and pepper	
	Grated nutmeg	
¼ lb	Beef marrow	125 g / 4 oz
1 tbsp	Flour	1 tbsp

1. Peel and slice the carrots and shallots; peel and crush the garlic. Place the beef in an earthenware pot or deep glass dish. Add the shallots, carrots, garlic and bouquet garni and pour over the olive oil and wine. Leave to marinate for 24 hours, turning the meat often.
2. The next day, cut the ham into small dice. Clean the cèpes and cut off the end of the stems. Rinse the cèpes under running water and slice thinly.
3. Heat half of the butter in a flameproof casserole, add the ham and cook until golden brown. Remove the ham with a slotted spoon and reserve.
4. Remove the meat from the marinade and wipe dry with paper towels. Set aside. Pour the marinade into the casserole and bring to a boil. Simmer over a gentle heat for 20 minutes, then strain, pressing all the solids well. You should have 1 cup [250 ml / 8 fl oz] liquid.
5. Place the meat in a frying pan without any fat and brown on all sides. Put it in the casserole and add the cèpes, diced ham, brandy and reduced marinade. Season with salt, pepper and a pinch of nutmeg. Bring to a boil quickly, then cover and cook over a low heat for about 35 minutes. Turn the meat once during cooking.
6. Meanwhile, dice the marrow. Drop into a pan of boiling

salted water and cook for 3 minutes. Drain well and set aside.

7. Mix the flour with the rest of the butter to a paste. About 10 minutes before the meat has finished cooking, add the flour and butter paste and stir well to thicken the liquid. Add the marrow.

8. Serve very hot.

Boeuf miroton
Beef in Onion Sauce

◣▷ 00:20   00:50 🍲

American	Ingredients	Metric/Imperial
¾ lb	Onions	350 g / 12 oz
1½ lb	Cooked beef	750 g / 1½ lb
3 tbsp	Oil	3 tbsp
2 cups	Beef stock	450 ml / ¾ pint
⅔ cup	Vinegar	150 ml / ¼ pint
2 tbsp	Sliced dill pickles [gherkins]	2 tbsp
	Salt and pepper	

1. Peel and thinly slice the onions. Slice the cooked beef. Heat the oil in a flameproof casserole, add the onions and cook until they are translucent but not colored.

2. Add the beef stock and vinegar and bring to a boil. Boil for 15 minutes, stirring occasionally, until the mixture has taken on the consistency of cream.

3. Add the beef slices. Cover and cook gently, without letting it boil, for 10 minutes.

4. Add the gherkins, and salt and pepper to taste.

Boeuf au gratin
Potato-Topped Beef Casserole

◣▷ 00:30   00:40 to 00:45 🍲

American	Ingredients	Metric/Imperial
2 lb	Potatoes	1 kg / 2 lb
2 tbsp	Butter	25 g / 1 oz
1 cup	Milk	250 ml / 8 fl oz
	Salt and pepper	
	Grated nutmeg	
2	Medium-size onions	2
1	Small garlic clove	1
2 tbsp	Lard	25 g / 1 oz
1 lb	Ground [minced] beef	500 g / 1 lb
1¼ cups	Tomato sauce	300 ml / ½ pint
1 tbsp	Chopped fresh parsley	1 tbsp
	Dried thyme	
2 tbsp	Golden raisins [sultanas]	2 tbsp
¼ cup	Grated gruyère cheese	50 g / 2 oz
2 tbsp	White bread crumbs	2 tbsp

1. Peel and quarter the potatoes. Place them in a saucepan of cold water, bring to a boil and cook for 20 minutes.

2. Preheat the oven to 425°F / 220°C / Gas Mark 7.

3. Drain and mash the potatoes, or purée them in a food mill. Put the potatoes back in the saucepan over a medium heat, add the butter and milk and beat to a smooth consistency. Season with salt, pepper and a very little nutmeg. Set aside.

4. Peel and chop the onions and garlic. Heat the lard in a frying pan, add the onions and cook until golden brown. Add the beef and cook until browned and crumbly. Add the tomato sauce, parsley, thyme and garlic. Season with salt and pepper. Simmer over a low heat for 7-10 minutes, then add the raisins and mix well.

5. Pour the beef mixture into a shallow baking dish and cover with the potatoes. Sprinkle with the gruyère mixed with the bread crumbs.

6. Bake for 20-25 minutes or until piping hot and the top is browned.

Boeuf à la ficelle
Beef Tied with String

◣▷ 00:30   03:00 🍲

American	Ingredients	Metric/Imperial
8	Carrots	8
7	Turnips	7
2	Onions	2
4	Cloves	4
9	Leeks	9
1¼ lb	Beef shank [shin]	625 g / 1¼ lb
2 lb	Beef bones	1 kg / 2 lb
5 quarts	Water	5 l / 9 pints
	Salt	
5	Black peppercorns	5
6	Potatoes	6
1	Stick of celery	1
6	Small pieces of beef marrow	6
1 (2½ lb)	Piece of top round [top rump] steak	1 (1.25 kg / 2½ lb)

1. Peel and dice 2 of the carrots and 1 turnip. Peel the onions and stud each with 2 cloves. Dice 3 of the leeks. Put these vegetables into a stewpot with the beef shank, bones and water. Add a handful of sea salt and the peppercorns and bring to a boil. Simmer for 2 hours.

2. Meanwhile, prepare the accompanying vegetables. Peel the remaining carrots and turnips and the potatoes. Trim the celery and separate the stalks. Tie the leeks and celery stalks into bundles with string. Place the turnips in a large square of cheesecloth or muslin and tie the four corners together; do the same with the carrots and the pieces of marrow. Tie up the steak, leaving a good length of string at each end.

3. When the stock is ready, strain it and return to the stewpot. Bring back to a boil and add the carrots. Cook for 10 minutes, then add the celery and leeks. Cook for another 10 minutes.

4. Tie the two ends of spare string on the steak to the two handles of the stewpot so that the meat is immersed in the stock without touching the bottom of the pot. Add the marrow. Simmer for 20 minutes, then remove from the heat and leave the meat in the stock for 20 minutes.

5. Meanwhile, cook the potatoes in boiling salted water for about 20 minutes or until tender.

6. To serve, drain the meat and place on a warmed serving dish. Unwrap or untie all the vegetables and arrange around the meat with the marrow. Skim the fat from the stock and serve in soup cups with the meat.

Boeuf en gelée
Beef in Aspic

	00:20 plus chilling	02:00

American	Ingredients	Metric/Imperial
1 (4 lb)	Piece of top round [top rump] steak	1 (2 kg / 4 lb)
1 tbsp	Oil	1 tbsp
1 lb	Carrots	500 g / 1 lb
4	Onions	4
1	Garlic clove	1
1	Bouquet garni	1
	Salt and pepper	
	Grated nutmeg	
⅔ cup	Dry white wine	150 ml / ¼ pint
⅔ cup	Water	150 ml / ¼ pint
1 envelope	Unflavored gelatin	1 sachet
1	Sugar cube	1
¾ lb (3 cups)	Fresh shelled peas	350 g / 12 oz

1. Trim all the fat from the beef and prick it all over with a fork. Heat the oil in a flameproof casserole, add the beef and brown all over on a medium heat for 5 minutes.
2. Peel and slice the carrots, onions and garlic. Add them to the meat with the bouquet garni. Season with salt, pepper and a pinch of nutmeg. Cover and cook over a low heat for 30 minutes.
3. Moisten with the wine and water. Cover again and leave to simmer over a very low heat for 1½ hours.
4. Take the meat and vegetables out of the casserole and set aside. Strain the cooking liquid and skim off any fat. Dissolve the gelatin in this liquid. Set the aspic aside.
5. Bring a saucepan of water to a boil. Add salt and the sugar cube, then the peas. Cook for 15 minutes or until the peas are tender but still firm. Drain.
6. Line the bottom of a cake pan or earthenware dish with a layer of peas and carrot slices. Cover with a little of the aspic and chill for about 20 minutes.
7. Slice the meat thinly and put back together in its original shape. Place the meat on top of the vegetables in the pan. Cover with the rest of the aspic, and then add the remaining vegetables. Cover and chill for 12 hours.
8. Unmold the beef in aspic and serve with a green salad.

Boeuf braisé
Braised Beef

	00:20	01:30

American	Ingredients	Metric/Imperial
3 lb	Shank [shin]	1.5 kg / 3 lb
3	Onions	3
1	Garlic clove	1
2 tbsp	Lard	25 g / 1 oz
1 cup	Dry white wine or water	250 ml / 8 fl oz
1	Bouquet garni	1
	Salt and pepper	
½ lb	Bacon	250 g / 8 oz
3	Uncooked pork and beef sausages flavored with herbs	3

1. Ask your butcher to tie up the beef like a roast but without barding fat, and to give you a few bones. Peel and chop the onions and garlic.
2. Heat the lard in a flameproof casserole, add the beef and brown gently on all sides. Moisten with the wine or water and add the bones, onions, garlic, bouquet garni, and salt and pepper to taste.
3. Cover and simmer over a very gentle heat for 1½ hours, turning the meat from time to time.
4. Cut the bacon into slices, about ½ in / 1 cm thick, and blanch for 5 minutes in boiling water. Drain. Brown the bacon slices in their own fat in a frying pan.
5. Prick the sausages so that they do not burst, then cook in barely simmering water for 10 minutes. Let them cool slightly in the water, then drain and slice fairly thickly.
6. About 20 minutes before the meat is cooked, add the bacon and sausage slices to the casserole.
7. Discard the bouquet garni and serve the meat sliced with the bacon, sausages and gravy.

Boeuf aux carottes
Beef with Carrots

	00:45	04:00

American	Ingredients	Metric/Imperial
3 lb	Carrots	1.5 kg / 3 lb
5 oz	Fresh bacon rind	150 g / 5 oz
¼ cup	Oil	4 tbsp
1 (3 lb)	Boneless chuck eye roast, [topside], larded and tied	1 (1.5 kg / 3 lb)
2 tbsp	Brandy	2 tbsp
¼ cup	Butter	50 g / 2 oz
	Salt and pepper	
1	Fresh thyme sprig	1
2	Bay leaves	2

1. Preheat the oven to 350°F / 180°C / Gas Mark 4.
2. Peel and thinly slice the carrots. Cut the bacon rind into strips.
3. Heat 3 tablespoons of the oil in a flameproof casserole, add the beef and brown on all sides for about 5 minutes.
4. Take out the meat and discard the cooking oil. Replace the meat in the casserole, sprinkle with the brandy and set alight. Shake the casserole until the flame goes out. Remove the meat and set aside.
5. Scatter the bacon rind over the bottom of the casserole. Place the meat on top.
6. Heat the rest of the oil and butter in a frying pan, add the carrot slices and cook for about 8 minutes without letting them brown. Season with salt and pepper.
7. Add the carrots, thyme and bay leaves to the casserole. Cover the casserole with a sheet of oiled wax [greaseproof] paper, place the casserole lid on top and put in the oven. Cook for about 4 hours.
8. To serve, slice the meat and arrange on the serving dish. Surround it with the carrots. Discard the herbs from the cooking liquid and serve with the meat.

Cook's tip: you can also serve this dish cold in aspic. Add 1 tablespoon unflavored gelatin dissolved in 1 cup [250 ml / 8 fl oz] water to the cooking liquid. Pour a ¼ in / 5 mm layer of this over the bottom of an earthenware dish, add a layer of carrots and then a little more aspic. Place the meat on top, surround with the rest of the carrots and pour on the rest of the aspic. Chill for 12 hours or until set. To serve, unmold onto a serving dish.

7. Transfer the casserole to the oven, and reduce the heat to 350°F / 180°C / Gas Mark 4. Cook for 3 hours.
8. Remove the meat and place it on a carving board. Strain the sauce. Slice the meat and serve with the sauce.

Carpaccio
Marinated Raw Beef

	00:35 plus marinating		00:00

American	Ingredients	Metric/Imperial
2 lb	Beef tenderloin [fillet]	1 kg / 2 lb
4	Lemons	4
1 cup	Olive oil	250 ml / 8 fl oz
	Salt and pepper	
1	Head of lettuce	1
	Chopped fresh parsley	

1. Cut the meat into very thin slices (about the thickness of Parma ham slices). Put them in a deep dish. Squeeze the lemons and pour the juice over the slices of meat – its acidity will 'cook' the raw meat. Then pour over the olive oil and season with salt and pepper.
2. Marinate for 1 hour in the refrigerator.
3. Wash the lettuce, keeping the leaves whole.
4. Serve the beef with the lettuce, sprinkled with parsley.

Braised beef with carrots

Boeuf mode
Braised Beef with Carrots

	00:25		03:00

American	Ingredients	Metric/Imperial
2 lb	Carrots	1 kg / 2 lb
3	Onions	3
1	Leek	1
2	Tomatoes	2
½ lb	Button mushrooms	250 g / 8 oz
2	Pieces of beef bone	2
¼ cup	Butter	50 g / 2 oz
1 (2 lb)	Piece of braising beef, larded	1 (1 kg / 2 lb)
1	Large piece of fresh pork rind	1
1 tbsp	Flour	1 tbsp
1 tbsp	Tomato paste [purée]	1 tbsp
	Salt and pepper	
½	Calf's foot, boned	½
1	Bouquet garni including a celery stalk	1
2 cups	Beef stock	500 ml / ¾ pint

1. Preheat the oven to 450°F / 260°C / Gas Mark 9.
2. Peel and dice the carrots and onions. Dice the leek. Peel the tomatoes (first plunging them in boiling water for 10 seconds), scoop out the seeds and chop the flesh. Trim the stems of the mushrooms and slice thinly.
3. Place the beef bones in the oven and bake until they crack.
4. Meanwhile, heat the butter in a frying pan, add the beef and a piece of the pork rind and brown on all sides. Discard the rind and put the beef on one side.
5. Add the onions, leek and mushrooms to the pan and cook until softened. Add the flour and cook until golden brown. Add the tomatoes and tomato paste; season to taste.
6. Cover the bottom of a flameproof casserole with the rest of the pork rind. Spread the cooked vegetables on top, then place the beef on the vegetables. Add the bones, calf's foot and carrots. Season well and add the bouquet garni and beef stock, which should come halfway up the meat. Cover the casserole and bring to a boil.

Filet de boeuf en croûte
Beef Fillet in a Pastry Case

	01:00 plus making dough	01:00 to 01:15	

American	Ingredients	Metric/Imperial
1 (3 lb)	Tenderloin [fillet]	1 (1.5 kg / 3 lb)
	Salt and pepper	
2 quantities	Brioche dough (see page 457)	2 quantities
1	Egg	1

1. Heat a heavy-based frying pan, add the meat without any fat and brown on all sides. Remove the meat from the pan and immediately sprinkle all over with salt and pepper. Allow to become completely cold.
2. Preheat the oven to 400°F / 200°C / Gas Mark 6.
3. Roll out the brioche dough to ¼ in / 5 mm thick. Put the meat in the center of the dough and wrap and fold so that the meat is completely enclosed.
4. Lightly beat the egg and brush over the edges of the dough. Press them together to seal well. Brush the dough all over with beaten egg. Place on a buttered baking sheet, joins on top.
5. Bake until the pastry becomes golden, then cover with foil and continue cooking for 54-60 minutes.
6. When the meat is cooked, turn off the oven and leave the meat inside for another 10 minutes before serving. Serve with madeira sauce (see page 130).

Boeuf aux olives

Beef with Olives

	00:20		03:00

American	Ingredients	Metric/Imperial
1 (¼ lb)	Piece of smoked bacon	1 (125 g / 4 oz)
2	Shallots	2
2	Carrots	2
10	Onions	10
1	Garlic clove	1
¼ lb	Button mushrooms	125 g / 4 oz
1 (2½ lb)	Chuck steak [brisket]	1 (1.25 kg / 2½ lb)
1	Bouquet garni	1
	Salt and pepper	
⅔ cup	Madeira or red wine	150 ml / ¼ pint
1½ cups	Green olives	250 g / 8 oz

1. Cut the bacon into strips. Peel and thinly slice the shallots, carrots and onions. Peel and crush the garlic. Quarter the mushrooms.
2. Cook the bacon strips in a flameproof casserole until they have rendered their fat, without browning. Remove the bacon with a slotted spoon. Add the piece of beef to the casserole with the onions and carrots and cook until the meat is browned on all sides. Add the bouquet garni and season with a little salt and plenty of pepper. Cook, covered, over a low heat for 20 minutes, turning the meat once.
3. Add the shallots, garlic, madeira or wine and bacon strips. Continue cooking, still covered, over a gentle heat for about 1½ hours.
4. Meanwhile, remove the pits [stones] from the olives. Blanch them in boiling water for 3 minutes, then drain.
5. Add the olives and mushrooms to the casserole. Continue cooking covered, over a gentle heat for 45 minutes longer.
6. Season and discard the bouquet garni before serving.

Boeuf en salade

Beef Salad

	00:20		00:25

American	Ingredients	Metric/Imperial
6	Potatoes	6
	Salt and pepper	
1¼ lb	Cooked beef	625 g / 1¼ lb
1	Large onion	1
4	Shallots	4
2	Garlic cloves	2
	Few fresh parsley sprigs	
1	Small bunch of fresh chives	1
1 tbsp	Prepared mustard	1 tbsp
2 tbsp	Vinegar	2 tbsp
¼ cup	Oil	4 tbsp
⅔ cup	White wine	150 ml / ¼ pint
6	Hard-cooked eggs	6

1. Scrub the potatoes and put them in a saucepan of cold water with a handful of sea salt. Bring to a boil and cook for about 20 minutes.

2. Meanwhile, cut the meat into small cubes. Peel and slice the onion and shallots and separate the slices into rings. Peel and chop the garlic. Chop parsley; snip chives into small pieces.
3. In a mixing bowl, combine the mustard with the vinegar, parsley, garlic, oil, onions and some pepper. Add the diced meat and mix well. Adjust the seasoning if necessary by adding a little salt, vinegar and pepper.
4. Drain the potatoes, then peel and slice them into a large salad bowl. Heat the wine in a small saucepan and when very hot, pour it over the hot potatoes. Sprinkle with the chives and shallots and season with salt and pepper. Fold together gently.
5. Put the meat mixture on top of the potatoes. Cut the eggs into quarters and arrange on top of the meat salad. Serve immediately.

Beef stroganoff

Boeuf strogonoff

Beef Stroganoff

	00:20		00:40

American	Ingredients	Metric/Imperial
1 tbsp	Mustard powder	1 tbsp
1½ tsp	Sugar	1½ tsp
	Salt and pepper	
8	Onions	8
1 lb	Button mushrooms	500 g / 1 lb
5 tbsp	Oil	5 tbsp
2½ lb	Beef tenderloin [fillet]	1.25 kg / 2½ lb
2 cups	Crème fraîche	500 ml / ¾ pint

1. Mix together the mustard, sugar and a pinch of salt. Add a little water to make a thick cream. Set aside.
2. Peel and thinly slice the onions. Thinly slice the mushrooms.
3. Heat 2 tablespoons of the oil in a frying pan, add the onions and mushrooms and season with salt and pepper. Cook, covered, over a gentle heat for about 20-30 minutes or until all the liquid has evaporated. Set aside.
4. Cut the beef into slices ¾ in / 1.5 cm thick and then cut these slices into strips ¼ in / 5 mm wide. Heat 2 tablespoons of the oil in another frying pan over a high heat, add one-third of the meat and cook, stirring, for about 2 minutes or until the meat strips are just brown. Remove these with a slotted spoon and place in the other pan on top of the onions and mushrooms. Brown the remaining beef strips, adding a little more oil if necessary, and add to the onions and mushrooms.

5. Heat all the ingredients over a gentle heat. Add the mustard mixture, stirring all the time. Cook, covered, over a very gentle heat for 2-3 minutes.
6. Stir in the crème fraîche and add seasoning to taste. Heat through gently and serve.

Côte de boeuf marchand de vin
Rib of Beef with Red Wine Sauce

	00:10	00:30

American	Ingredients	Metric/Imperial
3	Large onions	3
½ cup	Butter	125 g / 4 oz
1 tsp	Flour	1 tsp
1	Bouquet garni	1
2 cups	Full-bodied red wine	500 ml / ¾ pint
	Salt and pepper	
1 (3 lb)	Rib roast	1 (1.5 kg / 3 lb)

1. Preheat the broiler [grill].
2. Peel and thinly slice the onions. Heat half the butter in a saucepan, add the onions and cook until soft and translucent. Sprinkle with the flour and stir well, then add the bouquet garni and wine. Bring to a boil, stirring. Season to taste with salt and pepper. Cover and cook for 10-12 minutes.
3. Meanwhile, put the beef on the rack in the broiler pan and broil on one side for 10 minutes or until well browned. Turn and cook the other side for 15-20 minutes.
4. Strain the sauce into a clean saucepan. Add the rest of the butter, cut into small pieces, whisking well.
5. Carve the meat and serve with the sauce.

Côte de boeuf rôtie
Roast Rib of Beef

	00:03	00:45 to 01:00

American	Ingredients	Metric/Imperial
1 (3 lb)	Rib roast	1 (1.5 kg / 3 lb)
	Salt and pepper	
4 - 5 tbsp	Hot water	4 - 5 tbsp
2 tbsp	Butter	25 g / 1 oz

1. Remove the meat from the refrigerator 2 hours before cooking to bring it up to room temperature.
2. Preheat the oven to 450°F / 260°C / Gas Mark 9.
3. Place the meat on a rack in a roasting pan and sprinkle with salt and pepper. Roast for about 15 minutes or until the meat begins to brown, then reduce the temperature to 425°F / 220°C / Gas Mark 7. Add 3 tablespoons of hot water to the roasting pan and continue roasting for 30 minutes (for very rare meat), 35 minutes (for rare meat) or 45 minutes (for medium rare meat). Turn the meat 4 times while it is roasting and baste from time to time with the juices in the roasting pan.
4. Put the meat on a serving platter and keep hot in the oven with the door ajar. Add the remaining hot water to the roasting pan and boil to reduce over a brisk heat, scraping the bottom of the pan with a spatula. Add the butter and whisk in well.
5. Pour the sauce into a sauceboat and serve with the meat.

Palets du Poitou à la moelle
Poitou Meatcakes with Beef Marrow

	00:20	00:15

American	Ingredients	Metric/Imperial
1 cup	Milk	250 ml / 8 fl oz
2 cups	Bread crumbs	125 g / 4 oz
2	Medium-size onions	2
¼ cup	Butter	50 g / 2 oz
¾ lb	Beef marrow	350 g / 12 oz
1¼ lb	Lean ground [minced] beef	625 g / 1¼ lb
2	Eggs	2
	Grated nutmeg	
	Salt and pepper	
3 tbsp	Oil	3 tbsp
2 tbsp	White wine	2 tbsp
1	Lemon	1
1 tbsp	Chopped fresh parsley	1 tbsp

1. Heat the milk in a small saucepan and add the bread crumbs. Stir well to make a smooth, slightly sticky mixture. Remove from the heat and allow to cool.
2. Peel and chop the onions. Heat half the butter in a frying pan, add the onions and cook gently until slightly colored.
3. Mash the beef marrow in a bowl with a fork. Add the beef and mix well. Add the bread crumb mixture, onions, eggs, a pinch of nutmeg, and salt and pepper to taste. Mix all the ingredients thoroughly together with your hands.
4. Divide the mixture into 6 equal portions and shape into flat cakes or patties about ¾ in /1.5 cm thick.
5. Heat the oil with the rest of the butter in the frying pan. Add the patties and cook over a gentle heat for about 15 minutes or until golden brown on both sides. Arrange the patties on a warmed serving dish and keep hot.
6. Discard the fat from the pan. Add the wine to the pan and bring to a boil, scraping the bottom of the pan with a wooden spatula to detach the meat residue. Add the juice of the lemon and the parsley.
7. Pour the sauce over the meatcakes and serve immediately.

Côte de boeuf au gros sel
Rib of Beef in a Salt Crust

	00:05	00:30

American	Ingredients	Metric/Imperial
2 lb (5 cups)	Sea salt	1 kg / 2 lb
1 (2½ lb)	Rib roast	1 (1.25 kg / 2½ lb)

1. Preheat the oven to 450°F / 260°C / Gas Mark 9.
2. Cover the bottom of an ovenproof dish with two-thirds of the sea salt. Place the meat on top and cover it with the rest of the salt.
3. Put the meat in the oven and roast for 25 minutes. Turn the oven off and let the meat rest inside for 5 minutes. This will produce medium rare meat.
4. Crack the salty crust and remove it. Carve the meat and serve hot.

Chateaubriands au poivre et au madère
Pepper Steak in Madeira Sauce

American	Ingredients	Metric/Imperial
3 tbsp	Crushed black peppercorns	3 tbsp
6 (½ lb)	Boneless sirloin [fillet] steak	6 (250 g / 8 oz)
⅔ cup	Butter	150 g / 5 oz
	Salt	
¼ cup	Brandy	4 tbsp
1 tsp	Potato starch or flour or cornstarch [cornflour]	1 tsp
1 cup	Madeira wine	250 ml / 8 fl oz

1. Sprinkle a chopping board or worktop with the crushed peppercorns and press both sides of each steak into them. Press with the palm of the hand to ensure the peppercorns stick to the meat well.
2. Heat ¼ cup [50 g / 2 oz] of the butter in a large frying pan. When it has turned golden brown, reduce the heat and add the steaks. Cook for 2-4 minutes on each side according to individual taste. Sprinkle with a little salt.
3. Pour the brandy over the steaks and set alight, lifting the steaks up so that the flames burn all over them. Remove the steaks with a slotted spoon, arrange on a serving dish and keep hot.
4. Dissolve the potato starch or cornstarch in 1 tablespoon of the madeira. Pour the rest of the madeira into the frying pan and bring to a boil, scraping the bottom of the pan with a wooden spatula. Remove the pan from the heat and add the dissolved potato starch. Return to a medium heat and stir until the sauce is slightly thickened. Remove from the heat again and gradually add the rest of the butter, cut into small pieces, whisking constantly.
5. Pour the sauce over the steaks and serve.

Chateaubriands béarnaise
Chateaubriand with Béarnaise Sauce

American	Ingredients	Metric/Imperial
2	Shallots	2
2	Fresh tarragon sprigs	2
2	Fresh chervil sprigs	2
¾ cup + 1 tbsp	Butter	190 g / 6½ oz
1 tbsp	Oil	1 tbsp
⅔ cup	Vinegar	150 ml / ¼ pint
	Salt and pepper	
3	Egg yolks, at room temperature	3
2 tbsp	Water	2 tbsp
6 (½ lb)	Chateaubriand steaks (from thickest part of beef tenderloin or fillet)	6 (250 g / 8 oz)

1. Peel and finely chop the shallots. Chop the tarragon and chervil leaves.
2. Heat 1 tablespoon [15 g / ½ oz] of butter with the oil in a heavy saucepan. Add the shallots, half of the tarragon and chervil, the vinegar and pepper to taste. Reduce over a gentle heat for 20 minutes (put a heatproof mat under the pan to diffuse the heat) until only 1 tablespoon of vinegar remains.
3. Meanwhile, heat the rest of the butter in a bowl placed over a pan of hot water or in a double boiler. When the butter has melted you will see a whitish deposit at the bottom: this is the whey. Pour the melted butter very carefully into a bowl so as to leave the whey behind.
4. Preheat the broiler [grill].
5. Put the egg yolks into another bowl over the pan of hot water. Add the reduced vinegar mixture, beating with a whisk. Gradually whisk in the water, a pinch of salt and some pepper and whisk until the mixture becomes creamy. Remove from the heat and, still whisking, dribble in the melted butter. Strain the sauce, then stir in the rest of the tarragon and chervil. Keep warm over the pan of hot water.
6. Cook the steaks under the broiler for 3-5 minutes on each side, depending on whether you like them rare, medium or well done.
7. Serve the steaks accompanied by the hot béarnaise sauce.

Carbonade flamande
Flemish Beef Stew

American	Ingredients	Metric/Imperial
2½ lb	Chuck steak	1.25 kg / 2½ lb
¼ cup	Lard	50 g / 2 oz
5	Onions	5
1½ tbsp	Flour	1½ tbsp
1 tbsp	Brown sugar	1 tbsp
1 tbsp	Vinegar	1 tbsp
1	Bouquet garni	1
2 cups	Beef stock	500 ml / ¾ pint
2 cups	Light beer [pale ale]	500 ml / ¾ pint
	Salt and pepper	
6	Potatoes	6

1. Cut the beef into large cubes. Heat the lard in a flameproof casserole, add the beef cubes and brown on all sides, stirring from time to time. Meanwhile, peel and thinly slice the onions.
2. When the meat is browned, take it out with a slotted spoon and set aside. Add the onions to the pan and brown lightly, stirring occasionally.
3. Replace the meat in the casserole. Sprinkle over the flour and stir until the flour has turned golden brown. Add the brown sugar, vinegar, bouquet garni, beef stock, beer, and salt and pepper to taste. Cover and cook over a gentle heat for about 2½ hours.
4. Meanwhile, peel and halve the potatoes. Cook in boiling salted water for 20 minutes or until tender. Drain.
5. Pour the stew into a heated serving dish, surround with the potatoes and serve very hot.

Cook's tip: you can also cook the potatoes in the steam from the meat. To do this, cut them in quarters and place in a steaming basket over the meat 40 minutes before the end of the cooking period. Make sure that the steamer has a very well-fitting lid.

Entrecôtes bercy
Rib Steaks in Bercy Sauce

00:10　　　**00:20**

American	Ingredients	Metric/Imperial
6	Shallots	6
1 cup	Dry white wine	250 ml / 8 fl oz
	Salt and pepper	
6 (½ lb)	Boneless rib [sirloin or entrecôte] steaks	6 (250 g / 8 oz)
2 - 3 tbsp	Oil	2 - 3 tbsp
1	Bunch of fresh parsley	1
6 tbsp	Butter	75 g / 3 oz

1. Peel and finely chop the shallots. Put them in a small saucepan with the wine and salt and pepper. Cook over a medium heat until only 2-3 tablespoons of liquid remain.
2. Meanwhile, heat a steak or chop grill or griddle. Brush the steaks with the oil, lay them on the grill and cook for 3-4 minutes on each side. Season with salt and pepper.
3. Chop the parsley. When the shallot sauce has reduced, add the chopped parsley and the butter cut into small pieces, whisking well.
4. Serve the steaks coated with the sauce.

Cook's tip: add the salt to the steaks as each side is browned.

Émincé de boeuf
Beef Strips in Mustard Sauce

00:15　　　**00:20**

American	Ingredients	Metric/Imperial
2 lb	Boneless sirloin [rump] steak	1 kg / 2 lb
4	Shallots	4
¼ cup	Butter	50 g / 2 oz
1 cup	Crème fraîche	250 ml / 8 fl oz
1 tsp	Strong prepared mustard	1 tsp
	Salt and pepper	

1. Trim any fat from the steak, then cut into slices ¼ in / 5 mm thick. Cut these slices into strips ¼ in / 5 mm wide. Peel and finely chop the shallots.
2. Heat half of the butter in a frying pan and add half of the meat strips. Cook over high heat, stirring, until browned all over. Remove with a slotted spoon. Brown the rest of the meat strips and remove.
3. Melt the rest of the butter in the frying pan over a medium heat, add the shallots and cook until soft and translucent. Add 4 tablespoons of the crème fraîche and stir, scraping the bottom of the pan with a wooden spatula. Cook until the mixture is a golden color, then add the rest of the crème and the mustard. Season with salt and a lot of pepper. Bring to a boil and cook, stirring, to thicken the sauce.
4. Add the meat strips and any juices from the frying pan and heat through quickly, stirring. Do not let the mixture boil again. Serve immediately.

Entrecôtes bordelaise
Rib Steaks in Bordelaise Sauce

00:15　　　**00:05 to 00:10**

American	Ingredients	Metric/Imperial
1 tbsp	Oil	1 tbsp
⅔ cup	Butter	150 g / 5 oz
6 (½ lb)	Boneless rib [sirloin or entrecôte] steaks	6 (250 g / 8 oz)
6	Shallots	6
½	Bottle red wine (preferably Bordeaux)	½
1	Fresh thyme sprig	1
1	Bay leaf	1
	Salt and pepper	
1	Small bunch of fresh parsley	1
½	Lemon	½

1. Heat the oil with ¼ cup [50 g / 2 oz] of the butter in a frying pan. Add the steaks and cook over a high heat for 2-4 minutes on each side, according to taste. When they are cooked, arrange them on a warmed serving platter and keep hot.
2. Discard the fat left in the frying pan. Peel and finely chop the shallots. Put them in the frying pan with the wine, thyme, bay leaf, and salt and pepper to taste. Bring to a boil, scraping the bottom of the pan to loosen the sediment. Reduce by at least half over a high heat.
3. Chop the parsley. Squeeze the juice from the ½ lemon. Strain the sauce and add the lemon juice, parsley and the remaining butter, cut into small pieces. Whisk the sauce well.
4. Pour the sauce over the hot steaks and serve immediately.

Entrecôtes au roquefort
Rib Steaks with Roquefort Cheese

00:15　　　**00:06 to 00:10**

American	Ingredients	Metric/Imperial
6 tbsp	Butter	75 g / 3 oz
¼ cup	Flour	50 g / 2 oz
1 quart	Hot milk	1 l / 1¾ pints
6 (½ lb)	Boneless rib [sirloin or entrecôte] steaks	6 (250 g / 8 oz)
1 cup	Crème fraîche	250 ml / 8 fl oz
½ lb	Roquefort cheese	250 g / 8 oz

1. Melt ¼ cup [50 g / 2 oz] of the butter in a saucepan over a gentle heat. As soon as it begins to foam, add the flour and stir until completely absorbed. Add the milk and cook, stirring well, over a gentle heat for about 10 minutes.
2. Meanwhile, heat the remaining butter in a frying pan, add the steaks and cook for 3-5 minutes on each side.
3. Stir the crème fraîche into the sauce. Add two-thirds of the cheese and mix carefully.
4. Pour the sauce over the steaks. Crumble the rest of the cheese over the steaks and serve very hot.

Tajine aux oeufs d'or

Spiced Beef with Golden Eggs

| 00:30 | 04:00 |

American	Ingredients	Metric/Imperial
2 lb	Chuck steak	1 kg / 2 lb
1 lb	Shank [shin]	500 g / 1 lb
2	Garlic cloves	2
1 lb	Onions	500 g / 1 lb
¼ cup	Oil	4 tbsp
	Saffron powder	
2 tsp	Ground ginger	2 tsp
3 cups	Water	750 ml / 1¼ pints
	Salt	
1	Small bunch of fresh coriander	1
6	Hard-cooked eggs	6
1 tbsp	Butter	15 g / ½ oz
2 cups	Blanched almonds	250 g / 8 oz

1. Cut the beef into large chunks and set aside. Peel and chop the garlic. Peel and thinly slice the onions.
2. Heat the oil in a flameproof casserole. Remove from the heat and add the garlic, 2 pinches of saffron powder, the ginger and ⅔ cup [150 ml / ¼ pint] water. Sprinkle with salt and mix all these ingredients together.
3. Add the meat to the casserole, stirring so that it becomes well coated with the spices. Add the onion slices, remaining water and, finally, the bunch of coriander. Place the casserole on a medium heat and cover. When boiling point is reached, lower the heat and simmer the casserole for 4 hours over a very low heat.
4. Remove the meat with a slotted spoon and keep hot. Pour the cooking liquid into a small saucepan and reduce for about 10 minutes over a medium heat until thick.
5. Meanwhile, add 4 pinches of saffron powder to a pan of boiling water. Add the shelled eggs and stir until they have taken on a uniform golden color. Drain.
6. Heat the butter in a frying pan, add the almonds and cook until lightly browned.
7. Return the meat to the reduced sauce and reheat for a few minutes. Place in a deep serving dish and arrange the eggs on top. Sprinkle over the almonds.

Tournedos à la moelle

Steaks with Beef Marrow

| 00:10 | 00:04 to 00:12 |

American	Ingredients	Metric/Imperial
6 (5 oz)	Filets mignons [fillet steaks]	6 (150 g / 5 oz)
1 tbsp	Oil	1 tbsp
	Salt and pepper	
5 oz	Beef marrow	150 g / 5 oz
¼ cup	Butter	50 g / 2 oz
3 tbsp	Chopped fresh parsley	3 tbsp

1. About 30 minutes before cooking, brush the steaks with oil and sprinkle with pepper.
2. Cut the marrow into 6 slices ½ in / 1 cm thick. Cook them gently in simmering salted water for 3-4 minutes.
3. Meanwhile, cook the steaks. Use a frying pan with no extra fat, (or a little butter, if preferred), or a very hot steak or chop grill [griddle] or the broiler [grill]. Allow 2 minutes on each side for very rare meat, 4 minutes for rare meat, and 6 minutes for medium rare.
4. Arrange the steaks on a warmed serving dish and put a pat of butter on top of each. Place a drained slice of marrow on each steak and sprinkle with the chopped parsley.

Cook's tip: this delicious dish reaches the heights of haute cuisine if served with a burgundy sauce

Tournedos maître d'hôtel

Steaks with Parsley Butter Sauce

| 00:10 | 00:04 to 00:08 |

American	Ingredients	Metric/Imperial
½ cup	Butter	125 g / 4 oz
1 tsp	Lemon juice	1 tsp
1 tsp	Prepared mustard	1 tsp
2 tbsp	Chopped fresh parsley	2 tbsp
	Salt and pepper	
6 (5 oz)	Filets mignons [fillet steaks]	6

1. If you are using a steak or chop grill [griddle], preheat it until it is as hot as possible.
2. Melt the butter over a low heat and whisk until it takes on the consistency of cream. Remove from the heat and add the lemon juice and mustard, still whisking. Add the parsley and salt and pepper to taste and stir to mix.
3. Place the steaks on the very hot grill and cook for 2-4 minutes on each side, according to taste. Alternatively, cook the steaks in butter in a frying pan.
4. Arrange the steaks on a warmed serving dish, sprinkle with salt and serve the parsley butter sauce in a sauceboat.

Cook's tip: you can also serve the steaks with a béarnaise sauce.

Saffron: an essential ingredient for spiced beef with golden eggs

Braised Beef with Garlic

Rôti à l'ail en chemise

00:10   00:30 to 00:40

American	Ingredients	Metric/Imperial
1 (2½ lb)	Boneless rump [topside] or tip roast	1 (1.25 kg / 2½ lb)
5	Garlic cloves	5
3 tbsp	Oil	3 tbsp
	Salt and pepper	
3	Fresh rosemary sprigs	3
⅔ cup	Water	150 ml / ¼ pint

1. The piece of tied beef should be about 2½ in / 6 cm thick.
2. Remove all but the innermost layer of skin from the cloves of garlic. With a pointed knife, cut a groove the length of each clove.
3. Heat the oil in a flameproof casserole, add the meat, and cook for 3 minutes on each side over high heat, until it is well browned. Turn down the heat to the lowest possible setting. Season with salt and pepper, add the cloves of garlic and the rosemary and continue cooking for 25 minutes for rare meat, or 40 minutes for medium-rare meat. Turn the meat every 10 minutes using a spatula (do not prick it with a fork or the juices will run out).
4. Untie the meat and slice it thinly. Arrange the meat on a warmed serving dish and surround with the cloves of garlic. Keep hot.
5. Discard three-quarters of the cooking fat and pour the water into the casserole. Bring to a boil, scraping up the meat residue with a wooden spoon. Pour this gravy into a sauceboat and serve with the meat.

Chateaubriand – slices of beef fillet (see page 126)

Steaks with Truffle Sauce

Tournedos Rossini

00:10   00:20

American	Ingredients	Metric/Imperial
3 oz	Bacon	75 g / 3 oz
2	Shallots	2
1 tbsp	Oil	1 tbsp
2 tbsp	Flour	2 tbsp
1 tbsp	Tomato paste [purée]	1 tbsp
2 tbsp	Chopped fresh parsley	2 tbsp
⅔ cup	Beef broth	150 ml / ¼ pint
	Salt and pepper	
1	Small can of truffle peelings	1
2 tbsp	Butter	25 g / 1 oz
6 (5 oz)	Filets mignons [fillet steaks]	6 (150 g / 5 oz)

1. Cut the bacon into matchstick strips. Peel and finely chop the shallots. Heat the oil in a small heavy-based saucepan, add the bacon and shallots and cook until the bacon is golden brown. Remove the bacon and set aside.
2. Add the flour to the pan and cook, stirring, until the flour is golden. Add the tomato paste, parsley and cooked bacon. Gradually stir in the stock. Add salt and pepper to taste and simmer for a few minutes.
3. Remove the bacon with a slotted spoon and discard it. Purée the sauce in a blender or food processor. Add the drained truffles and keep warm.
4. Melt the butter in a frying pan, add the steaks and cook for 2-4 minutes on each side, according to taste.
5. Serve the steaks coated with the sauce.

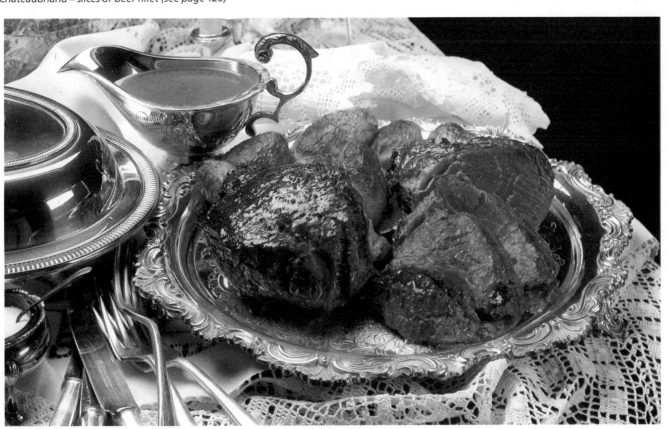

Côtes de veau normande

Normandy Veal Chops

⏱ 00:30   00:30 🍲

American	Ingredients	Metric/Imperial
⅔ cup	Butter	150 g / 5 oz
6 (6 oz)	Veal loin chops	6 (175 g / 6 oz)
	Salt and pepper	
1 cup	Crème fraîche	250 ml / 8 fl oz
6 tbsp	Calvados or applejack	6 tbsp
2 lb	Golden Delicious apples	1 kg / 2 lb
1 tbsp	Sugar	1 tbsp

1. Preheat the oven to 350°F / 180°C / Gas Mark 4.
2. Heat ¼ cup [50 g / 2 oz] of the butter in a frying pan. Add the chops a few at a time and brown on both sides. As they are browned, transfer them to an ovenproof dish. Season the chops with salt and pepper and put to one side.
3. Add the crème fraîche to the frying pan and stir to scrape up the meat residue from the bottom of the pan. Reduce by one-third over a medium heat. Stir in the calvados.
4. Pour the crème sauce over the chops. Place in the oven and bake for 15-20 minutes.
5. Meanwhile, peel the apples and cut into quarters. Remove the seeds and core. Heat the rest of the butter in a frying pan, add the apple quarters and cook until golden. Halfway through this cooking period, sprinkle with the sugar.
6. To serve, arrange the chops on a warmed serving dish and surround with the apples. Adjust the seasoning of the sauce and pour over the chops.

Chaussons au jambon et au fromage

Veal, Ham and Cheese Turnovers

⏱ 00:10   00:10 🍲

American	Ingredients	Metric/Imperial
6 (¼ lb)	Thin veal scaloppine [escalopes]	6 (125 g / 4 oz)
	Grated nutmeg	
12	Large fresh basil leaves	12
3	Thin slices of bayonne ham or cooked ham	3
¼ lb	Gruyère cheese	125 g / 4 oz
2 tbsp	Oil	2 tbsp
6 tbsp	Butter	75 g / 3 oz
	Salt and pepper	
5 tbsp	White wine	5 tbsp

1. Lay the slices of veal out flat and sprinkle with a little nutmeg. Lay 2 basil leaves on each one. Cut the ham slices in half and lay these on the veal. Cut the cheese into 6 thin slices and arrange these on top of the ham, making sure to leave a ½ in / 1 cm gap all around the edge of the meat.
2. Fold over each scaloppine in half and pin the edges together with a wooden toothpick.
3. Heat the oil in a frying pan and add the butter. As soon as the butter foams, add the veal turnovers and cook for 5 minutes on each side. Season with salt and pepper during cooking.

4. Transfer the veal to a warmed serving platter and keep hot.
5. Pour the wine into the frying pan and bring to a boil over a high heat, scraping up all the meat residue from the bottom of the pan. Reduce by about half, then spoon over the veal and serve hot.

Brochettes de veau

Veal Kebabs

⏱ 00:10 plus marinating   00:10 to 00:15 🍲

American	Ingredients	Metric/Imperial
2 lb	Boneless veal from the round [topside or cushion]	1 kg / 2 lb
2 tsp	Olive oil	2 tsp
	Paprika	
	Salt	
¼ lb	Smoked bacon slices	125 g / 4 oz

1. Cut the veal into 1½ in / 4 cm cubes. Put them in a mixing bowl and add the oil, a pinch of paprika and salt to taste. Marinate for 1 hour.
2. Preheat the broiler [grill] or heat a steak or chop grill.
3. Halve the bacon slices crosswise and roll them up loosely.
4. Thread the veal cubes and bacon rolls alternately onto 6 skewers. Cook the kebabs for 10-15 minutes. If cooking under the broiler, baste the kebabs with the marinating oil when you turn them.

Confit à la sauge

Veal Cooked in Goose Fat

⏱ 00:10 plus macerating   02:00 🍲

American	Ingredients	Metric/Imperial
3 tbsp	Sea salt	3 tbsp
2 tsp	Sugar	2 tsp
1 (2½ lb)	Piece of boneless veal round [topside or cushion], rolled, larded and tied	1 (1.25 kg / 2½ lb)
4	Garlic cloves	4
1 tsp	Pepper	1 tsp
4	Fresh sage leaves	4
3 lb (6 cups)	Goose fat	1.5 kg / 3 lb

1. Mix together the salt and sugar. Rub this mixture all over the veal so that it penetrates the meat. Leave to macerate for 12 hours.
2. The next day, rinse the veal under running water and pat dry with paper towels.
3. Peel the garlic cloves, cut each one in half and roll in the pepper. Cut the sage leaves in half. Make 8 deep incisions in the veal with a small pointed knife and insert in each one half a clove of garlic and half a sage leaf. If there is any pepper left over, sprinkle it over the meat.
4. Put the veal in a flameproof casserole and add the goose fat. Cover the casserole and cook over a gentle heat for 2 hours, never allowing the goose fat to boil — it should be just simmering.
5. Drain the veal and slice it. Serve hot, accompanied by noodles and a green vegetable.

Côtes de veau en papillotes

Veal Chops
Baked in Foil

00:10   00:40

American	Ingredients	Metric/Imperial
4	Onions	4
4	Shallots	4
1½ lb	Button mushrooms	750 g / 1½ lb
½ cup	Butter	125 g / 4 oz
	Salt and pepper	
6	Thin slices of bayonne ham or prosciutto	6
6 (6 oz)	Veal chops	6 (175 g / 6 oz)

1. Preheat the oven to 425°F / 220°C / Gas Mark 7.
2. Peel and finely chop the onions and shallots. Chop the mushrooms as finely as possible. Melt half of the butter in a frying pan, add the onions and shallots and cook for 5 minutes over a gentle heat until softened. Turn up the heat, add the chopped mushrooms and continue cooking for 10 minutes, stirring well, until no liquid remains. Remove from the heat, season with salt and pepper and set aside.
3. Cut the slices of ham in half. Set aside.
4. Melt the remaining butter in the frying pan, add the veal chops and cook for 4-8 minutes on each side to brown well. Remove from the pan and season with salt and pepper.
5. Cut 6 pieces of foil each large enough to wrap a chop. Butter each piece of foil. Place ½ slice of ham on each, then add a spoonful of the mushroom mixture. Put the chops on top. Add the remaining mushroom mixture and finally another ½ slice of ham to each. Seal the packages securely.
6. Place the packages on a rack in the oven and cook for 15 minutes. Serve very hot in the foil.

Blanquette de veau

Veal in a White Sauce

00:10   02:00

American	Ingredients	Metric/Imperial
2½ lb	Boneless breast of veal	1.25 kg / 2½ lb
2	Carrots	2
1	Onion	1
1	Shallot	1
1	Bouquet garni	1
	Salt and pepper	
5 oz	Button mushrooms (optional)	150 g / 5 oz
2 tbsp	Butter	25 g / 1 oz
2 tbsp	Flour	2 tbsp
1	Egg yolk	1
½ cup	Crème fraîche	125 ml / 4 fl oz
½	Lemon	½

1. Cut the veal into 1 in / 2.5 cm wide strips. Put them into a flameproof casserole and just cover with cold water. Bring to a boil, skimming off the froth.
2. Meanwhile, peel and slice the carrots, onion and shallot. Add to the casserole with the bouquet garni. Season with salt and pepper and simmer very gently for 2 hours.

3. Halfway through the cooking period, add the mushrooms, if used.
4. With a fork, mix the butter and flour together to a paste. Take the casserole off the heat and add this paste. Bring to a boil, stirring, and cook for 5 minutes.
5. Just before serving, mix the egg yolk with the crème fraîche. Remove the casserole from the heat and add the egg yolk mixture, stirring all the time. Add the juice of the ½ lemon. Discard the bouquet garni and serve.

Veal in white sauce

Coeurs de veau braisés

Braised Calves' Hearts

00:10   01:20

American	Ingredients	Metric/Imperial
2	Calves' hearts	2
2 lb	Carrots	1 kg / 2 lb
20	Small onions	20
6 tbsp	Butter	75 g / 3 oz
1 tbsp	Oil	1 tbsp
1	Bouquet garni	1
3	Garlic cloves	3
	Salt and pepper	
½	Bottle of dry white wine	½
⅔ cup	Chicken stock	150 ml / ¼ pint

1. Rinse the hearts to remove any blood clots and pat dry. Peel and thinly slice the carrots. Peel the onions.
2. Melt the butter with the oil in a large flameproof casserole. Add the hearts and brown all over. Add the onions and carrots and cook over a high heat for about 5 minutes or until golden brown.
3. Add the bouquet garni and peeled garlic. Season with salt and pepper and add the wine and stock. Cover and cook for at least 1 hour.
4. To serve, slice the hearts and surround with the vegetables. Reduce the cooking liquid by one-third over a fast heat, discard the bouquet garni and pour into a sauceboat.

Estouffade à la moutarde
Veal in Wine and Mustard Sauce

⏱ 00:20 — 02:15 🍲

American	Ingredients	Metric/Imperial
2 lb	Boneless breast of veal	1 kg / 2 lb
1 lb	Boned veal blade steaks [middle neck cutlets]	500 g / 1 lb
¼ lb	Lightly salted lean bacon	125 g / 4 oz
¼ lb	Bacon rind	125 g / 4 oz
4	Shallots	4
½ lb	Button mushrooms	250 g / 8 oz
½	Lemon	½
3 tbsp	Oil	3 tbsp
2 tbsp	Butter	25 g / 1 oz
1 tbsp	Flour	1 tbsp
1 cup	Dry white wine	250 ml / 8 fl oz
1 tbsp	Prepared mustard	1 tbsp
1	Fresh thyme sprig	1
1	Bay leaf	1
1 cup	Thin crème fraîche	250 ml / 8 fl oz
	Salt and pepper	

1. Preheat the oven to 350°F / 180°C / Gas Mark 4.
2. Cut all the veal into large cubes. Cut the bacon and bacon rind into matchstick strips. Peel and finely chop the shallots. Thinly slice the mushrooms. Sprinkle them with the juice of the ½ lemon and put to one side.
3. Heat the oil in a frying pan, add the veal and bacon and cook over a high heat for 5 minutes or until browned on all sides. Remove with a slotted spoon and place in a flameproof casserole.
4. Add the butter and shallots to the pan and cook over a medium heat for 3 minutes. Add to the casserole.
5. Sprinkle the flour over the casserole and mix in well. Add the wine, mustard, thyme, bay leaf, crème fraîche, mushrooms and their lemon juice, the bacon rind, and salt and pepper to taste. The meat should be completely covered; if it is not, add a little water. Mix everything together well.
6. Bring to a boil on top of the stove, then transfer the casserole to the oven. Cook for 2 hours or until the veal is tender.

Escalopes au cidre
Scaloppine with Cider Cream

⏱ 00:10 — 00:20 🍲

American	Ingredients	Metric/Imperial
3	Onions	3
6 (5 oz)	Veal scaloppine [escalopes]	6 (150 g / 5 oz)
	Salt and pepper	
3 tbsp	Butter	40 g / 1½ oz
2½ cups	Dry hard cider	600 ml / 1 pint
1½ cups	Crème fraîche	350 ml / 12 fl oz

1. Peel and finely chop the onions. Sprinkle the slices of veal with salt and pepper on both sides. Melt the butter in a frying pan, add the veal and cook for 4-5 minutes on each side, until golden brown. Remove and keep hot.
2. Add the onions to the pan and cook for about 5 minutes over a medium heat, scraping up the meat residue from the bottom of the pan with a wooden spatula. Pour in the cider and reduce over a high heat until only about 3 tablespoons of liquid remain.
3. Reduce the heat and add the crème fraîche. Reduce by half, stirring constantly. Season with salt and pepper.
4. Return the veal to the pan and reheat briefly in the sauce.

Foie de veau au bacon
Calves' Liver with Bacon

⏱ 00:05 — 00:06 🍲

American	Ingredients	Metric/Imperial
½ cup	Butter	125 g / 4 oz
6 (5 oz)	Slices of calves' liver	6 (150 g / 5 oz)
	Salt and pepper	
12	Thin bacon slices	12
½	Lemon	½
	Lemon wedges for serving	

1. Melt half of the butter in a frying pan over a high heat, add the liver slices and cook until browned on both sides. Season with salt and pepper when you turn them over. When they are cooked (still pink inside), arrange them on a warmed serving platter and keep hot.
2. Cook the slices of bacon in the frying pan until the fat becomes translucent. Lay them on the serving platter around the slices of liver.
3. Heat the rest of the butter in the frying pan until it foams. Add the juice of the ½ lemon and pour this sauce over the liver. Serve with lemon wedges.

Escalopes aux cèpes
Scaloppine with Cèpes

⏱ 00:15 (plus soaking) — 00:40 🍲

American	Ingredients	Metric/Imperial
9	Dried or canned medium-size cèpes	9
3	Ripe tomatoes	3
2	Medium-size onions	2
6 (5 oz)	Veal scaloppine [escalopes]	6 (150 g / 5 oz)
3 tbsp	Flour	3 tbsp
¼ cup	Oil	4 tbsp
1 cup	Red wine	250 ml / 8 fl oz
	Salt and pepper	
1	Lemon	1

1. If using dried cèpes, rinse them well and soak in warm water to cover for 30 minutes; drain. Drain canned cèpes. Slice the cèpes thinly.
2. Peel the tomatoes (first plunging them in boiling water for 10 seconds), quarter them and mash with a fork. Set aside. Peel and thinly slice the onions.

3. Coat the veal slices in the flour. Heat the oil in a frying pan, add the veal and cook for 4-5 minutes on each side over a medium heat. Remove from the pan and keep warm.
4. Add the onions to the pan and cook for 5 minutes over a moderate heat, scraping the bottom of the pan well. Add the wine, mashed tomatoes and cèpes. Add seasoning to taste. Wash the lemon, grate the lemon rind and add to the mixture. Cook for 15 minutes over a high heat, stirring well.
5. Return the veal to the pan and reheat briefly in the sauce before serving.

Foie de veau sauté aux raisins
Calves' Liver with Grapes

	00:30	00:15

American	Ingredients	Metric/Imperial
36	Large green grapes	36
1	Bunch of fresh parsley	1
6 (5 oz)	Slices of calves' liver	6 (150 g / 5 oz)
	Salt and pepper	
½ cup	Flour	50 g / 2 oz
½ cup	Butter	125 g / 4 oz
1¼ cups	Dry white wine	300 ml / ½ pint

1. Peel the grapes. Chop the parsley. Season the liver slices with salt and pepper and coat in the flour.
2. Heat the butter in a large frying pan, add the liver slices and cook over a high heat for 3-4 minutes on each side. Arrange on a warmed serving platter and keep hot.
3. Add the parsley and grapes to the frying pan and allow to color slightly over a medium heat, stirring gently. Pour over the wine. Reduce by half over a high heat, stirring often.
4. Pour the grape sauce over the liver and serve immediately.

Escalopes berrichonne
Scaloppine with Morels in Cream

	00:25	00:45

American	Ingredients	Metric/Imperial
7 tbsp	Butter	90 g / 3½ oz
6 (5 oz)	Veal scaloppine [escalopes]	6 (150 g / 5 oz]
	Salt and pepper	
¾ lb	Fresh morels or other mushrooms	350 g / 12 oz
5 oz	Bayonne ham or prosciutto	150 g / 5 oz
3	Shallots	3
1 cup	White wine	250 ml / 8 fl oz
1 cup	Crème fraîche	250 ml / 8 fl oz
1 cup	Grated gruyère cheese	125 g / 4oz

1. Preheat the oven to 425°F / 220°C / Gas Mark 7.
2. Heat 3 tablespoons [40 g / 1½ oz] of the butter in a frying pan, add the slices of veal and cook until golden brown on both sides, about 15 minutes. Season with salt and pepper and arrange in an ovenproof dish. Set aside.

3. Trim the morels and chop them if they are large. Cut the ham into thin strips. Peel and chop the shallots.
4. Heat the rest of the butter in the frying pan, add the mushrooms and shallots and cook until softened and the liquid produced by the mushrooms has evaporated. Add the ham and wine and stir well. Add the crème fraîche and salt and pepper to taste and reduce the sauce over a very gentle heat for about 10 minutes.
5. Cover the veal with the grated cheese, then pour over the sauce. Bake for 15 minutes.

Cook's tip: if fresh morels are not available, you can substitute 4 oz / 125 g dried morels or other wild mushrooms. Rinse these well, then soak in warm water to cover for 30 minutes. Drain and proceed as above. Drained canned morels may also be used.

Escalopes farcies
Stuffed Scaloppine in Madeira

	00:50	00:20

American	Ingredients	Metric/Imperial
4	Slices of stale bread	4
⅔ cup	Milk	150 ml / ¼ pint
3	Garlic cloves	3
5 oz	Chicken livers	150 g / 5 oz
5 oz	Pork sausage meat	150 g / 5 oz
1¼ cups	Madeira wine	300 ml / ½ pint
⅓ cup	Brandy	5 tbsp
	Salt and pepper	
	Grated nutmeg	
1	Small bunch of fresh parsley	1
6 tbsp	Butter	75 g / 3 oz
6	Veal scaloppine [escalopes]	6
¼ cup	Flour	50 g / 2 oz
⅔ cup	Dry white wine	150 ml / ¼ pint
1¼ cups	Veal or chicken stock	300 ml / ½ pint
1¼ cups	Crème fraîche	300 ml / ½ pint

1. Preheat the oven to 475°F / 250°C / Gas Mark 9.
2. Soak the bread in the milk in a bowl. Peel and chop one of the cloves of garlic. Chop the chicken livers. Mix together the bread, chopped garlic, sausage meat, chicken livers, half of the madeira and the brandy. Season with salt and pepper and a pinch of nutmeg. Chop the parsley finely and add it to the rest of the ingredients and mix.
3. Heat 2 tablespoons [25 g / 1 oz] butter in a frying pan, add the slices of veal and cook for 3-4 minutes on each side, until golden brown. Do not cook through. Transfer to an ovenproof dish.
4. Melt the rest of the butter and stir in the flour. Peel and chop the rest of the garlic and add to the pan with the wine and stock, stirring all the time. Season with salt, pepper and nutmeg. Cook for a few minutes, stirring constantly. Add the rest of the madeira and the crème fraîche. Bring to a boil, stirring.
5. Pile the chicken liver stuffing on top of the veal and pour over the sauce. Bake for about 20 minutes or until the veal is cooked through and serve piping hot.

Veal shanks with cheese

Jarret de veau gratiné
Veal Shanks [Knuckle] with Cheese

| | 00:30 | | 01:30 |

American	Ingredients	Metric/Imperial
2	Carrots	2
2	Onions	2
2	Large pieces of pork rind	2
6	Veal shank cross cuts [slices of knuckle]	6
	Salt and pepper	
1	Bouquet garni	1
2 tbsp	Brandy	2 tbsp
1¼ cups	Dry white wine	300 ml / ½ pint
½ cup	Crème fraîche	125 ml / 4 fl oz
1	Egg yolk	1
5 tbsp	Grated gruyère cheese	5 tbsp

1. Peel and thinly slice the carrots and onions. Place one of the pieces of pork rind on the bottom of a flameproof casserole, fatty side down. Cover this with the carrots and onions and lay the slices of veal on top. Season with salt and pepper and push the bouquet garni into the middle of the meat. Add the brandy and wine. Lay the other piece of rind on top.
2. Cover the casserole and simmer over a gentle heat for 1 hour 20 minutes.
3. Preheat the oven to 450°F / 230°C / Gas Mark 8.
4. Remove the rind, and place the drained meat and carrots in a shallow ovenproof dish. Set aside.
5. Strain the cooking liquid into a mixing bowl. Skim off the fat. Mix the crème fraîche with the egg yolk and add to the bowl. Stir well. Adjust the seasoning, pour over the meat and sprinkle with the grated cheese.
6. Bake for 15 minutes to brown the top.

Foie de veau lyonnaise
Calves' Liver with Onions

| | 00:10 | | 00:20 |

American	Ingredients	Metric/Imperial
6 (5 oz)	Slices of calves' liver	6 (150 g / 5 oz)
	Salt and pepper	
½ cup	Flour	50 g / 2 oz
6	Medium-size onions	6
3 tbsp	Butter	40 g / 1½ oz
1 tbsp	Wine vinegar	1 tbsp
2 tbsp	Chopped fresh parsley	2 tbsp

1. Season the liver slices with salt and pepper on both sides, and coat them in the flour. Peel and thinly slice the onions.
2. Melt 2 tablespoons [25 g / 1 oz] of the butter in a frying pan, add the slices of liver and cook for 3-4 minutes on each side over a high heat. Arrange on a warmed serving dish and keep hot.
3. Add the rest of the butter and the onions to the frying pan and cook over a gentle heat for 15 minutes. Add the vinegar and salt and pepper to taste. Stir well over a gentle heat for 1 minute without boiling, then pour this sauce over the liver slices.
4. Sprinkle with the parsley and serve immediately.

Grenadins au vermouth
Veal Steaks in Vermouth

| | 00:25 | 00:30 to 00:35 | |

American	Ingredients	Metric/Imperial
6 (5 oz)	Slices of veal tenderloin [fillet], about 1 in / 2.5 cm thick, wrapped in pork fat	6 (150 g / 5 oz)
2 tbsp	Flour	2 tbsp
¼ cup	Butter	50 g / 2 oz
1 cup	Dry red vermouth	250 ml / 8 fl oz
1 tsp	Grated lemon rind	1 tsp
4	Tomatoes	4
8	Medium-size onions	8
1	Bouquet garni	1
	Salt and pepper	
2 tbsp	Crème fraîche	2 tbsp

1. Lightly coat the veal steaks in the flour. Heat the butter in a frying pan, add the steaks and cook gently until they are golden on all sides. Do not let the butter burn.
2. Remove from the heat and pour over the vermouth. Add the lemon rind. Cover and leave to infuse for 5 minutes.
3. Meanwhile, quarter the tomatoes and remove the seeds. Peel the onions.
4. Replace the pan on a high heat and bring to a boil. Turn the heat down and add the tomatoes, onions and bouquet garni. Season with salt and pepper. Cover and simmer over a low heat for 25-30 minutes.
5. Arrange the steaks on a warmed serving dish and garnish with the onions. Keep hot. Add the crème fraîche to the sauce

and heat through, stirring. Strain the sauce, pressing the solids to extract all the liquid. Pour the sauce over the steaks.

Cook's tip: there should not be a lot of sauce, so if necessary, reduce it by boiling before adding the crème fraîche. If you do not like cream, substitute ¼ cup [50 g / 2 oz] butter. This should be added away from the heat, little by little, beating all the time.

Médaillons au porto

Veal Steaks with Port

	00:05		00:10

American	Ingredients	Metric/Imperial
6	Slices of veal tenderloin [fillet], about ½ in / 1 cm thick	6
6 tbsp	Flour	6 tbsp
¼ cup	Butter	50 g / 2 oz
6 tbsp	Port wine	6 tbsp
1 cup	Crème fraîche	250 ml / 8 fl oz
	Salt and pepper	
1	Lemon	1

1. Coat the veal steaks with the flour. Melt the butter in a frying pan, add the veal and cook over a medium heat for 3-4 minutes on each side, until golden. Remove and keep warm.
2. Add the port to the pan and bring to a boil. Stir in the crème fraîche and season with salt and pepper. Grate the lemon rind and add to the pan. Boil briskly for 2 minutes, then turn down the heat.
3. Replace the veal steaks in the pan and turn them over in the sauce so that they are coated with it. Reheat briefly.

Noix de veau rôtie

Roast Veal Round [Topside]

	00:02		01:15

American	Ingredients	Metric/Imperial
1 (3 lb)	Veal round roast [topside or cushion], at room temperature	1 (1.5 kg / 3 lb)
	Salt and pepper	
1 tbsp	Boiling water	1 tbsp
2 tbsp	Butter	25 g / 1 oz

1. Preheat the oven to to 425°F / 220°C / Gas Mark 7.
2. Rub the veal all over with salt and pepper. Place it on a rack in a roasting pan.
3. Roast until the meat browns, then turn it over and continue roasting for 1 hour, basting frequently with the pan juices.
4. Turn off the oven and leave the meat inside for 5 minutes. (With an electric oven, open the door and leave it ajar.)
5. Remove the meat from the pan and keep hot. Put the roasting pan over a gentle heat on top of the stove and cook until the meat juices color slightly without burning. Add the boiling water and butter and stir until melted. Add salt and pepper to taste.
6. Slice the meat and serve with the gravy.

Fricassée de foie de veau et de rognons

Fricassee of Calves' Liver and Kidneys

	00:30		00:30

American	Ingredients	Metric/Imperial
2	Calves' kidneys	2
3	Slices of calves' liver	3
2	Medium-size onions	2
¼ cup	Butter	50 g / 2 oz
3 tbsp	Vinegar	3 tbsp
1¼ cups	Red wine	300 ml / ½ pint
	Salt and pepper	

1. Quarter the kidneys. Remove the white parts and the fat in the center. Cut the kidneys into pieces. Cut the slices of liver into small pieces of the same size.
2. Peel and chop the onions. Heat 1 tablespoon of the butter in a frying pan, add the onions and cook until they begin to turn golden brown (after about 10 minutes). Add the vinegar and wine. Bring to a boil and reduce until the mixture is syrupy. Pour this sauce into a bowl.
3. Wipe out the frying pan out but do not wash. Melt the rest of the butter, add the pieces of liver and kidney and cook over a high heat for 3 minutes, stirring. Season with salt and pepper.
4. Pour over the sauce and reheat briefly.

Grenadins au poivre vert

Veal Steaks with Green Peppercorns

	00:20	00:20 to 00:30	

American	Ingredients	Metric/Imperial
6	Slices of veal tenderloin [fillet], about 1 in / 2.5 cm thick, wrapped in pork fat	6
2 tbsp	Flour	2 tbsp
2 tbsp	Butter	25 g / 1 oz
½ cup	Brandy	125 ml / 8 fl oz
1¼ cups	Dry white wine	300 ml / ½ pint
1 tbsp	Green peppercorns	1 tbsp
1 cup	Heavy [double] cream	250 ml / 8 fl oz
1 tsp	Tomato paste [purée]	1 tsp
	Salt	

1. Lightly coat the veal steaks all over in flour. Heat half of the butter in a frying pan, add the veal and cook gently, until they are golden on all sides. Do not let the butter brown.
2. Transfer the veal to another frying pan. Pour over the brandy, cover and leave to macerate.
3. Add the wine to the first frying pan and bring to a boil, scraping up the meat residue from the bottom of the pan. Add the green peppercorns, crushed with a mortar and pestle or put through a food mill. Reduce the liquid by half. Pour over the veal steaks.
4. Mix the cream with the tomato paste and add to the veal. Add salt to taste. Cook over a very low heat for 20 minutes, turning the veal steaks once halfway through and stirring the sauce occasionally.

Pieds de veau rémoulade
Calves' Feet with Rémoulade Sauce

	00:30	01:30

American	Ingredients	Metric/Imperial
6	Calves' feet	6
1	Carrot	1
2	Onions	2
3	Shallots	3
2	Garlic cloves	2
2	Cloves	2
2 quarts	Water	2 l / 3½ pints
1	Bouquet garni	1
	Salt and pepper	
1	Egg yolk	1
3	Hard-cooked egg yolks	3
1 tbsp	Mustard	1 tbsp
1 cup	Oil	250 ml / 8 fl oz
2 - 3	Gherkins	2 - 3
¼ cup	Capers	50 g / 2 oz
2	Fresh parsley sprigs	2

1. Split the calves' feet in half. Plunge them into a saucepan of boiling water and blanch for 5 minutes. Drain and cool.
2. Peel the carrot, onions, shallots and garlic. Stud the onions with the cloves. Pour the water into a large stewpot and add all the vegetables, the bouquet garni and salt and pepper to taste. Bring to a boil. Add the calves' feet, cover and cook over a low heat for at least 1½ hours.
3. Put the egg yolk in a bowl with the 3 hard-cooked egg yolks, the mustard, and salt and pepper to taste. Mix together to make a smooth paste. Add the oil little by little in a trickle, beating constantly until the mixture thickens and takes on the consistency of mayonnaise (but rather less smooth). Chop the gherkins, capers and parsley and add to the mayonnaise.
4. Serve the calves' feet hot with the rémoulade sauce.

Ris de veau jardinière
Sweetbreads with Spring Vegetables

	00:45 plus soaking	00:55

American	Ingredients	Metric/Imperial
2 (1½ lb)	Calves' sweetbreads	2 (750 g / 1½ lb)
½ lb	Lightly salted bacon	250 g / 8 oz
¼ cup	Butter	50 g / 2 oz
2	Shallots	2
2	Onions	2
	Grated nutmeg	
1	Bouquet garni	1
	Salt and pepper	
1 cup	Madeira wine	250 ml / 8 fl oz
1 lb	Fresh peas	500 g / 1 lb
8	Young carrots	8
1	Sugar cube	1

1. Soak the sweetbreads in cold water to cover for 10 hours, changing the water 2 or 3 times.
2. Drain the sweetbreads and place in a saucepan of fresh cold water. Bring to a boil slowly and boil for 4 minutes, then drain and rinse under cold running water. Take off the skin and all gristly parts.
3. Place the bacon in a saucepan of water, bring to a boil and simmer for 5 minutes. Drain and cut into strips.
4. Cook the bacon strips in a flameproof casserole until they start to brown. Remove with a slotted spoon and set aside. Add the sweetbreads to the casserole and cook over a moderate heat until golden all over. Remove the sweetbreads. Discard the fat in the casserole and wipe it out.
5. Heat 2 tablespoons [25 g / 1 oz] of the butter in the casserole, and replace the bacon and sweetbreads. Peel the shallots and onions and add to the casserole with a pinch of nutmeg, the bouquet garni, and salt and pepper to taste. Cook gently for 10 minutes. Add the madeira, cover and simmer for 25 minutes.
6. Meanwhile, shell the peas and cook in boiling salted water for 15 minutes. Peel the carrots and cook in boiling salted water for 10-15 minutes or until just tender.
7. Drain the carrots and peas and add them to the casserole, together with the sugar cube. Simmer for 15 minutes longer.
8. Add the rest of the butter. Remove and discard the bouquet garni, onions and shallots, and serve the sweetbreads, sliced, on top of the remaining vegetables.

Poitrine de veau roulée à l'oseille
Breast of Veal with Sorrel

	00:45	01:45

American	Ingredients	Metric/Imperial
5 oz	Fresh sorrel or spinach	150 g / 5 oz
6 tbsp	Butter	75 g / 3 oz
4	Shallots	4
1½ lb	Button mushrooms	750 g / 1½ lb
⅓ cup	Crème fraîche	5 tbsp
1 (3 lb)	Boneless breast of veal	1 (1.5 kg / 3 lb)
3	Thick slices of Bayonne ham or prosciutto	3
2	Onions	2
1	Carrot	1
2	Fresh rosemary sprigs	2
2	Fresh thyme sprigs	2
1	Small bunch of fresh parsley	1
1	Garlic clove	1
2 tbsp	Oil	2 tbsp
1 cup	Dry white wine	250 ml / 8 fl oz
1 - 2	Veal bones	1 - 2
	Grated nutmeg	
	Salt and pepper	

1. Remove the stalks from the sorrel and cut it into strips. Melt 2 tablespoons [25 g / 1 oz] of the butter in a frying pan, add the sorrel and cook for a few minutes or until it has softened. Remove the sorrel from the pan and put to one side.
2. Peel and finely chop the shallots. Chop the mushrooms. Melt another 2 tablespoons [25 g / 1 oz] of the butter in the frying pan, add the shallots and mushrooms and cook over a

moderate heat until the liquid produced by the mushrooms has evaporated. Add the crème fraîche, then remove the pan from the heat and mix well with the sorrel.

3. Spread the breast of veal out flat and lay the slices of ham on top. Spread the sorrel mixture on top of the ham. Roll up the breast and tie it into shape.

4. Peel and slice the onions. Peel and thinly slice the carrot. Tie the rosemary sprigs, thyme and parsley together. Peel the garlic.

5. Heat the oil and the rest of the butter in a flameproof casserole. Add the veal and brown all over for 10 minutes over a fairly high heat. Remove the meat and set aside. Discard the cooking fat.

6. Add the carrot and onions to the casserole and cook for a few minutes, stirring well with a wooden spoon. Replace the meat and add the wine, garlic and bouquet garni of herbs. Add the veal bones: they will add flavor to the sauce during cooking. Season with a pinch of nutmeg and salt and pepper to taste. Cook over a low heat for 1 hour, basting the meat frequently.

7. Halfway through the cooking period, prick the meat with a fork in 2-3 places so that the juices from the stuffing can mix with the sauce and flavor it.

8. To serve, untie the meat and slice it thinly. Serve the strained gravy separately. Stuffed veal breast can also be served cold.

Ragoût de veau aux olives
Veal Ragoût with Olives

| 00:30 | | 01:30 |
American	Ingredients	Metric/Imperial
2½ lb	Boneless breast of veal	1.25 kg / 2½ lb
¼ lb	Slightly salted bacon	125 g / 4 oz
50	Green olives, pitted [stoned]	50
1 tbsp	Butter	15 g / ½ oz
1 tbsp	Oil	1 tbsp
3	Carrots	3
1	Large onion	1
1	Celery stalk	1
½ lb	Shallots	250 g / 8 oz
1 tbsp	Flour	1 tbsp
1	Veal bone	1
	Pepper	
1¼ cups	Veal or chicken stock	300 ml / ½ pint
1¼ cups	White wine	300 ml / ½ pint
¾ lb	Canned cèpes	350 g / 12 oz

1. Cut the veal into 1 in / 2.5 cm wide strips. Set aside.
2. Place the bacon and olives in a large saucepan, cover with cold water and bring to a boil. Simmer gently for 5 minutes, then drain. Cut the bacon into small strips.
3. Heat the butter and oil in a large flameproof casserole, add the bacon strips and veal and brown lightly.
4. Peel and slice the carrots and onion. Slice the celery. Peel and chop the shallots. Add all these vegetables to the casserole and cook over a high heat for 2-3 minutes. Turn down the heat and sprinkle over the flour. Cook, stirring, until golden.
5. Add the olives, veal bone and a little pepper. Pour over the stock and wine, which should cover all the ingredients. Cook for about 1½ hours.
6. Drain the cèpes and add to the casserole. Heat through gently. Discard the bone before serving.

Rognons de veau aux champignons
Kidneys with Mushrooms

| 00:10 | | 00:35 |
American	Ingredients	Metric/Imperial
6	Shallots	6
14 oz	Button mushrooms	400 g / 14 oz
6 tbsp	Butter	75 g / 3 oz
3	Calves' kidneys	3
¼ cup	Brandy	4 tbsp
7 tbsp	Crème fraîche	7 tbsp
	Salt and pepper	
2 tbsp	Dijon mustard	2 tbsp

1. Peel and finely chop the shallots. Coarsely chop the mushrooms. Melt 2 tablespoons [25 g / 1 oz] of the butter in a frying pan, add the shallots and mushrooms and cook over a moderate heat, stirring often, until all the liquid produced by the mushrooms has evaporated. Remove the vegetables and set aside.
2. Add another 2 tablespoons [25 g / 1 oz] butter to the frying pan with the kidneys. Cook for 10 minutes over a moderate heat, turning the kidneys over halfway through to brown evenly.
3. Remove the kidneys from the frying pan. Quarter them lengthwise and cut out the tubes and fatty core with a small pointed knife. Cut each piece of kidney into slices about ¼ in / 5 mm thick. Set aside.
4. Add the brandy to the frying pan and reduce to about 1½ tablespoons. Return the shallots and mushrooms and add the crème fraîche and salt and pepper to taste. Reduce by half over a high heat, stirring often.
5. Remove from the heat and stir in the mustard. Put the kidneys back in the pan and add the remaining butter. Stir to coat the kidney slices with the sauce. Heat through gently without boiling.

Longe de veau

Roast Loin of Veal with Kidneys

	00:05	01:15
	plus standing time	

American	Ingredients	Metric/Imperial
1 (3 lb)	Boneless loin of veal	1 (1.5 kg / 3 lb)
1 - 2	Calves' kidneys	1 - 2
	Salt and pepper	
1 ¼ cups	Water	300 ml / ½ pint

1. Ask your butcher to tie the veal up around the kidneys. Rub the roast all over with salt and pepper and set aside, at room temperature, for 1 hour.
2. Preheat the oven to 400°F / 200°C / Gas Mark 6.
3. Put the veal on a rack in a roasting pan and roast until one side is golden brown. Turn the meat over and pour half of the water into the pan. Continue roasting for 1 hour, basting the meat with the juices in the pan towards the end of the cooking time.
4. Turn off the oven and leave the meat inside for 10 minutes. (With an electric oven, open the door and leave it ajar.)
5. Slice the meat and keep hot. Place the roasting pan over a gentle heat on top of the stove and cook until the meat juices color slightly without burning. Add the remaining water and scrape the bottom of the pan with a wood spoon to dissolve the caramelized juices. Reduce the liquid by half. Add salt and pepper to taste.
6. Serve the gravy in a sauceboat with the sliced meat.

Noix de veau aux cèpes et à la crème

Braised Veal with Cèpes and Cream

	00:05	01:30
	plus soaking	

American	Ingredients	Metric/Imperial
2 tbsp	Oil	2 tbsp
¼ cup	Butter	50 g / 2 oz
1 (3 lb)	Veal round roast [topside or cushion], barded and tied	1 (1.5 kg / 3 lb)
2	Medium-size onions	2
	Salt and pepper	
1 ¼ cups	Dry white wine	300 ml / ½ pint
¼ lb	Dried cèpes	125 g / 4 oz
1 tsp	Cornstarch [cornflour]	1 tsp
1 tbsp	Cold water	1 tbsp
⅔ cup	Crème fraîche (see page 122)	150 ml / ¼ pint

1. Heat the oil and butter in a flameproof casserole, add the veal roast and seal all over for 10 minutes over a moderate heat. Remove the meat and set aside.
2. Peel and chop the onions. Add to the casserole and cook for 5 minutes over a gentle heat, stirring well with a wooden spoon to detach the meat residue from the bottom of the casserole.
3. Replace the meat in the casserole. Season with the salt and pepper and add the wine. Cook for 45 minutes over a low

heat, turning the meat occasionally and adding a few spoonfuls of water from time to time as necessary so that the meat does not dry out.
4. Meanwhile, rinse the cèpes well and soak in warm water to cover for 30 minutes. Drain and slice thinly.
5. Add the cèpes to the casserole and cook for another 45 minutes.
6. Remove the meat from the casserole and keep warm. Dissolve the cornstarch in the cold water and add to the casserole with the crème fraîche. Cook over a moderate heat for 2-3 minutes, stirring, until the sauce thickens. Remove from the heat.
7. Remove the string and barding fat from the meat and carve into slices about 1 in / ½ cm thick. Arrange the slices in a deep serving dish and pour over the hot sauce.

Langue de veau braisée

Braised Tongue

	00:20	02:00
	plus soaking and parboiling	

American	Ingredients	Metric/Imperial
1	Fresh or cured calf's tongue	1
6	Carrots	6
3	Onions	3
1	Celery stalk	1
2	Garlic cloves	2
1 tbsp	Tomato paste [purée]	1 tbsp
2 cups	Beef stock	500 ml / ¾ pint
¼ cup	Butter	50 g / 2 oz
½	Calf's foot	½
1 ¼ cups	White wine	300 ml / ½ pint
1	Bouquet garni	1
	Salt and pepper	
⅔ cup	Vinegar	150 ml / ¼ pint
1 tbsp	Sugar	1 tbsp
1 tbsp	Flour	1 tbsp

1. If using a cured tongue, soak it in cold water for 24 hours, changing the water frequently. Drain.
2. Place the tongue (cured or fresh) in a saucepan, cover with fresh cold water and bring to a boil. Simmer for 10-20 minutes, depending on size. Drain.
3. Preheat the oven to 425°F / 220°C / Gas Mark 7.
4. Peel and dice the carrots, onions and celery. Peel and crush the garlic. Mix the tomato paste with the stock.
5. Heat 3 tablespoons [40 g / 1½ oz] of the butter in a flameproof casserole, add the carrot, onion, celery and the half calf's foot and cook until golden brown. Pour over the wine and the stock mixed with the tomato paste. Add the garlic, bouquet garni and salt and pepper. Place the tongue in the casserole.
6. Bring to a boil over a high heat, then cover the casserole and transfer to the oven. Cook for about 2 hours or until the tongue is tender.
7. Meanwhile, boil the vinegar and sugar in a small saucepan to make a liquid caramel. Mix together the rest of the butter with the flour to a paste.
8. Remove the tongue and plunge it into cold water. Drain and peel off the skin. Trim off any bones and gristle. Slice the tongue and keep hot.
9. Strain the cooking liquid into a saucepan and add the butter/flour paste and vinegar caramel. Cook, stirring, for 5 minutes or until thickened. Add the slices of tongue and heat through for 2-3 minutes.

Braised tongue

Ragoût aux pois frais et à la menthe
Veal with Peas and Mint

	00:15		01:35

American	Ingredients	Metric/Imperial
2½ lb	Boneless breast of veal	1.25 kg / 2½ lb
1 (2 oz)	Slice of Canadian [back] bacon	1 (50 g / 2 oz)
½ lb	Young carrots	250 g / 8 oz
2	Onions	2
1	Garlic clove	1
3 tbsp	Oil	3 tbsp
	Salt and pepper	
⅔ cup	Water	150 ml / ¼ pint
2 lb	Fresh peas	1 kg / 2 lb
1 lb	Fresh lima or broad beans	500 g / 1 lb
1 tbsp	Fresh mint cut into strips	1 tbsp

1. Cut the veal into large cubes. Cut the bacon into matchstick strips. Peel and slice the carrots and onions. Peel the garlic but do not crush it.
2. Heat the oil in a flameproof casserole, add the bacon and brown for 5 minutes over a medium heat. Add the veal cubes and brown all over for about 5 minutes.
3. Add the carrots, onions and garlic. Season with salt and pepper. Pour the water into the casserole and cook for 45 minutes over a medium heat.
4. Meanwhile, shell the peas. Shell the beans, removing the thin inner skin.
5. Add the beans to the casserole and continue cooking for 10 minutes. Add the peas and mix well. Cover the casserole and continue cooking for 30 minutes.
6. Add the mint. Cover again and cook for a further 10 minutes.

Rognons de veau bercy
Kidneys in Bercy Sauce

	00:15		00:15

American	Ingredients	Metric/Imperial
3	Calves' kidneys	3
1 cup	Butter	250 g / 8 oz
	Salt and pepper	
10	Shallots	10
1½ cups	Dry white wine	350 ml / 12 fl oz
1	Lemon	1
3 tbsp	Chopped fresh parsley	3 tbsp

1. Quarter the kidneys lengthwise. Cut out the tubes and the fatty core with a sharp pointed knife. Cut each piece of kidney into slices about ½ in / 1 cm thick.
2. Melt half the butter in a frying pan, add the kidneys and cook for 5 minutes over a high heat, stirring, to brown the kidney slices on both sides. Season with salt and pepper, then remove from the frying pan and put to one side.
3. Peel and chop the shallots. Add to the frying pan and cook for 3 minutes over a moderate heat, stirring. Add the wine and reduce it until only about 3 tablespoons are left. Add the juice of the lemon and return the kidneys. Cook for 2-3 minutes, stirring often. Remove from the heat.
4. Cut the rest of the butter into small pieces and gradually add to the sauce, beating well with a whisk. Taste and adjust the seasoning.
5. Serve hot, sprinkled with the parsley.

Noix de veau au lait
Veal Cooked in Milk

	00:10 plus macerating		03:15

American	Ingredients	Metric/Imperial
1 (3 lb)	Veal round roast [topside or cushion]	1 (1.5 kg / 3 lb)
1 quart	Milk	1 l / 1¾ pints
4	Garlic cloves	4
2 tbsp	Butter	25 g / 1 oz
½ tsp	Grated nutmeg	½ tsp
	Salt and pepper	
3 tbsp	Madeira wine	3 tbsp

1. Do not have the veal barded or tied. Place it in a large bowl and cover with the milk. Refrigerate for 12 hours. If the milk does not completely cover the meat, turn it occasionally.
2. Preheat the oven to 375°F / 190°C / Gas Mark 5.
3. Peel the garlic. Butter the inside of a flameproof casserole and place the meat, garlic and milk in it. Bake for 1½ hours.
4. Reduce the oven temperature to 350°F / 180°C / Gas Mark 4. Turn the meat over and season with the nutmeg and salt and pepper to taste. Continue cooking for 1½ hours.
5. Remove the meat from the casserole and place it on a warmed serving dish. Keep hot. Add the madeira to the casserole and cook over a high heat on top of the stove for about 5 minutes, beating until the milk, which will have curdled during cooking, takes on the consistency of cream. The sauce should be smooth and velvety.
6. Cut the meat into thin slices and serve the sauce separately in a sauceboat.

Côtelettes d'agneau provençale
Provençal Lamb Chops

00:05 plus marinating		00:25

American	Ingredients	Metric/Imperial
⅔ cup	Olive oil	150 ml / ¼ pint
1 tbsp	Dried thyme	1 tbsp
12 (3 oz)	Lamb chops	12 (75 g / 3 oz)
3	Eggplant [aubergines]	3
	Salt	
6	Tomatoes	6
1	Garlic clove	1
3 tbsp	Chopped fresh parsley	3 tbsp

1. Mix the oil in a bowl with the thyme and leave to infuse for 1 hour.
2. Brush each chop with the herby oil and leave to marinate for 30 minutes.
3. Meanwhile, peel and thickly slice the eggplant. Lay them on paper towels, sprinkle with salt and leave to drain for 30 minutes. Rinse and pat dry, then dice.
4. Preheat the broiler [grill].
5. Heat 2 tablespoons of the herby oil in a frying pan, add the eggplant and cook over a low heat until golden, about 25 minutes. Stir occasionally.
6. Meanwhile, cut the tomatoes in half and remove the seeds. Sprinkle with a few drops of herby oil and set aside. Peel and chop the garlic.
7. Arrange the chops on the broiler rack and cook for 3-5 minutes on each side. Add the tomatoes when you turn the chops and cook until golden brown and softened.
8. Spoon the eggplant into the center of a warmed serving platter and sprinkle with the garlic and half of the parsley. Arrange the chops around the eggplant and garnish with the tomatoes. Sprinkle the tomatoes with the remaining parsley.

Épaule d'agneau farcie
Kidney-Stuffed Shoulder of Lamb

00:20		00:40

American	Ingredients	Metric/Imperial
1	Shallot	1
¼ lb	Cooked ham	125 g / 4 oz
2	Fresh thyme sprigs	2
1	Small bunch of fresh parsley	1
2	Small lamb's kidneys	2
¼	Butter	50 g / 2 oz
	Salt and pepper	
6	Small firm tomatoes	6
1 (2 lb)	Boneless shoulder of lamb with shank (knuckle) attached	1 (1 kg / 2 lb)

1. Preheat the oven to 425°F / 220°C / Gas Mark 7.
2. Peel the shallot. Put it through a food mill or grinder [mincer] with the ham, thyme and parsley.
3. Halve the kidneys and cut out the cores. Melt 2 tablespoons [25 g / 1 oz] of the butter in a frying pan, add the kidneys and

cook for 3-4 minutes without letting them brown. Sprinkle with salt and pepper. Remove from the pan.
4. Add the shallot and ham mixture to the pan and cook until softened, scraping up the residue. Season with salt and pepper.
5. Spread the ham mixture in the cavity in the shoulder of lamb. Arrange the kidneys on top in a single layer. Roll up the meat in a long roll and tie. Place in an ovenproof dish.
6. Peel the tomatoes (first plunging them in boiling water for 10 seconds). Sprinkle with salt and pepper and arrange them around the meat.
7. Roast for about 40 minutes.
8. Turn off the oven. Add the remaining butter and a few drops of water. Leave the meat inside for 8-10 minutes. (With an electric oven, open the door and leave it ajar.)
9. Serve carved in slices with the tomatoes and pan juices.

Épaule de mouton berrichonne
Stuffed Shoulder of Lamb with Puréed Vegetables

00:30		01:20

American	Ingredients	Metric/Imperial
2	Onions	2
1 tbsp	Oil	1 tbsp
1 cup	Fresh white bread crumbs	50 g / 2 oz
½ lb	Pork sausage meat	250 g / 8 oz
2 tbsp	Chopped fresh parsley	2 tbsp
1	Egg	1
1	Garlic clove	1
	Grated nutmeg	
	Salt and pepper	
1 (2 lb)	Boneless shoulder of lamb	1 (1 kg / 2 lb)
1	Celeriac	1
2	Turnips	2
3	Carrots	3
4	Leeks	4
1	Bouquet garni	1
3	Medium-size potatoes	3
1 tbsp	Butter	15 g / ½ oz

1. Peel and thinly slice one of the onions. Heat the oil in a frying pan, add the onion and cook until golden. Tip the onion into a mixing bowl. Set aside.
2. Soak the bread crumbs in hot water for 2-3 minutes. Drain the bread crumbs and squeeze with your fingers to remove excess water. Add the bread to the bowl.
3. Add the sausage meat, parsley and egg. Peel and chop the garlic and add it. Season with a pinch of nutmeg and salt and pepper to taste. Mix well together.
4. Lay the lamb out on a working surface. Spread with the stuffing and roll up the meat. Tie into shape with string. Place the meat in a flameproof casserole and cover with water. Bring to a boil.
5. Meanwhile, peel and dice the celeriac, turnips and carrots. Finely chop the leeks. Peel and thinly slice the remaining onion. When the water in the casserole has reached boiling point, add all the vegetables and the bouquet garni. Season with salt and pepper. Simmer gently over a low heat for 1 hour.
6. Peel and dice the potatoes. Add to the casserole and simmer for 20 minutes longer.

7. Remove the vegetables from the casserole with a slotted spoon and purée them in a blender or food processor until coarse-fine. Do not blend until smooth. Reheat this purée in a saucepan over a very gentle heat, adding the butter in small pieces.
8. Drain the lamb and cut it into medium thick slices. Remove the string. Arrange the meat on a warmed serving platter and surround with the vegetable purée.

Épaule d'agneau en gigot
Shoulder of Lamb 'Leg-of-Mutton' Style

00:10   00:40

American	Ingredients	Metric/Imperial
1	Garlic clove	1
1	Boneless shoulder of lamb with the shank [knuckle] attached	1
¼ cup	Butter	50 g / 2 oz
	Salt and pepper	
1 tbsp	Boiling water	1 tbsp

1. Preheat the oven to 475°F / 250°C / Gas Mark 9. Preheat the broiler [grill].
2. Peel the garlic and cut into slices. With a small pointed knife, prick the meat here and there, sliding in a piece of garlic along the knife blade at each incision. Spread 1 tablespoon [15 g / ½ oz] of the butter all over the meat and sprinkle with salt and pepper.
3. Place the meat on a rack in a roasting pan. Put it in the oven and roast for 15 minutes, then transfer to the broiler, placing the meat as far as possible from the heat. Cook for 25 minutes, turning occasionally to brown evenly.
4. Remove the meat from the heat and leave to rest for 8 minutes.
5. Carve the meat, and pour the juices produced back into the roasting pan. Add the boiling water and then the rest of the butter, beating well. Heat gently.
6. Serve the meat with the gravy.

Shoulder of lamb 'leg-of-mutton' style

Épaule d'agneau rôtie
Roast Shoulder of Lamb with Herbs

00:20 plus seasoning   00:40

American	Ingredients	Metric/Imperial
1 (2 lb)	Boneless shoulder of lamb, rolled and tied	1 (1 kg / 2 lb)
	Salt and pepper	
2	Bay leaves	2
3	Fresh thyme sprigs	3
3	Fresh rosemary sprigs	3
⅓ cup	Water	5 tbsp
¼ cup	Butter	50 g / 2 oz

1. Sprinkle the meat with salt and pepper. Slide the bay leaf and thyme and rosemary sprigs under the string tying the meat.
2. Preheat the oven to 425°F / 220°C / Gas Mark 7.
3. Place the lamb on a rack in a roasting pan. Roast about 20 minutes, then turn the meat over. Add the water to the roasting pan and continue cooking for 20 minutes.
4. Turn off the oven and leave the lamb inside for 5 minutes. (With an electric oven, open the door and leave it ajar.)
5. Carve the meat, and pour the juices produced back into the roasting pan. Add 1 tablespoon of hot water and bring to a boil on top of the stove, scraping up the caramelized meat residue from the bottom of the pan. Reduce by half, then add the butter, stirring with a whisk to incorporate well.
6. Serve the meat with the gravy.

Épaule de mouton aux olives
Shoulder of Lamb with Olives

00:15   01:00

American	Ingredients	Metric/Imperial
1	Boneless shoulder of lamb, barded and tied	1 (1 kg / 2 lb)
	Salt and pepper	
3	Onions	3
4	Carrots	4
3 tbsp	Oil	3 tbsp
1	Bay leaf	1
1	Fresh thyme sprig	1
2	Cloves	2
⅔ cup	Hot water	150 ml / ¼ pint
¾ cup	Green olives	125 g / 4 oz

1. Sprinkle the meat with salt and pepper. Peel and thinly slice the onions and carrots.
2. Heat the oil in a flameproof casserole, add the meat and brown for 5 minutes on each side. Add the carrots, onions, bay leaf, thyme, cloves, and salt and pepper to taste. Add the hot water and mix the vegetables together well. Cover and cook over a medium heat for 30 minutes.
3. Meanwhile, plunge the olives into boiling water, then drain.
4. Add the olives to the casserole and cook over a gentle heat for 30 minutes longer.
5. Carve the meat into slices and serve with the vegetables and gravy.

Navarin de mouton
Lamb and Vegetable Stew

| | 00:15 | 01:30 to 02:00 |

American	Ingredients	Metric/Imperial
3 lb	Boneless shoulder of lamb	1.5 kg / 3 lb
2 tbsp	Flour	2 tbsp
¼ lb	Small onions	125 g / 4 oz
2 tbsp	Lard or goose fat	2 tbsp
⅔ cup	Dry white wine	150 ml / ¼ pint
1	Bouquet garni	1
	Grated nutmeg	
	Salt and pepper	
¾ lb	Fresh peas	350 g / 12 oz
½ lb	Green beans	250 g / 8 oz
1 lb	Carrots	500 g / 1 lb

1. Cut the lamb into 1½ in / 2 cm cubes and coat with the flour. Peel the onions.
2. Melt the lard or goose fat in a flameproof casserole, add the lamb and brown all over without letting the fat burn. Pour in the wine, then add the onions, bouquet garni, a pinch of nutmeg, and salt and pepper to taste. Cover. When the liquid comes to a boil, turn down the heat and simmer very gently for about 45 minutes.
3. Shell the peas. Trim the beans and remove strings if necessary. Peel the carrots.
4. Add the vegetables to the casserole and cook, covered, for 30 minutes longer over a very low heat.

Gigot aux légumes nouveaux
Leg of Lamb with Spring Vegetables

| | 01:00 | 01:00 |

American	Ingredients	Metric/Imperial
1	Garlic clove	1
1 (3 lb)	Leg of lamb	1 (1.5 kg / 3 lb)
2 tbsp	Oil	2 tbsp
	Salt and pepper	
1	Bouquet garni	1
1 lb	Small white turnips	500 g / 1 lb
2	Medium-size cucumbers	2
1 lb	Carrots	500 g / 1 lb
¾ lb	Small green beans	350 g / 12 oz
1	Small bunch of celery	1
1 lb	Fresh peas	500 g / 1 lb
1¼ lb	Potatoes	625 g / 1¼ lb
¾ lb	Onions	350 g / 12 oz
¼ cup	Butter	50 g / 2 oz

1. Peel the garlic and cut into small slivers. Prick the meat with a small pointed knife, sliding in a piece of garlic along the knife blade at each incision.
2. Heat 1 tablespoon of the oil in a flameproof casserole, add the lamb and brown all over. Sprinkle with salt and pepper and

add the bouquet garni. Cover and cook for 45-55 minutes.
3. Meanwhile, peel the turnips. Peel the cucumbers and carrots. Trim the beans and remove strings, if necessary. Cut all the vegetables, as well as the celery, into small dice. Shell the peas. Cook the vegetables separately in boiling salted water until tender but still firm: allow 10 minutes for the turnips, 10-15 minutes for the celery, 5 minutes for the cucumber, 10 minutes for the carrots, 20-25 minutes for the peas, and 5-10 minutes for the beans. Drain and set aside.
4. Peel and dice the potatoes. Peel and finely chop the onions. Heat 1 tablespoon [15 g / ½ oz] butter and the rest of the oil in a frying pan, add the potatoes and onions and cook gently for about 15 minutes.
5. Preheat the oven to 450°F / 230°C / Gas Mark 8.
6. Transfer the lamb to a roasting pan and roast for 10-12 minutes. Skim off and reserve the fat from the cooking liquid in the casserole. Use this fat to baste the lamb once or twice while it is roasting.
7. Put all the vegetables in the casserole with the cooking liquid from the meat. Add the rest of the butter and mix well. Cover and reheat quickly. Discard the bouquet garni, and season with salt and pepper.
8. Serve the meat sliced and surrounded by the vegetables.

Méchoui
Spit-Roasted Whole Lamb

| | 00:45 | 05:00 |

plus lighting fire and marinating
Serves 15–20

according to the size of the lamb

American	Ingredients	Metric/Imperial
2	Garlic bulbs	2
1	Fat lamb (without head)	1
12	Dried hot peppers [chillies]	12
10	Black peppercorns	10
	Sea salt	
1	Large bunch of fresh mint	1
4	Lemons	4
1½ cups	Melted butter	350 g / 12 oz
1 cup	Olive oil	250 ml / 8 fl oz
6 tbsp	Dried oregano	6 tbsp
¼ cup	Harissa or other hot chili-based sauce	4 tbsp
2 tbsp	Black pepper	2 tbsp
3 tbsp	Dried mint	3 tbsp
2 tbsp	Salt	2 tbsp

1. Peel all the cloves of one bulb of garlic and place inside the lamb, together with the hot peppers, peppercorns, a handful of sea salt and the bunch of fresh mint.
2. Peel all the cloves of the other bulb of garlic and crush them. Grate the rind from the lemons and squeeze out the juice. In a large bowl, combine the melted butter with the oil, crushed garlic, lemon rind and juice, oregano, harissa, black pepper, dried mint and 2 tablespoons of salt. Mix very well.
3. Brush the lamb with the lemon mixture and leave to marinate for 2 hours.
4. Meanwhile, prepare the barbecue: dig a hole in the ground 3 ft / 1 m long, 20 in / 50 cm wide and 16 in / 40 cm deep. Fill the hole with wood, either on its own or mixed with charcoal, and light the fire. Leave to burn until reduced to embers.
5. Tie the lamb firmly to a rotisserie spit, with its fore and hind

legs well stretched out. Place over the fire and cook the lamb, turning it constantly and basting with the lemon mixture. To check whether the lamb is cooked, insert a skewer — the juice which runs out should be clear, not pink.
6. Take the lamb off the spit and lay it on a large board. Carve it or let your guests help themselves.

Lamb-chop
Lamb Chops with Herb Butter

00:05   00:05 to 00:10

American	Ingredients	Metric/Imperial
½ cup	Butter, at room temperature	125 g / 4 oz
2 tbsp	Chopped fresh herbs (chives, parsley, tarragon)	2 tbsp
1	Garlic clove	1
6 (5 oz)	Thin lamb loin double chops	6 (150 g / 5 oz)
	Salt and pepper	

1. Mash all but 2 tablespoons (25 g / 1 oz) of the butter with the herbs and peeled and crushed garlic. Chill until firm.
2. Melt the remaining butter in a large frying pan. Add the chops to the pan — in one layer — and cook for 5-10 minutes according to taste, turning over halfway through. Keep a close eye on how the 'tails' of the chops are cooking; they should not be cooked as much as the thicker meat.
3. Arrange the chops on a warmed serving dish. Sprinkle with salt and pepper and top each chop with a spoonful of the seasoned butter. Serve hot.

Haricot de mouton
Lamb with White Beans

00:15 plus soaking   02:30

American	Ingredients	Metric/Imperial
3 cups	Dried navy (haricot) beans	750 g / 1½ lb
2½ lb	Boneless shoulder of lamb	1.25 kg / 2½ lb
2	Carrots	2
2	Onions	2
2	Garlic cloves	2
¼ cup	Lard or goose fat	50 g / 2 oz
1	Bouquet garni	1
	Salt and pepper	

1. Soak the beans overnight in cold water to cover.
2. Drain the beans and place them in a saucepan. Cover with fresh cold water. Bring to a boil and simmer for about 2 hours or until the beans are tender.
3. Meanwhile cut the lamb into 1 in / 2.5 cm cubes. Peel and slice the carrots and onions. Peel the garlic.
4. Heat the lard in a flameproof casserole, add the lamb cubes and brown on all sides. Add the carrots, onions, garlic and bouquet garni. Cover and simmer over a very low heat for 1 hour.

5. Drain the beans, reserving their cooking liquid. Add them to the meat and moisten with a few spoonfuls of the reserved cooking liquid. Season with salt and pepper. Cover and simmer for 15 minutes longer. Serve very hot.

Mixed grill
Mixed Grill

00:15   00:40

American	Ingredients	Metric/Imperial
½ cup	Butter	125 g / 4 oz
6	Small lamb rib chops	6
6 (3 - 4 oz)	Slices of calves' liver	6 (75 - 100 g / 3 - 4 oz)
6	Lambs' kidneys	6
6	Small sausages	6
3	Small tomatoes	3
6	Small button mushrooms	6
	Lemon juice	
	Salt and pepper	

1. Heat 3 tablespoons [40 g / 1½ oz] butter in each of two frying pans. Add the chops, slices of liver, kidneys, sausages and halved tomatoes and sauté quickly until browned but not cooked through. Remove from the heat.
2. Heat the rest of the butter in a saucepan, add the mushrooms and sprinkle with a few drops of lemon juice and salt and pepper to taste. Cook until all the liquid they produce has evaporated, stirring from time to time. Remove from the heat.
3. Preheat the broiler [grill].
4. To make serving easier, you could thread all the ingredients onto skewers in the following order: lamb chop, liver, kidney, sausage, mushroom. Sprinkle with salt and pepper.
5. Place the 'kebabs' under the broiler and cook for a few minutes. When one side starts to sizzle, turn them over. Heat through the tomato halves. Serve very hot.

Sauté d'agneau de lait
Sautéed Lamb with Parsley

00:10   00:45

American	Ingredients	Metric/Imperial
2½ lb	Boneless shoulder of baby lamb	1.2 kg / 2½ lb
¼ cup	Butter	50 g / 2 oz
1	Small bunch of fresh parsley	1
2	Garlic cloves	2
	Salt and pepper	

1. Cut the lamb into pieces. Melt the butter in a heavy frying pan, add the pieces of lamb and brown, without burning the butter, for about 20 minutes.
2. Meanwhile, chop the parsley. Peel and chop the garlic.
3. Add the parsley and the garlic to the pan. Season with salt and pepper. Cover and cook over a very low heat for about 25 minutes, stirring from time to time.

Aspic au jambon
Ham in Aspic

American	Ingredients	Metric/Imperial
¼ lb	Fresh peas	125 g / 4 oz
	Salt	
3	Hard-cooked eggs	3
2 cups	Aspic (see page 116)	500 ml / ¾ pint
½ lb	Prunes	250 g / 8 oz
12	Stuffed green olives	12
1 lb	Cooked ham	500 g / 1 lb

1. Shell the peas. Cook in boiling salted water for 15 minutes or until tender. Drain and set aside.
2. Shell the eggs. Dice the whites and mash the yolks.
3. Pour some of the liquid aspic into a decorative 1½ quart [1.5 l / 2½ pint] mold. Chill for 15 minutes or until set.
4. Meanwhile, remove the pits [stones] from the prunes with a small pointed knife. Quarter the prunes lengthwise.
5. Arrange 6 olives, 3 tablespoons of the peas and the diced white of one of the eggs on the layer of aspic in the mold. Cover with more aspic and chill for another 15 minutes.
6. Meanwhile, cut the ham into small dice.
7. As soon as the second layer of aspic has set well, layer the ham, remaining olives, remaining peas, the prunes, remaining egg whites and the mashed egg yolks in the mold. Cover with the rest of the aspic, and chill for 6 hours.
8. To serve, unmold onto a serving dish.

Andouillettes grillées sauce moutarde
Broiled [Grilled] Sausages with Mustard Sauce

American	Ingredients	Metric/Imperial
6	Andouillettes or other small cooked pork sausages	6
3 tbsp	Oil	3 tbsp
2	Fresh tarragon sprigs	2
¾ cup	Butter	175 g / 6 oz
3 tbsp	Strong prepared mustard	3 tbsp
3 tbsp	Lemon juice or wine vinegar	3 tbsp
	Salt and pepper	

1. Preheat the broiler [grill].
2. Brush the sausages with the oil. Do not prick them, but lay them on the rack of the broiler pan and cook for 20 minutes, turning to brown evenly.
3. About 5 minutes before the end of cooking, remove the leaves from the tarragon sprigs and chop them. Cut the butter into small pieces. Mix the mustard and lemon juice or vinegar together in a small saucepan and heat gently, stirring. When the mixture boils, add the pieces of butter. Continue stirring over a low heat without boiling. Add the tarragon and salt and pepper to taste and mix well. Pour into a sauceboat.
4. Serve the sausages with the sauce.

Andouille à la purée
Sausage with Creamed Potatoes

American	Ingredients	Metric/Imperial
½ lb	Andouille or other large cooked pork sausage	250 g / 8 oz
8	Medium-size potatoes	8
3 tbsp	Crème fraîche (see page 122)	3 tbsp
	Salt and pepper	
1	Small bunch of fresh parsley	1
2 tbsp	Dry bread crumbs	2 tbsp
2 tbsp	Butter	25 g / 1 oz

1. Cut the sausage into thin slices and remove the skin. Set aside.
2. Peel the potatoes and put them in a saucepan of cold water. Bring to a boil and cook for 20 minutes.
3. Preheat the oven to 425°F / 220°C / Gas Mark 7.
4. Drain the potatoes, then purée them using a potato ricer or food mill, or mash them. Add the crème fraîche and salt and pepper to taste. Chop the parsley. Add to the potato purée and mix in well.
5. Spread a layer of the potato purée on the bottom of a deep ovenproof dish. Cover with a layer of sausage slices, then add another layer of potato. Continue making layers until the ingredients are used up, finishing with a layer of potato.
6. Sprinkle with the bread crumbs and dot with the butter. Bake for 10 minutes or until the top is browned.

Boudin blanc aux pommes
White Sausage with Apples

American	Ingredients	Metric/Imperial
6	Apples	6
6 tbsp	Butter	75 g / 3 oz
2 tbsp	Sugar	2 tbsp
6	Boudins blancs (white pork and poultry sausage or pudding)	6
	Salt and pepper	

1. Peel the apples. Cut each into 8 wedges and remove the core and seeds. Heat half of the butter in a frying pan, add the apples and cook for a few minutes over a moderate heat. Sprinkle with the sugar and cook over a gentle heat for a further 10 minutes or until golden. Keep warm.
2. Remove all the skin from the sausages. Melt the rest of the butter in a large frying pan over a gentle heat. Lay the puddings in the pan side by side and cook very gently until golden (without the skin, white sausages do not color so much). Turn very carefully using two spatulas, and cook the other side. Sprinkle with salt and pepper during cooking.
3. Serve the sausages with the apples.

Andouillettes à l'échalote
Sausages with Shallots

	00:05		00:20

American	Ingredients	Metric/Imperial
2 tbsp	Lard or	25 g / 1 oz
2 tbsp	Oil	2 tbsp
6	Andouillettes or other small cooked pork sausages	6
3	Shallots	3
2	Lemons	2
	Salt and pepper	

1. Preheat the oven to 350°F / 180°C / Gas Mark 4.
2. Heat the lard or oil in a frying pan, add the andouillettes and brown all over on a medium heat, for 20 minutes. Drain and arrange on a warmed serving dish. Keep hot.
3. Peel and chop the shallots. Add to the frying pan and cook until soft and translucent. Add the juice of the lemons and salt and pepper to taste. Cook over a high heat, stirring well to scrape the sausage drippings from the bottom of the pan.
4. Pour this sauce over the sausages and serve immediately.

Carré de porc aux fruits
Loin of Pork with Fruit

	00:15		01:20

American	Ingredients	Metric/Imperial
½ cup	Butter	125 g / 4 oz
1 (2½ lb)	Pork loin (center cut)	1 (1.25 kg / 2½ lb)
	Salt and pepper	
	Cayenne pepper	
4	Fresh sage leaves	4
6	Apples	6
	Ground cinnamon	
3	Bananas	3
3 tbsp	Rum	3 tbsp
6	Canned pineapple rings with syrup	6

1. Heat 2 tablespoons [25 g / 1 oz] of the butter in a flameproof casserole, add the pork and brown all over. Season with salt and pepper to taste and a pinch of cayenne pepper. Add the sage leaves and 1 tablespoon water and cook, covered, over a gentle heat for about 1½ hours, adding a little more water during cooking if necessary.
2. Meanwhiie, peel the apples and cut into quarters. Remove the core and seeds. Heat 3 tablespoons [40 g / 1½ oz] of the butter in a frying pan, add the apples and cook, covered, over a gentle heat until golden. Sprinkle with a little cinnamon.
3. Peel the bananas and cut in half lengthwise. Heat the rest of the butter in another frying pan, add the banana halves and cook, covered, over a gentle heat until golden. Keep the bananas and apples warm.
4. When the meat is cooked, pour over the rum and set it alight. Lift up the meat so that the flame burns all over it. Transfer the meat to a warmed serving dish and surround with the apples, bananas and pineapple slices. Keep hot.

5. Pour ⅔ cup [150 ml / ¼ pint] pineapple syrup into the casserole and bring to a boil, scraping the bottom of the casserole with a wooden spatula. Reduce by half. Pour into a sauceboat and serve with the pork.

Cook's tip: in summer, you could use peaches instead of apples and bananas. Canned pineapple could be replaced by fresh pineapple cubes, sprinkled with sugar and fried in butter, or, if you want to be really original, cubes of fresh or canned mango.

Andouillettes au four
Baked Sausages

	00:05		00:30

American	Ingredients	Metric/Imperial
3 tbsp	Butter	40 g / 1½ oz
6	Andouillettes or other small cooked pork sausages	6
3	Shallots	3
2 cups	Dry white wine	450 ml / ¾ pint
	Salt and pepper	

1. Preheat the oven to 425°F / 220°C / Gas Mark 7.
2. Heat half the butter in a frying pan, add the sausages and brown quickly on all sides.
3. Meanwhile, peel and chop the shallots. Heat the remaining butter in a saucepan, add the shallots and cook until softened. Do not let them burn.
4. Lay the sausages in an ovenproof dish and add their cooking liquid, the shallots and the wine. Season with salt and pepper. Bake for 20 minutes, turning them over once.
5. Remove the sausages to a warmed serving dish and keep hot. Pour the cooking liquid into a saucepan and boil to reduce by two-thirds. Pour this sauce over the sausages.

Loin of pork with fruit

Cervelat [Saveloys] with Spinach

Cervelas aux épinards

	00:20		00:15

American	Ingredients	Metric/Imperial
6	Medium-size cervelat [saveloys] or other smoked cooked pork sausage	6
1 tbsp	Oil	1 tbsp
2 lb	Fresh spinach or	1 kg / 2 lb
14 oz	Frozen spinach	400 g / 14 oz
	Salt and pepper	
¼ cup	Butter	50 g / 2 oz
6	Eggs	6

1. Split the sausages ¾ of the way through their thickness. Heat the oil in a frying pan, add the sausages and heat gently for 10 minutes.
2. Meanwhile, remove the stalks from fresh spinach and cook in boiling salted water for 10 minutes. Drain and squeeze to extract all excess water. Chop the spinach. (Cook frozen spinach according to the instructions on the package.)
3. Heat 2 tablespoons [25 g / 1 oz] of the butter in a saucepan, add the spinach and heat through over a very low heat.
4. Meanwhile, break the eggs into a mixing bowl and beat for a few seconds with a fork. Season with salt and pepper. Melt the rest of the butter in a saucepan, add the eggs and cook over a very gentle heat, stirring, until the eggs are lightly scrambled.
5. Spoon the spinach into the center of a warmed serving dish. Surround with the sausages and fill them with scrambled eggs where they have been split down the middle. Serve very hot.

Blood Sausage [Black Puddings] with Creamed Potatoes

Boudin mousseline

	00:05		00:25

American	Ingredients	Metric/Imperial
4 lb	Potatoes	2 kg / 4 lb
	Salt and pepper	
6	Boudins noirs (blood sausages or black puddings)	6
⅔ cup	Boiling milk	150 ml / ¼ pint
½ cup	Butter	125 g / 4 oz
	Grated nutmeg	
	Prepared mustard	

1. Preheat the oven to 425°F / 220°C / Gas Mark 7.
2. Scrub the potatoes and cook them in boiling salted water for 20 minutes.
3. Meanwhile, prick the sausages with the point of a knife and lay them on the rack of a roasting pan. Bake for 20 minutes.
4. Drain the potatoes, peel them and return to the saucepan. Mash with a potato masher. Gradually beat the boiling milk

into the potatoes over a gentle heat. Add the butter, a large pinch of nutmeg and salt and pepper to taste. Beat the purée over the heat until piping hot.
5. Put the potatoes in the center of a warmed serving dish and arrange the sausages all around. Serve with the mustard.

Sausages in White Wine

Andouillettes à la lyonnaise

	00:10		00:20 to 00:30

American	Ingredients	Metric/Imperial
6 tbsp	Butter	75 g / 3 oz
6	Andouillettes or other small cooked pork sausages	6
¾	Bottle of dry white wine	¾

1. Preheat the oven to 450°F / 230°C / Gas Mark 8.
2. Generously grease an ovenproof dish with 2 tablespoons [25 g / 1 oz] of the butter and arrange the sausages in it. Cut the rest of the butter into small pieces and scatter these over the sausages. Pour ¼ of the wine over the sausages.
3. Bake for 20-30 minutes, gradually adding the rest of the white wine.
4. Serve the sausages in the ovenproof dish.

Pork Loin Charentaise

Filet de porc charentaise

	00:10 plus marinating		02:30

American	Ingredients	Metric/Imperial
½	Sugar cube	½
1 tbsp	Sea salt	1 tbsp
1 tsp	Black peppercorns	1 tsp
	Ground allspice	
1	Fresh thyme sprig	1
1	Bay leaf	1
⅓ cup	Brandy	5 tbsp
1 (2½ lb)	Boneless loin of pork, bones reserved	1 (1.25 kg / 2½ lb)
1	Onion	1
1	Carrot	1
1 quart	Hot water	1 l / 1¾ pints
	Salt and pepper	

1. Put the sugar, sea salt and peppercorns in a mortar and crush with the pestle. Put these spices in a mixing bowl. Add a pinch of allspice, leaves from the thyme sprig, bay leaf, crumbled, and the brandy. Put the meat in a dish and rub all over with this mixture; leave it to marinate for 12 hours.
2. Preheat the broiler [grill].
3. Peel and chop the onion and carrot. Put them with the pork bones and brown for 10 minutes under the broiler.
4. Transfer the bones and vegetables to a flameproof casserole. Add the meat. Pour over the hot water and season with salt and pepper. Simmer for 1 hour.
5. Preheat the oven to 425°F / 220°C / Gas Mark 7.
6. Drain the meat, reserving the stock, and place on a rack in a roasting pan. Roast for about 1½ hours, basting frequently with the strained stock.

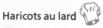

Haricots au lard

Bacon with White Beans

▿ 00:20 plus soaking		02:30 to 03:00 🍲

American	Ingredients	Metric/Imperial
2 cups	Dried navy [haricot] beans	500 g / 1 lb
1 (1½ lb)	Piece of bacon	1 (750 g / 1½ lb)
2	Onions	2
2	Tomatoes	2
1 tbsp	Lard	15 g / ½ oz
1	Bouquet garni	1
1	Garlic clove	1
	Salt and pepper	

1. Soak the beans in cold water to cover for 1 hour. Drain and place in a saucepan. Cover with fresh cold water, bring to a boil and simmer for 45 minutes over a low heat.
2. Meanwhile, put the bacon in a saucepan, cover with cold water and bring to a boil. Simmer for 5 minutes, the drain and set aside.
3. Peel and thinly slice the onions. Peel the tomatoes (first plunging them in boiling water for 10 seconds), remove the seeds and chop.
4. Add the bacon and bouquet garni. Peel and crush the garlic and add. Cover with boiling water. Cook, covered, for 45 minutes over a low heat.
5. Drain the beans, reserving the cooking liquid, and add to the tomato sauce. Add enough of the cooking liquid from the beans just to cover them. Cover and simmer for 1 hour. Add a little more of the liquid from the beans from time to time, so that they are always covered. At the end of the cooking period, boil to reduce the liquid.
6. Remove the bacon and cut it into thin slices. Arrange on a warmed serving dish.
7. Season the beans with salt and pepper and pour over the bacon.

Roast pork loin

Filet de porc rôti

Roast Pork Loin

This roast is cooked by first simmering in flavored water, then roasting in the oven. With this method, only about 10% of the weight of the meat is lost (as opposed to about 20% at least if cooked only in the oven), and results in very tender, juicy meat.

▿ 00:10		01:15 🍲

American	Ingredients	Metric/Imperial
2	Carrots	2
4	Shallots	4
4	Garlic cloves	4
2	Onions	2
1	Bouquet garni	1
3	Bay leaves	3
	Salt and pepper	
1 (2½ lb)	Boneless loin of pork	1 (1.25 kg / 2½ lb)
1 tbsp	Butter	15 g / ½ oz

1. Peel the carrots, shallots, garlic and onions. Slice the onions. Place the prepared vegetables in a casserole in which the meat will fit comfortably. Just cover these ingredients with water and add the bouquet garni, bay leaves, and salt and pepper to taste. Simmer for 10 minutes.
2. Add the meat and simmer for 45 minutes longer, turning the meat over halfway through.
3. Preheat the oven to 425°F / 220°C / Gas Mark 7.
4. Remove the casserole from the heat and cool for 5 minutes. Drain the meat and place it on a rack in a roasting pan. Roast for 20 minutes.
5. To serve, carve the meat, retaining all the juices. Add these juices to those in the roasting pan, together with the butter, to make a gravy.

Cook's tip: roast pork is just as delicious cold, so you could cook enough for two meals.

Jambon à la bourguignonne

Burgundy Ham

▿ 00:15		00:25 🍲

American	Ingredients	Metric/Imperial
6	Slices of cooked ham	6
2	Shallots	2
¼ cup	Butter	50 g / 2 oz
⅔ cup	Dry white wine	150 ml / ¼ pint
2 tbsp	Vinegar	2 tbsp
1 cup	Crème fraîche	250 ml / 8 fl oz
1 tbsp	Tomato paste [purée]	1 tbsp
1	Egg yolk	1
	Grated nutmeg	
	Salt and pepper	

1. Lay the slices of ham on a gratin dish or other flameproof serving dish. Set aside.
2. Peel and finely chop the shallots. Melt the butter in a saucepan, add the shallots and cook until golden brown. Add the wine and vinegar. Boil to reduce until only 3 tablespoons of liquid remain.
3. Add the crème fraîche and tomato paste. Heat through,

then add the egg yolk, a pinch of nutmeg and salt and pepper to taste. Cook, stirring with a whisk, until you have a smooth sauce. Do not boil.
4. Strain this sauce over the ham. Heat gently for 20 minutes. Do not allow to boil. Serve in the cooking dish.

Côtes de porc à la moutarde

Pork Chops with Mustard

◁	00:05		00:30 🍲
American	**Ingredients**		**Metric/Imperial**
½ cup	Crème fraîche (see page 122)		125 ml / 4 fl oz
3 tbsp	Prepared mustard		3 tbsp
1 tbsp	Capers		1 tbsp
¼ cup	Butter		50 g / 2 oz
6 (6 oz)	Pork chops		6 (175 g / 6 oz)
	Salt and pepper		

1. Mix the crème fraîche with the mustard and capers. Set aside.
2. Melt the butter in a large frying pan, add the pork chops and cook for 7-8 minutes on each side. Sprinkle with salt and pepper.
3. Pour the mustard sauce over the chops. Reduce the heat, cover and cook over a low heat for 10-12 minutes. Serve hot.

Jambon à la crème

Ham with Rich Cream Sauce

◁	00:10		00:25 🍲
American	**Ingredients**		**Metric/Imperial**
⅔ cup	Dry white wine		150 ml / ¼ pint
⅔ cup	Chicken stock		150 ml / ¼ pint
6	Medium-thick slices of cooked ham		6
5 oz	Button mushrooms		150 g / 5 oz
¾ cup	Crème fraîche		175 ml / 6 fl oz
	Salt and pepper		
2	Egg yolks		2
½	Lemon		½

1. Heat the wine and stock together in a deep frying pan. Add the ham slices and heat through very gently for 15-20 minutes.
2. Meanwhile, thinly slice the mushrooms. Put the crème fraîche in a saucepan and bring to a boil. Add the mushroom slices and cook for 5 minutes. Season with salt and pepper. Add the cooking liquid from the ham and remove from the heat.
3. Beat the egg yolks in a large bowl. Pour 1 tablespoon of the hot sauce over the eggs, beating constantly with a whisk. Add half of the sauce, still stirring. Finally add this mixture to the rest of the sauce in the pan. Put on a low heat and stir until thick, but do not allow to boil. Add the juice of the ½ lemon.
4. Arrange the slices of ham on a warmed serving dish and pour over the hot sauce. Serve immediately.

Jambon au champagne

Ham with Champagne Sauce

◁	00:30 plus soaking		03:00 🍲 Serves 10-12
American	**Ingredients**		**Metric/Imperial**
1 (6½ lb)	Piece uncooked country ham		1 (3 kg / 6½ lb)
2	Shallots		2
2	Onions		2
2	Garlic cloves		2
2	Carrots		2
1	Bouquet garni		1
1	Bottle of brut champagne		1
	Confectioners' [icing] sugar		
1 tbsp	Potato starch or flour or cornstarch [cornflour]		1 tbsp
1 tsp	Tomato paste [purée]		1 tsp
	Salt and pepper		

1. Soak the ham for 18-24 hours in cold water to cover, to remove excess salt, changing the water 2 or 3 times. Drain.
2. Peel the shallots, onions, garlic cloves and carrots. Place them in a large flameproof casserole, add the ham and bouquet garni, and cover with cold water. Cover, bring to a boil over a moderate heat and simmer for 1½ hours.
3. Preheat the oven to 425°F / 220°C / Gas Mark 7.
4. Drain the ham, discarding the cooking liquid and vegetables. Remove the rind and excess fat from the ham. Put the ham back in the casserole and pour over the champagne. Place in the oven and cook for 1-1½ hours, basting frequently. The ham will be cooked when the small shank [knuckle] bone can be pulled out but offers a slight resistance.
5. Remove the ham from the casserole. Place it in a roasting pan and sprinkle it with confectioners' [icing] sugar. Increase the oven temperature to 450°F / 230°C / Gas Mark 8, return the ham to the oven and cook until it is golden.
6. Meanwhile, boil to reduce the champagne in the casserole. Add the potato starch or cornstarch, dissolved in 1 tablespoon cold water, and the tomato paste and stir well. Taste the sauce and adjust the seasoning.
7. Serve the ham carved into slices, with a little sauce poured over. Serve the rest of the sauce in a sauceboat.

Ham with champagne sauce

Grillades de porc

Grilled Pork Steaks

	00:05 plus seasoning	00:15

American	Ingredients	Metric/Imperial
6 (6 oz)	Boneless pork chops or steaks	6 (175 g / 6 oz)
2 tbsp	Oil	2 tbsp
	Salt and pepper	

1. Trim all the fat from the meat and score the surface. Brush each side with oil and sprinkle with salt and pepper. Set aside for 1 hour.
2. Heat a steak or chop grill [griddle] over a moderate heat.
3. Place the steaks on the hot grill and cook for 10-15 minutes, turning over halfway through.

Échine de porc bourbonnaise

Roast Pork with Cabbage and Chestnuts

	00:20	01:20

American	Ingredients	Metric/Imperial
1	Red cabbage	1
2	Garlic cloves	2
1 (3 lb)	Boneless pork blade Boston roast [spare rib]	1 (1.5 kg / 3 lb)
	Salt and pepper	
1 (½ lb)	Piece of lightly salted bacon	1 (250 g / 8 oz)
6 tbsp	Butter	75 g / 3 oz
1	Bouquet garni	1
1 cup	Red wine	250 ml / 8 fl oz
1	Can or bottle of unsweetened chestnuts	1
1	Fresh thyme sprig	1

1. Preheat the oven to 425°F / 220°C / Gas Mark 7.
2. Remove any damaged outer leaves from the cabbage. Cut it into quarters and remove the center core. Cut each quarter into thin slices. Set aside.
3. Peel the garlic and cut into small slivers. Pierce the meat here and there with a small pointed knife and slide a garlic sliver along the knife blade into each incision.
4. Place the pork in an ovenproof dish. Sprinkle with salt and pepper and add 3 tablespoons of water. Roast for 1 hour 20 minutes, basting often with its own juices. Add 1 or 2 tablespoons of hot water if necessary during cooking.
5. Meanwhile, put the shredded cabbage in a stewpot. Cover with plenty of cold salted water and bring to a boil. Simmer for 5 minutes, then drain and rinse well under cold running water. Drain again well.
6. Cut the bacon into strips. Blanch in boiling water for 5 minutes, then rinse under cold running water and drain.
7. Heat 2 tablespoons [25 g / 1 oz] of the butter in a flameproof casserole, add the bacon and cook until lightly browned. Add the cabbage, bouquet garni, and salt and pepper to taste. Pour over the wine and leave to cook, covered, over a low heat until the pork is ready.
8. Drain the chestnuts, reserving their juice. Put them in a frying pan with 3 tablespoons of their juice, the rest of the

butter, the thyme, and salt and pepper to taste. Heat gently, covered.
9. When the pork is cooked, take the dish out of the oven and surround the meat with the chestnuts and the cabbage mixture. Serve immediately.

Côtes de porc au chou rouge

Pork Chops with Red Cabbage

	00:20	01:00

American	Ingredients	Metric/Imperial
3	Onions	3
1 tbsp	Butter	15 g / ½ oz
3	Bacon slices	3
6	Pork chops	6
1	Red cabbage	1
2	Small apples	2
6	Sugar cubes	6
3 cups	Red wine	750 ml / 1¼ pints

1. Peel and thinly slice the onions. Heat the butter in a flameproof casserole, add the bacon, pork chops and onions and cook for 15 minutes, turning the chops over half-way through.
2. Meanwhile, discard any damaged outer leaves from the cabbage. Cut it into quarters and remove the center core. Cut each quarter into thin slices. Peel the apples. Remove the core and seeds and cut the apples into matchstick strips.
3. Add the cabbage, apples, sugar cubes and wine to the casserole. Season with salt and pepper. Cover and simmer over a gentle heat for 1 hour, stirring occasionally.

Pork chops with cabbage

Daube de porc aux aubergines

Pork and Eggplant [Aubergine] Stew

	00:40		01:30

American	Ingredients	Metric/Imperial
2½ lb	Boneless pork shoulder or blade	1.25 kg / 2½ lb
2 tbsp	Flour	2 tbsp
2 tbsp	Oil	2 tbsp
4	Onions	4
2	Garlic cloves	2
	Salt and pepper	
2	Fresh thyme sprigs	2
2	Eggplant [aubergines]	2
1¼ cups	Hot water	300 ml / ½ pint

1. Cut the pork into 1½ in / 2 cm pieces. Coat with the flour. Heat the oil in a flameproof casserole, add the pork pieces and brown on all sides.
2. Peel and thinly slice the onions. Peel and crush the garlic. Add the onions and garlic to the casserole. Season with salt and pepper. Add the thyme. Cook over a low heat for 15 minutes, stirring often to brown the ingredients evenly.
3. Meanwhile, peel and slice the eggplant. Add to the casserole with the hot water. Simmer gently for 1¼ hours.

Filet de porc à l'ail

Loin of Pork with Garlic

	00:10 plus seasoning		01:30

American	Ingredients	Metric/Imperial
7	Garlic cloves	7
1 (2½ lb)	Boneless loin of pork, bones reserved	1 (1.25 kg / 2½ lb)
	Salt and pepper	
2	Onions	2
2	Fresh thyme sprigs	2
1	Bay leaf	1
⅔ cup	White wine	150 ml / ¼ pint
⅓ cup	Water	5 tbsp

1. Peel 2 of the garlic cloves and cut into slivers. Pierce the meat here and there with a small pointed knife and insert a sliver of garlic in each incision. Rub in some salt and pepper mixed together and leave for 1 hour.
2. Preheat the oven to 425°F / 220°C / Gas Mark 7.
3. Place the meat in a roasting pan with the bones. Roast for 10 minutes, turning the meat to brown it evenly.
4. Peel and quarter the onions. Add to the roasting pan with the rest of the garlic, unpeeled, the thyme and bay leaf. Pour over the wine and water. Lower the heat to 350°F / 180°C / Gas Mark 4 and continue cooking for 1¼ hours, basting and turning the meat twice.
5. Turn off the oven, leave the oven door ajar and leave the meat inside for 10 minutes. Transfer the pork to a warmed serving platter and keep hot.
6. Add 1 tablespoon of boiling water to the juices in the

roasting pan. Bring to a boil on top of the stove, scraping the meat residue from the bottom of the pan. Strain the gravy and serve with the pork.

Fromage de tête

Head Cheese [Brawn]

	00:15 plus chilling		02:30

American	Ingredients	Metric/Imperial
2	Carrots	2
2	Medium-size onions	2
3 quarts	Water	3 l / 5½ pints
	Salt and pepper	
½	Pig's head	½
1	Leek (white part only)	1
1	Bouquet garni	1
	Black peppercorns	
1	Garlic clove	1
2	Shallots	2
2	Small onions	2
1	Small bunch of fresh parsley	1

1. Peel the carrots and the 2 medium-size onions. Place the water in a large stewpot, add a little salt and bring to a boil. Add the ½ pig's head, peeled onions, carrots, leek, bouquet garni and a few peppercorns. Simmer very gently for 2½ hours.
2. Drain the pig's head. Strain the cooking liquid and reserve. Remove the bones from the head. Chop the meat and place in a deep round bowl or mold.
3. Peel the garlic, shallots and the 2 small onions. Mince these finely with the parsley.
4. Mix the minced vegetables with the meat. Season with salt and pepper and pour over 4 ladlefuls of the strained cooking liquid, or enough to cover. Chill for 12 hours.
5. To serve, unmold the head cheese by dipping the bowl or mold into hot water for a few seconds.

Côtes de porc poêlées

Fried Pork Chops

	00:00	00:14 to 00:18	

American	Ingredients	Metric/Imperial
2 tbsp	Oil	2 tbsp
6 (6 oz)	Pork chops	6 (175 g / 6 oz)
	Salt and pepper	
	Lemon juice	

1. Heat the oil in a frying pan, add the chops and cook over a medium heat for 8-10 minutes, according to thickness.
2. Season with salt and pepper and turn the chops over. Cook on the other side for 6-8 minutes longer. Season again with salt and pepper 3 minutes before the end of the cooking period.
3. Sprinkle the chops with a few drops of lemon juice and serve.

Cook's tip: you can also cook pork chops on a steak or chop grill [griddle]. Brush them first with oil on each side and cook on the very hot grill. Serve sprinkled with any fresh herbs you like.

Jambon Moivriot
Ham Slices in Red Wine

⏱ 00:15   00:25 🍲

American	Ingredients	Metric/Imperial
6	Slices of dried country ham or cooked ham about ¼ in / 5 mm thick	6
3	Onions	3
1	Garlic clove	1
2 tbsp	Lard	25 g / 1 oz
1 tbsp	Flour	1 tbsp
2 cups	Full-bodied red wine	450 ml / ¾ pint
7 tbsp	Water	7 tbsp
1	Bouquet garni	1
	Salt and pepper	

1. Simmer the ham slices in water to cover for 10 minutes.
2. Meanwhile, peel and chop the onions. Peel and crush the garlic. Heat the lard in a frying pan, add the onions and cook, stirring, until they become pale golden (about 10 minutes). Sprinkle with the flour and stir well, then add the wine, water, bouquet garni, garlic, and salt and pepper to taste. Cover and cook over a gentle heat for 10 minutes. If the sauce evaporates too much, add a little more wine.
3. Drain the ham slices and add to the sauce. Simmer for a few minutes, then turn the slices over and cook for a few minutes longer.
4. Remove the bouquet garni before serving.

Poule verte
Pork-Stuffed Cabbage Roll

⏱ 00:30   02:45 🍲

American	Ingredients	Metric/Imperial
1	Large green cabbage	1
2	Garlic cloves	2
2	Onions	2
1	Bunch of fresh parsley	1
¾ lb	Ground [minced] pork	350 g / 12 oz
1 cup	Fresh white bread crumbs	50 g / 2 oz
1	Egg	1
	Salt and pepper	
1 (¾ lb)	Piece of bacon	1 (350 g / 12 oz)
6	Carrots	6
2	Turnips	2
6	Black peppercorns	6
1 cup	Tomato sauce	250 ml / 8 fl oz

1. Remove any damaged outer leaves from the cabbage and put it whole into a large saucepan of cold water. Bring to a boil and simmer for 15 minutes. Remove the cabbage from the water, rinse under cold runnning water and drain.
2. Peel 1 clove of garlic and 1 onion. Mince the garlic and onion with the parsley. Place these ingredients in a mixing bowl and add the pork, bread crumbs, egg, and salt and pepper to taste. Mix together well.
3. Take off the large outer leaves of the cabbage. Remove the

thick central ribs and spread out the leaves flat in a line, overlapping them. Spread the pork stuffing on top. Roll up like a long loaf of bread, and tie like a roast of meat. Reserve the remaining cabbage.
4. Put the piece of bacon in a saucepan of cold water, bring to a boil and simmer for 10 minutes. Drain.
5. Peel the carrots, turnips and remaining onion and garlic. Place the vegetables in a stewpot with the cabbage roll, peppercorns and bacon. Cover with water. Bring to a boil, then cover and cook for 1¼ hours.
6. Remove the core and large ribs from the remaining cabbage and cut into strips. Add to the pot and cook for another hour.
7. Serve the cabbage roll and the bacon cut into slices, surrounded by the drained vegetables. Accompany with the tomato sauce.

Cook's tip: the stock, poured boiling hot over thick slices of stale bread, makes a delicious soup.

Pork-stuffed cabbage roll

Porc braisé au chou
Braised Pork with Cabbage

⏱ 00:20   02:15 🍲

American	Ingredients	Metric/Imperial
1 (¼ lb)	Piece of bacon	1 (125 g / 4 oz)
3 tbsp	Oil	3 tbsp
1 (2 lb)	Boneless pork roast	1 (1 kg / 2 lb)
1	Small green cabbage	1
	Salt and pepper	
1	Small bunch of fresh parsley	1
1¼ lb	Potatoes	625 g / 1¼ lb

1. Cut the bacon into small dice. Heat the oil in a flameproof casserole, add the bacon and cook until browned. Add the pork and brown on all sides. Cover and reduce the heat. Leave to cook gently.

2. Meanwhile, remove any damaged outside leaves of the cabbage. Cut into quarters and remove the hard stalk at the base of the leaves. Drop the cabbage quarters into a saucepan of boiling salted water and cook for 10 minutes.

3. Drain the cabbage and rinse under cold water, then add to the casserole. Add the parsley. Cook, covered, over a gentle heat for 1 hour.

4. Peel the potatoes and add to the casserole. Season with salt and pepper. Cover again and cook gently for 45 minutes longer.

5. To serve, cut the meat into slices and arrange on top of the cabbage in a deep dish. Surround by the potatoes. Pour over the cooking liquid.

Ragoût de porc
Pork Stew

	00:20		02:00

American	Ingredients	Metric/Imperial
3 lb	Boneless shoulder of pork	1.5 kg / 3 lb
2 tbsp	Oil	2 tbsp
1 tbsp	Flour	1 tbsp
3	Onions	3
2	Tomatoes	2
1	Bouquet garni	1
	Salt and pepper	
8	Potatoes	8

1. Trim excess fat from the pork, then cut the meat into 1½ in / 2 cm pieces. Heat the oil in a frying pan, add the pork and brown the pieces on all sides. Drain the pork and place in a flameproof casserole.

2. Sprinkle the flour over the meat and stir to coat the meat evenly with the flour.

3. Peel the onions and add to the casserole with the tomatoes (whole) and bouquet garni. Add enough water so that the meat is just covered. Season with salt and pepper. Bring to a boil, then simmer very gently for 1½ hours.

4. Peel the potatoes and put them on top of the other ingredients in the casserole. Cook for 25-30 minutes longer or until they are tender.

5. Discard the bouquet garni before serving.

Rôti de porc boulangère
Roast Pork with Potatoes

	00:20		01:45

American	Ingredients	Metric/Imperial
1 (3 lb)	Boneless loin of pork, bones reserved	1 (1.5 kg / 3 lb)
	Salt and pepper	
2	Garlic cloves	2
4 lb	Potatoes	2 kg / 4 lb
4	Fresh thyme sprigs	4
2	Bay leaves	2
	Grated nutmeg	
1 tbsp	Lard	15 g / ½ oz

1. Preheat the oven to 400°F / 200°C / Gas Mark 6.

2. Bring a large saucepan of water to a boil. Add the pork and bones and season with salt and pepper. Bring back to a boil and simmer, covered, for 20 minutes.

3. Meanwhile, peel 1 clove of garlic and rub the inside of an ovenproof dish. Discard the garlic. Peel and thinly slice the potatoes. Arrange them in the dish in 3 layers, seasoning each layer with the thyme, the bay leaves, crumbled, a large pinch of nutmeg, and the remaining garlic, peeled and crushed. Moisten with some of the liquid from the meat and add sufficient boiling water just to come up to the top of the potatoes. Dot with the lard.

4. Place in the oven and cook for 15 minutes.

5. Drain the pork, discard the bones and place on top of the potatoes. Continue cooking for 1½ hours, turning the pork occasionally so that it browns all over. This dish is cooked when the potatoes have absorbed nearly all the liquid.

Petit salé aux lentilles
Lentils with Salt Pork and Sausage

	00:20 plus soaking	02:30 to 03:00	

American	Ingredients	Metric/Imperial
2½ cups	Small green lentils	625 g / 1¼ lb
1 (1 lb)	Piece of salt pork	1 (500 g / 1 lb)
1 (2 lb)	Uncooked smoked pork loin [lean bacon joint]	1 (1 kg / 2 lb)
1	Large carrot	1
2	Onions	2
1	Bouquet garni	1
6	Montbéliard sausages or other smoked pork sausages	6
	Salt and pepper	
2 tbsp	Butter (optional)	25 g / 1 oz

1. Soak the lentils in cold water to cover for 2-3 hours. Soak the salt pork and pork loin in cold water to remove excess salt, if necessary. Drain.

2. Place the salt pork and pork loin in a saucepan and cover with fresh cold water. Simmer gently for about 2 hours.

3. Meanwhile, drain the lentils and put into another saucepan. Peel the carrot and onions and add to the pan with the bouquet garni. Cover with water. Bring to a boil very slowly and simmer very gently for about 30-40 minutes. It is important not to let the lentils boil fast, or their skins will burst. Green lentils have a very thin skin, and cook quickly.

4. Add the sausages, pricked so that they do not burst, to the meats and simmer gently for a further 10 minutes.

5. Add a little salt to the lentils and then drain as soon as they are cooked. (Reserve the cooking liquid together with the vegetables as this will make an excellent soup.)

6. Drain the meats, reserving the cooking liquid. Cut the meats into pieces or slices and place them in a heavy-based saucepan. Cover with the lentils and moisten with a small ladleful of the meat cooking liquid, taken from the top so as to include a little fat (or else with the fat skimmed off and the liquid enriched instead with the butter). Add a little pepper and cover. Cook over a very low heat for 15-20 minutes.

7. To serve, arrange the meat on a warmed platter and spoon over the lentils and sauce.

Jambonneau en potée

Ham Hotpot

	00:30		03:15

American	Ingredients	Metric/Imperial
1 (2½ lb)	Uncooked boneless ham [gammon joint]	1 (1.25 kg / 2½ lb)
4 quarts	Water	4 l / 7 pints
	Salt and pepper	
1 (½ lb)	Piece of bacon	1 (250 g / 8 oz)
1	Veal shank [knuckle]	1
2	Pigs' tails (optional)	2
1	Onion	1
3	Cloves	3
½ lb	Young carrots	250 g / 8 oz
½ lb	Young turnips	250 g / 8 oz
½ lb	New potatoes	250 g / 8 oz
1	Spring cabbage	1
¼ lb	Fresh broad or lima beans	125 g / 4 oz

1. Soak the ham in cold water to cover to remove excess salt, if necessary. Drain.
2. Place the ham in a large cooking pot and cover with the water. Add a little pepper. Bring to a boil and cook for 40 minutes over a moderate heat.
3. Cut the bacon into large pieces. Add to the pot with the veal shank and pigs' tails. Peel the onion and stud with the cloves. Add to the pot. Simmer, covered, for 2 hours.
4. Meanwhile, peel the carrots, turnips and potatoes. Remove the hard inner core from the cabbage to leave only the leaves. Shell and peel the beans, if necessary.
5. Add the whole carrots and cabbage leaves to the pot and cook for 10 minutes, then add the turnips and beans. Cook for 10 minutes longer and add the potatoes. Cook for a final 15 minutes.

Saucisse aux pois cassés

Sausages with Split Peas

	00:05		00:40 to 00:50

American	Ingredients	Metric/Imperial
2 cups	Split peas	500 g / 1 lb
1	Onion	1
1	Bouquet garni	1
6	Thick fresh sausages, 6 in / 15 cm long	6
¼ cup	Butter	50 g / 2 oz
	Grated nutmeg	
	Salt and pepper	

1. Rinse the split peas, put them in a saucepan and cover with plenty of cold water (1 in / 2.5 cm above the peas).
2. Peel the onion and add to the peas with the bouquet garni. Bring to a boil over a moderate heat and simmer for 40-50 minutes or until tender. Add more boiling water whenever the peas come above the surface of the water.
3. Meanwhile, prick the sausages with a fork, so that they do not burst while cooking. If a long sausage is used, roll it into a coil. Place in a frying pan and cook over a moderate heat for 25 minutes on each side. Add a little fat to the pan if necessary.
4. Drain the peas. Remove the onion and bouquet garni. Purée

the peas in a food mill, blender or food processor. Beat in the butter. Add a pinch of nutmeg and season with salt and pepper. If the purée is too thick, thin it with a little milk or warm water.
5. Serve the purée with the well-drained sausages.

Sauté de porc provençale

Provençal Pork Sauté

	00:25		01:30

American	Ingredients	Metric/Imperial
2 lb	Boneless shoulder of pork	1 kg / 2 lb
2 tbsp	Olive oil	2 tbsp
	Salt and pepper	
2	Onions	2
2	Garlic cloves	2
3	Shallots	3
1	Bouquet garni	1
2 tbsp	Flour	2 tbsp
1 cup	Dry white wine	250 ml / 8 fl oz
15	Young carrots	15
2	Sweet red peppers	2
½ lb	Fresh peas	250 g / 8 oz
1 cup	Green and black olives	150 g / 5 oz

1. Cut the pork into large pieces. Heat the olive oil in a flameproof casserole. Add the pieces of pork and brown on all sides. Sprinkle with salt and pepper.
2. Peel and thinly slice the onions, garlic and shallots. Add them to the casserole with the bouquet garni. Cook until the vegetables are golden, then add the flour and mix well. Cook until the flour turns a light golden color. Add the wine, stirring all the time. Bring to a boil.
3. Meanwhile, peel the carrots. Core and seed the red peppers and cut into thin strips. Shell the peas.
4. Add the carrots, pepper strips, peas and olives to the casserole. Cover and simmer over a low heat for 1 hour. Serve very hot.

Saucisses en croûtes

Sausages in Pastry

	00:30		00:15 to 00:18
		plus making or thawing pastry	

American	Ingredients	Metric/Imperial
½ lb	Puff pastry	250 g / 8 oz
3	Large fresh pork sausages	3
	Cayenne pepper	
1	Egg, beaten	1

1. If using frozen pastry, allow it to thaw.
2. Preheat the oven to 450°F / 230°C / Gas Mark 8.
3. Cut each sausage into 3 and sprinkle with a little cayenne.
4. Roll out the pastry to ⅛ in / 3 mm thick. Cut into 9 strips. Roll up each piece of sausage in a strip of pastry and seal the edges with egg. Score a few lines on the top of the pastry with the point of a knife, and brush the surface with egg.
5. Place on a baking sheet. Bake for 10-12 minutes, then turn down the heat to 400°F / 200°C / Gas Mark 6 and bake for 5 minutes longer. Serve hot.

Sausages are the basis of many French country dishes

Preserving raw meat

Meat	Preparation	Freezing
Steaks, fillets, chops, scaloppine [escalopes], tenderloin	Remove sinews and fat. **Cook's tip:** do not freeze ground [minced] meat, otherwise you run the risk of serious food poisoning.	1. Pack separately in foil. 2. Freeze for 6 hours. 3. Gather together in freezer bags, label and return to freezer. **To use:** thaw for 12 hours in refrigerator. Will keep 10 months.
Roasts	Remove excess fat and cut into pieces no heavier than 4 lb / 2 kg.	1. Wrap in foil. 2. Freeze for 24 hours. 3. Place in freezer bags, label and return to freezer. **To use:** thaw for 12 hours in refrigerator. Will keep 10 months.
Legs of mutton or lamb **Ribs of beef**	Remove fat and sinews.	1. To prevent perforations, wrap bones in foil to form protective buffers. 2. Wrap in foil and freeze for 12 hours. 3. Place in freezer bags, label and return to freezer. **To use:** thaw for 12 hours in refrigerator. Will keep 10 months.
Meat for stewing or braising	Cut into pieces.	1. Make up portions according to your requirements and proceed as for steaks. **To use:** thaw for 12 hours in refrigerator. Will keep 10 months.
Charcuterie: dried and smoked sausages, [black or white pudding], crépinettes, faggots, etc.	1. Blanch for 1 minute in boiling water. 2. Drain and dry carefully.	Place in aluminum trays or wrap in foil separately. Label and freeze. **To use:** thaw for 12 hours in refrigerator. Will keep 6 months.
Variety meats [offal]	Except for brains, they do not freeze very well. Eat as soon as you have bought them.	

Fish, meat, vegetables and crustaceans can be frozen and retain their quality

Vegetables

Côtes de bettes gratinées
Swiss Chard in Cheese Sauce

00:20   00:45

American	Ingredients	Metric/Imperial
1½ lb	Swiss chard	750 g / 1½ lb
1	Small celeriac	1
	Salt and pepper	
1	Lemon	1
2 cups	Cheese sauce	500 ml / ¾ pint
½ cup	Grated gruyère cheese	50 g / 2 oz
2 tbsp	Butter	25 g / 2 oz

1. Remove the green leaves from the chard as they are not used in this recipe. Scrape the white stems, wash well and cut into pieces 2½ in / 7 cm long. Slice into sticks a little thicker than matchsticks ('julienne' style, see page 411).
2. Peel, wash and cut the celeriac into sticks of the same size as the chard stems.
3. Bring some salted water to a boil in a saucepan. Add the juice of the lemon and the celeriac. Cook for 5-7 minutes and add the chard stems. Continue cooking until the chard is tender, but not soft.
4. Preheat the oven to 400°F / 200°C / Gas Mark 6.
5. Drain the vegetables well and arrange in a buttered gratin dish. Cover with the cheese sauce, sprinkle with the cheese and dot with the butter.
6. Bake for 20-30 minutes until the top is golden brown.

Brocolis au gratin
Broccoli in Cheese Sauce

00:20   00:40 to 00:50

American	Ingredients	Metric/Imperial
	Salt and pepper	
2 lb	Broccoli	1 kg / 2 lb
¼ cup	Butter	50 g / 2 oz
2 tbsp	Flour	25 g / 1 oz
2 cups	Milk	500 ml / ¾ pint
⅔ cup	Crème fraîche	150 ml / ¼ pint
	Grated nutmeg	
1 cup	Grated gruyère cheese	125 g / 4 oz

1. Boil some salted water in a saucepan.
2. Thoroughly wash the broccoli and trim. Add to the pan and cook for about 10 minutes or until just tender.
3. Drain well and chop into large pieces. Preheat the oven to 400°F / 200°C / Gas Mark 6.
4. Melt 2 tablespoons [25 g / 1 oz] of the butter in a frying pan. Add the broccoli and cook gently to evaporate any remaining water. Season with salt and pepper. Remove the pan from the heat.
5. Melt the remaining butter in a heavy-bottomed saucepan over a low heat. Add the flour and mix together until the butter has absorbed all the flour. Gradually add the milk and continue

stirring over a low heat for about 10 minutes or until the sauce thickens. Finally, stir in the crème fraîche, a pinch of nutmeg and half the gruyère and season with salt and pepper.
6. Arrange the broccoli in a gratin dish, pour over the cheese sauce and sprinkle with the remaining cheese. Bake for 20-30 minutes or until golden brown. Serve hot.

Carottes aux raisins
Carrots with Raisins

00:15   01:00
plus soaking

American	Ingredients	Metric/Imperial
1⅓ cups	Raisins	200 g / 7 oz
2 lb	Carrots	1 kg / 2 lb
½ cup	Butter	125 g / 4 oz
	Salt	
1 tsp	Sugar (optional)	1 tsp

1. Put the raisins in a bowl, cover with warm water and leave to soak.
2. Peel the carrots and cut them into thin slices. Melt the butter in a heavy-bottomed saucepan and add the carrots. Stir well then cover and cook over a very low heat for 40 minutes, taking care that they do not stick to the bottom of the pan.
3. Drain the raisins and mix with the carrots.
4. Cook for 10 minutes longer or until the carrots are tender. Add a little salt. If the carrots are not sweet enough, add the sugar. Serve very hot.

Broccoli in cheese sauce

Cèpes à la parisienne
Cèpes French Style

00:20   00:30 to 00:40

American	Ingredients	Metric/Imperial
4 lb	Cèpes or other fresh mushrooms	2 kg / 4 lb
¼ cup	Oil	4 tbsp
1	Lemon	1
3	Shallots or	3
2	Garlic cloves	2
1⅓ cups	Coarse dry bread crumbs	125 g / 4 oz
1 tbsp	Chopped fresh parsley	1 tbsp

1. Separate the mushroom caps from the stems. Slice the stems into quarters lengthwise.
2. Heat 1 tablespoon of the oil in a flameproof casserole. Add the juice of the lemon and the mushroom caps and stems. Cook over a low heat for about 10 minutes or until all the liquid has evaporated. Remove from the pan and cut the caps into even-sized pieces. Set aside one-third of the stems.
3. Heat the remaining oil in the casserole. Return the mushroom caps and remaining stems to the pan, season with salt and pepper and cook for a further 15-25 minutes.
4. Finely chop the shallots (or garlic) together with the reserved mushroom stems.
5. A few minutes before serving, add this mixture with the bread crumbs to the cèpes and stir quickly. Turn onto a warmed serving dish and sprinkle with the parsley.

Cardons béchamel

Cardoons in Béchamel Sauce

| | 00:10 | 00:40 to 00:50 | |

American	Ingredients	Metric/Imperial
1	Lemon	1
3 lb	Cardoons (with a few leaves)	1.5 kg / 3 lb
¼ cup	Flour	25 g / 1 oz
2 quarts	Water	2 l / 3½ pints
1 tbsp	Salt	1 tbsp
1 tbsp	Beef drippings or oil	1 tbsp
3 cups	Béchamel sauce	750 ml / 1¼ pints

1. Squeeze the lemon. Cut away the outer stems and leaves and wash and dry the cardoons. Cut them into 4 in / 10 cm pieces and sprinkle with a little lemon juice.
2. Mix the flour with a little of the water then put in a large saucepan with the rest of the water. Add the salt, the remaining lemon juice and the drippings or oil. Bring to a boil and add the cardoons. Cover and cook for 30-40 minutes until just tender.
3. Drain and dry the cardoons and place them in a deep frying pan. Coat them with the béchamel sauce and heat through over a low heat for 10 minutes. Serve very hot.

Artichauts au naturel

Globe Artichokes

| | 00:05 | 00:25 to 00:30 | |

American	Ingredients	Metric/Imperial
	Salt	
½	Lemon	½
6	Globe artichokes	6

Cook by either of the methods given below.
In a saucepan:
1. Bring a large saucepan of salted water to a boil. Add the juice of the half lemon.
2. Break the stems of the artichokes, pulling them to remove the strings. Remove any damaged or discolored outer leaves.
3. Place the artichokes in the boiling water and cook for about 30 minutes, or until a leaf pulls out easily.

4. Drain upside-down and serve warm with melted clarified butter or hollandaise sauce (see page 126).

In a steamer:
1. Prepare the artichokes as above.
2. Fill the bottom of the steamer with water. Put the artichokes in the top of the steamer, above the water, cover, and steam for 25-30 minutes (depending on the size of the artichokes).

Cook's tip: after cooking, the leaves and hairy choke can be removed, and the hearts cooked gently in a frying pan with a little butter.

Swiss chard in cheese sauce

Carottes forestière

Carrots with Mushrooms in Cream

| | 00:20 | 00:30 | |

American	Ingredients	Metric/Imperial
2 lb	Young carrots	1 kg / 2 lb
2 cups	Chicken stock	500 ml / ¾ pint
1 tbsp	Sugar	1 tbsp
6 tbsp	Butter	75 g / 3 oz
	Salt and pepper	
	Grated nutmeg	
¾ lb	Button mushrooms	350 g / 12 oz
⅔ cup	Crème fraîche	150 ml / ¼ pint
	Chopped fresh chervil	

1. Peel the carrots, cut them into small strips and place in a saucepan with the stock, sugar, half the butter, salt, pepper and a pinch of nutmeg. Cover and cook over a moderate heat until the liquid has completely evaporated.
2. Meanwhile, clean the mushrooms and trim the stems. Cut into thin slices. Heat the remaining butter in a frying pan, add the mushrooms and season with salt and pepper. Cook until the liquid from the mushrooms has evaporated. Add the mushrooms and the crème fraîche to the carrots once they are cooked, mix together and sprinkle with the chervil.

Choux de Bruxelles au lard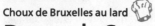

Brussels Sprouts with Chestnuts

	00:45		01:00

American	Ingredients	Metric/Imperial
	Salt and pepper	
1 lb	Chestnuts	500 g / 1 lb
1 quart	Chicken stock	1 l / 1¾ pints
1½ lb	Brussels sprouts	750 g / 1½ lb
½ lb	Lightly salted bacon	250 g / 8 oz
1 tbsp	Lard	1 tbsp

1. Heat a saucepan of salted water. With the point of a knife, pierce the rounded part of the chestnuts. Add to the pan and bring back to a boil. Cook for 30 minutes.
2. Remove the saucepan from the heat and shell the chestnuts one at a time, leaving the rest to keep hot in the water.
3. Heat the stock in a saucepan. Add the shelled chestnuts and simmer gently for 10-15 minutes. Take care that the chestnuts do not disintegrate during cooking.
4. Meanwhile, cut the stems and outer leaves from the sprouts. Cook the sprouts in boiling salted water for 10-15 minutes. Be sure not to overcook them — they should remain firm.
5. Place the bacon in a saucepan and cover with water. Bring to a boil and simmer for 10 minutes. Drain and cut into strips.
6. Heat the lard in a saucepan and add the bacon. Cook gently until golden brown, then add the sprouts and drained chestnuts. Season with salt and pepper and stir gently. Cook for a further 5 minutes until well heated through.

Chou-fleur gratiné

Cauliflower in Cheese Sauce

	00:10		00:30 to 00:35

American	Ingredients	Metric/Imperial
1	Large cauliflower	1
¼ cup	Butter	60 g / 2 oz
6 tbsp	Flour	40 g / 1½ oz
1 cup	Crème fraîche	250 ml / 8 fl oz
1 cup	Grated gruyère cheese	150 g / 5 oz
	Grated nutmeg	
	Salt and pepper	

1. Preheat the oven to 375°F / 190°C / Gas Mark 5.
2. Remove the outer leaves from the cauliflower. Cut into the hard stem and separate the cauliflower into large florets.
3. In a saucepan bring some salted water to a boil. Add the cauliflower and bring back to a boil. Lower the heat and simmer gently, without a lid, for 10-15 minutes. Pierce the cauliflower with the blade of a knife. The florets should be cooked but still firm.
4. Meanwhile, melt 3 tablespoons [40 g / 1½ oz] of the butter in a saucepan, add the flour and stir until it is absorbed. Gradually stir in the crème fraîche and cook, stirring, until thickened. Flavor with two-thirds of the grated cheese, a pinch of nutmeg, and salt and pepper to taste.

5. Drain the cauliflower well, arrange in a gratin dish and cover with the sauce. Sprinkle with the remaining cheese and dot with the remaining butter.
6. Bake for about 20 minutes, or until the surface is golden brown.

Choux de Bruxelles à l'étouffée

Braised Brussels Sprouts

	00:20		00:40

American	Ingredients	Metric/Imperial
1½ lb	Brussels sprouts	750 g / 1½ lb
1	Medium-sized onion	1
½ lb	Bacon	250 g / 8 oz
2 tbsp	Lard or oil	2 tbsp
2 tsp	Flour	2 tsp
2 cups	Chicken stock	500 ml / ¾ pint
	Salt and pepper	

1. Trim and wash the sprouts. Peel the onion and cut into thin slices. Cut the bacon into small strips.
2. Heat the lard or oil in a saucepan and brown the onion for 2-3 minutes. Add the strips of bacon and brown for 3-4 minutes, stirring constantly. Sprinkle with the flour, mix well, and add the stock a little at a time. Slowly bring to a boil. Add the sprouts and season with salt and pepper. Cover and cook over a low heat for 30 minutes.

Chou rouge braisé

Braised Red Cabbage

	00:25		02:00

American	Ingredients	Metric/Imperial
1 (3 lb)	Head of red cabbage	1 (1.5 kg / 3 lb)
¼ cup	Lard (or oil)	4 tbsp
2 tbsp	Sugar	2 tbsp
2 tbsp	Vinegar	2 tbsp
⅔ cup	Water	150 ml / ¼ pint
	Salt and pepper	
2	Crisp eating apples	2
¼ cup	Red currant jelly	4 tbsp

1. Preheat the oven to 325°F / 160°C / Gas Mark 3.
2. Wash the cabbage, remove any damaged outer leaves and cut into thin slices.
3. Place the lard or oil in a large flameproof casserole with the sugar, vinegar, water, salt and pepper. Bring to a boil and add the cabbage. Stir and bring back to a boil.
4. Cover the casserole and place in the oven. Cook for 2 hours.
5. After 1 hour, stir the cabbage and add a little water if necessary.
6. About 20 minutes before the end of the cooking time add the apples, cored and chopped, and the red currant jelly.
7. If the cabbage has produced a lot of water, reduce over a high heat on top of the stove, stirring constantly, before serving.

Cook's tip: serve with pork or ham.

Chou-fleur en soufflé

Cauliflower Soufflé

| | 00:20 | | 00:45 |

American	Ingredients	Metric/Imperial
1	Cauliflower	1
	Salt and pepper	
⅔ cup	Milk	150 ml / ¼ pint
1 cup	Bread crumbs	50 g / 2 oz
4	Eggs, separated	4
¾ cup	Grated gruyère cheese	75 g / 3 oz

1. Remove the leaves from the cauliflower. Cut into the hard stem and separate into large florets. Wash and drain.
2. Bring a pan of salted water to a boil and add the cauliflower. Bring back to a boil, lower the heat and simmer, without a lid, for 15-20 minutes.
3. Drain the cauliflower well and purée in a blender or food processor. Put the purée in a large bowl.
4. Preheat the oven to 350°F / 180°C / Gas Mark 4.
5. Heat the milk and pour it over the bread crumbs in a bowl. Leave to soak for a few minutes then squeeze out the bread and add to the cauliflower purée, along with the 4 egg yolks and the grated gruyère cheese. Season with salt and pepper and mix well.
6. Beat the egg whites until stiff and carefully fold them into the cauliflower mixture.
7. Butter a 6½ in / 16 cm soufflé dish. Fill it three-quarters full with the mixture. Bake for 10 minutes then increase the heat to 425°F / 220°C / Gas Mark 7. Bake for a further 15 minutes and serve immediately.

Chou-fleur

Cauliflower

| | 00:10 | | 00:08 to 00:15 |

American	Ingredients	Metric/Imperial
2	Medium-sized cauliflowers (or 1 large)	2
	Salt and pepper	
1 tbsp	Flour	1 tbsp
½ cup	Butter	125 g / 4 oz
1 cup	Bread crumbs	50 g / 2 oz
2 tbsp	Vinegar	2 tbsp
1 tsp	Prepared mustard	1 tsp
¼ cup	Oil	4 tbsp

1. Remove the outer leaves from the cauliflower. Cut into the hard stem and separate the cauliflower into large florets.
2. Bring a saucepan of salted water to a boil and add the cauliflower and the flour mixed with a little cold water. Bring back to a boil, lower the heat and simmer gently, without a lid, for 10-15 minutes. Drain well.
3. If you prefer to use a steamer or pressure cooker, keep the cauliflower whole. Steam for 15 minutes, or for 4 minutes from the moment the steam begins to flow in a pressure cooker.
4. When the florets are cooked, but still firm, remove from the heat and drain well.
5. The cauliflower can be sprinkled with parsley and served with lemon clarified butter (see page 113). Or with bread crumbs (à la chapelure): heat the butter with the bread crumbs in a small saucepan over a low heat. Reshape the cauliflower in

a serving dish and coat with the butter and bread crumb sauce. Or with vinaigrette dressing (à la vinaigrette): dissolve a pinch of salt in the vinegar. Mix in the mustard and season with pepper. Add the oil and mix well. Pour the vinaigrette over the cauliflower and serve hot or cold.

Chou pommé à la crème

Creamed Cabbage

| | 00:15 | | 01:00 |

American	Ingredients	Metric/Imperial
1 (3 lb)	Head of white cabbage	1 (1.5 kg / 3 lb)
	Salt and pepper	
1 tbsp	Lard (or oil)	1 tbsp
1	Garlic clove	1
1	Bouquet garni	1
⅔ cup	Chicken stock	150 ml / ¼ pint
3 tbsp	Crème fraîche	3 tbsp

1. Wash the cabbage and remove any damaged outer leaves. Cut into quarters and cut away the thick stem. Wash again, if necessary.
2. Bring a large saucepan of salted water to a boil. Add the cabbage and bring back to a boil. Cook for 10 minutes then drain.
3. Heat the lard or oil in a saucepan. Peel and chop the garlic clove and add to the pan. Stir, making sure that it does not brown.
4. Add the cabbage to the saucepan along with the bouquet garni. Moisten with the stock and season with salt and pepper. Cover and simmer for 45 minutes to 1 hour. Check from time to time that there is still some liquid in the bottom of the pan. Add a little more stock if necessary.
5. Remove the pan from the heat. Add the crème fraîche, stir well and serve immediately.

Chanterelles ou girolles au beurre

Buttered Chanterelles or Girolles

| | 00:10 | | 00:30 |

American	Ingredients	Metric/Imperial
1 lb	Fresh chanterelles or girolles	500 g / 1 lb
½	Lemon	½
¼ cup	Butter	50 g / 2 oz
3	Shallots	3
6	Fresh parsley sprigs	6
1	Garlic clove	1
	Salt and pepper	

1. Trim the mushrooms and sprinkle with a little lemon juice. Melt the butter in a frying pan, add the mushrooms and brown for 10 minutes over a moderate heat, stirring frequently and carefully with a wooden spatula.
2. Meanwhile, peel and finely chop the shallots and parsley. Add them to the frying pan, along with the peeled, but whole, garlic clove. Season with salt and pepper, cover and cook for 20 minutes.

Cèpes bordelaise

Stuffed Cèpes Bordelaise

	00:30		00:20

American	Ingredients	Metric/Imperial
2 lb	Cèpes or other fresh mushrooms	900 g / 2 lb
3	Shallots	3
3 or 4	Garlic cloves	3 or 4
1	Lemon	1
⅓ cup	Olive oil	6 tbsp
2 tbsp	Chopped fresh parsley	2 tbsp
	Salt and pepper	

1. Trim the stems of the cèpes and then separate from the caps. Shred the stems using a blender, vegetable mill or food processor. Peel and chop the shallots. Peel and crush the garlic. Squeeze the juice from the lemon.
2. Heat half the olive oil in a frying pan, add the shredded stems, shallots and parsley and season with salt and pepper. Cook over a low heat for about 10 minutes, or until the liquid has completely evaporated.
3. Heat the remaining oil in a large frying pan and add the mushroom caps. Cook for about 5 minutes on each side over a low heat.
4. Arrange the mushroom caps, stem side upwards, on a serving dish and fill with the mixture of stems, shallots and parsley. Sprinkle with lemon juice and serve immediately.

Céleri-rave en purée

Creamed Celeriac

	00:20 Serves 8	00:30 to 00:40	

American	Ingredients	Metric/Imperial
2	Lemons	2
3	Celeriac	3
1 lb	Potatoes	500 g / 1 lb
2 tbsp	Flour	2 tbsp
1 cup	Milk	250 ml / 8 fl oz
½ cup	Crème fraîche	125 ml / 4 fl oz
	Grated nutmeg	
2 tbsp	Butter	25 g / 1 oz
	Salt and pepper	

1. Squeeze the lemons, reserving the juice of one half. Peel the celeriac and rub with lemon juice immediately so that it does not discolor. Cut into slices. Peel the potatoes.
2. Mix the flour with the remaining lemon juice and add to a saucepan of water. Bring to a boil then add the celeriac and potatoes. Cook for 20-30 minutes until the celeriac is tender.
3. Drain the vegetables and put through a blender, vegetable mill or food processor. Put the purée in a saucepan, reduce for a few minutes over a gentle heat then add the milk. Stir until the purée has a good, smooth consistency. Add the crème fraîche and a pinch of nutmeg. Mix well and add the butter. Season with salt and pepper and serve very hot.

Cook's tip: this dish can be served as a first course, or to accompany roasts.

Aubergines à la catalane

Eggplant [Aubergines] with Tomatoes

	00:30		00:45

American	Ingredients	Metric/Imperial
4	Long eggplant [aubergines]	4
	Salt and pepper	
	Oil for deep frying	
3	Tomatoes	3
1	Small bunch of fresh parsley	1
2	Garlic cloves	2
1 tbsp	Bread crumbs	1 tbsp
1 tbsp	Olive oil	1 tbsp

1. Cut the eggplant into slices, lengthwise. Sprinkle each slice with a little salt, place in a colander and drain for 30 minutes.
2. Heat a deep-fryer to 330°F / 175°C. Rinse and dry the eggplant and plunge them into the fryer one at a time, to brown them without completely cooking them. Drain well and place in an ovenproof dish.
3. Preheat the oven to 400°F / 200°C / Gas Mark 6.
4. Halve the tomatoes, remove the seeds and place in the dish on top of the eggplant. Season with salt and pepper.
5. Finely chop the parsley. Peel and finely chop the garlic. Mix together in a bowl with the bread crumbs. Cover the tomatoes with three-quarters of the mixture.
6. Sprinkle with olive oil and bake for 30 minutes until the top is golden brown. Before serving, sprinkle with the remaining bread crumb mixture.

Champignons farcis

Stuffed Mushrooms

	00:40		00:25

American	Ingredients	Metric/Imperial
12	Large cup [open] mushrooms	12
6	Medium-sized mushrooms	6
6 tbsp	Butter	75 g / 3 oz
2	Thin slices of cooked ham	2
3 tbsp	Flour	40 g / 1½ oz
2 cups	Milk	500 ml / ¾ pint
¾ cup	Crème fraîche	200 ml / ⅓ pint
2	Egg yolks	2
	Grated nutmeg	
	Salt and pepper	
¾ cup	Grated gruyère cheese	75 g / 3 oz

1. Preheat the oven to 425°F / 220°C / Gas Mark 7.
2. Clean the mushrooms and trim the stems. Melt 2 tablespoons [25 g / 1 oz] of the butter in a frying pan. Remove the stems of the large mushrooms and place the caps in the pan. Cook over a very gentle heat for about 10 minutes, taking care not to break them.
3. Chop the stems from the large mushrooms with the

remaining mushrooms. Place them in a saucepan with 2 tablespoons [25 g / 1 oz] of butter and cook over a moderate heat until the liquid from the mushrooms has evaporated.

4. Chop the slices of ham and add to the chopped mushrooms.

5. Melt the remaining butter in a heavy-bottomed pan, add the flour and mix well. Gradually add the milk and stir over a gentle heat until the sauce thickens. Remove from the heat. Pour in the crème fraîche, the egg yolks and a pinch of nutmeg. Season with salt and pepper and stir.

6. Add half the sauce and a quarter of the grated cheese to the chopped mushrooms and ham. Taste, and adjust the seasoning if necessary.

7. Fill the large mushrooms with the mixture. Place the rest of the mixture in a gratin dish, and top with the stuffed mushrooms.

8. Coat with the rest of the sauce mixed with the remaining cheese and a little milk.

9. Bake for 15 minutes until the top is golden brown and serve very hot.

Mushrooms baked in cream

Champignons en gratin
Mushrooms Baked in Cream

	00:30		00:30	

American	Ingredients	Metric/Imperial
2 lb	Button mushrooms	1 kg / 2 lb
1	Lemon	1
2	Shallots	2
¼ cup	Butter	50 g / 2 oz
1	Garlic clove	1
¾ cup	Crème fraîche	200 ml / ⅓ pint
⅔ cup	Milk	150 ml / ¼ pint
1	Egg yolk	1
1 tbsp	Cornstarch [cornflour] or potato starch or flour	1 tbsp
	Salt and pepper	

1. Preheat the oven to 400°F / 200°C / Gas Mark 6.

2. Clean the mushrooms, trim the stems and cut into thin slices. Sprinkle with a little lemon juice.

3. Peel the shallots and chop finely. Melt three-quarters of the butter in a frying pan and add the mushrooms and the chopped shallots. Cook until the liquid from the mushrooms has evaporated, stirring frequently. Do not allow to dry out completely.

4. Rub a gratin dish with the garlic clove and discard.

5. Mix the crème fraîche in a bowl with the milk, the egg yolk and the cornstarch or potato starch. Season with salt and pepper.

6. Put the mushrooms and shallots into the gratin dish and pour over the mixture of egg, flour and crème fraîche. Dot with the remaining butter.

7. Bake for about 30 minutes, without allowing the mixture to boil.

Carottes glacées
Glazed Carrots

	00:10		00:20 to 00:30	

American	Ingredients	Metric/Imperial
4 lb	Young carrots	2 kg / 4 lb
½ cup	Butter	125 g / 4 oz
2 tbsp	Sugar	2 tbsp
	Salt and pepper	

1. Peel, wash and chop the carrots into equal lengths. Trim into the shape of large olives, if liked.

2. Melt the butter in a heavy-bottomed saucepan and add the carrots, sugar, and salt and pepper to taste. Cover with water.

3. Cook, uncovered, over a gentle heat for 20-30 minutes, until the water has evaporated and the carrots are coated with the golden, syrupy liquid.

Champignons sautés
Sautéed Mushrooms

	00:10		00:15 to 00:20	

American	Ingredients	Metric/Imperial
2 lb	Button mushrooms	1 kg / 2 lb
1	Lemon	1
6 tbsp	Butter	75 g / 3 oz
	Salt and pepper	
3 tbsp	Chopped fresh parsley	3 tbsp
1	Garlic clove (optional)	1

1. Clean the mushrooms and trim the stems. Leave the mushrooms whole if they are small; if not, cut them into slices and sprinkle with lemon juice.

2. Heat half the butter in a frying pan and add the mushrooms and the juice of half a lemon. Cook over a moderate heat, stirring frequently, until all the liquid from the mushrooms has evaporated.

3. Add the remaining butter, season with salt and pepper and cook gently over a very low heat until the mushrooms are cooked. Do not allow the butter to brown.

4. To serve, sprinkle with chopped parsley or with a mixture of parsley and peeled and crushed garlic.

Endives aurore
Belgian Endive [Chicory] with Cheese Sauce

⏱ 00:10 🍲 00:20

American	Ingredients	Metric/Imperial
12	Heads of Belgian endive [chicory]	12
	Salt and pepper	
2 tbsp	Butter	25 g / 1 oz
2 tbsp	Flour	2 tbsp
2 cups	Milk	500 ml / ¾ pint
6 oz	Cooked ham	175 g / 6 oz
1¼ cups	Grated gruyère cheese	150 g / 5 oz
2 tbsp	Tomato paste [purée]	2 tbsp
3	Egg yolks	3

1. Remove any damaged leaves from the endive and cut out the hard core using a small pointed knife. Wash and drain. Boil some salted water in a saucepan. Add the endive and cook for 10 minutes.
2. Meanwhile, melt the butter in a saucepan, sprinkle with the flour, stir for 3 minutes over a low heat then gradually add the milk. Cook for about 10 minutes, stirring often. Remove from the heat.
3. Preheat the broiler [grill].
4. Dice the ham and add to the sauce together with the grated cheese, the tomato paste, salt and pepper. Return to a low heat, stir until the cheese has melted and then remove from the heat. Mix in the egg yolks, stirring vigorously.
5. Drain the endive well and place in a gratin dish. Cover with the sauce and brown under the broiler for 6-7 minutes.

Endives en gratin
Gratin of Belgian Endive [Chicory]

⏱ 00:10 🍲 00:40

American	Ingredients	Metric/Imperial
4 lb	Belgian endive [chicory]	2 kg / 4 lb
⅓ cup	Butter	75 g / 3 oz
½	Lemon	½
1 tbsp	Flour	1 tbsp
¾ cup	Crème fraîche	200 ml / 7 fl oz
1 cup	Grated comté or gruyère cheese	125 g / 4 oz
	Salt and pepper	

1. Preheat the oven to 400°F / 200°C / Gas Mark 6.
2. Remove any damaged outer leaves from the endive and cut out the hard core using a small pointed knife. Rinse quickly and wipe dry. Cut into pieces ¾-1 in / 1½-2 cm long and place in a frying pan over a low heat with ¼ cup [50 g / 2 oz] of the butter and the juice of half a lemon. Stir well.
3. Cook until the endive is soft and all the liquid has evaporated, then sprinkle with the flour. Stir, and cook over a low heat for a further 10 minutes.

4. Add the crème fraîche and three-quarters of the grated cheese. Season with salt and pepper.
5. Pour into a buttered ovenproof dish and sprinkle with the remaining cheese. Dot with the rest of the butter. Bake for 20 minutes until the gratin is piping hot and the top is golden brown.

Endives braisées
Braised Belgian Endive [Chicory]

⏱ 00:10 🍲 00:20

American	Ingredients	Metric/Imperial
12	Heads of Belgian endive [chicory]	12
3 tbsp	Butter	40 g / 1½ oz
⅔ cup	Water	150 ml / ¼ pint
2 tsp	Sugar	2 tsp
½	Lemon	½
	Salt and pepper	

1. Remove any damaged outer leaves from the Belgian endive and then cut out the hard core using a small pointed knife. Wash and wipe dry.
2. Melt the butter in a frying pan and add the endive, the water, the sugar and the juice of the half lemon. Season with salt and pepper. Cover and cook for about 20 minutes over a low heat.
3. Place the endive in a serving dish and serve immediately.

Cook's tip: if the endive produces a lot of liquid during cooking, reduce over a high heat before serving.

Coulemelles en fricassée
Braised Mushrooms

⏱ 00:20 🍲 00:20

American	Ingredients	Metric/Imperial
2 lb	Large mushrooms	1 kg / 2 lb
2	Onions	2
1	Carrot	1
¼ cup	Butter	50 g / 2 oz
2 tbsp	Flour	25 g / 1 oz
1	Fresh thyme sprig	1
1	Fresh rosemary sprig	1
1	Bay leaf	1
	Salt and pepper	
1¼ cups	Water	300 ml / ½ pint
2	Egg yolks	2
1	Lemon	1

1. Remove the stems from the mushrooms, clean the caps carefully and chop them.
2. Peel and thinly slice the onions and carrots. Heat the butter in a frying pan and brown the onions. Sprinkle the flour into the pan, and add the chopped mushrooms, carrot, the thyme, rosemary and the bay leaf. Season with salt and pepper and add the water. Cover and cook over a low heat for 20 minutes.
3. Place the egg yolks in a bowl. Remove all the ingredients

from the frying pan using a slotted spoon so that only the cooking liquid is left, and keep them warm.
4. Add a tablespoon of the liquid to the egg yolks and stir with a wooden spoon. Add half the remaining liquid, stir well and then return this mixture to the liquid in the pan. Place over a low heat and add all the vegetables. Stir to thicken the sauce, but do not allow it to boil or the egg yolk will curdle. Squeeze the juice from the lemon over the top and serve hot.

Beignets de courgettes
Zucchini [Courgette] Fritters

	00:25 plus standing time		00:05 per batch of fritters

American	Ingredients	Metric/Imperial
2	Eggs	2
	Salt	
1 cup	Flour	150 g / 5 oz
2 tbsp	Oil	2 tbsp
⅔ cup	Beer	150 ml / ¼ pint
2 lb	Zucchini [courgettes]	1 kg / 2 lb
	Oil for deep frying	
1	Egg white	1

1. Beat the eggs in a bowl (or use a blender or food processor) and add a pinch of salt, the flour and 2 tablespoons of the oil. Beat together well and add the beer a little at a time. Leave to stand for 1 hour.
2. Peel the zucchini and cut them into thin slices or sticks. Spread out on a clean cloth and dry well.
3. Heat the oil in a deep pan to 340°F / 175°C.
4. Put some flour in a deep dish and coat the zucchini in it.
5. Beat the egg white until stiff and fold into the batter.
6. Dip the zucchini in the batter and plunge them in the oil, which should be hot, but not smoking. Cook for a few minutes until puffed and brown and then drain them on paper towels. Keep them warm while cooking the rest of the fritters. Serve hot with a garlic mayonnaise.

Crosnes sautés
Sautéed Chinese Artichokes

	00:15 Serves 4		00:20

American	Ingredients	Metric/Imperial
	Coarse salt	
2 lb	Chinese artichokes	1 kg / 2 lb
	Salt and pepper	
¼ cup	Butter	50 g / 2 oz
2 tbsp	Chopped fresh parsley	2 tbsp
½	Garlic clove	½

1. Sprinkle the coarse salt onto a cloth and place the artichokes on top. Rub them to remove the thin outer skin and then rinse them as quickly as possible.

2. Put the artichokes in a saucepan with just enough salted water to prevent them burning. Bring to a boil, cover and cook for about 10 minutes.
3. Melt the butter in a frying pan, add the artichokes, cover the pan and brown them over a low heat for a further 10 minutes. Season with pepper.
4. Serve sprinkled with a mixture of chopped parsley and finely chopped garlic. This dish is a good accompaniment to roasts.

Épinards béchamel
Spinach with Béchamel Sauce

	00:15		00:30

American	Ingredients	Metric/Imperial
5 lb	Fresh spinach	2.5 kg / 5 lb
	Salt and pepper	
3 cups	Béchamel sauce (see page 124)	750 ml / 1¼ pints
	Grated nutmeg	

1. Preheat the oven to 425°F / 220°C / Gas Mark 7.
2. Remove the stems from the spinach and wash the leaves thoroughly. Put in a large saucepan with a large pinch of salt (no extra water should be needed) and cook over a medium heat for 8 minutes, stirring occasionally. Drain well.
3. Butter an ovenproof dish. Put half the spinach in the bottom of the dish and cover with half the sauce. Add another layer of spinach and top with the remaining sauce.
4. Bake for 10 minutes until golden brown. Serve very hot.

Cook's tip: add a soft-boiled or poached egg to each serving for a quick lunch or supper dish; or sprinkle with grated gruyère cheese for extra goodness.

Gratin de courgettes
Baked Zucchini [Courgettes]

	00:05		00:25

American	Ingredients	Metric/Imperial
2 lb	Zucchini [courgettes]	1 kg / 2 lb
	Salt and pepper	
3	Eggs	3
1 cup	Crème fraîche	250 ml / 8 fl oz
1 cup	Grated gruyère cheese	125 g / 4 oz
	Grated nutmeg	

1. Preheat the oven to 425°F / 220°C / Gas Mark 7.
2. Wash the zucchini and cut into slices ½ in / 1 cm thick. Cook in a little boiling salted water for about 10 minutes then drain well.
3. Place the zucchini in a buttered ovenproof dish. Beat the eggs in a bowl with the crème fraîche, grated cheese, salt and pepper and a pinch of nutmeg. Pour over the zucchini. Brown in the oven for 15 minutes. Serve very hot.

Jardinière de légumes
Mixed Spring Vegetables

▷ 00:45   00:30 🍲

American	Ingredients	Metric/Imperial
¾ lb	Turnips	350 g / 12 oz
¾ lb	Carrots	350 g / 12 oz
¾ lb	New potatoes	350 g / 12 oz
¾ lb	Fresh peas	350 g / 12 oz
¾ lb	Green beans	350 g / 12 oz
	Salt and pepper	
1 tsp	Sugar	1 tsp
3 tbsp	Chopped fresh mixed herbs	3 tbsp
1 cup	Butter at room temperature	250 g / 8 oz

1. Peel and dice the turnips, carrots and potatoes. Shell the peas. String the beans, if necessary, wash and cut them into pieces ½ in / 1 cm long.
2. Boil some salted water in 3 separate saucepans.
3. Put the diced carrot in one saucepan and cook for 5 minutes before adding the turnips. Cook for a further 5 minutes, and drain well.
4. Add the beans to another saucepan, cook for 5 minutes and then add the peas and the sugar. Cook for a further 5-10 minutes and drain well.
5. Add the potatoes to the third saucepan, bring to a boil and cook for 10-15 minutes over a gentle heat so that the potatoes do not disintegrate. Drain well.
6. While the vegetables are cooking, mix the fresh herbs with three-quarters of the butter. Season with salt and pepper. Roll into a sausage shape and wrap in foil. Place in the refrigerator to harden.
7. Place the drained vegetables in a serving dish with the remaining butter. If you are not serving them immediately, keep them warm over a saucepan of boiling water so that the butter melts without cooking.
8. Serve very hot with the herb butter.

Marrons bouillis
Boiled Chestnuts

▷ 00:30   00:45 🍲

American	Ingredients	Metric/Imperial
3 lb	Chestnuts	1.5 kg / 3 lb
1 quart	Chicken stock	1 l / 1¾ pints
	Salt and pepper	
	Butter	

1. Using a small pointed knife, cut around the chestnuts, just piercing both skins. Place in a saucepan, cover with cold water and bring to a boil. Boil for 7 minutes and then remove from the heat.
2. Remove the chestnuts from the water one by one, peeling them as you go along. Put the chicken stock in a large saucepan, add the chestnuts, and a little water if necessary, so that the chestnuts are covered by the liquid. Bring to a boil and simmer gently for 25-35 minutes.
3. Drain the chestnuts and place in a warmed serving dish. Add salt, pepper and butter to taste.

Chicory loaf

Pain de chicorée
Chicory [Curly Endive] Loaf

▷ 00:30   01:00 🍲

American	Ingredients	Metric/Imperial
6	Heads of chicory [curly endive]	6
	Salt and pepper	
1 cup	Béchamel sauce	250 ml / 8 fl oz
4	Eggs	4
	Grated nutmeg	
1 (2 lb)	Can[s] tomato sauce	2 (400 g / 14 oz)
6 oz	Cooked ham	150 g / 6 oz

1. Preheat the oven to 350°F / 180°C / Gas Mark 4.
2. Remove the outer leaves from the chicory, wash thoroughly and drain.
3. Heat a large saucepan of salted water. Add the chicory, bring back to a boil and cook for 15 minutes. Drain well and chop coarsely.
4. Mix together the sauce and the chicory. Beat the eggs and add to the mixture together with a pinch of nutmeg. Taste and adjust the seasoning.
5. Grease a 1 quart [1 l / 2 pint] charlotte mold generously with butter and pour in the mixture. Place the mold in an ovenproof pan filled with water.
6. Bake for about 1 hour. The top of the loaf should hardly change color and the water in the pan should not boil. To check whether the loaf is cooked, pierce with a knife. If the blade comes out dry, then the loaf is ready.
7. Boil the tomato sauce to reduce it by one-third. Dice the ham and add to the sauce.
8. Remove the loaf from the oven and let cool 5 minutes before unmolding it onto a serving dish. Pour around the tomato sauce and serve.

Pain d'épinard
Spinach Loaf

	00:40		01:00

American	Ingredients	Metric/Imperial
6 lb	Fresh spinach	3 kg / 6 lb
	Salt and pepper	
3 tbsp	Butter	40 g / 1½ oz
3 tbsp	Flour	40 g / 1½ oz
¾ cup	Crème fraîche	200 ml / ⅓ pint
4	Eggs	4
	Grated nutmeg	

1. Preheat the oven to 350°F / 180°C / Gas Mark 6.
2. Remove the stems from the spinach and wash thoroughly.
3. Put the spinach in a large pan with a pinch of salt and cook for 5-8 minutes. Drain well then chop coarsely.
4. Melt the butter in a saucepan, add the flour and stir until it is absorbed. Gradually stir in the crème fraîche and cook, stirring, until thickened. Add the beaten eggs, a pinch of grated nutmeg, salt and pepper and mix well.
5. Mix together the sauce and the spinach. Taste, and adjust the seasoning. Pour into a buttered 1 quart [1 l / 2 pint] charlotte mold and place the mold in an ovenproof pan filled with water.
6. Bake for 1 hour, without allowing the mixture to brown. To check whether it is cooked, pierce the loaf with a knife. If the blade comes out dry then it is ready.
7. Serve with a cheese sauce.

Pain de laitue
Lettuce Loaf

	00:45		00:45

American	Ingredients	Metric/Imperial
	Salt and pepper	
3	Heads of soft-leaved lettuce	3
4	Eggs	4
2½ cups	Béchamel sauce	600 ml / 1 pint
	Grated nutmeg	
2	Slices of cooked ham	2

1. Preheat the oven to 350°F / 180°C / Gas Mark 4.
2. Bring a saucepan of salted water to a boil. Cut the heads of lettuce in half and plunge into the boiling water. Cook for 2 minutes. Drain well. Chop the lettuce finely.
3. Break the eggs into a bowl and beat well. Add the lettuce and half the sauce. Mix well.
4. Butter an 8 in / 20 cm savarin mold. Cut the slices of ham into triangles and arrange in the bottom of the mold. Pour the lettuce mixture into the mold and place in a large ovenproof dish. Fill the dish with water to halfway up the sides of the mold.
5. Bake for 45 minutes.
6. To serve, turn out of the mold and cover with the remaining béchamel sauce.

Oseille à la crème
Sorrel with Cream

	00:15		00:30

American	Ingredients	Metric/Imperial
2 lb	Sorrel	1 kg / 2 lb
	Salt and pepper	
⅓ cup	Butter	75 g / 3 oz
⅔ cup	Crème fraîche	150 ml / ¼ pint

1. Remove the stems from the sorrel and wash the leaves. Bring a saucepan of salted water to a boil. Add the sorrel and cook for 5 minutes. Drain well.
2. Melt the butter in a frying pan, add the sorrel and cook for 10-15 minutes, stirring constantly. Season with salt and pepper and add the crème fraîche. Stir over a moderate heat until the sauce thickens. Adjust the seasoning if necessary and serve immediately.

Petits pois surprise
Peas and Chicken in Aspic

	01:00		01:20

American	Ingredients	Metric/Imperial
2	Carrots	2
2	Onions	2
1	Leek	1
8 cups	Water	2 l / 3½ pints
2	Bouquets garnis	2
	Salt and pepper	
1 (2 lb)	Chicken	1 (1 kg / 2 lb)
1 envelope	Unflavored gelatin	20 g / 1 packet
4 lb	Fresh peas, shelled	2 kg / 4 lb
1 tbsp	Sugar	1 tbsp
3	Fresh mint sprigs	3

1. Peel the carrots and onions and place in a saucepan with the leek and water. Add one bouquet garni, salt and pepper, and bring to a boil. Cook for 20 minutes. Add the chicken and cook for 35-40 minutes.
2. Remove the chicken. Take the meat from the carcass and cut it into small pieces, discarding the skin. Leave to cool.
3. Strain the stock and reduce it to 3 cups [750 ml / 1¼ pints]. Sprinkle in the gelatin, stir well and set to one side to cool.
4. Place the peas in a saucepan with a little boiling water. Season with salt, pepper, the sugar, the remaining bouquet garni and the mint. Cook for 10-15 minutes. The peas should still be quite firm. Refresh under cold water and drain well.
5. Arrange ½ in / 1 cm of peas in the bottom of a 10 in / 26 cm savarin mold and add a little of the lukewarm aspic to cover. Leave in a cool place for 15 minutes.
6. Place the diced chicken on top of the peas and garnish the sides of the mold with peas as you go along.
7. Once the mold is full, moisten it with the remaining aspic until it reaches the top. Chill for 6 hours.
8. To remove from the mold, dip the mold in lukewarm water for a few seconds before turning out. Serve with mayonnaise or a vinaigrette dressing

Concombres au gratin
Cucumbers in Cheese Sauce

00:30   **00:30**

American	Ingredients	Metric/Imperial
3	Cucumbers	3
	Salt and pepper	
1	Onion	1
2 tbsp	Butter	25 g / 1 oz
2 tbsp	Flour	25 g / 1 oz
¾ cup	Crème fraîche	200 ml / 7 fl oz
½ cup	Grated gruyère cheese	50 g / 2 oz
	Grated nutmeg	

1. Preheat the oven to 425°F / 220°C / Gas Mark 7.
2. Peel the cucumbers and cut into quarters, lengthwise. Remove the seeds and dice the flesh.
3. Add the cubes of cucumber to a pan of boiling salted water and blanch for 10-12 minutes. Drain and place in a gratin dish.
4. Peel and finely chop the onion. Heat the butter in a saucepan, add the onion and cook over a low heat, without browning. Sprinkle in the flour, mix well and add the crème fraîche, stirring constantly until the mixture has thickened. Stir in the grated cheese, a small pinch of nutmeg and salt and pepper to taste.
5. Pour the sauce over the cucumber. Bake for 20 minutes until the top is golden brown.

Cook's tip: this is a delicious first course, but it also goes well with roasts.

Épinards en gâteau
Spinach Cake

00:15   **00:30**

American	Ingredients	Metric/Imperial
2 lb	Spinach	1 kg / 2 lb
2 cups	Flour	250 g / 8 oz
3	Medium-sized eggs	3
1 cup	Butter	250 g / 8 oz
⅓ cup	Crème fraîche	6 tbsp
1 cup	Ricotta or curd cheese	250 g / 8 oz
	Salt and pepper	
	Grated nutmeg	

1. Preheat the oven to 400°F / 200°C / Gas Mark 6.
2. Remove the stems from the spinach and wash the leaves thoroughly. Drain and dry in a clean cloth then place on a chopping board and chop coarsely.
3. Place the flour in a bowl, form a hollow and add to it the eggs, the butter, the crème fraîche, the cheese, salt, pepper and a pinch of nutmeg. Work the mixture together using your hands, as if making pastry.
4. Add the chopped spinach, mix together and place in a buttered ovenproof dish.
5. Bake for 30 minutes. Check whether the cake is cooked by inserting a knife – if it comes out dry the cake is ready.

Gratin de courgettes au riz
Zucchini [Courgettes] and Rice

00:25   **00:40**

American	Ingredients	Metric/Imperial
4 lb	Zucchini [courgettes]	2 kg / 4 lb
	Salt and pepper	
3 tbsp	Long-grain rice	3 tbsp
3	Eggs	3
1 cup	Crème fraîche	250 ml / 8 fl oz
1¾ cups	Grated cheese	200 g / 7 oz
	Grated nutmeg	

1. Preheat the oven to 350°F / 180°C / Gas Mark 4.
2. Cut the zucchini into thick slices. Cook for about 5 minutes in a little salted water and drain well.
3. Arrange in a gratin dish and sprinkle with the rice.
4. In a bowl beat the eggs with the crème fraîche and the grated cheese. Flavor with a pinch of nutmeg and season with salt and pepper.
5. Pour the sauce over the zucchini and mix well together.
6. Bake for 40 minutes or until the rice has absorbed the water from the zucchini and the top is lightly browned.

Épinards au gratin
Layered Spinach Casserole

00:40   **00:30**

American	Ingredients	Metric/Imperial
4 lb	Fresh spinach	2 kg / 4 lb
	Salt and pepper	
1½ lb	Button mushrooms	750 g / 1½ lb
1	Lemon	1
¼ cup	Butter	50 g / 2 oz
3 tbsp	Flour	40 g / 1½ oz
1¼ cups	Crème fraîche	300 ml / ½ pint
	Grated nutmeg	
½ cup	Grated gruyère cheese	50 g / 2 oz
3-4 tbsp	Milk	3-4 tbsp

1. Preheat the oven to 400°F / 200°C / Gas Mark 6.
2. Remove the stems from the spinach and wash the leaves thoroughly. Put in a large saucepan with a pinch of salt (no extra water should be needed) and cook over a medium heat for 8 minutes, stirring from time to time. Drain well.
3. Clean and slice the mushrooms and put them in a large saucepan with a little salted water, a few drops of lemon juice and a tablespoon [15 g / ½ oz] of butter. Cook until all the liquid has evaporated.
4. Melt the remaining butter in a saucepan, add the flour and stir until it is absorbed. Gradually stir in the crème fraîche and cook, stirring, until thickened. Season with salt and pepper and add a pinch of nutmeg. Pour 4 tablespoons of the sauce over the mushrooms, stir together and put through a blender, vegetable mill or food processor to make a purée.

5. Arrange 3 layers of spinach, alternating with 2 layers of mushroom purée in an ovenproof dish. Mix the remaining sauce with the grated cheese and, if necessary, dilute with a few tablespoons of milk. Pour over the spinach.
6. Bake for 30 minutes. The top should be brown but not burned.

Grind a little pepper over the top and bake for 20-30 minutes. Do not allow them to brown, and moisten from time to time with a little water, if necessary.
5. Sprinkle with the chopped parsley and serve as an accompaniment to any meat.

Fèves au lard
Broad or Lima Beans with Bacon

American	Ingredients	Metric/Imperial
00:30		00:25
4 lb	Fresh broad or lima beans	2 kg / 4 lb
½ lb	Bacon	250 g / 8 oz
2 tbsp	Butter	20 g / ¾ oz
	Salt and pepper	
5 tbsp	Crème fraîche	5 tbsp
2	Egg yolks	2

1. Shell the beans and cut the bacon into small strips. Heat the butter in a frying pan and brown the bacon for 3 or 4 minutes. Drain.
2. Place the beans in a saucepan with the bacon. Cover with a little water and season with pepper. Bring to a boil then lower the heat, cover, and cook for 10-15 minutes.
3. Meanwhile, place the crème fraîche in a bowl, add a pinch of salt and the egg yolks and mix well.
4. When the beans are cooked, remove the saucepan from the heat and add the egg and crème mixture. Return it to a very low heat and stir for 1 minute without letting it boil. Adjust the seasoning if necessary, and serve.

Fenouil meunière
Baked Buttered Fennel

American	Ingredients	Metric/Imperial
00:10		00:30 to 00:40
1	Lemon	1
	Salt and pepper	
6-9	Heads of fennel	6-9
⅓ cup	Butter	75 g / 3 oz
2 tbsp	Chopped fresh parsley	2 tbsp

1. Preheat the oven to 300°F / 150°C / Gas Mark 2.
2. Squeeze the juice from the lemon and add to a saucepan of water. Season with salt and bring to a boil.
3. Trim the heads of fennel and cut them in half. Rinse and add them to the pan. Cook for 10-15 minutes until just tender. The point of a knife should penetrate fairly easily when they are done. Take care not to overcook as this results in a loss of flavor.
4. Drain the fennel well and cut each piece in half again. Arrange in an ovenproof dish and dot with pieces of the butter.

Morilles à la crème
Morels with Cream

American	Ingredients	Metric/Imperial
00:10		00:20
3 lb	Fresh morels or other mushrooms	1.5 kg / 3 lb
5	Shallots	5
½ cup	Butter	125 g / 4 oz
	Salt and pepper	
1¼ cups	Dry white wine	300 ml / ½ pint
1¼ cups	Crème fraîche	300 ml / ½ pint

1. Trim the stems of the mushrooms, wash quickly and wipe dry. Peel and finely chop the shallots. Melt the butter in a large saucepan, add the mushrooms and cook over a moderate heat for 10 minutes, until all the liquid has evaporated.
2. Add the shallots and season with salt and pepper. When the shallots are translucent, add the wine. Cook, uncovered, over a moderate heat for 10 minutes, or until the wine has completely evaporated.
3. Add the crème fraîche, stir to thicken over a high heat and serve immediately.

Haricots verts frais
Green Beans with Garlic

American	Ingredients	Metric/Imperial
00:20		00:10 to 00:15
2 lb	Green beans	1 kg / 2 lb
	Salt and pepper	
⅓ cup	Butter	75 g / 3 oz
1	Onion	1
1	Garlic clove	1
1 tbsp	Chopped fresh parsley	1 tbsp

1. Trim the beans, stringing them if necessary. Rinse them in cold water.
2. Bring some salted water to a boil in a saucepan. Add the beans and cook, partially covered, for about 8 minutes or until barely tender.
3. Meanwhile, melt half the butter in a small pan. Peel and finely chop the onion and garlic and add to the pan. Cook until the onion is translucent.
4. When the beans are cooked, rinse them under cold water and drain.
5. Return to the saucepan and reheat gently, without a lid, with the rest of the butter.
6. Stir in the onion and garlic mixture and season with salt and pepper. Finally, stir in the chopped parsley and serve immediately.

Haricots Périgourdine
White Beans in Tomato Sauce

American	Ingredients	Metric/Imperial
2 cups	Dried navy [haricot] beans	500 g / 1 lb
3	Garlic cloves	3
½ lb	Bacon	250 g / 8 oz
1	Small bunch of fresh parsley	1
3	Tomatoes	3
1	Onion	1
2	Cloves	2
	Salt and pepper	

1. Soak the beans overnight in water to cover.
2. Drain the beans and place them in a saucepan. Cover with fresh water. Bring to a boil and simmer for 1 hour.
3. Peel the cloves of garlic and put them through a blender, vegetable mill or food processor with the bacon and parsley.
4. Peel the tomatoes (first plunging them into boiling water for 10 seconds), and remove the seeds. Peel the onion and stud with the cloves.
5. Add the tomatoes, onion and bacon mixture to the beans and stir well. Cook over a gentle heat for a further 30-45 minutes or until the beans are tender.
6. Discard the onion before serving. Serve as an accompaniment to spareribs with barbecue sauce .

Pieds-de-mouton en fricassée
Mushroom Fricassée

American	Ingredients	Metric/Imperial
2 lb	Mushrooms	1 kg / 2 lb
6	Shallots	6
6 tbsp	Butter	75 g / 3 oz
⅔ cup	Chicken stock	150 ml / ¼ pint
1	Garlic clove	1
1	Onion	1
1	Bouquet garni	1
	Salt and pepper	
1	Egg yolk	1
6	Slices of bread ½ in / 1 cm thick	6

1. Clean the mushrooms and trim the stems. Peel and finely chop the shallots.
2. Heat three-quarters of the butter in a saucepan. Brown the mushrooms and sprinkle with the shallots.
3. Heat the stock and pour over the mushrooms. Peel the garlic clove and cut it in half. Peel the onion and cut it into quarters. Add the garlic and onion to the saucepan along with the bouquet garni. Season with salt and pepper and cook for 30-45 minutes over a moderate heat.
4. At the end of this time, remove the vegetables using a slotted spoon and keep warm. Strain the cooking liquid.
5. Place the egg yolk in a bowl, and mix with 1 tablespoon of the strained cooking liquid. Gradually add half the remaining liquid, stirring constantly, and then pour this mixture into the

rest of the liquid. Place over a low heat and stir to thicken, without allowing the sauce to boil.
6. Cut the crusts from the bread and cut into triangles. Fry in the remaining butter until golden brown on both sides.
7. Place the mushrooms in a serving dish and cover with the sauce. Garnish with the bread triangles and serve very hot.

Petits pois à la Parisienne
Braised Peas

American	Ingredients	Metric/Imperial
1	Head of romaine [cos] lettuce	1
4	Onions	4
1	Bunch of fresh parsley	1
2	Scallions [spring onions]	2
¼ cup	Butter	50 g / 2 oz
1 tbsp	Flour	1 tbsp
2 cups	Water	500 ml / ¾ pint
2 lb	Fresh peas	1 kg / 2 lb
	Salt and pepper	
3	Egg yolks	3

1. Wash the lettuce. Drain. Cut into thin strips. Peel the onions and cut into thin slices. Finely chop the parsley and scallions.
2. Melt the butter in a saucepan, add the flour and stir until the butter has absorbed all the flour. Stir in the water, a little at a time, and bring to a boil. Add the peas, onions, lettuce, scallions and parsley and season with salt and pepper. Cover and cook over a low heat for 20-30 minutes.
3. To serve, remove the saucepan from the heat and add the egg yolks, one by one, stirring vigorously. Adjust the seasoning, if necessary, and serve immediately.

Poireaux gratinés
Leeks in Cheese Sauce

American	Ingredients	Metric/Imperial
18	Leeks	18
	Salt and pepper	
6 tbsp	Butter	75 g / 3 oz
¼ cup	Flour	50 g / 2 oz
3 cups	Milk	750 ml / 1 ¼ pints
1 ¼ cups	Grated gruyère cheese	150 g / 5 oz
	Grated nutmeg	

1. Preheat the oven to 425°F / 220°C / Gas Mark 7.
2. Trim the leeks to leave the white part only and wash well. Boil some salted water in a saucepan and add the leeks. Simmer, without a lid, for about 20 minutes, or until the leeks are just cooked.
3. Meanwhile, melt three-quarters of the butter in a heavy-bottomed saucepan, sprinkle with the flour and stir for 2-3 minutes over a low heat until the butter has absorbed all the

flour. Add the milk a little at a time and stir over a gentle heat, until the sauce thickens. Add two-thirds of the grated cheese, and season with salt, pepper and a little freshly grated nutmeg. Remove from the heat.

4. Drain the leeks carefully and arrange in a buttered gratin dish. Cover with the cheese sauce, sprinkle with the remaining cheese and dot with the rest of the butter.

5. Bake for about 15 minutes until golden brown.

Petits pois bonne femme

Peas with Ham and Onions

	00:20		00:50

American	Ingredients	Metric/Imperial
12	Small onions	12
¼ cup	Butter	50 g / 2 oz
1	Bouquet garni	1
	Salt and pepper	
2 lb	Fresh peas, shelled	1 kg / 2 lb
½ lb	Cooked ham	250 g / 8 oz
	Grated nutmeg	
2 tsp	Sugar	2 tsp
2	Egg yolks	2
1 tbsp	Water	1 tbsp

1. Peel the onions and place in à heavy-bottomed saucepan. Add half the butter, the bouquet garni and a little water. Cook over a low heat until the liquid has evaporated and the onions have softened.

2. Meanwhile, heat ½ in / 1 cm of salted water in a large saucepan. Add the peas and cook, covered for 15 minutes.

3. Dice the ham and add to the onions. Cook until the ham begins to brown.

4. When the peas are cooked, drain and add to the onions and ham with the remaining butter, a little freshly grated nutmeg and the sugar. Season with salt and pepper, cover and heat for 5 minutes over a low heat, stirring to mix well.

5. Discard the bouquet garni. Remove the saucepan from the heat and add the egg yolks mixed with the water. Stir well and serve very hot.

Purée de carottes

Creamed Carrots

	00:20	00:30 to 00:40	

American	Ingredients	Metric/Imperial
3 lb	Carrots	1.5 kg / 3 lb
	Salt	
1	Onion	1
6 tbsp	Butter	75 g / 3 oz
1 lb	Potatoes	500 g / 1 lb
½ cup	Crème fraîche	125 ml / 4 fl oz
1 tsp	Sugar (optional)	1 tsp
2	Egg yolks	2
	Grated nutmeg	

1. Peel the carrots and cut into thick slices. Heat a small amount of salted water in a saucepan. Add the carrots and cook for 10 minutes. Drain.

2. Peel and slice the onion. Heat half the butter in a saucepan and add the carrots and onion. Cover and cook over a low heat, without allowing either vegetable to brown, until the carrots are tender.

3. Meanwhile, peel the potatoes and cook in boiling salted water for 25 minutes or until soft. Drain.

4. Purée the vegetables using a blender, vegetable mill or a food processor, and place in a saucepan over a low heat. Stir in the crème fraîche a little at a time together with the sugar, if necessary. Finally, stir in the remaining butter and the egg yolks and season with a little freshly grated nutmeg. Serve very hot.

Cook's tip: a leek purée can be prepared and served at the same time.

Ratatouille (see page 172)

Poireaux braisés

Braised Leeks

	00:15		00:40

American	Ingredients	Metric/Imperial
18	Leeks	18
½ cup	Butter	125 g / 4 oz
	Salt and pepper	
½ lb	Bacon	250 g / 8 oz
1 tbsp	Oil	1 tbsp
¼ cup	Crème fraîche	4 tbsp

1. Trim the leeks, removing the roots and the very green leaves. Wash well under cold water and wipe dry.

2. Melt the butter in a saucepan, add the leeks, salt and pepper, cover and cook over a gentle heat for 30 minutes.

3. Meanwhile, cut the bacon into small strips. Heat the oil in a frying pan and brown the bacon over a moderate heat for 5 minutes, stirring constantly. Drain.

4. When the leeks are cooked, remove from the pan with a slotted spoon. Arrange in a serving dish and keep warm. Pour the crème fraîche into the saucepan together with the bacon and stir over a moderate heat for a few minutes until the sauce thickens. Cover the leeks with the sauce and serve immediately.

Potiron en gratin
Creamed Pumpkin

	00:20		00:30

American	Ingredients	Metric/Imperial
4 lb	Pumpkin	2 kg / 4 lb
7 tbsp	Butter	90 g / 4½ oz
2 tbsp	Flour	2 tbsp
1 cup	Milk	250 ml / 8 fl oz
1 cup	Crème fraîche	250 ml / 8 fl oz
	Salt and pepper	
	Grated nutmeg	
4	Eggs	4

1. Peel the pumpkin, discard the seeds and take out the stringy center. Cut the flesh into pieces. Place in a saucepan with ¼ cup [50 g / 2 oz] of the butter and cook for about 20 minutes over a moderate heat, stirring frequently, until the pumpkin is tender.
2. Purée in a blender, vegetable mill or food processor. The pumpkin purée should be quite thick. If it is too liquid, reduce by stirring it over a high heat.
3. Preheat the oven to 400°F / 200°C / Gas Mark 6.
4. Heat 2 tbsp [25 g / 1 oz] of the butter in a saucepan, sprinkle with the flour and cook for 2 or 3 minutes. Gradually stir in the milk and then the crème fraîche and cook for a few minutes until the sauce thickens. Add the puréed pumpkin and season with salt and pepper and a little freshly grated nutmeg. Stir in the eggs and leave to cool for a few minutes.
5. Butter an ovenproof dish and pour in the purée. Dot with the remaining butter and bake for 10 minutes.

Purée de chicorée
Chicory [Curly Endive] Purée

	00:20		00:25

American	Ingredients	Metric/Imperial
4 lb	Chicory [curly endive]	2 kg / 4 lb
	Salt and pepper	
2 tbsp	Butter	60 g / 2 oz
1½ cups	Béchamel sauce	350 ml / 12 fl oz
4	Slices of bread ½ in / 1 cm thick	4

1. Remove any damaged leaves from the chicory, cut into quarters and wash. Boil some salted water in a saucepan, add the chicory and simmer for 15 minutes.
2. Drain the chicory well and put it through a blender, vegetable mill or food processor. Add to the béchamel sauce. Taste and adjust the seasoning if necessary. Pour into a warmed serving dish and keep hot.
3. Melt the butter in a frying pan and fry the slices of bread until golden brown on both sides. Cut into small cubes and arrange on the chicory. Serve immediately.

Cook's tip: although this vegetable is more usually served raw in salads, it is equally good cooked. Try this delicious alternative as an accompaniment to crisp bacon.

Ratatouille Niçoise
Ratatouille

	00:40		01:30 to 02:00

American	Ingredients	Metric/Imperial
6	Eggplant [aubergines]	6
	Salt and pepper	
2	Sweet green or red peppers	2
6	Tomatoes	6
4	Medium-size onions	4
2	Garlic cloves	2
4	Zucchini [courgettes]	4
¼ cup	Olive oil	4 tbsp
1-2 tsp	Sugar	1-2 tsp
1	Bouquet garni	1

1. Preheat the broiler [grill].
2. Peel the eggplant and cut them into slices. Place them in a colander, sprinkle with salt and leave for 30 minutes to drain off the liquid.
3. Meanwhile, skin the peppers by placing them under the hot broiler until the skins are charred. The skin should then peel off easily under cold running water. Remove the seeds and cut the flesh into thin strips.
4. Peel the tomatoes (first plunging them into boiling water for 10 seconds). Cut in half and remove the seeds. Peel the onions and cut into slices. Peel and crush the garlic. Slice the zucchini.
5. Heat the olive oil in a large flameproof casserole and add the onions and garlic. Cook until soft but not browned.
6. Rinse the eggplant and dry on paper towels. Add to the pan together with the peppers. Cover and cook for 15 minutes over a medium heat.
7. Put in the zucchini and tomatoes and stir well. Season with salt, pepper and a little sugar. Add the bouquet garni and simmer, uncovered, over a moderate heat for about 50 minutes or until the vegetables are cooked and most of the cooking liquid has evaporated.
8. Serve hot or cold.

Purée de chou-fleur
Cauliflower Purée

	00:15		00:30

American	Ingredients	Metric/Imperial
1	Large cauliflower	1
¼ cup	Butter	50 g / 2 oz
¼ cup	Crème fraîche	4 tbsp
1 tsp	Sugar	1 tsp
	Salt and pepper	

1. Remove the leaves from the cauliflower, cut off the stem and wash carefully.
2. Cook the cauliflower in a saucepan, steamer or pressure cooker until it is just tender.
3. Drain the cauliflower thoroughly and purée it in a blender, vegetable mill or food processor. Place the purée in a saucepan over a gentle heat so that any excess water evaporates.
4. Add the butter, crème fraîche and sugar, season with salt and pepper and stir well.

Cook's tip: serve as an accompaniment to all roasts.

Poivrons farcis braisés
Stuffed Peppers

	01:00		00:45

American	Ingredients	Metric/Imperial
2 lb	Tomatoes	1 kg / 2 lb
1	Large onion	1
2 tbsp	Olive oil	2 tbsp
1	Bouquet garni	1
1	Garlic clove	1
	Salt and pepper	
2	Medium-size onions	2
½ cup	Butter	125 g / 4 oz
½ cup	Long-grain rice	125 g / 4 oz
1¼ cups	Water	300 ml / ½ pint
1 lb	Ground [minced] lamb or beef	500 g / 1 lb
	Cayenne pepper	
6	Sweet green or red peppers	6

1. Peel the tomatoes (first plunging them in boiling water for 10 seconds). Cut into quarters and remove the seeds. Peel the large onion and cut into thin slices. Place the tomatoes and onion in a frying pan with the oil and add the bouquet garni and peeled and crushed garlic. Season with salt and pepper. Reduce, uncovered, over a gentle heat for 15 minutes. Remove the bouquet garni and purée in a blender or food processor.
2. Peel the medium-size onions and chop finely. Soften, without browning, in a saucepan with ¼ cup [60 g / 2 oz] of the butter.
3. Add the rice to the saucepan and stir well. Add the water together with a pinch of salt. Cover and cook, without stirring, until the rice has absorbed all the liquid.
4. Melt the remaining butter in a frying pan and brown the ground lamb over a moderate heat. Add the meat to the rice, along with 3 tablespoons of the tomato sauce and a pinch of cayenne pepper. Cook for a further 10 minutes.

5. Heat a saucepan of salted water, add the peppers and boil for 5 minutes. Drain and wipe them dry. Carefully cut out the stems of the peppers and remove the seeds. Stuff with the rice and meat mixture. Replace the pepper stems.
6. Place the peppers upright in a flameproof casserole and pour in the rest of the tomato sauce. Cover and simmer gently for about 45 minutes or until the peppers are tender.

Artichoke hearts with herbs

Poivrade en ragoût
Artichoke Hearts with Herbs

	00:20		00:30

American	Ingredients	Metric/Imperial
12	Small globe artichokes	12
	Lemon juice	
12	Small white onions	12
1½ lb	Small new potatoes	750 g / 1½ lb
2 tbsp	Olive oil	2 tbsp
1	Bay leaf	1
2 tsp	Dried thyme	2 tsp
2	Garlic cloves	2
	Dried savory	
	Dried basil	
	Salt and pepper	

1. Cut the stems and outer leaves from the artichokes and remove the remaining leaves and hairy choke with a small pointed knife until only the hearts remain. Rub these with a little lemon juice so that they do not turn black.
2. Peel the onions and press one into each artichoke heart.
3. Scrape or peel the potatoes, wash and drain them. Heat the olive oil in a heavy pan and add the artichoke hearts and the potatoes along with the bay leaf, thyme, peeled and crushed garlic, a pinch each of savory and basil, salt and pepper. Add water just to cover the ingredients and cook over a gentle heat for 25-30 minutes.

Tchaktchouka

Baked Eggs in Pepper Ragoût

	00:40		00:45

American	Ingredients	Metric/Imperial
4	Sweet peppers	4
2	Onions	2
2	Garlic cloves	2
3 tbsp	Olive oil	3 tbsp
2 lb	Tomatoes	1 kg / 2 lb
	Cayenne pepper	
1	Bay leaf	1
2	Fresh thyme sprigs	2
	Salt	
6	Eggs	6

1. Preheat the broiler [grill]. Place the peppers under the hot broiler and cook, turning constantly, until the skin is charred. Wrap them in a damp cloth and let them cool for 10 minutes. Peel and remove the seeds, then cut the flesh into thin strips. Peel and finely chop the onions and garlic.
2. Preheat the oven to 425°F / 220°C / Gas Mark 7.
3. Heat the oil in a frying pan, add the peppers and onions and cook until softened.
4. Peel the tomatoes (first plunging them into boiling water for 10 seconds), remove the seeds and cut into pieces. Add the tomatoes to the peppers, along with a pinch of cayenne pepper, the garlic, crushed bay leaf and the thyme leaves. Cook over a moderate heat until the mixture becomes thick. Add salt to taste.
5. Place the vegetable mixture in an ovenproof dish. Make 6 hollows using the back of a soup spoon and break an egg into each.
6. Place in the oven and bake until the egg whites are set but the yolks still soft. Serve immediately.

Cook's tip: the pepper ragoût can also be served without the eggs as an accompaniment to meat dishes.

Salsifis sautés

Sautéed Salsify

	00:40		00:30 to 00:40

American	Ingredients	Metric/Imperial
1	Lemon	1
3 lb	Salsify or scorzonera	1.5 kg / 3 lb
2 tbsp	Flour	2 tbsp
	Salt and pepper	
⅓ cup	Butter	75 g / 3 oz
½	Garlic clove	½
3 tbsp	Chopped fresh parsley	3 tbsp

1. Fill a bowl with water and add the juice of the lemon. Peel the salsify, cut into 1-1½ in / 3-4 cm pieces and add to the bowl.
2. Mix the flour with a little cold water. Heat some salted water in a pan and add the flour paste as it is about to boil. Stir until it boils and add the drained salsify. Cook over a moderate heat for 15-20 minutes or until just soft. Drain and refresh under cold running water.

3. Melt the butter in a frying pan and add the salsify. Cook gently, stirring frequently, for about 20 minutes. Season with salt and pepper.
4. Peel and chop the garlic and mix with the chopped parsley. Sprinkle over the salsify a few minutes before serving.

Tomates à la provençale

Baked Tomatoes with Herbs

	00:05		00:25

American	Ingredients	Metric/Imperial
3 lb	Tomatoes	1.5 kg / 3 lb
	Salt and pepper	
2 tsp	Dried thyme	2 tsp
1 tsp	Dried rosemary	1 tsp
3 tbsp	Olive oil	3 tbsp
4	Garlic cloves	4
1	Small bunch of fresh parsley	1
2 tbsp	Bread crumbs	2 tbsp

1. Preheat the oven to 400°F / 200°C / Gas Mark 6.
2. Wash the tomatoes and cut in half. Place them, flat side up, in a buttered ovenproof dish. Sprinkle each half with salt, pepper, thyme and rosemary. Pour the olive oil over them and bake for 15-20 minutes.
3. Peel and finely chop the garlic, and chop the parsley. Mix together with the bread crumbs.
4. Take the tomatoes out of the oven and increase the heat to 475°F / 240°C / Gas Mark 9. Sprinkle each tomato half with a heaped teaspoon of the garlic, parsley and bread crumb mixture. Return to the oven for 5 minutes or until the tops are brown.

Cook's tip: this dish is usually served hot, but is equally delicious cold.

Tomates farcies au riz

Tomatoes Stuffed with Rice

	00:30		00:50

American	Ingredients	Metric/Imperial
6	Large tomatoes	6
	Salt and pepper	
1 cup	Long-grain rice	180 g / 6 oz
½ cup	Butter	125 g / 4 oz
1	Small bunch of fresh parsley	1
6	Fresh chives	6
2	Hard-cooked eggs	2
1 cup	Grated gruyère cheese	125 g / 4 oz
2	Fresh chervil sprigs	2

1. Wash the tomatoes, slice off the tops and scoop out the insides with a small spoon, being careful not to puncture the shells. Sprinkle inside the tomato shells with a little salt and place them upside-down on a plate.

2. Boil a large pan of salted water and add the rice. Bring back to a boil and simmer for 6 minutes. Drain the rice and mix with the butter. Return it to the saucepan, cover and cook for 25 minutes over a gentle heat.
3. Preheat the oven to 400°F / 200°C / Gas Mark 6.
4. Place the rice in a mixing bowl. Chop the parsley and the chives and add to the rice. Shell the hard-cooked eggs, mash them and stir into the mixture.
5. Tip the liquid from each tomato and fill with the rice mixture. Arrange in a buttered ovenproof dish. Sprinkle with the grated cheese and chopped chervil and put in the oven. Bake for 25 minutes. Serve hot.

Cook's tip: these could also be served as a hot hors d'oeuvre.

Purée de marrons

Chestnut Purée

⏱ 00:40   00:30 🍲

American	Ingredients	Metric/Imperial
3 lb	Chestnuts	1.5 kg / 3 lb
¼	Celeriac	¼
	Salt and pepper	
1 cup	Milk	250 ml / 8 fl oz
¼ cup	Butter	60 g / 2 oz
2 tbsp	Crème fraîche	2 tbsp

1. Using a small pointed knife, cut around the chestnuts, piercing the 2 skins. Place in a saucepan, cover with cold water and bring to a boil. Boil for about 7 minutes and remove from the heat.
2. Remove the chestnuts one by one, and peel them. Peel the celeriac.
3. Place the chestnuts in a saucepan with the celeriac and cover with cold salted water. Bring to a boil and cook for about 30 minutes then drain well.
4. Purée in a blender, vegetable mill or food-processor and pour the purée into a saucepan. Place over a gentle heat and stir in the milk a little at a time. Add the butter and crème fraîche. Adjust the seasoning if necessary and serve very hot.

Cook's tip: serve with roast goose or turkey.

Topinambours sauce béchamel

Jerusalem Artichokes with Béchamel

⏱ 00:15   00:40 🍲

American	Ingredients	Metric/Imperial
2 lb	Jerusalem artichokes	1 kg / 2 lb
	Salt and pepper	
2 cups	Béchamel sauce	500 ml / ¾ pint
	Grated nutmeg	

1. Peel the artichokes and cook in a small amount of boiling, salted water for 15-20 minutes.
2. Drain the artichokes and add to the sauce. Simmer gently for 10 minutes and serve very hot.

Soufflé aux épinards

Spinach Soufflé

⏱ 00:20   01:00 🍲

American	Ingredients	Metric/Imperial
3 lb	Fresh spinach	1.5 kg / 3 lb
	Salt and pepper	
¼ cup	Butter	50 g / 2 oz
¼ cup	Flour	50 g / 2 oz
2½ cups	Milk	600 ml / 1 pint
	Grated nutmeg	
½ cup	Grated gruyère cheese	50 g / 2 oz
4	Eggs, separated	4

1. Wash the spinach thoroughly and remove the stems. Put in a large saucepan with a large pinch of salt and cook over a medium heat for 8 minutes. Drain well. Leave to cool a little then press the leaves between the palms of the hands to extract all the water. Chop the spinach finely and set aside.
2. Preheat the oven to 425°F / 220°C / Gas Mark 7.
3. Melt the butter in a saucepan, add the flour and stir until it has been absorbed. Gradually stir in the milk and cook, stirring, until thickened. Season with salt and pepper and add a little freshly grated nutmeg and the grated cheese.
4. Add 2 tablespoons of the sauce to the egg yolks and beat well. Stir in the rest of the sauce. Add the spinach.
5. Beat the egg whites until they are stiff and carefully fold into the spinach mixture.
6. Pour into a buttered 8 in / 21 cm soufflé dish to fill it three-quarters full. Bake for 30 minutes without opening the oven door, then increase the temperature of the oven to 450°F / 240°C / Gas Mark 8 and bake for a further 5 minutes. Serve immediately.

Cook's tip: make this soufflé with tender young spinach leaves and serve with glazed carrots and a bowl of hollandaise sauce for an appetizing spring lunch.

Purée de navets

Turnip Purée

⏱ 00:20   00:25 🍲

American	Ingredients	Metric/Imperial
3 lb	Turnips	1.5 kg / 3 lb
	Salt and pepper	
⅓ cup	Butter	75 g / 3 oz
1 tbsp	Sugar	1 tbsp
3 tbsp	Crème fraîche	3 tbsp

1. Peel the turnips. Bring some salted water to a boil in a saucepan and add the turnips. Simmer gently, uncovered for 15 minutes or until tender.
2. Drain the turnips and purée in a blender, vegetable mill or food processor. Cook the purée in a saucepan over a low heat for 5 minutes so that any liquid evaporates.
3. Add the butter, sugar and crème fraîche. Adjust the seasoning, if necessary. Stir for 5 minutes over a low heat and serve very hot.

Cook's tip: serve with ham and bacon dishes.

Galettes de pomme de terre

Creamed Potato Cakes

	00:20	00:35

American	Ingredients	Metric/Imperial
1½ lb	Potatoes	750 g / 1½ lb
	Salt and pepper	
1 cup	Milk	250 ml / 8 fl oz
3 tbsp	Flour	3 tbsp
6	Eggs	6
5 tbsp	Crème fraîche	5 tbsp
⅔ cup	Butter	150 g / 5 oz

1. Peel and cut up the potatoes. Place in a saucepan, cover with cold salted water and cook over a brisk heat for 30 minutes. Drain.
2. Heat the milk in a saucepan. Mash the potatoes and add the hot milk. Season with salt and pepper to taste. Mix thoroughly with a wooden spatula and leave to cool.
3. When the potato is cold add the flour and mix well. Then work in the eggs one at a time together with the crème fraîche. Mix thoroughly. Take one tablespoon of the potato mixture at a time and shape into a flat cake.
4. Melt the butter in a frying pan. When the butter is very hot fry the potato cakes for 1 minute each side and serve immediately.

Cook's tip: use a floury variety of potato to make these cakes.

Pommes de terre boulangère

Boulangère Potatoes

	00:25	01:30

American	Ingredients	Metric/Imperial
3 lb	Waxy potatoes	1.5 kg / 3 lb
½	Garlic clove	½
1	Bay leaf	1
4	Fresh thyme sprigs	4
4	Fresh parsley sprigs	4
¼ cup	Goose fat, beef drippings or lard	50 g / 2 oz
	Salt and pepper	

1. Peel the potatoes and cut into very thin slices using a sharp knife or mandoline. Rinse under cold water to remove starch and drain in a colander.
2. Peel and crush the garlic. Crumble the bay leaf and thyme and chop the parsley. Mix the garlic and herbs together. Grease the bottom and sides of a shallow flameproof dish with half the fat.
3. Cover the bottom of the dish with one-third of the potatoes. Season with salt and pepper and sprinkle with half the herb mixture.
4. Add another layer of potatoes and season with salt and pepper and the remaining herbs.
5. Cover with the remaining potatoes and season once more.
6. Dot the top with the remaining fat and add hot water to the level of the potatoes.
7. Bring to a boil over a medium heat. Lower the heat and simmer for 1 hour until all the water has evaporated.

8. Preheat the oven to 425°F / 220°C / Gas Mark 7.
9. Put the potatoes in the oven to complete the cooking and to color the top. When the potatoes are golden brown, reduce the heat to 325°F / 160°C / Gas Mark 3 and cook for a further 20 minutes.

Pommes darphin

Baked Potato Cake

	00:20 plus standing time	00:40

American	Ingredients	Metric/Imperial
2 lb	Waxy potatoes	1 kg / 2 lb
6 tbsp	Oil	6 tbsp
½ cup	Butter	125 g / 4 oz
	Salt and pepper	

1. Peel the potatoes and leave to stand in cold water for 1 hour. Drain, then cut into fine strips with a coarse grater or mandoline. Dry thoroughly.
2. Preheat the oven to 400°F / 200°C / Gas Mark 6.
3. In the oven heat half the oil in a shallow pan. In a frying pan melt half the butter and then add half the grated potatoes. Season with salt and pepper and stir over a high heat for 5 minutes. Transfer the potatoes to the shallow pan with a slotted spoon. Press down firmly into the pan. Heat the remaining butter in the frying pan and cook the rest of the potatoes in the same way. Add to the shallow pan and press down well.
4. Sprinkle the potatoes with the remaining oil and bake for 20-25 minutes or until golden brown. Turn onto a round dish to serve.

Cook's tip: serve with eggs and bacon for lunch or supper.

Pommes de terre farcies

Potatoes Stuffed with Pork

	00:25	01:00

American	Ingredients	Metric/Imperial
2 lb	Medium-size potatoes	1 kg / 2 lb
1	Garlic clove	1
2	Shallots	2
¼ lb	Cooked ham	125 g / 4 oz
¼ lb	Pork sausage meat	125 g / 4 oz
1 tsp	Chopped fresh parsley	1 tsp
	Salt and pepper	
⅓ cup	Butter	75 g / 3 oz
2 tbsp	Oil	2 tbsp

1. Peel the potatoes and cut a lid off each.
2. With a small pointed knife carefully remove the inside of each potato, taking care not to cut through the outside. Reserve the inside flesh.
3. Peel the garlic and shallots. Grind [mince] these ingredients in a blender, vegetable mill or food processor with the ham and scooped-out potato.
4. In a mixing bowl work the sausage meat with a fork, then add the ham mixture and season with the chopped parsley and

salt and pepper. Stir well until the mixture is completely smooth.

5. Stuff the potatoes with this mixture. Heat the butter and oil in a flameproof casserole and brown the potatoes for a few minutes. Cover and continue cooking over a low heat for 1 hour. Serve very hot.

Pommes duchesse
Duchesse Potatoes

	00:25		00:40
American	**Ingredients**		**Metric/Imperial**
3 lb	Potatoes		1.5 kg / 3 lb
	Salt and pepper		
⅔ cup	Butter		150 g / 5 oz
7	Egg yolks		7
3	Egg whites		3

1. Peel the potatoes. Place in a pan, cover with cold salted water and cook over a brisk heat for 30 minutes.
2. Drain. Mash the potatoes and transfer to a mixing bowl. Add the butter in small pieces and season with salt and pepper to taste.
3. Add six of the egg yolks to the potato mixture. Beat the egg whites until stiff and fold into the mixture.
4. Preheat the oven to 425°F / 220°C / Gas Mark 7.
5. Form the potato mixture into a ball. Flour a pastry board and gently roll out the potato mixture to 2 in / 5 cm thick. Using a small, pointed knife, cut into squares or diamonds.
6. With a pastry brush coat each shape with the remaining egg yolk and transfer to a buttered baking sheet. Bake for 10 minutes and serve hot.

Pommes dauphine
Potato Puffs

	00:15		00:30
	plus making of choux pastry		plus 5 minutes per batch
American	**Ingredients**		**Metric/Imperial**
2 lb	Potatoes		1 kg / 2 lb
	Salt and pepper		
1 quantity	Choux pastry		1 quantity
	Grated nutmeg		
	Oil for deep frying		

1. Peel and cut up the potatoes. Place in a pan, cover with cold salted water and cook over a brisk heat for 30 minutes. Drain and mash the potatoes.
2. Return the mashed potato to the pan and warm over a low heat for a few minutes to evaporate the excess moisture. Remove from the heat and leave to cool.
3. Mix the choux pastry into the potato, adding two parts pastry mixture to one part potato. Season with salt, pepper and freshly grated nutmeg to taste.
4. Heat the oil to 340°F / 175°C. The oil should be hot but not smoking. Form the potato mixture into balls with a teaspoon and add 5 or 6 balls at a time to the hot oil. The potato balls will double in size in seconds. Drain on paper towels. Repeat until all the potato mixture has been cooked. Serve immediately.

Cook's tip: grated gruyère cheese makes a tasty addition.

Pommes chips
Potato Chips [Crisps]

	00:30	00:08 to 00:12	
		per batch	
American	**Ingredients**		**Metric/Imperial**
2 lb	Potatoes		1 kg / 2 lb
	Oil for deep frying		
	Salt		

1. Peel the potatoes and cut into very thin rounds.
2. Place the potato slices in a bowl of cold water to soak for 10 minutes and then drain and dry.
3. Heat the oil until it is hot but not smoking. Add the potato slices a handful at a time and cook until golden brown. Drain and season with salt immediately before serving.

Pommes frites
French Fried Potatoes

	00:25	00:12 to 00:15	
American	**Ingredients**		**Metric/Imperial**
3 lb	Potatoes		1.5 kg / 3 lb
	Oil for deep frying		
	Salt		

1. Peel the potatoes and cut into slices ½ in / 1 cm thick. Cut each slice into ½ in / 1 cm sticks. Rinse and dry on paper towels.
2. Heat the oil in a deep pan or deep fryer until hot but not smoking. Place the potatoes in the oil and fry until they are cooked but still white.
3. Remove the potatoes from the oil with a slotted spoon and keep warm.
4. Just before serving, reheat the oil and fry the potatoes once more for 2-5 minutes until golden brown. Drain well and sprinkle with salt. Serve immediately.

Pommes sautées
Sauté Potatoes

	00:05		00:45
American	**Ingredients**		**Metric/Imperial**
3 lb	Potatoes		1.5 kg / 3 lb
⅔ cup	Oil		150 ml / ¼ pint
3 tbsp	Butter		40 g / 1½ oz
3 tbsp	Chopped fresh mixed herbs		3 tbsp
	Salt		

1. Peel the potatoes. Leave whole if they are very small, otherwise cut into medium-sized slices.
2. Heat the oil in a frying pan.
3. Add the potatoes and cook for about 25 minutes over a low heat until they begin to color. Stir occasionally with a wooden spoon.
4. When they are golden, pour off any excess oil and add the butter. Cover the pan and finish cooking over a very low heat.
5. Serve with the butter from the pan and sprinkle with the chopped fresh herbs (parsley, chives or basil) and salt to taste.

Desserts, Cakes and Pastries

Creams and basic pastries

Crème aux amandes
Almond Custard

	00:30	00:15 to 00:20	

plus cooling and chilling
Makes about 1 quart 1 l / 1¾ pints

American	Ingredients	Metric/Imperial
1¼ cups	Milk	300 ml / ½ pint
¾ cup	Sugar	150 g / 5 oz
½ cup	Ground almonds	50 g / 2 oz
	Vanilla extract [essence]	
6	Egg yolks	6
1¼ cups	Butter	300 g / 10 oz

1. Put the milk and sugar in a saucepan and bring to a boil, stirring to dissolve the sugar. Add the ground almonds and a few drops of vanilla and warm over a very low heat for 2-3 minutes.
2. Place the egg yolks in a deep bowl and pour in the milk, stirring continuously.
3. Pour the mixture back into the pan and cook over a very low heat, stirring continuously. When the custard is thick enough to coat a spoon, remove the pan from the heat and leave to cool.
4. Whisk in the butter, a little at a time, and chill the custard until set.

Crème Chiboust
Alternative Filling for Saint-Honoré

	00:30	00:06	

plus chilling
Makes enough to fill a Saint-Honoré cake
to serve 6-8 (see page 498)

American	Ingredients	Metric/Imperial
½	Vanilla bean [pod]	½
1 cup	Milk	250 ml / 8 fl oz
3	Eggs, separated	3
½ cup	Sugar	125 g / 4 oz
¼ cup	Cornstarch [cornflour]	25 g / 1 oz
2 tbsp	Water	2 tbsp
1	Egg white	1

1. Split the half vanilla bean. Put it in a saucepan with the milk and bring to a boil.
2. In a bowl mix egg yolks with 2 tablespoons [25 g / 1 oz] of the sugar and the cornstarch. Remove the vanilla bean from the milk and gradually pour the boiling milk onto the egg yolks, whisking vigorously. Return to the pan and stir over a low heat for 1 minute to thicken the custard. Remove from the heat and cover the pan to keep the custard warm.
3. Put the remaining sugar in a small pan with the water. Bring to a boil and boil for 5 minutes.
4. Beat the 4 egg whites until stiff. Pour the sugar syrup in a slow trickle onto the egg whites, beating vigorously. When all

the syrup has been incorporated, add the hot custard and mix quickly together with a wooden spoon. Continue stirring until completely cold.

Crème anglaise
Vanilla Custard Sauce

	00:05	00:15	

plus cooling   Makes about 1 quart 1 l / 1¾ pints

American	Ingredients	Metric/Imperial
1 quart	Milk	1 l / 1¾ pints
1	Vanilla bean [pod] or	1
	Vanilla extract [essence]	
	Salt	
8 - 10	Egg yolks	8 - 10
¾ cup	Superfine [caster] sugar	150 g / 5 oz

1. Place the milk in a saucepan and add the vanilla bean, cut in half lengthwise, or a few drops of vanilla extract, and a pinch of salt. Bring to a boil, then remove from the heat and leave to infuse.
2. Beat together the egg yolks and sugar until the mixture becomes pale. Remove the vanilla bean from the milk and gradually whisk the milk into the eggs. Pour the mixture back into the pan and cook over a low heat for about 10 minutes, stirring constantly. On no account allow the custard to boil.
3. As soon as the custard is thick enough to coat a spoon, remove the pan from the heat and leave to cool, stirring from time to time to prevent a skin forming.

Cook's tip: if you are afraid of the custard separating, beat 1 teaspoon of flour or cornstarch [cornflour] with the egg yolks. This custard is the basis of many desserts and ice creams (see pages 463 and 511, 515).

Crème au caramel
Caramel Buttercream

	00:35	00:15	

plus chilling

American	Ingredients	Metric/Imperial
1 cup	Sugar	250 g / 8 oz
¼ cup	Water	4 tbsp
1 cup	Heavy [double] cream	250 ml / 8 fl oz
1 cup	Butter	250 g / 8 oz

1. Put the sugar in a thick-based saucepan with the water. Heat, stirring to dissolve the sugar, then stop stirring. Cook over a moderate heat for 6-8 minutes until you have a golden syrup.
2. Pour the cream into a mixing bowl and slowly add the caramel, whisking continuously. Pour the mixture back into the pan and cook over a low heat for 10 minutes, stirring occasionally, until a little of the mixture dropped into cold water will form a small, fairly firm ball between the fingers.
3. In a mixing bowl, cream the butter with a wooden spoon until softened. Vigorously beat the caramel cream into the butter until smooth. Leave to cool, then chill until ready to serve.

Cook's tip: serve with a sponge cake, almond slices, meringues or lady fingers [sponge fingers].

Caramel

	00:05	00:06 to 00:08
	Makes enough to coat a 7 in / 18 cm mold	

American	Ingredients	Metric/Imperial
½ cup	Sugar	125 g / 4 oz
¼ cup	Water	4 tbsp
1 tbsp	Wine vinegar	1 tbsp

1. Put the sugar into a small, thick-based pan and add the water. Bring to a boil, stirring to dissolve the sugar. Stop stirring and, watching carefully, cook until the syrup turns golden, or brown, depending on how you prefer it. On no account allow it to turn black or it will taste burnt and will be unusable.
2. Remove the pan from the heat and add the wine vinegar. This will stop any further cooking.
3. Tip the caramel into the mold and tilt the mold quickly until the bottom and sides are completely covered.

Cook's tip: for a more runny caramel which can be served as a sauce, dilute with a little hot water after adding the vinegar.

Crème au beurre
Buttercream

	00:15	00:06
	plus chilling	
	Makes enough to cover a cake to serve 6	

American	Ingredients	Metric/Imperial
4	Egg yolks	4
⅔ cup	Sugar	150 g / 5 oz
¼ cup	Water	4 tbsp
1 cup	Butter, at room temperature	250 g / 8 oz
	Vanilla extract [essence]	
¾ cup	Cocoa powder (optional)	75 g / 3 oz

1. Beat the egg yolks in a mixing bowl.
2. Put the sugar and water in a saucepan and heat, stirring to dissolve the sugar. Stop stirring and cook for about 6 minutes or until a drop of syrup forms a bead when dropped into cold water.
3. Pour the syrup in a fine stream into the egg yolks, beating vigorously. Continue beating until completely cold.
4. Add the butter a little at a time and continue to beat until the cream is smooth. Finally add vanilla to taste. Chill well.
5. If preferred, the cream can be flavored with cocoa. Dissolve the cocoa in a little hot water before adding to the cream.

Crème Chantilly
Chantilly Cream

	00:20	00:00
	plus chilling	

American	Ingredients	Metric/Imperial
2 cups	Thin crème fraîche	500 ml / ¾ pint
½ cup	Confectioners' [icing] sugar	50 g / 2 oz
	Vanilla extract [essence]	

1. The whole secret of this recipe's success lies in the correct temperature of the cream: place the crème fraîche in the bowl in which you intend to whip it, in the refrigerator 2 hours in advance.
2. Whip the cream gently until it doubles in volume and sticks to the blades of the beater. Do not whip too quickly or you risk turning the cream into butter.
3. With a wooden spoon slowly stir in the sugar, then a few drops of vanilla and mix well.
4. Chill until ready to serve.

Cook's tip: if you prefer to use thick crème fraîche, add some very cold milk (allowing 5 tablespoons milk to 1 cup [250 ml / 8 fl oz] crème fraîche).

Crème au kirsch
Kirsch Custard

	00:20	00:10
	plus cooling	

American	Ingredients	Metric/Imperial
1 quart	Milk	1 l / 1¾ pints
1	Vanilla bean [pod]	1
	Salt	
6	Egg yolks	6
1 cup	Flour	125 g / 4 oz
1 cup	Sugar	250 g / 8 oz
½ quantity	Chantilly cream	½ quantity
¼ cup	Kirsch	4 tbsp

1. Bring the milk to a boil with the halved vanilla bean and a pinch of salt. Remove from the heat and leave to infuse.
2. Meanwhile, beat the egg yolks with the flour and sugar. Remove the vanilla bean from the milk, and beat the milk into the egg yolk mixture. Return to the milk pan.
3. Return to a gentle heat and bring to a boil, stirring until the custard thickens.
4. Strain the custard into a bowl. Grease a piece of foil with butter and place on the surface of the custard to prevent a skin forming.
5. Just before serving fold in the chantilly cream and kirsch.

Crème au café
Baked Coffee Creams

	00:10	00:20
	plus chilling	

American	Ingredients	Metric/Imperial
3	Eggs	3
3	Egg yolks	3
⅔ cup	Superfine [caster] sugar	150 g / 5 oz
3 tbsp	Heavy [double] cream	500 ml / ¾ pint
5 tsp	Instant coffee powder	5 tsp
⅔ cup	Boiling water	150 ml / ¼ pint
2 cups	Milk	500 ml / ¾ pint

1. Preheat the oven to 325°F / 160°C / Gas Mark 3.
2. In a bowl beat together the eggs, yolks, sugar and cream.
3. Dissolve the coffee in the boiling water. Add the milk and slowly pour into the egg mixture, stirring continuously.
4. Pour into 6 ramekin dishes and place them in a shallow pan containing hot, but not boiling, water. Bake for about 20 minutes or until the cream has set.
5. Leave to cool, then chill for 1 hour before serving.

Crème pour choux au chocolat

Chocolate Custard for Choux Buns

	00:25		00:10

plus cooling
Makes enough to fill 12 large choux buns
(see choux pastry, page 457 and profiteroles, page 496)

American	Ingredients	Metric/Imperial
1 quart	Milk	1 l / 1¾ pints
4	Eggs, separated	4
2	Egg yolks	2
1 cup	Superfine [caster] sugar	250 g / 8 oz
¾ cup	Cornstarch [cornflour] *	75 g / 3 oz
2 tsp	Unflavored gelatin	4 tsp
	Salt	
7 oz	Semisweet [plain] chocolate	200 g / 7 oz

1. Bring the milk to a boil.
2. Cream the 6 egg yolks with the sugar and cornstarch until the mixture is pale. Gradually add the boiling milk, whisking continuously.
3. Return the mixture to the milk pan. Return the pan to the heat and cook gently, stirring, for 2-3 minutes or until the custard begins to simmer. Remove the pan from the heat. Dissolve the gelatin in a little water. Stir into the custard until smooth.
4. Add a pinch of salt to the 4 egg whites and beat until very stiff. Fold gently into the custard.
5. Break the chocolate into small pieces. Place in a thick-bottomed pan with a tablespoon of milk or water and stir over a low heat until melted. Leave to cool, then stir into the custard.

Cook's tip: chocolate custard can also be served as a dessert. Chill in the refrigerator for several hours and top each serving with a spoonful of crème fraîche.

Crème moka

Chilled Mocha Creams

	00:20		00:10

plus cooling

American	Ingredients	Metric/Imperial
¼ cup	Cornstarch [cornflour]	25 g / 1 oz
1¼ cups	Cold milk	300 ml / ½ pint
1 cup	Very strong coffee	250 ml / 8 fl oz
¼ cup	Sugar	50 g / 2 oz
	Vanilla extract [essence]	
½ cup	Crème fraîche	125 ml / 4 fl oz
2 tbsp	Confectioners' [icing] sugar	2 tbsp
6	Sugar coffee beans	6

1. In a saucepan, whisk the cornstarch gently into the cold milk. Gradually whisk in the cold coffee and the sugar. Bring to a boil, stirring continuously. Add a few drops of vanilla and continue boiling for a few seconds. Allow to cool.
2. Meanwhile whip the very cold crème fraîche in a chilled bowl. Add the confectioners' sugar and continue whipping until it doubles in volume. Set aside in the refrigerator.
3. Divide the coffee cream between 6 individual glasses and chill until ready to serve.
4. Decorate with the whipped crème fraîche and the sugar coffee beans.

Crème pâtissière

Pastry Cream or Confectioner's Custard

	00:05		00:15

plus chilling
Makes about 3 cups [750 ml / 1¼ pints]

American	Ingredients	Metric/Imperial
2 cups	Milk	500 ml / ¾ pint
½ cup	Flour	50 g / 2 oz
3	Egg yolks	3
1	Egg	1
6 tbsp	Sugar	75 g / 3 oz
3 tbsp	Kirsch or rum or	3 tbsp
1 tsp	Vanilla extract [essence]	1 tsp

1. Set ⅔ cup [150 ml / ¼ pint] of the milk to one side and bring the rest to a boil.
2. Put the flour in a mixing bowl and beat in the egg yolks, whole egg and sugar. Gradually add the reserved milk, stirring.
3. When the mixture is smooth and creamy, stir in the boiled milk and return the mixture to the saucepan. Place over a low heat and cook, stirring continuously, until the cream is thick.
4. Add the kirsch (or rum or vanilla) and chill.

Cook's tip: pastry cream is used for a variety of desserts: cakes, tarts, fruit, pastries, etc.

Pâte sablée

Rich Flan Pastry

	00:15		00:25

plus chilling
Makes enough to line a 10 in / 25 cm pan

American	Ingredients	Metric/Imperial
½ cup	Butter	125 g / 4 oz
6 tbsp	Superfine [caster] sugar	75 g / 3 oz
1	Egg yolk	1
	Salt	
	Vanilla extract [essence]	
2 cups	Flour	250 g / 8 oz

1. Cut the butter into small pieces and leave in a warm place to soften.
2. Place the sugar in a mixing bowl. Mix in the egg yolk, then add the softened butter, a pinch of salt and a drop of vanilla. Mix together, then add the flour. Quickly work all the ingredients together with your hands. Form into a ball and chill for 1 hour.
3. Roll out the dough and fold in three. Repeat the process twice more. This makes the pastry smooth and supple. Use the pastry to line a buttered and lightly floured pan. Prick the bottom with a fork and the pastry case is ready for use.

Cook's tip: this pastry can be used for any flan containing uncooked fruit such as strawberries or raspberries, or ready-cooked fruit, such as blackberries or pears. It is very fragile and will be difficult to remove from the pan unless you use one with a loose base. If you find the pastry difficult to roll, you can flatten it with the palm of your hand, place it in the pan and work it up the sides with your fingertips.

2. With a fork beat the egg white for 10 seconds, then add to the sugar and almonds and stir thoroughly with a wooden spoon until the paste is smooth.

Pâte brisée

Basic Short Pastry

00:15
plus chilling
Makes enough to line a 10 in / 25 cm pan

00:00

American	Ingredients	Metric/Imperial
½ cup	Butter	125 g / 4 oz
2 cups	Flour	250 g / 8 oz
2 tbsp	Sugar	25 g / 1 oz
	Salt	
1	Egg yolk	1
½ cup	Water	5 tbsp

1. Cut the butter into small pieces and leave to soften. Sift the flour into a mixing bowl, make a well in the center and into the well put the sugar, a pinch of salt, the egg yolk and the cold water. Work quickly together. Incorporate the softened butter into the pastry without over-working it. Roll into a ball and leave to chill in the refrigerator for 1 hour.
2. When the pastry is ready for use, roll it out to ¼ in / 5 mm thick and fold in three. Repeat the rolling and folding process twice more as for puff pastry. This will make the pastry smooth and supple.
3. If you are making pastry for a savory pie omit the sugar, use only 6 tbsp [75 g / 3 oz] butter and work the pastry with the palm of your hand until supple. Leave to stand. Pastry made like this is better for longer baking times.

Cook's tip: use as little flour as possible when rolling out.

Glaçage au fondant

Fondant Icing

00:15
Makes enough to ice a cake to serve 6

00:05

American	Ingredients	Metric/Imperial
½ cup	Sugar	125 g / 4 oz
⅓ cup	Water	75 ml / 3 fl oz
¾ lb	Fondant	350 g / 12 oz
	Food coloring (red, green, yellow)	
	Cocoa powder	

1. Put the sugar and water in a pan and bring to a boil, then remove from the heat and leave to cool.
2. Place the fondant in a heatproof bowl and put over a pan half filled with water. Heat until the fondant melts, adding the sugar syrup very gradually until the fondant is warm and supple.
3. Stir in a few drops of food coloring. Add it a drop at a time to avoid giving the icing too deep a color.
4. Spread the icing over the cake with a metal spatula. (If you are icing small choux buns, dip them directly into the icing and smooth the surface with your finger.)
5. For chocolate icing, gradually add cocoa powder to the fondant along with the syrup. For coffee icing, dissolve 2 teaspoons of instant coffee in 2 teaspoons boiling water. Gradually add to the fondant with the syrup.

Pâte à brioche

Brioche Dough

00:40
plus rising

00:30

American	Ingredients	Metric/Imperial
⅔ cup	Milk	5 tbsp
1 tbsp	Sugar	1 tbsp
1 package	Active dry yeast	½ sachet
⅔ cup	Butter	150 g / 5 oz
2¾ cups	Flour	300 g / 11 oz
5	Eggs	5
½ tsp	Salt	½ tsp

1. Warm the milk in a small saucepan and add ½ teaspoon of the sugar. Remove from the heat. Dissolve the yeast in the milk, and leave in a warm place for 15 minutes or until frothy.
2. Cream the butter with a wooden spoon until pale.
3. Sift the flour into a mixing bowl. Make a well in the center and pour in the milk and yeast mixture. Add the butter, 4 of the eggs, the remaining sugar and the salt. Work all the ingredients together thoroughly and shape the dough into a ball.
4. Knead the dough for about 20 minutes or until smooth and elastic. Leave in a warm place to rise for 6 hours or until doubled in bulk.
5. Punch down the dough to knock out the air, and knead again briefly.
6. Preheat the oven to 425°F / 220°C / Gas Mark 7.
7. To make a large brioche, take one-quarter of the dough and shape it into a ball with a 'tail'. Shape the remaining dough into a larger ball and place it in a buttered brioche mold. With your thumb, make a hole in the center of the dough in the mold, and place the smaller ball in it, tail downwards. Brush the surface with the remaining egg, beaten.
8. Bake for 30 minutes.

Cook's tip: the dough will keep well in the refrigerator, wrapped in foil. Allow the dough to come back to room temperature before using it.

Pâte à choux

Choux Pastry

00:20
Makes 15 choux buns or éclairs

00:10

American	Ingredients	Metric/Imperial
1½ cups	Water	250 ml / 8 fl oz
1 tbsp	Superfine [caster] sugar (for sweet choux)	1 tbsp
	Salt	
5 tbsp	Butter	65 g / 2½ oz
1¼ cups	Flour	125 g / 5 oz
4	Eggs	4

1. Pour the water into a large saucepan and add the sugar (if using), a pinch of salt and the butter. Warm the liquid until the butter has melted, then raise the heat and bring the mixture to a boil. When the liquid rises in the pan remove immediately from the heat and tip in the flour all at once.
2. Beat with a wooden spoon until smooth, then return the pan to the heat and stir gently for ½-1 minute.
3. When the pastry comes away from the sides of the pan, remove from the heat once more. Thoroughly beat in the eggs one at a time. The dough should be shiny and should just fall from the spoon.

Crêpe batter

6. Return the pastry to the refrigerator and chill for 10-20 minutes, then remove it and repeat the rolling out, folding and turning as before. You have now completed 4 turns. (If you are not using the pastry immediately, it will keep for 6 days in the refrigerator or 2 months in the freezer, wrapped in foil or a plastic bag.)
7. Before using frozen pastry, thaw for 12 hours in the refrigerator in its wrapper, or for 3 hours at room temperature.
8. The more turns you give your puff pastry, the finer it will be. It may be as many as 6 (for very fine pastry), and is never less than 4, as for croissants.

Pâte à crêpes

Crêpe Batter

	00:10 plus standing time Makes 15 crêpes	00:03 per crêpe

American	Ingredients	Metric/Imperial
3	Eggs	3
2 cups	Flour	250 g / 8 oz
2½ cups	Milk (or half milk and half beer)	500 ml / ¾ pint
2 tbsp	Oil	2 tbsp
	Salt	
3 tbsp	Rum, Grand Marnier or Cointreau	3 tbsp
3 tbsp	Warm water	3 tbsp
	Butter fo	

1. Beat the eggs in a mixing bowl or in a blender or food processor. Add the flour. Beat until smooth then gradually beat in the milk (or milk and beer), the oil and a pinch of salt.
2. Leave the batter to stand for at least 2 hours, then add the rum or orange liqueur.
3. When you are ready to cook the crêpes, thin the batter with the warm water so that it is runny enough to cover the bottom of the pan immediately.
4. Put a pat of butter in a crêpe or frying pan and heat. Pour a ladle of batter into the pan and tip so that the batter is thinly spread. Cook for 2 minutes or until golden brown on the underside, then turn with a spatula and brown the other side. Slide the crêpe out of the pan and repeat with the remaining batter.

Cook's tip: crêpes can be cooked in advance. Wrapped in foil they will keep well in the refrigerator for 2-3 days. The batter itself will keep up to 24 hours in the refrigerator. Take care to store it in a container with a tight lid.

Pâte feuilletée quatre tours

Puff Pastry

	01:30 to 02:00 including chilling Makes about 2 lb / 1 kg	00:00

American	Ingredients	Metric/Imperial
4 cups	Flour	500 g / 1 lb
2 tsp	Salt	2 tsp
1½ cups	Water	250 ml / 8 fl oz
1¾ cups	Butter	400 g / 14 oz

1. The quantity of butter used for puff pastry can vary considerably, from equal quantities flour and butter to one-third the weight of flour. The more butter you use, the richer the pastry.
2. Sift the flour onto the worktop. Make a well in the center and into it tip the salt, the water and one eighth of the butter. Chill the remaining butter. Mix together into a smooth, firm pastry. Roll into a ball and chill for 30 minutes.
3. Roll out the pastry into a round about ¾ in / 2 cm thick. In the center place the remaining butter, cut into small pieces. Flatten the butter with the rolling pin, avoiding touching it with your hands, until it is spread thickly over the pastry.
4. Fold the pastry into three over the butter (stretching it a little if necessary) and seal the edges with the rolling pin.
5. Roll out again to ensure that the butter is evenly distributed. Fold into three and roll out into a rectangle. Fold the pastry into three once again. Turn the pastry a quarter turn to the right and again roll out into a rectangle. Fold in three again. You have now completed 2 turns, so make 2 finger marks in the pastry to remind yourself.

Praline aux amandes

Almond Praline

	00:05 plus cooling	00:25 to 00:30

American	Ingredients	Metric/Imperial
1 cup	Sugar	250 g / 8 oz
¼ cup	Water	4 tbsp
1¼ cup	Whole almonds	150 g / 5 oz

1. Place the sugar and water in a heavy-based saucepan and bring to a boil, stirring to dissolve the sugar. Stop stirring and boil over moderate heat until the syrup reaches 248°F / 120°C. This will take about 5 minutes.

2. Remove from the heat and add the nuts. Stir until the syrup starts to turn grainy. Return to the heat and cook, stirring, until the mixture becomes white and hardened. Continue cooking, stirring, until the crystallized syrup becomes liquid again. Cook for 10-15 minutes or until the syrup is a dark caramel color. Do not let the caramel burn or it will be bitter.

3. Remove the pan from the heat and pour the mixture onto an oiled marble or formica surface. Allow to cool completely, when the mixture will be totally hard.

4. Break up the praline and put it into a blender or food processor. Blend to a coarse powder, but not too fine. Store the praline in an airtight container.

Crème pour Paris-Brest

Praline Cream for Paris-Brest

	00:20		00:05
	Makes enough to fill a Paris-Brest (see page 492)		

American	Ingredients	Metric/Imperial
½ cup	Superfine [caster] sugar	125 g / 4 oz
3 tbsp	Water	3 tbsp
2	Egg whites	2
½ cup	Butter at room temperature	125 g / 4 oz
⅓ cup	Ground praline	65 g / 2 oz

1. Put the sugar in a pan and add the water. Bring to a boil, stirring to dissolve the sugar, and cook for 5 minutes until a drop of syrup forms a bead in cold water.

2. Beat the egg whites until very stiff. Trickle the boiling sugar syrup slowly onto the egg whites, beating vigorously. When all the syrup has been incorporated, continue beating until completely cold.

3. Cream the butter with the praline. Blend with the egg whites until completely smooth. Transfer the mixture to an icing bag and use to fill the Paris-Brest.

Pâte à beignets

Sweet Fritter Batter

	00:10		00:05
	plus standing time Makes 20 fritters (2 lb / 1 kg fruit)		per batch of fritters

American	Ingredients	Metric/Imperial
3 tbsp	Butter	40 g / 1 ½ oz
3	Eggs	3
	Salt	
2 cups	Flour	250 g / 8 oz
2 tbsp	Sugar	2 tbsp
	Vanilla extract [essence]	
1 ½ cups	Milk	250 ml / 8 fl oz
⅔ cup	Beer	150 ml / ¼ pint
3 tbsp	Rum or Grand Marnier (optional)	3 tbsp
2	Egg whites	2

1. Melt the butter. In a mixing bowl, beat together the whole eggs, a pinch of salt, the flour, melted butter, sugar and a few drops of vanilla.

2. Gradually add the milk and beer. The batter should be runny. Leave the batter to stand for 2 hours.

3. Just before use, add the rum or Grand Marnier if used. Beat the egg whites until stiff and fold into the batter.

Cook's tip: for a savory batter for meat or vegetables, omit the sugar, vanilla and rum.

Pâte à foncer

Rich Egg Pastry

	00:20		00:00
	plus standing time Makes enough to line a 10 in / 25 cm pan		

American	Ingredients	Metric/Imperial
2 cups	Flour	250 g / 8 oz
¼ cup	Superfine [caster] sugar	50 g / 2 oz
2	Eggs	2
½ tsp	Salt	½ tsp
7 tbsp	Butter	100 g / 3 ½ oz

1. Sift the flour onto the worktop and make a well in the center. Into the well put the sugar, beaten eggs, a pinch of salt and the butter, cut into small pieces. Work the ingredients together with your fingertips, gradually adding cold water until you obtain a smooth, supple pastry. The pastry is best if left to stand for 30 minutes at this stage, although it can be used immediately if necessary.

2. Roll out the pastry to about ¼ in / 5 mm thick. Use to line a buttered and floured pan, then chill for 30 minutes to prevent the pastry shrinking during cooking. Prick the bottom of the pastry case with a fork before filling.

Cook's tip: this pastry is suitable for 2 crust pies or flans. It can be used with fruits such as apples, plums, apricots.

Pâte à frire

Frying Batter

	00:10		00:05
	plus standing time Makes 15 fritters		

American	Ingredients	Metric/Imperial
1 ¼ cups	Flour	150 g / 5 oz
1 tbsp	Oil	1 tbsp
	Salt	
½ cup	Water	4 tbsp
1	Egg white (from a large egg)	1
	Oil for deep frying	

1. Sift the flour into a mixing bowl and make a well in the center. Add the oil, a pinch of salt and the water. Beat thoroughly and leave to stand for 2 hours.

2. Beat the egg white until very stiff and gently fold into the batter.

3. Heat the oil for frying until hot but not smoking (340°F / 175°C). Add the fritters a few at a time and fry until golden.

Cook's tip: to check the temperature of the frying oil, drop in 1 teaspoon of batter. If it sticks to the bottom of the pan the oil is not hot enough. If it turns golden and rises to the top immediately the oil is too hot. If the batter takes 30 seconds to rise, the oil is the right temperature. All modern deep-fat fryers can be set at the required temperature.

Crème caramel
Baked Caramel Custard

00:20 plus cooling   01:00

American	Ingredients	Metric/Imperial
1¼ cups	Sugar	300 g / 10 oz
3 tbsp	Water	3 tbsp
1	Vanilla bean [pod]	1
1 quart	Milk	1 l / 1¾ pints
	Salt	
10	Eggs	10

1. Place ½ cup [125 g / 4 oz] of the sugar in a small pan with the water. Melt the sugar over a moderate heat and cook until the caramel is golden. Quickly remove from the heat and pour the caramel into a dry, hot 6 in / 15 cm diameter dish or mold. Tilt the dish or mold to coat all over and leave to cool.
2. Preheat the oven to 350°F / 180°C / Gas Mark 4.
3. Cut the vanilla bean in half lengthwise and put in a large saucepan with the milk and a pinch of salt. Bring to a boil, then stir in the remaining sugar.
4. Beat the eggs in a large mixing bowl. Gradually beat in the milk. Strain the mixture into the caramel mold and place in a shallow ovenproof dish. Fill the dish with water to halfway up the mold.
5. Bake for 1 hour. Test that the custard is ready by piercing with a knife. The blade should come out clean.
6. Remove the mold from the ovenproof dish and leave to cool. Just before serving, unmold the custard onto a serving plate.

Cook's tip: this dessert should be cooked at least 4 hours before it is required. Care should be taken not to overcook the custard.

Mont blanc
Chestnut Cream Cake

01:30   00:30

American	Ingredients	Metric/Imperial
¾ cup + 2 tbsp	Butter	200 g / 7 oz
3	Eggs, separated	3
1	Egg yolk	1
6 tbsp	Superfine [caster] sugar	75 g / 3 oz
¾ cup	Flour	75 g / 3 oz
¼ cup	Rum	4 tbsp
1½ lb	Canned sweetened chestnut purée	750 g / 1½ lb
1 tbsp	Cocoa powder	1 tbsp
½ cup	Granulated sugar	125 g / 4 oz
⅓ cup	Water	5 tbsp
1 quantity	Chantilly cream	1 quantity

1. Preheat the oven to 450°F / 230°C / Gas Mark 8.
2. Melt 2 tablespoons [25 g / 1 oz] butter. Set aside. Beat the 4 egg yolks with half the superfine sugar. When pale, quickly work in the flour. Beat the 3 egg whites until very stiff and gradually beat in the remaining superfine sugar. Beat the egg whites and melted butter into the egg yolk mixture.
3. Pour the batter into a buttered 10 in / 25 cm cake pan. Bake for about 10 minutes or until a skewer inserted into the center

of the cake comes out clean. Remove the cake from the oven, unmold and leave to cool.
4. Mix half the rum with the chestnut purée in a warm bowl. Add the remaining butter and the cocoa. Beat well until smooth.
5. Put the chestnut paste into a pastry bag fitted with a plain ¼ in / 5 mm nozzle. Pipe over the sides of an oiled 10 in / 25 cm savarin mold in successive rings. Leave in the refrigerator to set.
6. Cut the cake into 2 layers.
7. Dissolve the granulated sugar in the water and remaining rum. Bring to a boil and boil for 2 minutes. Moisten the two cake layers with this syrup, and break one layer into pieces.
8. Place the whole cake layer on a flat serving plate. Slide the chestnut case out of the savarin mold and place the case on the cake layer. Fill the chestnut case with alternate layers of broken cake and chantilly cream. Place the rest of the chantilly cream in a pastry bag fitted with a plain ½ in / 1 cm nozzle and pipe the cream over the whole cake. Serve at once.

Chocolate mousse

Mousse au chocolat
Chocolate Mousse

00:20 plus chilling   00:05

American	Ingredients	Metric/Imperial
3	Eggs, separated	3
½ cup	Superfine [caster] sugar	125 g / 4 oz
8 oz	Semisweet [plain] chocolate	250 g / 8 oz
2 tbsp	Water	2 tbsp
¼ cup	Butter	50 g / 2 oz
1	Egg white	1
	Salt	

1. Beat the egg yolks and sugar together until the mixture becomes pale.
2. Break the chocolate into another bowl and add the water. Place over a saucepan of hot water to melt. Remove the bowl from the heat and stir in the butter.
3. Add the chocolate to the egg yolk mixture. Beat the 4 egg whites with a pinch of salt until they form firm peaks, then gently fold into the chocolate mixture.
4. Spoon the mousse into a shallow dish or into 6 individual glasses and chill for at least 3 hours before serving.

Oeufs au lait

Baked Egg Custard

American	Ingredients	Metric/Imperial
00:10 plus cooling		01:00
1	Vanilla bean [pod]	1
1 quart	Milk	1 l / 1¾ pints
8	Egg yolks	8
⅔ cup	Superfine [caster] sugar	150 g / 5 oz

1. Preheat the oven to 325°F / 160°C / Gas Mark 3.
2. Cut the vanilla bean in half lengthwise and put in a saucepan with the milk. Bring to a boil.
3. In a mixing bowl, whisk the egg yolks and sugar together until the mixture is pale. Remove the vanilla bean from the milk and gradually whisk the milk into the egg yolks.
4. Pour the custard into a porcelain baking dish. Place the dish in a roasting pan and fill the pan with water to halfway up the sides of the dish.
5. Bake for 1 hour, without allowing the water in the pan to boil, or until a skewer inserted into the center of the custard comes out clean.
6. Remove the dish from the roasting pan in the oven and leave to cool. Serve the custard from the porcelain dish.

Nègre en chemise

Cream-coated Chocolate Mousse

American	Ingredients	Metric/Imperial
00:30 plus chilling		00:10
7 oz	Semisweet [plain] chocolate	200 g / 7 oz
1 tbsp	Milk	1 tbsp
1 cup	Butter	200 g / 7 oz
⅓ cup	Superfine [caster] sugar	75 g / 3 oz
4	Eggs, separated	4
2 cups	Crème fraîche	150 ml / ¾ pint
	Vanilla extract [essence]	
½ cup	Confectioners' [icing] sugar	50 g / 2 oz

1. Break the chocolate into a pan, add the milk and melt over a low heat. Cut the butter into small pieces and soften in a bowl with a wooden spoon. Beat in the superfine sugar and then the egg yolks one at a time. Finally beat in the melted chocolate.
2. Beat the egg whites until very stiff. Gently fold into the chocolate mixture with a wooden spoon. Spoon into a greased 1 quart [1 l / 2 pint] charlotte mold. Chill for 12 hours.

3. Chill the crème fraîche and just before serving, pour it into a chilled mixing bowl. Add a few drops of vanilla extract and the confectioners' sugar and whip until the cream has doubled in quantity.
4. Unmold the chocolate mousse onto a serving plate and cover it completely with the whipped cream.

Soufflé au citron

Lemon Soufflé

American	Ingredients	Metric/Imperial
00:30		00:15
4	Eggs, separated	4
1	Egg yolk	1
¼ cup	Superfine [caster] sugar	4 tbsp
1 tbsp	Potato starch or flour	1 tbsp
1	Lemon	1

1. Preheat the oven to 400°F / 200°C / Gas Mark 6.
2. Whisk the 5 egg yolks with 2 tablespoons of the sugar until light and frothy. Add the potato starch and the finely grated rind of the lemon and whisk in lightly.
3. Beat the egg whites until very stiff, gradually incorporating the remaining sugar. Carefully fold the whites into the yolks.
4. Generously butter 6 4 in / 10 cm diameter ramekins and sprinkle inside with sugar. Fill each ramekin to the top with the soufflé mixture and bake for 15 minutes. Serve immediately.

Cook's tip: the ramekins can be filled before you start the meal and then put in the oven 15 minutes before they are to be served.

Soufflé au chocolat

Chocolate Soufflé

American	Ingredients	Metric/Imperial
00:30		00:30
7 oz	Semisweet [plain] chocolate	200 g / 7 oz
1 tbsp	Water	1 tbsp
6	Eggs, separated	6
	Vanilla extract [essence]	
⅓ cup	Potato starch or flour	40 g / 1½ oz
½ cup	Superfine [caster] sugar	125 g / 4 oz
	Confectioners' [icing] sugar	

1. Preheat the oven to 425°F / 220°C / Gas Mark 7.
2. Break the chocolate into a bowl and place over a pan of hot water. Add the water and melt the chocolate over a low heat. Remove the bowl from the pan of water and beat in the egg yolks, 2 at a time, a few drops of vanilla extract and the potato starch mixed with three-quarters of the sugar.
3. Beat the egg whites until very stiff, then gradually beat in the remaining sugar. Fold the whites into the chocolate mixture.
4. Butter a 6 in / 15 cm soufflé dish and sprinkle with sugar. Fill the soufflé dish to the top with the chocolate mixture. Bake for 30 minutes. Serve sprinkled with confectioners' sugar.

Cook's tip: to make this soufflé at the last minute, prepare the chocolate mixture (step 2), then beat the whites and fold in just before you are ready to bake the soufflé.

Mousse aux marrons

Chestnut Mousse

	00:30 plus chilling	00:45

American	Ingredients	Metric/Imperial
2 lb	Chestnuts	1 kg / 2 lb
⅔ cup	Sugar	150 g / 5 oz
1	Vanilla bean [pod]	1
1 quart	Milk	1 l / 1¾ pints
	Salt	
1½ cups	Crème fraîche	350 ml / 12 fl oz
½ cup	Broken marrons glacés	150 g / 5 oz

1. With a pointed knife make an incision around each chestnut, cutting through both layers of skin, and place them in a saucepan. Cover with plenty of cold water. Bring to a boil and boil for about 5 minutes. Peel the chestnuts one at a time.
2. Place the peeled chestnuts in a pan with the sugar, the vanilla bean, cut in half lengthwise, the milk and a pinch of salt. Bring to a boil, then cover the pan and cook over a low heat for 40 minutes.
3. Remove the vanilla bean and purée the chestnut mixture in a vegetable mill, blender or food processor. Transfer the purée to a mixing bowl.
4. Pour the cold crème fraîche into a chilled mixing bowl and whip until it has doubled in quantity. Fold the whipped crème gently into the chestnut purée.
5. Spoon the chestnut mousse into a glass bowl. Decorate with pieces of marrons glacés and chill until ready to serve.

Riz à l'impératrice

Empress Rice Mold

	00:30 plus chilling	00:30

American	Ingredients	Metric/Imperial
	Salt	
1 cup	Round-grain rice	250 g / 8 oz
1 quart	Milk	1 l / 1¾ pints
1	Vanilla bean [pod]	25 g / 1 oz
2 tbsp	Butter	25 g / 1 oz
1 envelope	Unflavored gelatin	½ sachet
3 tbsp	Water	3 tbsp
¼ quantity	Vanilla custard sauce	¼ quantity
1 cup	Sugar	250 g / 8 oz
1¼ cups	Crème fraîche (see page 122)	300 ml / ½ pint
⅔ cup	Fruit jelly (apricot or gooseberry)	150 ml / ¼ pint
1 tbsp	Kirsch or rum	1 tbsp

1. Bring a large pan of lightly salted water to a boil. Add the rice; blanch for 2 minutes and drain.
2. Place the milk and vanilla bean, halved lengthwise, in a heavy saucepan and bring to a boil. Stir in the rice and butter. Cover the pan and simmer over a low heat for 25 minutes.
3. Meanwhile, dissolve the gelatin in the water. Stir into the custard sauce. Strain into a bowl and set aside.
4. When the rice is cooked, remove the vanilla bean. Stir in the sugar and leave to cool.
5. Whip the cold crème fraîche in a chilled bowl until it doubles

in volume. Stir the rice into the custard, then fold in the whipped cream.
6. Transfer the mixture to a charlotte or savarin mold and chill for 3 hours or until set.
7. To serve, warm the fruit jelly with the kirsch until melted. Turn the rice mold onto a plate and spoon over the melted jelly.

Oeufs à la neige

Snow Eggs

	00:35 plus chilling	00:30

American	Ingredients	Metric/Imperial
	Salt	
8	Eggs, separated	8
1½ quarts	Milk	1.5 l / 2½ pints
1	Vanilla bean [pod]	1
⅔ cup	Superfine [caster] sugar	150 g / 5 oz
½ cup	Granulated sugar	125 g / 4 oz
2 tbsp	Water	2 tbsp

1. Add a pinch of salt to the egg whites and beat until firm. Set aside for 20 minutes, then beat again until very stiff.
2. Pour 5 cups [1.25 l / 2 pints] milk into a saucepan and add the vanilla bean, halved lengthwise, and half the superfine sugar. Bring to a boil, then lower the heat so that the milk is just simmering.
3. Take a large tablespoonful of egg white, float it on the surface of the milk and cook for 1 minute. Turn the poached meringue over and cook for a further minute. Remove the meringue with a slotted spoon and transfer to a cloth to drain. Repeat the process until all the egg white has been used.
4. Add enough milk to the pan to bring the quantity back to 1 quart [1 l / 1¾ pints]. Bring to a boil.
5. Add the remaining superfine sugar to the egg yolks and whisk until pale. Slowly add the boiling milk, whisking vigorously, then pour the mixture back into the pan. Stir over a low heat for about 10 minutes or until the custard is thick enough to coat the spoon. Pour the custard into a shallow dish and stir until just warm. Leave until completely cold.
6. When the custard is cold, carefully place the poached meringues on top.
7. Place the granulated sugar in a small pan with the water and melt over a moderate heat. Cook until the syrup turns to a golden brown caramel. Pour the caramel over the meringues and chill for 1 hour before serving.

Empress rice mold

Orange Liqueur Soufflé

Soufflé à l'orange

| | 00:25 | 00:40 |

American	Ingredients	Metric/Imperial
2	Oranges	2
½ quantity	Vanilla custard sauce	½ quantity
1¼ cups	Mandarin or orange liqueur	300 ml / ½ pint
½ quantity	Pastry cream	½ quantity
4	Egg whites	4
12	Ladyfingers [sponge fingers]	12

1. Preheat the oven to 425°F / 220°C / Gas Mark 7.
2. Thinly pare the rind from 1 orange. Add to the custard sauce with 4 tablespoons of the liqueur. Set aside in the refrigerator.
3. Finely grate the rind from the remaining orange and squeeze out the juice. Stir the grated rind and juice into the pastry cream.
4. Beat the egg whites until stiff and fold carefully into the pastry cream.
5. Moisten the lady fingers with the remaining liqueur.
6. Butter a 6 in / 15 cm soufflé dish. Cover the bottom with a layer of ladyfingers, then add a layer of pastry cream. Continue the layers until you have used all the ingredients, finishing with a layer of the cream.
7. Bake for 25-30 minutes.
8. Remove the orange rind from the custard sauce and serve with the soufflé immediately it is removed from the oven.

Grand Marnier Soufflé

Soufflé au Grand Marnier

| | 00:15 | 00:30 to 00:35 |

American	Ingredients	Metric/Imperial
1 cup	Milk	250 ml / 8 fl oz
¼ cup	Superfine [caster] sugar	50 g / 2 oz
¼ cup	Butter	50 g / 2 oz
2 tbsp	Flour	50 g / 2 oz
2 tbsp	Potato starch or flour	15 g / ½ oz
	Vanilla extract [essence]	
4	Eggs, separated	4
5 tbsp	Grand Marnier	5 tbsp
1	Ladyfinger [sponge finger]	1
	Confectioners' [icing] sugar	

1. Preheat the oven to 400°F / 200°C / Gas Mark 6.
2. Place the milk in a saucepan with the sugar and bring to a boil. Melt the butter in another saucepan and stir in the 2 tablespoons each of flour and potato starch or 4 tablespoons flour. Add the boiling milk and a few drops of vanilla extract. Cook, stirring, for about 3 minutes. Remove from the heat.
3. Carefully stir the egg yolks, one at a time, into the sauce, then add 4 tablespoons of the Grand Marnier.
4. Beat the egg whites until very stiff and fold gently into the mixture. Butter a 6 in / 15 cm soufflé dish and sprinkle with sugar. Half-fill the dish with the soufflé mixture.
5. Crumble the ladyfinger into a cup and moisten with the remaining Grand Marnier. Sprinkle over the soufflé mixture in

the dish, then fill the dish with the remaining soufflé mixture.
6. Bake for about 30 minutes (on no account open the oven door during this time) or until well risen. Serve immediately, sprinkled with a little confectioners' sugar.

Burgundy Pudding

Pudding de Bourgogne

| | 00:25 plus cooling and chilling | 01:00 |

American	Ingredients	Metric/Imperial
⅔ cup	Sugar	150 g / 5 oz
2½ tbsp	Water	2½ tbsp
1	Lemon	1
3 cups	Milk	750 ml / 1¼ pints
6 tbsp	Butter	75 g / 3 oz
6 tbsp	Flour	75 g / 3 oz
4	Eggs, separated	4

1. Put ¼ cup [50 g / 2 oz] of the sugar and 1½ tablespoons of the water into a deep cake pan. Cook over a moderate heat for 6-10 minutes or until the caramel is golden brown. Add the remaining water and stir to stop the caramel cooking further. Leave to cool.
2. Preheat the oven to 400°F / 200°C / Gas Mark 6.
3. Thinly pare the rind from the lemon and place in a saucepan with the milk and the rest of the sugar. Bring the milk slowly to a boil, then remove the pan from the heat. Cover the pan and leave to infuse for about 10 minutes.
4. Melt the butter in another saucepan, add the flour and stir for 3 minutes over a low heat. Remove the lemon rind from the milk and stir the milk, a little at a time, into the butter and flour roux. Bring to a boil, stirring, then remove the pan from the heat. Leave the sauce to cool for 5 minutes.
5. Stir the egg yolks into the sauce, one at a time. Beat the egg whites until very stiff and gently fold into the mixture.
6. Spoon into the cake pan and place in a shallow roasting pan containing about 1 in / 2.5 cm water. Bake for 1 hour.
7. Leave the pudding to cool until warm, then unmold onto a serving dish. Leave to cool completely, then chill before serving.

Grand Marnier soufflé

Tarts and flans

Pie aux pommes
Apple Pie

	00:30	
	plus thawing or making pastry	00:30

American	Ingredients	Metric/Imperial
14 oz	Puff pastry (see page 458 or use frozen)	400 g / 14 oz
3 large	Cooking apples	3 large
⅔ cup	Golden raisins [sultanas]	125 g / 4 oz
½ cup	Sugar	125 g / 4 oz
⅓ cup	Butter	75 g / 3 oz
1	Egg	1
1 cup	Crème fraîche	250 ml / 8 fl oz

1. If using frozen pastry, allow it to thaw.
2. Preheat the oven to 450°F / 230°C / Gas Mark 8.
3. Peel the apples and cut each into 8 segments. Cut out the cores and seeds. Arrange in layers in a deep pie dish with the raisins and sugar Dot with the butter.
4. Roll out the pastry to ¼ in / 5 mm thick. Cut a strip the same width as the rim of the dish, roll out to ⅛ in / 3 mm thick and stick to the rim of the dish with beaten egg. Brush the pastry strip with beaten egg.
5. Cover the dish with the remaining pastry, pressing firmly around the rim, after brushing the rim once more with egg. Cut off any excess pastry. Press with the tines of a fork all around the rim. Make a hole in the center and insert a roll of card to keep it open. Brush the surface of the pie with beaten egg.
6. Bake for 30 minutes or until golden brown. Turn off the oven and wait a few minutes before removing the pie. Serve hot with crème fraîche.

Pie à la rhubarbe
Rhubarb Pie

	00:20	
	plus making or thawing pastry	01:00

American	Ingredients	Metric/Imperial
1 lb	Puff pastry (see page 458 or use frozen) or	500 g / 1 lb
1 quantity	Basic short pastry	1 quantity
1½ lb	Rhubarb	750 g / 1½ lb
3	Apples	3
2 cups	Sugar	500 g / 1 lb

1. If using frozen pastry, allow it to thaw.
2. Preheat the oven to 450°F / 230°C / Gas Mark 8.
3. Cut the sticks of rhubarb into ½ in / 1 cm lengths. Heat a little water in a saucepan and gently cook the rhubarb for 6-7 minutes. Drain.
4. Peel the apples. Cut each into 8 segments and cut out the core and seeds.
5. Arrange the fruit in a deep pie dish and stir in the sugar.
6. Roll out the pastry to ¼ in / 5 mm thick. Cut a strip the same width as the rim of the dish and stick it onto the rim with beaten egg.

7. Cut a few slits in the remaining pastry with the point of a knife and then cover the dish, sticking the lid to the pastry on the rim with beaten egg. Cut off any excess and press the edge down firmly with the tines of a fork. Brush the top of the pie with egg and brush again after a few minutes.
8. Bake for 45 minutes or until golden brown, pricking the pastry with the point of a knife when it rises.

Cook's tip: serve hot or cold with thick cream and sugar.

Pie aux fruits mélangés
Mixed Fruit Pie

	00:30	
	plus making or thawing pastry	00:45

American	Ingredients	Metric/Imperial
14 oz	Puff pastry (see page 458 or use frozen)	400 g / 14 oz
1½ lb	Fresh fruit (apricots, grapes, cherries, plums, etc)	750 g / 1½ lb
⅔ cup	Sugar	150 g / 5 oz
1	Egg	1
1 cup	Crème fraîche	250 ml / 8 fl oz

1. If using frozen pastry, allow it to thaw.
2. Preheat the oven to 450°F / 230°C / Gas Mark 8.
3. Remove the pits [stones] or seeds from the fresh fruit and arrange in a deep pie dish. Sprinkle with the sugar.
4. Roll out the pastry to ¼ in / 5 mm thick. Cut a strip of pastry the same width as the rim of the dish, roll it out to ⅛ in / 3 mm thick and stick to the rim of the dish with beaten egg. Brush the strip of pastry with beaten egg.
5. Cover the dish with the remaining pastry and press down firmly around the rim. Make a hole in the center and insert a piece of rolled card or a pie funnel to keep it open. Brush the surface of the pie with egg.
6. Bake for 10 minutes. When the pastry begins to rise, lower the heat to 350°F / 180°C / Gas Mark 4 and bake for a further 30 minutes.
7. Serve hot with crème fraîche.

Pie aux abricots
Apricot Pie

	00:35	
	plus making or thawing pastry	00:45

American	Ingredients	Metric/Imperial
14 oz	Puff pastry (see page 458 or use frozen)	400 g / 14 oz
1½ lb	Apricots	750 g / 1½ lb
⅔ cup	Sugar	150 g / 5 oz
1	Egg	1
1 cup	Crème fraîche	250 ml / 8 fl oz

1. If using frozen pastry, allow it to thaw.
2. Preheat the oven to 450°F / 230°C / Gas Mark 8.
3. Wash, drain and pit [stone] the apricots. Cut into quarters or sixths depending on size and arrange in a deep pie dish. Sprinkle with the sugar.
4. Roll out the pastry to ¼ in / 5 mm thick. Cut a strip the

same width as the rim of the pie dish and roll out to ⅛ in / 3 mm thick. Stick this strip to the rim of the dish with beaten egg, then brush the top of the strip with egg.

5. Cover the dish with the remaining pastry and press it down firmly around the rim. Make a hole in the center of the pastry lid and insert a piece of rolled card or a pie funnel to prevent it closing. Brush the top of the pie with beaten egg.

6. Bake for 15 minutes. When the pastry begins to rise, turn down the oven to 350°F / 180°C / Gas Mark 4 and bake for a further 30 minutes.

7. Serve hot with crème fraîche.

Apricot pie

Flan aux cerises

Cherry Flan

	00:25		01:00
	plus making or thawing pastry		

American	Ingredients	Metric/Imperial
14 oz	Puff pastry (see page 458 or use frozen)	400 g / 14 oz
2½ cups	Milk	500 ml / ¾ pint
4	Eggs	4
	Vanilla extract [essence]	
½ cup	Superfine [caster] sugar	125 g / 4 oz
½ cup	Flour	50 g / 2 oz
1 tbsp	Butter, at room temperature	15 g / ½ oz
½ lb	Pitted [stoned] cherries, fresh or bottled	250 g / 8 oz

1. If using frozen pastry, allow it to thaw.
2. Preheat the oven to 425°F / 220°C / Gas Mark 7.
3. Roll out the pastry and use to line a buttered 10 in / 25 cm tart or flan pan. Prick the bottom of the pastry case with a fork. Set aside.
4. Heat the milk. Put 2 whole eggs and 2 egg yolks into a bowl, add a few drops of vanilla extract and the sugar and beat until pale. Mix in the flour and butter, then stir in the hot milk.
5. Beat the 2 egg whites until stiff and fold into the mixture.
6. Arrange the cherries in the pastry case and pour on the mixture. Bake until the top is golden brown, then reduce the oven temperature to 400°F / 200°C / Gas Mark 6. Cover the

flan with foil and continue baking until the flan has cooked for a total of 1 hour.

Far aux pruneaux

Prune Pudding

	00:25		01:15
	plus soaking and cooling		

American	Ingredients	Metric/Imperial
1 cup	Prunes	125 g / 4 oz
3 cups	Milk	750 ml / 1 ¼ pints
½ cup	Sugar	125 g / 4 oz
1 cup	Flour	150 g / 5 oz
3	Eggs	3
3 tbsp	Rum	3 tbsp

1. Soak the prunes in water to cover for 12 hours.
2. Preheat the oven to 350°F / 180°C / Gas Mark 4.
3. Heat the milk. In a mixing bowl stir together the sugar and flour. Make a well in the center and add the eggs. Beat well, then gradually stir in the hot milk.
4. Drain the prunes and remove the pits [stones]. Add to the batter with the rum.
5. Pour the batter into a buttered 10 in / 25 cm cake pan or shallow ovenproof dish. Bake for about 1¼ hours. The pudding is cooked when the point of a knife inserted in the center comes out clean.
6. Leave to cool before removing from the pan.

Flan aux pruneaux

Prune Flan

	00:15		00:35
	plus making pastry and soaking prunes		

American	Ingredients	Metric/Imperial
3 cups	Pitted [stoned] prunes	400 g / 14 oz
2 cups	Weak tea	500 ml / ¾ pint
1 quantity	Basic short pastry (see page 457)	1 quantity
⅔ cup	Thick crème fraîche (see page 122)	150 ml / ¼ pint
2	Eggs	2
5 tbsp	Superfine [caster] sugar	65 g / 2½ oz
1 tbsp	Potato starch or flour	1 tbsp
⅔ cup	Milk	150 ml / ¼ pint
2 tbsp	Orange liqueur	2 tbsp
2 tbsp	Butter	25 g / 1 oz

1. Place the prunes in a bowl, cover with the weak tea and leave to soak for 4 hours.
2. Preheat the oven to 400°F / 200°C / Gas Mark 6.
3. Roll out the pastry to ¼ in / 5 mm thick and use to line a buttered 10 in / 25 cm tart or flan pan. Prick the bottom of the pastry case with a fork.
4. Drain the prunes and arrange in the pastry case.
5. Whip the crème fraîche with the eggs and sugar until thick. Dissolve the potato starch in the milk and orange liqueur and stir into the egg mixture. Pour over the prunes and dot the top with the butter.
6. Bake for 35 minutes. Remove from the pan and cool on a wire rack.

Tarte aux cerises
Cherry Tart

	00:30 plus making pastry		00:50

American	Ingredients	Metric/Imperial
1 quantity	Basic short pastry	1 quantity
1½ lb	Bottle pitted cherries (preferably morello)	625 g / 1½ lb
⅓ cup	Red currant jelly	100 g / 4 oz

1. Preheat the oven to 350°F / 180°C / Gas Mark 4.
2. Roll out the pastry and use to line a buttered 10 in / 25 cm tart pan. Prick with a fork.
3. Drain the cherries and arrange in the pastry case, starting from the outside edge and squeezing them closely together.
4. Bake for 30 minutes, then reduce the heat to 325°F / 160°C / Gas Mark 3 and bake for a further 20 minutes. The tart is cooked when the base is firm. Remove the tart from the pan and leave to cool.
5. Meanwhile, warm the red currant jelly over a low heat in a small pan until melted. Pour the jelly over the cherries and the sides of the tart.

Long pineapple tart

Tarte aux framboises
Raspberry Tart

	00:20 to 00:30 plus making pastry		00:20

American	Ingredients	Metric/Imperial
1 quantity	Basic short pastry	1 quantity
1 lb	Raspberries	500 g / 1 lb
⅓ cup	Red currant jelly	125 g / 4 oz
	Confectioners' [icing] sugar	

1. Preheat the oven to 400°F / 200°C / Gas Mark 6.
2. Roll out the pastry to ¼ in / 5 mm thick. Use to line a buttered 10 in / 25 cm tart pan. Prick the bottom of the pastry case with a fork. Bake 'blind' for 20 minutes.
3. Meanwhile, rinse and drain the raspberries and pat dry with paper towels. Remove any stalks.
4. Remove the pastry case from the pan and place it on a plate.
5. Melt the red currant jelly in a small pan over a low heat and

brush over the bottom of the tart case. Cover with the raspberries, then brush with the remaining jelly. Sprinkle with confectioners' sugar and serve chilled.

Clafoutis aux cerises
Baked Cherry Pudding

	00:15 plus standing time		00:35

American	Ingredients	Metric/Imperial
½ cup	Superfine [caster] sugar	125 g / 4 oz
	Salt	
6	Eggs	6
1¼ cups	Milk	250 ml / 8 fl oz
¾ cup	Flour	100 g / 3½ oz
1½ lb	Black cherries	750 g / 1½ lb

1. Place three quarters of the sugar and a pinch of salt in a mixing bowl. Beat in the eggs and then the milk. Add the flour and beat vigorously, then leave the batter to stand for 10 minutes.
2. Preheat the oven to 425°F / 220°C / Gas Mark 7.
3. Wash and dry the cherries and remove the stalks. Remove the pits [stones].
4. Spread out the cherries in a buttered 10 in / 25 cm cake pan or ovenproof dish and fill with the batter.
5. Bake for 35 minutes.
6. Leave to cool, then sprinkle with the remaining sugar.

Cook's tip: other soft fruit, such as apricots, can be used successfully in this dish.

Tarte longue à l'ananas
Long Pineapple Tart

	00:40 plus thawing or making pastry		00:40

American	Ingredients	Metric/Imperial
14 oz	Puff pastry	400 g / 14 oz
1	Egg	1
1	Fresh pineapple	1
1 quantity	Pastry cream	1 quantity
5 tbsp	Apricot jam	5 tbsp

1. If using frozen pastry, allow it to thaw.
2. Preheat the oven to 450°F / 230°C / Gas Mark 8.
3. Roll out the puff pastry into a rectangle about 6 in / 15 cm wide and about ¼ in / 5 mm thick. From each long side cut a strip of pastry about ¾ in / 2 cm wide.
4. Dampen a large baking sheet and place the rectangle of pastry on it. Brush the long edges with beaten egg and stick on the two narrow strips of pastry. Cut slits in the outside of this border with a knife at ¾ in / 2 cm intervals. Prick the pastry base with a fork. Bake for 12 minutes.
5. Meanwhile, cut off the two ends of the pineapple. Place the pineapple on a board and peel from top to bottom with a large knife. Cut out the eyes with a small pointed knife. Slice the pineapple crosswise and cut out the core. Cut each slice in half.
6. Remove the pastry case from the oven. Cover it with pastry cream, then arrange the pineapple slices on top. Reduce the heat of the oven to 400°F / 200°C / Gas Mark 6 and bake for a further 30 minutes.
7. Warm the apricot jam. Remove the tart from the oven and brush with hot apricot jam.

Cook's tip: if you prefer to make a round tart, proceed in exactly the same way, but cut the pastry using a large plate as a guide. Cut out a ¾ in / 2 cm border. Place the pastry base in a round tart pan and stick on the border with beaten egg. For the round tart cut the pineapple slices into quarters.

Tarte au fromage blanc
Cheese Tart

	00:30	00:45 to 00:50
	plus making pastry	

American	Ingredients	Metric/Imperial
1 quantity	Basic short pastry	1 quantity
2½ cups	Cream cheese	600 g / 1¼ lb
½ cup	Thick crème fraîche	125 ml / 4 fl oz
2	Eggs	2
2	Egg yolks	2
¾ cup	Superfine [caster] sugar	175 g / 6 oz
1 tbsp	Flour	1 tbsp
	Vanilla extract [essence] or	
1	Lemon	1
	Salt	
	Confectioners' [icing] sugar	

1. Preheat the oven to 425°F / 220°C / Gas Mark 7.
2. Roll out the pastry to ¼ in / 5 mm thick. Use to line a buttered and floured 10 in / 25 cm tart pan. Prick the bottom of the pastry case with a fork.
3. Beat the cream cheese until smooth, then beat in the crème fraîche. Add the whole eggs, one at a time, and then the egg yolks. Stir in the sugar mixed with the flour and a few drops of

vanilla extract or the finely grated rind of the lemon. Finally add a pinch of salt.
4. Pour the cheese mixture into the pastry case. Bake for 20 minutes, then lower the oven temperature to 350°F / 180°C / Gas Mark 4. If necessary, prick the filling with a fork to reduce bubbling and bake for a further 25 minutes. Serve hot or cold, sprinkled with confectioners' sugar.

Tarte aux poires
Pear Tart

	00:20	00:20
	plus making pastry	

American	Ingredients	Metric/Imperial
1 quantity	Basic short pastry	1 quantity
4	Large ripe pears	4
3	Eggs	3
1 cup	Crème fraîche	250 ml / 8 fl oz
1 tbsp	Cornstarch [cornflour]	1 tbsp
½ cup	Superfine [caster] sugar	125 g / 4 oz

1. Preheat the oven to 400°F / 200°C / Gas Mark 6.
2. Roll out the pastry to ¼ in / 5 mm thick and use to line a buttered 10 in / 25 cm tart pan.
3. Peel and quarter the pears. Remove the cores and cut into very thin slices.
4. Beat the eggs together and stir in the crème fraîche, cornstarch and sugar.
5. Arrange the sliced pears in the pastry case and cover with the egg mixture. Bake for about 20 minutes.
6. Remove the tart from the oven and allow to cool before removing from the pan.

Pear tart

Tarte à la rhubarbe

Rhubarb Tart

	00:30	01:45
	plus making pastry	

American	Ingredients	Metric/Imperial
1 quantity	Basic short pastry	1 quantity
1 cup	Hazelnuts	125 g / 4 oz
2 lb	Rhubarb	1 kg / 2 lb
½ cup	Granulated sugar	125 g / 4 oz
⅓ cup	Water	5 tbsp
5	Egg whites	5
1 cup	Superfine [caster] sugar	250 g / 8 oz

1. Preheat the oven to 350°F / 180°C / Gas Mark 4.
2. Roll out the pastry to ¼ in / 5 mm thick and use to line a buttered 10 in / 25 cm tart pan. Prick the bottom of the pastry case with a fork. Bake 'blind' for 20 minutes.
3. Grind the hazelnuts and toast without fat in a frying pan or in the oven.
4. Cut the rhubarb into short lengths and cook with the granulated sugar and water for about 15 minutes or until very soft. Purée in a vegetable mill, blender or food processor.
5. Remove the pastry case from the oven and reduce the temperature to 275°F / 120°C / Gas Mark 1. Fill the pastry case with the rhubarb purée.
6. Beat the egg whites until stiff, then gradually beat in the superfine sugar. Spread the meringue over the rhubarb purée.
7. Sprinkle the toasted hazelnuts over the meringue and bake for about 45 minutes. Serve warm.

Tarte à la vergeoise

Brown Sugar Tart

	00:30	00:15 to 00:18
	plus rising time	

American	Ingredients	Metric/Imperial
1½ cups	Milk	150 ml / ¼ pint
2 packages	Active dry yeast	1 sachet
2 tbsp	Granulated sugar	2 tbsp
4 cups	Flour	500 g / 1 lb
2	Eggs	2
	Salt	
½ cup	Melted butter	125 g / 4 oz
1⅓ cups	Light brown sugar	250 g / 8 oz

1. Heat the milk in a small pan over a low heat until lukewarm. Remove from the heat. Add the yeast and granulated sugar and stir well. Leave in a warm place for 15-20 minutes or until frothy.
2. Sift the flour onto a worktop and make a well in the center. Add the eggs and a pinch of salt. Work in with your fingertips. Moisten with the yeast mixture and add all but 2 tablespoons [25 g / 1 oz] of the melted butter. Knead the dough until it no longer sticks to your fingers or the worktop. Roll into a ball and leave to rise in a warm place for about 1 hour.
3. Preheat the oven to 400°F / 200°C / Gas Mark 6.
4. Roll out the dough into a round ½ in / 1 cm thick. Trim the edges, using a plate as a guide, to make the round neat. Place on a buttered and floured baking sheet.
5. Cover the top with the brown sugar, leaving a border ¾ in / 2 cm all the way around. Sprinkle with the remaining melted butter and bake for 15-18 minutes. Serve hot.

Redcurrant meringue tart

Tarte à la mirabelle

Plum Tart

	00:25	00:30 to 00:40
	plus making pastry	

American	Ingredients	Metric/Imperial
1 quantity	Basic short pastry	1 quantity
2 lb	Plums	1 kg / 2 lb
¼ cup	Sugar	50 g / 2 oz
⅓ cup	Apricot jam	125 g / 4 oz

1. Preheat the oven to 400°F / 200°C / Gas Mark 6.
2. Roll out the pastry to ¼ in / 5 mm thick and use to line a buttered 10 in / 25 cm tart pan. Prick the bottom of the pastry case with a fork. Bake 'blind' for 15 minutes.
3. Remove from the oven and increase the temperature to 425°F / 220°C / Gas Mark 7.
4. Remove the pits [stones] from the plums. Arrange in the tart case in a circular pattern and sprinkle with the sugar. Bake for 30 minutes. Remove from the oven and allow to cool.
5. When the tart is cold, warm the apricot jam in a small pan and pour over the plums.

Tarte meringuée aux groseilles

Red Currant Meringue Tart

	00:30	01:30
	plus making pastry	

American	Ingredients	Metric/Imperial
1 quantity	Basic short pastry	1 quantity
1 cup	Hazelnuts	125 g / 4 oz
¾ lb	Ripe red currants	250 g / 12 oz
6	Egg whites	6
1 cup	Superfine [caster] sugar	250 g / 8 oz
	Confectioners' [icing] sugar	

1. Preheat the oven to 400°F / 200°C / Gas Mark 6.
2. Roll out the pastry to ¼ in / 5 mm thick and use to line a 10 in / 25 cm tart pan. Prick the bottom of the pastry case with a fork. Bake 'blind' for about 20 minutes.
3. Remove the pastry case from the oven. Reduce the oven temperature to 275°F / 120°C / Gas Mark 1.
4. Grind the hazelnuts and toast them in a frying pan (or in the oven) without fat for a few minutes. Remove the stalks from the currants.
5. Beat the egg whites, gradually adding the sugar, until very stiff. Keep 4 or 5 tablespoons of egg white to one side, and fold the currants into the remaining whites.
6. Sprinkle the bottom of the pastry case with the hazelnuts. Cover with the currant meringue, then top with the plain meringue. Smooth over with a wooden spatula and sprinkle generously with confectioners' sugar.
7. Bake for 1 hour without allowing the meringue to brown. Serve hot or cold.

Tarte aux pommes
Apple Tart

	01:00 plus making pastry	00:35 to 00:40	

American	Ingredients	Metric/Imperial
3 lb	Apples	1.5 kg / 3 lb
1	Lemon	1
3 tbsp	Sugar	3 tbsp
1 quantity	Rich flan pastry	1 quantity
¼ cup	Fruit jelly (currant, apricot, etc)	4 tbsp

1. Preheat the oven to 400°F / 200°C / Gas Mark 6.
2. Set aside 5 apples of similar size. Peel and core the remaining apples and purée them in a vegetable mill, blender or food processor. Add the juice of ½ lemon and 2 tablespoons sugar. Stir well.
3. Roll out the pastry and use to line a buttered 10 in / 25 cm tart pan. Prick the bottom of the pastry case with a fork and cover with the apple purée.
4. Peel the reserved apples. Cut into quarters, remove the cores and slice as thinly as possible. Arrange the apple slices in overlapping layers on the purée and sprinkle with the remaining sugar.
5. Bake for 35-40 minutes or until the pastry case is firm and golden.
6. Warm the fruit jelly and brush over the apple slices as soon as the tart is removed from the oven.

Tarte aux fraises
Strawberry Tart

	00:30 plus making pastry	00:25	

American	Ingredients	Metric/Imperial
1 quantity	Rich flan pastry	1 quantity
⅔ cup	Red currant or raspberry jelly	250 g / 8 oz
¼ cup	Water	4 tbsp
1 lb	Strawberries	500 g / 1 lb
2 tbsp	Sugar	2 tbsp
½	Lemon	½

1. Preheat the oven to 350°F / 180°C / Gas Mark 4.
2. Roll out the pastry and use to line a buttered 10 in / 25 cm tart pan. Prick the bottom of the pastry case, then bake 'blind' for 20 minutes.
3. Meanwhile, combine the red currant or raspberry jelly and water in a small pan and cook for 10 minutes over a low heat to give a smooth syrup.
4. Rinse, drain and hull the strawberries.
5. Remove the pastry case from the pan and place it on a plate. Sprinkle with the sugar mixed with the grated rind of the ½ lemon and then fill with the strawberries. Just before serving glaze with the jelly syrup.

Brown sugar tart

Tarte au citron
Lemon Tart

	00:40 plus making pastry	00:30	

American	Ingredients	Metric/Imperial
1 quantity	Basic short pastry	1 quantity
3	Lemons	3
2	Eggs	2
1 cup	Superfine [caster] sugar	250 g / 8 oz
1 cup	Ground almonds	125 g / 4 oz
1 cup	Water	250 ml / 8 fl oz
1	Vanilla bean [pod]	1
3	Glacé cherries	3

1. Preheat the oven to 350°F / 180°C / Gas Mark 4.
2. Roll out the pastry to ¼ in / 5 mm thick and use to line a buttered 10 in / 25 cm tart pan. Prick the bottom of the pastry case with a fork.
3. Finely grate the rind and squeeze the juice from 1 lemon. Beat the eggs with ¼ cup [50 g / 2 oz] of the sugar until pale, then stir in the ground almonds and lemon rind and juice.
4. Pour the mixture into the pastry case and bake for 30 minutes or until the filling is golden brown.
5. Meanwhile, thinly slice the remaining lemons. Dissolve the rest of the sugar in the water and add the vanilla bean, cut in half lengthwise. Boil for 10 minutes. Add the lemon slices and cook for 10 minutes longer. Drain, reserving the syrup.
6. Arrange the lemon slices in the tart case and garnish with halved glacé cherries. Pour over the syrup.

Cook's tip: if liked, cover the cooked tart with 2 egg whites stiffly beaten with ½ cup [125 g / 4 oz] superfine sugar and a pinch of salt. Brown in a cool oven.

Tarte Tatin
Upside-down Apple Tart

	00:25 plus making pastry	00:30

American	Ingredients	Metric/Imperial
1 lb	Firm apples	500 g / 1 lb
½ cup	Butter	125 g / 4 oz
¾ cup	Sugar	150 g / 5 oz
1 quantity	Basic short pastry	1 quantity
1 cup	Crème fraîche	250 ml / 8 fl oz

1. Preheat the oven to 350°F / 180°C / Gas Mark 4.
2. Peel, core and thickly slice the apples.
3. Butter a 9 in / 22 cm tart pan with 2 tablespoons [25 g / 1 oz] of the butter and sprinkle with half of the sugar. Arrange the apple slices in the pan and sprinkle with the remaining sugar. Cut the remaining butter into small pieces and dot over the apples.
4. Roll out the pastry to ¼ in / 5 mm thick and cut out an 11 in / 28 cm round. Place the pastry round over the apples and press the edges down well.
5. Put the pan over a high heat on top of the stove for 3 minutes to caramelize the sugar, then transfer to the oven and bake for 30 minutes.
6. To serve, turn the tart out of the pan onto a plate with the caramelized apples on top. Serve with crème fraîche.

Tarte aux myrtilles
Bilberry Tart

	00:40 plus making pastry	00:20

American	Ingredients	Metric/Imperial
1 quantity	Basic short pastry	1 quantity
¾ lb	Bilberries or blueberries	350 g / 12 oz
½ cup	Sugar	125 g / 4 oz
1 cup	Water	250 ml / 8 fl oz
2 tbsp	Apricot jam	2 tbsp

1. Preheat the oven to 400°F / 200°C / Gas Mark 6.
2. Roll out the pastry and use to line a 10 in / 25 cm tart pan. Prick the bottom of the pastry case with a fork. Bake 'blind' for 20 minutes.
3. Meanwhile, remove the stalks from the berries, and rinse and drain them.
4. Dissolve the sugar in the water and bring to a boil. Boil for 5 minutes over a moderate heat. Remove the pan from the heat and add the berries. Leave to infuse for 2 minutes, then return the pan to a low heat and cook the berries for 2 minutes or until they have absorbed the syrup.
5. Melt the apricot jam with 1 tablespoon of water over a low heat.
6. Pour the berries into the tart case and glaze with the jam. Leave to cool and then refrigerate for at least four hours before serving.

Cook's tip: bilberries are attractive mixed with other berries, such as raspberries, strawberries or red and black currants in an open tart.

Tarte rustique aux abricots
Country Style Apricot Tart

	00:30 plus making pastry	00:45 to 00:50

American	Ingredients	Metric/Imperial
1 quantity	Basic short pastry	1 quantity
2 tbsp	Superfine [caster] sugar	25 g / 1 oz
2 lb	Apricots	1 kg / 2 lb
	Confectioners' [icing] sugar	

1. Preheat the oven to 425°F / 220°C / Gas Mark 7.
2. Roll out the pastry to ¼ in / 5 mm thick and use to line a buttered 10 in / 25 cm tart pan. Prick the bottom of the pastry case with a fork and sprinkle with 1 tablespoon of sugar.
3. Cut the apricots in half and remove the pits [stones]. Arrange the apricots in the pastry case, cut side uppermost, and overlapping each other.
4. Bake for 20 minutes, then lower the temperature to 350°F / 180°C / Gas Mark 4. Sprinkle the apricots with the remaining sugar and bake for a further 20-25 minutes or until the pastry case is firm.
5. Serve hot or cold, sprinkled with confectioners' sugar.

Red, white and black currants are delicious in tarts and flans

Apple tart

Crêpes soufflées
Soufflé Crêpes

	00:25	00:15 to 00:20
	plus making crêpes	

American	Ingredients	Metric/Imperial
1 cup	Milk	250 ml / 8 fl oz
6	Eggs, separated	6
6 tbsp	Superfine [caster] sugar	75 g / 3 oz
¼ cup	Flour	25 g / 1 oz
	Vanilla extract [essence]	
2 tbsp	Orange liqueur	2 tbsp
15	Crêpes	15
2 tbsp	Melted butter	25 g / 1 oz
	Confectioners' [icing] sugar	

1. Preheat the oven to 400°F / 200°C / Gas Mark 6.
2. Heat the milk in a saucepan. Beat the egg yolks and sugar together until frothy. Beat in the flour, then stir in the hot milk.
3. Pour into the milk saucepan and heat, stirring, until thickened. Do not boil. Add a few drops of vanilla extract and the orange liqueur and leave to cool until warm.
4. Beat the egg whites until very stiff and fold gently into the mixture.
5. Cover half of each crêpe with 3 tablespoons of the mixture and fold over the other half. Arrange the crêpes in a buttered ovenproof dish. Brush with melted butter and bake until risen.
6. Remove from the oven, sprinkle with confectioners' sugar and serve at once.

Croissants
Croissants

	00:30	00:20
	plus rising and chilling	Makes 20

American	Ingredients	Metric/Imperial
4 cups	Flour	500 g / 1 lb
2 packages	Active dry yeast	1 sachet
⅓ cup	Warm water	5 tbsp
¼ cup	Superfine [caster] sugar	50 g / 2 oz
2 tsp	Salt	2 tsp
2½ cups	Milk	450 ml / ¾ pint
½ cup	Butter, chilled	125 g / 4 oz
1	Egg	1

1. Put 1 cup [125 g / 4 oz] flour in a bowl. Dissolve the yeast in the warm water and stir into the flour. Work to form a soft dough, adding more warm water, if necessary. Leave in a warm place for 20 minutes or until doubled in volume.
2. Mix the remaining flour with the sugar, salt and milk to make a dough. Add the yeast dough and mix well.
3. Cut the chilled butter into pieces. Roll out the dough thinly and dot with the pieces of butter. Fold the dough into 3, to enclose the butter. Roll out again, then fold into 3 and chill for 25 minutes. Make 2 further 'turns' (rolling out and folding).
4. Finally roll out the dough to ¼ in / 5 mm thick. Cut into strips 5 in / 12 cm wide and then into triangles 4 in / 10 cm along the base. Roll each into a tube from the base, stretching the top over slightly.
5. Place on an ungreased baking sheet and stretch the rolls slightly to shape into crescents.
6. Cover with a linen towel and leave to rise in a warm place until tripled in volume.

7. Preheat the oven to 475°F / 240°C / Gas Mark 9.
8. Brush the risen croissants with beaten egg and bake for 20 minutes.

Crêpes suzette

Éclairs
Chocolate and Coffee Éclairs

	00:30	00:30
	Makes 12 large or 36 small éclairs	

American	Ingredients	Metric/Imperial
1 quantity	Choux pastry	1 quantity
1 quantity	Pastry cream	1 quantity
2 tbsp	Instant coffee powder	2 tbsp
2 tbsp	Cocoa powder	2 tbsp
1 lb	Fondant icing	500 g / 1 lb

1. Preheat the oven to 400°F / 200°C / Gas Mark 6.
2. Put the choux pastry into a pastry bag fitted with a ¾ in / 15 mm nozzle. Pipe the pastry in 3 in / 7 cm lengths onto a buttered baking sheet, leaving plenty of room for them to swell. Bake for 20 minutes, or until they have risen well.
3. Remove the éclairs from the oven and pierce each on the side to allow the steam to escape. Leave until cold.
4. Divide the pastry cream in half. Flavor one-half with 1 tablespoon of instant coffee powder and the rest with 1 tablespoon of cocoa.
5. Put the chocolate cream into a pastry bag fitted with a ½ in / 1 cm nozzle. Make a hole in the end of each éclair and fill half the éclairs with chocolate cream. Fill the remaining éclairs with coffee cream.
6. Warm the fondant over a low heat in a pan, stirring until smooth. Flavor half the fondant with the remaining coffee powder and the other half with the remaining cocoa.
7. Dip the top of each chocolate éclair into the chocolate fondant and place on a serving plate. Repeat with the coffee éclairs and coffee fondant.

Cornes de gazelle
Almond Croissants

	00:30 Makes 15	00:15 to 00:20	

American	Ingredients	Metric/Imperial
2¾ cups	Ground almonds	300 g / 11 oz
½ cup	Superfine [caster] sugar	125 g / 4 oz
¼ cup	Melted butter	50 g / 2 oz
1½ tbsp	Orange-flower water	1½ tbsp
1¼ cups	Flour	175 g / 6 oz
1 cup	Flaked almonds	125 g / 4 oz

1. Mix together the ground almonds and sugar. Add half the melted butter and ½ tablespoon of the orange-flower water, drop by drop, mixing well. Set the almond paste aside.
2. Combine the flour with the remaining melted butter and orange-flower water. Add a little water, if necessary, to give a supple dough.
3. Preheat the oven to 350°F / 180°C / Gas Mark 4.
4. Divide both mixtures into 15 equal portions. Roll out each portion of dough to form a small square. Roll the 15 portions of almond paste into sticks, slightly shorter than the diagonal of the 15 squares of pastry.
5. Tip the flaked almonds onto a plate. Place the squares of dough one at a time on the plate and place a stick of almond paste across them. Roll up and curve the points around to resemble a small croissant.
6. Arrange the croissants on a buttered baking sheet. Bake until golden brown (15-20 minutes).
7. Leave the croissants to dry out for a few minutes with the oven door open before serving.

Crêpes Suzette
Crêpes Suzette

	00:20 plus making batter	00:40	

American	Ingredients	Metric/Imperial
1 quantity	Crêpe batter (see page 458)	1 quantity
1 cup	Orange liqueur	200 ml / ⅓ pint
	Butter for frying	
½ cup	Butter	125 g / 4 oz
1	Orange	1
½ cup	Sugar	125 g / 4 oz
⅔ cup	Brandy	150 ml / ¼ pint

1. Crêpes Suzette are finished just before serving, but the crêpes should be made in advance.
2. Prepare the crêpe batter, flavoring it with 4 tablespoons of orange liqueur.
3. Melt a little butter in a frying pan. Pour in a ladle of batter and tip the pan in all directions until the bottom is covered evenly with batter. Cook over a moderate heat until the underside of the crêpe is golden brown. Turn it over and cook the other side. Remove the crêpe. Repeat until you have used all the batter. Pile up the crêpes (interleaved with wax [greaseproof] paper) and set aside until ready to serve.
4. Cream the butter with the grated rind of the orange.
5. Just before serving, melt a little of the orange butter in a frying pan over a moderate heat (or in a chafing dish at the table). Add a crêpe and turn it immediately to coat both sides. Sprinkle with a little sugar. Fold in 4 and transfer the crêpe to a hot plate.

6. Repeat for all the crêpes, then return them all to the pan. Pour over the brandy and remaining orange liqueur and sprinkle with the rest of the sugar. Heat, then set alight and serve flaming.

Crêpes au miel
Honey Crêpes

	00:10 plus making crêpes	00:10 Makes 15	

American	Ingredients	Metric/Imperial
⅔ cup	Liquid honey	250 g / 8 oz
¾ cup	Chopped nuts	75 g / 3 oz
½ cup	Ground almonds	50 g / 2 oz
15	Freshly made crêpes	15

1. Preheat the oven to 375°F / 190°C / Gas Mark 5.
2. Warm the honey with the nuts and ground almonds.
3. Brush a little of the honey mixture over each crêpe, roll up and arrange in a buttered ovenproof dish. Reheat in the oven for a few minutes and serve hot.

Diplomate au moka
Coffee Diplomat

	01:00 plus chilling	00:20	

American	Ingredients	Metric/Imperial
2 cups	Milk	500 ml / ¾ pint
1	Vanilla bean [pod]	1
6	Egg yolks	6
¾ cup	Superfine [caster] sugar	150 g / 5 oz
2 tsp	Unflavored gelatin	2 tsp
1 tsp	Coffee flavoring	1 tsp
16	Ladyfingers [sponge fingers]	16
1 cup	Thin crème fraîche	250 ml / 8 fl oz
2 tbsp	Confectioners' [icing] sugar	2 tbsp
	Vanilla extract [essence]	

1. Bring the milk to a boil with the vanilla bean, split in half. Remove the pan from the heat, cover and leave to infuse for 10 minutes.
2. Meanwhile, beat the egg yolks with the sugar until pale. Remove the vanilla bean from the milk and beat the milk into the egg mixture. Pour the mixture back into the pan and cook over a low heat, stirring, until thickened. Do not allow the custard to boil. Remove from the heat.
3. Dissolve the gelatin in a little water, and stir into the custard. Add the coffee flavoring. Leave until cold and beginning to set.
4. Cover the bottom and sides of a buttered 1 quart [1 l / 2 pint] charlotte mold with the ladyfingers, curved side to the mold. Cut the tops to be level with the top of the mold.
5. Whip the crème fraîche in a chilled bowl with the confectioners' sugar and a few drops of vanilla extract. Fold the whipped crème into the coffee custard and pour into the mold. Chill for 2 hours or until set.
6. Unmold the coffee diplomat onto a serving dish. It will be easier to turn out if you dip the mold in hot water for a few moments as this melts the butter that sticks the ladyfingers to the mold.

Macarons
Macaroons

	00:30	00:12 to 00:15
	Makes 36 single or 18 double macaroons	

American	Ingredients	Metric/Imperial
6	Egg whites	6
2 lb	Uncooked almond paste	1 kg / 2 lb
3 cups	Confectioners' [icing] sugar	350 g / 12 oz
	Salt	
	Vanilla extract [essence]	

1. Preheat the oven to 350°F / 180°C / Gas Mark 4.
2. Mix 1 egg white into the almond paste until completely absorbed and the paste is firm and supple. Add a further egg white and work until well blended. Then add, all together, the sugar, a pinch of salt, a few drops of vanilla extract and the remaining egg whites. Work the ingredients together until smooth.
3. Cover a baking sheet with wax [greaseproof] paper. Put the mixture into a pastry bag fitted with a ½ in / 1 cm nozzle. Pipe 36 small blobs, about 1½ in / 4 cm in diameter, onto the paper.
4. Bake for 12-15 minutes or until golden. Remove the baking sheet from the oven and immediately remove the macaroons from the paper.

Mascotte
Buttercream Sponge Cake

	00:30	00:25 to 00:30
	plus making cake and buttercream	

American	Ingredients	Metric/Imperial
½ cup	Ground praline	80 g / 3 oz
1 quantity	Buttercream	1 quantity
1 cup	Flaked almonds	100 g / 4 oz
½ cup	Sugar	100 g / 4 oz
2 tbsp	Water	2 tbsp
¼ cup	Rum	4 tbsp
1 (10 in)	Sponge cake	1 (25 cm / 10 in)

1. Add the ground praline to the buttercream and mix well. Set aside.
2. Toast the flaked almonds under the broiler [grill] or in a frying pan, stirring continuously until light brown. Leave to cool.
3. Bring the sugar and water to a boil, stirring to dissolve the sugar. Remove from the heat and add the rum.
4. Cut the sponge cake into 3 equal layers and brush each with the rum syrup. Cover each layer with buttercream, spreading it with a spatula, then place them one on top of the other. Cover the sides of the cake with the remaining buttercream.
5. Sprinkle the toasted almonds over the cake. Cut several strips of paper ½ in / 1 cm wide and arrange them on the top of the cake at regular intervals. Sprinkle generously with confectioners' sugar, then slide the strips of paper carefully off the cake. Chill until ready to serve.

Millefeuille
Napoleons or Cream Slices

	00:30	00:35 to 00:40
	plus making or thawing pastry	

American	Ingredients	Metric/Imperial
1 lb	Puff pastry	500 g / 1 lb
1 tbsp	Sugar	1 tbsp
½ quantity	Pastry cream	½ quantity
	Confectioners' [icing] sugar	

1. If using frozen pastry, allow it to thaw.
2. Preheat the oven to 400°F / 200°C / Gas Mark 6.
3. Roll out the pastry to ⅛ in / 3 mm thick and place on a buttered baking sheet. Leave to stand for 10 minutes.
4. Moisten the pastry slightly with water and sprinkle with sugar, then prick all over with a fork. Bake for 20-25 minutes or until dry and crisp. Leave to cool.
5. Cut the pastry sheet into 4 equal widths, each about 12×4 in / 30×10 cm. Spread 3 with pastry cream and place one on top of the other. Put the fourth piece of pastry on top. Sprinkle generously with confectioners' sugar and, if liked, decorate with criss-crossed lines.

Paris-Brest
Praline Filled Choux Ring

	00:15	00:30 to 00:45
	plus making pastry	

American	Ingredients	Metric/Imperial
1 quantity	Choux pastry	1 quantity
2	Eggs	2
½ cup	Flaked almonds	50 g / 2 oz
1 cup	Milk	250 ml / 8 fl oz
1	Egg yolk	1
½ cup	Sugar	100 g / 4 oz
¼ cup	Cornstarch [cornflour]	30 g / 1 oz
⅔ cup	Butter	125 g / 5 oz
½ cup	Ground praline	75 g / 3 oz
	Confectioners' [icing] sugar	

1. Preheat the oven to 350°F / 180°C / Gas Mark 4.
2. Put the choux pastry into a pastry bag fitted with a plain ¾ in / 2 cm nozzle. Place an 8 in / 20 cm diameter plate upside-down on a baking sheet and pipe a ring of pastry ½ in / 1 cm from the rim of the plate. Remove the plate.
3. Beat 1 egg and brush the ring of pastry with beaten egg. Sprinkle with the flaked almonds and bake for 20-25 minutes. If the pastry begins to get too brown cover it with foil. When cooked remove the pastry ring from the oven, cut a slit in the side to allow the steam to escape and leave to cool.
4. Bring the milk to a boil in a saucepan. Beat the egg yolk with the remaining whole egg and add the sugar and cornstarch. Gradually whisk in the boiling milk, then pour the mixture into the pan. Cook, stirring, until the custard thickens. Remove from heat. Stir in half the butter, in small pieces, and leave until cold.

5. Cream the remaining butter and mix in the praline. Add this mixture to the cold custard and stir until smooth.

6. Cut across the ring of pastry to make two equal layers. Put the custard into a pastry bag fitted with a large fluted nozzle and pipe onto the bottom half of the ring. Replace the top half. Sprinkle with confectioners' sugar and chill until ready to serve.

Petits fours

Petits Fours

	01:00		00:00

American	Ingredients	Metric/Imperial
2 lb	Almond paste	1 kg / 2 lb
	Food colorings: red, green and yellow	
	Rum or kirsch	
1	Egg white	1
1 cup	Whole hazelnuts	125 g / 4 oz
1 cup	Blanched almonds	125 g / 4 oz
1 cup	Shelled walnuts	125 g / 4 oz

1. Divide the almond paste into 3 equal portions.

2. Hazelnut petits fours: place one portion of almond paste on a pastry board, make a hollow in the center and add 3 drops of red food coloring. Knead the paste using the palms of your hands until of uniform color. Add 1 teaspoon of rum or kirsch and knead once more. Roll the paste into a tube of ¾ in / 1.5 cm diameter and cut into ½ in / 1 cm slices. Stir, but do not beat, the egg white in a bowl and tip in the hazelnuts. Shape the slices of almond paste to resemble olives and decorate each with 3 hazelnuts.

3. Almond petits fours: color the second portion of almond paste with 3 drops of green food coloring and flavor with 1 teaspoon of rum or kirsch. Roll into a tube of ¾ in / 1.5 cm diameter and cut into 1½ in / 4 cm lengths. Dip the almonds in the egg white and decorate each piece of paste with 1 almond on top.

4. Walnut petits fours: color the remaining almond paste with 3 drops of yellow food coloring and flavor with 1 teaspoon of rum or kirsch. Roll the paste into a tube ¾ in / 1.5 cm in diameter and cut into slices. Shape each slice into a ball. Dip the walnuts in the egg white and place a walnut on opposite sides of each ball of paste.

Cook's tip: all these petits fours can be candied (see pages 30, 31). If you candy them, they should be eaten within 24 hours, otherwise they will keep for anytime up to 2 weeks in an airtight container.

Napoleons or cream slices

Oreillettes
Fried Cookies [Biscuits]

⏱ 00:30 (plus standing time) — 00:03 to 00:04 (per batch) Makes 45-50

American	Ingredients	Metric/Imperial
4 cups	Flour	1 kg / 2 lb
2 tsp	Baking powder	2 tsp
2	Eggs	2
	Vanilla extract [essence]	
½ tsp	Salt	½ tsp
2 cups	Milk	300 ml / ½ pint
½ cup	Butter	100 g / 4 oz
	Oil for frying	
	Confectioners' [icing] sugar	

1. Sift the flour and baking powder onto a worktop. Make a well in the center, and add the eggs, a few drops of vanilla extract and the salt. Work the ingredients together, gradually adding the cold milk. When all the ingredients are mixed, lightly flour the dough and knead until supple. Add the butter a little at a time and leave to stand for 2 hours.
2. Roll out the dough very thinly and cut into diamond shapes.
3. In a frying pan heat 1 in / 3 cm oil until hot but not smoking. Add a few diamonds at a time and fry until golden on both sides. Drain on paper towels.
4. Sprinkle with confectioners' sugar before serving.

Profiteroles
Profiteroles

⏱ 00:20 (plus making pastry) — 00:40

American	Ingredients	Metric/Imperial
1 quantity	Choux pastry	1 quantity
½ lb	Semisweet [plain] chocolate	250 g / 8 oz
⅓ cup	Milk	5 tbsp
2 tbsp	Butter	25 g / 1 oz
1¼ cups	Thick crème fraîche	300 ml / ½ pint
3 cups	Vanilla ice cream	750 ml / 1¼ pints
1 quantity	Chantilly cream	1 quantity

1. Preheat the oven to 400°F / 200°C / Gas Mark 6.
2. Put the pastry into a pastry bag fitted with a plain ¼ in / 5 mm nozzle. Pipe small balls of pastry onto a buttered baking sheet.
3. Bake for 20 minutes or until light golden brown and crisp. Make a small slit in each choux bun to allow steam to escape and cool on a wire rack.
4. Break the chocolate into a bowl and place over a pan of hot water. Add the milk and stir until the chocolate melts. Add the butter and stir until smooth, then mix in the crème fraîche. Keep warm over the pan of hot water.
5. Halve the choux buns and fill with vanilla ice cream or chantilly cream. Arrange in individual glasses.
6. Pour on the chocolate sauce and serve immediately.

Petits fours glacés
Candied Petits Fours

⏱ 01:00 (plus drying) — 00:20 Makes 80

American	Ingredients	Metric/Imperial
1½ cups	Prunes	250 g / 8 oz
1½ cups	Dates	250 g / 8 oz
⅔ cup	Glacé cherries	125 g / 4 oz
2 lb	Almond paste	1 kg / 2 lb
	Food coloring: red, green and yellow	
4 cups	Sugar	1 kg / 2 lb
⅔ cup	Water	150 ml / ¼ pint
2 tbsp	White vinegar	2 tbsp

1. Halve the prunes and dates and remove the pits [stones]. Halve the glacé cherries.
2. Divide the almond paste into 4 equal portions. Knead the first portion until very white and supple, then roll it into a tube ¾ in / 1.5 cm in diameter. Cut into ½ in / 1 cm slices. Roll each slice into a ball and garnish each side with ½ glacé cherry.
3. Color the other 3 portions of almond paste (see recipe for petits fours page 493): the first with 3 drops of red food coloring, the second with 3 drops of green food coloring and the third with 3 drops of yellow food coloring. Roll each portion into a tube ¾ in / 1.5 cm in diameter and cut into ½ in / 1 cm slices. Shape to resemble olives. Use these 'olives' to stuff the prunes and dates and close up the fruit.
4. Leave for 24 hours to dry.
5. Dissolve the sugar in the water with the vinegar and cook over a moderate heat until the syrup begins to color.
6. Thread the fruit one at a time onto a skewer and dip in the caramel. Drain and place on a buttered baking sheet. Leave until quite dry.
7. Place each fruit in a paper case. Eat within 24 hours.

Pain perdu
French Toast

⏱ 00:10 — 00:04 (per batch)

American	Ingredients	Metric/Imperial
1 cup	Milk	250 ml / 8 fl oz
½ cup	Sugar	100 g / 4 oz
	Vanilla extract [essence]	
5	Eggs	5
1 cup	Butter	250 g / 8 oz
12	Slices brioche (fresh or stale)	12

1. Warm the milk. Add the sugar and a few drops of vanilla extract and stir until dissolved.
2. Beat the eggs in a shallow dish.
3. Melt the butter in a bowl over a pan of hot water and leave to cool. A whitish deposit will form in the bottom of the bowl. Carefully pour the butter into a dish, leaving the deposit behind.
4. Dip the slices of brioche in the sweetened milk, then in the beaten eggs. Pour 1 tablespoon of the clarified butter into a frying pan and, when hot, add a batch of brioche. Fry until golden on both sides. Fry the remaining brioche, adding more clarified butter to the pan as necessary.
5. Serve hot with sugar and apricot jam.

Profiteroles

Négrillons aux noix

Chocolate and Nut Cakes

	00:30		00:15
	Makes 20		

American	Ingredients	Metric/Imperial
1 cup	Shelled walnuts	120 g / 4 oz
¼ cup	Butter	60 g / 2 oz
½ cup	Superfine [caster] sugar	120 g / 4 oz
3 oz	Semisweet [plain] chocolate	90 g / 3 oz
3	Egg whites	3
½ cup	Blanched almonds	50 g / 2 oz
⅓ cup	Glacé cherries	50 g / 2 oz

1. Preheat the oven to 350°F / 180°C / Gas Mark 4.
2. Finely grind the walnuts. Set aside.
3. Cream the butter and sugar together until pale and fluffy.
4. Break the chocolate into a bowl and place over a pan of hot water. Melt the chocolate and cool until just warm, then gradually stir it into the butter and sugar mixture. Add the ground walnuts.
5. Beat the egg whites until stiff and fold into the mixture.
6. Half fill 20 buttered tartlet pans with the mixture. Decorate the top of each with an almond and a few pieces of glacé cherry.
7. Bake for 15 minutes.
8. Remove from the pans immediately as this mixture tends to stick when cool.

Petits gâteaux à l'anis

Small Aniseed Cakes

	00:25	00:25 to 00:30	
	plus cooling	Makes about 20	

American	Ingredients	Metric/Imperial
1 cup	Butter	250 g / 8 oz
2½ cups	Confectioners' [icing] sugar	280 g / 10 oz
2	Eggs yolks	2
	Rosewater	
3½ cups	Flour	400 g / 14 oz
½ tsp	Baking powder	½ tsp
1 tbsp	Ouzo or Pernod	1 tbsp
½ cup	Ground almonds	60 g / 2 oz
20	Cloves	20

1. Preheat the oven to 300°F / 150°C / Gas Mark 2.
2. Cream the butter in a mixing bowl, then beat in two-thirds of the sugar, the egg yolks, one at a time, and 6 drops of rosewater. Beat the mixture well, then add the flour, baking powder and ouzo or Pernod.
3. Toast the almonds in a dry pan for about 5 minutes, stirring continuously until golden. Add to the mixture and stir until smooth.
4. Using a teaspoon make 20 small heaps of the mixture on a baking sheet. Stick a clove in each. Bake for about 30 minutes without allowing the cakes to brown.
5. Roll each cake in the remaining confectioners' sugar while still hot and leave on a wire rack to cool. When cold roll once more in the sugar.

Mousse à l'orange
Orange Mousse

American	Ingredients	Metric/Imperial
	00:10 plus chilling	00:10
3 tbsp	Flour	25 g / 1 oz
3	Eggs, separated	3
½ cup	Superfine [caster] sugar	100 g / 4 oz
4	Oranges	4

1. In a saucepan stir together the flour, egg yolks, three quarters of the sugar and the finely grated rind of 1 orange. Place the pan on a low heat.
2. Squeeze the juice from all the oranges and add to the pan. Cook, stirring, for about 10 minutes or until the custard is thick enough to coat the spoon. Do not boil. Remove the pan from the heat and leave to cool, stirring from time to time to prevent a skin forming.
3. Beat the egg whites with the remaining sugar until stiff. Carefully fold the whites into the orange custard.
4. Pour the mousse into a large bowl and chill for at least 1 hour.

Cook's tip: this mousse is excellent to follow a filling main course. It can be served with petits fours (see page 493).

Mousse au citron
Lemon Cheese Mousse

American	Ingredients	Metric/Imperial
	00:10 plus soaking and chilling	00:00
1 cup	Currants	150 g / 6 oz
6	Petit suisse cheeses	6
¾ cup	Sugar	150 g / 6 oz
3	Lemons	3
⅔ cup	Thin crème fraîche	150 ml / ¼ pint
¼ cup	Confectioners' [icing] sugar	30 g / 1 oz

1. Put the currants in a bowl of warm water and leave to soak for 1 hour.
2. Put the cheeses, sugar, flesh of 2 lemons (without seeds) and the juice of the third lemon into a blender or food processor and blend to give a thick cream.
3. Whip the crème fraîche in a chilled bowl, gradually adding the confectioners' sugar, until stiff and doubled in volume.
4. Gently fold the cream and drained currants into the lemon cream.
5. Divide between 6 individual glasses and chill for 1 hour.

Mousse au citron vert
Lime Mousse

American	Ingredients	Metric/Imperial
	00:20 plus cooling and chilling	00:10
6	Eggs, separated	6
1 cup	Superfine [caster] sugar	200 g / 8 oz
3	Limes	3

1. Beat the egg yolks with the sugar until frothy, then add the juice of the limes.
2. Place the bowl over a pan of hot water and heat gently, stirring constantly, for 10 minutes or until the mixture will coat a spoon. Remove the bowl and leave until cold.
3. Beat the egg whites until very stiff and gently fold into the lime mixture.
4. Divide the mousse between 6 individual glasses and chill for 1 hour.

Cook's tip: the cooking over the pan of hot water is necessary for the success of this recipe.

Fruits rafraîchis
Fruit Salad with Liqueur

American	Ingredients	Metric/Imperial
	00:20 plus chilling	00:10
2	Oranges	2
2	Pears	2
2	Apples	2
½ lb	Pineapple (canned or fresh)	250 g / 8 oz
1 cup	Sugar	250 g / 8 oz
1 ¼ cups	Water	300 ml / ½ pint
½ lb	Strawberries	250 g / 8 oz
	Kirsch or maraschino liqueur	

1. Peel the oranges and cut into slices. Peel, core and slice the pears and apples. Cut the pineapple into chunks. Transfer all this fruit to a serving bowl.
2. Boil the sugar and water over a moderate heat for 10 minutes. Pour the syrup over the fruit and chill.
3. Just before serving, decorate the salad with strawberries or other seasonal fruit (raspberries, grapes, etc) and add a dash of kirsch or maraschino liqueur.

Pruneaux au Vouvray
Prunes in White Wine

American	Ingredients	Metric/Imperial
	01:00 plus soaking and chilling	00:10
1 lb	Semi-dried prunes	500 g / 1 lb
3	Lemons	3
1	Bottle of white wine	1
½ cup	Sugar	100 g / 4 oz
1	Vanilla bean [pod]	1
	Grated nutmeg	

1. Soak the prunes in a bowl of warm water for 1 hour.
2. Meanwhile, thinly pare the rind from the lemons. Pour the wine into a pan and add the sugar, vanilla bean split lengthwise, a pinch of nutmeg and the lemon rind. Bring to a boil and simmer for 10 minutes. Cool.
3. Drain the prunes and transfer to a serving bowl. Cover with the spiced wine and chill for at least 3 hours (or, better still, for 2-3 days).

Cook's tip: add a pinch of ground cinnamon to the wine and serve with chantilly cream (see page 455).

Melon cups

Oranges meringuées
Meringue Oranges

| ⊳ | 00:50 plus chilling | 00:20 to 00:25 🍲 |

American	Ingredients	Metric/Imperial
6	Oranges	6
1 cup	Raspberries (or pitted [stoned] cherries)	100 g / 4 oz
2	Bananas	2
2	Apples	2
1	Pear	1
½ cup	Granulated sugar	100 g / 4 oz
3	Egg whites	3
⅔ cup	Superfine [caster] sugar	150 g / 5 oz
1 cup	Crème fraîche oz chantilly cream	250 ml / 8 fl oz

1. Cut a lid off each orange and remove the flesh without breaking the skins. Dice the flesh. Place the skins in an ovenproof dish and set aside.
2. Rinse, drain and hull the raspberries (or cherries). Peel and slice the bananas. Peel, core and slice the apples and pear. Place all the fruit in a bowl and sprinkle with the granulated sugar. Leave to steep in the refrigerator for 2 hours.
3. Preheat the oven to 275°F / 120°C / Gas Mark 1.
4. Pile the fruit salad into the orange skins.
5. Beat the egg whites, gradually adding the superfine sugar, until stiff. Transfer the meringue to a pastry bag and pipe onto the tops of the oranges. Take care that the fruit is completely covered.
6. Bake for about 25 minutes, without allowing the meringue to brown. Serve at once with crème fraîche or chantilly cream.

Cook's tip: if you would prefer to serve the oranges cold, use ¾ cup [180 g / 6 oz] sugar to make the meringue and bake for 1 hour. Allow to cool before serving.

Melon d'espagne fourré
Melon Cups

| ⊳ | 00:30 plus chilling | 00:00 🍲 |

American	Ingredients	Metric/Imperial
1	Large cantaloupe melon	1
2 lb	Mixed fresh fruit: grapes, pears, strawberries, oranges	1 kg / 2 lb
½ cup	Sugar	100 g / 4 oz
¼ cup	Kirsch or maraschino liqueur	4 tbsp
1 cup	Thick crème fraîche oz chantilly cream	250 ml / 8 fl oz

1. Cut a lid off the melon and scoop out the fruit in balls using a ball-cutter or a teaspoon. Discard the seeds.
2. Wash the fresh fruit and peel, dice and remove seeds where necessary. Place the fruit in a bowl with the melon balls and sprinkle with the sugar and liqueur. Leave to steep in the refrigerator for 1 hour.
3. Just before serving, fill the melon shell with the fruit salad. Serve well chilled with the crème fraîche or chantilly cream.

Coupe aux pommes et aux mûres
Blackberry and Apple Cup

| ⊳ | 00:15 plus chilling | 00:10 to 00:15 🍲 |

American	Ingredients	Metric/Imperial
¾ lb	Blackberries (or raspberries)	350 g / 12 oz
3 tbsp	Water	3 tbsp
1 cup	Sugar	250 g / 8 oz
1½ lb	Apples	750 g / 1½ lb
1 cup	Thin crème fraîche	250 ml / 8 fl oz
½ cup	Confectioners' [icing] sugar	50 g / 2 oz

1. Rinse the blackberries (or raspberries) and place in a pan with the water and ½ cup [125 g / 4 oz] sugar. Cook without boiling for 10-15 minutes.
2. Set aside the blackberries (or raspberries) which are still whole after cooking (about half). Purée the remainder with the juice in a blender or food processor and then strain to remove the seeds.
3. Peel and core the apples. Cut into quarters and place in a pan. Just cover with water and add the remaining sugar. Cook without boiling for 10-15 minutes and leave to cool in the juice.
4. Divide the blackberry purée between 6 individual glasses and garnish with apple segments and whole blackberries. Chill.
5. Whip the crème fraîche in a chilled bowl, gradually adding the confectioners' sugar until it has doubled in volume.
6. Remove the glasses from the refrigerator and pipe a whirl of cream onto each.

Melon aux framboises
Melon with Raspberries

	00:20 plus chilling		00:00

American	Ingredients	Metric/Imperial
1 large or 2 medium	Cantaloupe melon(s)	1 large or 2 medium
½ lb	Raspberries	250 g / 8 oz
½ cup	Sugar	100 g / 4 oz
¼ cup	Kirsch	4 tbsp
1 pint	Raspberry ice cream	500 ml / 1 pint

1. Cut a zig-zag around the top of the melon and remove the lid. Remove the seeds and scoop out the flesh in balls using a ball-cutter or a teaspoon.
2. Rinse and hull the raspberries.
3. Mix the melon balls and raspberries. Sprinkle with the sugar and kirsch and leave to steep for 1 hour in the refrigerator, so that the flavors can mingle.
4. To serve, half fill melon with ice cream and top with fruit.

Pears Belle-Hélène

Fondue de pommes
Stewed Apples

	00:15 plus cooling		00:20

American	Ingredients	Metric/Imperial
1	Lemon	1
3 lb	Apples	1.25 kg / 3 lb
1 cup	Sugar	200 g / 8 oz
1	Vanilla bean [pod]	1
	Ground cinnamon	
⅔ cup	Water	150 ml / ¼ pint

1. Squeeze the juice from the lemon into a large bowl. Peel, core and thinly slice the apples. Add to the bowl and stir to coat with the lemon juice.
2. Transfer the apples and lemon juice to a pan and add the sugar, the vanilla bean split lengthwise, a good pinch of cinnamon and the water. Cover the pan and cook over a low heat for 15 minutes without stirring, then remove the lid and allow the water to evaporate (still over a low heat) for 5 minutes. Remove the vanilla bean.
3. Pour the stewed apples into a serving dish and leave to cool. Serve well chilled.

Poires Belle-Hélène
Pears Belle-Hélène

	00:30 plus chilling	00:20

American	Ingredients	Metric/Imperial
1 cup	Sugar	200 g / 8 oz
1 cup	Water	250 ml / 8 fl oz
6 medium or 3 large	Ripe pears	6 medium or 3 large
	Lemon juice	
½ lb	Semisweet [plain] chocolate	250 g / 8 oz
3 cups	Vanilla ice cream	750 ml / 1¼ pints

1. In a thick-bottomed pan dissolve the sugar in ¾ cup [175 ml / 6 fl oz] of the water. Bring to a boil over a high heat and boil for 5 minutes.
2. Peel and halve the pears lengthwise, then remove the cores. Immerse the pears in the boiling syrup, without overlapping them if possible. Add a few drops of lemon juice. When the syrup returns to a boil, remove the pan from the heat. Leave the pears to cool in the syrup until just warm, then drain and chill them.
3. Break the chocolate into a bowl and add the rest of the water. Place the bowl over a pan of hot water and melt the chocolate to a thick cream. Keep hot.
4. Place a portion of vanilla ice cream in each of 6 chilled serving glasses and cover with 1 or 2 pear halves. Pour the hot chocolate sauce over the pears at the table.

Croûtes aux pêches
Peach Toasts

	00:25 plus chilling	00:25

American	Ingredients	Metric/Imperial
6	Large yellow peaches	6
1¼ cups	Sugar	300 g / 10 oz
2 cups	Water	500 ml / ¾ pint
¼ cup	Butter	60 g / 2 oz
6	Thick slices brioche	6
	Raspberry jelly	
	Few pieces candied angelica	

1. Blanch the peaches in boiling water for 30 seconds, then drain and peel them.
2. Put 1 cup [250 g / 8 oz] of the sugar and water in a saucepan and bring to a boil, stirring to dissolve the sugar. Add the peaches and simmer for 5 minutes. Remove the pan from the heat and leave the peaches to cool in the syrup.
3. Preheat the oven to 400°F / 200°C / Gas Mark 6.
4. Butter the slices of brioche. Sprinkle with the remaining sugar and arrange in an ovenproof dish. Brown the bread in the oven for about 10 minutes. Spread each slice with raspberry jelly and arrange on a serving dish.
5. Remove the peaches from their syrup using a slotted spoon. Add 2 tablespoons of raspberry jelly to the syrup and thicken over a low heat. Put the peaches back in the syrup and cook for 1 minute, turning them gently, then place the peaches on the brioche slices. Pour on the syrup. Decorate with angelica and leave until cold. Chill until ready to serve.

Poires Bourdaloue
Pears in Almond Custard

	00:15 plus chilling	00:20 to 00:25

American	Ingredients	Metric/Imperial
6	Pears	6
1	Lemon	1
2 cups	Milk	500 ml / ¾ pint
1 cup	Sugar	250 g / 8 oz
	Vanilla extract [essence]	
¼ cup	Cornstarch [cornflour]	25 g / 1 oz
½ cup	Ground almonds	50 g / 2 oz
5	Egg yolks	5
1 tbsp	Kirsch	1 tbsp
2 tbsp	Water	2 tbsp

1. Carefully peel the pears without removing the stalks, and sprinkle with the juice of the lemon.
2. Place the pears in a flameproof casserole, cover with cold water and top with wax [greaseproof] paper to prevent the pears going brown. Simmer gently for 12-15 minutes. Remove from the heat and leave to cool. When cold, drain the pears and arrange upright in a serving dish.
3. Bring the milk to a boil with ¾ cup [150 g / 6 oz] of the sugar and a few drops of vanilla extract.
4. Thoroughly beat the cornstarch and ground almonds with the egg yolks. Beat until the mixture has increased in volume. Add the boiling milk and pour back into the pan. Cook gently, stirring, for about 10 minutes or until the custard coats the spoon. Do not boil. Leave to cool, then flavor with the kirsch. Pour the custard around the pears.
5. Place the remaining sugar in a pan with the water and dissolve over a moderate heat. Cook until the syrup is golden brown. Cover the top of each pear with this caramel and chill until ready to serve.

Mousse aux marrons
Chestnut Cream

	00:20 Serves 8–10	00:00

American	Ingredients	Metric/Imperial
1 cup	Butter	200 g / 8 oz
¾ cup	Superfine [caster] sugar	150 g / 6 oz
¼ cup	Rum	4 tbsp
2 lb	Canned sweetened chestnut purée	1 kg / 2 lb
1¼ cups	Thin crème fraîche	300 ml / ½ pint
1½ cups	Broken marrons glacés	200 g / 8 oz
6	Marrons glacés (candied chestnuts)	6

1. Cream the butter until softened, then beat in the sugar and rum. Add the chestnut purée, a little at a time, and beat until well blended.
2. Whip the crème fraîche until thick and fold carefully into the chestnut mixture. Gently stir into the mixture the broken marrons glacés.
3. Divide the mousse between 8-10 individual glasses. Decorate with the whole marrons glacés and chill.

The Best Of
Italian Cooking

Antipasti

Flagship-style anchovies

Acciughe in salamoia
Anchovies in Brine

	00:60	00:00

American	Ingredients	Metric/Imperial
2 lb	Anchovies	1 kg / 2 lb
	Fine salt	

1. Remove the heads from the anchovies and wash in salted water and allow to drain thoroughly.
2. In the bottom of a wide-necked glass vessel put a layer of salt, place on the salt a layer of anchovies with the tails radiating from the centre, cover with a layer of salt and continue until the ingredients are used up. The last layer must be of salt.
3. Place a glass disc on the layered anchovies with a weight on top. Close the mouth of the vessel and return it to a cold store-room. After several months if the anchovies are too dry, pour over some salted water. To prepare the salted water, put as much cold water as you need, together with some salt and dissolve it very thoroughly. Immerse a small raw potato in the water; if the potato comes to the surface it means that the water is salted to the right degree.

Acciughe alla piemontese
Piedmont-Style Anchovies

	00:25	00:00

American	Ingredients	Metric/Imperial
½ lb	Fresh anchovies	225 g / 8 oz
3 tbsp	Vinegar	2 tbsp
Scant ¼ cup	Olive oil	3 tbsp
1	Truffle	1
	Parsley sprigs	

1. Wash the anchovies, bone and divide them into fillets. Soak in vinegar for 10 minutes.
2. Drain and arrange the anchovies in a serving dish. Cover with olive oil.
3. Slice a truffle very finely and sprinkle over the anchovies. Keep in a cool place, but not in the refrigerator. Serve the dish garnished with sprigs of parsley.

Acciughe alla ammiraglia
Flagship-Style Anchovies

	00:20 plus 12 hours standing Serves 4–6	00:00

American	Ingredients	Metric/Imperial
1 lb	Fresh anchovies	450 g / 1 lb
2	Lemons	2
3 tbsp	Oil	2 tbsp
	Salt and pepper	
	Oregano or chopped parsley	

1. Thoroughly clean the fresh anchovies, remove bones, head and tail them and divide into fillets. Wash the fillets in cold water and then drain well. Arrange on a serving dish.
2. Completely cover the anchovies with plenty of well-strained lemon juice and leave to stand for 12 hours. Just before serving beat oil with a little salt and pepper in a cup and sprinkle over anchovies before serving. The lemon causes the anchovies to have a cooked effect and they appear very white. According to taste, complete the dish with a sprinkling of fresh oregano or chopped parsley.

Acciughe con peperoni gialli
Anchovies with Yellow Peppers

	00:15 Serves 6–8	00:05

American	Ingredients	Metric/Imperial
1 lb	Anchovy fillets	450 g / 1 lb
3	Yellow peppers	3
½ cup	Oil	6 tbsp
¼ lb	Capers	100 g / 4 oz
2	Eggs	2
1	Lemon	1
	Black pepper	
1 tbsp	Chopped parsley	1 tbsp

1. Arrange rows of anchovy fillets on a serving dish.
2. Deseed peppers and cut into thin strips. Heat 3 tablespoons oil in a frying pan and cook the strips of pepper over a medium heat for 5 minutes.
3. Arrange the anchovies and peppers in alternate rows. Sprinkle with chopped capers and decorate with rounds of hard-cooked (boiled) eggs.
4. Mix the strained juice of the lemon with 3 tablespoons oil, freshly ground black pepper and chopped parsley. Pour over the anchovies and peppers.

Scodelline di granchi cinesi
Little Bowls of Crabs

	00:25	00:15

American	Ingredients	Metric/Imperial
1 lb	Canned crab flesh	450 g / 1 lb
1	Small onion	1
1 tbsp	Butter	1 tbsp
1¼ cups	Béchamel sauce	300 ml / ½ pint
1 tbsp	Cognac	1 tbsp
3 tbsp	Cream	2 tbsp
1 tbsp	Tomato purée	1 tbsp
	Salt and pepper	

1. Drain the canned crab.
2. Peel and finely chop a small onion. Heat the butter and cook over a low heat until transparent.
3. Make the béchamel sauce, add onion, cognac, cream and tomato purée, season with salt and pepper. Add the crab flesh, turn off the heat. Arrange in small dishes and decorate with basil leaves and triangles of hot toast.

Conchiglie al cartoccio
Clams in Parcels

▭◣   00:20   00:12 ⊆

American	Ingredients	Metric/Imperial
4	Clams	4
1	Bunch of parsley	1
2	Lemons	2
	Salt and pepper	
3 tbsp	Cognac	2 tbsp
4	Egg yolks	4
1 tbsp	Grated parmesan cheese	1 tbsp

1. Preheat the oven to 350°F / 180°C / Gas Mark 4.
2. Wash the clams thoroughly without detaching the mollusc from the valve. Chop the parsley finely, mix with the strained lemon juice, a little salt, pepper and cognac.
3. Arrange 4 ovenproof saucers or china dishes, such as ramekins, each on a large square of foil. Place a clam in each dish and divide the lemon juice and parsley mixture equally amongst the clams.
4. Break an egg into a cup to ensure the yolk remains whole, slip the egg yolk into the centre of each clam, sprinkle with the parmesan cheese.
5. Wrap each clam in a square of foil leaving a little crown of foil at the top of the dish where the square has been gathered together. Place on a baking sheet and cook in the oven for 12 minutes.
6. Remove the foil and serve hot.

Ostriche vellutate
Velvet Oysters

▭◣   00:10   00:50 ⊆

American	Ingredients	Metric/Imperial
24	Oysters	24
½ cup	Red wine	125 ml / 4 fl oz
6 tbsp	All-purpose (plain) flour	40 g / 1½ oz
3 tbsp	Butter	40 g / 1½ oz
1 cup	Fish stock	300 ml / ½ pint
	Salt and pepper	
	Lemon rind	
3 tbsp	Cream	2 tbsp
1 tbsp	Chopped parsley	1 tbsp

1. Place the shelled oysters with the liquid from the shells in a saucepan, add red wine, bring to the boil and simmer for 10 minutes. Strain the liquid through a sieve lined with muslin into another pan and reduce by half. Arrange the oysters in a serving dish.
2. Prepare a savory white sauce with flour, butter and stock (see page 164), blend with the oyster juice, add salt and pepper, a little grated lemon rind and cook slowly for 10 minutes. Add the cream.
3. Pour the sauce over the oysters, garnish with chopped parsley. Place in the refrigerator to chill before serving.

Clams in parcels

Charente Oysters

Ostriche charenteises

	00:20		00:08

American	Ingredients	Metric/Imperial
24	Oysters	24
12	Small sausages	12
1 tbsp	Oil	1 tbsp
8	Sprigs of parsley	8

1. Remove oysters from the shells, scald in boiling water for a few minutes, then keep on one side.
2. Place the sausage in boiling water for 1 minute, pat dry with kitchen paper.
3. Heat the oil in a frying pan and fry sausages until golden brown.
4. Arrange the sausages and the oysters on a heated serving dish and garnish with parsley sprigs.

Napoleon-Style Oysters

Ostriche alla Napoleone

	00:15		00:00

American	Ingredients	Metric/Imperial
24	Oysters	24
	Ice	
	Lettuce leaves	
	Freshly ground white pepper	
1	Lemon	1
Scant ¼ cup	Cognac	3 tbsp
	Salt	
Scant ¼ cup	Olive oil	3 tbsp

1. Arrange the oysters on a serving dish covered by a bed of finely chopped ice. Cover with well washed and drained lettuce leaves.
2. In a small bowl beat some freshly ground white pepper, the juice of a lemon, good quality cognac and a little salt. Beat until you have a smooth mixture, then add a drop at a time of fine olive oil. Pour the seasoning over the oysters and serve them immediately at table.

Canapés with Oysters

Canapés con le ostriche

	00:60		00:00

American	Ingredients	Metric/Imperial
½ cup	Butter, softened	100 g / 4 oz
4 tbsp	Mild mustard	3 tbsp
12	Slices of bread	12
12	Oysters	12
3 tbsp	White wine	2 tbsp
1 cup	Mayonnaise	225 ml / 8 fl oz

1. Beat the butter until it becomes creamy. Add half the mustard and mix well.
2. Place the slices of bread without crusts in the oven for a few minutes, then spread with the butter.
3. Wash and brush the oyster shells thoroughly, then open the oysters, add a sprinkling of white wine, put in an earthenware dish with some mayonnaise flavored with the remaining mustard.
4. Place an oyster on each slice of bread, arrange on a large serving dish and decorate all around with the best shells containing a little finely chopped ice.

Crayfish Cups

Coppe di gamberoni

	00:25		00:08

American	Ingredients	Metric/Imperial
2 lb	Crayfish	1 kg
1 ¼ cups	Mayonnaise	300 ml / ½ pint
2 tsp	Tomato purée	2 tsp
¼ tsp	Tabasco sauce	¼ tsp
1 tbsp	Cognac	1 tbsp
	Lettuce	

1. Cook the crayfish in boiling water for 5 minutes, then drain and shell.
2. Prepare the mayonnaise and flavor it with tomato purée, Tabasco sauce and a little cognac. Mix the crayfish with the pink sauce.
3. Arrange leaves of well washed and drained fresh lettuce in 4 cups. Place a few crayfish all around the rim of the cup. Serve cold.

Cocktail of Dublin Bay Prawns

Cocktail di scampi

	00:60		00:10
	Chilling time 02:00		

American	Ingredients	Metric/Imperial
1	Leek	1
1	Lemon	1
1	Head of lettuce	1
3 tbsp	Vinegar	2 tbsp
1 lb	Dublin Bay prawns	450 g / 1 lb
1 cup	Coffee (single) cream	225 ml / 8 fl oz
3 tbsp	Rum	2 tbsp

1. Wash the leek and remove any discolored leaves. Chop into thin slices and blanch in boiling water for 4 minutes, drain well and allow to cool. Sprinkle with lemon juice.
2. Place a few washed lettuce leaves in an earthenware dish and add the leek.
3. Place some water with vinegar in a saucepan, bring to the boil and drop in the prawns, bring back to the boil and cook for 5 minutes, drain and allow to cool, then remove shells.
4. Put the prawns in the dish, mix thoroughly with the cream and rum.
5. Divide the mixture between 4 glasses, and garnish with some more lettuce leaves torn or cut into strips. Place in the refrigerator for 2 hours, then serve.

Sandwiches esotici

Whole Meal Avocado

◄▽	00:15		00:00 ▭

American	Ingredients	Metric/Imperial
1 or 2	Avocado pears	1 or 2
5 tbsp	Mayonnaise	4 tbsp
1 tbsp	Lemon juice	1 tbsp
Scant ¼ cup	Soy (soya) sauce	3 tbsp
	Salt and pepper	
1 tbsp	Chopped parsley	1 tbsp
8 slices	Slices whole wheat (wholemeal) bread	8 slices

1. Cut avocado pear in half, take out the stone and remove the flesh with a spoon. Put the flesh in a bowl and add the mayonnaise, lemon, soy sauce and season with a pinch of salt, pepper and chopped parsley.
2. Beat ingredients thoroughly and spread the smooth mixture on slices of whole wheat bread, plain or toasted. Cut into strips.

Avocado saporito

Savory Avocado

◄▽	00:20		00:00 ▭
	Cooling time 00:10		

American	Ingredients	Metric/Imperial
2	Ripe avocado pears	2
1	Lemon	1
2	Onions	2
1 tbsp	Vinegar	1 tbsp
½ lb	Goat's milk cheese	225 g / 8 oz
1 tbsp	Oil	1 tbsp
	Salt and pepper	

1. Cut the avocado in two lengthwise, remove the stones and sprinkle them with lemon juice to prevent them turning black.
2. Cut the peeled onions into very thin slices and put to soak in a little vinegar and water to allow them to become less pungent.
3. Mix the goat's milk cheese in bowl with oil, salt, pepper and the drained onions. Blend into a cream.
4. Fill the avocados with goat's milk cheese. Leave in the refrigerator for 10 minutes and serve.

Avocado in coppa

Avocado Pear in a Cup

◄▽	00:30		00:00 ▭
	Cooling time 02:00		

American	Ingredients	Metric/Imperial
2	Ripe avocado pears	2
¼ lb	Gruyère cheese	100 g / 4 oz
¼ lb	Cooked ham in a single slice	100 g / 4 oz
2 oz	Smoked salmon	50 g / 2 oz
⅔ cup	Mayonnaise	150 ml / ¼ pint
3 tbsp	Coffee (single) cream	2 tbsp
¼ tsp	Paprika	¼ tsp
1	Small lettuce	1

1. Peel and cut the avocado pears, the cheese and cooked ham into very small dice. Cut the salmon into little pieces.
2. Place everything in a bowl and add the mayonnaise softened with the cream and flavored with the paprika. Mix gently.
3. Line 4 small dishes or wine glasses with choice washed and drained lettuce leaves and divide the mixture into each dish. Put in the refrigerator for 2 hours before serving.

Avocado in insalata

Avocado Pear in Salad

◄▽	00:30		00:00 ▭

American	Ingredients	Metric/Imperial
4	Celery stalks	4
1	Lemon	1
2	Ripe avocado pears	2
2 oz	Fresh almonds, shelled	50 g / 2 oz
1	Lettuce	1
2	Hard-cooked (boiled) eggs	2
Scant ¼ cup	Oil	3 tbsp
1 tbsp	Wine vinegar	1 tbsp
	Salt and pepper	
3 tbsp	Coffee (single) cream	2 tbsp
	A small piece of horseradish root	
½ tsp	Tomato ketchup	½ tsp

1. Trim the celery and cut the stalks into matchstick slices. Peel the avocado pear and cut the flesh into small dice. Sprinkle with lemon juice.
2. Skin the almonds and halve them. Line 4 small plates with the leaves from the heart of the lettuce, arrange on them the celery, avocado and almonds and surround with segments of hard-cooked (boiled) eggs.
3. Mix oil, vinegar, salt and pepper and cream in a bowl, add the freshly grated horseradish, a dash of tomato ketchup and pour the well mixed sauce over the prepared salad.

Coppe di cozze

Mussel Cups

◄▽	00:40		00:20 ▭
	Cooling time 01:00		

American	Ingredients	Metric/Imperial
3 lb	Mussels	1.5 kg / 3 lb
2	Small onions	2
1 oz	Parsley	1 oz / 25 g
⅔ cup	White wine	150 ml / ¼ pint
	Freshly ground black pepper	
1	Aspic cube	1
⅔ cup	Mayonnaise (see page 175)	150 ml / ¼ pint
1 tbsp	Cream	1 tbsp
½ tsp	Strong mustard	½ tsp
1	Lemon	1

Mussel cups

1. Wash the mussels well under cold running water, remove beards and scrape clean with a knife. Discard any open shells which do not close when tapped with a knife.

2. Chop the onions finely and add half of them to a large saucepan with a few sprigs of parsley and half the wine. Add the mussels, shake the pan well, cover with a lid and cook over a fairly high heat for about 10 minutes until the shells open, shaking the pan from time to time. Cool and remove the mussels from the shells.

3. Strain the mussel liquor through a sieve lined with muslin, pour into a saucepan with the remaining white wine, chopped onion and freshly ground black pepper, reduce the liquid until you have ⅔ cup [150 ml / ¼ pint] left. Strain again and dissolve the aspic in the hot liquid. (If using granules follow directions on the packet.)

4. When the mixture has cooled add the mayonnaise, cream, mustard and lemon juice, mix well. Line the 4 serving dishes with some of the sauce, divide the mussels equally in the dishes. Pour the remaining sauce over the mussels and sprinkle with chopped parsley. Refrigerate for at least 1 hour or until the sauce is set before serving.

Pizzette al basilico

Little Pizzas with Basil

◢ 00:05   00:07 ⌐⊡

American	Ingredients	Metric/Imperial
1 tbsp	Milk	1 tbsp
Scant ¼ cup	Tomato purée	3 tbsp
	A few sprigs of basil	
8	Slices of bread	8
4	Small processed cheeses	4
	Freshly ground pepper	

1. Preheat the oven to 400°F / 200°C / Gas Mark 6.
2. Mix a little milk with tomato purée and half the chopped basil.
3. Remove crusts from bread and spread with cheese, put on a baking sheet in a moderately hot oven for 5-7 minutes. Serve sprinkled with chopped basil and freshly ground black pepper.

Pizzette rapide

Quick Pizzas

◢ 00:10   00:15 ⌐⊡

American	Ingredients	Metric/Imperial
8	Slices of bread	8
3 tbsp	Oil	2 tbsp
8	Slices large tomato	8
	Salt and pepper	
1 tsp	Oregano	1 tsp
8	Slices of cheese	8
8	Anchovy fillets (optional)	8

1. Preheat the oven to 425°F / 210°C / Gas Mark 7.
2. Cut the crust from the slices of bread, sprinkle with a few drops of oil, and on each slice place a slice of tomato, a pinch of salt and pepper, sprinkle with oregano and top with a slice of cheese which will melt easily.
3. Arrange the little pizzas on a baking sheet greased with oil and put in a very hot oven for a quarter of an hour. If liked add 2 halved anchovy fillets to each slice.

Little pizzas with basil

Pizzette di San Gennaro

Little Pizzas from San Gennaro

▱ 01:30   00:10 🍲

American	Ingredients	Metric/Imperial
½ lb	Pizza dough (see page 156)	225 g / 8 oz
3 tbsp	Oil	2 tbsp
3	Tomatoes	3
4	Anchovies	4
¼ cup	Green olives	40 g / 1½ oz
	Freshly ground pepper	
1 tsp	Oregano	1 tsp

1. Prepare a dough bread and allow to rise. Roll it out thinly and once it has risen, cut out some rounds with a 3 in / 7.5 cm cutter or glass.
2. Preheat the oven to 450°F / 220°C / Gas Mark 8.
3. Brush each round with oil and place on an oiled baking sheet.
4. Slice the tomatoes and arrange on the round with anchovy fillets and green olives. Sprinkle with fresh oregano, if possible, and brush over with oil.
5. Cook in a hot oven for 8-10 minutes. Serve hot.

Toast con germogli e salsa di soia

Toasted Sandwiches with Bean Sprouts and Soya

▱ 00:10   00:15 🍲

American	Ingredients	Metric/Imperial
2	Eggs	2
¼ cup	Flour	25 g / 1 oz
8-12	Slices of bread	8-12
½ cup	Oil	125 ml / 4 fl oz
1	Garlic clove	1
	Paprika	
4 cups	Bean sprouts	225 g / 8 oz
¼ lb	Fontina cheese	100 g / 4 oz
¼ lb	Lean cooked ham	100 g / 4 oz
	Soy sauce	

1. Beat the eggs in a plate and sieve the flour on to another plate.
2. Dip each slice of bread in egg and flour, coating each side. Heat three-quarters of the oil in a frying pan and fry the bread over a good medium heat until golden brown both sides. Remove the bread, arrange on the serving dish and season.
3. In another frying pan heat the rest of the oil and sauté a clove of garlic with the paprika and bean sprouts.
4. Make toasted sandwiches with the slices arranged on the plate, placing on top of each other and filling them with a slice of fontina, a slice of ham, the bean sprouts and a sprinkle of soy sauce.
5. Before serving reheat for 1 minute in the oven.

Tramezzini al gorgonzola e noci

Sandwiches with Gorgonzola and Walnuts

▱ 00:10   00:00 🍲

American	Ingredients	Metric/Imperial
8	Slices of bread	8
5 tbsp	Butter	65 g / 2½ oz
	Salt	
7 oz	Gorgonzola cheese	200 g / 7 oz
10	Walnuts	10
¼ lb	Cooked ham	100 g / 4 oz

1. Cut some triangles of medium sliced bread, spread them with butter worked with a pinch of salt and some gorgonzola, then sprinkle on a few chopped walnuts.
2. Top with a slice of cooked ham, a little more gorgonzola, and another of chopped walnuts. Two triangles may be sandwiched together or leave them single.

Pane ripieno
Baked Filled Bread

▱ 00:20   00:15 🍲

American	Ingredients	Metric/Imperial
8	Slices of bread	8
¼ lb	Cooked ham	100 g / 4 oz
¼ lb	Fresh mozzarella cheese	100 g / 4 oz
2	Eggs	2
3 tbsp	Milk	2 tbsp
	Salt and pepper	
2 tbsp	Butter	25 g / 1 oz

1. Preheat the oven to 400°F / 200°C / Gas Mark 6.
2. Slice a sandwich loaf, discarding the crusts. Cut the cooked ham into thin strips and slice the mozzarella finely.
3. Separately, beat eggs with milk, salt and pepper. Then butter a baking tin with sides. Arrange in it a layer of bread dipped in egg, one of ham and mozzarella, another of bread and so on until the ingredients are used up. Pour over the remaining egg, finish with dabs of butter and cook in the oven for about 15 minutes.

Piadine al pomodoro

Tomato Rolls

These 'piadine' rolls are found near the Adriatic and are popular seaside fare.

00:10 | 00:00

American	Ingredients	Metric/Imperial
4	Piadine (type of roll)	4
1 lb	Creamy soft cheese	225 g / 8 oz
1 tbsp	Chopped parsley	1 tbsp
¼ lb	Chopped cooked ham	100 g / 4 oz
2 or 3	Tomatoes	2 or 3
	Salt	
2 4	Gherkins or Fresh scallion (spring onion)	2 4

1. Use some long rolls, cut in half and fill with a mixture of cream cheese blended with chopped parsley and chopped ham. Top with slices of tomato, a little salt and a few rounds of gherkin or, if preferred, fresh scallions.

Tartine rustiche

Rustic Canapés

00:15 Standing time 01:00 | 00:00

American	Ingredients	Metric/Imperial
1 tbsp	Parsley	1 tbsp
1 tsp	Basil	1 tsp
½ tsp	Bay leaf	½ tsp
5 oz	Fresh ricotta cheese	150 g / 5 oz
4	Slices of whole wheat (wholemeal) bread	4
2 tbsp	Butter	25 g / 1 oz
	Freshly ground pepper	

1. Finely chop the parsley, basil and bay leaf. Use a wooden spoon to work the ricotta and the chopped herbs together until it is a soft cream, then put it in the refrigerator and allow to stand for at least 1 hour.

2. Toast four thick slices of whole wheat or sandwich bread. Serve the bread very hot, spread with butter and then ricotta mixture with freshly ground pepper.

Tartine di pollo

Chicken Canapés

00:45 | 00:00

American	Ingredients	Metric/Imperial
¾ lb	Left over boiled or roasted chicken	350 g / 12 oz
1 cup	Mayonnaise	225 ml / 8 fl oz
1 tsp	Pale mustard	1 tsp
	Salt	
8	Slices of bread	8
8 oz	Can of asparagus	225g / 8 oz
	Small crisp lettuce leaves	

1. Bone the chicken and remove the skin. Prepare mayonnaise and mix with 1 teaspoonful of pale mustard and salt.
2. Cut the chicken into small pieces and season it with the sauce.
3. Lightly toast the slices of bread, remove crusts, then place on each slice some heaped chicken with plenty of sauce.
4. To garnish, use some well drained canned asparagus. Place the chicken canapés on a large serving dish, decorate around them with asparagus alternated with small crisp lettuce leaves.

Tartine fantasia

Fancy Canapés

00:15 plus 01:00 starting time | 00:10

American	Ingredients	Metric/Imperial
3	Eggs	3
6 tbsp	Butter	75 g / 3 oz
¾ cup	Grated parmesan cheese	75 g / 3 oz
4 tsp	Mustard	3 tsp
	Salt and pepper	
¼ lb	Cooked or raw ham	100 g / 4 oz
1 tbsp	Chopped parsley	1 tbsp
1 tbsp	Capers	1 tbsp
1 small	Cucumber	1 small
8	Slices of bread	8
	Pickles	

1. Hard-cook (boil) 2 eggs and rinse in cold water before removing shells.
2. Cream the butter in a bowl until it becomes foamy, then add the grated parmesan, 1 raw egg yolk, a little mustard, salt, pepper and some ham chopped together with parsley, capers and cucumbers. Thoroughly blend the ingredients then spread on the slices of bread, which can be cut into squares, rectangles or triangles.
3. Garnish each slice with a little piece of hard-cooked egg and pickles. Before serving, refrigerate for at least 1 hour.

Goufietti
Puffs

American	Ingredients	Metric/Imperial
2 cups	All purpose (plain) white flour	225 g / 8 oz
	Salt	
1/3 cup	Milk	4 tbsp
1/2 cup	Butter	100 g / 4 oz
1/2 lb	Fontina cheese	225 g / 8 oz
	Cayenne pepper	

1. Sieve the flour and salt onto a clean pastry board or work surface. Make a well in the centre, add the warmed milk and the butter, cut into dice.
2. Work into a dough and knead the pastry on a floured board. Roll out with a floured rolling pin until a sheet the thickness of a coin is obtained.
3. Cut the fontina into cubes. Cut the pastry into rounds using a 2 in / 5 cm cutter.
4. In each round, place the cubes of cheese and fold over, sealing the edges well. Allow to rest for 20 minutes in refrigerator. Sprinkle pastry rounds with cayenne pepper.
5. Heat the oil until hot (350°F / 180°C) and fry the half moon shapes until golden brown on each side. Serve hot.

Polenta e chiodini
Polenta and Chiodini Mushrooms

Chiodini are mushrooms which appear around November. They grow in clusters and in Italy are often called famigliole, little families.

00:60 Serves 8 — **00:60**

American	Ingredients	Metric/Imperial
2 lb	Mushrooms	1 kg / 2 lb
	Butter	25 g / 1 oz
3 tbsp	Oil	2 tbsp
2	Garlic cloves	2
1 1/4 cups	Meat extract or stock cube	300 ml / 1/2 pint
	Salt and pepper	
1 tbsp	Chopped parsley	1 tbsp
1 1/4 lb	Diced cooked veal or cooked veal or sausages	600 g / 1 1/4 lb
	Polenta	

1. Separate the mushrooms from each other, scrape and soak them. Leave them for a while until any earth is deposited at the bottom of the bowl.
2. Drain then place on a tea towel, dab to remove excess moisture but take care not to crush them. If they are very small, cook them whole, but if they are large, remove the hard, woody stalks and boil the rest for about 30 minutes in salted water.
3. Heat the butter and oil in a frying pan and add the garlic. Fry slowly until the garlic begins to brown. Then put in the mushrooms and sauté over a very gentle heat for a few

minutes. Dissolve a little meat extract or stock cube in boiling water and from time to time splash over the mushrooms. Season with salt and pepper. Sprinkle with chopped parsley.
4. This can be served as a dish on its own, or, to make it a main meal, add diced veal, chicken pieces or sausage. Serve as an accompaniment to a dish of steaming polenta.

Crespelle
Fritters

American	Ingredients	Metric/Imperial
1/2 cup	All purpose (plain) White flour	50 g / 2 oz
2	Eggs	2
1 cup	Milk	225 ml / 8 fl oz
	Salt and pepper	
1/4 cup	Butter	50 g / 2 oz
1	Small onion	1
3 tbsp	Oil	2 tbsp
1 lb	Peeled tomatoes	500 g / 1 lb
2	Mozzarella cheeses	2
1 tbsp	Grated parmesan cheese	1 tbsp
1 tsp	Oregano	1 tsp

1. Sieve the flour in a bowl, make a well in the centre of the flour, add two eggs and beat with a whisk, taking care that lumps do not form.
2. Pour into the beaten mixture, a little at a time, the milk with a little salt added to it. Heat a little butter in a frying pan, tip in enough batter to cover the bottom and form a small fritter. Lightly brown it on both sides. Remove from the frying pan and make other fritters in the same way.
3. Prepare the sauce separately. Chop the onion and brown it in the heated oil. Add the tomatoes, salt and pepper, cook for about 20 minutes.
4. Preheat the oven to 350°F / 180°C / Gas Mark 4.
5. Cut the mozzarella into cubes. Place the fritters on a surface and fill them with the cheese, roll them up and cut them into points to make small diamonds.
6. Pour a little sauce into a fireproof dish. Arrange the fritters in the dish and cover with the sauce. Sprinkle with the cheese and oregano. Put in a moderate oven for about 15 minutes.

Fagottini
Cheese Puff Turnovers

00:15 Serves 6 — **00:15**

American	Ingredients	Metric/Imperial
1/2 lb	Frozen puff pastry	225 g / 8 oz
7 oz	Fontina cheese	200 g / 7 oz
	Butter	
1	Egg	1

1. Preheat oven to 425°F / 210°C / Gas Mark 7.
2. Roll out the thawed pastry into a fairly thin layer. Cut out 6 medium-sized shapes from the pastry with a round saucer.
3. Cut all the cheese into dice. Place on each round of pastry the same quantity of cheese and a knob of butter. Fold over the dough, damp the edges and form 6 turnovers. Glaze with beaten egg. Place in the oven for 15 minutes or until golden brown.

Panini nonno Ati
Grandfather Ati's Rolls

◢ 00:10   00:10 🍲

American	Ingredients	Metric/Imperial
1	Egg	1
8	Small milk rolls	8
3-4	Pieces of mozzarella cheese	3-4
3 oz	Tuna fish in oil	75 g / 3 oz
3 tbsp	Oil	2 tbsp
1 tsp	Chopped oregano, basil and sage	1 tsp

1. Hard-cook the egg and then rinse in cold running water. Remove shell.
2. Open the rolls and divide in half. Fill with a slice of mozzarella, a teaspoonful of tuna fish in oil, a round slice of hard-cooked egg, a drop of oil, and finally the chopped oregano, basil and sage. Close and serve.

Panini alla frutta
Fruit Sandwiches

◢ 00:15   00:05 🍲

American	Ingredients	Metric/Imperial
8	Slices of bread	8
¼ lb	Fontina cheese, cut thinly	100 g / 4 oz
¼ lb	Smoked ham	100 g / 4 oz
2	Orange segments	2
2	Slices of apple	2
2	Bananas	2
3 tbsp	Cognac	2 tbsp

1. Toast the slices of bread under the grill, place on 4 slices the fontina, the ham, the orange segments (without peel and without pips), the slices of apple and banana, or any other fruit in season.
2. Sprinkle with cognac and cover with the other slices of bread.
3. Alternatively preheat the oven to 350°F / 180°C / Gas Mark 4 and heat the sandwiches for 5 minutes.

Panini dorati
Golden Rolls

◢ 00:20   00:10 🍲

American	Ingredients	Metric/Imperial
16	Bread Rolls	16
2 tbsp	Butter	25 g / 1 oz
¼ lb	Liver sausage	100 g / 4 oz
2 or 3	Tomatoes	2 or 3
¼ lb	Cooked ham	100 g / 4 oz
1 tbsp	Oil	1 tbsp
1 tsp	Oregano	1 tsp
	Salt	

1. Preheat the oven to 350°F / 180°C / Gas Mark 4.
2. Cut the rolls in half, leaving them joined on one side.
3. In a bowl, mix the butter with the sausage. Remember, when buying the sausage, that it must be fine paste. When a very smooth mixture has been obtained, spread it on the rolls.
4. Wash the tomatoes and having sliced and salted them, leave to drain for 5 minutes.
5. Cover the rolls with slices of tomato, a slice of ham, oil, oregano and top with more tomato and a pinch of salt. Close the rolls and, when they are all prepared arrange on an ovenproof dish. Just before serving, place in the oven for 10 minutes.

Stuzzichini al gruyère
Gruyère Titbits

◢ 00:45   00:10 🍲

American	Ingredients	Metric/Imperial
2 cups	White flour	225 g / 8 oz
1 cup	Butter	225 g / 8 oz
2	Eggs	2
2 cups	Gruyère cheese, grated	225 g / 8 oz

1. Preheat the oven to 400°F / 200°C / Gas Mark 6.
2. Tip the flour onto a pastry-board and make a hollow in it. Add the butter and eggs to the flour, then work into dough.
3. Grate the gruyère and blend with the dough. Wrap the mixture in a clean cloth or plastic bag and leave it to stand in a cool place for about 30 minutes.
4. Roll out the paste into a layer about ⅛ in / 3 mm thick and cut out little crescent shapes from it with a cutter or the rim of a glass. Butter and flour a large baking tray, then arrange the crescents on it. Place in a hot oven until the surface is quite golden. Serve hot or cold.

Crostini al gorgonzola
Gorgonzola Toasts

◢ 00:30   00:40 🍲

American	Ingredients	Metric/Imperial
12	Slices of cold polenta	12 slices
½ cup	Oil or lard for frying	125 ml / 4 fl oz
½ lb	Strong gorgonzola cheese	225 g / 8 oz
½ cup	Butter	100 g / 4 oz

1. Preheat the oven to 350°F / 180°C / Gas Mark 4, if using oven method.
2. Cut the cold polenta into 1 in / 2½ cm thick slices.
3. Heat oil or lard in a very large frying pan. Fry the slices of polenta on both sides, they must be really crisp, then take them out of the frying pan, drain on absorbent kitchen paper.
4. Prepare a cheese mixture by creaming the strong gorgonzola and softened butter until smooth.
5. Spread fried polenta with the cheese mixture. Remove the cooking fat from the frying pan, arrange the slices in the pan, cover with a lid and heat over a very low heat until the cheese has completely melted. Serve really hot. Alternatively arrange slices on a baking sheet and put into a preheated oven.

Rice croquettes

Suppli di riso

Rice Croquettes

	00:60	00:25	
	each batch		
	Serves 6–8		

American	Ingredients	Metric/Imperial
1	Onion	1
¾ cup	Butter	175 g / 6 oz
1 ½ cups	Rice	300 g / 11 oz
1 ½ quarts	Meat stock	1.5 litres / 2 ½ pints
4	Eggs	4
¼ tsp	Nutmeg	¼ tsp
1 cup	Grated parmesan cheese	100 g / 4 oz
	Salt	
4 tbsp	All purpose (plain) flour	3 tbsp
	Bread crumbs	
1 ¼ cups	Oil	300 ml / ½ pint

1. Chop the onion finely and cook in ½ cup (100 g / 4 oz) heated butter in a pan until golden. Add the rice to the lightly fried onion and baste from time to time with hot stock stirring all the time.

2. When cooking is completed add the rest of the butter, mix briskly and leave to cool slightly.

3. Add 2 eggs to the rice and mix thoroughly, sprinkle with nutmeg and grated parmesan.

4. Butter a baking sheet and pour the mixture onto it, roll it out and flatten thoroughly with a spoon. Wait until it is cold and compact, and then with a round cutter or with a glass, cut out several small discs.

5. Beat the other eggs and add salt to them. Dip the discs (which will be about ¾ inch / 2 cm thick) on both sides first in the flour, next in the beaten eggs, then in the bread crumbs.

6. Heat the oil in a frying pan. When it is hot (190°F / 90°C), fry the croquettes until golden. Drain well and serve hot.

Cook's tip: this dish can be prepared in advance and finished just before serving.

Rainbow vegetables

Pasta

 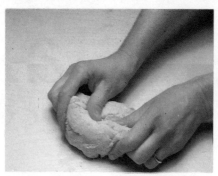 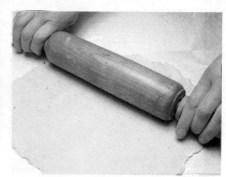

To make pasta
1. Sift the flour onto the board, mix with some beaten egg and salt (add any other ingredients such as sieved spinach or grated cheese). Knead with floured hands.

2. Add more beaten egg and knead again until the dough is smooth. Continue in this way until all the eggs are added. Divide into several pieces, knead each piece well and then re-shape all together to form a ball.

3. Leave in a cool place to rest for 30 minutes to 1 hour. Roll out thinly and cut into noodles, lasagne or use for filled pasta shapes such as agnolotti, ravioli or cappelleti.

Pasta con semolino
Pasta with Semolina

	01:00		00:05
	plus 00:30 in refrigerator		

American	Ingredients	Metric/Imperial
1 lb	Semolina, finely ground or all purpose (strong white) flour	450 g / 1 lb
5	Eggs	5
1 tbsp	Salt	1 tbsp
	Flour	

1. Put semolina in a heap on the pastry board, make a hole in the centre and put in eggs beaten with salt. Begin to knead with your hands, forming a ball-shaped mixture. Work until dough is smooth and even. Continue kneading dough firmly until bubbles form on the surface. Wrap ball of dough in foil and put in the bottom of the refrigerator for 30 minutes.
2. Remove and knead again for about 10 minutes. Flour pastry board and roll out dough, not too thinly. Leave dough to dry, turn over and dry on the other side, then cut into shape.
3. Cook in plenty of boiling salted water with a few drops of oil until 'al dente', cooking time according to shape.

Cook's tip: unless you can get very finely ground semolina it is better to use plain white flour. Allow 3-4 oz / 75-125 g of pasta per person.

Pasta al formaggio
Pasta with Cheese

	01:30	00:03 to 00:08

American	Ingredients	Metric/Imperial
2 cups	Reggiano or parmesan cheese	225 g / 8 oz
2 cups	Flour	225 g / 8 oz
5	Eggs	5
1 tsp	Salt	1 tsp

1. Finely grate cheese and mix with the flour, then tip onto a pastry board. Make a well in the centre. In a bowl beat one of the eggs with salt and pour into the well.
2. Flour hands, begin to knead mixture, add another beaten egg, knead again and continue this process until all eggs are added, to produce a smooth even dough.

3. Break dough into several pieces kneading each piece well, then reshape all pieces together to form a smooth ball. Wrap in transparent film or seal in a plastic bag and leave in a cool place (not the refrigerator) for 1 hour.
4. Flour pastry board, put dough in centre, flatten with a rolling pin and turning over the dough frequently, roll into a thickish rectangle. Cut into required shape and cook immediately in plenty of boiling salted water. Cooking time will depend on shape and thickness of the pasta.

Pizzoccheri
Pizzoccheri

A typical dish from the mountain pastures of Valtellina.

	01:00		00:20

American	Ingredients	Metric/Imperial
3 cups	Buckwheat flour	350 g / 12 oz
1 ½ cups	White flour	175 g / 6 oz
4	Eggs	4
½ cup	Milk	125 ml / 4 fl oz
	Salt	
½ lb	Potatoes	225 g / 8 oz
½ lb	French beans	225 g / 8 oz
½ cup	Butter	100 g / 4 oz
1 tsp	Sage	1 tsp
5 oz	Bitto or any fresh dairy cheese	150 g / 5 oz
1 tbsp	Grated parmesan cheese	1 tbsp
	Pepper	

1. Combine flours together and tip onto a pastry board. Make a well in the centre, break eggs into the middle with the milk, salt and a few drops of tepid water.
2. Knead ingredients well together to form a smooth dough, shape into a ball then wrap in transparent film or put in to a plastic bag and seal. Leave in a cool place for 30 minutes.
3. Roll the dough into a thickish rectangle, cut into strips ½ in / 1 cm wide by 1 in / 2.5 cm long.
4. Peel and dice potatoes. Bring a pan of salted water to the boil, add potatoes and beans to the pan and cook for about 10 minutes, then add the pizzoccheri pasta and cook a further 5 minutes. Drain vegetables and pasta, add butter, sage, chunks of bitto, parmesan and pepper.
5. Spoon onto a hot serving dish and put under a medium grill to melt cheese. Serve immediately.

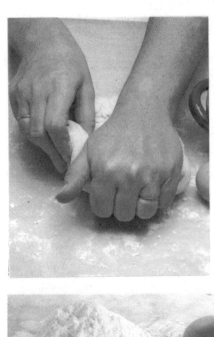

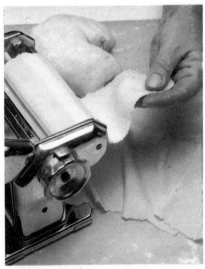

If you enjoy making pasta it is well worth investing in a machine that will cut your pasta into interesting different shapes

Pasta alla toscana
Tuscan-Style Pasta

00:10   01:10

American	Ingredients	Metric/Imperial
1	Onion	1
1	Sweet yellow pepper	1
1	Carrot	1
1	Celery stalk	1
2 oz	Bacon	50 g / 2 oz
	Oil	
2	Garlic cloves	2
¾ lb	Tomato purée	350 g / 12 oz
1	Bunch of basil	1
½ cup	Dry white wine	125 ml / 4 fl oz
1 oz	Capers	25 g / 1 oz
	Pepper	
¼ tsp	Oregano	¼ tsp
14 oz	Spaghetti	400 g / 14 oz
¼ cup	Grated pecorino cheese	25 g / 1 oz

1. Peel and chop onion, sweet yellow pepper, carrot and celery. Dice bacon. Heat oil in a saucepan and cook prepared vegetables, bacon, garlic, tomato purée and basil for 5 minutes. Pour over the wine and simmer over a low heat for about 1 hour. Add capers, pepper and oregano 5 minutes before the end of cooking time.
2. Cook spaghetti in plenty of boiling salted water until 'al dente', drain and mix pasta into vegetable mixture.
3. Spoon onto a serving dish and sprinkle over the grated cheese. Serve immediately.

Pasta alla sbirraglia
Policeman's Pasta

00:05   00:50

American	Ingredients	Metric/Imperial
14 oz	Fresh lasagne	400 g / 14 oz
1 tsp	Cornstarch (cornflour)	1 tsp
½ cup	Whipping (double) cream	125 ml / 4 fl oz
½ cup	Cognac	125 ml / 4 fl oz
	Nutmeg	
	Salt and pepper	
1	Truffle	1
2 tbsp	Butter	25 g / 1 oz
1 tbsp	Grated cheese	1 tbsp

1. Preheat oven to 350°F / 180°C / Gas Mark 4. Grease an oblong ovenproof serving dish.
2. Cook lasagne a few pieces at a time in boiling salted water until 'al dente'. Drain and leave to dry on a clean tea towel or kitchen paper.
3. Meanwhile blend cornstarch with a little of the cream. Pour remaining cream into a saucepan, add blended cornstarch, cognac, nutmeg, pepper, salt and thinly sliced truffle, and bring to the boil stirring all the time. Simmer for 2 minutes.
4. Layer cooked lasagne in serving dish, add butter and pour over sauce. Sprinkle over grated cheese and bake in the oven for 25 minutes. Serve piping hot.

Pappardelle del cacciatore
Huntsman's Noodles

00:10   00:30

American	Ingredients	Metric/Imperial
½ lb	Mushrooms or dried mushrooms, softened	225 g / 8 oz
Scant ¼ cup	Olive oil	3 tbsp
1	Garlic clove	1
	Salt and pepper	
14 oz	Pappardelle	400 g / 14 oz
1 cup	Coffee (single) cream	225 ml / 8 fl oz
1 tbsp	Tomato sauce	1 tbsp
1 tbsp	Grated parmesan cheese	1 tbsp

1. Rinse fresh mushrooms under hot water then slice thinly. (Reconstitute dried mushrooms in water).
2. Heat oil in a pan, fry garlic for 1-2 minutes then remove. Add mushrooms to the pan and sauté for 2 minutes, then allow to simmer for about 20 minutes. Season with salt and pepper.
3. Meanwhile cook the pappardelle in boiling salted water until 'al dente', drain and put on a hot serving dish.
4. Add cream and tomato sauce to mushroom sauce, stir well then pour over pasta, sprinkle with the parmesan cheese.

Pappardelle con la lepre
Noodles with Hare

00:20   02:10

American	Ingredients	Metric/Imperial
	Legs and back of a hare with liver and lights	
1	Onion	1
1	Garlic clove	1
Scant ¼ cup	Oil	3 tbsp
¼ tsp	Thyme	¼ tsp
¼ tsp	Sweet marjoram	¼ tsp
¼ tsp	Rosemary	¼ tsp
½ cup	Red wine (or more as required)	125 ml / 4 fl oz
1 cup	Meat stock	225 ml / 8 fl oz
¼ tsp	Nutmeg	¼ tsp
	Pepper	
14 oz	Pappardelle	400 g / 14 oz

1. Remove meat from the hare and cut into small pieces. Chop liver and lights and reserve.
2. Peel and chop onion, peel garlic. Heat half the oil in a large pan, fry onion, garlic, thyme, marjoram and rosemary together for 2-3 minutes.
3. Add hare meat to the pan and brown quickly. Pour over the wine and stock, bring to the boil, then reduce heat. Cover and simmer for about 2 hours.
4. Pour hare sauce into a blender and purée. Heat remaining oil in a pan and fry the prepared liver and lights together for 3-4 minutes. Pour hare purée into pan and mix ingredients together. Add nutmeg and pepper.
5. Cook pappardelle in boiling salted water until 'al dente', drain and stir into hare sauce.
6. Spoon on to a heated serving dish and serve.

Maccheroni Trinacria al forno

Sicilian Baked Macaroni

⏱ 00:45   🍳 01:00

American	Ingredients	Metric/Imperial
2	Large eggplant (aubergines)	2
	Salt and pepper	
2	Garlic cloves	2
14 oz can	Tomatoes	400 g / 14 oz can
⅔ cup	Oil	150 ml / ¼ pint
14 oz	Pilchards	400 g / 14 oz
¾ lb	Macaroni	350 g / 12 oz
	Oregano	
½ cup	Grated cheese	50 g / 2 oz
1 tbsp	Butter	1 tbsp

1. Preheat oven to 350°F / 180°C / Gas Mark 4. Grease an ovenproof serving dish.
2. Slice eggplant thinly, place in a colander and sprinkle with salt. Leave for 30 minutes, then rinse under cold water and dry well.
3. Peel garlic and chop finely. Heat 1 tablespoon of the oil in a large saucepan and add garlic and fry gently until golden. Add tomatoes and juice from can. Season with salt and pepper and simmer for 15 minutes.
4. Meanwhile clean pilchards. Slit to open but leave halves joined, wash under cold running water and add to sauce. Cover and leave to cook a further 10 minutes.
5. Heat remaining oil in a large pan and fry slices of eggplant until lightly browned, then drain on kitchen paper.
6. Cook macaroni in boiling salted water until 'al dente', drain and add a dash of oil to prevent it sticking together. Arrange pasta on the base of the dish, top with pilchard sauce, then the eggplant.
7. Add freshly ground pepper and oregano to grated cheese and scatter dabs of butter over surface. Bake for about 30 minutes until lightly browned. Serve piping hot.

Pasta alla livornese

Leghorn-Style Pasta

⏱ 00:15   🍳 00:20

American	Ingredients	Metric/Imperial
¼ lb	Lean raw ham	100 g / 4 oz
¼ lb	Neck of pork	100 g / 4 oz
1	Onion	1
Scant ¼ cup	Oil	3 tbsp
2	Garlic cloves	2
1	Bunch of basil	1
	Salt and pepper	
¼ tsp	Thyme	¼ tsp
¼ tsp	Paprika	¼ tsp
¼ cup	Best quality cognac	50 ml / 2 fl oz
14 oz	Semolina pasta	400 g / 14 oz

1. Chop ham and pork into small pieces. Peel and chop onion. Heat oil and fry meat and onion together with the crushed garlic, basil, thyme, paprika and cognac for 10 minutes, stirring from time to time. Add salt and freshly ground pepper.
2. Meanwhile cook pasta in boiling salted water until 'al dente', drain and stir into the meat sauce, mixing well.
3. Spoon on to a hot serving dish and serve immediately.

Pasta alla potentina

Potentina Pasta

⏱ 00:10   🍳 00:50

American	Ingredients	Metric/Imperial
6	Eggs	6
	Salt and pepper	
3 tbsp	Flour	2 tbsp
3 tbsp	White wine	2 tbsp
14 oz	Cooked fine macaroni	400 g / 14 oz
Scant ¼ cup	Oil	3 tbsp
1 tbsp	Butter	1 tbsp
1 tbsp	Bread crumbs	1 tbsp
¾ lb	Mozzarella cheese	350 g / 12 oz

1. Preheat oven to 400°F / 200°C / Gas Mark 6. Grease a large ovenproof serving dish.
2. Beat eggs with salt and pepper, add the flour, whisk well, and then the white wine. Mix in the macaroni.
3. Heat remaining oil in an iron frying pan. When just beginning to smoke, slide mixture into it, as for making normal omelette, cook for about 10 minutes, turn and cook the other side for 5 minutes. Place cooked omelette in dish, dot with butter, sprinkle with bread crumbs and cover with thin slices of mozzarella. Bake for about 25 minutes. Serve hot.

Pasta alla panna e funghi

Pasta with Cream Mushrooms

⏱ 00:15   🍳 00:15

American	Ingredients	Metric/Imperial
½ lb	Mushrooms	225 g / 8 oz
	Salt and pepper	
1 tsp	Oil	1 tsp
14 oz	Pasta	400 g / 14 oz
1 cup	Whipping (double) cream	225 ml / 8 fl oz
1 tsp	Powdered truffle	1 tsp
	Nutmeg	
1 oz	Fontina or melting cheese	25 g / 1 oz
1	White truffle	1

1. Rinse mushrooms under hot water then remove stalks, slice tops and put into a bowl. Add salt, pepper and oil to mushrooms and leave to stand.
2. Put pasta to cook in boiling salted water until 'al dente'.
3. Meanwhile pour cream into a saucepan, add the truffle, the nutmeg and the mushrooms and leave to simmer for about 10 minutes. Slice cheese and white truffle thinly.
4. Drain pasta, mix in the cheese and spoon on to a serving dish. Cover with the mushroom sauce and garnish with slices of white truffle.

Fisherman's penne

Penne del pescatore
Fisherman's Penne

⊿ 00:10   00:25 🍲

American	Ingredients	Metric/Imperial
1¾ lb	Fresh prawns	800 g / 1¾ lb
5 or 14 oz can	Tomatoes	5 or 400 g / 14 oz can
3 tbsp	Oil	2 tbsp
2 or 3	Bay leaves	2 or 3
	Salt and black pepper	
¾ lb	Penne pasta (smooth, short-cut pasta tubes)	350 g / 12 oz
1 tbsp	Chopped parsley	1 tbsp

1. Plunge prawns into a pan of boiling salted water, cover, remove from the heat and leave to cool, then shell.
2. Peel and quarter tomatoes and remove seeds; if using canned tomatoes, use juice and fruit.
3. Heat oil in a large pan, add bay leaves, tomatoes and cook for 5-10 minutes, until mixture is reduced to a pulp.
4. Stir prawns gently into tomato sauce and season with salt and freshly ground black pepper. Leave to simmer over a low heat for 5 minutes.

5. Meanwhile cook penne pasta in plenty of boiling salted water until 'al dente'. Drain well.
6. Add the pasta to the prawn sauce over a medium heat and discard the bay leaves.
7. Spoon onto a hot serving dish, season with black pepper and garnish with chopped parsley.

Pasta alla cipolla
Onion Pasta

⊿ 00:10   00:25 🍲

American	Ingredients	Metric/Imperial
2	Large onions	2
¼ cup	Butter	50 g / 2 oz
	Salt	
2	Eggs	2
14 oz	Bavette (thin noodles)	400 g / 14 oz
1 tbsp	Grated parmesan cheese	1 tbsp

1. Peel and thinly slice onions. Melt butter and cook onions slowly for about 10 minutes until soft without browning, then remove from the heat.
2. Add salt and beaten eggs to the pan and mix ingredients thoroughly.
3. Cook bavette in boiling salted water until 'al dente', drain, add the onion sauce and top with grated cheese. Serve immediately.

Corzetti alla rivierasca
Coastal-Style Corzetti

This dish is famous throughout the Riviera.

⏱ 00:30   00:45 🍲

American	Ingredients	Metric/Imperial
1 (½ lb)	Fresh salmon slice	1 (225 g / 8 oz)
Scant ¼ cup	Oil	3 tbsp
1	Onion	1
½ cup	Dry white wine	125 ml / 4 fl oz
½ cup	Stock	125 ml / 4 fl oz
5 tbsp	Tomato purée	4 tbsp
1 tsp	Fresh, chopped basil	1 tsp
2	Walnuts	2
14 oz	Corzetti (spiral pasta shapes)	400 g / 14 oz
	Salt	

1. Cut the fresh salmon into thin strips.
2. Heat the oil, add the chopped onion, cook for 4 minutes then add the salmon strips. Cook for about 10 minutes, add the white wine, the stock and the tomato purée, allow to simmer over a very low heat, so that the sauce remains very thick.
3. Pass through the blender. Chop the fresh basil and walnuts finely, retain a quarter for the garnish and mix the rest with the sauce.
4. Heat a saucepan with plenty of salted water and when it boils cook the corzetti. Drain, season at once with the fish sauce and serve hot. Add extra chopped basil and walnuts sprinkled on top.

Maccheroni di primavera
Springtime Macaroni

⏱ 00:15   00:50 🍲

American	Ingredients	Metric/Imperial
2 lb	Asparagus or frozen packets of asparagus	1 kg / 2 lb
½ cup	Butter	100 g / 4 oz
¾ lb	Roman ricotta or piedmontese cheese	350 g / 12 oz
¼ cup	Milk	50 ml / 2 fl oz
	Salt and pepper	
14 oz	Macaroni	400 g / 14 oz
¼ cup	Grated parmesan cheese	25 g / 1 oz
2	Eggs	2
¼ tsp	Nutmeg	¼ tsp
3 tbsp	Grated cheese	2 tbsp

1. Preheat oven to 375°F / 190°C / Gas Mark 5. Grease an ovenproof serving dish.
2. Clean asparagus and cook for 5 minutes in boiling salted water, drain well. Cut into small pieces discarding hard stems.
3. In a large pan, melt a quarter of the butter add asparagus and cook until golden.
4. In a bowl beat ricotta with the milk, salt and pepper to obtain a smooth cream.

5. Cook macaroni until 'al dente', then drain. Add the rest of the butter and parmesan to the pasta, and spoon over the base of the dish.
6. Top with the asparagus and half the ricotta. Continue layering in this way finishing with a layer of macaroni.
7. Beat eggs with salt, pepper, nutmeg and grated cheese and pour over macaroni. Bake for 30 minutes until golden. Serve piping hot.

Maccheroni con la piovra
Macaroni with Octopus

⏱ 00:10   00:40 🍲

American	Ingredients	Metric/Imperial
1¼ lb	Octopus	600 g / 1¼ lb
2	Bay leaves	2
Scant ¼ cup	Oil	3 tbsp
3	Garlic cloves	3
3 tbsp	Chopped parsley	2 tbsp
14 oz	Macaroni	400 g / 14 oz
	Salt	

1. Clean octopus thoroughly, beat and put in a saucepan, with plenty of water; do not add salt. Add bay leaves, bring to the boil and cook until the octopus becomes red, drain and cool.
2. In a frying pan heat oil, peel and crush 2 cloves of garlic, add to the pan with most of the chopped parsley.
3. Cut octopus into small pieces, add to the pan, stirring for about 10 minutes.
4. Meanwhile boil macaroni until 'al dente' in plenty of lightly salted water, drain well and stir into the octopus and its cooking juices, until thoroughly mixed.
5. Spoon onto a hot serving dish and garnish with chopped parsley and crushed garlic.

Maccheroni alla vodka
Macaroni with Vodka

⏱ 00:05   00:30 🍲

American	Ingredients	Metric/Imperial
1	Large onion	1
1 oz	Sausage	25 g / 1 oz
3 tbsp	Butter	2 tbsp
½ cup	Vodka	125 ml / 4 fl oz
2 cups	Whipping (double) cream	450 ml / 16 fl oz
	Salt and pepper	
14 oz	Macaroni	400 g / 14 oz

1. Peel and chop onion, skin sausage and slice into small pieces.
2. Melt butter and cook the onion and sausage for about 5 minutes over a medium heat. Pour over three-quarters of vodka and bring to the boil. Reduce heat and simmer for 8-10 minutes. Finally stir in all but 2 tablespoons [25 ml / 1 fl oz] of the cream, simmer for a further 3-5 minutes, then season.
3. Boil macaroni in salted water until 'al dente', drain and stir into the vodka cream sauce.
4. Spoon onto a large serving plate, pour over the remaining vodka and cream and serve immediately.

Maccheroni alla siciliana
Sicilian-Style Macaroni

00:10   00:25

American	Ingredients	Metric/Imperial
1	Small onion	1
½	Sweet pepper	½
1	Garlic clove	1
Scant ¼ cup	Oil	3 tbsp
1	Bay leaf	1
Scant ¼ cup	Tomato purée	3 tbsp
8	Black olives	8
½ tsp	Anchovy paste	½ tsp
¼ tsp	Oregano	¼ tsp
¼ tsp	Basil	¼ tsp
	Salt and pepper	
½ lb	Fine macaroni	225 g / 8 oz
¼ cup	Grated pecorino cheese	25 g / 1 oz

1. Chop onion and sweet pepper, peel garlic. Heat oil in a pan and sauté these with a bay leaf for 3 minutes.
2. Add tomato purée, black olives, anchovy paste, oregano and basil. Season with salt and pepper, cover and cook over a low heat for 8-10 minutes.
3. Cook macaroni in boiling salted water until 'al dente', drain and add to the sauce, stirring both ingredients carefully until

thoroughly mixed. Sprinkle with fresh pepper and grated pecorino and serve immediately.

Maccheroni alla chitarra
Guitar Macaroni

00:35   00:25

American	Ingredients	Metric/Imperial
¼ lb	Bacon	100 g / 4 oz
Scant ¼ cup	Oil	3 tbsp
1	Sweet red pepper	1
6	Tomatoes, peeled	6
3 cups	Flour	350 g / 12 oz
4	Eggs	4
	Salt and pepper	

1. Cube the bacon, heat oil in a pan and cook bacon for 2 minutes. Add chopped sweet pepper and tomatoes, stir with a wooden spoon and cook over a low heat until of a thickish consistency.
2. Sift flour onto a pastry board, make a well in the centre and tip in beaten eggs to obtain a firm dough and draw out with a rolling-pin over a guitar (a frame on which wires are stretched) to obtain thin strips of pasta, or cut into thin strips.
3. Cook these in plenty of boiling salted water until 'al dente'. Drain, season with hot sauce and serve.

Guitar macaroni

Pasta e bisi
Pasta and Peas

⏱ 00:10   00:25 🍲

American	Ingredients	Metric/Imperial
2¼ cups	Small new peas, or frozen peas	350 g / 12 oz
½ cup	Butter	100 g / 4 oz
½ lb	Chicken livers	225 g / 8 oz
2	Sage leaves	2
14 oz	Pasta	400 g / 14 oz
1 tbsp	Grated parmesan cheese	1 tbsp
	Cognac (optional)	

1. Boil peas for 10 minutes then drain. Melt butter in a frying pan, add peas and washed chopped chicken livers and brown slightly, stirring frequently. Add sage leaves, and continue cooking a further 5 minutes.
2. Bring a large saucepan of salted water to the boil, add chosen pasta and cook until 'al dente'.
3. Drain and sprinkle with grated parmesan, then stir in the chicken liver sauce. Add a little cognac if desired and serve.

Maccheroni gratinati
Macaroni au Gratin

⏱ 00:15   01:05 🍲

American	Ingredients	Metric/Imperial
5 oz	Thick slice of cooked ham	150 g / 5 oz
7 oz	Mushrooms	200 g / 7 oz
14 oz can	Peeled tomatoes	400 g / 14 oz can
2	Garlic cloves	2
Scant ¼ cup	Oil	3 tbsp
	Salt and pepper	
14 oz	Macaroni	400 g / 14 oz
3 tbsp	Cornstarch (cornflour)	2 tbsp
1¼ cups	Milk	300 ml / ½ pint
3 tbsp	Butter	2 tbsp
¼ tsp	Nutmeg	¼ tsp
1 tbsp	Grated cheese	1 tbsp

1. Preheat oven to 350°F / 180°C / Gas Mark 4. Grease an oblong serving dish.
2. Dice ham, wash mushrooms and slice, peel tomatoes and roughly chop. Peel garlic.
3. In a large frying pan, heat oil and cook mushrooms and crushed garlic for 1-2 minutes, stirring all the time. Add ham, season with salt and pepper and cook for a few minutes.
4. Add tomatoes to the pan, cover and simmer for 10 minutes.
5. Meanwhile cook macaroni in plenty of boiling salted water until 'al dente', drain and rinse under cold water, then stir into the tomato sauce.
6. Make a sauce by blending cornstarch with a little milk, add remainder of milk and heat in a pan until boiling, stirring all the time. Add half the butter, salt, pepper and nutmeg.
7. Spoon the macaroni and tomato sauce over the base of the serving dish, cover with the white sauce, sprinkle with grated cheese and scatter remaining butter in knobs over the top.
8. Bake for 35-40 minutes until golden and serve hot.

Pasta and peas

Bigoli con sardelle
Bigoli with Sardines

This is a typical Lombard recipe.

⏱ 00:20   00:20 🍲

American	Ingredients	Metric/Imperial
¼ lb	Sardines	100 g / 4 oz
14 oz	Bigoli pasta	400 g / 14 oz
	Salt	
3 tbsp	Olive oil	2 tbsp
2	Garlic cloves	2

1. Clean, bone and wash the fish and place them on a board.
2. Cook the bigoli pasta in a large saucepan with plenty of salted water.
3. Heat the oil, add the garlic, and when the garlic turns golden, put in the sardines. While they are cooking squash them with a wooden fork without frying them.
4. Drain the bigoli when firm to the bite and put them in an earthenware dish, pour over the fish sauce and serve very hot.

Spaghetti in foil

fairly large space above, so that the steam may circulate inside.
5. Bake in the oven for 10 minutes, then serve parcel of spaghetti at the table.

Note: the shellfish may be cooked with or without valves.

Spaghetti all'arrabbiata
Arrabbiata-Style Spaghetti

	00:30		00:20

American	Ingredients	Metric/Imperial
14 oz	Chitterlings mixed with pork	400 g / 14 oz
10	Shelled walnuts	10
½ cup	Vegetable oil	125 ml / 4 fl oz
4	Garlic cloves	4
¼ tsp	Red paprika	¼ tsp
	Salt and pepper	
⅓ cup	Raisins	50 g / 2 oz
14 oz	Spaghetti	400 g / 14 oz
1 tbsp	Grated pecorino cheese	1 tbsp

1. Clean chitterlings and chop, blend walnuts to a purée with a little of the oil. Heat remaining oil in a frying pan and when very hot fry chopped chitterlings with pork, crushed garlic, red paprika and pepper for 5 minutes.
2. Blanch raisins, drain and add to pan with walnut purée and wine. Stir well then purée sauce in a food processor or blender, return to pan and leave over a very low heat.
3. Meanwhile cook spaghetti in plenty of boiling salted water until 'al dente' and drain.
4. Stir grated pecorino into spaghetti and then mix pasta and cheese into sauce in frying pan and continue to cook over a low heat for 5 minutes.
5. Spoon onto a hot serving dish, sprinkle over fresh pepper and serve hot.

Spaghetti al cartoccio
Spaghetti in Foil

	00:15		00:15

American	Ingredients	Metric/Imperial
1¼ lb	Shellfish (mussels, clams, limpets) weighed with the shell	600 g / 1¼ lb
⅓ cup	Vegetable oil	5 tbsp
2	Garlic cloves	2
1	Bunch of parsley	1
Scant ¼ cup	Chopped tomatoes	3 tbsp
14 oz	Spaghetti	400 g / 14 oz
	Salt and pepper	
	Aluminium foil	

1. Preheat oven to 400°F / 200°C / Gas Mark 6.
2. Clean shell fish thoroughly. Heat oil in a frying pan, and when very hot, add shellfish, garlic, chopped parsley, and chopped tomatoes. Cook for 5 minutes, stirring all the time, then leave sauce to thicken over a low heat.
3. Half cook spaghetti in boiling salted water, then drain and pass under running cold water. Stir into shellfish sauce, mixing well.
4. Spread a big sheet of aluminum foil over a baking sheet. In the centre place the seasoned spaghetti, sprinkle the top with a thin trickle of oil, add pepper and close up the foil, leaving a

Spaghetti alle vongole
Spaghetti with Clams

	00:20		00:20

American	Ingredients	Metric/Imperial
1¼ lb	Clams	600 g / 1¼ lb
Scant ¼ cup	Vegetable oil	3 tbsp
6	Sprigs of parsley	6
14 oz can	Peeled tomatoes	400 g / 14 oz can
	Salt and pepper	
1¼ lb	Spaghetti	600 g / 1¼ lb

1. Wash clams in several changes of water until water remains clear, then wipe dry. Heat oil in a pan, add clams, cover and cook for 5 - 8 minutes until shells open, discarding any that remain closed.
2. Add the parsley and the tomatoes to the pan and cook for a further 7 minutes. Taste and adjust seasoning.
3. Cook spaghetti in plenty of boiling salted water until 'al dente', drain and spoon onto a hot serving dish. Pour over clam sauce and serve immediately.

Spaghetti with clams

Fusilli grande estate
High Summer Fusilli

	00:25 plus 00:30 in refrigerator	00:25

American	Ingredients	Metric/Imperial
½ lb	Frozen or shelled fresh peas	225 g / 8 oz
1⅓ cups	Shelled, cooked prawns	225 g / 8 oz
2	Ripe but firm pear-shaped tomatoes	2
3 tbsp	Pickled capers	2 tbsp
7 oz can	Tuna	200 g / 7 oz can
Scant ¼ cup	Oil	3 tbsp
1	Lemon	1
½ lb	Fusilli pasta	225 g / 8 oz
	Salt and pepper	
¼ tsp	Oregano ·	¼ tsp

1. Cook the frozen or fresh peas, drain and place into an earthenware dish.
2. Cut the prawns in half and add them to the peas.
3. Plunge the tomatoes into boiling water, skin them, remove their seeds and cut into small pieces. Add the tomatoes to the other ingredients with pickled capers.
4. Drain the oil from a small can of tuna fish, break it up with a fork and then add it to the dish, mixing gently. Season with oil and the juice of a lemon.
5. Cook the fusilli in plenty of boiling salted water, drain and pass under cold water. Drain well and season with a small amount of oil. Allow to cool.
6. Mix the pasta with the other ingredients, add pepper, salt and sprinkle with oregano. Cover and chill in the refrigerator for about 30 minutes before serving.

Bucatini alla gaetana
Gaeta-Style Bucatini

This is a typical recipe of Gaeta and dates back to the time of wild boar hunting in southern Italy.

	00:20	00:20

American	Ingredients	Metric/Imperial
14 oz	Young wild pig meat or pork	400 g / 14 oz
Scant ¼ cup	Oil	3 tbsp
1	Onion	1
2 or 3	Mint leaves	2 or 3
1	Garlic clove	1
½ lb	Green olives	225 g / 8 oz
½ cup	Dry white wine	125 ml / 4 fl oz
¼ lb	Wild boar or calf's liver	100 g / 4 oz
Scant ¼ cup	Stock	3 tbsp
14 oz	Bucatini pasta	400 g / 14 oz
	Salt	
1 tbsp	Pecorino (ewe's milk cheese)	1 tbsp
¼ tsp	Oregano	¼ tsp

1. Finely chop the pork. Heat the oil in a frying pan, and brown the meat. Lower the heat and add the finely chopped onion, mint leaves and crushed garlic. Cook for 5 minutes.

2. Mix well, add the green olives and white wine.
3. Chop the liver into small pieces and add to the sauce with the stock. Allow to simmer for 10 minutes.
4. Cook the pasta in boiling salted water until 'al dente', drain and toss it with the pecorino and oregano. Mix with the sauce and serve.

Pasta con ragù al tonno
Pasta with Tuna Sauce

	00:10	00:40

American	Ingredients	Metric/Imperial
1	Onion	1
1	Garlic clove	1
3	Anchovies in oil	3
¼ lb	Tuna fish in oil	100 g / 4 oz
3 tbsp	Olive oil	2 tbsp
¼ cup	Butter	50 g / 2 oz
½ lb	Peeled tomatoes	225 g / 8 oz
2 or 3	Basil leaves	2 or 3
	Salt and pepper	
¾ lb	Pasta (sedani rigati)	350 g / 12 oz

1. Peel and finely chop onion and garlic. Pound anchovies to a pulp and break up tuna fish and stir into anchovies with half of the oil.
2. Heat oil and butter together in a pan and when foaming sauté onion and garlic for 2-3 minutes. Add peeled tomatoes, basil, salt and pepper and pounded fish. Cook for 2-3 minutes, stirring all the time, cover and allow to simmer over a low heat for 30 minutes.
3. Cook pasta in boiling salted water until 'al dente', drain and stir into tuna sauce.
4. Spoon onto a hot serving dish and serve immediately.

Pasta con le verdure piccanti
Pasta with Spicy Vegetables

	00:10	00:25

American	Ingredients	Metric/Imperial
2	Sweet yellow peppers	2
1	Onion	1
Scant ¼ cup	Vegetable oil	3 tbsp
1½ cups	Spinach, boiled and squeezed	350 g / 12 oz
2	Garlic cloves	2
1	Bunch of basil	1
½ tsp	Red paprika	½ tsp
	Pepper	
1 cup	Dry white wine	225 ml / 8 fl oz
¾ lb	Pasta	350 g / 12 oz
	Grated pecorino cheese	

1. Deseed and slice peppers, peel and chop onion.
2. Heat oil and add the cooked spinach and garlic and sauté for 5 minutes stirring all the time. Add peppers, onion and basil to pan and cook for a further 2 minutes.
3. Finally stir in paprika, pepper and white wine. Cover and simmer for 10 minutes.

4. Meanwhile cook pasta in boiling salted water until 'al dente'. Drain and stir into vegetable sauce.
5. Spoon onto a hot serving dish, sprinkle a little oil over surface and grated pecorino and serve at once.

Pasta e ricotta sprint
Pasta with Two Cheeses

◁▷ 00:05   00:15 🍲

American	Ingredients	Metric/Imperial
½ lb	Very fresh ricotta cheese	25 g / .8 oz
½ cup	Coffee (single) cream	100 ml / 3½ fl oz
4 tbsp	Butter	50 g / 2 oz
	Pepper	
3 tbsp	Grated parmesan cheese	2 tbsp
14 oz	Pasta	400 g / 14 oz
1 tsp	Grated parmesan cheese	1 tsp
1 tsp	Grated pecorino cheese	1 tsp

1. Sieve ricotta into a saucepan. Stir in cream with butter, season with pepper and add parmesan. Heat gently over a low heat. Do not allow to boil.
2. Cook pasta in boiling salted water until 'al dente', drain and tip into the ricotta sauce.
3. Spoon onto a heated serving dish, mix together the teaspoon of parmesan and pecorino cheeses and sprinkle over the top.

Pasta con le sarde
Pasta with Sardines

◁▷ 00:30   00:45 🍲

American	Ingredients	Metric/Imperial
1	Head of wild fennel	1
2	Onions	2
14 oz	Sardines	400 g / 14 oz
4	Anchovies	4
Scant ¼ cup	Vegetable oil	3 tbsp
2 oz	Pine kernels	50 g / 2 oz
⅓ cup	Sultanas	50 g / 2oz
	Salt	
1 lb	Macaroni	450 g / 1 lb

1. Preheat oven to 350°F / 180°C / Gas Mark 4. Grease an oblong ovenproof serving dish.
2. Trim and thinly slice the fennel, cook in boiling salted water for 10 minutes, drain. Peel and chop onions, clean and pound sardines, clean and bone anchovies.
3. Heat the oil in a large pan, add the onions and cook for 2-3 minutes. Add fennel, half the sardines and anchovies to pan. Cook for 3 minutes stirring all the time, add pine nuts, sultanas and ⅔ cup [150 ml / ¼ pint] of vegetable water to the pan, cover and simmer over a low heat for 10 minutes.
4. Put the remaining sardines in a bowl and add salt and oil. Leave to stand. Cook macaroni in boiling salted water until 'al dente'.
5. Drain and spoon half the cooked pasta over the base of the serving dish. Mix the remaining macaroni with half the fennel sauce. Spoon the sardines over the pasta then top with the mixed pasta and sauce.
6. Bake for 20 minutes and serve with a crunchy salad.

Conchiglie alla spagnola
Spanish-Style Shells

◁▷ 00:30   01:15 🍲

American	Ingredients	Metric/Imperial
4 tbsp	Butter	50 g / 2 oz
Scant ¼ cup	Oil	3 tbsp
2	Onions	2
2	Carrots	2
1	Celery stalk	1
1 lb	Lean veal pieces	500 g / 1 lb
3 tbsp	Flour	2 tbsp
¼ cup	White wine	50 ml / 2 fl oz
1 cup	Stock	225 ml / 8 fl oz
½ lb	Peeled tomatoes	225 g / 8 oz
2	Large sweet peppers	2
1 tsp	Oregano	1 tsp
	Salt and pepper	
¾ lb	Durum wheat shells	350 g / 12 oz
½ lb	Mozzarella cheese	225 g / 8 oz

1. Preheat the oven to 400°F / 200°C /Gas Mark 6.
2. Heat half the butter and oil in a frying pan, add thinly sliced onions, carrots and celery, cook over a medium heat.
3. Push the vegetables to one side after 5 minutes.
4. Cut the veal into small pieces, toss in flour and add to the pan and fry on both sides until brown.
5. Sprinkle with white wine and when it has evaporated, continue the cooking moistening with stock, with the lid on the pan. Stir occasionally and after 10 minutes add 2 peeled and squashed tomatoes.
6. In a separate pan, heat remaining oil and butter and lightly fry a large diced onion. When the onion becomes transparent, add the deseeded sweet peppers which have been cut into fairly small slices, and the peeled tomatoes, season with salt and pepper, sprinkle with oregano and leave to cook. After 20 minutes add the onion and sweet pepper sauce to the meat mixture, mix well and adjust seasoning. Continue cooking until pasta is ready.
7. Cook the shells in plenty of salted and boiling water. Drain the pasta, mix with meat mixture, and sauce. Turn into an ovenproof dish, sprinkle the surface with oregano and mozzarella cut into small pieces. Place in hot oven for 15 minutes and serve immediately.

Dashing bucatini

Bucatini alla brava
Dashing Bucatini

	00:20		00:30

American	Ingredients	Metric/Imperial
¼ cup	Butter	50 g / 2 oz
1	Onion	1
1 cup	Cooked prawns	175 g / 6 oz
½ cup	Whipping (double) cream	125 ml / 4 fl oz
¼ tsp	Chopped thyme	¼ tsp
¼ tsp	Chopped sweet marjoram	¼ tsp
1 tsp	Curry powder	1 tsp
1 tsp	Fine-grain semolina	1 tsp
	Salt	
14 oz	Bucatini pasta	400 g / 14 oz

1. In a small saucepan, melt the butter, add the finely chopped onion, the peeled prawns, cream, thyme, marjoram and the curry powder, mix well over a low heat.
2. Sprinkle on the semolina, keeping the heat low and mixing carefully.
3. Heat plenty of salted water in a large saucepan, when it boils toss in the bucatini pasta stirring frequently. When cooking is completed, drain and season at once with the sauce. Cheese is not necessary. You may use other types of pasta, from macaroni to spaghetti, according to taste.

Pasticcio alla Bambi
Bambi-Style Pie

	00:15		00:55

American	Ingredients	Metric/Imperial
3 cups	Béchamel sauce (see page 162)	700 ml / 1 ¼ pints
3 tbsp	Grated parmesan cheese	2 tbsp
⅓ cup	Butter	75 g / 3 oz
1 ½ oz	Dried mushrooms	40 g / 1 ½ oz
14 oz	Canned peas	400 g / 14 oz
7 oz	Fontina cheese	200 g / 7 oz
2 oz	Slice of cooked ham	50 g / 2 oz
1 lb	Conchiglioni (large shell-shaped pasta)	450 g / 1 lb
¼ cup	Butter	50 g / 2 oz

1. Preheat oven to 350°F / 180°C / Gas Mark 4. Grease an oblong ovenproof serving dish.
2. Make béchamel sauce and stir in half the grated parmesan.
3. Heat the butter, sauté the mushrooms and the drained peas for 3 minutes. Cut the fontina and the ham into small pieces and put in a bowl. Add the cooked mushrooms and the peas and mix well.
4. Cook conchiglioni in plenty of boiling salted water until 'al dente', drain and spoon half the pasta over base of dish. Top with half the mushroom sauce then a layer of béchamel. Continue to layer remaining pasta sauce and béchamel. Sprinkle over remaining parmesan, add dabs of butter and bake for 30 minutes until golden brown.

Pasta con la ricotta
Pasta with Ricotta

	00:10		00:10

American	Ingredients	Metric/Imperial
7 oz	Ricotta cheese	200 g / 7 oz
1 cup	Whipping (double) cream	225 ml / 8 fl oz
	Salt and pepper	
¼ tsp	Paprika	¼ tsp
1 tbsp	Sugar	1 tbsp
1 tbsp	Cinnamon	1 tbsp
14 oz	Hard-grain semolina pasta, e.g. spaghetti, macaroni, zite, or rigatoni	400 g / 14 oz

1. In a bowl mix the ricotta with cream, pepper, salt, paprika, sugar and cinnamon.
2. In a large saucepan cook the pasta till 'al dente', in plenty of salted water. Drain well and stir in the ricotta sauce over a low heat, then serve.

Variations: other cheeses may be used such as romand or piedmont ricotta, ligurian curd cheese or strong apulian ricotta.

Penne con le zucchine crude
Penne with Raw Gourds

	00:15		00:15

American	Ingredients	Metric/Imperial
4	Coastal gourds	4
¼ cup	Refined lard	50 g / 2 oz
2	Garlic cloves	2
⅔ cup	Ripe black olives	100 g / 4 oz
1 lb	Penne pasta	450 g / 1 lb
	Salt and pepper	

1. Wash gourds carefully and slice finely.
2. Heat lard until hot, add the crushed cloves of garlic and cook for 1-2 minutes, then add black olives and cook for a further 2 minutes, stirring all the time.
3. Cook pasta in boiling salted water until 'al dente', then drain and add olive sauce to pasta and stir in the gourds. Season with pepper and serve immediately.

Pasticcio di fegatini e maccheroni
Chicken Livers and Macaroni Pie

American	Ingredients	Metric/Imperial
	◢ 00:30	00:40
1	Onion	1
1	Celery	1
2	Leeks	2
2	Carrots	2
⅓ cup	Butter	65 g / 2½ oz
	Salt and pepper	
1¼ cups	Tomato sauce	300 ml / ½ pint
8	Chicken livers	8
2 cups	Béchamel sauce	450 ml / ¾ pint
1 lb	Macaroni	450 g / 1 lb
¼ cup	Grated parmesan cheese	25 g / 1 oz

1. Preheat oven to 375°F / 190°C / Gas Mark 5. Grease an overproof serving dish.
2. Peel and chop onion, slice celery, leeks and carrots. Heat most of the butter and, when foaming, sauté the vegetables for 5 minutes, season and stir in tomato sauce.
3. Chop trimmed chicken livers into small pieces and add to the pan. Cook for 5 minutes stirring from time to time. Remove pan from heat.
4. Make a béchamel sauce. Cook macaroni in boiling salted water until 'al dente', drain and spoon half over the base of dish. Top with half the liver and vegetable mixture. Continue layering pasta and liver sauce, then cover with béchamel.
5. Sprinkle with parmesan, dot with dabs of remaining butter and bake for 30 minutes until golden brown. Serve hot.

Spaghetti al dolce
Sweet-Style Spaghetti

American	Ingredients	Metric/Imperial
	◢ 00:15	00:10
14 oz	Thin spaghetti (fidelini)	400 g / 14 oz
Scant ¼ cup	Vegetable oil	3 tbsp
2 tbsp	Vinegar	1½ tbsp
	Salt and pepper	
1	Red beetroot, cooked	1
3	Medium-sized carrots	3
2	White celery stalks	2
1 cup	Mayonnaise	225 ml / 8 fl oz

1. Cook spaghetti in boiling salted water until 'al dente'. Beat the oil, vinegar, salt and pepper together. Drain pasta and toss in some of the dressing.
2. Peel beetroot, dice into small cubes and put in a bowl. Scrape carrots, grate finely and add to the beetroot; slice celery thinly and add to bowl. Toss vegetables in prepared dressing and mayonnaise and stir into spaghetti. Mix carefully and serve cold.

Variation: canned white tuna fish may be added with the vegetables.

Pasta con coniglio alla sarda
Sardinian-Style Rabbit with Pasta

American	Ingredients	Metric/Imperial
	◢ 00:25	00:30
¾ lb	Rabbit meat, raw or cooked	350 g / 12 oz
2 tbsp	Oil	1½ tbsp
1	Sprig of sage	1
1	Sprig of myrtle	1
½ cup	White wine	125 ml / 4 fl oz
½ cup	Stock	125 ml / 4 fl oz
	Salt and pepper	
14 oz	Pasta	400 g / 14 oz
1 cup	Coffee (single) cream	225 ml / 8 fl oz

1. Grind (mince) rabbit meat finely. Heat oil and quickly brown meat with sage and myrtle. Pour over wine and stock, season, cover and simmer for 20 minutes.
2. Meanwhile cook pasta in boiling salted water until 'al dente', then drain.
3. Purée rabbit sauce in a blender or food processor, stir in cream, add drained pasta, and mix well. Serve immediately.

Pasta alla veneziana
Venetian-Style Pasta

American	Ingredients	Metric/Imperial
	◢ 00:15	00:50
1¼ lb	Well-filleted fish in a slice or whole	600 g / 1¼ lb
1	Onion	1
⅓ cup	Butter	65 g / 2½ oz
3 tbsp	White wine	2 tbsp
5 tbsp	Tomato concentrate	4 tbsp
¼ lb	Pine kernels	100 g / 4 oz
1 cup	Béchamel sauce	225 ml / 8 fl oz
1 tbsp	Grated parmesan cheese	1 tbsp
14 oz	Spaghetti	400 g / 14 oz
	Bread crumbs as required	
	Salt	

1. Preheat the oven to 400°F / 200°C / Gas Mark 6. Grease an ovenproof dish.
2. Poach fish in simmering water for about 10 minutes, then drain, and chop up flesh into bite-size pieces. Peel and finely chop onion.
3. Melt half the butter in a pan and when foaming add onion and fish and sauté for 2 minutes. Add white wine, tomato concentrate, pine kernels. Simmer for 5 minutes, uncovered.
4. Prepare a béchamel sauce with the rest of the butter, ¼ cup [25 g / 1 oz] flour and 1 cup [225 ml / 8 fl oz] milk. Stir in the parmesan.
5. Cook spaghetti in boiling salt water until 'al dente' then drain and add to the fish sauce mixing gently.
6. Sprinkle bread crumbs over base of serving dish, spoon a layer of spaghetti sauce over base, top with some béchamel. Continue layering in this way finishing with béchamel.
7. Bake in the oven for 15 minutes until golden. Serve at once.

Penne e beccacce
Penne Pasta and Woodcocks

American	Ingredients	Metric/Imperial
2	Oven-ready woodcocks	2
1	Onion	1
¼ cup	Vegetable oil	50 ml / 2 fl oz
½ cup	Butter	100 g / 4 oz
¼ tsp	Sage	¼ tsp
¼ tsp	Thyme	¼ tsp
¼ tsp	Sweet marjoram	¼ tsp
¼ tsp	Rosemary	¼ tsp
¼ tsp	Chervil	¼ tsp
2	Garlic cloves	2
	Salt and pepper	
¼ cup	Cognac	50 ml / 2 fl oz
½ lb	Strained tomato pulp	225 g / 8 oz
14 oz	Penne pasta	400 g / 14 oz
6 oz	Fresh fontina cheese	175 g / 6 oz
	Truffle	

1. Cut all flesh from woodcocks into small pieces. Peel and chop onion.
2. Heat oil and butter together and, when foaming, brown meat, stirring all the time. Add onion, herbs, garlic, salt, pepper and cognac to the pan with the tomato pulp. Cook for a further 45 minutes until woodcock is done.
3. Cook pasta in boiling salted water until 'al dente', then drain. Cut fontina into thin slices and mix into the pasta with the woodcock sauce.
4. Serve on a hot serving dish garnished with grated truffle.

Pizzoccheri ai colombacci
Pizzoccheri with Wood Pigeons

American	Ingredients	Metric/Imperial
2	Oven-ready wood pigeons	2
1	Onion	1
¼ cup	Lard	50 g / 2 oz
½ cup	Red wine	125 ml / 4 fl oz
2 or 3	Sage leaves	2 or 3
1 cup	Coffee (single) cream	225 ml / 8 fl oz
14 oz	Pizzoccheri	400 g / 14 oz
10 oz	Bitto cheese	275 g / 10 oz

1. Remove all flesh from the bones of the pigeons, and cut into even-sized pieces. Peel and chop onion, heat lard and when hot brown pigeon flesh lightly, stirring from time to time.
2. Pour the red wine into the pan, add onion and sage leaves, cover and simmer a further 45 minutes. Cool slightly, then stir in cream and keep warm over a low heat.
3. Cook pizzoccheri in boiling unsalted water until 'al dente'. Drain, stir in the bitto cheese, and cream sauce. Serve immediately.

Sformato di maccheroncelli
Small Macaroni Mold

American	Ingredients	Metric/Imperial
1	Bread roll	1
	Milk as required	
1¾ cups	Ground (minced) meat	400 g / 14 oz
2	Eggs	2
3 tbsp	Grated cheese	2 tbsp
	White flour, as required	
½ cup	Vegetable oil	125 ml / 4 fl oz
1	Large onion	1
6 - 7	Plum tomatoes (fresh or canned)	6 - 7
2	Garlic cloves	2
½ tsp	Oregano	½ tsp
½ tsp	Basil	½ tsp
	Salt and pepper	
¾ lb	Small macaroni	350 g / 12 oz
1	Scamorza cheese	1

1. Preheat oven to 375°F / 190°C / Gas Mark 5.
2. Soak inside of roll in milk, then squeeze out excess liquid. Mix ground meat with beaten eggs, the soaked bread crumbs and grated cheese. Mix all ingredients well, divide mixture into even-sized small balls and toss in flour.
3. Heat all but 2 tablespoons of the oil in a frying pan and, when very hot, fry meat balls until evenly browned — about 5-8 minutes, then drain on absorbent paper.
4. Peel and slice onion, sieve tomatoes. Heat remaining oil in another pan and cook onion and crushed garlic for 5 minutes until golden brown. Add tomatoes, oregano, basil and pepper, then the meat balls. Cover and simmer for about 20 minutes.
5. Meanwhile cook small macaroni until 'al dente' in boiling salted water, drain then add meat balls and sauce. Skin and dice scamorza cheese and stir into pasta mixture.
6. Spoon pasta and sauce into an ovenproof serving dish. Bake for 25 minutes until a golden brown crust forms. Serve with grated cheese.

Pennette alla contadina
Peasant Quills

American	Ingredients	Metric/Imperial
8	Tomatoes	8
3 tbsp	Olive oil	2 tbsp
1	Garlic clove	1
1 tbsp	Oregano	1 tbsp
	Salt and pepper	
14 oz	Pennette pasta	400 g / 14 oz
	Grated cheese as required	

1. Skin tomatoes and quarter. Heat oil in a pan and when hot fry crushed garlic, tomatoes and oregano for 5 minutes. Season and simmer for 10 minutes.
2. Cook pennette in boiling salted water until 'al dente', drain and stir into tomato sauce.
3. Spoon onto a serving dish, sprinkle with black pepper and grated cheese. Serve very hot.

Pasta del pirata Barbanera
Pirate Barbanera's Pasta

⊳ 00:10　　　01:15

American	Ingredients	Metric/Imperial
1	Onion	1
4	Garlic cloves	4
3 tbsp	Olive oil	2 tbsp
¼ tsp	Rosemary	¼ tsp
1	Chilli pepper	1
¾ lb	Ripe plum tomatoes	350 g / 12 oz
	White wine as required	
14 oz	Spaghetti or trenette (long narrow noodles)	400 g / 14 oz
4	Garlic cloves (optional)	4

1. Peel and finely chop onion and garlic. Heat oil in a pan and when hot add onion, garlic, rosemary and deseeded, chopped chilli and cook for 3 minutes.
2. Purée tomatoes and add to pan. Cover and simmer over a very low heat for 1 hour, adding white wine if sauce becomes too thick.
3. Cook spaghetti or trenette in boiling salted water until 'al dente', drain and put in a serving bowl. If liked add a further 4 cloves of crushed garlic to sauce, pour tomato sauce over pasta, stir well and serve.

Bucatini al garganello
Bucatini with Teal

⊳ 00:35　　　00:60

American	Ingredients	Metric/Imperial
1	Small teal (wild duck)	1
2	Lemons	2
4	Anchovies	4
1 oz	Capers	25 g / 1 oz
½ cup	Butter	100 g / 4 oz
3 tbsp	Flour	2 tbsp
½ cup	Concentrated clear soup	125 ml / 4 fl oz
½ cup	Strong red wine	125 ml / 4 fl oz
	Salt and pepper	
¼ tsp	Nutmeg	¼ tsp
14 oz	Bucatini pasta	400 g / 14 oz

1. Clean the teal with water and rub over with a slice of lemon, then cut into pieces.
2. Chop anchovies and capers, sprinkle with lemon juice.
3. Melt 2 tablespoons [25 g / 1 oz] butter in a saucepan, add the white flour, mix well and add the mixture of soup and red wine. Add the chopped anchovies and capers, mix well and then add pieces of teal. Cook over a moderate heat until tender.
4. Remove the teal and take off all the flesh. Chop finely or blend the meat in an electric food blender or processor, add the sauce, season, mix well and warm again.
5. Cook the bucatini pasta in boiling salted water, drain when 'al dente' and dress the pasta with the teal sauce.

Spaghetti with a selection of sauces

Tagiatelle alle cozze
Noodles with Mussels

00:25   00:25

American	Ingredients	Metric/Imperial
2 lb	Mussels	1 kg / 2 lb
2	Garlic cloves	2
1 tbsp	Chopped parsley	1 tbsp
Scant ¼ cup	Vegetable oil	3 tbsp
½ cup	Whipping (double) cream	100 ml / 3½ fl oz
	Salt and pepper	
14 oz	Noodles	400 g / 14 oz
¼ cup	Butter	50 g / 2 oz
2	Egg yolks	2

1. Preheat oven to 325°F / 160°C / Gas Mark 3. Butter a large piece of foil and place on a heatproof serving dish.
2. Wash and scrub mussels individually in three changes of water and remove beards. Put in a large pan of water, bring to the boil and cook for 8-10 minutes until all the mussel shells have opened. Discard any closed mussel shells. Remove the moluscs carefully from the shells and leave on one side. Retain the cooking liquid.
3. Finely chop garlic and parsley. Heat oil in a pan and when very hot add garlic and parsley and cook for 1 minute then add mussels, seasoning and half the cooking water used for the mussels. Boil until liquid has reduced by half, then stir in cream and simmer for 3 minutes.
4. Cook noodles in boiling salted water until 'al dente', drain and put in a serving bowl. Add mussel sauce and butter and stir in well with the beaten egg yolks.
5. Spoon noodle mixture over foil in dish, close up foil to form a parcel. Bake for 10 minutes and serve 'parcel' in the dish at the table.

Tagliatelle alle cipolle e porro
Noodles with Onions and Leek

00:05   00:15

American	Ingredients	Metric/Imperial
2	Onions	2
1	Leek	1
1	Bunch of chives	1
1	Bunch of parsley	1
½ cup	Vegetable oil	125 ml / 4 fl oz
14 oz	Noodles	400 g / 14 oz
	Salt	
1 tbsp	Grated pecorino cheese	1 tbsp

1. Finely chop onions and leek with chives and parsley. Heat oil and cook half the vegetable and herb mixture for 3-5 minutes, stirring all the time.
2. Cook the noodles in the boiling salted water until 'al dente', drain and stir in the grated pecorino cheese and the hot vegetable mixture.
3. Finally stir in remaining raw chopped vegetables.
4. Spoon onto a hot serving dish and serve immediately.

Rigatoni con le zucchine
Rigatoni with Gourds

00:10   00:40

American	Ingredients	Metric/Imperial
14 oz	Gourds	400 g / 14 oz
Scant ¼ cup	Vegetable oil	3 tbsp
1	Garlic clove	1
	Salt and pepper	
1 tbsp	Chopped parsley	1 tbsp
14 oz	Rigatoni	400 g / 14 oz
¼ cup	Grated parmesan cheese	25 g / 1 oz

1. Wash gourds and slice thinly.
2. Heat oil and, when hot, add crushed garlic and cook for 1 minute. Put prepared gourds in pan, season, add chopped parsley, cover and cook for 40 minutes over a low heat, stirring from time to time.
3. Cook rigatoni in plenty of boiling salted water until 'al dente', drain and put in a serving bowl. Stir in the cooked gourds and sprinkle over parmesan cheese, just before serving.

Bavette e pesce
Noodles and Fish

This delicious pasta dish is eaten throughout Versilia, but even more in the south. It is essential to use fresh fish or left-over boiled fish, sieved carefully. A typical seaside dish which has several names and is often enjoyed near the Mediterranean.

00:40   00:60

American	Ingredients	Metric/Imperial
1½ lb	Fish	600 g / 1½ lb
1	Piece of skate	1
1	Piece of octopus	1
¼ cup	Oil	3 tbsp
2	Onions	2
1	Red chilli pepper	1
1 tbsp	Parsley	1 tbsp
¼ tsp	Basil	¼ tsp
2	Garlic cloves	2
1 cup	Strained tomato pulp	225 ml / 8 fl oz
1	Sweet yellow pepper	1
⅔ cup	Shelled, cooked prawns	100 g / 4 oz
	Salt and pepper	
14 oz	Noodles	400 g / 14 oz

1. Boil the fish in salted water, drain when firm, cool and remove the bones.
2. Pass the fish flesh through the blender, then tip it into a large saucepan with oil and peeled chopped onions.
3. Add chopped chilli pepper already deseeded, some chopped parsley and basil and 2 crushed cloves of garlic. Cook for about 10 minutes, mixing thoroughly, add the strained tomato pulp and a sweet yellow pepper cut into thin strips. Continue to cook the sauce, stirring from time to time. Add prawns and season well.
4. Cook the noodles in plenty of salted water. Drain them well while still firm and add to the sauce, stir for a few moments, increasing the heat, then serve, if possible in the cooking pot.

Gratinated green noodles

Tagliatelle verdi gratinate
Gratinated Green Noodles

	00:10	00:45

American	Ingredients	Metric/Imperial
¾ lb	Noodles	350 g / 12 oz
1 cup	Béchamel sauce	225 ml / 8 fl oz
5 oz	Mushrooms	150 g / 5 oz
½ lb	Ham cut into dice	225 g / 8 oz
	Butter as required	
1 tbsp	Bread crumbs	1 tbsp
2	Eggs	2
	Salt and pepper	
1 tbsp	Grated parmesan cheese	1 tbsp
1 cup	Cream	225 ml / 8 fl oz
2 tsp	Curry powder	2 tsp
	Black or powdered truffle (optional)	

1. Heat oven to 350°F / 180°C / Gas Mark 4.
2. Parboil noodles for 5 minutes, then drain and rinse under cold water. Prepare a cup of béchamel.
3. Add mushrooms and ham to the béchamel, blend with the noodles, mixing carefully.
4. Butter an ovenproof dish, scatter with bread crumbs and slip mixture into it. Beat eggs with salt, pepper and parmesan and pour over the noodle mixture.

5. Place dish in centre of the oven and bake for 20-25 minutes until a golden crust forms.
6. Meanwhile beat cream with the curry powder. Add grated black truffle (or powdered form) to sauce. Pour into a sauceboat and serve cold as an accompaniment to the dish of hot gratinated noodles.

Tagliatelle al caviale e panna
Noodles with Caviar and Cream

	00:05	00:15

American	Ingredients	Metric/Imperial
1 cup	Coffee (single) cream	225 ml / 8 fl oz
1	Small jar of caviar or substitute	1
1 tbsp	Butter	1 tbsp
2 or 3	Sage leaves	2 or 3
¼ cup	Cognac (optional)	50 ml / 2 fl oz
14 oz	Egg noodles	400 g / 14 oz
3 tbsp	Grated parmesan cheese	2 tbsp

1. Pour cream into a saucepan, add caviar and simmer over a low heat for 10 minutes, stirring all the time, but do not allow to boil. Add butter, sage and cognac and cook for a further 2 minutes.
2. Cook noodles in plenty of boiling salted water until 'al dente', drain and stir into caviar sauce with grated parmesan.
3. Spoon onto a hot serving dish and serve immediately.

Fettuccine dorate
Golden Noodles

	00:10		00:20

American	Ingredients	Metric/Imperial
	Salt	
14 oz	Noodles	400 g / 14 oz
4 tbsp	Margarine	50 g / 2 oz
3 tbsp	Bread crumbs	2 tbsp
1 tsp	Chopped basil	1 tsp
	Pepper	
	Pecorino cheese as desired	

1. Bring to the boil a large saucepan of salted water, drop in the egg noodles, drain when cooked 'al dente'.
2. Heat the margarine in a frying pan, lightly brown the bread crumbs and the very finely chopped basil in the fat, add the drained noodles and cook till golden over a brisk heat. Season and sprinkle with grated strong pecorino.

Bavette alla livornese
Leghorn-Style Noodles

	00:25		00:35

American	Ingredients	Metric/Imperial
3 tbsp	Oil	2 tbsp
4	Red rock mullet	4
1	Onion	1
1	Garlic clove	1
½ lb	Peeled tomatoes	225 g / 8 oz
	Salt and pepper	
1½ tsp	Chopped basil	1½ tsp
14 oz	Noodles, fresh or dried	400 g / 14 oz

1. Heat the oil in a frying pan, add the well-cleaned mullet, a chopped onion, crushed garlic, peeled tomatoes, salt, pepper, and 1 teaspoon of basil and cook gently; turn the fish over only once. (The fish will be cooked when the eyes appear white.)
2. Remove the fish without breaking, open and bone carefully.
3. Beat the fish flesh with the cooking liquid, then return to a small saucepan to thicken well.
4. Heat plenty of salted water in a large saucepan, add the noodles when the water is boiling and cook until firm. Drain and season at once with the mullet sauce. Sprinkle with basil.

Agnolotti alla parmense
Parmesan Ravioli

	00:60		00:12 to 00:18
			depending on size

American	Ingredients	Metric/Imperial
½ cup	Grated stale bread	50 g / 2 oz
1 cup	Grated parmesan cheese	100 g / 4 oz
	Salt and pepper	
½ tsp	Nutmeg	½ tsp
1 lb	Pasta dough	450 g / 1 lb

1. Mix the bread, grated parmesan, salt and pepper with the nutmeg, blending together well.
2. Prepare the pasta by halving the dough, rolling 2 pieces out thinly on the table.
3. Place little heaps of filling on one half, cover with the remaining half of the dough and shape some perfectly round agnolotti with a small glass or cutter.
4. Heat plenty of salted water in a saucepan and when the water comes to the boil, toss in ravioli and serve them with meat sauce or in clear soup.
5. Serve grated parmesan separately with this delicately flavored dish.

Agnolotti
Small Ravioli

	00:30	00:08 to 00:10	
	The pasta dough 01:00		

American	Ingredients	Metric/Imperial
¼ cup	Butter	50 g / 2 oz
¼ lb	Veal	100 g / 4 oz
5 oz	Lean pork	150 g / 5 oz
	Salt and pepper	
5 oz	Chopped raw ham	150 g / 5 oz
1	Truffle (optional)	1
1	Egg, beaten	1
¼ cup	Grated parmesan cheese	25 g / 1 oz
	A little dry white wine (if required)	
	A sheet of fresh pasta dough	
	Grated parmesan cheese	
2 tbsp	Butter for seasoning	25 g / 1 oz

1. Melt butter in a saucepan, add the ground (minced) veal, pork, salt, pepper, chopped ham, half the truffle cut in fine slices, cook over a low heat.
2. Add the beaten egg and the grated cheese, mix all the ingredients thoroughly, cooking and moistening only if necessary with a little dry white wine. Allow to cool.
3. Make the pasta according to the basic recipe for fresh pasta (see page 94). Roll out the dough in two equal pieces, on one half place spoonfuls of prepared filling in little heaps. Fold over and cut with the ravioli cutter to give the desired shape.
4. Continue with remaining dough and mixture. Leave the filled ravioli for 30 minutes.
5. Boil plenty of salted water in a large saucepan and as soon as it reaches boiling point, toss the pasta in.
6. The ravioli will be ready when they rise to the surface. Take out of the water with a slotted spoon, arrange on a hot serving dish. Toss in butter and sprinkle with grated parmesan cheese. Finally, scatter with fine slices of the remaining truffle and serve.

Preparing small ravioli
1. When you have cooked the filling of veal, pork, seasoning ham and truffle over low heat, transfer it to a bowl and add the egg and grated parmesan cheese. Mix thoroughly, moistening if necessary with a little dry wine. Cool.
2. Roll the pasta dough out into two equal pieces. On one half place teaspoonfuls of prepared filling.
3. Fold the rest of the dough over and press down between the rows of filling. Cut out with the ravioli cutter.
4. Cook the pasta in a saucepan of boiling salted water.
5. Serve tossed in butter and sprinkled with grated parmesan.

Green ravioli with ricotta

Raviolini al gratin
Little Ravioli au Gratin

00:15   **01:00**

American	Ingredients	Metric/Imperial
1	Small onion	1
3 tbsp	Butter	2 tbsp
5 oz	Ham cooked in a single slice	150 g / 5 oz
1 cup	Frozen peas	150 g / 5 oz
	Salt and pepper	
3	Peeled tomatoes	3
14 oz	Ravioli	400 g / 14 oz
¼ lb	Sliced fontina	100 g / 4 oz
1 tbsp	Grated cheese	1 tbsp

1. Preheat oven to 400°F / 200°C / Gas Mark 6. Grease an ovenproof dish.
2. Peel and slice onion. Melt half the butter and fry the onion for 2 - 3 minutes. Dice ham, add to pan and cook a further minute, then add the peas, salt, pepper and crushed tomatoes. Cook for 10 minutes.
3. Meanwhile cook the ravioli in the boiling salted water for 6-8 minutes. Remove with a slotted spoon. Put half ravioli over the base of the dish, top with slices of fontina cheese and pour over half the tomato sauce. Continue layering in this way with ravioli and sauce, then sprinkle top with grated cheese and add dabs of butter.
4. Bake for 30 minutes until golden and crusty. Serve piping hot.

Ravioli verdi alla ricotta
Green Ravioli with Ricotta

01:15   **00:12**

American	Ingredients	Metric/Imperial
3½ cups	Flour	400 g / 14 oz
4	Eggs	4
	Salt	
7	Sprigs of parsley	7
2 or 3	Basil leaves	2 or 3
¾ lb	Ricotta cheese	350 g / 12 oz
½ cup	Grated parmesan cheese	50 g / 2 oz
¼ tsp	Nutmeg	¼ tsp
	Butter and nutmeg for seasoning	

1. Prepare pasta dough according to basic recipe using flour, eggs, a few drops green colouring and salt (see page 94) and leave to stand, wrapped in foil.
2. Finely chop parsley, basil and ricotta and put in a bowl with remaining egg, parmesan, salt and nutmeg. Stir to mix well, then beat to a smooth mixture.
3. Roll out pasta dough into 4 equal thin oblongs. On one sheet drop tiny mounds of filling 1½ in / 4 cm apart. Brush water between mounds and place a sheet of dough evenly over the top. Press dough firmly down between mounds of filling to form 2 in / 5 cm squares. Cut into squares using pastry wheel or cutter. Repeat with remaining dough and filling.
4. Bring a pan of salted water to the boil and drop in ravioli. Boil 5-6 minutes. Remove carefully with a slotted spoon, place on a hot serving dish and dot with butter and nutmeg.

Ravioli alla Val Passiria
Passer Valley Ravioli

01:00   **00:15**

American	Ingredients	Metric/Imperial
1 lb	Pasta dough	450 g / 1 lb
2	Potatoes	2
2	Eggs	2
1	Bunch of mint	1
¼ lb	Ricotta cheese	100 g / 4 oz
	Salt and pepper	
¼ tsp	Nutmeg	¼ tsp
1 tsp	Bread crumbs	1 tsp
1¼ lb	Tender green beans	600 g / 1¼ lb
1 tbsp	Butter	1 tbsp
1 tbsp	Grated parmesan cheese	1 tbsp

1. Prepare pasta dough using basic recipe.
2. Peel the potatoes and boil until tender, drain and mash. Add 2 beaten eggs, mint, ricotta, salt, pepper, nutmeg and bread crumbs and mix to form a firm mixture.
3. Prepare ravioli using potato and ricotta filling following procedure opposite for 'Port Maurice little ravioli'.
4. Put on a large wide pan of salted water and bring to the boil, then cook beans until just tender, drain and keep warm. Drop in ravioli, simmer for 6-8 minutes until tender when ravioli will rise to surface.
5. Remove carefully using a slotted spoon and put on a hot serving dish. Mix in beans, dot with butter, sprinkle with parmesan and serve immediately.

Ravioli alla mantovana
Mantuan-Style Ravioli

⏱ 00:40   00:20 🍲

American	Ingredients	Metric/Imperial
¾ lb	Mixed herbs	350 g / 12 oz
1 cup	Grated parmesan cheese	100 g / 4 oz
¾ lb	Ricotta cheese	350 g / 12 oz
1	Egg	1
	Salt and pepper	
	Meat sauce	
	Grated parmesan cheese	
14 oz	Pasta dough	400 g / 14 oz

1. Wash and boil herbs in salted water for 5 minutes, drain and squeeze out well, then chop finely. Mix herbs with parmesan, ricotta and egg to obtain a smooth mixture. Season with salt and pepper.
2. Roll out the dough very finely and make ricotta filled ravioli, following procedure for 'Port Maurice little ravioli'.
3. Prepare a large wide pan with a plenty of boiling salted water and drop in ravioli. Simmer until tender for 6-8 minutes when ravioli will rise to surface.
4. Remove carefully with a slotted spoon and place on a hot serving dish. Serve with a meat sauce and parmesan.

Raviolini alla Porto Maurizio
Port Maurice
Little Ravioli

⏱ 00:30   00:45 🍲

American	Ingredients	Metric/Imperial
Scant ¼ cup	Vegetable oil	3 tbsp
1 ½ cups	Ground (minced) meat or left-over roast or boiled meat	350 g / 12 oz
½ tsp	Sage	½ tsp
½ tsp	Rosemary	½ tsp
½ tsp	Thyme	½ tsp
½ tsp	Sweet marjoram	½ tsp
½ tsp	Basil	½ tsp
2	Bay leaves	2
	Salt and pepper	
1	Egg	1
1 tbsp	Grated cheese	1 tbsp
¼ tsp	Nutmeg	¼ tsp
For the pasta		
3 ½ cups	White flour	400 g / 14 oz
4	Eggs	4
1 tsp	Fine salt	1 tsp

1. Heat oil until very hot, fry meat until lightly browned all over. Add sage, rosemary, thyme, sweet marjoram, basil, bay, salt and pepper. Allow to simmer for 30 minutes stirring from time to time, then remove from heat and leave to cool.
2. Grind meat and herb mixture in a food processor until very fine. Add beaten egg, cheese, nutmeg and seasoning to forcemeat and mix thoroughly to obtain a smooth mixture.
3. Prepare pasta according to basic recipe (see page 94).

4. Roll out pasta on a floured board into 4 equal thin oblongs. On one sheet drop tiny mounds of filling 1½ in / 4 cm apart in straight lines. Brush water in straight lines between mounds. Place a sheet of dough evenly over the top. Working quickly press down between each mound of filling along wetted line to form 2 in / 5 cm squares. Cut pasta into squares using a pastry cutter or wheel. Separate squares and put on a floured tea towel. Repeat with remaining pasta and filling.
5. Prepare a large wide pan with plenty of boiling salted water and drop in ravioli. Simmer for 6-8 minutes, when ravioli will rise to surface. Remove with a slotted spoon and place on a hot serving dish.
6. Serve with a tomato sauce poured over ravioli.

Ravioli alle noci
Ravioli with Walnuts

⏱ 00:20   00:10 🍲

American	Ingredients	Metric/Imperial
½	Bread roll	½
	Milk	
20	Shelled walnuts	20
½	Garlic clove	½
Scant ¼ cup	Vegetable oil	3 tbsp
¼ cup	Grated cheese	25 g / 1 oz
¼ tsp	Marjoram	¼ tsp
	Salt and pepper	
¼ cup	Coffee (single) cream	50 ml / 2 fl oz
1 ¼ lb	Ravioli (without meat)	600 g / 1 ¼ lb
1 tbsp	Butter	1 tbsp

1. Soak bread crumbs from roll in milk, then squeeze and put in blender with walnuts, garlic, oil, cheese, marjoram, salt, pepper and cream. Blend until a thick purée is formed, then put in a pan over a low heat to heat through whilst ravioli cooks.
2. Cook ravioli in boiling salted water for 6 - 8 minutes then carefully remove with a slotted spoon and place on a hot serving dish.
3. Pour walnut sauce over pasta, add a few dabs of butter and serve immediately.

Gnocchi fritti senza ripieno
Fried Gnocchi
without Filling

⏱ 00:20   00:05 🍲

American	Ingredients	Metric/Imperial
2 cups	White flour or finely ground semolina	225 g / 8 oz
½ tsp	Salt	½ tsp
2 tbsp	Lard	25 g / 1 oz
	Oil for deep frying	

1. Knead flour with a little water, salt, and the lard and roll out paste to a very thin layer. Cut into squares and prick with a fork.
2. Heat oil in a large heavy based pan, fitted with a basket and fry squares for 2 minutes, then drain on absorbent paper.
3. Fried gnocchi can be served as an hors d'oeuvre with cold dishes such as cooked pressed pork, mortadella, ham or various kinds of sausages.

Gnocchi verdi

Green Gnocchi

◢ 00:25   00:25 🍲

American	Ingredients	Metric/Imperial
1 lb	Spinach	500 g / 1 lb
	Salt and pepper	
14 oz	Very fresh ricotta cheese	400 g / 14 oz
2	Egg yolks	2
	All purpose (plain) flour	
2 tbsp	Butter	25 g / 1 oz
1 tbsp	Grated parmesan cheese	1 tbsp

1. Cook the spinach in boiling, salted water, for a few minutes.
2. Work the ricotta in an earthenware dish, mixing continuously with a wooden spoon.
3. Drain the spinach, chop and pass through a food processor or vegetable mill. Add the purée obtained to the ricotta and blend. Mix in the two egg yolks. Allow the mixture to stand for a few minutes then make it into many little gnocchi, with the aid of a spoon.
4. Flour a large pastry-board and, for convenience, lay the little gnocchi on it as you make them.
5. Heat a large saucepan of salted water, when it is boiling tip the gnocchi into it a few at a time. Leave them to cook for about 2 minutes. Drain them, without breaking.
6. Melt the butter and when it turns golden, remove from the heat and pour it over the gnocchi. Sprinkle with grated cheese, freshly-ground pepper, and serve. If there should be any left over, remember that they are also excellent browned in butter.

Gnocchi gialli

Yellow Gnocchi

◢ 00:60   00:20 🍲

American	Ingredients	Metric/Imperial
1¾ lb	Pumpkin pulp	800 g / 1¾ lb
¾ cup	Butter	175 g / 6 oz
	Salt and pepper	
¼ lb	Emmental cheese	100 g / 4 oz
¼ lb	Gouda cheese	100 g / 4 oz
¼ lb	Bergkase cheese	100 g / 4 oz
2	Eggs	2
1 cup	White flour	100 g / 4 oz
3	Sage leaves	3

1. Cut the pumpkin into small pieces. In a large saucepan melt about ½ cup [100 g / 4 oz] of butter, thin with a little water and add the pieces of pumpkin. Season with salt and sprinkle with freshly-ground pepper, allow to cook until, by stirring briskly, you succeed in obtaining a thick and smooth cream from the pumpkin. Remove from the heat and allow to stand.
2. Chop up all the cheeses and mix them together. Then add them to the pumpkin. Add the eggs and the flour and work until you obtain a fairly stiff mixture. Make many little gnocchi from the mixture.
3. Bring a large saucepan of salted water to the boil. Tip the gnocchetti in the water, in batches, for about 3 minutes and when they begin to float, take them out on a slotted spoon.
4. In a frying pan melt the rest of butter and flavour by adding sage leaves. Season the gnochetti with melted butter.

Yellow gnocchi

Veronese-style gnocchi

Gnocchi alla veronese
Veronese-Style Gnocchi

◢▭ 01:20   01:10 ◥

American	Ingredients	Metric/Imperial
2 oz	Dried mushrooms	50 g / 2 oz
5 oz	Brains	150 g / 5 oz
3 tbsp	Vinegar	2 tbsp
½ cup	Butter	100 g / 4 oz
1	Onion	1
¼ cup	Brandy	50 ml / 2 fl oz
	Salt and pepper	
½ cup	Stock	125 ml / 4 fl oz
1 lb	Gnocchi or pasta	450 g / 1 lb
2½ cups	Béchamel sauce	600 ml / 1 pint
¼ cup	Grated parmesan cheese	25 g / 1 oz
¼ cup	Bread crumbs	25 g / 1 oz

1. Preheat the oven to 400°F / 200°C / Gas Mark 6.
2. Steep the mushrooms in hot water for 1 hour, drain well.
3. Soak the brains in vinegar and water.
4. Heat the butter in a pan over a low heat, add the chopped onion and the mushrooms.
5. Drain the brains, pat dry with absorbent kitchen paper. Cut into small pieces, add to the mixture in the frying pan with the brandy, season with salt and pepper, mix in the stock and cook for about 45 minutes, pouring in additional stock if necessary.

6. Cook the gnocchi in a saucepan with plenty of salted water, drain them and place them in a buttered ovenproof dish. Cover with the béchamel sauce and sprinkle them with a generous amount of grated parmesan and bread crumbs. Place in the oven for about 20 minutes and serve immediately.

Gnocchi filanti
Stringy Gnocchi

◢▭ 00:15   00:30 ◥

American	Ingredients	Metric/Imperial
	Salt	
7 oz	Fontina cheese	200 g / 7 oz
1 cup	Coffee (single) cream	225 ml / 8 fl oz
½	Vegetable stock cube	½
	Pepper	
2 lb	Potato gnocchi	1 kg / 2 lb
4 tbsp	Grated parmesan cheese	3 tbsp

1. Bring to the boil a large saucepan of salted water.
2. Cut the fontina into small cubes. Heat the cream in a little pan and flavour it with half a stock cube and freshly-ground pepper. Add the fontina and remove it immediately after from the heat. Pour into a soup tureen.
3. Cook the gnocchi in the boiling water. When they begin to float to the surface, drain with a slotted spoon. Tip into the soup tureen, stir and serve sprinkled with plenty of grated parmesan.

Potato gnocchi
Sieving the potatoes, adding the egg and sausage mixture and the flour.
Bottom from left to right: Shaping the gnocchi, arranging the cheese and sage in an ovenproof dish and adding the cooked gnocchi.

Gnocchetti di semola alle zucchine

Little Semolina Gnocchi with Gourds

00:35   00:30

American	Ingredients	Metric/Imperial
4	Gourds	4
1 cup	Cream	225 ml / 8 fl oz
½ cup	Butter	100 g / 4 oz
¼ tsp	Nutmeg	¼ tsp
	Salt and pepper	
½ tsp	Cornstarch (cornflour)	½ tsp
14 oz	Pasta gnocchi	400 g / 14 oz
1 tbsp	Grated parmesan cheese	1 tbsp
1	Bunch of mint, chopped	1

1. Boil 2 gourds until they are 'al dente', then pass through the vegetable mill or blender.
2. Add the cream and put in a small saucepan with the butter (retaining a little for the pasta), nutmeg, salt and pepper. Gradually thicken this sauce, adding the cornstarch mixed with a few drops of water.
3. Boil the little gnocchi in salted water until 'al dente'. Drain and season them with cheese and a little butter.
4. Wash separately two raw tender gourds, and slice finely, if possible with a slicing machine. Slightly heat the sauce made with the sieved gourds and mix with the gnocchetti, complete with the slices of raw gourds, sprinkle with mint and serve.

Gnocchi di patate

Potato Gnocchi with Cheese

00:40   00:45

American	Ingredients	Metric/Imperial
2 lb	Potatoes	1 kg / 2 lb
3 cups	All purpose (plain) flour	350 g / 12 oz
1	Egg	1
¼ lb	Mortadella sausage	100 g / 4 oz
¼ tsp	Nutmeg	¼ tsp
	Salt	
¼ lb	Mozzarella cheese	100 g / 4 oz
24	Sage leaves	24
1 tbsp	Butter	15 g / ½ oz
½ cup	Grated cheese	100 g / 4 oz

1. Preheat the oven to 400°F / 200°C / Gas Mark 6.
2. Boil the potatoes in cold salted water. When they are tender, drain and remove the skins and put through a ricer or food mill or coarse sieve.
3. Sprinkle some of the sifted flour on to the board, place the heap of potatoes in the centre and make a well in the centre. Add the egg, mixed with the finely chopped mortadella, nutmeg and salt, sprinkle in a little flour and mix together to be a fairly firm dough.
4. Roll the strips into thin sausage shapes and then cut off pieces 1½ in / 4 cm long. Mark on the rough side of a grater.
5. Cook in boiling salted water or stock for about 5 minutes until they start floating to the surface.
6. Arrange some slices of mozzarella on the bottom of a buttered ovenproof dish, sprinkle with grated cheese and arrange some leaves of sage on top.
7. Drain the gnocchi onto the cheese and sprinkle with the remaining cheese, bake in the oven for 20 minutes. Serve piping hot with a tomato sauce.

Romans' Pinches

Pizzicotti dei romani

◣▱ 00:30		00:20 ▱
American	**Ingredients**	**Metric/Imperial**
1½ lb	Spinach	700 g / 1½ lb
	Salt and pepper	
¾ lb	Ricotta cheese	350 g / 12 oz
3	Eggs	3
Scant ¼ cup	Grated parmesan cheese	3 tbsp
¼ tsp	Nutmeg	¼ tsp
	Flour as required	
4 tbsp	Butter	50 g / 2 oz
Scant ¼ cup	Whipping (double) cream	3 tbsp
¼ tsp	Sage	¼ tsp
¼ tsp	Basil	¼ tsp
Scant ¼ cup	Grand Marnier	3 tbsp
3 tbsp	Grated cheese	2 tbsp

1. Clean spinach in several changes of water, put in a pan and cook for about 5 minutes over a medium heat. Season with salt and then press spinach well to remove all excess water.
2. Sieve spinach and ricotta cheese together into a bowl or blend in a food processor.
3. Add beaten eggs, parmesan cheese, salt, pepper and nutmeg and blend all ingredients well together with the hands adding sufficient flour to form a smooth paste.
4. Grease hands and divide paste into small pieces the size of a cherry and roll each into a ball.
5. To make sauce, melt butter in a pan, add salt, pepper and cream and boil for 5 minutes. Stir in sage, basil and Grand Marnier, then the grated cheese.
6. Bring a pan of salted water to the boil and drop in balls of gnocci, poach until they rise and float on the water. Carefully remove with a slotted spoon.
7. Put the gnocchi in a serving bowl, top with the cream sauce and serve at once.

Magdalene's Little Gnocchi

Gnocchetti alla Maddalena

◣▱ 00:30		01:10 ▱
American	**Ingredients**	**Metric/Imperial**
3	Artichokes	3
1	Lemon	1
⅓ cup	Butter	75 g / 3 oz
½ cup	Oil	125 ml / 4 fl oz
	Salt and pepper	
2	Large chicken breasts	2
2	Garlic cloves	2
¼ tsp	Rosemary	¼ tsp
¼ tsp	Sage	¼ tsp
1	Stock cube	1
¾ lb	Little gnocchi made with hard-grain wheat or other pasta	350 g / 12 oz
¼ cup	Grated cheese	25 g / 1 oz

1. Preheat oven to 400°F / 200°C / Gas Mark 6.
2. Carefully clean the artichokes, removing the hardest leaves, chokes and the spines, cut into thin slices and place them in water and lemon juice.
3. Melt half the butter in a large frying pan, add 3 tablespoons of oil and, when it begins to brown, add the well-drained artichokes, season with salt and pepper and cover with a lid. Cook on a very low heat, check from time to time and if the pan should become too dry, add a little hot water.
4. Clean the chicken breasts, cut them in small pieces. Heat the oil, garlic, rosemary and sage. When they are nicely browned, add salt and pepper and continue cooking, moistening with a little water and stock cube. Cook the chicken and the artichokes for about 45 minutes.
5. Heat a saucepan with plenty of salted water, bring it to the boil and cook the little gnocchi till 'al dente'. Drain the pasta well and season it with the artichokes and the chicken, mix and tip into an ovenproof dish. Sprinkle the surface with small dabs of the remaining butter and grated cheese. Place in the moderately hot oven and cook for about 15 minutes, until the surface is golden.

Spicy Lasagne

Lasagne piccanti

◣▱ 00:15		01:45 ▱
American	**Ingredients**	**Metric/Imperial**
1	Onion	1
1	Garlic clove	1
¼ lb	Sausage	100 g / 4 oz
1 oz	Dried mushrooms	25 g / 1 oz
Scant ¼ cup	Oil	3 tbsp
½ cup	Ground (minced) beef	100 g / 4 oz
1	Chilli pepper	1
½ cup	Red wine	125 ml / 4 fl oz
½ lb	Peeled tomatoes	225 g / 8 oz
	Salt and pepper	
6 tbsp	Flour	65 g / 1½ oz
3 tbsp	Butter	65 g / 1½ oz
2½ cups	Milk	600 ml / 1 pint
½ cup	Grated parmesan cheese	50 g / 2 oz
7 oz	Lasagne	200 g / 7 oz
7 oz	Noodles	200 g / 7 oz

1. Peel and chop onion, crush garlic clove, chop sausage and soften mushrooms in warm water for 10 minutes.
2. Heat half the oil in a pan, sauté the onions and the garlic for 2 minutes, add meat, sausage and drained mushrooms. Cook a further 2-3 minutes. Add chopped deseeded chilli.
3. Pour in red wine, add tomatoes, season with salt and pepper and cook over a low heat for about 1 hour in an uncovered pan.
4. Preheat the oven to 350°F / 180°C / Gas Mark 4.
5. Meanwhile make béchamel sauce with the flour, butter and milk (see page 162). Finally stir in parmesan cheese.
6. Cook lasagne, a few sheets at a time, in boiling salted water with a dash of oil added until 'al dente'. Remove and rinse with cold water then dry on a tea towel.
7. Cook noodles in boiling salted water with a dash of oil added until 'al dente', drain and stir in the tomato sauce. Spoon mixture onto an oblong ovenproof serving dish.
8. Top with a layer of lasagne and finally pour over the béchamel sauce.
9. Bake in the oven for 30 minutes, then serve with a salad.

Lasagne primavera
Springtime Lasagne

⏲ 00:30   00:45 🍲

American	Ingredients	Metric/Imperial
3½ cups	Flour	400 g / 14 oz
4	Eggs	4
	Salt	
1 lb	Asparagus	500 g / 1 lb
½ tsp	Basil	½ tsp
1 cup	Coffee (single) cream	225 ml / 8 fl oz
2 tbsp	Butter	25 g / 1 oz
	Pepper	
1 cup	Béchamel	225 ml / 8 fl oz

1. Preheat the oven to 350°F / 180°C / Gas Mark 4.
2. Prepare pasta dough using flour, egg and salt (see page 94), and cut out lasagne, then cook in boiling salted water until 'al dente'. Rinse under cold water and dry. Put half the lasagne into a rectangular ovenproof serving dish.
3. Cook asparagus until just softened, then drain. Meanwhile add chopped basil, half the cream, half the butter, salt and pepper to the béchamel sauce. Stir in asparagus and spoon over lasagne in serving dish.
4. Top with remaining lasagne, pour over remaining cream and dab with butter.
5. Bake for 25-30 minutes and serve immediately.

Lasagnette e lumache
Small Lasagne and Snails

⏲ 00:10   00:45 🍲

American	Ingredients	Metric/Imperial
2 lb	Snails with the shell	1 kg / 2 lb
Scant ¼ cup	Oil	3 tbsp
1	Bunch of parsley	1
2	Garlic cloves	2
½ cup	White wine	125 ml / 4 fl oz
14 oz	Small lasagne	400 g / 14 oz
	Salt and pepper.	

1. Preheat oven to 325°F / 170°C / Gas Mark 3.
2. Toss snails in boiling salted water for 10 minutes, drain and carefully remove snails from shells using a sharp-pronged fork.
3. Heat half of the oil in a pan, chop parsley and add to pan with crushed garlic. Cook for 1 minute, then add snails and cook a further 2-3 minutes to brown.
4. Pour in the wine and cook for 10 minutes. Cook lasagne in boiling salted water until 'al dente', drain, then add snail sauce to pasta with remaining oil.
5. Spoon into 4 individual ovenproof serving dishes, reheat in the oven for 15 minutes and serve.

Lasagne verdi alla ligure
Ligurian-Style Green Lasagne

⏲ 00:40   00:40 🍲

American	Ingredients	Metric/Imperial
1 lb	Basic mixture for fresh pasta	500 g / 1 lb
1 lb	Nettles or beet	500 g / 1 lb
1	Egg	1
1 lb	Meat sauce	500 g / 1 lb
2½ cups	Béchamel	600 ml / 1 pint

1. Preheat oven to 350°F / 180°C / Gas Mark 4.
2. Make pasta.
3. Finely chop nettles or beet, boil in a little water then squeeze thoroughly to remove all water.
4. Blend the pressed vegetables with the pasta, adding a beaten egg. Roll out pasta dough thinly, cut out lasagne in desired shape.
5. Cook lasagne in boiling salted water, a few pieces at a time until 'al dente'. Lay pasta on a clean teatowel to dry thoroughly.
6. Grease an oblong ovenproof serving dish, place a layer of lasagne over base, top with a layer of meat sauce. Cover with more lasagne then sauce, ending with a layer of pasta.
7. Pour over béchamel and bake for 25 minutes. Serve hot.

Variation: lasagne can be cooked and served at once with garlic and basil sauce, fresh tomato or meat sauce, without baking.

Ligurian-style green lasagne

Fresh and dried herbs

Cannelloni alla siciliana
Sicilian-Style Cannelloni

▸▽ 00:30   00:40 🍲

American	Ingredients	Metric/Imperial
2 cups	Coffee (single) cream	450 ml / 16 fl oz
¾ lb	Ricotta cheese	350 g / 12 oz
2 oz	Softened pine nuts	50 g / 2 oz
⅓ cup	Raisins	50 g / 2 oz
1	Onion	1
	Salt and pepper	
½ tsp	Red paprika	½ tsp
½ lb	Cooked ham	225 g / 8 oz
½ cup	Dry marsala	125 ml / 4 fl oz
1 lb	Cannelloni	500 g / 1 lb
	Butter	
½ cup	Grated pecorino cheese	50 g / 2 oz
½ tsp	Cumin seeds	½ tsp

Preheat oven to 400°F / 200°C / Gas Mark 6.
1. Prepare the sauce by heating the cream over a low heat. Add the crumbled ricotta, pine nuts, raisins, finely chopped onion, salt, pepper, red paprika, the cooked ham, diced, and dry marsala. Allow the sauce to simmer over a very low heat.
2. Boil the cannelloni in salted water till firm to the bite, drain.
3. In a well-buttered ovenproof dish arrange a layer of cannelloni, cover with a little sauce, then sprinkle with grated pecorino. Continue with a layer of cannelloni, one of sauce and one of pecorino. Finish with a layer of sauce, sprinkle with plenty of pecorino and finally scatter with cumin seeds. Put in oven to cook for 25 minutes.

Cannelloni della nonna
Granny's Cannelloni

▸▽ 00:40   00:40 🍲

American	Ingredients	Metric/Imperial
¾ lb	Spinach	350 g / 12 oz
¾ lb	Braised meat	350 g / 12 oz
2	Eggs	2
7 tbsp	Grated cheese	5½ tbsp
	Salt and pepper	
¼ tsp	Nutmeg	¼ tsp
2½ cups	Béchamel	600 ml / 1 pint
12	Cannelloni or squares of fresh pasta	12
2 tbsp	Butter	25 g / 1 oz

1. Preheat the oven to 375°F / 190°C / Gas Mark 5.
2. Cook the spinach in very little salted water, drain and squeeze well, then pass through a vegetable mill, collecting the purée in an earthenware dish.
3. Chop the braised meat, removing any fat from it and add to the spinach, mix and blend with two egg yolks and most of the grated cheese. Season the filling with salt and pepper and a little grated nutmeg.
4. Cook the cannelloni in boiling salted water, drain on a table napkin or on absorbent kitchen paper.
5. Use a spoon to fill the cannelloni with the mixture of meat and spinach and arrange them in an ovenproof dish.
6. Prepare separately the béchamel sauce and pour over the cannelloni. Scatter with little dabs of butter, sprinkle with grated cheese and place in the oven for 30 minutes.

Rice

Rice Navarre

Rice Navarre

Riso al Marquis de Navarra

⏱ 00:15   00:20 🍲

American	Ingredients	Metric/Imperial
1	Sweet red pepper	1
1	Garlic clove	1
½ lb	Mushrooms	225 g / 8 oz
¾ lb	Scampi	350 g / 12 oz
¼ cup	Vegetable oil	50 ml / 2 fl oz
1⅔ cups	Rice	350 g / 12 oz
3 cups	Stock	750 ml / 1 ¼ pints
½ envelope	Saffron	½ sachet
	Pepper	
	Lemon wedges	

1. Preheat oven to 400°F / 200°C / Gas Mark 6. Grease a large piece of foil and place on a baking sheet.
2. Deseed and chop pepper with garlic, rinse mushrooms in hot water then slice, wash scampi.
3. Heat oil and, when very hot, cook pepper and garlic for 2 minutes. Add rice to pan, cook a further minute stirring briskly. Pour over the stock, cover and simmer for 10 minutes.
4. Add scampi, mushrooms and saffron to rice, season with pepper. Spoon onto foil, parcel up rice in foil and bake for 10 minutes.
5. Place rice parcel on serving dish, open foil, garnish with lemon wedges and serve hot.

Precious Salad

Insalata preziosa

⏱ 00:35   00:15 🍲

American	Ingredients	Metric/Imperial
⅔ cup	Vegetable oil	150 ml / ¼ pint
½	Onion	½
1 ½ cups	Rice	300 g / 11 oz
½ cup	Dry white wine	125 ml / 4 fl oz
2 ¼ cups	Meat stock	500 ml / 18 fl oz
3 oz	Smoked cooked ham	75 g / 3 oz
3 oz	Smoked salmon	75 g / 3 oz
3 oz	Cooked tongue	75 g / 3 oz
3 oz	Prawns, cooked and shelled	75 g / 3 oz
½	Lemon	½
Scant ¼ cup	Vinegar	3 tbsp
1 tbsp	Vodka	1 tbsp
	White pepper	
1 tbsp	Caviar	1 tbsp

1. Heat 4 tablespoons [50 ml / 2 fl oz] of the oil in a large pan and cook the onion until it is golden brown, tip the rice into it and sprinkle it with the wine and stir. Cook for 3 minutes.
2. Prepare about 2¼ cups [500 ml / 18 fl oz] of boiling stock. Pour it over the rice and cook over a low heat for 10 minutes, when 'al dente' cool and drain.
3. Cut the ham, smoked salmon and the tongue into cubes. Add the prawns to the other ingredients in a large bowl.
4. Add the rice and stir. Sprinkle the mixture with the juice of half a lemon. Season with remainder of oil, vinegar, vodka and white pepper. Mix and finally top with the caviar.

Precious salad

Risi e bisati
Rice and Little Eels

◣◥ 00:10   00:20 🍲

American	Ingredients	Metric/Imperial
1 lb	Small eels	500 g / 1 lb
2	Garlic cloves	2
Scant ¼ cup	Vegetable oil	3 tbsp
1 tbsp	Parsley	1 tbsp
3	Bay leaves	2
1	Lemon	1
2 cups	Rice	400 g / 14 oz
3¾ cups	Stock	900 ml / 1 ½ pints
½ cup	Grated parmesan cheese	50 g / 2 oz

1. Cut eels into small pieces and crush the garlic. Heat the oil in a pan and, when very hot, brown pieces of eel quickly with garlic, parsley and bay leaves.
2. Sprinkle over with lemon juice, add rice and stir into mixture. Pour over stock, cover and cook for about 15 minutes, until all stock is absorbed.
3. Remove pan from heat, stir in parmesan cheese, spoon onto a hot serving dish, and serve hot.

Riso alla Sandokan
Sandokan Rice

◣◥ 00:05   00:15 🍲

American	Ingredients	Metric/Imperial
3¾ cups	Water or stock	900 ml / 1 ½ pints
2 cups	Rice	400 g / 14 oz
1 tsp	Curry powder	1 tsp
	Salt and pepper	
1½ oz	Prawns	40 g / 1 ½ oz
3 tbsp	Butter	40 g / 1 ½ oz
½ cup	Grated parmesan cheese	50 g / 2 oz

1. Pour the measured quantity of boiling water or stock over rice in pan. Add curry powder, bring to boil. Reduce heat, cover and simmer for 10 minutes. Season well.
2. Add well washed prawns to the rice and cook a further 5 minutes. Tip rice and prawn mixture into individual bowls. Add knobs of butter to each bowl, and sprinkle with cheese.

Riso alla salsiccia
Rice with Sausage

◣◥ 00:10   00:25 🍲

American	Ingredients	Metric/Imperial
1⅔ cups	Rice	350 g / 12 oz
1	Large onion	1
½ lb	Sausage	225 g / 8 oz
4	Pear-shaped tomatoes	4
3 tbsp	Butter	40 g / 1 ½ oz
3	Sprigs of rosemary	3
¼ cup	Dry white wine	50 ml / 2 fl oz
	Salt and pepper	

1. Cook rice in boiling salted water for 15 minutes. Meanwhile peel and chop onion, chop sausage. Skin and quarter tomatoes.
2. Heat butter and when foaming sauté onion for 2-3 minutes to soften. Add sausage to the pan with rosemary and cook a further 2-3 minutes. Pour over the wine, add tomatoes, season and simmer for 10 minutes.
3. Stir sausage and tomato mixture into cooked rice. Spoon onto a hot serving dish and serve at once.

Riso al salto
Sautéed Rice

◣◥ 00:10   00:30 🍲

American	Ingredients	Metric/Imperial
1	Onion	1
1 envelope	Saffron	1 sachet
3 cups	Stock	750 ml / 1 ¼ pints
¾ cup	Butter	175 g / 6 oz
2 cups	Rice	400 g / 14 oz
½ cup	Red wine	125 ml / 4 fl oz
	Salt and pepper	
¼ cup	Grated parmesan cheese	25 g / 1 oz

1. Chop onion finely, dissolve saffron in a tablespoon of boiling stock. Heat a third of the butter in a pan and when hot sauté the onion for 2 minutes. Add rice to pan and cook a further minute, stirring briskly.
2. Pour over the red wine and stock, stir in saffron and season. Cover and simmer for 15 minutes until rice is cooked. Remove from heat, add a knob of butter and stir in parmesan and leave to cool.
3. Heat another third of butter in a frying pan, spread rice over the base of pan to form a flat cake and cook for 5 minutes over a medium heat. Invert onto a plate placed over pan. Heat remaining butter in frying pan, slip rice cake back in pan to brown the other side. Cook a further 5 minutes.
4. Turn the rice cake onto a hot serving dish and serve immediately.

Riso al caviale
Rice with Caviar

◣◥ 00:15   00:25 🍲

American	Ingredients	Metric/Imperial
1	Onion	1
¼ cup	Butter	50 g / 2 oz
1⅔ cups	Rice	350 g / 12 oz
1 cup	Dry white wine	225 ml / 8 fl oz
2½ cups	Stock	600 ml / 1 pint
2 oz	Jar caviar	50 g / 2 oz
	or	
⅓ cup	Lumpfish cream	60 ml / 2 ½ fl oz

1. Chop the onion. Heat butter and when hot sauté onion for 2 minutes to brown lightly. Add rice to the pan and cook briskly for 1 minute all the time.
2. Pour over the wine and stock. Bring to the boil, then reduce heat, cover and simmer for about 15-20 minutes, until rice is cooked.
3. Remove pan from heat, stir in caviar and spoon into a hot serving dish and serve immediately.

Riso con castrato
Rice with Mutton

⏱ 00:10   00:45 🍲

American	Ingredients	Metric/Imperial
1	Onion	1
¾ lb	Peeled tomatoes	350 g / 12 oz
1 lb	Lean lamb	500 g / 1 lb
½ cup	Butter	100 g / 4 oz
1 tsp	Cinnamon	1 tsp
3 cups	Stock	750 ml / 1¼ pints
1½ cups	Rice	300 g / 11 oz
	Oil	
	Parsley sprigs	

1. Chop onion and tomatoes, cut lamb into small pieces. Heat butter and when hot, brown meat all over, then add onion to pan and cook a further minute. Stir in tomatoes and cinnamon and pour over the stock. Cover and simmer for about 30 minutes.

2. Add rice to the pan, add more stock if needed, cover and cook for 15 minutes, until rice is tender.

3. Lightly oil a 3 cup [750 ml / 1¼ pint] ring mold, spoon rice mixture into mold, pressing down well. Leave for 5 minutes, then turn out onto a serving plate and garnish with sprigs of parsley.

Cook's tip: if you wish, the mold may also be served cold.

Pizza di riso
Rice Pizza

⏱ 00:15   00:35 🍲

American	Ingredients	Metric/Imperial
½	Small onion	½
1	Sweet yellow pepper	1
2	Tomatoes	2
⅓ cup	Vegetable oil	4 tbsp
¼ cup	Butter	50 g / 2 oz
1⅓ cups	Rice	250 g / 9 oz
2½ cups	Stock	600 ml / 1 pint
	Salt	
½ cup	Grated parmesan cheese	50 g / 2 oz
1	Egg yolk, beaten	1

1. Preheat oven to 425°F / 220°C / Gas Mark 7. Grease a baking sheet.

2. Chop the onion, clean and deseed pepper and cut into thin strips. Slice the skinned tomatoes.

3. Heat half the oil and half the butter in a pan, sauté the onion for 2 minutes and add rice to pan, cook for 1-2 minutes, stirring briskly.

4. Pour over stock, add salt, cover and cook for 15 minutes.

5. Remove pan from the heat, stir in grated cheese, egg yolk and remaining butter. Mix together well then divide mixture into 4.

6. Smooth each portion into rounds to form pizzas and place on baking sheet. Heat remaining oil and fry pepper strips for 5 minutes.

7. Arrange tomatoes and peppers on pizza bases to form wheel shapes. Bake for 10 minutes and serve immediately.

Rice with mutton

Nido di riso giallo
Yellow Rice Nest

⏱ 00:10   01:00 🍲

American	Ingredients	Metric/Imperial
1	Onion	1
½ lb	Chicken livers	225 g / 8 oz
½ cup	Butter	100 g / 4 oz
1 cup	Risotto rice	200 g / 7 oz
¼ cup	White wine	50 ml / 2 fl oz
2 cups	Stock	450 ml / ¾ pint
1 envelope	Saffron	1 sachet
1 tsp	Dried sage	1 tsp
2 tbsp	Brandy	1½ tbsp
½ cup	Water	125 ml / 4 fl oz
	Salt and pepper	
½ lb	Frozen peas	225 g / 8 oz
1 cup	Grated cheese	100 g / 4 oz
2 oz	Gruyère cheese	50 g / 2 oz

1. Slice onion, chop chicken livers into small pieces. Heat half the butter and, when foaming, sauté onion for 1 minute then add rice and sauté for a further minute. Pour over the wine, increase heat and cook for 5 minutes to allow the wine to evaporate.

2. Add stock to the rice, then cover and simmer for about 15 minutes. Soak saffron in a little water in a cup.

3. Preheat oven to 375°F / 190°C / Gas Mark 5.

4. Meanwhile melt butter in another pan, add livers and sage, cook for a few minutes to brown all over. Pour in the brandy, water, salt and pepper, cover and simmer over a low heat for about 10 minutes, then add peas.

5. Remove risotto from heat, taste and adjust seasoning, add saffron and half the grated cheese and stir well. Grease an ovenproof serving dish, spoon half the risotto over the base, pour over the peas and chicken livers, sprinkle over diced gruyère and cover with remaining risotto.

6. Sprinkle surface with grated cheese and dab with knobs of butter. Bake for 25-30 minutes until golden brown, and serve very hot.

Timballo di riso
Rice Mold

| | 00:25 | | 01:30 | |

American	Ingredients	Metric/Imperial
¼ lb	Dried mushrooms	100 g / 4 oz
½ lb	Chicken livers	225 g / 8 oz
½ lb	Sweetbreads	225 g / 8 oz
1⅔ cups	Rice	300 g / 12 oz
¼ cup	Butter	50 g / 2 oz
2	Beaten egg yolks	2
½ cup	Grated cheese	50 g / 2 oz
8	Sage leaves	8
	Salt and pepper	
¼ cup	White wine	50 ml / 2 fl oz
Scant ¼ cup	Oil	3 tbsp
2	Garlic cloves	2
¼ lb	Sausages	100 g / 4 oz
¼ cup	Brandy	50 ml / 2 fl oz
2 tbsp	Butter	25 g / 1 oz

1. Soak mushrooms in hot water for 30 minutes, drain and chop. Clean chicken livers, slice sweetbreads.
2. Cook rice in plenty of boiling salted water for 15 minutes, drain and rinse under cold water, stir in half the butter, beaten egg yolks and 1 tablespoon grated cheese.
3. Preheat oven to 425°F / 220°C / Gas Mark 7. Grease an ovenproof dish.
4. Melt the remaining butter and, when foaming, add chicken livers and sage leaves, season with salt and pepper, sauté for 2-3 minutes, then pour over wine. Cover and cook over a low heat for 10 minutes.
5. In another pan, heat oil and, when very hot, sauté garlic and mushrooms for 5 minutes, reduce the heat and simmer for 10 minutes, then add to chicken livers in pan.
6. Lightly fry sausages until evenly browned, pour over brandy and simmer for 10 minutes. Pour juices into chicken liver mixture, taste and adjust seasoning.
7. Cover base of ovenproof dish with a layer of rice, top with half the chicken liver filling, then the sausages and half the cheese. Continue layering ingredients in this way, finishing with a rice layer.
8. Sprinkle remaining cheese over surface, add knobs of butter and bake for 30 minutes until golden brown. Serve hot accompanied by a tomato sauce if wished.

Riso in 'cagnun'
'Cagnun' Rice

A true Milanese recipe.

| | 00:10 | | 00:15 | |

American	Ingredients	Metric/Imperial
1⅔ cups	Rice	350 g / 12 oz
¼ lb	Back bacon	100 g / 4 oz
2	Garlic cloves	2
3 tbsp	Butter	40 g / 1½ oz
3	Plum tomatoes, peeled	3
	Salt and pepper	
	Grated cheese	

1. Cook rice in boiling salted water for 15 minutes. Remove rind from bacon and dice. Chop garlic.
2. Melt the butter, lightly fry the bacon, add the tomatoes, sieved to a purée, and a pinch of pepper. Cook for 5 minutes, then remove garlic.
3. Drain rice, and stir tomato sauce into rice. Spoon onto a hot serving dish and serve grated cheese separately.

Riso e ossibuchi
Rice and Marrow Bones

| | 00:10 | | 01:10 | |

American	Ingredients	Metric/Imperial
1	Celery stalk	1
1	Carrot	1
1	Garlic clove	1
3 tbsp	Olive oil	2 tbsp
½ cup	Butter	100 g / 4 oz
¾ lb	Peeled tomatoes	350 g / 12 oz
4	Large marrow bones	4
3 tbsp	White flour	2 tbsp
½ cup	Dry white wine	125 ml / 4 fl oz
	Salt and pepper	
4	Sprigs of parsley	4
1½ cups	Rice	300 g / 11 oz

1. Clean and finely chop celery, carrot and garlic. Heat oil and butter and, when foaming, fry the prepared vegetables for 3-4 minutes, stirring from time to time.
2. Add tomatoes to pan and cook for a further 2 minutes. Dip marrow bones in flour and add to pan. Pour over the wine, add seasoning and parsley, cover and cook for about 1 hour.
3. Cook rice in boiling salted water for 15 minutes, then drain. Border a large hot serving dish with rice, place the marrow bones in centre, pour over sauce and serve hot.

Risotto con gli scampi
Risotto with Prawns

| | 00:10 | | 00:22 | |

American	Ingredients	Metric/Imperial
1 lb	Cooked prawns, shelled	450 g / 1 lb
½	Onion	½
2	Small sage leaves	2
½ cup	Butter	100 g / 4 oz
½ lb	Canned peas	225 g / 8 oz
1⅔ cups	Rice	350 g / 12 oz
3 cups	Stock	750 ml / 1¼ pints
	Grated cheese	

1. Wash and rinse prawns well, then dry on a kitchen towel. Chop onion and sage leaves.
2. Heat half the butter and, when foaming, sauté onion and sage for 3 minutes to lightly brown. Add drained peas to pan with prawns and cook for a further 5 minutes, stirring all the time until prawns are lightly browned.
3. Tip rice into pan, sauté for 1 minute, pour over stock, cover and cook for 15 minutes. Off the heat stir in remaining butter and spoon onto a hot serving dish. Serve grated cheese separately.

Riso verde freddo
Cold Green Rice

⊲ 00:10 00:15 🍲

American	Ingredients	Metric/Imperial
1⅔ cups	Rice	350 g / 12 oz
12	Basil leaves	12
1 tbsp	Grated pecorino cheese	1 tbsp
1 tbsp	Pine kernels	1 tbsp
	Salt	
½ cup	Olive oil	125 ml / 4 fl oz
1	Medium-sized can tuna	1
6	Pickled gherkins	6

1. Cook rice in boiling salted water for 15 minutes then drain and leave to cool in a large serving bowl.
2. Put all but 4 basil leaves, the pecorino, pine nuts, salt and all but 1 tablespoon of olive oil into a blender goblet. Blend to a purée, adding water if mixture is too thick.
3. Drain the tuna and flake. Quarter and slice the gherkins. Mix with the rice and add remaining oil. Spoon into a serving dish, pour over the sauce and garnish with basil leaves.

Riso tricolore
Three-colored Rice

⊲ 00:10 00:20 🍲

American	Ingredients	Metric/Imperial
1⅔ cups	Rice	350 g / 12 oz
1	Small onion	1
15	Basil leaves	15
¼ cup	Butter	50 g / 2 oz
5 tbsp	Tomato purée	4 tbsp
	Salt and pepper	
1¼ cups	Grated hard cheese	150 g / 5 oz

1. Cook rice in plenty of boiling salted water for 15 minutes. Finely slice onion, chop 10 basil leaves.
2. Heat butter and, when foaming, sauté onion for 2 minutes, stir in tomato purée, add chopped basil and seasoning and cook for 5 minutes. Add remaining whole basil leaves, and simmer a further 5 minutes.
3. Drain rice and add to basil sauce in pan. Stir well and cook over a low heat for 2-3 minutes.
4. Spoon onto a hot serving dish, sprinkle over grated cheese and serve.

Risotto con le lumache
Risotto with Snails

⊲ 00:15 03:15 🍲

American	Ingredients	Metric/Imperial
1 tbsp	Cornmeal	1 tbsp
Scant ¼ cup	Vinegar	3 tbsp
48	Fresh snails	48
1	Onion	1
1	Celery stalk	1
2	Garlic cloves	2
¼ cup	Dry white wine	50 ml / 2 fl oz
2 cups	Rice	400 g / 14 oz
3 cups	Stock	750 ml / 1¼ pints
1	Bunch of parsley	1
1 cup	Grated cheese	100 g / 4 oz

1. Prepare a saucepan of salted water, add cornmeal and vinegar, put snails in and leave to boil for 3 hours. Drain and shell, then wash under a jet of hot running water.
2. Chop onion, celery and garlic. Heat oil and lightly fry onion, celery and garlic, then add snails and cook until brown. Pour over white wine, leave to evaporate, then add rice and pour over stock. Cover and cook for 15 minutes.
3. Spoon rice onto a hot serving dish, garnish with parsley and serve grated cheese separately.

Cold green rice

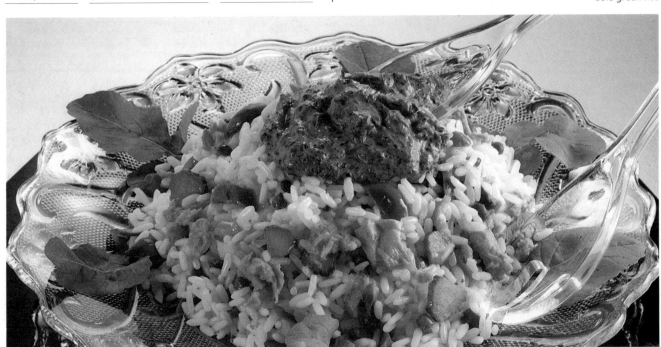

Venetian-style risotto

Risotto con carciofi
Risotto with Artichokes

⏱ 00:10   00:30 🍲

American	Ingredients	Metric/Imperial
4	Globe artichokes	4
1 tbsp	Lemon juice	1 tbsp
2	Slices of raw ham	2
⅓ cup	Butter	65 g / 2½ oz
1 tbsp	Chopped parsley	1 tbsp
1	Garlic clove	1
2 cups	Rice	400 g / 14 oz
¼ cup	White wine	50 ml / 2 fl oz
3 cups	Stock	750 ml / 1¼ pints
	Salt and pepper	
½ cup	Grated cheese	50 g / 2 oz

1. Trim artichokes, cut each one into 8 and cover with water and lemon juice. Chop ham.
2. Heat ¼ cup [50 g / 2 oz] butter and when foaming add ham, parsley and garlic and cook for 2 minutes. Stir artichokes into mixture in pan and cook gently for 10 minutes.
3. Tip rice into pan, cook for 1 minute to brown lightly. Pour over wine and stock and cook covered for 15 minutes.
4. Just before serving, taste and adjust seasoning. Stir in remaining butter and grated cheese, spoon onto a hot serving dish and serve immediately.

Risotto delicato alla veneta
Venetian-Style Risotto

⏱ 00:15   00:45 🍲

American	Ingredients	Metric/Imperial
2	Fennel bulbs	2
1	Chicken breast	1
1	Onion	1
2 tbsp	Butter	25 g / 1 oz
¼ cup	Dry white wine	50 ml / 2 fl oz
1 quart	Stock	1 litre / 1¾ pints
	Salt and pepper	
1⅔ cups	Rice	350 g / 12 oz
½ cup	Grated parmesan cheese	50 g / 2 oz

1. Clean fennel, removing outer leaves, wash thoroughly and cut into thin segments. Trim chicken of skin and bone, chop coarsely. Thinly slice onion.
2. Heat butter and, when foaming, sauté onion for 3-4 minutes to brown lightly. Add fennel and chicken, cover and cook over a low heat for 5 minutes. Pour over wine, add stock. Season with salt and pepper, cover and cook for about 30 minutes until fennel is almost falling apart.
3. Add rice to pan, cover and simmer a further 15 minutes. Before taking off the heat, stir butter into risotto with grated parmesan cheese, then spoon onto a hot serving dish and serve piping hot.

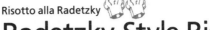

Wagon Risotto

Risotto del vagone

⏱ 00:10   00:50 🍲

American	Ingredients	Metric/Imperial
1 tbsp	Vinegar	1 tbsp
1	Sage leaf	1
8	Sausages	8
	Salt and pepper	
14 oz	Brussels sprouts	400 g / 14 oz
½ cup	Butter	100 g / 4 oz
2 cups	Coffee (single) cream	450 ml / ¾ pint
1	Stock cube	1
¼ cup	Brandy	50 ml / 2 fl oz
½ lb	Peeled tomatoes	225 g / 8 oz
1 tsp	Chopped basil	1 tsp
1⅔ cups	Rice	300 g / 12 oz
½ cup	Dry white wine	125 ml / 4 fl oz
1 quart	Stock	1 litre / 1¾ pints
½ cup	Grated parmesan	50 g / 2 oz

1. Heat a saucepan with a little water, vinegar and a sage leaf. Prick sausages and cook in the water for about 20 minutes.
2. Trim and wash the sprouts. Boil in lightly salted water for 8 minutes then drain. Melt half the butter in a pan and when foaming lightly brown sprouts. Remove from heat, pour over cream, sprinkle in stock cube and stir.
3. Drain sausages, return to heat, pour over brandy and cook a further 15 minutes.
4. Prepare sauce. Break down tomatoes to form thick purée. Melt butter in a pan, add tomato pulp and chopped basil. Cook for 5 minutes. Tip in rice, pour over wine and stock, cover and simmer for 15 minutes. Reheat sprouts in sauce but do not boil.
5. Remove rice from heat, add pepper and stir in parmesan cheese. Spoon onto the centre of a hot serving dish, arrange sausages around border of plate with the brussels sprouts and sauce. Serve hot.

Wagon risotto

Radetzky-Style Risotto

Risotto alla Radetzky

A recipe dedicated to Marshal Radetzky as he particularly liked this Milanese dish.

⏱ 00:10   00:40 🍲

American	Ingredients	Metric/Imperial
1	Small onion	1
1 oz	Beef marrow	25 g / 1 oz
¼ lb	Chicken giblets	100 g / 4 oz
½ lb	Small peas	225 g / 8 oz
2 oz	Hard cheese	50 g / 2 oz
¼ lb	Gorgonzola	100 g / 4 oz
2 oz	Dried mushrooms	50 g / 2 oz
⅓ cup	Butter	65 g / 2½ oz
1⅔ cups	Rice	350 g / 12 oz
2¼ cups	Stock	500 ml / 18 fl oz
	Salt and pepper	
2 cups	Barolo wine	450 ml / ¾ pint
1¼ cups	Béchamel sauce	300 ml / ½ pint

1. Preheat the oven to 400°F / 200°C / Gas Mark 6. Butter an ovenproof serving dish.
2. Chop onion, beef marrow and chicken giblets. Shell or defrost peas. Slice hard cheese and dice gorgonzola. Clean dried mushrooms.
3. Heat butter and, when foaming, sauté onion for 3-5 minutes to brown lightly. Add rice to pan and cook a further minute stirring all the time, then add beef marrow pieces. Pour over stock, cover and simmer for about 8 minutes.
4. Add peas, three quarters of the mushrooms, and chicken giblets to pan, season with salt and pepper, pour over wine, cover and cook a further 8 minutes until rice is just cooked.
5. Spoon rice mixture into ovenproof dish, cover with cheese slices and dabs of butter. Bake for 20 minutes until golden.
6. Meanwhile prepare sauce. Stir the rest of the mushrooms into prepared béchamel sauce with gorgonzola chunks. Stir and cook in a double saucepan until sauce is smooth and thickened. Serve with the baked risotto.

Preparing rice

There are many varieties of rice available now and it is essential for the inexperienced cook to read the manufacturer's instructions to find out if it is plain rice or one of the pre-cooked varieties. If you have bought easy-cook rice follow the instructions for best results.

- Only wash non-processed rice before cooking or when using a microwave oven.
- To boil rice, use the correct amount of water or stock and add boiling liquid to the rice.
- Take care not to over salt as the rice absorbs the liquid.
- Stir a risotto from time to time while it is cooking.

- To keep rice white when cooking in hard water, add 1 teaspoon lemon juice or 1 tablespoon vinegar.
- Only stir boiled rice when it goes into the saucepan but not during the cooking process.
- Cover the rice tightly with a lid and do not remove until the cooking time is nearly finished.
- It is not wise to leave the cooked rice in a saucepan for more than 10 minutes as it will continue to cook and form a solid mass. It is best to fork it into a heated serving dish.
- A wooden fork is useful for fluffing cooked rice, try not to use a spoon.
- Browning rice in a pan — with or without fat — prior to cooking with moisture, helps to keep the grains separate and gives the rice a good flavor.

Polenta, Pizzas and Soufflés

Polenta

To make this traditional dish Italian cooks use a 'paiolo' which is rather like a copper cauldron with a rounded bottom. This pan is not lined with tin. It is better to cook polenta in a copper pan but it can be made in any heavy saucepan.

There is now available in Italy an automatic polenta cooker with an electric beater. It is a very good purchase for a dish which requires such a long time to cook and a lot of attention from the person cooking it.

Polenta is made from maize flour which is not unlike American cornmeal. The consistency varies from region to region. In Bergamo, the home of polenta, a coarse grain cornmeal is used; in Verona it is less coarse whereas in Padua and Venice finely ground meal is much favoured. Polenta Taragna is made from equal quantities of cornmeal and wheat flour.

There are a few basic rules that you should remember when you are preparing polenta:

1. The meal should be added to the water as soon as it reaches boiling point in a steady flow.

2. Stirring is always done in a clockwise direction with a wooden spoon. A special polenta spoon is used for this and is a slightly different shape from the usual wooden spoon.

3. The polenta must be cooked for at least 50 minutes in an ordinary saucepan. It will take at least 1½ hours in a double boiler and must be stirred constantly.

Polenta
Polenta

▭◿ 00:05   00:50 ◖⊐

American	Ingredients	Metric/Imperial
2 quarts	Boiling water	2 litres / 3½ pints
2 tsp	Salt	2 tsp
3 cups	Coarsely ground cornmeal (maize)	450 g / 1 lb

1. Bring the water up to the boil with the salt in a large saucepan. Bring a kettle of water to the boil for later, if needed.
2. When the water has just boiled, sprinkle in half the cornmeal stirring always in a clockwise direction with a wooden spoon. Reduce the heat and as the mixture thickens, add a little more boiling water.

3. When the mixture is smooth, sprinkle in remaining meal continuing to stir in a clockwise direction. Add a little boiling water when the mixture becomes too thick.
4. Cook for about 45-50 minutes when the mixture should leave the sides of the pan clean. Turn onto a marble slab or clean board and form the polenta into a dome shape.
5. Serve the polenta hot or allow to cool and use as required.

Cook's tip: polenta can be eaten when it is just cooked and still hot with many of the sauces that are given in the sauce section. Alternatively, it can be allowed to cool and harden, arranged in a dish with butter and cheese with or without a savory sauce and baked in the oven. Sliced cold polenta can be served in place of bread with stews or dishes which have a rich gravy.

Polenta falcadina
Falcadina Polenta

This is a quick and very tasty method of using left-over polenta and scraps of cheese thought up by the mountain-dwellers of Falcade.

▭◿ 00:20   00:20 ◖⊐

American	Ingredients	Metric/Imperial
½ lb	Left-over cheese	225 g / 8 oz
¼ cup	Butter	50 g / 2 oz
¼ cup	Cream	50 ml / 2 fl oz
1	Basic quantity of cold polenta	1
	Salt and pepper	

1. Cut the cheese (use more if it is available) in small pieces or grate if possible.
2. Heat the butter in a pan over a low heat in a double boiler, add the cheese and allow to melt into the butter to form a cream. Add a little cream if liked.
3. Cut the polenta into little cubes slightly larger than a walnut and toss them in salted boiling water. After a few minutes, just enough time to heat the polenta, drain and season with salt and pepper.
4. Arrange the polenta in a heated serving dish and pour the creamy cheese over it.

Polenta
1. Pour the cornmeal into boiling salted water and stir clockwise with a wooden spoon.
2. When too thick to be stirred, gradually add more boiling water.
3. After about 50 minutes turn the polenta out onto a clean board.
4. Serve the hot polenta cut in slices to accompany a main meal.
5. When the polenta is cold, it can be easily cut with a cheese wire.

Polenta fritta con erbe e funghi
Fried Polenta with Herbs and Mushrooms

00:25   01:00

American	Ingredients	Metric/Imperial
1	Onion	1
Scant ¼ cup	Oil	3 tbsp
½ lb	Mushrooms	225 g / 8 oz
1 tsp	Chopped tarragon	1 tsp
	Salt	
¼ tsp	Red paprika	¼ tsp
12	Slices of polenta (see recipe opposite)	12
3 tbsp	Flour	40 g / 1½ oz
	Vegetable oil for frying	
1	Sprig of rosemary	1

1. In a frying pan lightly brown the sliced onion with a little oil, add the washed, sliced mushrooms and cook for 5 minutes over a low heat. Add chopped tarragon, salt and red paprika.
2. Prepare the polenta and halfway through cooking tip in the fried mixture.
3. When the polenta is cooked, turn out onto a suitable chopping-board and leave to cool, flattened as much as possible.
4. Cut the polenta into slices, dip it in the flour.
5. Heat the oil until hot with a little rosemary. Fry the floured slices until golden on each side. Drain and serve hot.

Polenta in bianco al forno
Baked Polenta in White Sauce

00:25   01:30

American	Ingredients	Metric/Imperial
1 lb	Cornmeal (maize)	500 g / 1 lb
¼ cup	Butter	50 g / 2 oz
¼ lb	Fontina cheese	100 g / 4 oz
	Salt and pepper	
1	Mozzarella cheese	1
1 tsp	Oregano	1 tsp
1 cup	Grated parmesan cheese	100 g / 4 oz
¼ lb	Taleggio cheese	100 g / 4 oz
1 cup	Cream	225 ml / 8 fl oz

1. Prepare a polenta, following the basic recipe for polenta (see opposite), let it cool and cut it into slices.
2. Preheat the oven to 375°F / 190°C / Gas Mark 5.
3. Butter an ovenproof dish and arrange in it a layer of polenta slices and add the finely chopped fontina. Sprinkle with freshly milled pepper and add a few knobs of butter.
4. Cover with more slices of polenta, then the thinly sliced mozzarella and sprinkle with oregano and salt. Cover with more slices of polenta, sprinkle with grated parmesan, pepper and a few knobs of butter. Cover the final layer of polenta with slices of taleggio cheese.
5. Pour the cream over the dish, moistening the surface thoroughly, place in the oven and cook for at least 30 minutes.

Pizza

It has been said that the pizza was the invention of bakers in the back streets of Naples. The poverty in this city was so great that it was a way of making a very little food stretch a long way and fill hungry stomachs.

On the other hand historians record that it was served at the palace of Casenta. King Ferdinand IV had it specially cooked in the ovens of the famous porcelaine works at Capodimarte.

Whatever historians say about pizza it has now travelled world wide and is one of the most popular 'fast foods'. It is available on most high streets all over the USA, Australia, Great Britain and many other European countries. Home-made pizzas have a slightly different texture from those cooked in a special pizza oven but are delicious because of the innumerable amount of fillings or toppings which can be used to suit the individual diner.

Pizza

Pizza Dough

	00:00	00:00
	Make 4 × 8 in / 20 cm pizza bases Rising time 01:00	

American	Ingredients	Metric/Imperial
1½ lb	All purpose (plain) flour	650 g / 1½ lb
	Salt	
1 tbsp	Dry active yeast	15 g / ½ oz
1 cup	Water	225 ml / 8 fl oz
1 tsp	Sugar	1 tsp
2 tsp	Oil	2 tsp
½ cup	Milk	125 ml / 4 fl oz

1. Sieve the flour into a large bowl with the salt, leave covered in a warm atmosphere, e.g. in the airing cupboard or above the cooker but do not allow to become hot.
2. Activate the yeast by mixing half the water with dissolved sugar at hand-hot temperature, 140°F / 43°C, and allow to ferment. Packet yeast, which can be mixed directly with the flour, requires no reconstituting. Read directions on dried yeast packets carefully.
3. Make a well in the centre of the slightly warmed flour and pour in the liquid with yeast and 1 teaspoon oil. Mix the milk with the water (tepid temperature), add gradually, mixing well to ensure the dough becomes soft and pliable, but not sticky because too much liquid has been added.
4. Knead the dough for 10 minutes, place in a bowl covered with a clean cloth or in an oiled plastic bag. Leave in a warm place to double in size (never near direct heat). This means warm room temperature rather than warm cooking temperature. The yeast cells will be killed if the temperature is too hot.
5. Knock back the dough and use as pizza bases.
6. This quantity will make 4 to 6 8 in / 20 cm pizza bases, depending on thickness or 3 larger thin bases.

Pizza alla napoletana

Neapolitan Pizza

	01:20	00:20

American	Ingredients	Metric/Imperial
¼	Pizza dough recipe	¼
1 tbsp	Olive oil	1 tbsp
6	Ripe tomatoes	6
1	Garlic clove	1
	Salt and pepper	
2	Sprigs of oregano or	2
1 tsp	Dried oregano	1 tsp
6	Basil leaves	6

1. Preheat the oven to 450°F / 220°C / Gas Mark 7.
2. Knock back the risen dough, roll it into the shape of a pizza pan or 8 in / 20 cm tart pan or even a flan ring on an oiled baking sheet. Brush pan well with olive oil.
3. Work the dough until the pan is lined and if liked make a round edge.
4. Skin the tomatoes by plunging into boiling water, blend or sieve the tomatoes to make a purée, mix with crushed garlic. Use canned plum tomatoes if fresh are unavailable or expensive. Season well.
5. Brush the dough with olive oil, spread with tomato and garlic purée. Sprinkle with chopped oregano and basil and brush with oil.
6. Bake in a very hot oven for 15-20 minutes until cooked. Serve hot.

Variations

Pizza bases can be filled with toppings to suit the individual taste. Use the basic tomato base with the following toppings:

Anchovies, olives and parmesan cheese
Anchovies and mozzarella cheese
Mushrooms, fried onion and parmesan cheese
Blanched green sweet peppers and salami with cheese
Chopped chilli with cheese
Tuna fish, capers and anchovies
Ham, mortadella or any spicy sausage or salami
Use a béchamel sauce (see page 162) in place of the tomato filling
Top with ham and various cheeses (mozzarella is the most suitable)
Mushrooms and chopped parsley
Lightly fried onions with herbs
Sliced tomatoes and sweet peppers
Bacon with cheese
Prawns with cheese

1

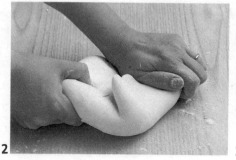

2

3

Pizza

1. Make a well in the centre of the flour, add sugar, water, yeast, oil and milk.

2. Knead dough for 10 minutes and leave to double in size.

3. Roll out the dough to fit the pizza pan or spread it out with your knuckles.

4. Spoon tomato purée over the base and sprinkle with herbs.

5. Add diced cheese and a light covering of olive oil.

Bake in a hot oven for 15-20 minutes until cooked.

Sauces

Ragu alla cacciatora
Beef Sauce for Pasta and Gnocchi

00:10   01:40

American	Ingredients	Metric/Imperial
1	Onion	1
1	Carrot	1
1	Celery stalk	1
¼ cup	Butter	50 g / 2 oz
⅓ cup	Oil	5 tbsp
1 oz	Dried mushrooms	25 g / 1 oz
1	Garlic clove	1
1 cup	Ground (minced) beef	225 g / 8 oz
	Salt and pepper	
½ cup	Red wine	125 ml / 4 fl oz
1 lb	Peeled tomatoes	450 g / 1 lb
1	Bay leaf	1

1. Finely chop onion, carrot and celery. Melt butter and oil and sauté vegetables for 2 minutes. Soak mushrooms in hot water and when soft, chop coarsely and add to the pan with a peeled crushed clove of garlic.
2. Cook these ingredients together for about 5 minutes then add the meat, salt and pepper and brown thoroughly.
3. Pour in the wine, then add the tomatoes. Crush a bay leaf and add to the sauce. Cover and simmer over a low heat for about 1½ hours.

Cook's tip: this sauce can be frozen for up to 6 months.

To freeze: cool, quickly pour into small containers, cover, seal and label.

To reheat: from frozen put in a moderate oven for 45 minutes or reheat in a saucepan over a very low heat.
In a microwave, select thaw or defrost setting and stir from time to time. Cook on 'High' for 3-4 minutes.

Carbonara
Egg and Bacon Sauce

00:10   00:15

American	Ingredients	Metric/Imperial
5 oz	Streaky bacon	150 g / 5 oz
2	Eggs	2
2	Egg yolks	2
¾ cup	Grated pecorino cheese	75 g / 3 oz
	Pepper	
1 lb	Spaghetti	450 g / 1 lb

1. Cut bacon into thin strips and brown gently over a low heat. Break eggs into a bowl with the egg yolks and whisk lightly. Grate the pecorino and add to the eggs. Continue whisking with a fork to ensure the mixture is smooth.
2. Put spaghetti on to cook in boiling salted water with a dash of oil added. When pasta is 'al dente', drain and put straight into the pan with the bacon.
3. Pour the egg and cheese mixture on top of the spaghetti and mix quickly, keeping the pan over the heat to keep the pasta hot.

4. Season generously with pepper and serve.

Variations
1. Fry a clove of crushed garlic in a tablespoon of oil, and then add the bacon.
2. Add 2 tablespoons cream to the eggs for a creamier sauce.

Sughi per bollito misto
Green and Red Sauces for Mixed Meat Dishes

00:35   00:00
Standing time 02:00 to 03:00

American	Ingredients	Metric/Imperial
Green sauce		
1	Large bunch of parsley	1
1	Hard-cooked (boiled) egg	1
	The inside of a bread roll	
3 tbsp	Vinegar	2 tbsp
½	Sweet red pepper	½
½	Sweet yellow pepper	½
4	Anchovies in salt	4
	Salt	
½ cup	Virgin olive oil	125 ml / 4 fl oz
1	Garlic clove	1
Red sauce		
1 lb	Tomatoes	500 g / 1 lb
1	Onion	1
1	Sweet green pepper	1
1	Carrot	1
1	Celery stalk	1
1 tbsp	Basil	1 tbsp
	Salt	
1	Chilli pepper	1
1 tsp	Olive oil	1 tsp

Green Sauce
1. Clean parsley, remove stalks, rinse thoroughly and dry. Shell the egg, soak bread in vinegar and when the vinegar has been absorbed, squeeze it out by hand. Wash and cut sweet peppers into thin strips, and remove filaments and seeds. Wash and fillet anchovies, then chop all the ingredients together on a board.
2. Transfer to a bowl, add salt, stir in the olive oil to obtain the right consistency and then add the halved garlic. Leave for a few hours and then remove garlic. Chop garlic finely with the other ingredients if it is to be retained in sauce.

Red Sauce
1. Clean, wash and coarsely chop the tomatoes, onion, sweet pepper, carrot, celery and basil.
2. Heat all these ingredients together in a covered pan over a low heat, adding a little water if there is not enough liquid from the tomatoes.
3. When cooked, rub through a sieve, return to pan and continue cooking, stirring frequently. Season with salt. Just before serving, remove from heat, crumble in the chilli and stir in a trickle of oil.
4. Serve thickened sauce either hot or cold.

Cook's tip: if you wish, the ingredients for the green sauce can be finely chopped in a blender or food processor before adding the olive oil.

Green and red sauces

Ragu
Bolognese Sauce

⏱ 00:15   🍲 01:15

American	Ingredients	Metric/Imperial
1	Carrot	1
1	Medium-sized onion	1
1	Celery stalk	1
2½ oz	Bacon	65 g / 2½ oz
2 tbsp	Butter	25 g / 1 oz
Scant ¼ cup	Olive oil	3 tbsp
5 oz	Sausage meat	150 g / 5 oz
1 cup	Ground (minced) beef	225 g / 8 oz
½ cup	Red wine	125 ml / 4 fl oz
1 cup	Tomato sauce	225 ml / 8 fl oz
½ cup	Stock	125 ml / 4 fl oz
	Salt and pepper	

1. Finely chop the carrot, onion, celery and bacon. Heat the butter and oil in a saucepan over a low heat, and sauté prepared vegetables until golden brown.
2. Break the sausage meat up with a fork and add to the beef and stir thoroughly. After a few minutes, pour in red wine and allow to evaporate, keeping the heat turned low.
3. When all the wine has evaporated, pour in the tomato sauce and the hot stock. Stir in and leave to simmer for at least 1 hour over a low heat, stirring from time to time with a wooden spoon. If the sauce becomes too dry, add more stock.
4. Finally taste and adjust seasoning, adding salt if necessary and freshly milled pepper and cook for a further 5 minutes.
5. Serve with tagliatelle (made with eggs), spaghetti and other pasta. Coarsely chopped mushrooms may be added to the chopped vegetables if wished.

Salsa al vino rosso
Red Wine Sauce

⏱ 00:10   🍲 00:30

American	Ingredients	Metric/Imperial
1 cup	Stock	225 ml / 8 fl oz
½ cup	Red wine	125 ml / 4 fl oz
1	Bay leaf	1
1 tbsp	Chopped onion	1 tbsp
1 tbsp	Chopped parsley	1 tbsp
	Salt and pepper	
4 tbsp	Butter	50 g / 2 oz
½ cup	Flour	50 g / 2 oz

1. Bring the stock to the boil together with the wine. Simmer very gently for a few minutes, add the bay leaf, chopped onion and parsley. Season with salt and freshly milled pepper.
2. Melt the butter in another saucepan and as soon as it begins to sizzle, blend in the flour, stirring vigorously to obtain a smooth mixture.
3. Add the boiling stock to the butter and flour, pouring in gradually. Continue stirring and simmer for a further 20 minutes until the sauce has thickened. Red wine sauce should be served hot. Serve with steak, chops or poached eggs.

Salsa per pasta
Hot Sauce for Pasta

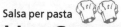

⏱ 00:20   🍲 00:20

American	Ingredients	Metric/Imperial
1	Large onion	1
¼ cup	Butter	50 g / 2 oz
	Pinch of salt	
1 tsp	Flour	1 tsp
1 cup	Whipping (double) cream	225 ml / 8 fl oz
¼ cup	Brandy	50 ml / 2 fl oz
1	Red chilli pepper	1
2 lb	Ripe tomatoes	1 kg / 2 lb
1 lb	Shell pasta	450 g / 1 lb
½ cup	Grated parmesan cheese	50 g / 2 oz
	Few fresh basil leaves	

1. Finely chop the onion, heat butter and sauté the onion until soft but not brown. Sprinkle with salt, add the flour and cook for 2 minutes, stirring with a wooden spoon.
2. Allow to cool slightly then mix in the cream and bring to the boil, stirring with a wooden spoon until the sauce thickens, then add the brandy and deseeded chopped chilli.
3. Peel and sieve all but 6 of the tomatoes, adding the sieved mixture to the sauce.
4. Meanwhile, cook the pasta in boiling salted water. When the pasta is 'al dente', drain and pour into the pan containing the sauce, add parmesan, cut the remaining tomatoes into strips and add these with the chopped basil leaves to the sauce. Allow the pasta to absorb the sauce for a few minutes over a low heat, then serve.

Salsa di pomodoro con fegatini
Tomato and Chicken Liver Sauce

⏱ 00:20   🍲 00:35

American	Ingredients	Metric/Imperial
½	Onion	½
2 oz	Raw ham	50 g / 2 oz
2 tbsp	Butter	25 g / 1 oz
1 cup	Fresh mushrooms	100 g / 4 oz
2 oz	Chicken livers	50 g / 2 oz
1 cup	Tomato sauce	225 ml / 8 fl oz
	Salt and pepper	
1	Small bunch of parsley	1
½ cup	Dry red wine	125 ml / 4 fl oz

1. Finely chop the onion and cut the ham into thin strips. Heat these in the butter in a saucepan and cook over a very low heat for about 10 minutes.
2. Thickly slice the mushrooms, add to the pan and cook for a few minutes stirring with a wooden spoon.
3. Coarsely chop the chicken livers and add to the other ingredients together with the tomato sauce and a little pepper. Stir and bring to the boil. Boil for a few seconds then turn down the heat again and simmer for 15 minutes, stirring constantly.
4. Chop the parsley. Heat the wine in another saucepan and reduce by a half. Add this to the sauce with the parsley.
5. Serve with cooked tagliatelle or any other pasta.

Al tonno e ai piselli
Tuna and Pea Sauce

 00:20   00:20

American	Ingredients	Metric/Imperial
1	Medium-sized onion	1
Scant ¼ cup	Olive oil	3 tbsp
1 cup	Tomato juice	225 ml / 8 fl oz
14 oz	Fresh peas, unshelled	400 g / 14 oz
¼ lb	Tuna	100 g / 4 oz
1 cup	Stock	225 ml / 8 fl oz
	Salt and pepper	

1. Peel and finely chop the onion. Heat oil and sauté onion until it begins to turn golden. Add the tomato juice and simmer for a few minutes.
2. Shell the peas, add to the pan and continue to simmer for 15 minutes, adding a little stock if tomato juice has reduced too much. Stir from time to time.
3. When the peas are cooked, break up drained tuna fish with a fork and add to the pan. Cook for 5 minutes then taste and adjust seasoning.
4. Serve with boiled rice.

Salsa per beccaccia e tordi
Sauce for Woodcock

 00:20   00:10

American	Ingredients	Metric/Imperial
2	Anchovy fillets	2
1	Small onion	1
1	Shallot	1
1	Small bunch of parsley	1
¼ tsp	Basil	¼ tsp
¼ tsp	Sage	¼ tsp
¼ tsp	Rosemary	¼ tsp
¼ tsp	Thyme	¼ tsp
½ lb	Spinach	225 g / 8 oz
½ lb	Endive	225 g / 8 oz
4 tbsp	Butter	50 g / 2 oz
3 tbsp	Oil	2 tbsp
⅔ cup	Reduced meat stock or diluted stock cube	150 ml / ¼ pint
1	Egg yolk	1
1 oz	Capers	25 g / 1 oz
1	Lemon	1

1. Clean and finely chop anchovy fillets. Chop onion, shallot, parsley, basil, sage, rosemary and thyme. Wash and chop spinach and endive and add these to the other chopped ingredients.
2. Heat butter and oil together, then sauté prepared ingredients for a few minutes, and stir in a little reduced stock. Remove from heat, stir in the egg yolk, rinsed and dried capers and lemon juice. Mix again and heat over a bain-marie before serving in a sauceboat.

Cook's tip: woodcock should be hung for up to a week before plucking and cooking. They are considered to be a special delicacy when cooked with all their innards (apart from the gizzard but including the brain). They are roasted undrawn.

Salsa al pomodoro
Tomato Sauce

 00:30   00:50

American	Ingredients	Metric/Imperial
2 lb	Tomatoes	1 kg / 2 lb
1 tbsp	Oil	1 tbsp
2 tbsp	Butter	25 g / 1 oz
1	Onion	1
2	Garlic cloves	2
1	Carrot	1
1 tbsp	Flour	1 tbsp
2 lb	Tomatoes	1 kg / 2 lb
½ tsp	Basil	½ tsp
1	Bay leaf	1
½ tsp	Thyme	½ tsp
½ tsp	Sugar	½ tsp
	Salt and pepper	
1 tbsp	Tomato purée	1 tbsp
½ cup	White wine (optional)	125 ml / 4 fl oz

1. Plunge the tomatoes into boiling water, remove the skins and drain.
2. Heat the oil and butter in a pan over a low heat, add the peeled and finely chopped onion and the crushed garlic. Allow to cook for 5 minutes, stirring from time to time. Add the grated carrot, stir for 1 minute then add the flour and stir well until the vegetables have absorbed it.
3. Add the remaining ingredients with 1 cup [225 ml / 8 fl oz] water and the wine, allow to simmer for 45 minutes on a low heat. Remove bay leaf and sprigs of herbs before serving or using in other dishes.

Cook's tip: for a smooth tomato sauce, pass through a sieve, blender or food processor.

Salsa di prugne
Prune Sauce

 00:10   00:35

American	Ingredients	Metric/Imperial
½	Onion	½
1 oz	Raw ham	25 g / 1 oz
2 tbsp	Butter	25 g / 1 oz
¼ cup	Vinegar	50 ml / 2 fl oz
10	Prunes	10
	Salt	
1	Bay leaf	1
4	Sprigs of thyme	4

1. Chop the onion and ham, heat the butter and sauté onion and ham over a moderate heat until onion is transparent. Pour over the vinegar and boil until half of it has evaporated.
2. Meanwhile stone the prunes, and add to the onions and ham. Pour in enough water to cover, add salt, bay leaf and thyme. Cover the pan and cook over a low heat until the prunes have softened, about 20 minutes.
3. Rub the prunes through a sieve and mix thoroughly with the juices from the pan. Reheat and serve as an accompaniment to loin of pork.

Paté di tonno
Tuna Butter

◢ 00:20   00:00 🍲

American	Ingredients	Metric/Imperial
¼ lb	Tuna	100 g / 4 oz
⅔ cup	Softened butter	150 g / 5 oz
3 tbsp	Brandy	2 tbsp

1. Drain can of tuna and break up fish with a fork or vegetable chopper to produce a smooth paste.
2. Beat butter until creamy, then beat in the tuna until the ingredients are well mixed. Finally pour in brandy and mix again.
3. Use for canapés or on grilled fish.

Salsa esotica Pili Pili
Exotic Chilli Sauce

◢ 00:10   00:00 🍲
Standing time 5-6 days

American	Ingredients	Metric/Imperial
20	Small red dried chilli peppers	20
3 tbsp	Coarse salt	2 tbsp
1 tbsp	Unrefined sugar	1 tbsp
	White vinegar	
	Oil	

1. Put the chillies in a glass jar. Sprinkle with salt and sugar. Pour over the white vinegar until the chillies are completely covered and then pour on a layer of oil about ¼ in / 1 cm deep to keep the air out. Cover and leave to marinate for at least 5 or 6 days. The longer you leave it to marinate, the hotter the chilli sauce will be.
2. Serve with Creole rice, couscous or with raw fish.

Pesto alla genovese
Garlic and Basil Sauce

◢ 00:30   00:00 🍲

American	Ingredients	Metric/Imperial
¼ lb	Fresh basil	100 g / 4 oz
1 oz	Marjoram	25 g / 1 oz
1 oz	Parsley	25 g / 1 oz
1	Garlic clove	1
¼ cup	Mixed grated pecorino and parmesan cheeses	25 g / 1 oz
6 tbsp	Olive oil	5 tbsp

1. Crush basil, marjoram, parsley and garlic using a pestle and mortar, blender or food processor. Add pecorino and parmesan. Continue to crush and add oil in a thin trickle. Taste and adjust seasoning.

Variation: the marjoram can be omitted, and parsley reduced to half the quantity.

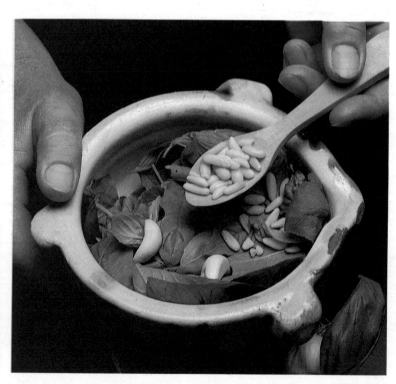

Garlic and basil sauce

Salsa con acciughe
Anchovy Sauce

⊿ 00:20   00:00 🍲

American	Ingredients	Metric/Imperial
2	Fresh anchovies	2
1 tbsp	Vinegar	1 tbsp
10	Black olives	10
	Pepper	
6 tbsp	Olive oil	5 tbsp

1. Thoroughly wash and fillet the anchovies then finely chop them and put them in a bowl. Pour over the vinegar and crush with a fork (the vinegar will gradually soften the anchovy).
2. Stone the olives and finely chop, then add to the anchovy. Mix in a little freshly grated pepper and finally pour over the olive oil, a little at a time, combining it with the other ingredients.
3. Continue stirring the mixture to obtain a thick, tasty sauce and serve as an accompaniment for veal, and grilled chicken breast.

Salsa menta
Mint Sauce

⊿ 00:15   00:00 🍲

American	Ingredients	Metric/Imperial
2 oz	Mint leaves	50 g / 2 oz
	The inside of a bread roll	
½ cup	White vinegar	125 ml / 4 fl oz
½ cup	Confectioner's (icing) sugar	50 g / 2 oz
	Salt	

1. Finely chop the mint leaves. Soak the bread in the vinegar in a bowl. Strain and reserve the vinegar. Squeeze the bread and rub it through a sieve.
2. Add sugar, a pinch of salt and vinegar to the bread crumbs in a bowl and stir in the mint. Mix thoroughly to obtain a smooth creamy sauce.
3. Pour into a sauceboat and serve with spit roast lamb.

Crema al limone
Lemon Sauce

⊿ 00:15   00:00 🍲

American	Ingredients	Metric/Imperial
¼ cup	Softened butter	50 g / 2 oz
¼ cup	Cream cheese	50 g / 2 oz
1	Lemon	1
	Salt	

1. Beat butter to a soft paste, then beat in the cream cheese. Grate the lemon, squeeze juice and add rind and juice to cheese mixture with salt.
2. Use to stuff celery stalks or to accompany crudités.

Salsa di ciliege
Cherry Sauce

⊿ 00:05   00:15 🍲

American	Ingredients	Metric/Imperial
1	Orange	1
½ cup	Marsala wine	125 ml / 4 oz
¼ tsp	Cinnamon powder	¼ tsp
⅓ cup	Redcurrant jelly	100 g / 4 oz
1½ cups	Cherries in syrup	350 g / 12 oz

1. Cut the orange peel into matchsticks, then squeeze to obtain the juice. Heat peel and juice in a saucepan with the marsala. Cook over a low heat until half the liquid has evaporated. Add cinnamon and the redcurrant jelly.
2. When the jelly has dissolved, drain the cherries and add to the pan. As soon as the sauce begins to boil pour it into a sauceboat.
3. Serve with venison or fillet of pork.

Salsa di mirtilli
Cranberry Sauce

⊿ 00:20   00:10 🍲

American	Ingredients	Metric/Imperial
2 cups	Cranberries	225 g / 8 oz
	Sugar to taste	

1. Wash the cranberries well. Remove leaves and stalks and put the berries in a saucepan. Cover with water and boil for a few minutes.
2. Remove the cranberries with a slotted spoon, retaining the liquid, strain and rub them through a fine sieve, a few at a time. Pour the purée back into the pan and dilute with the cooking water, adding 1 tablespoon at a time, until the sauce has the desired consistency. Add sugar to taste.
3. Serve with roast turkey.

Salsa alla mela
Apple Sauce

⊿ 00:15   00:00 🍲

American	Ingredients	Metric/Imperial
1	Large apple	1
¼ lb	Fontina cheese	100 g / 4 oz
2 oz	Cooked ham	50 g / 2 oz
¼ cup	Walnuts	25 g / 1 oz
5 tbsp	Olive oil	4 tbsp
	Salt and pepper	
½	Lemon	½

1. Peel and dice apple. Put into a bowl and add diced fontina, strips of ham, and peeled and coarsely chopped walnuts.
2. Season with oil, salt, pepper and lemon juice, mix and pour over boiled, well-drained rice. Serve cold.

Herbs play an important part in flavoring sauces. In the basket left to right: Rosemary, parsley, thyme, chives, fennel, bay leaves, chervil, sage, coriander, marjoram, basil.

Soups

Zucchini soup

Minestra di zucchine

Zucchini [Courgette] Soup

00:15   00:35

American	Ingredients	Metric/Imperial
3 tbsp	Vegetable oil	2 tbsp
1	Sliced onion	1
6	Zucchini (courgettes)	6
2	Potatoes	2
12	Peeled tomatoes	12
2 quarts	Stock	2 litres / 3½ pints
¾ lb	Pasta	350 g / 12 oz
¼ tsp	Nutmeg	¼ tsp
3	Sprigs of parsley	3

1. Heat the oil in a large saucepan, add the chopped onion and cook for 3 minutes.
2. Wash and dice the zucchini, peel and dice the potatoes.
3. Add the tomatoes to the onion and then stir in the zucchini and the potatoes, allow to brown over a medium heat for a few minutes.
4. Add the stock and cook for 10 minutes, throw in the pasta and cook until it is 'al dente'.
5. Serve the soup sprinkled with a little grated nutmeg and finely chopped parsley.

Minestrone al pesto

Minestrone with Garlic and Basil Sauce

00:40   00:60
Soaking time 12:00

American	Ingredients	Metric/Imperial
5 oz	Haricot beans	150 g / 5 oz
1 oz	Dried mushrooms	25 g / 1 oz
2	Eggplant (aubergines)	2
¼ lb	Green beans	100 g / 4 oz
3	Potatoes	3
1	Red cabbage	1
¼ lb	Zucchini (courgettes)	100 g / 4 oz
2 oz	Pumpkin	50 g / 2 oz
4	Peeled tomatoes	4
3 tbsp	Vegetable oil	2 tbsp
2 oz	Pasta or rice	50 g / 2 oz
	Garlic and basil sauce	

1. Allow beans to soak overnight and soak dried mushrooms.
2. Bring 2 quarts [2 litres / 3½ pints] water to the boil and put in the beans and cook for 40 minutes. Dice the eggplant and green beans. Peel and dice the potatoes, and slice and chop the red cabbage. Slice the zucchini and dice the pumpkin. Add the vegetables, the peeled tomatoes, oil and dried mushrooms to the beans. Season well. When the ingredients are almost cooked, put in the pasta or rice, according to choice.
3. Before serving the soup, add a good helping of the garlic and basil sauce to the pan. Serve very hot.

Cook's tip: this also makes an excellent cold dish, which will keep for several days.

Minestrone toscano

Tuscan Minestrone

00:30   01:40

American	Ingredients	Metric/Imperial
11 oz	Shelled white beans	300 g / 11 oz
2 oz	Parsley	50 g / 2 oz
1	Small onion	1
1	Celery stalk	1
2	Small carrots	2
1	Sprig of rosemary	1
2	Basil leaves	2
1	Garlic clove	1
2 oz	Bacon	50 g / 2 oz
½ cup	Olive oil	125 ml / 4 fl oz
4	Tomatoes	4
½	Savoy cabbage	½
2 or 3	Thyme leaves	2 or 3
	Salt and pepper	
5 oz	Pasta	150 g / 5 oz

1. Boil the beans in plenty of water and add salt towards the end of the cooking time. When they are cooked, drain, reserving the cooking water, and sieve or blend half of them.
2. While the beans are cooking, prepare the other ingredients. Chop the parsley, onion, celery, peeled carrots, sprig of rosemary and the basil together with the garlic clove and the bacon.
3. Heat the oil in a large pan, add the vegetable and herb mixture, cook gently over a low heat for 5 minutes, then add the peeled and chopped tomatoes, shredded cabbage, thyme, the sieved and whole beans.
4. Add 2 quarts [2 litres / 3¼ pints] cooking water from the beans made up with water or stock. Season lightly with salt and pepper. Cook on a slow heat for 40 minutes, then add the cabbage and the pasta. Serve without cheese when the pasta is cooked.

Cook's tip: if using dried haricot beans, soak overnight before cooking.

Garlic and basil sauce

Minestra di bue
Beef Stew

	00:10		01:30

American	Ingredients	Metric/Imperial
1 lb	Spinach	500 g / 1 lb
1 lb	Stewing beef	500 g / 1 lb
2 quarts	Stock	2 litres / 3½ pints
1	Egg	1
1 tbsp	Grated parmesan cheese	1 tbsp
⅔ cup	Rice	150 g / 5 oz
	Salt and pepper	
¼ tsp	Nutmeg	¼ tsp

1. Wash and cook the spinach for 4 minutes, drain well then chop finely.
2. Slice the beef and bring to the boil in the stock or water, then simmer until well cooked.
3. Add the spinach, the egg and the parmesan to the stock and continue cooking until the meat is very well cooked. Break up the larger pieces of meat with a fork or whisk, place on the heat again and bring the stock to the boil.
4. Add the rice and continue cooking until the rice is tender and the stock reduced.
5. Season with salt and add a pinch of nutmeg. Pour into a soup tureen and serve piping hot.

Minestrone alla milanese
Milanese-Style Minestrone

	01:00		02:00
	Soaking time for beans 12:00		

American	Ingredients	Metric/Imperial
2	Carrots	2
2	Celery stalks	2
3	Leeks	3
2	Potatoes	2
1	Small zucchini (courgette)	1
½	Cabbage	½
2 oz	French beans	50 g / 2 oz
4	Ripe plum tomatoes	4
¼ lb	Spinach	100 g / 4 oz
1	Onion	1
1	Bunch of basil leaves	1
1	Small bunch of parsley	1
¼ lb	Bacon	100 g / 4 oz
5 tbsp	Butter	65 g / 2½ oz
6 tbsp	Vegetable oil	5 tbsp
2 oz	Haricot beans (soaked)	50 g / 2 oz
2 quarts	Stock	2 litres / 3½ pints
1 cup	Rice	200 g / 7 oz
	Salt and pepper	
⅓ cup	Frozen peas	50 g / 2 oz
	Parmesan cheese	

1. Scrape and dice the carrots. Slice the celery and the leeks. Peel, wash and dice the potatoes. Halve the zucchini and cut it first into slices, then into small cubes. Strip the leaves from the cabbage and cut into strips. Trim the beans and cut into two or three pieces. Wash the tomatoes and cut into pieces. Wash the spinach well and cut it into strips. Peel the onion and chop it finely together with the basil and parsley.
2. Cut the bacon into very small strips or cubes and fry it with the onion and herbs in a large saucepan in the heated butter and oil for 5 minutes. Add the tomatoes. After a few minutes, put all the prepared vegetables in the pot together with the soaked haricot beans.
3. Stir and allow the flavors to mingle; then moisten with the hot stock, season with salt and pepper and cook gently for 1½ hours, covered.
4. At the end of this time, pour in the rice and cook for 15 minutes; it should still be quite firm. Then add the peas, cook for 10 minutes, switch off the heat, cover and allow to rest for 5 minutes. Serve with grated parmesan.

Minestrone alla genovese
Genoese Minestrone

	01:00		01:00
	Soaking time for dried beans 12:00		

American	Ingredients	Metric/Imperial
¼ lb	Dried beans	100 g / 4 oz
4 tbsp	Olive oil	3 tbsp
1	Onion	1
1	Celery stalk	1
1	Slice of raw ham	1
1	Small savoy cabbage	1
2	Carrots	2
6	Swiss chard leaves	6
6	Lettuce leaves	6
1 tbsp	Tomatoe purée	1 tbsp
2 quarts	Stock	2 litres / 1¾ pints
2	Garlic cloves	2
5	Sprigs of parsley	5
3	Basil leaves	3
3	Rosemary leaves	3
½ cup	Grated parmesan cheese	50 g / 2 oz
1	Chilli pepper	1
½ lb	Pasta	225 g / 8 oz

1. Boil the beans in lightly salted water; if using dried beans, leave them soaking in warm water for 12 hours.
2. Pour half the oil into a soup pan over a low heat and put in the chopped onion, celery and the ham cut into thin strips and allow to cook until golden.
3. Add cabbage, chopped carrots, chard and the washed lettuce cut into thin strips, the boiled beans and finally 1 tablespoon of tomato purée. Pour the stock into the pan, bring to the boil and simmer.
4. Meanwhile chop some garlic with the parsley and a few leaves of basil and rosemary, then add grated parmesan, chilli pepper and remaining oil. Reduce these ingredients to a pulp by crushing vigorously and then sieve them. (This can be done in a blender or food processor.)
5. As soon as the vegetables are ready, add the pasta, also mixing in the 'pulp'. Stir, and when the pasta is still rather firm, sprinkle with parmesan. Serve after a few minutes.

Crema del pellegrino
Pilgrims' Soup

00:30   00:45

American	Ingredients	Metric/Imperial
4	Carrots	4
⅓ cup	Butter	75 g / 3 oz
	Salt and pepper	
4	Chicken livers	4
1 tbsp	Port	1 tbsp
1 quart	Chicken stock	1 litre / 1¾ pints
3 tbsp	Semolina	2 tbsp
½ cup	Grated parmesan cheese	50 g / 2 oz

1. Scrape the carrots and cut into even slices. Melt half the butter in a saucepan, stir in the carrots, adding salt and pepper to taste. Cover with water and cook for 30 minutes. Drain and pass through a sieve or food processor, collecting the purée in a bowl.
2. Clean the chicken livers and dice. Melt the remaining butter in a frying pan and brown the livers over a brisk heat. Season with a pinch of salt, moisten with the port and allow to evaporate.
3. Bring the chicken stock to the boil and sprinkle over the semolina, stirring continuously. After 10 minutes cooking, add the carrot purée and continue cooking for a further 5 minutes, stirring all the time. Finally mix in the chicken livers and the grated parmesan.

Zuppa di cipolle
Onion Soup

This is a more sophisticated version of the popular 'soupe a l'oignon'.

00:45   01:10

American	Ingredients	Metric/Imperial
4	Onions	4
⅓ cup	Butter	75 g / 3 oz
5 tbsp	Flour	4 tbsp
2 quarts	Stock	2 litres / 3½ cups
2	Egg yolks	2
	Salt	
4	Slices of bread	4
½ cup	Grated parmesan cheese	50 g / 2 oz
½ cup	Emmental cheese	50 g / 2 oz

1. Peel and wash the onions, slice thinly. Heat some of the butter, add onion and allow to fry gently in a saucepan. Cook the onions slowly until they are transparent, stirring very frequently.
2. Add the white flour, mix well and dissolve it by pouring in the stock, a little at a time to avoid lumps forming. Bring to the boil and simmer for about 1 hour.
3. Sieve, and use just the cooking water if you like a delicately flavored soup. If, on the other hand, you prefer a stronger taste, sieve the onions and put them back in the stock.
4. Put the egg yolks in a bowl, break them with a fork, add salt, stirring all the time, then add the soup a little at a time.
5. Preheat the oven to 400°F / 200°C / Gas Mark 6.

6. Slice a homemade loaf, or use a sliced loaf, and brown the slices in butter in a frying pan; drain and use them to line the bottom of four small pottery ovenproof dishes, preferably with a handle.
7. Sprinkle grated parmesan cheese over the bread, pour over some soup, then sprinkle over with more cheese, but this time it should be emmental cut into flakes.
8. Dust with a generous twist of pepper and then place the dishes in a hot oven until the cheese has melted.

Zuppa all'aglio
Garlic Soup

00:25   00:60

American	Ingredients	Metric/Imperial
16	Garlic cloves	16
1	Clove	1
1	Sprig of thyme	1
1	Sprig of sage	1
16	Bread	16
½ cup	Grated cheese	50 g / 2 oz
	Salt and pepper	
	Slices of bread	

1. Put the peeled garlic, clove, thyme and sage in 1 quart [1 litre / 1¾ pints] of water, season with salt and pepper and bring to the boil. Simmer briskly for 30 minutes.
2. Preheat the oven to 400°F / 200°C / Gas Mark 6.
3. Butter an oven tray and place on it the slices of bread sprinkled with grated cheese; brown them in the oven.
4. Soak 8 of the crisp slices until they are thoroughly saturated in the soup, after it has been taken from the heat, then purée the mixture in a blender or food processor.
5. Arrange the remaining 8 slices of bread in individual bowls, cover with the purée and serve.

Zuppa della Valsesia
Valsesia Soup

This is a well-loved soup eaten by the shepherds of Valsesia; many of the ingredients grown and produced in the valleys are used in this dish.

00:35   01:00

American	Ingredients	Metric/Imperial
2	Potatoes	2
1	Onion	1
1	Leek	1
2	Celery stalks	2
1	Garlic clove	1
1	Stock cube	1
2 slices	Rye bread	2 slices
¼ lb	Toma or fontina cheese	100 g / 4 oz

1. Peel the potatoes and cut them into small pieces; chop the onion, the washed leek, celery and a clove of garlic.
2. Put all the ingredients into a pot, season well. Pour over 1 quart [1 litre / 1¾ pints] of water, with a crumbled stock cube. Cover the pot and cook for 1 hour.
3. When the soup is ready to serve, add some cubes of rye bread and cheese.

Fresh ingredients for soup

Minestra di fagioli alla bolognese

Bolognaise Bean Soup

	02:00	01:30
	Soaking time 12:00	

American	Ingredients	Metric/Imperial
7 oz	Dried beans	200 g / 7 oz
	Salt and pepper	
2 or 3	Garlic cloves	2 or 3
3 tbsp	Olive oil	2 tbsp
1	Small bunch of parsley	1
¾ lb	Very ripe tomatoes, puréed or	350 g / 12 oz
1¼ cups	Tomato sauce	300 ml / ½ pint
¾ lb	Pasta	350 g / 12 oz
½ cup	Grated grana cheese	50 g / 2 oz

1. Soak the dried beans overnight in cold water. The following day put them in 2 quarts [2 litres / 3½ pints] of cold water and boil, adding salt at the end of cooking. When beans are quite tender, drain and reserve the water.
2. Fry garlic in a pan with heated olive oil. As soon as the garlic is browned, add a little chopped parsley, the tomato purée and the boiled beans. Cook for 15 minutes, then add the cooking water from the beans.
3. At this point you can proceed in different ways, either sieve or blend (liquidize) everything, or leave the beans whole. Alternatively, sieve only half of them; this is a matter of personal taste.
4. When the soup begins to boil, throw in the pasta. Allow to cook, pour into a soup tureen and accompany it with a generous portion of grated cheese, chopped parsley and pepper to taste.

Zuppa del diavolo

Devil's Soup

	00:45	01:00

American	Ingredients	Metric/Imperial
2 quarts	Stock	2 litres / 3½ pints
¾ lb	Cooked ham	350 g / 12 oz
¾ lb	Mortadella	350 g / 12 oz
2	Garlic cloves	2
1	Onion	1
5	Sprigs of parsley	5
2 or 3	Basil leaves	2 or 3
1¼ cups	Spinach	250 g / 9 oz
¾ lb	Noodles	350 g / 12 oz
1 cup	Cream	225 ml / 8 fl oz
½ cup	Cognac	125 ml / 4 fl oz
¼ lb	Peas	100 g / 4 oz
½ cup	Butter	100 g / 4 oz
	Grated cheese	

1. Prepare the stock and put in the diced ham and mortadella, the whole garlic cloves, the peeled onion, chopped with the parsley and basil.
2. Add the well washed spinach to the soup, and simmer for 10 minutes or so.
3. Throw in the pasta, add the cream and the cognac and the peas; for a fairly thick soup, it is best to use small peas, which will break down.
4. When cooking is almost finished, remove garlic cloves, add butter, stir well, and remove from the heat as soon as the butter is dissolved but not cooked.
5. Pour into bowls, garnish with plenty of grated cheese.

Minestrone alla coda di bue

Minestrone with Oxtail

00:45   04:15

American	Ingredients	Metric/Imperial
1	Oxtail	1
1	Calf's knuckle	1
1	Calf's foot	1
¼ cup	Butter	50 g / 2 oz
2	Onions	2
2	Carrots	2
2	Leeks	2
2	Celery stalks	2
2	Cloves	2
3	Sprigs of parsley	3
1	Sprig of thyme	1
2	Bay leaves	2
3 tbsp	Tomato purée	2 tbsp
	Salt and pepper	
1 tbsp	Potato flour	1 tbsp
3 tbsp	Madeira wine	2 tbsp
	Grated cheese	

1. Cut the washed oxtail into eight pieces. Bone and cut up the calf's knuckle and foot. Melt the butter in a large pan and fry the meat with 2 peeled chopped onions for 7 minutes.
2. Wash and cut all the vegetables into medium-sized pieces, add to meat and on a low heat cook for a further 5 minutes, stirring all the time.
3. Add 2 quarts [2 litres / 3½ pints] of water, the cloves, herbs and the tomato purée. Add salt and pepper and cook on a low heat for about 4 hours.
4. Remove meat and cut it up into smaller pieces. Strain the stock, return it to the pan on the heat and bring to the boil. Blend in 1 tablespoon of potato flour dissolved in the madeira and mixed with a little hot stock. Add the meat, season well and pour into the tureen. Accompany with grated cheese.

Cook's tip: the butcher will usually cut up the oxtail, knuckle and foot for you.

Zuppa alla monzese

Monza-Style Soup

00:15   00:20

American	Ingredients	Metric/Imperial
1	Garlic clove	1
1 tbsp	Dripping (roast beef fat)	1 tbsp
	Sliced homemade bread	
1 cup	Grated parmesan cheese	100 g / 4 oz
2 quarts	Stock	2 litres / 3½ pints

1. Rub the sides and bottom of a soup tureen thoroughly with the clove of garlic, put the dripping in the bottom, alternating with slices of homemade bread, and sprinkle over the grated parmesan.
2. Cover with plenty of very hot meat stock, or stock made from a cube, and keep hot for 10 minutes. If necessary you can add more stock, but it must be hot. Stir just before serving, and ladle into bowls. Sprinkle with more grated parmesan.

Minestra di riso e verze

Rice and Cabbage Soup

00:15   00:30

American	Ingredients	Metric/Imperial
2	Stock cubes	2
1 lb	Cabbage	500 g / 1 lb
1	Onion	1
1 tbsp	Vegetable oil	1 tbsp
1 cup	Rice	200 g / 7 oz
1 cup	Grated parmesan cheese	100 g / 4 oz

1. Heat 1½ quarts [1.5 litres / 2½ pints] of water in a pan, add stock cubes. Wash the cabbage and trim it, removing the tougher leaves. Removing the remaining leaves one by one, lay them one on top of another and cut them into thin strips.
2. Chop the onion. Put the oil in a frying pan on a medium heat, fry the onions until golden. Add 4 tablespoons of hot stock, then the cabbage, braise for 5 minutes. Tip into the stock. Bring to the boil and simmer for 10 minutes.
3. Pour the rice into the cabbage stock and leave on the heat until cooked.
4. When cooking is finished pour the soup into plates and sprinkle generously with the grated parmesan.

Minestra di pasta e carciofi

Pasta and Artichoke Soup

01:00   00:25

American	Ingredients	Metric/Imperial
6	Jerusalem artichokes	6
½	Lemon	½
2 tbsp	Butter	25 g / 1 oz
1	Small onion	1
1	Slice of lean bacon	1
2	Peeled tomatoes	2
	Salt and pepper	
5 oz	Fresh pasta	150 g / 5 oz
1 tbsp	Chopped parsley	1 tbsp
½ cup	Grated parmesan cheese or pecorino	50 g / 2 oz

1. Peel the artichokes and cut in half vertically and then into slices about 1 in / 2½ cm, then throw them into water made acid with lemon juice.
2. In a saucepan heat the butter, fry the chopped onion and bacon in the butter over a gentle heat. When they are transparent and only lightly colored, add the slices of artichoke, well drained. Fry on a moderate heat.
3. Add well crushed peeled tomatoes, allow the flavors to mingle for a couple of minutes and moisten with 1 quart [1 litre / 1¾ pints] of water, adding salt.
4. Bring to the boil, drop in the fresh pasta, and complete cooking over a fairly even heat, adding a little water if necessary. Remove from the heat, season, add chopped parsley. Serve parmesan separately.

Minestra campagnola
Country Soup

American	Ingredients	Metric/Imperial
00:15		00:45
3	Plum tomatoes, fresh or canned	3
1	Onion	1
Scant ¼ cup	Vegetable oil	3 tbsp
	Salt and pepper	
2½ cups	Stock	600 ml / 1 pint
14 oz	Fresh pasta	400 g / 14 oz
2	Eggs	2
½ cup	Grated parmesan cheese	50 g / 2 oz
1 tbsp	Chopped parsley	1 tbsp

1. Scald the tomatoes in boiling water, drain them, peel and cut into strips, removing the seeds. Peel and finely chop the onion.
2. Heat the oil in a large pan, sweat the onion until transparent over a low heat, add tomatoes, seasoning, 1 cup [225 ml / 8 fl oz] water and continue cooking gently for 20 minutes.
3. Add the stock to the pan, bring to the boil and throw in the pasta. Cook for 8 minutes, lower heat.
4. Whisk the eggs, flavor with a pinch of seasoning, the parmesan and the chopped parsley. Add some hot soup to the egg then mix together and pour into the pan with the pasta a few moments before removing from the heat. Stir, allow the eggs to thicken the soup, then transfer to a heated tureen.

Minestra della massaia
Housewife's Soup

American	Ingredients	Metric/Imperial
00:20		00:40
2 oz	Smoked bacon	50 g / 2 oz
1	Garlic clove	1
1	Onion	1
5	Sprigs of parsley	5
3 tbsp	Lard	40 g / 1½ oz
14 oz	Fresh or canned plum tomatoes	400 g / 14 oz
	Salt and pepper	
1 quart	Stock	1 litre / 1¾ pints
3	Potatoes	3
1 cup	Rice	200 g / 7 oz
1 cup	Grated emmental cheese	100 g / 4 oz

1. Finely chop or mince the smoked bacon together with the garlic, onion and parsley. Alternatively all the ingredients may be chopped in a food processor. Heat the lard and cook the bacon mixture over a low heat.
2. Scald the tomatoes in boiling water (if using fresh), drain, peel and cut them into strips, removing the seeds, add to the bacon. Stir, season with salt and pepper and after a few minutes cover with stock or water. Bring to the boil.
3. Peel and wash the potatoes, dice and throw into the boiling soup; after 5 minutes also add the rice. Cook over a low heat for a further 20 minutes, stirring gently with a wooden spoon. Transfer the soup to heated serving bowls and sprinkle with grated emmental. Serve hot.

Minestra di asparagi
Rice and Asparagus Soup

American	Ingredients	Metric/Imperial
00:30		00:40
¼ cup	Butter	50 g / 2 oz
1	Onion	1
1	Garlic clove	1
1 tbsp	Tomato purée	1 tbsp
14 oz	Asparagus, green and slender	400 g / 14 oz
1 quart	Meat stock	1 litre / 1¾ pints
1 cup	Rice	200 g / 7 oz
	Salt and pepper	
½ cup	Grated parmesan cheese	50 g / 2 oz

1. Heat the butter in a saucepan, cook the peeled, diced onion and garlic over a medium heat until onion is golden brown. Add 1 cup [225 ml / 8 fl oz] of water mixed with tomato purée and put in the asparagus tips. Cover and cook on a moderate heat for 10 minutes.
2. Heat the stock in a large pot and when it comes to the boil, throw in the rice and cook until tender. Add the fried onion and asparagus mixture, season well. Stir on the heat for a few minutes longer. Serve the soup accompanied with the grated parmesan cheese.

Minestra di broccoli alla romana

Roman-Style Broccoli Soup

American	Ingredients	Metric/Imperial
00:30		01:00
14 oz	Broccoli	400 g / 14 oz
2 oz	Bacon	50 g / 2 oz
1	Garlic clove	1
1 tsp	Lard	1 tsp
1 tbsp	Tomato purée	1 tbsp
2 cups	Stock	450 ml / 16 fl oz
	Salt and pepper	
¼ lb	Pork rind	100 g / 4 oz
7 oz	Spaghetti	200 g / 7 oz
	Grated parmesan cheese	

1. Divide the broccoli into small pieces, wash well and drain.
2. Mince or finely chop the bacon with a clove of garlic. Heat the lard in a saucepan, add the bacon and garlic and brown for a few minutes. Add tomato purée, the broccoli pieces, 2 cups [450 ml / 16 fl oz] of stock or water, salt and pepper, and cook on a low heat.
3. Meanwhile scrape the pork rind thoroughly, cover with water and heat in a saucepan, boil for 1 minute, drain and cut the rind into thin strips. Return to the heat, add 1 cup [225 ml / 8 fl oz] of water and boil until soft.
4. When the pieces of broccoli are still firm, add the rind together with its cooking juices and continue cooking for another 10 minutes. Taste and add salt and pepper if necessary. When the soup comes to the boil, add the spaghetti broken into small pieces. Serve with parmesan.

Fonduta

Cheese Fondue

02:00 00:30

American	Ingredients	Metric/Imperial
¾ lb	*Fontina cheese*	*350 g / 12 oz*
2¼ cups	*Milk*	*½ litre / 18 fl oz*
6 tbsp	*Butter*	*75 g / 3 oz*
3	*Egg yolks*	*3*
	Grated black truffle	

1. Cut the cheese into small cubes and cover it with milk in the top of a double boiler, allow to soak in the milk for 2 hours. Add butter and egg yolks to cheese.
2. Place the pan in the base of the double boiler containing water which has been brought to the boil.
3. Work the cheese with a large wooden spoon. At first the cheese will become rather stringy, then it will become more liquid, and finally thicken. When the mixture has thickened and is perfectly smooth, remove from the heat and serve piping hot. Garnish the fondue with the grated black truffle. Vegetables such as chard or fennel, cooked and puréed with butter can also be added to the fondue.

Crema Aurora

Cream Aurore

00:20 00:40

American	Ingredients	Metric/Imperial
1 lb	*Fleshy, ripe tomatoes*	*500 g / 1 lb*
5 tbsp	*Vegetable oil*	*4 tbsp*
2	*Medium sized onions*	*2*
1	*Small bunch of thyme*	*1*
7	*Parsley sprigs*	*7*
	Salt and pepper	
1 quart	*Vegetable stock*	*1 litre / 1¾ pints*
3 tbsp	*Cream*	*2 tbsp*

1. Scald the tomatoes, remove the skin and pips, and put the chopped flesh on one side.
2. Heat the oil in a saucepan. Thinly slice the onion and gently fry until transparent, then add the flesh of the tomatoes, the thyme and parsley, tied together in a bundle.
3. Stir, season with salt and pepper, add the stock and cook for about 30 minutes over a medium heat. Remove the herbs, allow to cool and put through a blender or food processor.
4. Return the purée to a gentle heat with enough stock to make a fairly smooth cream, if liked stir in 2-3 tbsp cream. The soup can be accompanied by small pieces of bread fried in butter and sprinkled with grated parmesan cheese.

Cheese fondue

Minestra di gianchetti
Anchovy Soup

00:15   00:45

American	Ingredients	Metric/Imperial
14 oz	Anchovy fry (whitebait)	400 g / 14oz
1 quart	Vegetable stock	1 litre / 1¾ pints
2	Garlic cloves	2
1	Bunch of fragrant minestrone herbs	1
½ lb	Spinach	225 g / 8 oz
	Salt and pepper	
⅔ cup	Fresh cream	150 ml / 5 fl oz
4 tsp	Cornstarch (cornflour)	4 tsp
3 tbsp	Milk	2 tbsp
	Croûtons	

1. Put the anchovy fry in a thin mesh sieve and wash under running cold water until the water runs clean.

2. Heat a pot with 1 quart [1 litre / 1¾ pints] of vegetable stock, put in the anchovy, 2 finely chopped cloves of garlic, a bunch of fragrant herbs, chopped, and a handful of raw chopped spinach.

3. Bring to a slow boil, seasoning with salt and pepper during cooking. Simmer for 30 minutes.

4. Pour a quarter of the cream into the soup, together with 4 teaspoons of cornstarch mixed in a little milk. Thicken over a low heat until it has a creamy consistency.

5. Correct the seasoning, then pour into soup bowls and serve with a garnish of croûtons.

Different garnishes for soup

Shellfish
and Fish

Scampi con riso pilaff
Scampi with Rice Pilaff

⏱ 00:20   🍲 01:00

American	Ingredients	Metric/Imperial
1 lb	Scampi	500 g / 1 lb
½ cup	Vegetable oil	125 ml / 4 fl oz
	White flour	
1	Onion	1
½ cup	Butter	100 g / 4 oz
3 tbsp	Cognac	2 tbsp
⅔ cup	Coffee (single) cream	150 ml / ¼ pint
	Salt	
1 quart	Stock	1 litre / 1¾ pints
2 cups	Rice	400 g / 14 oz

1. Preheat oven to 375°F / 190°C / Gas Mark 5.
2. Shell the scampi and wash them in running water, drain and dry them in a clean cloth. Heat the oil in a frying pan.
3. Dip the scampi in flour and fry over a medium heat until golden. Remove them from the oil and drain on kitchen towels to absorb the oil.
4. Finely chop half the onion and brown in half the butter. Add the scampi and allow the flavors to mingle for a few minutes. Sprinkle with cognac. When the cognac has evaporated, pour the cream over the scampi, season with salt and cook for a further 10 minutes over a low heat.
5. Heat stock to make a rice pilaff. In a large pan fry half an onion in a little butter until it is dry. Pour in the rice, stir and cover with the stock. Put the lid on the pan and put in the oven. Leave the rice in the oven, without opening the door, for 20 minutes.
6. When cooked, the rice will have completely absorbed the stock. Combine remainder of the butter with the rice. Heat the scampi and serve with the rice pilaff.

Granchi alla bordolese
Crabs in White Wine

⏱ 00:30   🍲 01:00

American	Ingredients	Metric/Imperial
1	Carrot	1
1	Onion	1
1	Shallot	1
2 tbsp	Chopped parsley	1½ tbsp
½ cup	Butter	100 g / 4 oz
2	Sprigs of thyme	2
2	Bay leaves	2
20	Crabs	20
½ cup	Chopped tomatoes	125 ml / 4 fl oz
¼ cup	Cognac	50 ml / 2 fl oz
	Salt and pepper	
1 cup	Dry white wine	225 ml / 8 fl oz
2	Egg yolks	2

1. Finely chop the carrot, onion, shallot and parsley, mix together.
2. Heat half the butter in a pan and when it starts to foam, add the chopped vegetables, thyme and bay, cook over a low heat

for about 15 minutes. The vegetables should be very soft. Remove the pan from the heat and put aside.
3. Clean the crabs, removing the inedible parts, and put them into a pan containing remaining hot butter. Cover and cook, shaking continuously, until they have turned red (about 10 minutes). Purée the tomatoes and keep hot.
4. When the crabs are ready, pour in the cognac and flame. Add the tomatoes, the cooked vegetable mixture, season with pepper, tip in wine, cover and cook for 20 minutes.
5. Arrange the crabs on a heated serving dish. Reduce the contents of the pan by boiling for 5-6 minutes. Stir in the egg yolks and a little water. Add the remaining butter to the sauce, let it melt and then pour all the sauce over the crabs.

Granceola gratinata
Spider-Crab au Gratin

⏱ 00:30   🍲 00:30

American	Ingredients	Metric/Imperial
4	Spider-crabs	4
¼ cup	Cognac	50 ml / 2 fl oz
1 cup	Béchemal sauce	225 ml / 8 fl oz
2	Egg yolks	2
¼ cup	Butter	50 g / 2 oz
½ cup	Grated emmental cheese	50 g / 2 oz

1. Preheat the oven to 400°F / 200°C / Gas Mark 6.
2. Poach the crabs in plenty of salted water for 15 minutes. Cut open with a knife, scoop out the insides and put the edible parts (meat and roe) into a bowl with the cognac. Wash the shells thoroughly.
3. Prepare a béchamel sauce and add the egg yolks and the crabmeat soaked in cognac.
4. Butter the shells, pile the crabmeat preparation inside them, top with dabs of butter and the grated cheese and place in a hot oven for 10 minutes. Serve very hot.

Mitili ripieni
Stuffed Mussels

⏱ 00:30   🍲 00:30

American	Ingredients	Metric/Imperial
1¾ lb	Mussels	800 g / 1¾ lb
2	Garlic cloves	2
5	Sprigs of parsley	5
¼ cup	Bread crumbs	25 g / 1 oz
1	Egg	1
	Salt and pepper	
3 tbsp	Vegetable oil	2 tbsp

1. Preheat the oven to 425°F / 220°C / Gas Mark 7.
2. Carefully wash the very fresh mussels, scraping them well. Then open the shellfish by plunging in boiling water until shells open, discard any which remain closed.
3. Crush the garlic and parsley, add the bread crumbs, egg, salt and pepper and mix with the oil. Stuff the mussels with this mixture, and close them again.
4. Put the stuffed mussels in a large foil bag, close and cook in a very hot oven for 25 minutes. Serve hot.

Gamberoni in agrodolce

Prawns in Sweet and Sour Sauce

⊳ 00:45   00:20 🍲

American	Ingredients	Metric/Imperial
20	Large prawns	20
	Salt	
2	Slices of lemon	2
1	Anchovy in oil	1
2 tbsp	Vegetable oil	1½ tbsp
2 tbsp	Butter	25 g / 1 oz
1	Garlic clove	1
3 tbsp	Capers	2 tbsp
3 tbsp	White vinegar	2 tbsp
2 tsp	Sugar	2 tsp
2 tbsp	Chopped parsley	1½ tbsp

1. Wash the prawns thoroughly in running water, then place into a saucepan with cold water to cover, salt and 2 slices of lemon. Bring to the boil and cook for about 15 minutes.
2. Prepare the sauce, sauté the anchovy lightly in heated oil and butter, add the crushed garlic and chopped capers, and then vinegar and sugar. Bring to the boil, stir, then turn off the heat and allow to cool slightly.
3. Drain the prawns, arrange on a dish, pour the sauce over the top and sprinkle liberally with chopped parsley. Refrigerate for 30 minutes before serving.

Aragosta all'arancia

Lobster in Orange Cream

⊳ 00:30   00:35 🍲
Chilling time 02:00

American	Ingredients	Metric/Imperial
1 (2 lb)	Lobster	1 (1 kg / 2 lb)
1	Onion	1
1	Carrot	1
1	Celery stalk	1
1	Bunch of herbs	1
½ cup	Dry white wine	125 ml / 4 fl oz
¼ cup	Butter	50 g / 2 oz
¼ cup	Cognac	50 ml / 2 fl oz
	Salt and pepper	
2	Eggs	2
3	Oranges	3
1 cup	Whipping (double) cream	225 ml / 8 fl oz

1. Wash the live lobster. Put the vegetables into a saucepan containing enough water to cover the lobster well, add herbs, salt, white wine and bring to the boil. Drop in the lobster and cook for 20 minutes. Allow to cool slightly in liquid.
2. Drain, remove the meat from the shell and cut into fairly thin slices. Melt butter in a saucepan, add the slices of lobster, shake the pan, add cognac, set alight. Shake again over the heat, then season with salt and pepper.
3. Beat the eggs with the juice of the oranges until frothy, add this to the saucepan, then add the cream; whisk over a low heat. Arrange the lobster on a serving dish and refrigerate for at least 2 hours. Serve cold.

Prawns in sweet and sour sauce

Capesante gratinate
Scalloped Mussels

00:25   00:25

American	Ingredients	Metric/Imperial
¾ lb	Sweetbreads	350 g / 12 oz
	Flour	
1	Small onion	1
2 tbsp	Butter	25 g / 1 oz
⅓ cup	Olive oil	75 ml / 3 fl oz
1 lb	Mussels	450 g / 1 lb
1	Bay leaf	1
1	Garlic clove	1
	Salt and pepper	
¼ cup	Dry white wine	50 ml / 2 fl oz
½ tsp	Cornstarch (cornflour)	½ tsp
⅓ cup	Whipping (double) cream	75 ml / 3 fl oz

1. Skin the sweetbreads then scald in boiling water for 5 minutes; drain, cut into small pieces and toss in flour.
2. Preheat the oven to 425°F / 220°C / Gas Mark 7.
3. Chop the onion and sauté in butter and oil; when it has colored slightly, add the sweetbreads and cook until golden, then the mussels (with shells properly scrubbed and washed), the bay leaf and clove of garlic. Sauté these for a few minutes, shake over the heat, then season with a little salt and pour in the wine. Cook for another 5 minutes.
4. Remove the bay leaf and garlic and thicken the sauce with cornstarch. Pour in the cream, add freshly ground black pepper, stir well and spoon the preparation into scallop shells. Crisp in a very hot oven for 10 minutes. The mussels may be removed from the shells before being cooked in the oven.

Frittura di pesce
Fried Seafood Platter

01:00   00:30

American	Ingredients	Metric/Imperial
4	Small lemon sole	4
4	Mullet	4
5 oz	Whitebait	150 g / 5 oz
½ lb	Scampi	225 g / 8 oz
1 lb	Mussels	500 g / 1 lb
½ lb	Sea-strawberries (tiny squid)	225 g / 8 oz
1	Bunch of parsley	1
1	Garlic clove (optional)	1
1 cup	Vegetable oil	225 ml / 8 fl oz
¼ cup	Butter	50 g / 2 oz
3 tbsp	Cognac	2 tbsp
2	Lemons	2

1. Skin, gut, wash and drain the soles. Remove the scales from the mullet and gut, wash and drain. Clean and wash the whitebait and squeeze to remove the innards. Shell the scampi.
2. Scrub the mussels, put them into boiling water until they open, then remove the meat and discard the shells. Clean and wash the sea-strawberries.
3. Wash and chop the parsley with the clove of garlic.
4. Flour all the fish and toss in a sieve to remove any excess.

5. Heat plenty of oil in a large frying pan until very hot, then fry the fish one batch at a time. When the first batch is cooked, transfer to a sheet of absorbent kitchen paper to drain. Sprinkle with salt and keep warm while the remainder of the fish is being cooked.
6. When all the fish have been fried, keep warm.
7. Heat the butter and a little oil in a small pan and sauté most of the bunch of parsley, chopped, add cognac and a few drops of lemon juice.
8. Arrange the fish on a heated serving dish, keeping the varieties separate, pour the sauce over them and serve very hot garnished with lemon slices and sprigs of parsley.

Fried seafood platter

Gamberi della Camargue
Crayfish Poached in Wine

00:20   00:25

American	Ingredients	Metric/Imperial
2 (¾ lb)	Crayfish	2 (350 g / 12 oz)
3 cups	Dry white wine	700 ml / 1 ¼ pints
¼ cup	Calvados	50 ml / 2 fl oz
	Salt and pepper	
8	Slices of crusty bread	8

1. Wash the crayfish very carefully and dry with a clean cloth.
2. Heat the wine and calvados in a saucepan with salt and pepper to taste. When the liquid boils, throw in the crayfish, reduce the heat, cover and simmer for at least 15 minutes.
3. Remove, drain and arrange on a dish. Serve with toasted slices of crusty bread.

Cook's tip: retain cooking liquid to use as stock for cooking other fish or for a fish soup.

Seppie in umido con riso
Stewed Cuttlefish with Rice

▱ 00:25   00:30 🍲

American	Ingredients	Metric/Imperial
1 lb	Cuttlefish	500 g / 1 lb
⅓ cup	Vegetable oil	5 tbsp
1 tbsp	Chopped parsley	1 tbsp
1	Garlic clove	1
½ lb	Peeled tomatoes, fresh or canned	225 g / 8 oz
	Salt and pepper	
1½ cups	Long grain rice	300 g / 11 oz

1. Skin and wash the cuttlefish, discard the sac containing the inky liquid. Cut lengthways into a large number of strips.
2. Heat the oil, finely chop the parsley and garlic, and brown in the oil. Add the cuttlefish. Crush the peeled tomatoes with a fork and add to the fish. Season with salt, sprinkle with pepper and cook for 20 minutes.
3. Meanwhile cook the rice 'al dente' in lightly salted water, drain and arrange in a large soup-tureen or heated casserole. Pour the cuttlefish and sauce over the rice.

Seppie ripiene alla Corsaro Nero
Stuffed Cuttlefish Corsaro Nero

▱ 00:30   00:50 🍲

American	Ingredients	Metric/Imperial
1½ lb	Cuttlefish	700 g / 1½ lb
Scant ¼ cup	Vegetable oil	3 tbsp
1	Onion	1
1	Garlic clove	1
2 tbsp	Chopped parsley	1½ tbsp
2 oz	Crustless bread	50 g / 2 oz
¼ cup	Milk	50 ml / 2 fl oz
½ cup	Dry white wine	125 ml / 4 fl oz
	Salt and pepper	
1¼ cups	Béchamel sauce	300 ml / ½ pint
2	Hard-cooked (boiled) eggs	2
3 tbsp	Grated cheese	2 tbsp
4	Tomatoes	4

1. Using scissors, cut open the belly side of the cuttlefish and clean thoroughly. Discard the sac of inky liquid, the eyes and mouth. Wash carefully under cold running water and drain, belly downwards on a cloth.
2. Heat the oil in a saucepan and brown the chopped onion, crushed garlic and parsley. Soak the crustless bread in milk, squeeze it, crumble and add to the fried onion. Sprinkle with the dry white wine, season with salt and allow the sauce to thicken.
3. Prepare a béchamel sauce, season well, remove from the heat, add finely chopped hard-cooked eggs to the sauce

together with the grated cheese. Stir thoroughly, adjusting the seasoning.
4. Preheat the oven to 350°F / 180°C / Gas / Mark 4.
5. Fill the cuttlefish with this mixture. Wash the tomatoes and cut in half. Close the opening of each cuttlefish with half a tomato and arrange them in an ovenproof dish.
6. Pour béchamel sauce over the fish, cover with oiled parchment (greaseproof paper) and cook in a moderate oven for about 40 minutes. If the cuttlefish becomes rather dry, add a little stock or dry white wine.

Palombo ai piselli
Dogfish with Peas

▱ 00:10   00:25 🍲

American	Ingredients	Metric/Imperial
1	Onion	1
2 tbsp	Vegetable oil	1½ tbsp
2 tbsp	Butter	25 g / 1 oz
4	Dogfish (rock salmon) slices	4
	Salt and pepper	
6	Tomatoes	6
¼ tsp	Oregano	¼ tsp
1 cup	Garden peas	150 g / 5 oz

1. Slowly fry a very finely chopped onion in a large frying pan with oil and butter. As soon as it begins to turn brown, add the slices of dogfish and season with salt and pepper.
2. Skin the tomatoes (canned tomatoes may be used) and chop up finely. Add tomatoes, oregano and drained peas to the fish. Cover and cook over a moderate heat for 20 minutes.

Palombo fritto
Fried Dogfish

▱ 00:15   00:15 🍲

American	Ingredients	Metric/Imperial
1	Small bunch of parsley	1
4	Dogfish (rock salmon) slices	4
½ cup	Milk	125 ml / 4 fl oz
½ cup	Flour	50 g / 2 oz
	Oil for frying	
1	Lemon	1

1. Wash and drain the parsley. Wash and fry the fish and immerse in milk for 5 minutes. Dip the fish slices in flour, shake to remove any excess.
2. Heat plenty of oil in a fryer or in a large frying pan. When it begins to haze, put in the slices of dogfish. Brown the fish on both sides. Drain and wipe off the excess oil with kitchen towels.
3. Pick good sprigs of parsley and toss them in the boiling oil for a few seconds. Serve the fried dogfish on a serving dish garnished with the fried parsley (be careful not to burn it) and slices of lemon.

Trancio di nasello alla toscana
Hake Tuscan-Style

00:15		00:20

American	Ingredients	Metric/Imperial
1 lb	Hake fillets	500 g / 1 lb
	Salt	
¼ cup	Butter	50 g / 2 oz
1	Sprig of sage	1

1. Steam or boil the hake fillets for about 10-15 minutes until cooked, season with salt, then drain and arrange on a serving dish.

2. In a frying pan heat butter until brown with a few chopped sage leaves and pour over the fillets. This is a dish with a delicate flavor and it is essential to serve it very hot.

Aringa affumicata alla bismarck
Smoked Herring Fillets on Garlic Bread

00:15		00:00

American	Ingredients	Metric/Imperial
¾ lb	Smoked herring	350 g / 12 oz
¾ lb	Brown bread	350 g / 12 oz
2 tbsp	Butter	25 g / 1 oz
2	Garlic cloves	2
	Chilli sauce or pickle	

1. Cut each herring into half and divide into fillets, removing the bone.

2. Slice the bread. Mix crushed garlic with butter, spread on the slices of bread, lay the herring fillets on top with skin and roe. Serve cold, accompanied by chilli sauce or pickle.

Coda di rospo con pomodoro e olive
Monkfish Tail with Tomato and Olives

00:20		00:40
		using a pressure cooker

American	Ingredients	Metric/Imperial
¼ cup	Vegetable oil	50 ml / 2 fl oz
14 oz	Monkfish tail	400 g / 14 oz
Scant ¼ cup	Chopped tomatoes (no seeds or juice)	3 tbsp
⅓ cup	Green olives, stoned	50 g / 2 oz
	Salt	

1. Put 1 cup [225 ml / 8 fl oz] of water into the pressure cooker. Into the pan supplied with the cooker, put some oil and then the fish, surround the fish with the chopped tomatoes and halved green olives and season with a little salt.

2. Close the cooker and bring up to pressure on a high heat, reduce the heat when pressure has been reached and continue to cook over minimum heat, for 10 minutes.

3. Reduce the pressure, remove the pan and thicken the sauce by boiling, uncovered, for a few minutes.

Triglie al cartoccio Portofino
Mullet Portofino-Style

00:10		00:35

American	Ingredients	Metric/Imperial
4 (7 oz)	Mullet	4 (200 g / 7 oz)
1	Roll	1
2 tbsp	Vinegar	1½ tbsp
6 oz	Capers	175 g / 6 oz
1	Hard-cooked (boiled) egg	1
½ tsp	Chopped sage	½ tsp
½ tsp	Chopped rosemary	½ tsp
	Salt and pepper	
2 tbsp	Vegetable oil	1½ tbsp
½ lb	Peeled shrimps	225 g / 8 oz
½ lb	Shelled mussels	225 g / 8 oz
8	Basil leaves	8
4	Sprigs of parsley	4
12	Black or green olives	12

1. Clean the mullet, removing the scales and make an incision under the belly. Wash and remove the guts.

2. To make the stuffing soak the inside of a bread roll with a little vinegar. Add some chopped capers, a crumbled hard-cooked egg, a generous pinch of chopped sage and rosemary, salt, pepper and a little oil; mix well. Fill the bellies of the mullet with this mixture and press down gently.

3. Preheat the oven to 400°F / 200°C / Gas Mark 6.

4. Spread out 4 sheets of foil or buttered wax paper (grease-proof) on the chopping board. On each sheet, lay one stuffed mullet, a few raw washed shrimps and mussels, and a few basil leaves. Close the cases, leaving a loose parcel to enable the steam to circulate. When the fish are wrapped, lay them on a baking sheet and put in a hot oven for 35 minutes.

5. Take out the cases, put on a heated serving dish. Each diner can open a case. Garnish with sprigs of parsley and if desired, some black or green olives. Serve with a mixed salad or boiled potatoes with parsley.

Triglie alla livornese
Mullet Leghorn-Style

00:30		00:35

American	Ingredients	Metric/Imperial
12	Mullet	12
	Flour	
	Salt and pepper	
½ cup	Vegetable oil	125 ml / 4 fl oz
3 tbsp	Chopped parsley	2 tbsp
3	Garlic cloves	3
1¼ cups	Tomato sauce	300 ml / ½ pint

1. Preheat oven to 400°F / 200°C / Gas Mark 6.

2. Clean, wash and dry the mullet, dip in seasoned flour. Heat the oil in a roasting pan, arrange the fish in the hot oil and brown in the oven for 10 minutes. Remove and turn the fish over carefully with a fish slice.

3. Season with salt, pepper, chopped parsley and crushed garlic. Return to the oven for 10 minutes, then add tomato sauce and cook for a further 15 minutes.

4. Serve piping hot with some sauce on each fish.

Mullet Leghorn-Style

Anchovy bake

Alici in tortiera
Anchovy Bake

American	Ingredients	Metric/Imperial
1½ lb	Fresh whole anchovies	700 g / 1½ lb
¼ cup	Vegetable oil	50 ml / 2 fl oz
½ cup	Fresh bread crumbs	25 g / 1 oz
1 tsp	Oregano	1 tsp
	Salt and pepper	
1 lb	Sieved fresh tomatoes	450 g / 1 lb
8	Garlic cloves	8

1. Preheat oven to 350°F / 180°C / Gas Mark 4.
2. Prepare the anchovies by removing the heads, slitting along the underside and opening flat; remove guts and bones, wash and dry.
3. Arrange an even layer of anchovies in a well-oiled pie dish; sprinkle with bread crumbs, oregano, salt and pepper. Spoon some of the sieved or blended tomatoes over the top. Repeat these layers until the dish is full and top with plenty of oil and several cloves of garlic.
4. Bake the anchovies in the oven for 40 minutes, remove garlic and serve hot.

Acciughe in cotoletta
Anchovy Cutlets

American	Ingredients	Metric/Imperial
1 lb	Fresh anchovies	450 g / 1 lb
1	Egg	1
	Salt and pepper	
	Flour	
1 cup	Lard	225 g / 8 oz
2	Garlic cloves	2
1 tbsp	Chopped basil	1 tbsp
4	Walnuts (shelled)	4
1 oz	Pine kernels	25 g / 1 oz
¼ cup	Vegetable oil	50 ml / 2 fl oz
3 tbsp	White wine vingar	2 tbsp
3 tbsp	Cognac (optional)	2 tbsp

1. Wash and dry the anchovies. Remove the heads and tails, split open and remove the backbone and all the smaller bones from the anchovies.
2. Coat in the beaten egg seasoned with salt and pepper, then drain and dip in flour.
3. Melt the lard or heat frying oil in a pan and when the fat is smoking hot, fry the anchovies and cook on both sides. Lift out with a fish slice and drain thoroughly on absorbent kitchen towels.
4. Meanwhile, chop the garlic and basil together, preferably in a blender or food processor and combine into a sauce with the walnuts, pine kernels, a little oil and the vinegar and cognac if desired.
5. Lay the anchovies in a single layer on a china (not metal) plate, spread the sauce over them, cover the dish with film and put in a cool place for 24 hours.

Cook's tip: this is a very good luncheon dish.

Leccia del Golfo Paradiso
Rudderfish (Amberjack) in Garlic and Lemon

American	Ingredients	Metric/Imperial
½ cup	Oil	125 ml / 4 fl oz
1¾ lb	Rudderfish (amberjack)	800 g / 1¾ lb
½ tsp	Chopped parsley	½ tsp
½ tsp	Sage	½ tsp
2	Garlic cloves	2
	Pepper	
2	Lemons	2
¼ cup	Dry white wine	50 ml / 2 fl oz

1. Brush oil all over the thick slice of fish.
2. Chop parsley and sage leaves with the cloves of garlic and sprinkle these into the fish-kettle with a thin layer of oil. Lay the fish on top and sprinkle with freshly-ground pepper. Leave for 2 hours, then turn, sprinkle again with pepper and leave for a further 2 hours.
3. Pour the juice of 2 lemons over the fish and commence cooking over a very low heat. If the fish shows any signs of sticking, put in some of the white wine which you may have chosen to serve with the meal. After 15 minutes, turn the fish and cook for a further 15 minutes.
4. Serve very hot, straight from the pan. The rudderfish is a very fine fish with a delicate flavor, no salt is needed when it is cooked by this method.

Cook's tip: moray eel can be cooked in exactly the same way making the tender white flesh delicious.

Alborelle in carpione
Soused Sprats

American	Ingredients	Metric/Imperial
2 lb	Sprats	1 kg / 2 lb
	Flour	
½ cup	Vegetable oil	125 ml / 4 fl oz
	Salt	
1 cup	Wine vinegar	225 ml / 8 fl oz
2	Medium-sized onions	2
1	Celery stalk	1
4	Basil leaves	4
½ tsp	Chopped thyme	½ tsp
2	Bay leaves	2

1. Cut, wash and dry the fish; coat with flour, eliminating the excess by tossing in a large sieve.
2. Heat some oil in a frying pan and cook the fish over a high heat for 2 minutes each side.
3. Drain on absorbent paper then put into a deep bowl and season with salt, shaking to ensure an even distribution.
4. Slice the onions into thin rings, put into a saucepan with the vinegar, ⅔ cup [150 ml / ¼ pint] water and bring to the boil. Add the celery (with leaves), basil, thyme, bay leaves and any other herbs you choose. Allow the vinegar to boil until the vegetables are cooked, then strain, still boiling hot, over the fish and cover immediately. Leave for at least 2 days before serving.

Alborelle arrosto
Fried Sprats

	00:20		00:25

American	Ingredients	Metric/Imperial
2 lb	Sprats	1 kg / 2 lb
2 tbsp	Butter	25 g / 1 oz
½ cup	Olive oil	125 ml / 4 fl oz
2	Sprigs of rosemary	2
	Salt and pepper	
½ cup	Dry white wine	125 ml / 4 fl oz
2	Lemons	2

1. Gut and clean the fish, wash well under the tap and dry with a cloth. Heat the oil and butter in a shallow pan with a sprig of rosemary.
2. Make some small transverse cuts on the backs of the fish and fry on all sides.
3. Season with salt and pepper. When the fish are crisp and golden, sprinkle the wine over them and allow it to evaporate completely.
4. Arrange the fish on a dish, garnish with lemon slices and serve with a crisp salad.

Sarde caramellate alla giapponese
Caramelized Sprats Japanese-Style

	00:20		00:30

American	Ingredients	Metric/Imperial
½ cup	Vegetable oil	125 ml / 4 fl oz
1 lb	Sprats	450 g / 1 lb
1 cup	Sugar	225 g / 8 oz
⅓ cup	Soy sauce	5 tbsp

1. Preheat oven to 350°F / 180°C / Gas Mark 4.
2. Put the oil in a frying pan, add the sprats and cook until golden brown, drain on kitchen towels.
3. Put the sugar in a saucepan, cook over a low heat until caramelized. Add the soy sauce, combine with the caramel and continue to cook over a low heat for a few minutes. Immerse the sprats in the caramel, then lay each fish on a foil lined baking sheet. Cook in the oven for 15 minutes and serve.

Frittata di bianchetti
Whitebait Frittata

	00:15		00:15

American	Ingredients	Metric/Imperial
½ cup	Flour	50 g / 2 oz
	Salt and pepper	
4	Eggs	4
¼ cup	Milk	50 ml / 2 fl oz
¾ lb	Whitebait (or bianchetti)	350 g / 12 oz
2 cups	Vegetable oil	450 ml / ¾ pint

1. Sift flour with salt and pepper, make a well in the centre, drop in the eggs and milk, mix well.
2. Beat the egg mixture together with the whitebait.
3. Pour into a large pan containing plenty of boiling oil. When one side is cooked, either turn the *frittata* (difficult and dangerous!) or remove from the pan and slide it under the broiler (grill) to brown the top.
4. This delicious *frittata* can be served either hot or cold, cut into thin slices.

Anguilla alla veneta
Venetian Eel

This is a traditional Venetian dish which appealed so much to the Austrians during their occupation of the region that they 'adopted' it.

	00:45 Marinating time 2 days		01:00

American	Ingredients	Metric/Imperial
¾ lb	Eel	350 g / 12 oz
4 tbsp	Flour	25 g / 1 oz
½ cup	Vegetable oil	125 ml / 4 fl oz
1	Onion	1
1	Carrot	1
1	Garlic clove	1
2	Sprigs of sage	2
1 cup	Wine vinegar	225 ml / 8 fl oz
	Salt and pepper	

1. Clean the eel and wipe it well with a damp cloth. Remove the internal organs and the gills, wash thoroughly then chop into pieces and coat with flour, shake off excess.
2. Using a cast-iron pan, heat a generous half of the oil and when this is very hot, add the eel and cook, stirring frequently. Drain and transfer to a bowl.
3. Slice the scraped carrot and peeled onion thinly, chop the garlic and sage and sauté all together in remaining heated oil.
4. Allow to brown slightly, add a little vinegar, a small quantity of water and some freshly ground pepper. Simmer for 20 minutes then pour over the eel. Marinate for 2 days, then serve cold.

Anguilla allo spiedo
Spit-Roasted Eel

	00:25		00:15

American	Ingredients	Metric/Imperial
1 (1½ lb)	Eel	1 (700 g / 1½ lb)
8	Slices of crusty bread	8
8	Bay leaves	8
	Salt and pepper	
4 tbsp	Vegetable oil	3 tbsp

1. Clean and wash the eel thoroughly, then chop into pieces about 2½ in / 6 cm long.
2. Thread the rotisserie skewers with small thick slices of bread, bay leaves and pieces of eel, season with salt and pepper, brush with oil and cook under a hot broiler (grill) until the eel is well done, brushing with oil from time to time during cooking.

Traditional Italian eel

rum. Flame, and when this dies down add the wine and a little cream. Continue to cook for 15 minutes over a low heat. Serve very hot, garnished with sprigs of parsley.

Capitone marinato

Marinated Eel

00:30 Marinating time 2 days		00:40

American	Ingredients	Metric/Imperial
1 (2 lb)	Eel	1 (1 kg / 2 lb)
1	Garlic clove	1
	Salt and pepper	
2 or 3	Bay leaves	2 or 3
1 cup	Vegetable oil	225 ml / 8 fl oz
1 cup	Wine vinegar	225 ml / 8 fl oz

1. Skin the eel by hanging up by the head, make a slit around the neck and then roll the skin downwards, using a coarse cloth to help grip. Gut, wash and dry, then coil the body around the head and lay it in a casserole pot. The coiled up eel should fit into the base of the casserole.
2. Sprinkle with salt, pepper, crushed garlic and a few bay leaves, then pour the oil and vinegar over, making sure that the eel is completely immersed.
3. Cover and cook over very low heat. When the eel is cooked, the juices should have been almost absorbed. Cool in the liquor and leave to marinate for several days before serving.

Capitone alla livornese

Leghorn Eel

00:30		00:30

American	Ingredients	Metric/Imperial
1	Onion	1
1	Carrot	1
1	Celery stalk	1
1	Lemon	1
1 (2 lb)	Eel	1 (1 kg / 2 lb)
	Salt and pepper	
2 tbsp	Wine vinegar	1½ tbsp
1 tbsp	Tomato paste	1 tbsp
4	Slices of bread	4
2 tbsp	Butter	25 g / 1 oz
2 tbsp	Oil	1½ tbsp

1. Prepare, wash and chop the vegetables into even-sized pieces. Cook in 1¼ cup [300 ml / ½ pint] water, adding the rind of a lemon.
2. Clean, wash and slice the eel.
3. When the vegetables are cooked, drain, retaining the vegetable water. Place alternate layers of eel and vegetables into a large pan until all ingredients are used. Season with salt and pepper, pour over vegetable water, add more warm water if necessary to cover, and simmer gently for about 20 minutes.
4. When the eel is cooked, add vinegar and tomato paste. Continue to simmer for 5 minutes.
5. Fry the slices of bread in butter and oil, then lay them on a heated serving dish and spoon the eel on top.

Capitone della tradizione italiana

Traditional Italian Eel

00:15		00:40

American	Ingredients	Metric/Imperial
1 (2 lb)	Eel	1 (1 kg / 2 lb)
¼ cup	Vegetable oil	50 ml / 2 fl oz
2 tbsp	Butter	25 g / 1 oz
4	Anchovy fillets	4
½ tsp	Chopped rosemary	½ tsp
2	Bay leaves	2
¼ cup	Rum	50 ml / 2 fl oz
½ cup	Dry white wine	125 ml / 4 fl oz
1 cup	Cream	225 ml / 8 fl oz
	Sprigs of parsley	

1. Clean and wash the eel and chop it into pieces about 4 in / 10 cm.
2. Heat a little oil and butter in a frying pan and sauté together the anchovy fillets and pieces of eel. Add the herbs and the

Squid in ink

Calamari neri
Squid in Ink

◣▽ 00:40   00:45 🍲

American	Ingredients	Metric/Imperial
2 lb	Squid (inkfish)	1 kg / 2 lb
	Salt and pepper	
	Flour	
¼ cup	Corn oil	50 ml / 2 fl oz
1	Onion	1
½ cup	Dry white wine	125 ml / 4 fl oz
2	Garlic cloves	2
1	Sweet red pepper	1
	Sprigs of parsley	
1	Lemon	1

1. Prepare the squid by removing the head with a sharp knife. Open the body and discard the internal organs, retain the ink sac.
2. Wash the squid, cut into strips and dip in seasoned flour.
3. Heat the oil in a frying pan and sauté the peeled chopped onion lightly; add the squid, stir for 3 minutes, pour in the white wine and season with salt and pepper, cook gently for 30 minutes.
4. Crush the garlic, deseed and chop sweet pepper and add with the ink-sac to the pan. Stir well, cook for a further 10 minutes and serve garnished with sprigs of parsley and lemon wedges.

Calamari in salsa rossa
Squid in Tomato Sauce

◣▽ 01:00   02:10 🍲

American	Ingredients	Metric/Imperial
2 lb	Squid	1 kg / 2 lb
2	Garlic cloves	2
1	Sprig of rosemary	1
½ cup	Vegetable oil	125 ml / 4 fl oz
1¼ lb	Ripe tomatoes	600 g / 1¼ lb
	Salt and pepper	
¼ cup	Butter	50 g / 2 oz
	Cornstarch (cornflour)	

1. Clean the squid carefully (retaining the ink sacs), wash and cut into strips then allow to drain in a colander.
2. Chop the garlic and rosemary finely, then put into a saucepan with the oil. Heat the oil and sauté the herbs for 2 minutes, then add the squid and continue to cook, stirring frequently over a moderate heat.
3. Wash and sieve or blend the tomatoes and add them to the pan together with the ink sacs, some salt and a few twists of pepper. Cover with really tight-fitting lid and simmer very gently for 2 hours (the liquid should only just bubble). Open the saucepan as little as possible, but from time to time to check that the pan is not drying up.
4. Add the butter and if the sauce is too thin, thicken it slightly with a little flour, check the seasoning and serve very hot.

Cacciucco alla livornese

Leghorn Fish Stew

Suitable fish for this recipe include conger eel, dog fish, sea hen, *cicale di mare, scorfani* or similar North Sea varieties.

	01:00		01:00

American	Ingredients	Metric/Imperial
4½ lb	Coarse fish plus squid and octopus	2 kg / 4½ lb
1	Red chilli pepper	1
1	Onion	1
1	Celery stalk	1
2 tbsp	Chopped parsley	1½ tbsp
½ tsp	Chopped basil	½ tsp
1 cup	Olive oil	225 ml / 8 fl oz
2	Garlic cloves	2
	Salt and pepper	
½ cup	Dry white wine	125 ml / 4 fl oz
¾ lb	Peeled tomatoes	350 g / 12 oz
8-12	Slices of crusty bread	8-12

1. Wash and generally prepare all the fish. Cut the squid and octopus into strips.
2. Chop the deseeded chilli pepper, onion, celery, parsley and basil.
3. Heat the olive oil in a large, deep pan with 1 clove of garlic, the deseeded chilli pepper and the chopped vegetable and a little salt and pepper. Cook lightly, then add strips of squid and octopus, cover and simmer until tender.
4. Stir in the white wine and allow this to evaporate. Add the peeled tomatoes, 1¼ cups [300 ml / ½ pint] water, stir well and then add the rest of the fish and cook until tender.
5. Prepare 2-3 slices of bread per person, rubbing with crushed garlic and either frying in oil, toasting under the broiler (grill) or in the oven. Put the bread on the individual plates and pour over the fish stew.

Moscardini alla camoglina

Octopus Camoglina-Style

	01:00		01:30

American	Ingredients	Metric/Imperial
1¾ lb	Octopus	800 g / 1¾ lb
⅓ cup	Vegetable oil	75 ml / 3 fl oz
3	Garlic cloves	3
⅓ cup	White wine	75 ml / 3 fl oz
5 oz	Chopped tomatoes	140 g / 5 oz
1 tbsp	Tomato purée	1 tbsp
2	Bay leaves	2
½	Chilli pepper	½
1	Sweet red pepper	1
	Salt and pepper	

1. Carefully clean the octopus. If they are rather large, cut them in half. Wash thoroughly, drain and brown in a large frying pan with heated oil and crushed cloves of garlic.
2. Cook until all the water has disappeared, sprinkle with white wine, evaporate and add the tomatoes and purée, bay leaves, a large piece of chilli, the deseeded sweet red pepper cut in four, salt and pepper. Cover and cook very gently for about 1¼ hours. During cooking, ensure that the juice does

not dry up too much and, if necessary, add a little water.
3. When the cooking is over, the juice must be thick and very red. Remove the garlic, red pepper and chilli.

Cook's tip: this dish is also suitable for freezing.

Polipi alla Marianna

Octopus Marianna

	00:15		02:30

American	Ingredients	Metric/Imperial
1¾ lb	Octopus	800 g / 1¾ lb
¾ cup	Vinegar	175 ml / 6 fl oz
2	Onions	2
2	Garlic cloves	2
2	Cloves	2
¼ cup	Vegetable oil	50 ml / 2 fl oz
	Salt and pepper	
3 tbsp	Brandy	2 tbsp

1. Preheat oven to 350°F / 180°C / Gas Mark 4.
2. Clean the octopus, remove eyes and vesicles. Wash them thoroughly under a cold tap and then in a mixture of cold water and a ¼ cup [50 ml / 2 fl oz] vinegar. Cut the octopus into large pieces.
3. Finely chop the onion and garlic. Put the octopus in an ovenproof dish, add the chopped garlic and onion, 2 cloves, the oil and the rest of the vinegar. Season generously with salt and pepper, add just enough water to cover all the ingredients. Cover with the lid and then cook in a moderate oven for about 2 hours.
4. Turn the oven up to 425°F / 220°C / Gas Mark 7.
5. Remove the casserole from the oven, sprinkle the brandy over the octopus, put the lid back on the casserole and return to the oven for 20 minutes.

Polipetti e seppioline affogati

Stewed Octopus and Cuttlefish

	00:10		00:30

American	Ingredients	Metric/Imperial
1¼ lb	Octopus and cuttlefish	600 g / 1¼ lb
2	Garlic cloves	2
¼ cup	Vegetable oil	50 ml / 2 fl oz
5	Fresh tomatoes	5
½	Sweet pepper	½
	Salt and pepper	
5 tbsp	White wine (optional)	4 tbsp
1 tbsp	Chopped parsley	1 tbsp

1. Buy the octopus and cuttlefish ready cleaned or frozen. In a stew pot or casserole lightly fry the cloves of garlic in oil, remove the garlic and add the cuttlefish and octopus (if the cuttlefish are large, cut them into rings).
2. Allow fish to cook for a few minutes in the oil, add the tomatoes, peeled and seeded, a piece of sweet pepper, salt and a pinch of pepper, and if liked the white wine. Cover, lower the heat and cook for at least 20 minutes. Serve sprinkled with chopped parsley.

Carpa alla birra
Carp Cooked in Beer

	00:30	00:25

American	Ingredients	Metric/Imperial
1 (1¾ lb)	Carp (freshwater fish)	1 (800 g / 1¾ lb)
¼ cup	Butter	50 g / 2 oz
2 tbsp	Vegetable oil	1½ tbsp
¼ tsp	Chopped rosemary	¼ tsp
¼ tsp	Chopped sage	¼ tsp
¼ tsp	Mixed herbs	¼ tsp
¼ tsp	Chopped bay leaves	¼ tsp
¼ tsp	Chopped thyme	¼ tsp
¼ tsp	Chopped marjoram	¼ tsp
1 quart	Beer	1 litre / 1¾ pints

1. Clean the carp thoroughly, removing the fins and gutting it. Wash and dry.
2. Heat the butter and oil in a pan, add chopped rosemary, sage and herbs and then add the carp.
3. Chop the bay leaves, thyme and marjoram. Turn up the heat under the pan, add the chopped herbs and all the beer together. Reduce the heat to moderate and continue to cook, turning the fish once only.
4. When the fish is cooked, the liquid in the pan should have reduced by half.
5. Transfer the carp to a heated serving dish, sieve the sauce, reheat and pour over the fish. Serve either hot or cold.

Carpa alla Chaplin con riso e salsa
Carp in Sauce with Rice

	01:00	01:00

American	Ingredients	Metric/Imperial
1 (2 lb)	Carp	1 (1 kg / 2 lb)
	Salt and pepper	
3	Garlic cloves	3
2	Cloves	2
¼ tsp	Powdered bay leaves	¼ tsp
¼ tsp	Powdered thyme	¼ tsp
4	Lemons	4
1	Onion	1
1	Carrot	1
2 tbsp	Chopped parsley	1½ tbsp
2 tbsp	Butter	25 g / 1 oz
¼ cup	Flour	25 g / 1 oz
1 cup	Rice	200 g / 7 oz

1. Clean the carp, remove the scales, wash and cut into slices, lay these in a deep dish and sprinkle with salt.
2. In a mortar, pound 1 clove of garlic, 1 clove and the powdered bay and thyme, gradually add the juice of 1 lemon and pour this mixture over the fish. Leave for 20 minutes, stirring from time to time.
3. Chop the other clove of garlic, the onion, carrot and parsley and put into a pan with 2½ cups [600 ml / 1 pint] of water. Add 1 clove, the juice of a lemon, some shavings of lemon peel and a little pepper, bring to the boil and simmer until the vegetables are cooked. Add 2½ cups [600 ml / 1 pint] of cold water and strain into a heatproof casserole. Transfer the fish

from the marinade into the casserole, bring the liquid to the boil and simmer for 15 minutes.
4. Remove the fish and place on a heated serving dish, taking care that it does not break. Remove half the liquid, reduce the remainder and thicken by adding the butter mixed with flour in small pieces, whisk until smooth.
5. Surround the fish with boiled or steamed rice, pour some of the sauce over the fish and serve the rest separately in a sauceboat.

Conchiglie di pesce gratinato
Scalloped Dentex au Gratin

	00:30	00:20

American	Ingredients	Metric/Imperial
14 oz	Dentex (perch)	400 g / 14 oz
¼ cup	Butter	50 g / 2 oz
¼ cup	Cognac	50 ml / 2 fl oz
1 cup	Béchamel sauce	225 ml / 8 fl oz
1	Egg yolk	1
2 tbsp	Grated parmesan cheese	1½ tbsp
½ cup	Bread crumbs	50 g / 2 oz
4	Scallop shells	4

1. Preheat oven to 400°F / 200°C / Gas Mark 6.
2. Poach the fish, drain and remove the skin and bones.
3. Dice the flesh and sauté lightly in butter. Sprinkle with a little cognac.
4. Prepare the béchamel sauce, then stir in an egg yolk and the grated cheese.
5. Butter the scallop shells and spoon a little béchamel into each; then lay the fish on it and cover with another layer of sauce. Top with bread crumbs and crisp in the oven for a few minutes.

Dentici alle mandorle
Dentex with Almonds

	00:20	01:00

American	Ingredients	Metric/Imperial
2	Dentex (perch)	2
2	Lemons	2
12	Peppercorns	12
	Salt	
1	Carrot	1
1	Celery stalk	1
1	Small bunch of parsley	1
½ cup	Flaked almonds	50 g / 2 oz
¼ cup	Vegetable oil	50 ml / 2 fl oz
1	Onion	1
2 tbsp	Flour	15 g / ½ oz
Scant ¼ cup	Tomato paste	3 tbsp
1½ cups	Green olives	225 g / 8 oz
2 tbsp	Capers	1½ tbsp
½ tsp	Anchovy paste	½ tsp
¼ cup	Wine vinegar	50 ml / 2 fl oz
1 tsp	Sugar	1 tsp

Scalloped dentex au gratin

1. Clean and wash the fish, put in a fish kettle with 1 lemon (cut in half), peppercorns, chopped carrot and celery, a bunch of parsley, some salt and plenty of water. Bring the water to the boil, then reduce the heat and cook gently for about 30 minutes. Turn off the heat and allow the fish to cool in the liquor.

2. Start preparing the sauce by toasting the almonds lightly in the oven.

3. Slice the onion into rings and sauté gently in oil; remove the pan from the heat, stir in the flour and the tomato paste, add a little warm water and bring to the boil. Stone the olives, add to the pan with the chopped capers and cook for 20 minutes. Stir in a very little anchovy paste, the vinegar, sugar and finally, the chopped almonds. Allow to cool but do not chill in the refrigerator.

4. Lay the fish on an oval dish, pour the cool sauce over it and garnish with slices of lemon and toasted almonds arranged alternately.

Perch rolls

Involtini di pesce persico
Perch Rolls

◤ 00:30   00:30 ◖

American	Ingredients	Metric/Imperial
8	Perch	8
4	Salted anchovies	4
1	Small bunch of parsley	1
1	Garlic clove	1
	Salt and pepper	
16	Sage leaves	16
¼ cup	Flour	25 g / 1 oz
¼ cup	Butter	50 g / 2 oz
¼ cup	Vegetable oil	50 ml / 2 fl oz
1	Lemon	1

1. Clean the perch carefully, split each one into half and remove all the bones.
2. Wash, split and bone the anchovies, then cut each half into two.
3. Chop the garlic with half the parsley and sprinkle this mixture onto the fish halves. Add pepper, a leaf of sage and a piece of anchovy. Roll the perch around the anchovy and herb filling and secure with a toothpick. Flour the rolls.

4. Heat the oil and butter in a heavy pan, then slip in the fish rolls and cook over medium heat.
5. When the fish are cooked on all sides, sprinkle with the remaining chopped parsley, the juice of a lemon, salt and pepper. Leave them in the pan for 1 minute, then serve hot.

Cotolette di pesce persico
Fried Fillets of Perch

◤ 00:30   00:10 ◖
   Marinating time 02:00

American	Ingredients	Metric/Imperial
1	Egg	1
1	Lemon	1
4	Fillets of perch	4
1	Large bunch of sage	1
¼ cup	Butter	50 g / 2 oz
¼ cup	Vegetable oil	50 ml / 2 fl oz
1 cup	Bread crumbs	100 g / 4 oz
2	Sweet red peppers	2

1. Beat the egg and lemon juice together until the mixture becomes a pale yellow cream. Immerse the fillets of perch in this mixture, completely cover with sage leaves and marinate for 2 hours, turning once only.
2. Heat the butter and oil in a frying pan, sauté some sage leaves for 1-2 minutes, then discard the sage.
3. Coat the marinated fillets, one at a time, with bread crumbs, slip them into the pan and cook for 8-9 minutes, only turning once.
4. Serve hot with the deseeded sliced sweet red peppers.

Salmone in salsa verde
Salmon in Green Sauce

02:00   01:00

American	Ingredients	Metric/Imperial
1 cup	White wine	225 ml / 8 fl oz
	Bouquet garni	
2	Carrots	2
1	Onion	1
4	Slightly crushed peppercorns	4
2 lb	Salmon	1 kg / 2 lb
5 tsp	Gelatin	5 tsp
3 tbsp	Port	2 tbsp
4	Eggs	4
1	Bunch of parsley	1
1	Bunch of watercress	1
1	Small bunch of tarragon	1
1	Gherkin	1
1	Anchovy fillet	1
½ cup	Butter	100 g / 4 oz
¼ cup	Vegetable oil	50 ml / 2 fl oz
2 tbsp	Vinegar	1½ tbsp
	Salt and pepper	
2	Tomatoes	2

1. Prepare a court-bouillon by bringing the white wine and an equal quantity of water to the boil with bouquet garni, sliced carrots, onions and peppercorns. Lower the heat, cover and simmer for 30 minutes, then allow to cool.
2. Clean and wash the pieces of salmon and put them in a saucepan with the court-bouillon. Cover and bring back to the boil. Lower the heat and simmer for 30 minutes
3. Lift the fish carefully from the liquid using a fish slice and place on a serving dish. Strain the liquid through a fine sieve or muslin and retain.
4. Prepare a gelatin by sprinkling on top of 3 tablespoons boiling water; dissolve completely. Add to this 2½ cups [600 ml / 1 pint] of the fish liquid, with the port; mix well.
5. Hard-cook (boil) 3 eggs, rinse in cold water, separate yolk from white in remaining egg.
6. Wash the parsley, watercress and tarragon and chop in a blender with the gherkin and anchovy fillet.
7. Soften the butter and add to the blender gradually with 1 raw egg yolk and 1 hard-cooked egg yolk. Switch on the machine again, add the oil, vinegar, salt and pepper, blending all together. Transfer to a sauceboat.
8. Cover the fish with the jelly allowing it to run on to the serving dish. Coat fish several times with wine jelly.
9. Garnish the serving dish and fish with slices of tomato, sliced hard-cooked eggs and the jelly, on the plate, roughly chopped with a knife.

Salmone del ghiottone
Salmon Filler

00:30   00:15

American	Ingredients	Metric/Imperial
½ lb	Potatoes	225 g / 8 oz
Scant ¼ cup	Milk	3 tbsp
2 tbsp	Butter	25 g / 1 oz
7 oz can	Salmon	200 g / 7 oz can
	Salt and pepper	
⅔ cup	Mayonnaise	150 ml / ¼ pint
2	Hard-cooked (boiled) eggs	2
4	Gherkins	4
1 tsp	Capers	1 tsp
6	Olives	6

1. Peel, quarter and cook 2 large potatoes, drain and mash with milk and a knob of butter.
2. Drain the salmon and remove the bones. Put the mashed potatoes and salmon together in a bowl, add salt and pepper and combine until the mixture is smooth and uniform. Cover and cool.
3. Choose an oval dish, shape the mixture into the form of a fish and garnish with mayonnaise, slices of hard-cooked (boiled) egg, gherkins, capers and olives. Serve with rice or potato salad and green salad.

Trotelle salmonate
Young Salmon Trout

00:35   00:40

American	Ingredients	Metric/Imperial
4	Young trout	4
1	Celery stalk	1
1	Onion	1
2	Carrots	2
	Salt	
¼ cup	Cream	50 ml / 2 fl oz
1 cup	Béchamel sauce	225 ml / 8 fl oz
1 tsp	Herb mustard	1 tsp
1 cup	Mayonnaise	225 ml / 8 fl oz
1	Lemon	1
1	Sprig of parsley	1

1. Wash, gut and clean the fish. Place in a saucepan.
2. Pour enough cold water to cover the fish into the saucepan and put in all the washed roughly chopped vegetables. Season with salt.
3. Bring to the boil and simmer gently for 15 minutes, remove from the water carefully with a fish slice, place on a serving dish and allow to cool.
4. Make a thick cream by mixing together the cream, béchamel sauce, mustard and the mayonnaise.
5. Remove the skin from the young trout and cover completely with the savoury sauce. The fish can be garnished with slices of lemon and sprigs of parsley. Serve with boiled potatoes and sliced zucchini (courgettes) or green beans.

Tinche alla piemontese
Piedmontese Tench

⊳ 00:15   00:35 🍲

American	Ingredients	Metric/Imperial
6	Tench (freshwater fish)	6
¾ cup	Flour	75 g / 3 oz
	Salt and pepper	
3 tbsp	Butter	40 g / 1 ½ oz
1	Onion	1
½ tsp	Sage	½ tsp
3 tbsp	Vinegar	2 tbsp
3 tbsp	Grape juice	2 tbsp

1. Thoroughly clean the tench and dip in flour, season with salt and pepper.
2. In a frying pan heat the butter, fry the fish on both sides and keep warm.
3. Put the finely chopped onion and the sage in the cooking juices, cook for 4 minutes until the onion is soft and transparent, add the vinegar and grape juice. Boil for 4 minutes, pour the sauce over the fish and serve hot.

Tench Piedmontese

Trout in cases

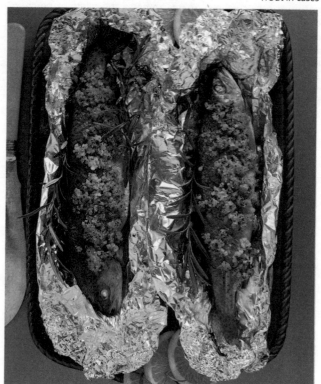

Trota al cartoccio
Trout in Cases

⊳ 00:20   00:35 🍲

American	Ingredients	Metric/Imperial
4	Trout	4
½ tsp	Chopped thyme	½ tsp
½ tsp	Chopped marjoram	½ tsp
½ tsp	Chopped rosemary	½ tsp
	Salt and pepper	
1	Lemon	1
2	Garlic cloves	2
½ cup	Olives, stoned	75 g / 3 oz
1 tbsp	Chopped parsley	1 tbsp
¼ cup	Butter	50 g / 2 oz
½ lb	Tomatoes	225 g / 8 oz
½ cup	Flour	50 g / 2 oz
½ cup	Dry white wine	125 ml / 4 fl oz

1. Clean, gut and wash the trout, then stuff the stomachs with a mixture of thyme, marjoram, rosemary, salt, pepper and the juice of the lemon.
2. Crush the garlic, chop the olives and mix with the chopped parsley.
3. Heat 1 tablespoon [15 g / ½ oz] butter in a pan and add the garlic, parsley and olives with the peeled chopped tomatoes and cook gently for 10 minutes.
4. Dip the trout in flour, shake off excess, heat the remaining butter, cook the trout until golden on each side.
5. Preheat the oven to 350°F / 180°C / Gas Mark 4.
6. Place each trout on a sheet of foil, sprinkle with white wine, cover with the olive and tomato sauce and season with salt and pepper. Close the foil cases, arrange on a baking sheet and cook in the oven for about 20 minutes.
7. Unwrap the foil cases and serve on heated plates.

Trotelle ripiene

Stuffed Young Trout

⏱ 01:00   00:35 🍲

American	Ingredients	Metric/Imperial
4	Young trout	4
3 oz	Mild provolone cheese	75 g / 3 oz
1	Small bunch of parsley	1
4	Crayfish tails	4
	Salt and pepper	
4 drops	Worcester sauce	4 drops
3 tbsp	Cognac	40 ml / 1½ fl oz
1	Egg	1
4	Whole crayfish	4
¼ cup	Dry white wine	50 ml / 2 fl oz
1 tbsp	Vegetable oil	1 tbsp
½	Lemon	½
⅔ cup	Cream	150 ml / ¼ pint
2 tbsp	Flour	15 g / ½ oz
1 tbsp	Tomato purée	1 tbsp
3 tbsp	Butter	40 g / 1½ oz

1. Clean the trout, cut them half open with scissors, then remove the backbone with all the bones, being careful not to remove the head.

2. Grate the cheese. Chop the parsley. Thoroughly wash all the crayfish and remove just the flesh from the shell of the four tails.

3. In an earthenware dish put the provolone, the parsley, a little salt, a good pinch of pepper, 2 drops of Worcester sauce, 2 teaspoons of cognac and a little less than a whole egg. Stir well and blend together. Spread the prepared mixture onto each trout, and place a crayfish tail on top, then roll up the trout, starting with the tail, keeping it tightly against the crayfish.

4. Preheat the oven to 400°F / 200°C / Gas Mark 6.

5. Arrange the fish in a high-sided container, add the remaining crayfish, season with salt and pepper, sprinkle with white wine and 1 tablespoon of oil. Add remaining cognac and the juice of half a lemon. Put a sheet of oiled parchment paper or foil over the container and bake in a hot oven for 25 minutes. When cooked, lift the trout on to a serving dish and keep warm.

6. Strain the remaining juice of the fish container into a pan, add the cream in which 2 tablespoons [15 g / ½ oz] flour, has been blended. Put the pan on the heat and stirring continuously, bring to the boil. Add 1 tablespoon of tomato purée and a few drops of Worcester sauce. Taste and if necessary, add salt. Blend in the butter, pour the sauce into a sauceboat and serve with the fish.

Stuffed young trout

Selecting and cooking fish

Make sure that fish and shellfish are really fresh when purchased. Look for bright eyes, stiff flesh and a shiny carpace in shellfish. Dull eyes accompanied by limp flesh and even the faintest whiff of ammonia indicate staleness.

Try to buy fish on the day it is going to be cooked and eaten. If storing in the refrigerator, cover loosely. It is best to cook and eat the fish within 24 hours.

Cooking fish

Deep frying

Many of the fish recipes in this book use this method as it is a popular way of eating fish in Italy. As frying requires boiling oil there are some simple but essential points to keep in mind.

- Use a deep pan and do not fill with oil. The oil should come no more than two-thirds of the way up the pan.
- Do not allow naked flames to lick up the side of the pan as even a splash of fat can cause a fire.
- If, by any unfortunate chance, the fat does catch fire never use water to douse flames. Turn off the heat immediately and cover the flames and pan, to exclude air, with a metal lid. Try not to move the pan as this can result in injury.

Food is usually coated before frying to prevent the fish breaking up and the fat soaking through the food. This can be done with flour or egg and breadcrumbs used as a coating, or by dipping the fish in batter. The fat must be heated to a high temperature to seal the outside or the result will be unappetizing. Heat the oil to 325°-375°F / 170°-190°C depending on the amount of fish which is being cooked at one time. Do not fill the pan with too much food as this lowers the temperature of the oil.

To test the temperature of the oil without a thermometer, drop a cube of stale bread into the oil; it should rise to the surface evenly browned in 1 minute.

Shallow frying or sautéing

This is a method of cooking food in a shallow frying pan with oil which reaches half way up the food to be cooked. Again the oil must be hot to seal the fish.

Broiling (grilling)

This is a good and fast method of cooking whole fish, large fillets and fish steaks. Heat the broiler (grill) before starting to cook the fish, brush with oil before cooking. It is better to make slits across the backs of whole fish such as trout before cooking, as this allows the heat to cook the fish evenly. Cooking time will depend on the size and thickness of the fish, an average-sized fish ¾ lb / 350 g will take about 10 minutes.

Poaching

This method is used for cooking whole fish, fish fillets and fish steaks in liquid which can be water, fish stock or milk. Poached fish is gently cooked over a low heat to ensure that the fish keeps its delicate flavor. It should not be boiled.

Baking

Whole fish and fish fillets can be baked in the oven with oil butter and herbs at 350°F / 180°C / Gas Mark 4. Sometimes wine or sauce is added during cooking.

Fish stock

Any liquid which has been used to cook fish becomes a stock and should be retained for use in sauces or cooking other fish. It is worth freezing if not required within a short time.

To make a good fish stock trimmings are used, so it is wise to ask the fishmonger to give you the trimmings if you are having fish filleted. Bring the fish trimmings to the boil with a chopped onion, carrot, bay leaf, bouquet garni, a few peppercorns, some white wine or white wine vinegar and 1 quart [1 litre / 1¾ pints] water. Lower the heat when the mixture boils and simmer for 25-30 minutes. Unlike beef stock, fish stock should not be cooked for hours otherwise it becomes bitter. Strain the stock and use as required.

Useful equipment for cooking fish: thermostatically controlled fryer, deep fat pan with basket, thick frying pans, fish slice.

Meat

3. Remove all the fat from the pan and pour in the wine used for marinating. When this has evaporated, add the chicken stock and simmer for 2 hours. Alternatively cook in the oven at 375°F / 190°C / Gas Mark 5.
4. Remove the capon to a heated dish, allow to stand for 10 minutes before carving.
5. Add the cognac to the sauce and stir well, sieve and serve in a sauceboat.

Braised capon

Cappone al brunello

Capon Braised in Red Wine

	00:20		02:15
	Marinating time 06:00		

American	Ingredients	Metric/Imperial
1 (4½ lb)	Medium-sized young capon	1 (2 kg / 4½ lb)
1	Onion	1
2	Carrots	2
1	Celery stalk	1
1	Bay leaf	1
1	Sprig of thyme	1
2	Cloves	2
	Salt and pepper	
1 (70 cl)	Bottle of red wine	1 (70 cl)
3 tbsp	Butter	40 g / 1½ oz
2 oz	Bacon	50 g / 2 oz
1 cup	Chicken stock	225 ml / 8 fl oz
3 tbsp	Cognac	2 tbsp

1. Wash and dry the capon. Prepare a marinade with sliced onion, carrots and celery, bay leaf, sprig of thyme, 2 cloves, pepper and the wine. Put the capon in a large plastic bag with the marinade and leave for 5 to 6 hours.
2. Remove from the marinade and transfer to a large, heavy saucepan containing melted butter and the diced bacon. Brown the capon, add the strained vegetables from the marinade.

Cappone ripieno

Stuffed Capon

	00:30		01:30
	Serves 6		

American	Ingredients	Metric/Imperial
1 (4½ lb)	Capon	1 (2 kg / 4½ lb)
¼ lb	Stale bread	100 g / 4 oz
⅔ cup	Milk	150 ml / ¼ pint
2 oz	Cooked ham	50 g / 2 oz
1 oz	Capers	25 g / 1 oz
½ tsp	Chopped sage	½ tsp
¼ tsp	Chopped rosemary	¼ tsp
1	Egg	1
	Salt and pepper	
1	Lemon	1
¼ cup	Butter	50 g / 2 oz
½ cup	Red wine	125 ml / 4 fl oz

1. Preheat the oven to 375°F / 190°C / Gas Mark 5.
2. Wash and dry the capon. Soak the bread in the milk, squeeze out the excess moisture and combine it with the diced ham and the capon's liver, washed and chopped. Chop the capers and a little sage and rosemary together and add with a beaten egg to the bread and milk mixture. Season well.
3. Stuff the capon carefully, sew up the aperture and sprinkle with a mixture of lemon juice and chopped sage.
4. Heat the butter in a large casserole, brown the capon well on all sides, pour in the red wine and cook in the oven for 1½ hours. Carve and keep warm.
5. Make a gravy with the cooking juices and little water if necessary, season and serve in a sauceboat.

Timballo di caccia

Timbale of Game

	00:30		02:00

American	Ingredients	Metric/Imperial
14 oz	Ground (minced) game or chicken	400 g / 14 oz
¼ lb	Chicken livers	100 g / 4 oz
5 oz	Raw ham	150 g / 5 oz
4	Eggs	4
1½ cups	Grated parmesan cheese	175 g / 6 oz
	Salt and pepper	
½ tsp	Nutmeg	½ tsp
1	Truffle	1
8	Slices of fat bacon to line the mold	8

1. Preheat the oven to 325°F / 170°C / Gas Mark 3.
2. Put the ground meat into a bowl, add washed, chopped chicken livers and chopped raw ham. Mix well adding the egg yolks, the grated cheese, salt, pepper, nutmeg and truffle. Finally; add the egg whites beaten to a stiff froth.
3. Line a small loaf pan with slices of fat bacon, so that they adhere properly. Pour the mixture into the pan, cover with the ends of fat bacon linings and a piece of foil.
4. Place the loaf pan in a roasting pan, pour boiling water carefully into the roasting pan until it reaches half way up the loaf pan.
5. Cook for 2 hours, remove from oven and allow to cool. Turn out and serve with crusty bread or toast.

Ruspante alla sabinese
Sabine-Style Chicken

00:25   01:15

American	Ingredients	Metric/Imperial
1 (3 lb)	Chicken	1 (1.4 kg / 3 lb)
2	Whole salt-cured anchovies	2
⅓ cup	Green olives, stoned	50 g / 2 oz
1	Red chilli pepper	1
1 tbsp	Capers	1 tbsp
Scant ¼ cup	Olive oil	3 tbsp
½ cup	Dry frascati	125 ml / 4 fl oz
	Salt	
½	Stock cube	½

1. Preheat the oven to 375°F / 190°C / Gas Mark 5.
2. Prepare the chicken, wash and dry thoroughly.
3. Wash and bone the anchovies and chop together with the olives, deseeded chilli and capers.
4. Heat the oil in a casserole until very hot, then add the whole chicken, turning to brown evenly.
5. Pour in the frascati and allow to bubble for 2 minutes. Turn down the heat and add the chopped anchovies, olives, chilli and capers. Season lightly with salt.
6. Cover and transfer to the oven for 30 minutes. Check to see if juice is drying out, add ½ cup [125 ml / 4 fl oz] chicken stock. Cook for a further 30 minutes.
7. Carve and serve with olive sauce poured over.

Pollo alla birra
Chicken Braised in Ale

00:25   01:10

American	Ingredients	Metric/Imperial
1 (3 lb)	Chicken	1 (1.4 kg / 3 lb)
3 tbsp	Flour	2 tbsp
2 tbsp	Vegetable oil	1½ tbsp
3 tbsp	Butter	40 g / 1½ oz
	Salt and pepper	
2 oz	Pork fat	50 g / 2 oz
2	Onions	2
3 cups	Light ale	700 ml / 1¼ pints

1. Wash the chicken, then cut into quarters and flour lightly.
2. Heat the oil and butter and sauté the chicken until brown on all sides. Season with a sprinkling of salt and pepper.

3. Preheat the oven to 350°F / 180°C / Gas Mark 4.
4. Chop the pork fat into small pieces and slice the onions finely. Put all the pork fat and some of the onions into a casserole, dust lightly with flour and lay the chicken on top, followed with another layer of onions.
5. Heat the ale in a pan with the cooking juices from the chicken, pour over the chicken. Cover and cook in the oven for about 45 minutes. Check for seasoning.
6. Transfer the chicken to a heated serving dish and keep warm. Sieve the sauce, thicken if necessary, pour into a sauceboat and serve with the chicken.

Pollo al cartoccio
Chicken Baked in Foil

00:15   01:25

American	Ingredients	Metric/Imperial
1 (3 lb)	Chicken	1 (1.4 kg / 3 lb)
1	Garlic clove	1
1	Sprig of rosemary	1
2 or 3	Sage leaves	2 or 3
¼ cup	Olive oil	50 ml / 2 fl oz
	Salt and pepper	
3 or 4	Slices of fat tuscany ham	3 or 4
¼ cup	Sherry or brandy	50 ml / 2 fl oz

1. Preheat the oven to 350°F / 180°C / Gas Mark 4.
2. Wash and dry the chicken thoroughly. Place the garlic and herbs inside, rub all over with olive oil, sprinkle lightly with salt and pepper and cover with the slices of ham, securing with thread or fine string.
3. Place on a sheet of foil, moisten with sherry or brandy, close the foil and bake in a moderate oven for about 1¼ hours or until cooked.
4. Carve and serve hot or cold with a mixed salad.

Fegatini al pompelmo in coppa
Liver in Grapefruit Cups

00:30   00:30

American	Ingredients	Metric/Imperial
4	Large grapefruits	4
1¾ lb	Chicken livers	800 g / 1¾ lb
	Salt	
1 tbsp	Flour	1 tbsp
Scant ¼ cup	Olive oil	3 tbsp
2 tbsp	Butter	25 g / 1 oz
2 tbsp	Marsala	1½ tbsp
	Pepper	

1. Cut off the top quarter of the grapefruits. Hollow out the insides and scrape out all the flesh without breaking the peel, which will subsequently act as a cup. Squeeze juice from grapefruit flesh.
2. Clean the livers, chop into pieces, season with salt and dip in the flour.
3. Heat the oil in a pan with butter, brown the chicken livers.
4. Sprinkle with marsala and pepper, turn from time to time, then add the juice of the grapefruit.
5. Serve liver mixture in the grapefruit cups.

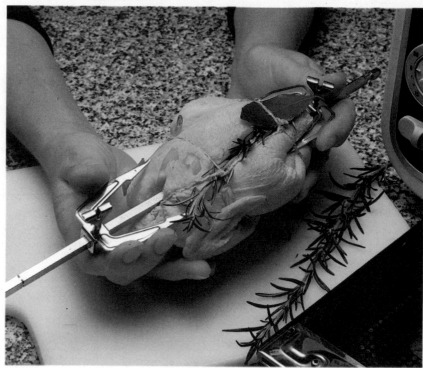

Spit-roasted spring chicken

Prosciuttini di pollo
Chicken Hams

This delicious recipe comes from Sergio Lorenzi who uses it with great success in his Pisa restaurant 'Da Sergio', which is very popular for its excellent cuisine.

00:40   01:00

American	Ingredients	Metric/Imperial
8	Chicken thighs	8
1 cup	Ground (minced) veal	225 g / 8 oz
¼ lb	Parma ham	100 g / 4 oz
½ cup	Grated parmesan cheese	50 g / 2 oz
	Salt and pepper	
Scant ¼ cup	Olive oil	3 tbsp
¼ cup	Dry white wine	50 ml / 2 fl oz
1 cup	Cream	225 ml / 8 fl oz

1. Bone the thighs, (this is a tricky job that requires some patience). Use a very sharp, slim knife and slide it between the bone and the flesh, turning the flesh back on itself as you loosen it and taking great care not to cut the skin. Hopefully there will be 8 little empty bags at the end of this operation ready for the stuffing.
2. Preheat the oven to 350°F / 180°C / Gas Mark 4.
3. Make a stuffing for the chicken thighs by mixing together the ground veal, chopped parma ham and grated parmesan. Add salt and pepper and mix well.
4. Stuff the thighs and sew them up carefully to resemble miniature hams.
5. Flour the 'little hams' (prosciuttini). Heat the olive oil in a shallow frying pan and sauté the chicken thighs until golden on each side. Season with salt and a few twists of freshly ground black pepper.
6. When golden transfer to a roasting pan and put in the moderate oven for 30 minutes to complete the cooking.

7. Transfer the chicken to a heated serving dish and keep warm. Reheat the pan juices, add the wine and cream, stir over a low heat until the sauce has acquired a good consistency.
8. Pour the sauce over the chicken and serve with green peas or carrots tossed in butter.

Galletti allo spiedo
Spit-Roasted Spring Chicken

00:25   01:00 to 01:25

American	Ingredients	Metric/Imperial
2 (3¼ lb)	Spring chickens	2 (1.5 kg / 3¼ lb)
2	Small onions	2
4	Cloves	4
1 tsp	Sage	1 tsp
2	Bay leaves	2
½ tsp	Rosemary	½ tsp
	Salt and pepper	
Scant ¼ cup	Vegetable oil	5 tbsp

1. Buy the chickens with the giblets, wash thoroughly.
2. Stick the onions with cloves and place in the stomach cavity of each chicken.
3. Chop the giblets, add sage, bay leaves and rosemary; stuff the chicken crop end with this mixture, season with salt and pepper. Close the openings with skewers or sew with kitchen thread.
4. Thread the birds onto the spit, sprinkle liberally with salt and pepper and brush with oil. While roasting, continue to baste or brush with oil to crisp the skin.
5. Test by inserting a skewer into the thigh joint, if juice is still pink, continue cooking until it is clear.
6. Remove from spit and carve.

Corona di pollo e olive
Chicken and Olive Ring

🔻 02:00　　　　01:15 🍲

American	Ingredients	Metric/Imperial
1 (3¼ lb)	Small chicken	1 (1.5 kg / 3¼ lb)
Scant ¼ cup	Vegetable oil	3 tbsp
2 tbsp	Butter	25 g / 1 oz
2	Sprigs of rosemary	2
2	Eggs	2
5 oz	Piece of tongue	150 g / 5 oz
1¼ cups	Gelatin	300 ml / ½ pint
¼ lb	Green olives	100 g / 4 oz
¼ lb	Black olives	100 g / 4 oz
1	Lettuce	1
1	Bunch of watercress	1

1. Pot-roast the chicken with oil, butter and rosemary for 1¼ hours.
2. Remove from the pot, allow to cool slightly, skin and remove flesh from the bones.
3. Hard-cook (boil) eggs, cool in cold water, remove shells. Cut the tongue into strips, discarding any fat.
4. Prepare the gelatin according to the maker's instructions and put a little of it in a mold (preferably a ring mold with a hole in the middle) and refrigerate. When the gelatin in the mold has set, arrange on it the chicken, tongue, olives and the sliced or quartered eggs. Top up with the cool gelatin and refrigerate. To serve, plunge the mold quickly into water and then turn onto a serving dish lined with lettuce leaves and watercress and remove the mold.

Budellette di pollo al limone
Chicken Livers with Lemon

🔻 00:30　　　　00:40 🍲

American	Ingredients	Metric/Imperial
1 lb	Chicken giblets and chicken livers	450 g / 1 lb
1	Onion	1
1	Carrot	1
1	Celery stalk	1
¼ lb	Mortadella	100 g / 4 oz
¼ cup	Butter	50 g / 2 oz
	Salt and pepper	
2½ cups	Chicken stock	600 ml / 1 pint
2	Egg yolks	2
1	Lemon	1
3 tbsp	Chopped parsley	2 tbsp

1. Wash the giblets well in hot water, chop finely.
2. Slice the onion, carrot and celery and cut the mortadella into thin strips; sauté in the heated butter. Add the giblets and season with salt and pepper. Cover with stock, bring to the boil then lower the heat and simmer for about 35 minutes.
3. Beat the egg yolks, add lemon juice and a little of the cooking liquid, mix well. Pour into the pan with the livers.
4. Stir well, remove from the heat and serve immediately, sprinkled with chopped parsley. Serve with rice or toast.

Pollo al formaggio
Chicken in Cheese Sauce

🔻 00:40　　　　01:00 🍲

American	Ingredients	Metric/Imperial
1 (3 lb)	Chicken	1 (1.4 kg / 3 lb)
	Flour	
3 tbsp	Olive oil	2 tbsp
2 tbsp	Butter	25 g / 1 oz
	Salt	
1 tsp	Paprika pepper	1 tsp
2 cups	Stock	450 ml / ¾ pint
1 cup	Dry white wine	225 ml / 8 fl oz
5 oz	Emmental cheese	150 g / 5 oz
¼ tsp	Nutmeg	¼ tsp
1 tbsp	Chopped parsley	1 tbsp

1. Wash the chicken, dry carefully and cut into quarters. Flour lightly.
2. Heat the oil and butter in a pan, add the chicken, brown all over, and sprinkle with a little salt and paprika pepper. As soon as the chicken has colored, cover with stock, turn down the heat to moderate and simmer, covered, for 30 minutes.
3. Add the wine, vaporize and continue to cook until the meat is tender, taking care that the liquor neither dries up nor darkens. Transfer the chicken to a dish and keep warm.
4. Grate the emmental and add it to the pan, away from the heat, then replace the pan on the stove over a gentle heat and add the rest of the wine. Stir the sauce, which should remain liquid and smooth. Check the seasoning and, at the last moment, add a pinch of grated nutmeg and a spoonful of chopped parsley. Serve immediately poured onto the chicken.

Coppette Stefania
Chicken and Cream Salad

🔻 00:35　　　　00:15 🍲

American	Ingredients	Metric/Imperial
2	Filleted chicken breasts	2
¼ cup	Butter	50 g / 2 oz
½ tsp	Chopped sage	½ tsp
2 cups	Beanshoots	100 g / 4 oz
¼ lb	Gruyère cheese	100 g / 4 oz
1 cup	Mayonnaise	225 ml / 8 fl oz
3 tbsp	Brandy	2 tbsp
2 tbsp	Tomato purée	1½ tbsp
½ cup	Cream	125 ml / 4 fl oz
	Salt and pepper	
1	Lettuce	1

1. Sauté the chicken breasts in butter and sage for 6 minutes each side on a gentle heat. Cool and cut into narrow strips.
2. Plunge the beanshoots into boiling water for 1 minute then drain well. Cut the gruyère into matchstick pieces.
3. Place the chicken, beanshoots and cheese in a bowl.
4. Prepare the sauce by blending the mayonnaise, brandy, tomato paste and cream together until the mixture is light and frothy, then fold into the other ingredients and season.
5. Cover the bowl and refrigerate until required. Serve in individual bowls each lined with a few crisp leaves of lettuce.

Chicken and lobster

Pollo con aragostina
Chicken and Lobster

	01:00		01:20

American	Ingredients	Metric/Imperial
1 (3 lb)	Young chicken	1 (1.4 kg / 3 lb)
2 tbsp	Vegetable oil	1½ tbsp
½ cup	Butter	100 g / 4 oz
1	Onion	1
1	Garlic clove	1
	Salt and pepper	
1	Bay leaf	1
¼ cup	Dry white wine	50 ml / 2 fl oz
4	Ripe tomatoes	4
1	Sprig of rosemary	1
¼ cup	Pine kernels	25 g / 1 oz
1 cup	Green peas	150 g / 5 oz
1 (1¼ lb)	Cooked lobster	1 (600 g / 1¼ lb)
3 tbsp	Cognac	2 tbsp

1. Wash and dry a prepared chicken, cut into pieces of roughly equal size. Heat the oil and half the butter and sauté the chicken joints for 5 minutes each side.
2. Add the onion, chopped and crushed clove of garlic, season with salt and pepper, add the bay leaf, pour in the wine, bubble for 2 minutes, then lower the heat. Add the chopped tomatoes and rosemary. Cover and cook for 45 minutes.
3. Add the chopped pine kernels and the peas. Complete the cooking, check the seasoning, remove from the heat and keep warm.
4. Extract the meat from the boiled lobster, using a sharp knife to remove the meat from the tail. Break the claws with a small hammer and remove the meat with a skewer. Chop all the meat.
5. Heat the remaining butter in a pan, sauté the lobster pieces then douse with cognac, set alight, and season with salt and pepper. Combine the chicken and lobster in the pan with all the juices and serve hot with boiled rice.

Pollo alla boscaiola
Chicken with Mushrooms and Tomatoes

	00:30		01:00

American	Ingredients	Metric/Imperial
1 (4½ lb)	Large chicken	1 (2 kg / 4½ lb)
3 tbsp	Flour	2 tbsp
1	Onion	1
2	Garlic cloves	2
Scant ¼ cup	Oil	3 tbsp
⅓ cup	Butter	75 g / 3 oz
½ cup	Dry white wine	125 ml / 4 fl oz
	Salt and pepper	
2	Sprigs of thyme	2
14 oz	Ripe tomatoes	400 g / 4 oz
1	Stock cube	1
½ lb	Mushrooms	225 g / 8 oz
1 tbsp	Chopped parsley	1 tbsp

1. Preheat the oven to 350°F / 180°C / Gas Mark 4.
2. Wash and dry the chicken, then joint into 6 pieces (see page 313) and flour lightly.
3. Chop the onion into dice, crush 1 clove of garlic and sauté in half the heated oil and butter.
4. As soon as they have colored slightly, remove to a casserole. Add the chicken pieces to the pan, brown lightly on all sides then pour in the wine and turn up the heat to reduce the wine. Season with salt and pepper and add to the casserole with the pan juices and thyme.
5. Skin the tomatoes, remove the seeds and chop coarsely, add them to the chicken with 1¼ cups [300 ml / ½ pint] stock, made from the cube, then cover and put in the oven for 30 minutes.
6. Wash and slice the mushrooms and cook in remaining oil and butter with 1 crushed clove of garlic for 10 minutes; add half the chopped parsley.
7. Remove the chicken from the oven, add the cooked mushrooms, stir well and return for a further 30 minutes.
8. Remove sprigs of thyme and serve piping hot, sprinkled with remaining parsley.

Pollanca ripiena arrosto
Stuffed and Roasted Spring Chicken

	00:30 Serves 6		02:00

American	Ingredients	Metric/Imperial
1 (4½ lb)	Spring chicken	1 (2 kg / 4½ lb)
3	Slices of bread (less crust)	3
1 cup	Stock	225 ml / 8 fl oz
	Chicken livers	
2 oz	Bacon	50 g / 2 oz
2 oz	Italian sausage	50 g / 2 oz
1	Garlic clove	1
1	Shallot	1
1	Small onion	1
1	Egg	1
	Salt and pepper	
2 tbsp	Butter	25 g / 1 oz
2 tbsp	Vegetable oil	1½ tbsp
½ cup	Dry white wine	125 ml / 4 fl oz

1. Preheat oven to 400°F / 200°C / Gas Mark 6.
2. Wash and dry the chicken thoroughly.
3. Prepare a stuffing by soaking the bread in the stock. Chop the chicken liver, the bacon, sausage, garlic, shallot and onion very finely. Mix all together in a bowl and add the soaked bread (squeezed out), egg, salt and pepper. The stuffing can be made in the food processor to save time. Mix thoroughly and stuff the chicken.
4. Sprinkle a little salt on the chicken and rub with butter and oil, place on roasting pan brushed with oil and roast in the oven for 1 hour.
5. Turn the heat down to 325°F / 170°C / Gas Mark 3. Remove the bird from the oven and baste with the wine and stock. Return and cook for a further 1 hour, basting from time to time.
6. Remove the bird to a board and leave to stand for 10 minutes before carving.
7. Make a gravy with the pan juices to serve with the roast chicken.

Petti di pollo allo sherry

Chicken Breasts in Sherry Sauce

⏱ 00:35   00:25 🍲

American	Ingredients	Metric/Imperial
4	Chicken breasts	4
	Salt	
1 tbsp	Flour	1 tbsp
3 oz	Parma ham	75 g / 3 oz
3 oz	Fontina cheese	75 g / 3 oz
1	Black truffle	1
2 tbsp	Olive oil	1½ tbsp
2 tbsp	Butter	25 g / 1 oz
1	Small onion	1
½ cup	Dry sherry	125 ml / 4 fl oz
1 cup	Stock	225 ml / 8 fl oz

1. Choose 4 plump breasts of chicken. Using a thin, sharp knife, open up each breast laterally to form a pouch. Flatten by pounding, season with salt and flour lightly.
2. Place 2 slices of ham (cut to fit), a thin slice of fontina and a sliver of truffle inside each one. Close and secure with toothpicks.
3. Heat the oil and butter in a large frying pan, chop the onion and sauté for 4 minutes. When the onion starts to color, add the chicken breasts and brown on both sides.
4. Pour in the sherry and allow to evaporate. Continue to cook, moistening the chicken from time to time with a little stock for a further 15 minutes. Make a gravy to serve with the chicken, using the juices from the pan.

Petti di pollo fritti

Chicken Breasts Fried in Batter

⏱ 00:30   00:08 🍲
Marinating time 01:30

American	Ingredients	Metric/Imperial
½ tsp	Chopped bay leaves	½ tsp
½ tsp	Chopped rosemary	½ tsp
1	Garlic clove	1
⅔ cup	Olive oil	150 ml / ¼ pint
1	Lemon	1
	Salt and pepper	
4	Chicken breasts	4
½ cup	All purpose (plain) flour	50 g / 2 oz
1	Egg	1
½ cup	Milk	125 ml / 4 fl oz
	Vegetable oil for frying	
	Lemon wedges	

1. Chop bay leaves and rosemary, crush the garlic and put in a bowl with the olive oil, lemon juice, salt and pepper.
2. Immerse the chicken breasts and marinate for 1½ hours turning from time to time.
3. Prepare a fairly thick batter by whisking flour, beaten egg and milk with a pinch of salt.
4. Coat the chicken breasts with batter. Heat some vegetable oil in a deep frying pan and when it is really hot slip in the

chicken breasts and cook until crisp and brown. Drain on absorbent kitchen towels.
5. Serve hot with lemon wedges and grilled tomatoes.

Pollo in gelatina

Chicken in Home-Made Aspic Jelly

⏱ 00:40   04:00 🍲

American	Ingredients	Metric/Imperial
2	Calves' feet	2
1 or 2	Celery stalks	1 or 2
2	Carrots	2
2	Onions	2
1	Egg white	1
1 (3 lb)	Chicken	1 (1.4 kg / 3 lb)
1½ oz	Pistachio nuts	40 g / 1½ oz
⅔ cup	Black and green olives	100 g / 4 oz
	Pickled onions	
	Gherkins	

1. You can buy aspic granules ready prepared, but the home-made variety is always superior.
2. Boil 2 calves' feet, celery, carrots and onions in 2 quarts [2 litres / 3½ pints] of water for 3 hours. When the liquid has reduced by half, strain through a cloth; add slightly beaten egg white and crushed shell, boil for another 5 minutes, strain through muslin again, this time into a bowl. Cool and refrigerate.
3. Cook the chicken by boiling or roasting depending on type. Allow 20 minutes to each 1 lb / 450 g plus 20 minutes over for roasting. A genuine boiling fowl of this size will take 2 hours.
4. Cool completely and carve with an eye to the appearance. Arrange on a serving dish and garnish with green and black olives and pistachio nuts.
5. Pour the cold jelly over the meat and decorate with pickled onions and gherkins.

Galletti al vino

Spring Chicken in Red Wine

⏱ 00:25   01:20 🍲

American	Ingredients	Metric/Imperial
1 (3 lb)	Spring chicken	1 (1.4 kg / 3 lb)
2 oz	Bacon	50 g / 2 oz
¼ cup	Vegetable oil	50 ml / 2 fl oz
¾ lb	Button onions	350 g / 12 oz
	Salt and pepper	
	Flour	
¼ cup	Butter	50 g / 2 oz
3 tbsp	Cognac	2 tbsp
½ cup	Red wine	125 ml / 4 fl oz
2	Bay leaves	2
2	Cloves	2
1 cup	Chicken stock	225 ml / 8 fl oz
1 tbsp	Chopped parsley	1 tbsp

Chicken in aspic jelly

1. Wash and dry the chicken thoroughly and joint into small pieces (see page 313).
2. Chop the bacon and sauté in a little oil; add the button onions and season with salt and pepper.
3. Flour the chicken pieces lightly. Melt most of the butter in a second pan, add the chicken and sauté until golden on all sides.
4. Transfer the onions and bacon to the pan with the chicken, stir and check seasoning. Add the cognac; flame, then add the wine, bay leaves and cloves.

5. As soon as the wine boils, add the stock, lower the heat and simmer gently for about 45 minutes.
6. When the chicken is cooked, transfer to a heated serving dish with the onions using a slotted spoon.
7. Thicken the sauce by gradually adding 2 teaspoons flour mixed with the remaining butter, beat until smooth and creamy.
8. Pour over the chicken and arrange the onions around it. Sprinkle with parsley.

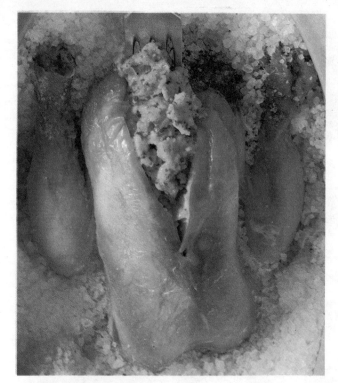

Stuffed and boiled chicken

Coscette di pollo alla boscaiola
Chicken Thighs Braised with Mushrooms

	00:15		00:50

American	Ingredients	Metric/Imperial
4	Chicken thigh portions	4
¼ lb	Bacon	100 g / 4 oz
½ tsp	Chopped thyme	½ tsp
½ tsp	Chopped rosemary	½ tsp
	Salt and pepper	
2 tbsp	Vegetable oil	1 ½ tbsp
¼ cup	Butter	50 g / 2 oz
1	Onion	1
1	Carrot	1
1	Celery stalk	1
¼ cup	Dry white wine	50 ml / 2 fl oz
1 cup	Stock	225 ml / 8 fl oz
¾ lb	Mushrooms	350 g / 12 oz
14 oz	Peeled plum tomatoes	400 g / 14 oz
1 cup	Coffee (single) cream	225 ml / 8 fl oz
1 tbsp	Parsley	1 tbsp

1. Bone the chicken portions carefully, wash and dry; insert a slice of bacon into each with a pinch of thyme and rosemary and a little pepper. Secure with a toothpick.
2. Sauté gently in heated oil and butter until golden.
3. Chop the onion, carrot and celery and add these to the pan on a medium heat, cook for 6 minutes.
4. Moisten with white wine, allow to bubble for 1 minute and then add the stock and the sliced mushrooms, stir well. After a few minutes add the pulped tomatoes. Cook over medium heat for 30 minutes.
5. Remove the toothpicks and check the seasoning. (This part of the dish can be prepared well ahead of time.)
6. To serve, heat through very gently, adding a little extra pepper if necessary and pour the cream into the sauce a few moments before serving. Sprinkle with chopped parsley.

Gallina ripiena
Stuffed and Boiled Chicken

	00:30		01:30

American	Ingredients	Metric/Imperial
1 (3 lb)	Small chicken	1 (1.4 kg / 3 lb)
	Chicken giblets	
¼ cup	Butter	50 g / 2 oz
½ tsp	Chopped sage	½ tsp
7 oz	Cooked ham	200 g / 7 oz
¼ lb	Italian sausage	100 g / 4 oz
2	Slices of bread	2
¼ cup	Milk	50 ml / 2 fl oz
1	Egg	1
3 tbsp	Grated parmesan cheese	2 tbsp
	Salt and pepper	
¼ tsp	Nutmeg	¼ tsp
1	Carrot	1
1	Onion	1
1	Celery stalk	1
1	Bouquet garni	1
4	Tomatoes	4

1. Wash and dry the chicken inside and out.
2. Sauté the liver and heart in heated butter and sage. Finely chop the ham, skin the sausage and soak the bread in the milk. Put all the chopped ingredients together, add the bread (well squeezed out), the egg, grated cheese, salt, pepper and a pinch of nutmeg. Mix thoroughly.
3. Stuff the chicken with this mixture and sew up to secure.
4. Place the carrot, onion, celery and bouquet garni in a large pan of boiling salted water, add the chicken and boil for about 1 hour. Drain, slice and serve garnished with tomato slices.

Tacchino alla salvia
Turkey with Sage

	00:25		00:35

American	Ingredients	Metric/Imperial
3 tbsp	Seedless raisins	2 tbsp
1 lb	Turkey breast	500 g / 1 lb
2 oz	Sliced bacon	50 g / 2 oz
4	Sage leaves	4
3 tbsp	Butter	40 g / 1 ½ oz
2 tbsp	Vegetable oil	1 ½ tbsp
	Salt and pepper	

1. Preheat the oven to 350°F / 180°C / Gas Mark 4.
2. Put the raisins to soak in warm water.
3. Stretch the turkey out flat and lay the sliced bacon and sage leaves on top. Roll and tie.
4. Heat the butter and some oil in a pan, add the turkey and brown well all over.

5. Transfer to a small casserole dish, season with salt and pepper and add the raisins. Cover with foil or a lid and cook for 15 minutes. Remove the cover and cook for a further 15-20 minutes.
6. Cut into slices and serve hot.

Cotolette di tacchino e speck
Turkey Rissoles

	00:30 Plus chilling	00:16

American	Ingredients	Metric/Imperial
3	Thick slices of white bread	3
¼ cup	Milk	50 ml / 2 fl oz
1¼ lb	Turkey meat	600 g / 1¼ lb
3 oz	Fat bacon	75 g / 3 oz
2	Eggs	2
1 tbsp	Grated parmesan cheese	1 tbsp
1 tsp	Worcester sauce	1 tsp
½ tsp	Cayenne pepper	½ tsp
½ tsp	Mixed herbs	½ tsp
1 tbsp	Flour	1 tbsp
½ cup	Dried bread crumbs	50 g / 2 oz
⅔ cup	Frying oil	150 ml / ¼ pint
	Salt and pepper	

1. Soak the bread in the milk, squeeze out the excess moisture.
2. Grind (mince) the turkey and the bacon fat together, add 1 beaten egg, grated parmesan cheese, Worcester sauce, cayenne pepper, mixed herbs and mix well with the bread. Form into 8 rissoles using floured hands.
3. Now beat the remaining egg with 2 tablespoons [1½ tablespoons] water on a flat plate and sprinkle the bread crumbs on another plate. Dip the rissoles in the egg and then in bread crumbs and chill in the refrigerator for 30 minutes.
4. Heat the oil in a frying pan over a high heat, slip in 4 rissoles and reduce heat slightly. Fry for 4 minutes each side, drain onto absorbent kitchen towels and keep warm. Reheat the oil and fry the remaining rissoles. Season and serve with lemon wedges.

Cook's tip: A quick dish which can be made from left-over pieces of turkey, chicken or game. Mix in the food processor to save time.

Tacchino fiorito
Turkey Flower

	02:00	00:45

American	Ingredients	Metric/Imperial
1	Rolled turkey breast	1
	Salt	
1	Carrot	1
1	Onion	1
1	Celery stalk	1
1	Sprig of parsley	1
2½ tsp	Gelatin	2½ tsp
8	Radishes	8
1	Bunch of watercress	1

1. Place the turkey in a saucepan just covered with slightly salted water containing a roughly chopped carrot, onion, stalk of celery and sprig of parsley.
2. Bring to the boil and simmer for 45 minutes or until cooked, cool and then cut into 6 even slices.
3. With scissors cut each slice into a petal shape.
4. Strain the vegetables and reserve the stock. Heat a few tablespoons until boiling, add gelatin, make up to 1¼ cups [300 ml / ½ pint] with remaining stock and cool.
5. Chill in ice-making compartment of the refrigerator or in the freezer for 15 minutes.
6. Arrange the turkey slices on a large plate in the shape of a flower, brush them several times over with the gelatin and decorate with radishes cut into flowers. Chop the rest of the gelatin and pile between the petals. Garnish with watercress.

Cook's tip: the turkey petals can be decorated with canned pimentos cut into petals, small flowers and cucumber peel for stalks. Surround with thinly sliced cucumber for a special, eye-catching buffet dish.

Rotolo di tacchino ripieno
Stuffed Turkey Roll

	00:35 Plus cooling time Serves 6	01:30

American	Ingredients	Metric/Imperial
1 (3 lb)	Roll of turkey meat	1 (1.4 kg / 3 lb)
¼ lb	Sliced mortadella	100 g / 4 oz
2	Eggs	2
1 tbsp	Grated parmesan cheese	1 tbsp
1 tbsp	Milk	1 tbsp
	Salt and pepper	
3	Slices of cheese	3
2	Sprigs of rosemary	2
¼ tsp	Nutmeg	¼ tsp
3 tbsp	Vegetable oil	2 tbsp
¼ cup	Butter	50 g / 2 oz
4	Sage leaves	4
½ cup	Dry white wine	125 ml / 4 fl oz
1 cup	Stock	225 ml / 8 fl oz
4	Tomatoes	4
12	Olives	12
8	Gherkins	8

1. Discard the string around the turkey roll, open out the meat and cover with slices of mortadella (with the skin removed).
2. Beat the eggs with the grated cheese, milk, salt and pepper; cook, as for an omelette, on both sides. The safest way of cooking the upper side is to slide the pan under a hot broiler (grill) for a few seconds.
3. Cool the omelette completely then lay it on the slices of mortadella, cover with the sliced cheese and sprinkle with chopped rosemary and a pinch of nutmeg. Roll up tightly and tie securely with kitchen string. Sew up the ends so that the melting cheese will not ooze out or cover with foil.
4. Preheat the oven to 375°F / 190°C / Gas Mark 5.
5. Heat some oil and butter in a large casserole, add rosemary and a few sage leaves. Brown the roll over a low heat, turning to achieve an even color. Pour wine over the meat, then continue to cook in a moderate oven basting with a little stock from time to time for 1½ hours.
6. Remove from the pan, cool completely. Slice and lay on a large serving dish. Garnish with tomatoes, olives and gherkins.

Cedrone al barolo
Grouse in Barolo Wine

� 00:20　　　　01:00 🍲

American	Ingredients	Metric/Imperial
2	Dressed wood grouse	2
1	Onion	1
1	Carrot	1
1	Celery stalk	1
1	Shallot	1
¾ lb	Mushrooms	350 g / 12 oz
¼ cup	Vegetable oil	50 ml / 2 fl oz
1 quart	Barolo wine	1 litre / 1¾ pints
¼ tsp	Cinnamon	¼ tsp
	Salt and pepper	
4	Cloves	4

1. Cut grouse in half, peel and chop onion, carrot, celery and shallot. Wash mushrooms in warm water and drain.
2. Heat oil and, when very hot, brown grouse, then drain and put on one side. Add onion to pan and sauté for 2 minutes. Pour over wine, remaining vegetables (not mushrooms) cinnamon, salt, pepper and cloves. Return grouse to pan, cover and cook on hob over a low heat for 1 hour.
3. Add mushrooms 10 minutes before end of cooking time, then arrange grouse on a dish, spoon over sauce and serve.

Faraona alla Giobatta
Guinea-Fowl in Walnut Sauce

� 00:30　　　01:00 to 01:15 🍲

American	Ingredients	Metric/Imperial
1 (2 lb)	Guinea-fowl	1 (1 kg / 2 lb)
¼ cup	Vegetable oil	50 ml / 2 fl oz
1 oz	Capers	25 g / 1 oz
2	Garlic cloves	2
¼ tsp	Chopped rosemary	¼ tsp
¼ tsp	Chopped sage	¼ tsp
¼ tsp	Chopped basil	¼ tsp
1 cup	Dry red wine	225 ml / 8 fl oz
	Salt and pepper	
1 cup	Stock	225 ml / 8 fl oz
¼ cup	Butter	50 g / 2 oz
1 tbsp	Cognac	1 tbsp
¼ cup	Flour	25 g / 1 oz
½ cup	Walnuts, shelled and chopped	50 g / 2 oz
½ cup	Milk (optional)	125 ml / 4 fl oz

1. Wash and dry the guinea-fowl, put into a large saucepan with oil and brown quickly over a fairly high heat.
2. Chop the capers, garlic, rosemary, sage and basil and sprinkle over the bird, then add the wine and season with salt and pepper.
3. Lower the heat, add stock and simmer until tender.
4. Prepare the sauce by melting the butter in small pan, then, away from the heat, add the cognac, flour, chopped walnuts and a pinch of salt. Return the pan to the heat and cook this

mixture for a few minutes adding stock from the bird and the milk. Mix well and heat through for a further 2 minutes.
5. Arrange the guinea-fowl on a heated serving dish, carve and pour the walnut sauce over the bird.

Faraona nel coccio
Guinea-Fowl Casseroled in Terracotta

This dish is regularly prepared by Giorgio Gioco at the '12 Apostles' restaurant in Verona; for an accompanying vegetable he suggests roasted or plain boiled potatoes.

� 00:30　　　　01:20 🍲

American	Ingredients	Metric/Imperial
1 (3 lb)	Guinea fowl	1 (1.4 kg / 3 lb)
⅓ cup	Butter	75 g / 3 oz
	Salt	
24	Button onions	24
¼ lb	Button mushrooms	100 g / 4 oz
½ cup	Port wine	125 ml / 4 fl oz

This dish requires a terracotta casserole that is fireproof.
1. Draw, singe, wash and dry the fowl, cut into quarters.
2. Heat half the butter in the casserole, sauté the bird until golden brown all over, add salt and cover. Lower the heat and cook gently for 15 minutes.
3. Sauté peeled onions with some butter in one pan and mushrooms in yet another. Add both, with their juices, to the casserole. Pour in the port wine, bubble for 2 minutes, adjust the seasoning. Cover and continue to cook gently until done.

Faraona arrosto tartufata
Roast Guinea-Fowl with Truffles

▮merge 00:20　　　　01:00 🍲

American	Ingredients	Metric/Imperial
1 (3 lb)	Guinea-fowl	1 (1.4 kg / 3 lb)
2	Black truffles	2
2 tbsp	Butter	25 g / 1 oz
	Salt and pepper	
Scant ¼ cup	Marsala wine	3 tbsp
1	Lemon	1

1. Preheat the oven to 400°F / 200°C / Gas Mark 6.
2. Rinse the inside of the guinea-fowl under running water.
3. Peel the truffles thinly and slice. Put a few raw slices in the cavity of the fowl and under the skin.
4. Sauté the remaining slices in butter with salt and pepper, moistening with marsala. Remove the pan from the heat and allow the mixture to cool before using it to stuff the fowl. Sew up both apertures.
5. Butter a sheet of baking foil, place the fowl on it, sprinkle lightly with salt, pepper and lemon juice. Wrap in the foil and cook in a moderately hot oven.
6. After 45 minutes, unwrap the foil and allow the bird to brown. Remove to a carving board, allow to stand for 10 minutes and carve.

Faraona alla panna
Guinea-Fowl in Fresh Cream Sauce

00:25   01:30

American	Ingredients	Metric/Imperial
1 (3¼ lb)	Guinea-fowl	1 (1.5 kg / 3¼ lb)
¼ lb	Bacon or parma ham with fat	100 g / 4 oz
½ cup	Butter	100 g / 4 oz
1	Celery stalk	1
2	Small carrots	2
1	Onion	1
¼ tsp	Chopped rosemary	¼ tsp
¼ tsp	Chopped thyme	¼ tsp
¼ tsp	Chopped marjoram	¼ tsp
2	Bay leaves	2
	Salt and pepper	
½ cup	Dry white wine	125 ml / 4 fl oz
1 cup	Stock	225 ml / 8 fl oz
1 cup	Coffee (single) cream	225 ml / 8 fl oz

1. Wash and dry the guinea-fowl and wrap the bacon or ham around it.
2. Melt the butter in a large, heavy pan, add the fowl and brown on all sides.
3. Chop the vegetables finely and add them, with the herbs to the pan. Season with salt and pepper. After a few minutes, add the wine and let it bubble, then add a little stock, lower the heat, cover and simmer for about 1¼ hours.
4. When the bird is cooked, transfer to a board, carve and then arrange on a heated serving dish.
5. Pour the cream into the pan, allow the sauce to thicken but not boil; sieve or blend, reheat and pour over the guinea-fowl.

Faraona alla panna e al marsala
Guinea-Fowl with Cream and Marsala

00:10   01:20

American	Ingredients	Metric/Imperial
1 (3 lb)	Guinea-fowl hen	1 (1.4 kg / 3 lb)
¼ cup	Butter	50 g / 2 oz
½ cup	Marsala wine	125 ml / 4 fl oz
	Salt and pepper	
1¼ cups	Coffee (single) cream	300 ml / ½ pint

1. Singe the guinea-fowl, wash and dry thoroughly both inside and outside.
2. Melt the butter in a heavy pan, add the fowl and brown all over, moistening with the marsala, a little at a time.
3. Allow the marsala to vaporize; season with salt and pepper and cook on a low heat for 50 minutes, adding the cream very gradually.
4. Remove guinea fowl and keep warm. Reduce the liquid in the pan slightly.
5. Cut the bird into 4 pieces, arrange on a heated serving dish and top with the fragrant sauce.

Starne arrosto
Roast Partridge

00:20   01:00 to 01:25

American	Ingredients	Metric/Imperial
2	Partridges	2
	Salt and pepper	
¼ lb	Chicken livers	100 g / 4 oz
1	Slice of ham	1
2 tbsp	Butter	25 g / 1 oz
1 tbsp	Cognac	1 tbsp
¼ tsp	Chopped thyme	¼ tsp
2	Thin slices of fat bacon	2
2	Vine leaves	2
	Fried bread	

1. Wipe the partridges and season the cavity.
2. Prepare the stuffing for the partridges by washing and chopping the chicken livers with those of the partridges.
3. Chop the ham, mix with the butter, chicken livers, the cognac, a pinch of thyme, salt and pepper. Put half of this mixture in each partridge and sew it up.
4. Wrap the birds in a thin slice of fat bacon and a vine leaf, then truss the partridges and cook on the spit or in a very hot oven (475°F / 240°C / Gas Mark 9.) When the partridges are almost cooked, remove the binding and bacon and brown over a brisk heat.
5. Cut in half and serve on slices of crisp fried bread.

Composta di piccioni
Pigeon Compote

00:25   01:15

American	Ingredients	Metric/Imperial
4	Pigeons	4
7 oz	Pork fat	200 g / 7 oz
	Butter	
2 tbsp	White flour	15 g / ½ oz
1 cup	Stock	225 ml / 8 fl oz
2	Bay leaves	2
2	Sprigs of thyme	2
5	Sprigs of parsley	5
	Salt and pepper	
16	Small onions	16
¼ lb	Dried mushrooms	100 g / 4 oz
1⅓ cup	Green olives, stoned	225 g / 8 oz

1. Wash the prepared pigeons. Heat the diced pork fat and butter, brown the pigeons.
2. Stir in the flour, allow it to color slightly then add the stock, bay leaves and sprigs of thyme and parsley; season with salt and pepper.
3. Add the onions, stir, cover and simmer on a low heat for about 40 minutes.
4. Wash the dried mushrooms and soak for at least 15 minutes in warm water. Add to the pigeons with the green olives, simmer for a further 20 minutes and remove herbs.
5. Serve the pigeons with boiled rice or pasta accompanied by a salad made from several different kinds of lettuce.

Partridges in sauce

Starne fra due fuochi

Partridges Between Two Fires

00:35   **01:55**

American	Ingredients	Metric/Imperial
2	Partridges	2
	Salt and pepper	
2	Slices of veal fat	2
2	Slices of ham fat	2
¼ cup	Butter	50 g / 2 oz
¼ cup	Vegetable oil	50 ml / 2 fl oz
1	Onion	1
½ cup	Dry white wine	125 ml / 4 fl oz
1 cup	Stock	225 ml / 8 fl oz
¼ cup	Flour	25 g / 1 oz
1	Seville orange	1
2 oz	Chicken livers	50 g / 2 oz

1. Preheat the oven to 350°F / 180°C / Gas Mark 4.
2. Prepare the partridges, season with salt and pepper and surround them with the veal fat and slices of ham fat.
3. Heat the butter and oil in a casserole and brown the birds, add onion, chopped. After 10 minutes, pour in the dry white wine, a little stock and cook slowly in the oven for 1½ hours.
4. Remove the veal and ham fat and keep the birds warm in a low oven.
5. Add washed chopped partridge and chicken livers to the cooking juices in the casserole, cook stirring for 3 minutes.
6. Add the stock and cook for a few minutes. Mix a knob of butter with the flour, whisk to thicken the sauce then add the juice of the orange. Bring to the boil, stirring all the time and strain into a sauceboat. Carve partridges and serve with sauce.

Pernici alla salsa

Partridges in Sauce

00:50   **01:30**

American	Ingredients	Metric/Imperial
2	Partridges	2
	Salt and pepper	
½ cup	Butter	100 g / 4 oz
½ cup	Dry white wine	125 ml / 4 fl oz
1	Carrot	1
1	Onion	1
	Partridge giblets	
1	Bay leaf	1
1	Garlic clove	1
1	Truffle	1
1¼ cups	Chicken stock	300 ml / ½ pint
1	Lemon	1
	Fried bread	

1. Preheat the oven to 350°F / 180°C / Gas Mark 4.
2. Clean and wash the partridges, truss them, season with salt and pepper.
3. Heat half the butter and brown the birds evenly in a large casserole, pouring a few tablespoons of wine over them and turning them so that they cook evenly all over.

4. Cook in the oven for 45 minutes basting and turning from time to time. Allow to cool and remove the wing tips and the skin. Add these to the cooking juices in the casserole with the diced carrot, chopped onion, the heart and liver of the partridges. Add the bay leaf, the clove of garlic, salt and pepper and half of the remaining butter.
5. Brown on a medium heat, pouring over the remaining wine a little at a time. Add the truffle in slices and 1 cup [225 ml / 8 fl oz] stock.
6. Cook over a moderate heat, stirring frequently, for about 30 minutes. Strain the sauce. Rub the remains through a sieve or blend and add to the sauce.
7. Cut the partridges in half, add to the sauce with a little more stock or wine if necessary and cook for 15 minutes over a low heat. Stir frequently.
8. Drain the birds on to a heated serving dish with a slotted spoon. Add the rest of the butter and lemon juice to the sauce, stir well and pour over the birds. Serve hot.

Pasticcio di fagiano

Pheasant Pie

01:00   **01:45**

American	Ingredients	Metric/Imperial
1 (2 lb)	Pheasant	1 (1 kg / 2 lb)
	Salt and pepper	
¼ cup	Vegetable oil	50 ml / 2 fl oz
⅓ cup	Butter	75 g / 3 oz
2 tbsp	Chopped parsley	1½ tbsp
1	Celery stalk	1
1	Carrot	1
1	Onion	1
¼ cup	White wine	50 ml / 2 fl oz
1 cup	Béchamel sauce	225 ml / 8 fl oz
3	Eggs	3
2 tsp	Gelatin	2 tsp
1¼ cups	Stock	300 ml / ½ pint
1	Truffle	1
1 oz	Canned tongue	25 g / 1 oz
1	Lettuce	1

1. Preheat the oven to 350°F / 180°C / Gas Mark 4.
2. Clean the pheasant, season with salt and pepper and brown in a mixture of half oil and half butter in a frying pan.
3. In a casserole put the parsley, some chopped celery, carrot, onion, sprinkle with wine and cook for 1 hour until the meat is tender.
4. Remove the pheasant meat from the bone and grind (mince) or put through a food processor.
5. Add the béchamel sauce to the ground meat, together with 3 egg yolks, blend well, then fold in 2 egg whites beaten to a very stiff froth.
6. Grease a pie mold with butter and line the inside with strips of parchment paper greased with butter. Pour in the mixture, so that the mold is three-quarters full, and shake it well. Cook over a bain-marie in a preheated oven and, when the mixture has solidified, allow it to cool in the mold. Turn out and remove the strips of paper.
7. Dissolve the gelatin in the stock. Clean the mold and pour in dissolved gelatin in a layer two fingers thick and refrigerate.
8. When the gelatin has set, garnish with slices of truffle and small cubes of tongue. Fill with more gelatin, set slightly and return the pie carefully on to the gelatin. Leave in the refrigerator to set. Unmold on to a bed of lettuce.

Fagiano alla piemontese

Pheasant Piedmont-Style

◧▽ 00:25   01:30 🍲

American	Ingredients	Metric/Imperial
1 (2 lb)	Pheasant	1 (1 kg / 2 lb)
1/3 cup	Butter	75 g / 3 oz
1	Sprig of rosemary	1
	Salt and pepper	
6	Slices of bacon	6
1/4 cup	Marsala wine	50 ml / 2 fl oz
7 oz	Black olives	200 g / 7 oz

1. Preheat the oven to 350°F / 180°C / Gas Mark 4.
2. Clean the pheasant, wash carefully and dry.
3. Mix half the butter with the rosemary and season, place inside the pheasant. Wrap the bird in the slices of bacon and truss it. Put in an ovenproof dish with the remaining butter, cut into pieces. Cook until golden brown in the oven, basting occasionally with marsala wine and the cooking juices.
4. Remove the stones from the olives, take the bird from the oven, add the olives and cook for a further 30 minutes over a moderate heat on the stove.
5. Remove the pheasant, untie and carve on a board. Cut the bacon into pieces. Arrange the bird and bacon on a heated serving dish, add the olives and serve.

Fagiano alla cacciatora

Hunter's Pheasant

◧▽ 00:20   02:00 🍲

American	Ingredients	Metric/Imperial
1/4 lb	Fat bacon	100 g / 4 oz
1	Carrot	1
2	Celery stalks	2
1/4 lb	Raw ham	100 g / 4 oz
1	Onion	1
2 oz	Dried mushrooms	50 g / 2 oz
Scant 1/4 cup	Vegetable oil	3 tbsp
1 tbsp	Butter	1 tbsp
2	Oven-ready well hung pheasants	2
1/2 cup	Brandy	125 ml / 4 fl oz
	Stock if needed	

1. Chop bacon, carrot, celery and ham finely, and slice onion. Soften dried mushrooms in tepid water, then drain.
2. Heat oil and butter in a large pan and sauté onion for 2 minutes. Add pheasants to pan and brown all over. Pour over brandy and add bacon, carrot, celery and ham to pan, with mushrooms.
3. Cover and cook over a low heat for about 2 hours, adding stock to the pan to prevent the ingredients drying out.
4. Transfer pheasants to a hot serving dish using a slotted spoon. Place vegetables around birds, pour juices over pheasants serve accompanied by puréed green vegetables tossed in butter.

Fagiano arrosto

Roast Pheasant

◧▽ 00:25   01:25 🍲

American	Ingredients	Metric/Imperial
1	Pheasant	1
1/4 lb	Fat bacon	100 g / 4 oz
1/2 cup	Butter	100 g / 4 oz
1 cup	Milk	225 ml / 8 fl oz
3	Slices of white bread	3
3	Cloves	3
	Salt	
1	Onion	1

1. Pluck and singe the pheasant. Lard the breast and legs with the bacon, and put on the spit, moistening continually with melted butter.
2. Serve the pheasant accompanied simply by its cooking juices or by the following bread sauce.
3. Boil the milk and add the bread, the onion studded with cloves, salt, 1 tablespoon [15 g / 1/2 oz] of butter and cook for 15 minutes. Stir well, remove the onion and mix well.
4. Carve the pheasant and serve with the bread sauce, roast potatoes and steamed broccoli.

Fagiano alla romana

Roman-Style Pheasant

This dish can be served hot or cold.

◧▽ 00:25   01:30 to 02:00 🍲

American	Ingredients	Metric/Imperial
7 oz	Sweetbreads	200 g / 7 oz
1	Onion	1
7 oz	Chopped veal	200 g / 7 oz
1/4 cup	Melted butter	50 g / 2 oz
1/2 tsp	Chopped sage	1/2 tsp
1/2 tsp	Chopped rosemary	1/2 tsp
1 tbsp	Grated parmesan cheese	1 tbsp
1	Egg, beaten	1
2	Pheasants	2
5 oz	Fat bacon	150 g / 5 oz
1/2 cup	Vegetable oil	125 ml / 4 fl oz
1 lb	Boiled potatoes	450 g / 1 lb

1. Preheat oven to 350°F / 180°C / Gas Mark 4.
2. Chop sweetbreads and onion and combine in a bowl with chopped meat, melted butter, sage, rosemary, parmesan and bind together with beaten egg. Stuff cavity of pheasants with forcemeat.
3. Cover pheasant breasts with fat bacon, place in a roasting pan, brush with oil and cook for about 1½ hours, basting with oil from time to time.
4. Pierce flesh of birds to check juices are clear, then remove stuffing in one piece. Joint pheasants into four, slice stuffing thickly. Place pheasant joints on a hot serving dish, surround with stuffing slices and boiled potatoes and pour over cooking juices. Serve hot.

Cook's tip: The dish can be refrigerated overnight and served cold the next day accompanied by a salad of several different kinds of lettuce and crusty bread.

Roast pheasant

Pheasant Vatel-style

Fagiano alla Vatel

Pheasant Vatel-Style

00:10   00:50

American	Ingredients	Metric/Imperial
1	Onion	1
1	Oven-ready pheasant and liver	1
¼ cup	Softened butter	50 g / 2 oz
1	Canadian apple	1
¼ cup	White vinegar	50 ml / 2 fl oz
¼ cup	Red wine	50 ml / 2 fl oz
	Salt and pepper	

1. Preheat oven to 350°F / 180°C / Gas Mark 4.
2. Chop onion and liver and mix in with half the butter. Place the stuffing inside bird and cover opening with apple. Place in a roasting tin.
3. Melt the remaining butter and use to brush bird. Combine vinegar and red wine and pour over pheasant. Season with salt and pepper and roast in the oven for about 50 minutes until cooked.
4. Transfer pheasant to a hot serving dish and serve with boiled rice or a potato purée.

Fagiano e cavolo

Pheasant and Cabbage

00:20   02:00

American	Ingredients	Metric/Imperial
1	Firm white cabbage	1
¼ cup	Vegetable oil	50 ml / 2 fl oz
¼ lb	Fat bacon	100 g / 4 oz
	Salt and pepper	
2	Oven-ready pheasants	2
¼ lb	Sliced bacon	100 g / 4 oz
¼ cup	Whipping (double) cream	50 ml / 2 fl oz

1. Wash and shred cabbage, par boil for 5 minutes, then drain. Heat half the oil in a pan and add cabbage and chopped fat bacon. Season with salt and pepper and cook for 30 minutes.
2. Truss pheasants, heat remaining oil in a large frying pan and brown birds all over. Cover breasts with bacon slices, then pour over thick cream, add cabbage to pan, cover and cook over a low heat for about 1½ hours.
3. Transfer pheasants to a hot serving dish, remove bacon, spoon cabbage around birds, pour creamy sauce over breasts, and serve.

Fantasia di pollo e quaglie

Chicken and Quail Surprise

00:25   00:45

American	Ingredients	Metric/Imperial
4	Quails	4
4	Chicken breasts	4
¼ cup	Butter	50 g / 2 oz
¼ cup	Vegetable oil	50 ml / 2 fl oz
2 oz	Bacon	50 g / 2 oz
½ tsp	Chopped rosemary	½ tsp
2 cups	Mushrooms	200 g / 7 oz
2 cups	Béchamel sauce	450 ml / ¾ pint

1. Cut the quails in half and cook with the chicken breasts, in a large pan with the heated butter and oil. Turn from time to time until golden on each side and cooked through. Add the chopped bacon and rosemary.
2. Wash the mushrooms, slice thinly and sauté in a small pan with a little butter for 5-6 minutes.
3. Prepare a béchamel sauce, add the mushrooms.
4. Arrange the chicken and quails on a serving dish, top with mushroom sauce and serve very hot surrounded by a garnish of triangles of toast.

Schidionata di quaglie

Quails on the Spit

00:35   00:15

American	Ingredients	Metric/Imperial
8	Quails	8
1 tsp	Chopped basil	1 tsp
1 tsp	Chopped rosemary	1 tsp
1	Onion	1
¼ cup	Butter	50 g / 2 oz
	Salt and pepper	
8	Slices of bacon	8
¼ cup	Vegetable oil	50 ml / 2 fl oz
	Rice	

1. Clean, singe and wash the quails. Dry and stuff with chopped basil, rosemary and onion mixed with butter.
2. Lightly season the quails with salt and pepper, then lard them by wrapping in thin slices of bacon secured with thread.
3. Put them on the spit and paint with vegetable oil. Brown the quails over a high heat, brush with the fat that falls into the dripping pan.

4. Remove from the spit at the end of the cooking time and serve with boiled rice, seasoning with the dripping pan juices.

Cook's tip: The same recipe can be used for cooking small pigeons and other small birds.

Quaglie alla cacciatora
Huntsman's Quails

◁▱ 00:30   00:45 ⬜🍲

American	Ingredients	Metric/Imperial
8	Large quails	8
½ cup	Butter	100 g / 4 oz
1 tsp	Chopped sage	1 tsp
8	Cloves	8
½ tsp	Nutmeg	½ tsp
4	Garlic cloves	4
8	Slices of bacon	8
¼ cup	Brandy	50 ml / 2 fl oz
8	Slices of polenta	8

1. Clean the quails, singe and remove their intestines.
2. Mix half the butter with the chopped sage, cloves, nutmeg and chopped garlic, divide into 4.
3. Place a portion inside each bird. Wrap the quails in the slices of bacon and secure with toothpicks.
4. Sauté them in a frying pan with butter, browning them evenly. Sprinkle with brandy, cover the pan and continue cooking for 15 minutes.
5. When the cooking is completed, put a lighted match to the pan and allow the excess alcohol to burn off completely.
6. Serve the quails immediately on slices of hot polenta on a heated serving dish.

Quaglie alla pavese
Quails Pavia-Style

◁▱ 00:30   01:00 ⬜🍲

American	Ingredients	Metric/Imperial
12	Quails	12
	Salt and pepper	
8	Slices of bacon	8
½ cup	Vegetable oil	125 ml / 4 fl oz
4	Garlic cloves	4
½ cup	Red wine	125 ml / 4 fl oz
1⅔ cups	Rice	350 g / 12 oz
1½ quarts	Chicken stock	1.5 litres / 2½ pints
2 oz	Ox marrow	50 g / 2 oz

1. Clean and singe the quails, season and cover them with slices of bacon.
2. Heat the oil, cook the birds with the crushed garlic until golden, sprinkle with the red wine as they turn brown.
3. Remove the quails after 25 minutes cooking and put them to one side.
4. Brown the rice in the pan juices from the quails, stirring frequently. As soon as the rice has browned, sprinkle with boiling stock and add the ox marrow. Continue cooking the rice so that it is 'al dente', then arrange it on the bottom of an ovenproof dish. Lay the quails on top of the rice, put in the oven or under the broiler (grill) for 5 minutes and serve immediately.

Quaglie arrosto alla foglia di vite
Roast Quails with Vine Leaves

◁▱ 00:40   00:25 ⬜🍲

American	Ingredients	Metric/Imperial
1 lb	Grapes	450 g / 1 lb
8	Vine leaves	8
8	Large, unhung quails	8
½ cup	Butter	100 g / 4 oz
	Salt and pepper	
8	Thin slices of bacon	8
1 cup	White wine	225 ml / 8 fl oz

1. Wash and dry grapes, halve and deseed them.
2. Wash the vine leaves very gently and dry them, taking care not to break them.
3. Pluck and draw the quails, singe, wash and dry them carefully. Brush all over with a little melted butter and season with a pinch of salt and pepper.
4. Put one grape, or more if they are small, inside each quail and wrap them first in a slice of bacon and then in a vine leaf. Truss them with white string.
5. Preheat the oven to 400°F / 200°C / Gas Mark 6.
6. Heat the remaining butter in a frying pan and cook the quails over a brisk heat for 5 minutes.
7. Arrange in a casserole, pour over the wine and 1 tablespoon water for each quail, season and cook for 20 minutes covered with foil. Add remaining grapes after 10 minutes.
8. Remove string, arrange quails on a serving dish surrounded by grapes. Pour over the pan juices. Serve accompanied by boiled rice.

Piccioni e piselli
Squab with Green Peas

◁▱ 00:15   01:15 ⬜🍲

American	Ingredients	Metric/Imperial
4	Squab	4
5 oz	Pork fat	150 g / 5 oz
2 tbsp	Vegetable oil	1½ tbsp
1	Stock cube	1
1 tbsp	Cornstarch (cornflour)	1 tbsp
1 lb	Fresh (shelled) or frozen peas	450 g / 1 lb
16	Button onions	16
	Salt and pepper	
2 tbsp	Chopped parsley	1½ tbsp

1. Prepare and wash the squab. Cut the pork fat into strips and fry in the heated oil; add the squab and brown all over.
2. After 10 minutes, remove the squab from the pan, add 1¼ cups [300 ml / ½ pint] stock made with the stock cube and stir in the cornstarch mixed with a little water. Bring to the boil, then add the peas, onions, salt and pepper.
3. Cover and simmer for 15 minutes, add the squab and simmer for a further 30 minutes. Add chopped parsley immediately before serving.

Cook's tip: serve these fledgling pigeons with a purée of potatoes seasoned with nutmeg or boiled potatoes.

Leprotto alla siciliana
Sicilian Hare

◢▷ 00:30   01:00 to 01:30 ▭

American	Ingredients	Metric/Imperial
1	Young hare	1
¼ lb	Grated ewe's milk cheese	100 g / 4 oz
⅔ cup	Sultanas	100 g / 4 oz
7 oz	Black olives	200 g / 7 oz
½ cup	Vegetable oil	125 ml / 4 fl oz
	Bilberry sauce (optional)	
Sauce		
1 lb	Bilberries	225 g / 8 oz
1 tsp	Mustard	1 tsp
1	Egg yolk	1

1. Preheat the oven to 400°F / 200°C / Gas Mark 6.
2. Thoroughly clean a young hare.
3. Chop up the usable intestines, add ewe's milk cheese and washed sultanas. Stir the pitted (stoned) black olives into the mixture and fill the belly of the hare. Cooking can take place in a hot oven for 1 hour or on the spit for 1½ hours, whichever is preferred, basting with the oil.
4. The hare is served sprinkled with the very hot pan juices and accompanied by a sweet spicy bilberry sauce. Rub bilberries through a strainer with mustard and egg yolk and serve in a sauceboat.

Lepre alla cacciatora
Huntsman's Hare

◢▷ 00:20   00:45 ▭

American	Ingredients	Metric/Imperial
1 (2 lb)	Saddle of hare	1 (1 kg / 2 lb)
½ cup	Vegetable oil	125 ml / 4 fl oz
¼ cup	Butter	50 g / 2 oz
2 oz	Bacon	50 g / 2 oz
	Basil	
5	Sprigs of parsley	5
½ tsp	Chopped rosemary	½ tsp
12	Juniper berries	12
1	Carrot	1
1	Celery stalk	1
1	Onion	1
2 cups	Stock	450 ml / ¾ pint
4	Peeled tomatoes	4
1 tbsp	Cornstarch (cornflour)	1 tbsp
1 cup	White wine	225 ml / 8 fl oz
	Salt and pepper	

1. Cut the saddle into joints, wash and dry thoroughly. Heat a mixture of oil and butter in a large casserole, add cubed bacon, basil, parsley, rosemary, juniper berries, carrot, celery, onion. When the mixture has turned golden, push to one side and add the pieces of hare.
2. Continue cooking, turning occasionally. Add the stock and the tomatoes, thicken with cornstarch (cornflour) and finally put in the wine, salt and pepper. Cover and complete the cooking.
3. Serve piping hot sprinkled with parsley.

Lepre casalinga in salmi
Hare Marinaded in Red Wine

◢▷ 00:30   02:30 ▭
Marinating time 24:00

American	Ingredients	Metric/Imperial
1 (4½ lb)	Hare, jointed	1 (2 kg / 4½ lb)
1 (70 cl)	Bottle red wine	1 (70 cl)
3	Onions	3
1	Carrot	1
1	Head of celery	1
2	Sprigs of thyme	2
¾ cup	Flour	75 g / 3 oz
	Salt and pepper	
⅓ cup	Butter	75 g / 3 oz
	Vegetable oil	
2 oz	Cooked ham	50 g / 2 oz

1. Wash the pieces of hare very carefully and steep in red wine with a piece of onion and a finely chopped carrot.
2. Add half the chopped celery and thyme, make sure the pieces of hare are completely covered and remain in the marinade for at least 24 hours, in a cool place.
3. Drain the hare joints and dust with seasoned flour.
4. Heat the oil and butter in a large frying pan, cook the pieces of meat until golden on each side.
5. Add finely chopped onion, the remaining chopped celery, season with salt and pepper. Continue cooking until no more blood can be seen, about 15 minutes on a low to medium heat. Sprinkle with marinade, then add the chopped ham. Cover and cook over a low heat for 2 hours.
6. Remove hare joints on to a heated serving dish and keep warm. Strain or blend the sauce, reheat and pour over the hare.

Cosciotto di cervo alla aostana
Haunch of Venison Aosta-Style

◢▷ 00:25   03:00 ▭

American	Ingredients	Metric/Imperial
1	Haunch of venison	1
8	Garlic cloves	8
12	Slices of bacon	12
⅔ cup	Vegetable oil	150 ml / ¼ pint
	Salt and pepper	
½ cup	Cognac	125 ml / 4 fl oz

1. Prepare fire for spit roasting, or preheat oven to 400°F / 200°C / Gas Mark 6.
2. Stud a haunch of venison with garlic and small pieces of fat bacon, brush with oil and put on the spit, start cooking, allowing 1½ hours per 2 lb / 1 kg of meat, turning from time to time. Sprinkle with pepper and a little salt, since meat is already flavored, and use fat oozing out to baste.
3. When half-cooked, pour over cognac, then baste again. The meat is cooked when the juices run clear when it is pierced with a fork.
4. Serve the haunch whole, on a large wooden chopping board or on a broad metal dish. Carve at the table.

Daino alla castellana

Venison Castelli-Style

� 00:20   02:00 🍲

American	Ingredients	Metric/Imperial
2 lb	Venison	1 kg / 2 lb
1	Onion	1
2	Garlic cloves	2
¼ lb	Bacon	100 g / 4 oz
½ cup	Vegetable oil	125 ml / 4 fl oz
3	Celery stalks	3
3	Carrots	3
2 tbsp	Chopped parsley	1½ tbsp
3	Tomatoes	3
1	Leek	1
1 quart	Red Barbera or Barola wine	1 litre / 1¾ pints

1. Preheat oven to 300°F / 150°C / Gas Mark 2.
2. Cut meat into bite-size pieces, chop onion, garlic and bacon. Heat oil in a fireproof casserole dish and when very hot add meat to pan and brown all over. Add onion, garlic and bacon to pan and cook a further 2 minutes, stirring briskly. Remove from heat.
3. Finely chop celery, carrots, parsley, tomatoes and leeks, add to pan and cook for 10 minutes. Pour over wine, cover and cook in the oven for about 1½-2 hours and serve piping hot.

Capriolo alla crema

Venison with Cream

▬▬▷ 00:25   03:00 🍲

American	Ingredients	Metric/Imperial
1	Onion	1
1	Celery stalk	1
2 tbsp	Vegetable oil	1½ tbsp
½ cup	Butter	100 g / 4 oz
2	Garlic cloves	2
1	Haunch of venison	1
	Salt and pepper	
6	Sage leaves	6
2 cups	Dry white wine	450 ml / ¾ pint
2 cups	Stock	450 ml / ¾ pint
3 tbsp	Flour	2 tbsp
½ cup	Whisky	125 ml / 4 fl oz
½ cup	Coffee (single) cream	125 ml / 4 fl oz

1. Peel and slice onion, chop celery. Heat oil and butter together in a large pan and brown vegetables with garlic for 2-3 minutes, then remove from pan and keep on one side.
2. Add venison haunch to pan and over a brisk heat brown all over, seasoning with salt and pepper. Add sage leaves, wine and sautéd vegetables and cook for about 2 hours, or cook in the oven at 350°F / 180°C / Gas Mark 4.
3. Add stock to pan, cover and simmer for a further hour, then remove haunch and put on a hot plate.
4. Strain stock into a saucepan, blend flour and whisky together using a fork to remove lumps, pour into stock and bring to the boil stirring all the time. Off the heat, stir in cream.
5. Carve haunch and arrange on a hot serving dish. Pour over cream sauce and serve hot with a purée of potato.

Daino con riso

Venison with Rice

▬▬▷ 00:25   02:00 🍲

American	Ingredients	Metric/Imperial
1	Shoulder of venison	1
1	Onion	1
1	Garlic clove	1
2 oz	Belly pork	50 g / 2 oz
½ cup	Vegetable oil	125 ml / 4 fl oz
1 cup	Stock	225 ml / 8 fl oz
1	Head of celery	1
1	Carrot	1
1	Bay leaf	1
¼ tsp	Chopped basil	¼ tsp
	Salt and pepper	
2	Plum tomatoes, peeled	2
⅔ cup	Rice	150 g / 5 oz
¼ cup	Grated cheese	25 g / 1 oz
1 tbsp	Chopped parsley	1 tbsp
1	Black truffle, sliced	1

1. Cut the meat into bite-size pieces. Chop onion very finely together with the garlic clove. Dice belly pork. Heat oil and, when very hot, brown meat all over.
2. Add the onion, garlic and the belly pork to pan and cook a further 2 minutes, stirring briskly. Pour over stock, add chopped celery, carrot, bay leaf, basil, salt, pepper and sieved tomatoes.
3. Cover pan and cook for about 2 hours over a low heat. Meanwhile, boil rice and drain, then put into pan with venison.
4. Spoon venison and rice mixture onto a hot serving dish, sprinkle with grated cheese and parsley, garnish with black truffle and serve.

Capriolo in salsa di menta

Venison in Mint Sauce

▬▬▷ 00:20   01:00 🍲

American	Ingredients	Metric/Imperial
1¾ lb	Venison	800 g / 1¾ lb
½ cup	Vegetable oil	125 ml / 4 fl oz
	Salt and pepper	
1 tbsp	Chopped mint	1 tbsp
1 tbsp	Chopped basil	1 tbsp
2	Garlic cloves	2
2	Egg yolks	2
1 tsp	Vinegar	1 tsp
1 tbsp	Butter	15 g / ½ oz
	Chopped parsley	

1. Preheat oven to 400°F / 200°C / Gas Mark 6.
2. Cut venison into bite-size pieces and put into a roasting pan. Pour over oil, season, cover and bake for about 1 hour.
3. Chop mint and basil with garlic and put into a bowl. Add beaten egg yolks, vinegar and beat until frothy. Place bowl over a pan of water and cook over a medium heat, beating butter into sauce. When thickened pour into a sauceboat.
4. Spoon cooked venison onto a hot serving dish, garnish with chopped parsley and serve with herb sauce.

Bollito freddo alla ligure
Ligurian Cold Boiled Beef

	00:30		03:00
	Serves 6		

American	Ingredients	Metric/Imperial
3¼ lb	Beef brisket	1.5 kg / 3¼ lb
1	Carrot	1
1	Celery stalk	1
1	Onion	1
1	Bunch of parsley	1
6	Hard crackers (biscuits)	6
1 cup	Red wine	225 ml / 8 fl oz
¼ cup	Vegetable oil	50 ml / 2 fl oz
2 tbsp	Vinegar	1½ tbsp
4	Anchovies	4
1 tbsp	Capers	1 tbsp
Scant ¼ cup	Olive oil	3 tbsp
1 tbsp	Mustard	1 tbsp
1	Hard-cooked (boiled egg)	1
	Salt and pepper	
	Pickled onions	
	Gherkins	

1. Put the rolled beef in a saucepan with the peeled carrot, celery, onion and a bunch of parsley, cover with water, bring to the boil and simmer for about 3 hours (or 40 minutes in a pressure cooker). When cooked, drain the beef from the stock (use stock for soup) and cool.
2. Cut the beef into small pieces and put it in a large pot. Crumble the hard crackers (biscuits) over and cover with strong red wine.
3. Beat the oil and vinegar together in a cup as for making a salad dressing, and pour over the meat. Return to the heat and simmer slowly until all the liquid has reduced; then cool.
4. Prepare a sauce by chopping and pounding (or make in a blender or food processor) the desalted and boned anchovy fillets and the capers, and dilute with olive oil. Add mustard, chopped hard-cooked (boiled) egg, salt and pepper and blend until you obtain a smooth sauce.
5. Remove the meat from the pot, place it on a serving dish and cover it with the sauce; allow to stand in a cool place but do not chill. Serve the beef decorated with pickled onions and gherkins.

Roast beef classico
Sirloin of Beef Pan-Roasted

	00:15		00:32

American	Ingredients	Metric/Imperial
3¼ lb	Beef tip (sirloin) joint	1.5 kg / 3¼ lb
	Salt and pepper	
1 cup	Olive oil	225 ml / 8 fl oz
1	Sprig of rosemary	1
2	Garlic cloves	2

1. Wipe the meat well, roll and tie with string or ask the butcher to do this for you. Season with salt and pepper.

2. Put the olive oil into a heavy frying pan with rosemary and the cloves of garlic, remove these as soon as they have colored.
3. When the oil begins to smoke, add the meat and turn continuously for exactly 30 minutes, turn heat down to moderate after 5 minutes each side.
4. Remove and stand between two plates with a weight on top. Leave for 10 minutes to allow the juices to drain out, collect and return juice to the pan. Heat gently to boiling point and tip into a sauceboat.
5. Remove the string from the joint, carve into wafer-thin slices and serve immediately.

Arrosto vecchio Piemonte
'Old Piedmont' Roast

	00:30		00:40

American	Ingredients	Metric/Imperial
¾ lb	Shortcrust pastry	350 g / 12 oz
1¼ lb	Sirloin beef, in a single slice	600 g / 1¼ lb
7 oz	Prague ham	200 g / 7 oz
¼ cup	Béchamel sauce	50 ml / 2 fl oz
1 tsp	Mixed spice	1 tsp
½ cup	Butter	100 g / 4 oz
2 or 3	Sage leaves	2 or 3

1. Preheat the oven to 350°F / 180°C / Gas Mark 4.
2. Roll out the pastry and lay the well beaten slice of beef on top. Put the ham on top of the meat, spread over a little béchamel and sprinkle with spice. Roll up the pastry with the meat filling. Damp and press the edges so that they are well sealed.
3. Place in a buttered baking pan, pour over the melted butter and add a few sage leaves. Put in a preheated oven and cook for 40 minutes, occasionally turning the roll carefully until it has taken on a good rosy color. If the cooking juice becomes too dry, add a little more butter.
4. Remove from the oven, let it cool, then cut into thick slices, putting two or three slices on each plate. Put the plates in a hot oven for a few moments before serving.

Costata alla campagnola
Country Sirloin

This is a stew of country origin, where the pot in the centre of the table invites drinking and lively conversation.

	00:10		01:00 to 01:30

American	Ingredients	Metric/Imperial
Scant ¼ cup	Vegetable oil	3 tbsp
¼ cup	Butter	50 g / 2 oz
1	Onion	1
1	Bunch of parsley	1
1	Celery stalk	1
1	Carrot	1
3 lb	Piece of sirloin	1 kg / 3 lb
	Salt and pepper	
⅔ cup	Dry white wine	150 ml / ¼ pint
1	Stock cube	1

Country sirloin

1. Put oil and butter into a high sided heatproof pan, prepare and chop the vegetables; add the sirloin, boned and rolled. Brown on all sides.

2. Season with salt and pepper and moisten with good dry white wine. Add about 1 cup [225 ml / 8 fl oz] of stock made from a cube and boil on a vigorous heat until the wine and stock are almost absorbed.

3. Reduce the heat and cook for about 1 hour, turning the meat from time to time and, if necessary, adding more stock.

4. When the meat is cooked, place on a dish, return the pan to the heat with the strained sauce, add a little more white wine and reduce the heat to low. Cut the meat into thick slices, put it back into the sauce and serve immediately in the pan or casserole.

Brasato alle salsicce

Braised Meat with Sausages

▱▷ 00:30   01:30 🍲

American	Ingredients	Metric/Imperial
2 lb	Topround (topside) beef	1 kg / 2 lb
Scant ¼ cup	Vegetable oil	3 tbsp
¼ cup	Butter	50 g / 2 oz
4	Onions	4
1	Garlic clove	1
1	Bouquet garni	1
4	Sausages	4
¾ lb	Small onions	350 g / 12 oz

1. Ask the butcher to prepare beef or roll the boned meat tightly, tying it with string or thread, and brown it in oil and butter on a medium heat. When it is well browned on all sides add the finely chopped onions, the crushed garlic, and the bouquet garni.
2. Moisten with a ladleful of water and continue cooking for 1¼ hours with the heat low and the lid on the pan.
3. Meanwhile begin cooking the sausages in another pan. Brown on both sides, then plunge into boiling water and simmer for 3 minutes. Discard the cooking water. Peel, if necessary, and cut them into fairly thick slices, adding to the meat while it is cooking.
4. Now scald and peel the small onions, then add them to the meat and leave until they are cooked. Test the meat and season. Serve when tender.

Cook's tip: This dish is excellent eaten immediately but even better the next day! You can make this dish with braising beef, or with pork, even if it is fatty, as this cooking method uses up the meat fat. If using pork, remember that it should be served very hot.

Pilau sardo 🧑‍🍳

Beef with Rice

▱▷ 00:10   02:00 🍲

American	Ingredients	Metric/Imperial
2 lb	Joint of beef brisket	1 kg / 2 lb
⅔ cup	Oil	150 ml / ¼ pint
¼ tsp	Chopped thyme	¼ tsp
¼ tsp	Chopped bay leaf	¼ tsp
¼ tsp	Chopped rosemary	¼ tsp
¼ tsp	Garlic powder	¼ tsp
½ cup	Dry white wine	125 ml / 4 fl oz
Scant 2 cups	Stock	450 ml / ¾ pint
1	Egg yolk	1
1	Lemon	1
	Salt and pepper	

1. Put the meat into a saucepan containing heated oil, add a ¼ teaspoon of thyme, bay, rosemary and garlic powder; pour over the wine gradually; when this has evaporated completely, add the stock. Cover and simmer until the meat is tender, which will take 1½-2 hours.

2. Remove from the pan. Strain the cooking juices, mix in the egg yolk and lemon juice and taste for seasoning.
3. Slice the meat, pour over some gravy, serving the rest in a sauceboat and serve with boiled rice.

Polpa alla bourguignonne 🧑‍🍳🧑‍🍳

Italian Beef Bourgignon

▱▷ 00:30   01:15 🍲

American	Ingredients	Metric/Imperial
1 lb	Shallots or small onions	500 g / 1 lb
Scant ¼ cup	Oil	3 tbsp
¼ cup	Butter	50 g / 2 oz
1¼ lb	Chuck eye beef (chuck) cubed	600 g / 1¼ lb
	Salt and pepper	
½ cup	Full-bodied red wine	125 ml / 4 fl oz
½ lb	Peeled plum tomatoes	225 g / 8 oz
1	Bay leaf	1
1	Stock cube	1

1. Wash the onions, plunge into boiling water for 5 minutes, drain and skin. Transfer to a saucepan containing heated oil and butter. Brown lightly then add the cubed meat and plenty of salt and pepper. When the meat is slightly browned, add the red wine and allow to evaporate.
2. Add the tomatoes with the bay leaf and moisten with 2½ cups [600 ml / 1 pint] hot water in which the stock cube has been dissolved, taking care that the sauce does not stick to the pan.
3. Cook for at least 1 hour: the meat should then be tender and the sauce very thick. Serve with polenta or thick slices of crusty bread.

Cook's tip: This dish may be prepared in large quantities and will freeze well for up to 6 months.

Magatello in salsa del Don

Beef in 'Don' Sauce

▱▷ 00:30   00:00 🍲

American	Ingredients	Metric/Imperial
1¼ lb	Fillet steak	600 g / 1¼ lb
Sauce		
2	Egg yolks	2
¼ cup	Oil	50 ml / 2 fl oz
1	Lemon	1
3 tbsp	Chopped black olives	2 tbsp
½ tsp	Anchovy paste	½ tsp
1 tsp	Mustard	1 tsp
	Salt and pepper	

1. Have your butcher slice the beef very thinly (with the meat slicer) and then arrange the slices on a serving dish.
2. Put the egg yolks into the blender, switch on, add oil gradually and when you can see that it is well beaten, add the lemon juice, the chopped black olives, the anchovy paste, the mustard, and salt and pepper to taste. Blend again to obtain a smooth sauce. Transfer to a bowl and place in the refrigerator for 30 minutes.
3. Cover the fillet of beef with the sauce and garnish the dish with black olives.

Beef in 'Don' sauce

Meat, egg and spinach roll

Rollé verde e giallo
Meat, Egg and Spinach Roll

	00:40		00:55

American	Ingredients	Metric/Imperial
1½ lb	Top round (topside) beef, in a slice	700 g / 1½ lb
1½ cups	Cooked spinach	300 g / 11 oz
¼ cup	Butter	50 g / 2 oz
¼ cup	Grated parmesan cheese	25 g / 1 oz
1 cup	Thick béchamel sauce (see page 162)	225 ml / 8 fl oz
5	Eggs — 3 hard-cooked (boiled)	5
11 oz	Ricotta (curd cheese)	300 g / 11 oz
1	Lemon	1
	Salt and pepper	
¼ tsp	Nutmeg	¼ tsp
2 or 3	Sprigs of rosemary	2 or 3
1	Onion	1
½ cup	Dry white wine	125 ml / 4 fl oz

1. Preheat the oven to 350°F / 180°C / Gas Mark 4.
2. Beat the beef flat, taking care not to tear it.
3. Mix the spinach with the butter, grated parmesan, béchamel sauce, 2 whole eggs, ricotta and grated rind of lemon. Season with salt, pepper and nutmeg.
4. Spread this mixture on the steak to within ¾ — 1¼ in / 2 — 3 cm of the edge. Place the 3 hard-cooked (boiled) eggs in the middle. Roll up carefully, ensuring that the filling stays in place and tie with kitchen string. Insert a few sprigs of fresh rosemary under the string.
5. Melt some butter in a casserole, add a chopped onion and then the meat roll; turn frequently so that the roll browns evenly. Sprinkle with white wine.
6. Transfer to the oven and bake, turning from time to time, for 45 minutes. To serve, cut the roll into fairly thick slices, arrange on a serving dish, strain and re-heat the cooking juices to pour over the meat.

Filetto in salsa
Beef Fillet in Sauce

	00:25		00:20 to 00:30

American	Ingredients	Metric/Imperial
1½ lb	Fillet beef	700 g / 1½ lb
1	Garlic clove	1
1 oz	Bacon	25 g / 1 oz
2 tbsp	Chopped parsley	1½ tbsp
3 tbsp	Butter	40 g / 1½ oz
1 tsp	Curry powder	1 tsp
½ cup	Cream	125 ml / 4 fl oz

1. Spread out and beat the open fillet to form a single slice, lay on top a crushed clove of garlic, a little bacon cut into strips and a little chopped parsley. Roll up the slice of meat, then sew it with white thread or secure with toothpicks.
2. Melt a little butter in a frying pan and cook for about 20 minutes, finally adding the curry powder, the parsley and a little cream. Place on a heated serving dish and serve very hot.

Bollito misto
Boiled Mixed Meats

This famous dish comes from Piedmont and is ideal for a large family party.

	01:00		03:00 to 04:00

Serves 10
Plus 06:00 soaking

American	Ingredients	Metric/Imperial
2 lb	Short ribs of beef	1 kg / 2 lb
2 lb	Bottom round of beef	1 kg / 2 lb
1 lb	Breast of veal, trimmed	450 g / 1 lb
1½ lb	Shoulder of lamb	700 g / 1½ lb
1	Calf's foot	1
½ lb	Belly of pork, trimmed	225 g / 8 oz
½ lb	Sausage	225 g / 8 oz
1	Ox tongue, soaked for 6 hours	1
1	Onion	1
2	Cloves	2
1	Garlic clove	1
2	Tomatoes, peeled and drained	2
2	Sprigs of parsley	2
8	Sprigs of thyme	8
2	Bay leaves	2
	Salt and pepper	
1 lb	New potatoes	450 g / 1 lb
24	Small onions	24
1 lb	Cabbage	450 g / 1 lb
1 lb	Zucchini (courgette)	450 g / 1 lb
1 lb	Carrots	450 g / 1 lb
1 lb	Green beans	450 g / 1 lb
1 quart	Béchamel sauce	1 litre / 1¾ pints
2½ cups	Green sauce	600 ml / 1 pint

1. Place all the meat in a very large pot with the soaked tongue, do not add the sausage at this stage. Cover with cold water, add the onion stuck with cloves, garlic, tomatoes, parsley, thyme and bay leaves.
2. Bring to the boil slowly and remove the scum as it rises to the surface.
3. Season with salt and pepper and simmer for 2-3 hours. Remove each joint of meat as it becomes tender; the veal and lamb will be cooked first. Add the sausage. Continue to skim the fat and scum from the surface as cooking progresses. The tongue will take longest to cook; drain it and skin when cooked.
4. At the end of 2½ hours start cooking the vegetables in a little stock from the meat or water, as preferred. Make sure that the vegetables are crisp. Keep warm.
5. Make the béchamel sauce with half meat broth and half and half milk and cream. Make the green sauce.
6. Carve the meats on a large heated serving platter and keep warm covered with foil in a low oven, adding a little meat stock from time to time. Garnish with parsley sprigs.
7. Serve the cooked vegetables on several platters covered with the béchamel sauce. Serve the green sauce separately, in a sauceboat.

Cook's tip: allow the stock to cool and skim for use in soups and sauces. Left-over meat can be served with a selection of salads for other meals.

Manzo brasato al barolo
Beef Braised in Red Wine

◣▱▱▱ 00:30   02:00 ⬛

American	Ingredients	Metric/Imperial
1½ oz	Cooked ham	40 g / 1½ oz
3 lb	Brisket beef	1.4 kg / 3 lb
2 tbsp	Lard	25 g / 1 oz
Scant ¼ cup	Oil	3 tbsp
3 tbsp	Butter	40 g / 1½ oz
	Salt and pepper	
1 (70 cl)	Bottle of Barolo wine	1 (70 cl)
2	Carrots	2
2	Onions	2
4	Celery stalks	4
1	Stock cube	1
	Potatoes	

1. Dice the ham and insert it around the outside of the beef. Rub all over with lard.
2. Choose a heavy saucepan with a lid, add the oil and butter, allow to bubble and then lay the meat in the pan. Season with salt and pepper, pour in the wine, which should cover the meat completely.
3. Prepare and chop the vegetables, and when most of the wine has evaporated add them to the saucepan together with a stock cube made up with 2½ cups [600 ml / 1 pint] of water. Cover and braise for at least 2 hours.
4. Prepare boiled potatoes to serve with the meat. Remove the beef to a carving board, slice it and arrange on a heated dish, surrounded by the vegetables. Serve hot with cooking liquid in a sauceboat.

Brasato all'acciuga
Braised Beef with Anchovies

◣▱▱▱ 00:15   02:00 ⬛

American	Ingredients	Metric/Imperial
3	Slices of bacon	3
Scant ¼ cup	Vegetable oil	3 tbsp
1¾ lb	Chuck steak	800 g / 1¾ lb
	Salt and pepper	
½ tsp	Nutmeg	½ tsp
3	Anchovies, desalted and boned	3
1	Stock cube	1
2 or 3	Sprigs of parsley	2 or 3

1. Chop the bacon into small pieces and put it in a pan with the heated oil, brown slightly, then add the piece of meat, season with salt and pepper and sprinkle with nutmeg. When the meat is browned on all sides, lower the flame and begin cooking.
2. Add the chopped anchovies and the parsley, mix in the 2½ cups [600 ml / 1 pint] stock made from the cube, cover and cook on a slow heat for about 2 hours.
3. Turn from time to time, add more stock if necessary, and check seasoning. Serve the meat in slices with boiled rice.

Carpaccio alla toscana
Lemon Steak

◣▱▱▱ 01:00   00:00 ⬛

American	Ingredients	Metric/Imperial
1¼ lb	Thin slices of fillet steak	600 g / 1¼ lb
3	Lemons	3
	Salt and pepper	
8	Small mushrooms (porcino)	8
2 oz	Grana cheese	50 g / 2 oz
2 tbsp	Chopped parsley	1½ tbsp

1. The meat must be sliced very thinly, as if it was ham; it is advisable to have the butcher cut it on a machine.
2. Arrange the thin slices of steak on a serving dish. Beat juice of lemons in a cup with salt and pepper and sprinkle the steak with the mixture.
3. After 30 minutes, when the meat has absorbed the dressing, slice the flesh of well cleaned raw mushrooms and lay them on top of the meat with some slices of grana cheese and chopped parsley. Serve immediately.

Filetto all'uva
Fillet Steak with Grapes

◣▱▱▱ 00:30   00:45 ⬛

American	Ingredients	Metric/Imperial
1¾ lb	Fillet steak	800 g / 1¾ lb
3 oz	Raw ham, cut into strips	75 g / 3 oz
¼ cup	Butter	50 g / 2 oz
1 lb	Ripe white grapes	500 g / 1 lb
Scant ¼ cup	Brandy	3 tbsp
½ cup	Coffee (single) cream	125 ml / 4 fl oz
2	Cloves	2
1 cup	Stock	225 ml / 8 fl oz
	Salt and pepper	
1	Sugar lump	1
½	Lemon	½

1. Lard the meat with small pieces of raw ham. Then tie the meat as for preparing a roast.
2. Melt the butter in a casserole, put in the piece of meat and brown it on all sides. Remove stones from grapes or use a seedless variety.
3. Blend grapes (or mash with a fork) together with brandy, sieve the mixture and pour the sauce over the meat. Add the cream, the cloves, ⅔ cup [150 ml / ¼ pint] stock, salt and pepper. Cover the pan, lower the heat and cook for about 20 minutes.
4. Put a sugar lump in a small pan and caramelize it, dilute with the juice of half a lemon and a little hot stock, then pour over the meat. Continue cooking, still covered, for a further 10 minutes.
5. Remove the meat, slice it (remember to remove all the string) and place it onto a heated serving dish. Return the pan to the heat with the sauce, add butter and heat on a high flame so that it thickens; then pour it onto the meat. Garnish the edge of the dish with white grapes which can be fried in butter. Serve with sauté potatoes and a green salad.

Lemon steak

Fegato all'italiana in salsa

Italian-Style Liver in Sauce

00:15   00:20

American	Ingredients	Metric/Imperial
1 lb	Calf's liver	500 g / 1 lb
	Flour	
	Salt and pepper	
¼ cup	Butter	50 g / 2 oz
3 oz	Raw ham	75 g / 3 oz
1	Small onion	1
2 or 3	Sage leaves	2 or 3
1	Bunch of parsley	1
2 tsp	Cornstarch (cornflour)	2 tsp
1	Stock cube	1
3 tbsp	Marsala	2 tbsp

1. Cut the liver into slices and dip in seasoned flour, shake off excess.
2. Heat the butter, add the liver and fry for 5 minutes. Remove the slices and keep warm.
3. Chop the ham, a small onion, a few sage leaves and a bunch of parsley, and fry them in the same butter over a low heat for 6 minutes.
4. Add cornstarch dissolved in 1¼ cups [300 ml / ½ pint] stock with a small glass of marsala, and simmer for 10 minutes. Put the liver back in the sauce for a few minutes. Serve hot, adding seasoning at the last minute.

Cotolettine di vitello gratinate

Veal Cutlets au Gratin

00:20   00:25
Soaking time 01:00

American	Ingredients	Metric/Imperial
8	Small veal loin steaks (cutlets)	8
3 tbsp	White flour	2 tbsp
2	Eggs	2
1 cup	Bread crumbs	100 g / 4 oz
½ cup	Butter	100 g / 4 oz
8	Slices of ham	8
8	Slices of fontina cheese	8
½ tsp	Nutmeg	½ tsp
	Salt and pepper	

1. Beat the cutlets on either side, flour lightly and soak in beaten egg for 1 hour. Coat in bread crumbs, pat the crumbs with the flat of the hand.
2. Heat the butter in a pan and fry the meat until golden brown each side, drain on absorbent kitchen towels.
3. Cool the cutlets and arrange in an ovenproof dish, place a slice of raw ham, without the fat, and a very thin slice of fontina on each cutlet.
4. Preheat the oven to 425°F / 220°C / Gas Mark 7.
5. Sprinkle with nutmeg, pepper and salt, and dot with butter. Place in a hot oven for 15 minutes and serve as soon as the cheese has melted.

Vitello al curry

Veal in a Curry Sauce

00:10   01:40

American	Ingredients	Metric/Imperial
2 lb	Veal loin	1 kg / 2 lb
	Seasoned flour	
1	Onion	1
1	Apple	1
¼ cup	Butter	50 g / 2 oz
2	Cloves	2
1 tbsp	Flour	1 tbsp
1 tsp	Curry powder	1 tsp
2 cups	Stock	450 ml / ¾ pint
½	Lemon	½
	Salt	

1. Dice veal and toss in seasoned flour. Chop onion, peel and dice apple, melt butter and when foaming, sauté apple and onion for 2-3 minutes, add meat and cloves and brown meat all over, then lower the heat.
2. Blend flour and curry powder with a little water to a smooth paste, and add to pan. Pour over stock, stirring all the time, cover and simmer gently for 1½ hours. When meat is tender, add juice of lemon and salt.
3. Serve piping hot with apple chutney and a potato purée seasoned with a pinch of nutmeg.

Frittata di vitello alla salvia

Veal Omelette with Sage

00:15   00:18

American	Ingredients	Metric/Imperial
1 lb	Roast veal	450 g / 1 lb
5	Eggs	5
1	Bunch of sage leaves	1
1 tbsp	Milk	1 tbsp
1 tsp	Flour	1 tsp
1 tbsp	Cognac	1 tbsp
	Salt and pepper	
1 cup	Vegetable oil	225 ml / 8 fl oz
2 – 3 tbsp	Béchamel sauce	1½ – 2 tbsp

1. Chop the roast meat very finely or grind (mince) or put through a food processor. Add the beaten egg yolks, the stiffly whipped whites, and a handful of whole sage leaves. Beat with milk and flour to obtain a smooth mixture. Mix in the cognac and season with salt and pepper to taste.
2. Put oil in a frying pan and when it is smoking pour in the mixture, lowering the flame and shaking the pan so that it does not stick. Turn as for an ordinary omelette or if preferred cook the top under the broiler (grill) under a high heat.
3. Preheat the oven to 350°F / 180°C / Gas Mark 4.
4. Transfer the omelette to an ovenproof serving dish lined with aluminium foil. Close the foil by folding and place in the oven for 12 minutes. Pour béchamel over the omelette.

Cook's tip: if using a food processor, chop meat and mix the egg yolks, sage, milk, flour, cognac, salt and pepper. Fold in stiffly beaten egg whites after the other ingredients have been processed.

Veal in a curry sauce

Kidneys in cream sauce

1. Skin kidneys, slice and remove cores.
2. Wash and soak for a few minutes in cold salt water. Remove the kidneys and pat dry in absorbent kitchen towels. Toss in seasoned flour.
3. Fry the floured kidneys in butter over medium heat for 6 minutes. Add chopped onion, garlic and thyme.
4. Add the wine and raise the heat for 2 minutes. Reduce the heat and add cream.
5. Add the juniper berries, cook for 8 minutes, season well and add parsley.

Rognoni di vitello

Kidneys in Cream Sauce

00:20 | 00:15

American	Ingredients	Metric/Imperial
1½ lb	*Veal or lamb's kidneys*	*700 g / 1½ lb*
3 tbsp	*Flour*	*2 tbsp*
½ cup	*Butter*	*50 g / 2 oz*
2	*Medium-sized onions*	*2*
1	*Small garlic clove*	*1*
¼ tsp	*Thyme*	*¼ tsp*
½ cup	*Red wine*	*125 ml / 4 fl oz*
	Salt and pepper	
½ cup	*Cream*	*6 tbsp*
12	*Slices small crusty loaf*	*12*
	Oil for frying	
1 tbsp	*Chopped parsley*	*1 tbsp*
1 tsp	*Juniper berries*	*1 tsp*

1. Prepare the kidneys by removing the skin and the core.
2. Flour the kidneys and fry in butter over medium heat. Add chopped onion, garlic and thyme. Cook for 6 minutes.
3. Add the wine, raise the heat for 2 minutes. Reduce the heat to low and stir in cream and juniper berries. Cook for a further 8 minutes and season well.
4. Fry the sliced bread in oil until crisp, drain on absorbent kitchen towels. Wash the parsley, chop finely and add to the kidneys.
5. Pour the kidneys into a heated serving dish, surround with fried bread and garnish with sprigs of parsley.

Rognone e riso in umido

Braised Calves' Kidneys with Rice

00:40 | 00:35

American	Ingredients	Metric/Imperial
1 lb	*Calves' kidneys*	*500 g / 1 lb*
3 tbsp	*Vinegar*	*2 tbsp*
½ cup	*Butter*	*100 g / 4 oz*
	Salt and pepper	
½ cup	*Dry white wine*	*125 ml / 4 fl oz*
2	*Garlic cloves*	*2*
1 tbsp	*Chopped parsley*	*1 tbsp*
1 tsp	*Rosemary*	*1 tsp*
1 cup	*Rice*	*200 g / 7 oz*

1. Slice the kidneys finely and remove all the fat; soak in vinegar and water for about 30 minutes.
2. Melt the butter in a heavy pan and when it is hot add the kidneys, brown and season.
3. Add the wine and allow it to evaporate, continue to cook for 15 minutes over a low heat.
4. Crush the garlic, chop the parsley and rosemary and mix.
5. Cook the rice in salted water until 'al dente', drain.
6. Place the kidneys in the middle of a heated serving dish, sprinkle with the garlic and rosemary mixture, surround with the rice and serve.

Panada del fattore

Veal and Whole Wheat Bread Stew

00:25 | 01:00

American	Ingredients	Metric/Imperial
11 oz	*Crusty whole wheat bread*	*300 g / 11 oz*
14 oz	*Veal shoulder or breast, cubed*	*400 g / 14 oz*
2 cups	*Stock*	*450 ml / ¾ pint*
2 tbsp	*Oil*	*1½ tbsp*
½ tsp	*Cinnamon*	*½ tsp*
	Salt and pepper	
2 tbsp	*Grated parmesan cheese*	*1½ tbsp*
2	*Eggs yolks*	*2*

1. Lay the bread, sliced thickly, in a saucepan, distribute the pieces of veal on the bread and pour on stock.
2. Cook over a medium heat, add oil, cinnamon, salt and pepper but do not stir.
3. Turn heat to low and allow the pan to cook slowly at an even temperature for about 50 minutes.
4. Towards the end of the cooking time test the meat with a fork, when tender, turn off the heat and sprinkle with grated parmesan.
5. Before serving, add the egg yolks, stir vigorously and serve in heated bowls.

Scaloppe alla Carlo Porta

Veal Scallopine Cooked in Foil with Spinach

00:25 | 00:30

American	Ingredients	Metric/Imperial
8	*Veal scallopine (escalopes)*	*8*
8	*Slices of fontina cheese*	*8*
8	*Slices of parma ham*	*8*
¼ tsp	*Chopped sage*	*¼ tsp*
1	*Shallot or small onion*	*1*
¼ cup	*Butter*	*50 g / 2 oz*
Scant 2 cups	*Cooked spinach*	*400 g / 14 oz*
1 cup	*Fresh cream*	*225 ml / 8 fl oz*
¼ cup	*Grated parmesan cheese*	*25 g / 1 oz*

1. Preheat the oven to 350°F / 180°C / Gas Mark 4.
2. Pound the scallopine flat and cover each one with a slice of fontina cheese and one of parma ham; add a small pinch of sage and roll up, securing with a toothpick.
3. Chop the shallot and fry in the butter, add the veal rolls and brown on a medium heat.
4. Put the spinach into another pan, add the cream and heat through gently. Sprinkle with parmesan cheese and stir well.
5. Spread the spinach mixture on a sheet of baking foil, lay the rolls of veal on top, close the foil and bake in the oven for 15 minutes.

Hamburger alla Bismarck
Rissoles with Meat and Anchovies

00:20 Serves 6   00:25 to 00:30

American	Ingredients	Metric/Imperial
1¼ lb	Mixed raw meats (veal, pork, beef)	600 g / 1¼ lb
7 oz	Bread crumbs, soaked in milk	200 g / 7 oz
1	Anchovy fillets or	1
¼ tsp	Anchovy paste	¼ tsp
2	Egg yolks	2
5 tbsp	Bread crumbs	4 tbsp
¼ cup	Oil	50 ml / 2 fl oz
2 tbsp	Butter	25 g / 1 oz
¼ tsp	Chopped sage	¼ tsp
¼ tsp	Chopped rosemary	¼ tsp
2 tbsp	Chopped parsley	1½ tbsp
4	Eggs	4
	Salt and pepper	

1. Grind (mince) the meat twice. Add to the bread crumbs and anchovy and mix well.
2. Place in a bowl, add egg yolks and enough extra bread crumbs to make a firm mixture; shape into 4 round, flat rissoles.
3. Heat some oil and butter in a frying pan, adding a little sage and rosemary.
4. Place the rissoles in the hot fat and cook for 3 minutes each side to brown and then reduce heat to low or medium to cook for another 7 minutes on each side.
5. Preheat the oven to 400°F / 200°C / Gas Mark 6.
6. Transfer to an oven-to-table dish, sprinkle with parsley and place a raw egg upon each rissole, taking care not to break the yolk. Cover immediately and put in the oven for 5 minutes or until the eggs are ready.
7. Serve immediately, adding salt and pepper at the table.

Ossobuc
Stewed Shin of Veal

00:30   02:00

American	Ingredients	Metric/Imperial
6 x 3 in	Veal shin bones	6 x 7½ cm / 3 in
¼ cup	Flour	25 g / 1 oz
½ cup	Butter	100 g / 4 oz
1	Onion	1
1	Carrot	1
1	Celery stalk	1
2	Garlic cloves	2
3 – 4	Sprigs of marjoram	3 – 4
1	Bay leaf	1
1	Lemon	1
½ cup	Dry white wine	125 ml / 4 fl oz
6	Ripe or canned tomatoes	6
1¼ cups	Stock	300 ml / ½ pint
	Salt and pepper	
½ cup	Chopped parsley	6 tbsp

1. Ask the butcher to saw the shin of veal into the correctly sized pieces, dip in flour and shake off the excess.
2. Melt the butter over a medium heat in a large heavy pan and brown the veal shin on all sides. Remove onto a plate.
3. Chop the onion, carrot and celery into fine dice and crush the cloves of garlic. Cook in the pan over a low heat in the butter used for the veal for 5 minutes.
4. Stand the veal on its end, upright to prevent the marrow in the bone coming out. Add the marjoram and bay leaf with a small piece of lemon peel and the dry white wine. Cook on a high heat for 5 minutes.
5. Add the chopped tomatoes and stock, season well, bring to the boil, lower the heat, cover and cook for 1½ hours on a low heat. Add a little boiling water if the pan seems to be drying out during cooking.
6. Prepare the 'gremolata' which is an essential part of this dish by grating the remaining lemon peel finely, crush the other clove of garlic, mix with the lemon rind and the chopped parsley. When the dish is cooked, sprinkle with the lemon and parsley mixture.

Cook's tip: this dish is traditionally served with risotto Milanese.

Ossibuchi della festa
Braised Shin of Veal

00:30   01:30

American	Ingredients	Metric/Imperial
1	Shin of veal sawn into 4 sections of 2 in / 5 cm	1
3 tbsp	Flour	2 tbsp
¼ cup	Oil	50 ml / 2 fl oz
3 tbsp	Butter	40 g / 1½ oz
1	Onion	1
½ cup	Dry white wine	125 ml / 4 fl oz
2 lb	Italian tomatoes fresh or canned	1 kg / 2 lb
	Salt and pepper	
	Ground nutmeg	
½ lb	Petit pois	225 g / 8 oz
¼ lb	Dried mushrooms	100 g / 4 oz

1. Remove the skin surrounding the shins, flour them lightly, shaking off the excess.
2. Put oil and butter into a wide, heavy pan with a close fitting lid, heat and add the onion chopped very fine.
3. Turn the heat to low and add a little water if necessary to prevent the onion coloring too much. Slip in the shin bones and brown on both sides, taking care that they do not stick to the pan. Sprinkle with a little white wine and add the tomatoes, peeled and mashed with a fork.
4. Season with salt, pepper and a pinch of nutmeg, cover and cook for about 1 hour.
5. Meanwhile, soak the dried mushrooms in warm water for at least 15 minutes, remove from the water and squeeze gently.
6. Drain the peas and add them to the contents of saucepan. After 10 minutes, add the dried mushrooms. Continue to cook slowly with the lid on for a further 15 minutes.
7. The veal may either be left in the saucepan to serve or transferred to a container suitable for the refrigerator and any excess fat removed when cold.
8. Reheat very gently, stirring carefully to avoid separating the marrow from the bone. Serve hot.

Roast loin of veal

Punta di vitello arrosto
Roast Loin of Veal

Lombardy produces excellent veal and roast veal is a traditional dish of the district around Pavia.

⏱ 00:10   01:30 🍲

American	Ingredients	Metric/Imperial
5 oz	Bacon	150 g / 5 oz
½ cup	Oil	125 ml / 4 fl oz
1	Onion	1
1	Garlic clove	1
3¼ lb	Loin of veal (boned and rolled)	1.5 kg / 3¼ lb
2 cups	Stock	450 ml / ¾ pint
½ cup	Dry white wine	125 ml / 4 fl oz
8	Thin slices of fat pork for larding	8
	Pepper to taste	

1. Preheat the oven to 400°F / 200°C / Gas Mark 6.
2. Chop the bacon into small pieces and fry in a casserole with heated oil and finely chopped onion. Add the crushed clove of garlic and continue to fry over gentle heat until the bacon begins to brown.
3. When the bacon has browned, turn up the heat and add the joint of veal, browning quickly on all sides. Add the stock (which can be made using stock cubes, if you wish) a little at a time, then the wine.
4. Lard the meat by placing 4 thin strips of fat pork over the joint.
5. Roast in the oven for 1 hour, turning the joint once and larding again with the remaining slices of fat pork to ensure a good color.
6. Sprinkle with pepper and add a little water if the meat shows signs of sticking to the pan.
7. Roast veal can be served either hot, garnished with strips of cooked mixed vegetables such as carrot, onion and green pepper, or cold with a variety of salads.

Pancetta di vitello in gelatina
Jellied Breast of Veal

◀ 00:45   02:10 🍲

American	Ingredients	Metric/Imperial
¼ lb	Cooked ham	100 g / 4 oz
¼ lb	Mortadella	100 g / 4 oz
3	Eggs	3
2 tbsp	Grated parmesan cheese	1½ tbsp
	Salt and pepper	
2 lb	Breast of veal	1 kg / 2 lb
3	Carrots	3
1	Onion	1
1	Celery stalk	1
1	Bunch of chopped parsley	1
5 tsp	Gelatin	5 tsp

1. Chop the ham and mortadella, put into a bowl with the eggs, parmesan, salt and pepper and mix well.
2. Wipe and trim excess fat from breast of veal, open out flat.
3. Stuff the breast of veal with the ham mixture, press down firmly and sew up with fine string, or secure with skewers.
4. Chop the carrots, onion, celery and parsley and put them in a large saucepan with plenty of water. Bring to the boil.
5. Wrap the breast of veal in a clean boiled cloth or muslin and secure firmly, lower into the boiling water and allow to cook for about 2 hours.
6. Remove from the pan, drain reserving 2½ cups [600 ml / 1 pint] stock. Unwrap the veal and put between 2 plates with a weight on top while it is cooling.
7. Dissolve the gelatin by sprinkling it on to 4-5 tablespoons boiling meat stock. Mix into the reserved stock and cool. Replace the vegetables.
8. Slice the veal and arrange on a deep serving dish, spoon gelatin and vegetables over the slices and refrigerate. Serve when meat and jelly have set. Some jelly can be chopped for decoration.

Costolette di agnello con patate al vino

Lamb Cutlets with Potatoes in Wine

	00:40		00:20
	Serves 6		

American	Ingredients	Metric/Imperial
12	Lamb cutlets	12
¼ cup	Flour	25 g / 1 oz
½ cup	Butter	100 g / 4 oz
4	Garlic cloves	4
4	Sage leaves	4
½ cup	Dry white wine	125 ml / 4 fl oz
2 lb	Potatoes	1 kg / 2 lb
¾ cup	Olive oil	175 ml / 6 fl oz
2	Onions	2
	Salt	
½ tsp	Hot paprika	½ tsp

1. Coat the cutlets in flour, heat the butter in a pan and fry until golden brown for about 3 minutes each side.
2. Add the crushed garlic and sage, pour in the wine and cook on a low heat for 10 minutes.
3. Peel the potatoes and cut into thick slices (alternatively if they are small to medium-sized, cut into quarters), cook in boiling salted water until tender but firm.
4. Heat the oil in a pan over a medium heat and cook the thinly sliced onions for 4 minutes.
5. Add the potatoes to the onion and fry, turning from time to time, without breaking the potatoes too much. Sprinkle with salt and paprika.
6. Serve the cooked cutlets on a heated serving dish garnished with potatoes and onions.

Frittura mista

Fried Mixed Grill

	00:40		00:20

American	Ingredients	Metric/Imperial
1 ¼ cups	Flour	150 g / 5 oz
3 tbsp	Olive oil	2 tbsp
2	Eggs	2
	Salt and pepper	
3 tbsp	Dry white wine	2 tbsp
3	Artichokes	3
½	Lemon	½
5 oz	Calf's brains	150 g / 5 oz
5 oz	Calf's liver	150 g / 5 oz
¾ lb	Zucchini (courgettes)	350 g / 12 oz
4	Lamb chops	4
½ tsp	Curry powder	½ tsp
1 ¼ cups	Vegetable oil for frying	300 ml / ½ pint
1	Bay leaf	1
1	Sage leaf	1

1. Prepare the batter, putting the flour in a large bowl, add olive oil, the egg yolks and a pinch of salt. Mix carefully and add the white wine and sufficient water so that the batter is not too thick.

2. Clean the artichokes and cook them for 5 minutes in water with a little lemon juice. Immerse the carefully cleaned calf's brains and liver in boiling water; steep for 5 minutes.
3. Cut all the meat and vegetables into thin slices or small pieces. Whip the egg whites until they are stiff and fold them gently into the batter, taking care that they do not collapse, add a little curry powder, tip in the meat and vegetables and mix so that they are all well covered.
4. Heat the oil in a large deep frying pan with a bay leaf and a leaf of sage and put the ingredients into the pan in batches and fry until golden brown. Drain on absorbent kitchen towels.

Montone del capraio

Mutton with Bread and Onions

Traditionally, this dish was cooked in a low-burning wood-fired range using a copper pan with a very tight-fitting lid. Nowadays the pressure cooker makes an ideal substitute.

	00:10		00:30
			in a pressure cooker

American	Ingredients	Metric/Imperial
¼ cup	Butter	50 g / 2 oz
1	Onion	1
2 lb	Stewing mutton	1 kg / 2 lb
	Salt and pepper	
8	Slices of crusty bread	8

1. Melt the butter in the pressure cooker, fry the chopped onion. Cut the meat into small pieces, add to the onion, season with salt and pepper. Pour over 1 cup [225 ml / 8 fl oz] water, close the cooker lid, bring to pressure and cook for 20 minutes over moderate heat.
2. De-pressurize the cooker, remove the meat and serve on thick slices of toast with all the juices poured over it.

Fondue all'abbacchio

Lamb Fondue

	02:30		01:00

American	Ingredients	Metric/Imperial
11 oz	Fontina cheese	300 g / 11 oz
2 cups	Milk	450 ml / ¾ pint
⅓ cup	Butter	75 g / 3 oz
3	Egg yolks	3
6	Lamb cutlets	6
½ cup	Stock	125 ml / 4 fl oz
1 tbsp	Lemon juice	1 tbsp
3 tbsp	Gin	2 tbsp

1. Prepare the fondue in the usual way using the basic recipe.
2. Heat half the butter in a pan, add the cutlets and fry gently for 3 minutes each side, then moisten with hot stock. Finish cooking with the pan covered for about 20 minutes. Add the gin and the lemon juice.
3. Arrange the cutlets on a metal dish and place on a hotplate, cover with the fondue and serve hot.

Fried mixed grill

Kidneys in Mustard Sauce

Rognoni alla senape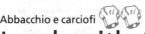

	00:20	00:00

American	Ingredients	Metric/Imperial
8	Lambs' kidneys	8
¼ cup	Butter	50 g / 2 oz
2	Garlic cloves	2
1 cup	Dry white wine	225 ml / 8 fl oz
1 tbsp	Mustard	1 tbsp
4 drops	Worcester sauce	4 drops
Scant ¼ cup	Chopped parsley	3 tbsp

1. Skin and core the kidneys, scald in boiling water for a few minutes and drain. Slice or halve the kidneys.
2. Heat the butter in a heavy pan with the garlic, add kidneys and fry over a medium heat for 5 minutes, then add the white wine and turn the heat up to allow it to evaporate.
3. Reduce the heat to moderate and continue cooking for another 10 minutes, add the mustard and a few drops of Worcester sauce. Stir well, sprinkle with parsley and serve hot with a purée of potatoes.

Lamb with Artichokes

Abbacchio e carciofi

	01:00	01:00

American	Ingredients	Metric/Imperial
2	Whole lamb loins	2
¼ cup	Butter	50 g / 2 oz
¼ cup	Vegetable oil	50 ml / 2 fl oz
6	Sage leaves	6
6	Sprigs of rosemary	6
	Salt and pepper	
1 cup	Dry white wine	225 ml / 8 fl oz
8	Small artichokes	8
2	Eggs	2
1 cup	Bread crumbs	100 g / 4 oz
½	Lemon	½
	Oil for deep frying	

1. Preheat the oven to 400°F / 200°C / Gas Mark 6.
2. Wash and thoroughly dry the lamb. Heat the butter and oil in a roasting pan, adding a few sage leaves, rosemary and seasoning with salt and pepper. Put the lamb in the pan and brown on all sides in the oven.
3. Moisten the lamb with the white wine, adding a little at a time so that one amount is absorbed before adding another.
4. While the lamb is cooking, clean the artichokes, remove the tough leaves, chokes and thorns, and boil them for 10 minutes or so. Remove them from the heat and drain upside down on a wire rack to extract all the water.
5. Cut the artichokes in two, dry them well, then coat them with the beaten eggs and the bread crumbs. Fry them on a brisk heat in plenty of oil.
6. Squeeze a few drops of lemon juice onto the artichokes, when cooked, then remove them from the pan and put to dry on a sheet of kitchen towel which will soak up the excess grease; then sprinkle with grated lemon rind.

Kidneys in mustard sauce

7. Finish cooking the lamb; there should be no juices left at the end of cooking. Place in the centre of a heated serving dish and surround with the fried artichokes.

Lamb with Lemon

Agnello al limone

	00:30	01:00
	Marinating time 02:00	
	Serves 6	

American	Ingredients	Metric/Imperial
3 lb	Leg of lamb	1.4 kg / 3 lb
2	Garlic cloves	2
2	Lemons	2
	Salt and pepper	
¾ cup	Vegetable oil	175 ml / 6 fl oz
½ tsp	Chopped sage	½ tsp
½ tsp	Chopped rosemary	½ tsp
2½ cups	White wine	600 ml / 1 pint
½ cup	Wine vinegar	125 ml / 4 fl oz
14 oz	Plum tomatoes, fresh or canned	400 g / 14 oz
1 cup	Black olives	175 g / 6 oz
	New potatoes	

1. Cut meat into 1 in / 2½ cm cubes, mix with the crushed garlic and lemon juice and pour over the lamb with salt and pepper. Marinate for 2 hours.
2. Heat the oil in a large frying pan, add the chopped sage and rosemary. When the fat is hot, brown the pieces of lamb well on all sides. Moisten a little at a time with the white wine mixed with the vinegar, then cover with the tomatoes, which can be broken down with a wooden spoon, and add the black olives.
3. Cook over a low heat, or continue cooking in the oven at 325°F / 170°C / Gas Mark 3.
4. Remove the meat from the pan when it is well cooked with a slotted spoon. Sieve the sauce, if necessary thickening it with a little flour or thinning with a little wine. Reheat and serve very hot, surrounded by boiled new potatoes.

Umido alla pugliese

Lamb Stew with Pasta

00:15　　　　　　01:30

American	Ingredients	Metric/Imperial
1¾ lb	Stewing lamb	800 g / 1¾ lb
2	Onions	2
1¼ lb	Tomatoes	600 g / 1¼ lb
3 tbsp	Vegetable oil	2 tbsp
1 tbsp	White flour	1 tbsp
⅔ cup	Red wine	150 ml / 5 fl oz
2	Lemons	2
1 lb	Orecchiette or other pasta	450 g / 1 lb
	Sprigs of parsley	
	Salt and pepper	

1. Dice meat, peel and chop onions, peel tomatoes. Heat oil and sauté meat and onions for 3-4 minutes until meat is brown.
2. Add flour to pan then cook for 1 minute. Remove from the heat and pour over wine, lemon juice and stir in tomatoes. Return to heat, cover and simmer for about 1¼ hours, stirring from time to time.
3. Meanwhile cook pasta in plenty of boiling salted water until 'al dente'. Stir cooked pasta into stew.
4. Spoon stew into an earthenware dish, garnish with sprigs of parsley, add a sprinkling of black pepper or powdered capsicum and serve.

Agnello arrosto del Nilo

Roast Lamb

01:00　　　　　　01:00
Marinating time 01:00

American	Ingredients	Metric/Imperial
3¼ lb	Leg of lamb	1.5 kg / 3¼ lb
1 cup	Vegetable oil	225 ml / 8 fl oz
	Salt and pepper	
¼ cup	Butter	50 g / 2 oz
2	Onions	2
½ cup	White wine	125 ml / 4 fl oz
	Stock	
4	Potatoes	4
1 lb	Artichokes	450 g / 1 lb
1	Lemon	1
3 tbsp	Chopped parsley	2 tbsp

1. Cut the leg of lamb into 1 in / 2½ cm cubes and marinate in oil, salt and pepper for 1 hour.
2. Heat the butter and oil from the marinade in a large pan, sweat thinly sliced onions over a low heat. Remove the onions to a plate, raise the heat and fry the meat until brown.
3. Return the onions to the lamb, mix well and moisten with the white wine and stock. Continue cooking on a moderate heat, covered, for about 30 minutes. When the lamb is cooked through, turn off the heat, leaving the pan covered.
4. Peel the potatoes and cut them into thin wedges; peel and trim the artichokes and cut them into slices after coating them with lemon juice. Slowly heat the lamb and add the potatoes and artichokes as soon as the cooking juices are hot. Cook for a further 30 minutes or until the vegetables are tender. Serve sprinkled with chopped parsley.

Abbacchio aglio e aceto

Lamb with Garlic and Vinegar

00:30　　　　　　01:30

American	Ingredients	Metric/Imperial
2 lb	Lamb (neck, shoulder, breast)	1 kg / 2 lb
¼ cup	Vegetable oil	50 ml / 2 fl oz
6	Garlic cloves	6
6	Sprigs of rosemary	6
	Salt and pepper	
2	Boned anchovies	2
½ cup	Vinegar	125 ml / 4 fl oz

1. Preheat the oven to 350°F / 180°C / Gas Mark 4.
2. Wash and thoroughly dry the meat, cut in pieces, then put in an ovenproof dish to brown with oil, 2 crushed cloves of garlic and rosemary in the oven for 15 minutes, turning from time to time. Season with pepper and a very little salt.
3. Crush the anchovies in a mortar or blender with 4 cloves of garlic, dilute the pulp with red or white vinegar, according to taste, to obtain a generous quantity of sauce.
4. When the lamb is well browned on all sides, pour over the sauce with 1 cup [225 ml / 8 fl oz] water and continue cooking on a medium heat on the stove or in the oven, as you wish.
5. Remove the meat from the pan to a heated serving dish. Dilute the sauce with a little water if it has reduced too much, pour into a sauceboat and serve separately with the lamb.

Agnello con le melanzane

Lamb Stew with Eggplant

00:30　　　　　　02:00
Serves 6

American	Ingredients	Metric/Imperial
3½ lb	Lamb, shoulder or breast	1.6 kg / 3½ lb
1 cup	Vegetable oil	225 ml / 8 fl oz
¼ lb	Chopped bacon	100 g / 4 oz
2	Garlic cloves	2
5	Eggplant (aubergines)	5
	Salt and pepper	
1 cup	Light red wine	225 ml / 8 fl oz
2 tbsp	Chopped parsley	1½ tbsp

1. Trim and cut the lamb into pieces.
2. Heat oil in a frying pan, add chopped bacon, crushed garlic, cook for 2 minutes, then put in the lamb and cook until brown on a medium heat.
3. Slice the eggplant (aubergines) lengthwise to obtain slices which are not too thin, salt and put the slices between two plates at an angle to drain. Place oil in another pan over a high heat and fry the slices until golden. Drain on kitchen towels.
4. Lower the heat under the pan with the lamb and pour in the wine and the same amount of water a little at a time, turning the meat to stop it sticking.
5. Drain any excess grease from the eggplant and, when the lamb is cooked, mix it with the fried eggplant slices, add plenty of chopped parsley and switch off the heat. Leave covered for a further 10 minutes, then serve, giving the dish a final stir.

Maialetto di Paolo
Cold Loin of Pork with Tuna Sauce

00:20   01:00

American	Ingredients	Metric/Imperial
2 lb	Loin of pork without bones or fat	1 kg / 2 lb
9 oz	Tuna in oil	250 g / 9 oz
1	Onion	1
4	Anchovies	4
	Salt and pepper	
2 cups	White wine	450 ml / ¾ pint
2 tsp	Cognac	2 tsp
¼ cup	Vegetable oil	50 ml / 2 fl oz
2	Lemons	2

1. Bone the loin of pork or buy one boned and discard all the fat. (The bones may be used next day for stock and pork fat is always useful for frying.)
2. Put the meat into a large saucepan with the chopped tuna, the thinly sliced onion, the washed, boned and broken up anchovies, salt, pepper, white wine and cognac. Cover and cook over moderate heat. Test the pork by inserting a toothpick, when it enters easily, the meat is cooked.
3. Transfer the pork, sliced, to a large serving dish and tip the remaining contents of the saucepan into a large bowl, mix oil and lemon juice and pour over the meat. Decorate with chopped gherkins.

Cook's tip: This dish must be prepared at least 12 hours in advance to allow the pork to absorb the flavor of the sauce. It will keep well in the refrigerator for several days.

Maiale alla bresciana
Pot-Roast of Pork with Artichoke Hearts

00:30   01:30

American	Ingredients	Metric/Imperial
1	Onion	1
1	Celery stalk	1
1	Carrot	1
¼ cup	Oil	50 ml / 2 fl oz
¼ cup	Butter	50 g / 2 oz
8	Artichoke hearts	8
¼ tsp	Chopped rosemary	¼ tsp
3 lb	Loin of pork, boned and rolled	1.4 kg / 3 lb
1 cup	Red wine	225 ml / 8 fl oz
	Salt and pepper	
14 oz	Small potatoes	400 g / 14 oz
1	Stock cube	1
Sauce (optional)		
2 tbsp	Mustard	1½ tbsp
1	Egg yolk	1
4	Anchovy fillets	4
1 cup	Coffee (single) cream	225 ml / 8 fl oz

1. Chop the onion, celery and carrot and fry lightly in oil and butter. Add the artichoke hearts and a little rosemary. Remove and set the vegetables aside on a plate, put the meat into the pan; brown quickly over a high heat, turning constantly.
2. Pour some red wine over the meat and allow to evaporate, season with salt and pepper. Now tip the vegetables into the pan with the meat and add the peeled potatoes; reduce the heat and add some stock made with the stock cube dissolved in boiling water.
3. Cook for about 1 hour, adding a small quantity of wine from time to time.
4. When the meat is cooked, cut it into thick slices and place on a heated serving dish. Arrange the potatoes around it and sieve or blend the vegetables and remaining liquid which can either be served separately or poured over the meat.
5. Serve with mustard or, if preferred, with a sauce made from mustard, egg yolk, a few chopped anchovy fillets and single cream beaten together.

Carré della Maremma
Loin of Pork 'Maremma'

00:30   01:30

American	Ingredients	Metric/Imperial
2 lb	Loin of pork, boned	1 kg / 2 lb
¼ lb	Fat bacon	100 g / 4 oz
	Salt and pepper	
3 or 4	Cloves	3 or 4
¼ cup	Vegetable oil	50 ml / 2 fl oz
6	Sage leaves	6
3	Sprigs of rosemary	3
½	Onion	½
1	Celery stalk	1
1 tbsp	Chopped parsley	1 tbsp
¼ cup	Butter	50 g / 2 oz
½ cup	Red wine	125 ml / 4 fl oz
1	Stock cube	1
1	Garlic clove	1
¼ lb	Canadian (lean) bacon	100 g / 4 oz
1 lb	Plum tomatoes	500 g / 1 lb
2 lb	Swiss chard	1 kg / 2 lb

1. Have the butcher bone the pork for you, stick in pieces of fat bacon dipped in salt and pepper and a few cloves. Paint with oil, coat with coarse salt, sage and rosemary. Tie it tightly with white thread.
2. Chop the onion with a little celery and parsley. Heat oil and butter, cook vegetables gently on a low heat in a large casserole, adding the meat. Moisten with dry full-bodied red wine. Allow the wine to evaporate, add some stock made from the cube and continue cooking, adding more stock from time to time.
3. Fry crushed cloves of garlic in a small pan with a little oil, add a little finely chopped bacon and some chopped, peeled, tomatoes with the seeds removed; pour in a little hot water and cook very gently until a reduced sauce has formed.
4. Separately boil some Swiss chard, using only the white part. When cooked, drain and mix the chard with the tomato sauce, seasoning well.
5. Cut the meat into slices and arrange it on a heated dish covered with the cooking sauce and with the chard around it.

Arista alla francese
Loin of Pork

00:20 **01:20**

American	Ingredients	Metric/Imperial
2 tbsp	Butter	25 g / 1 oz
¼ cup	Vegetable oil	50 ml / 2 fl oz
1½ lb	Loin of pork (chine)	700 g / 1½ lb
1	Onion	1
2	Potatoes	2
6	Sage leaves	6
2	Sprigs of rosemary	2
2	Garlic cloves	2
3	Juniper berries	3
¼ tsp	Chopped thyme	¼ tsp
2 cups	Milk	450 ml / ¾ pint
1	Stock cube	1
1	Zest of lemon	1
1 tbsp	Mustard	1 tbsp
1	Egg yolk	1
1 tbsp	Worcester sauce	1 tbsp
	Salt and pepper	

1. Heat butter and oil in a large pan, add the pork ribs with the onion cut into four, potatoes cut into wedges, sage, rosemary, crushed cloves of garlic, juniper berries and a pinch of thyme. Brown slowly on all sides.
2. Add the milk and the stock cube dissolved in a little boiling water and cook slowly for 1 hour. Strain the cooking juices. Remove the meat and keep warm.
3. Return to the heat adding the lemon zest, and reduce. Slice the meat and place it on a heated ovenproof dish.
4. Add mustard, the egg yolk and Worcester sauce to the cooking juices and mix well; adjust the seasoning and pour the sauce over the meat.

Cosciotto di maiale alla grappa
Leg of Pork with Grappa

00:25 **02:00**

American	Ingredients	Metric/Imperial
1	Carrot	1
1	Celery stalk	1
1	Bay leaf	1
4	Sprigs of parsley	4
3	Garlic cloves	3
¼ cup	Vegetable oil	50 ml / 2 fl oz
2 tbsp	Butter	25 g / 1 oz
10 oz	Leeks	275 g / 10 oz
2 lb	Loin of pork (chine)	1 kg / 2 lb
½ cup	Vinegar	125 ml / 4 fl oz
½ cup	Dry white wine	125 ml / 4 fl oz
1	Stock cube	1
	Pepper	
¼ cup	Grappa	50 ml / 2 fl oz

1. Prepare a bouquet garni with carrot, celery, bay leaf and parsley tied together. Put the whole cloves of garlic in a large saucepan and fry them in the oil and the butter; add the vegetables which you have tied together, the leeks cut into rings and finally the meat. Brown and moisten with a little vinegar and then the dry white wine.
2. When the vegetables have softened and the wine has evaporated, add stock made with a cube and 2½ cups [600 ml / 1 pint] water and plenty of pepper.
3. Cover the pan and cook on a very low heat for about 2 hours, adding a little hot water from time to time whenever the sauce becomes too dry.
4. When the meat is quite tender, remove it from the heat and place it on one side. Strain the sauce and return it to the pan together with the meat. On a medium heat add the grappa; cook for another 10 minutes.
5. When the pork is cooked, cut it into thick slices and serve it with the sauce and an accompaniment of steamed potatoes or white rice.

Arrosto di maiale all'arancia
Roast Pork with Orange

00:35 Serves 6 **02:10**

American	Ingredients	Metric/Imperial
1	Onion	1
1	Garlic clove	1
½ cup	Vegetable oil	125 ml / 4 fl oz
1 tsp	Lard	1 tsp
1	Sweet red pepper	1
4-6	Oranges	4-6
	Salt	
1 tsp	Sugar	1 tsp
4 lb	Boned leg of pork	2 kg / 4 lb
½ tsp	Powdered thyme	½ tsp
½ tsp	Chopped rosemary	½ tsp
½ tsp	Chopped mint	½ tsp
¼ tsp	Cayenne pepper	¼ tsp
1⅓ cups	Rice	250 g / 9 oz
⅓ cup	Olives	50 g / 2 oz
3 tbsp	Rum	2 tbsp

1. Preheat the oven to 350°F / 180°C / Gas Mark 4. Prepare the sauce, which will be used to moisten the roast.
2. Finely chop the onion and garlic and put in half the heated oil and the lard to brown for 4 minutes. Add the deseeded, chopped red sweet pepper, the grated peel of 2 oranges and the juice of 4 ripe oranges. Season with a little salt and sugar.
3. Rub the pork with a mixture of salt, remaining oil, powdered thyme, chopped fresh rosemary, chopped mint and a little cayenne pepper. Place the spiced meat on an oiled rack in a preheated oven.
4. During cooking brush the meat frequently with the sauce. If it becomes too thick add a little more orange juice. Cook for about 2 hours.
5. Cook rice until 'al dente', drain and keep warm in the oven.
6. When the roast is well cooked, remove from the oven and leave for 10 minutes, then cut into slices about ¼ in / 5 mm in thickness and arrange them on a serving dish. Garnish with slices of 2 oranges and olives and cover with the sauce, diluted with a little orange juice and a little rum. Serve surrounded by boiled rice.

Cassoeula o posciandra o bottaggio

Pork and Sausage Casserole

	00:00		03:00

American	Ingredients	Metric/Imperial
1	Onion	1
1	Large slice of fat bacon	1
2 tbsp	Vegetable oil	25 ml / 1 fl oz
2 tbsp	Butter	25 g / 1 oz
1	Carrot	1
1	Celery stalk	1
1 lb	Pork ribs	500 g / 1 lb
1	Pig's head (snout and ear)	1
7 oz	Pork rind	200 g / 7 oz
1 tbsp	Tomato purée	1 tbsp
1	Stock cube	1
	Salt and pepper	
2	Savoy cabbages	2
7 oz	Thin budello sausage	200 g / 7 oz
½ tsp	Spices (optional)	½ tsp

1. Chop the onion finely and brown it with chopped fat bacon or with oil and butter.
2. When the ingredients have softened, add the carrot and celery, also chopped very finely, and cook on a gentle heat, moistening with water if it is really necessary.
3. Boil separately the ribs, snout and rind until tender then cut into large pieces. Retain stock.
4. When the vegetables have softened, add the ribs, the snout and the rind, add the tomato purée diluted with a little warm water, pour in 2½ cups [1 pint / 600 ml] of stock made with the cube and cook through on a low flame, covered.
5. Preheat the oven to 325°F / 160°C / Gas Mark 3.
6. Strip the leaves from the cabbages, eliminating the tougher parts, rinse the leaves under running water, shred coarsely and mix with the meat, a little at a time. Season with salt and pepper and spices.
7. Cut the sausage into pieces, put it into a baking pan adding a drop of water and place it in the oven, covered and at a low heat. When the fat has melted, add the sausage to the casserole, cook for 1 hour in the oven. Serve piping hot with crusty bread.

Lonza profumata

Pork in Brandy Sauce

	00:20		00:15

American	Ingredients	Metric/Imperial
1¾ lb	Loin of pork	800 g / 1¾ lb
8	Round slices of bacon	8
20	Sage leaves	20
½ tsp	Rosemary leaves, chopped	½ tsp
¼ cup	Butter	50 g / 2 oz
3 tbsp	Oil	2 tbsp
¼ cup	Brandy	50 ml / 2 fl oz
½	Stock cube	½

1. Cut the pork in thin slices, (about 2 per head) removing all excess fat. Lay a slice of bacon and two sage leaves on each piece of meat, roll up and secure with a toothpick.
2. Put the butter and oil into a wide pan and add remaining sage and the rosemary; as soon as the fat has heated, add the meat and pour on the brandy. Allow to cook for 10 minutes, moistening from time to time with boiling water in which a stock cube has been dissolved.
3. Strain the cooking juices into a sauceboat and serve with the meat and accompany with purée potatoes.

Rognoni trifolati alla panna

Kidneys in Cream Sauce

	00:20		00:35
	Soaking time 02:00		

American	Ingredients	Metric/Imperial
3	Pigs' kidneys	3
¼ cup	Vinegar	50 ml / 2 fl oz
½ cup	Butter	100 g / 4 oz
1	Onion	1
	Salt and pepper	
¾ lb	Mushrooms	350 g / 12 oz
1	Bunch of parsley	1
⅔ cup	Single (coffee) cream	150 ml / ¼ pint

1. Skin and wash the kidneys, cut in half lengthwise and discard the fat. Place in a bowl with plenty of water and vinegar and leave to soak for 2 hours. Rinse well under the tap, dry and cut into fairly small pieces.
2. Melt the butter in a saucepan and fry the finely chopped onion for 4 minutes, add the kidneys and cook for 10 minutes, uncovered, over a medium heat. Season with salt and freshly ground black pepper.
3. Add the mushrooms, washed and sliced, continue cooking for a further 15 minutes and remove the pan from the heat. Chop the parsley, sprinkle over and then add the cream.
4. Put the kidneys on a low heat, do not allow to boil but reheat thoroughly. Serve very hot.

Maiale alla ciociara

Pork Pasties

A speciality of the Frosinone region, this dish is filling and very tasty.

	00:30		00:40

American	Ingredients	Metric/Imperial
3 tbsp	Oil	2 tbsp
¾ lb	Ground (minced) pork	350 g / 12 oz
2	Eggs	2
2	Italian sausages	2
1 cup	Grated parmesan cheese	100 g / 4 oz
2	Potatoes, boiled and mashed	2
¼ tsp	Nutmeg	¼ tsp
4	Sage leaves	4
½ lb	Short crust pastry	225 g / 8 oz
½ cup	Butter	100 g / 4 oz

Kidneys in cream sauce

1. Preheat the oven to 400°F / 200°C / Gas Mark 6.

2. Heat the oil in a pan and cook the pork for 8 minutes, drain on to a plate and allow to cool.

3. Put the ground (minced) pork, eggs, sausages, (skinned and chopped), parmesan and potatoes into a bowl and mix thoroughly. Add a little grated nutmeg and a few chopped sage leaves.

4. Divide the pastry into 4 portions. Roll each into a round. Divide the pork mixture into 4 and heap onto each pastry round. Damp and seal the edges.

5. Grease a baking tray, lay the pasties on the tray and bake in a hot oven for 15 minutes. Reduce the oven temperature to 325°F / 170°C / Gas Mark 3 and cook for a further 15 minutes. These pasties need only to be served with a green salad.

Meat

The most tender cuts of meat come from those sections of the animal where the least movement occurs, the hindquarters, and these are usually cooked by dry heat methods, such as roasting, broiling (grilling), pan roasting, sautéing and shallow frying. The parts of the animal which have the most muscular work to do in moving around are the forequarters. Tenderize these cuts with moist heat methods such as stewing, braising and poaching or deep frying.

Beef should be of a bright red color perhaps with a slight brownish tinge. Dark red meat may have been exposed to the air for some time but it could also be because it comes from an older animal. Look for firm flesh with a slight marbling of fat and this should be cream to dark cream depending on the feeding methods.

Veal should have pale pink flesh and firm, white fat.

Lamb should have reddish pink flesh with white to cream fat.

Pork will have pale pink flesh and white fat.

Avoid any flabby cuts of meat tinged with gray.

Vegetables

Spinach and mushroom salad

Spinach and Mushroom Salad

Insalata di spinaci e funghi

▱ 00:15   00:00 🍲

American	Ingredients	Metric/Imperial
14 oz	Fresh spinach	400 g / 14 oz
1-1½ cups	Mushrooms	150 g / 5 oz
1	Red onion	1
2½ oz	Strong gorgonzola cheese	65 g / 2½ oz
1	Garlic clove	1
1	Sprig of thyme	1
½ tsp	Salt	½ tsp
½ cup	Olive oil	125 ml / 4 fl oz
3 tbsp	White vinegar	2 tbsp
	Freshly ground white pepper	

1. Trim the spinach, wash in several changes of water and dry. Tear into pieces.
2. Wash the mushrooms, dry them and cut them into small slices.
3. Cut the onion into rings, crumble the gorgonzola and crush the garlic.
4. In a salad bowl put the spinach, the mushrooms, the onion and gorgonzola.
5. In a small glass jar with a screw-top lid put the garlic, the thyme, the salt, the oil and vinegar. Shake it vigorously and then pour the dressing over the salad. Mix gently to save crumpling the spinach leaves. Grind some pepper over and serve at once.

Tempting Rice Salad

Insalata di riso golosa

▱ 00:30   00:15 🍲

American	Ingredients	Metric/Imperial
2	Heads of lettuce	2
1 cup	Rice	200 g / 7 oz
4	Eggs	4
Scant ¼ cup	Vegetable oil	3 tbsp
2 tbsp	Vinegar	1½ tbsp
	Salt and pepper	
4	Sardines in oil	4

1. Carefully clean the lettuce removing the toughest leaves and cut the hearts in half. Cut most of the leaves into thin strips keeping a few large ones intact for garnishing the dish when it is served.
2. Boil the rice till 'al dente' and drain and rinse in cold water, drain again.
3. Hard-cook (boil) 4 eggs, cool in cold water and remove the shells.
4. Put the rice, strips of lettuce and the hearts in a salad bowl, mix and season with oil, vinegar, salt and pepper. Arrange the rice in the shape of a dome on a serving dish. Place the sardines on the rice.
5. Cut the eggs in half lengthways and place them around the rice. Arrange the large lettuce leaves between one piece of egg and the next.

Mushrooms with Tomato

Funghi con pomodoro

▱ 00:20   00:30 🍲

American	Ingredients	Metric/Imperial
1¾ lb	Mushrooms	800 g / 1¾ lb
1	Garlic clove	1
1	Onion	1
5 tbsp	Vegetable oil	4 tbsp
¼ cup	Dry white wine	50 ml / 2 fl oz
1 lb	Peeled tomatoes	450 g / 1 lb
	Salt and pepper	
1 tbsp	Chopped parsley	1 tbsp

1. Remove the stalks from the mushrooms (use in a sauce), wipe or wash the caps with a damp cloth and cut them into fairly thick slices.
2. Chop the garlic and the onion and brown them in a pan with the oil over a moderate heat. Add the mushrooms and when the pan juice has evaporated pour in the white wine and, over a moderate heat, leave it to evaporate.
3. Add the tomatoes, chopped up or passed through a vegetable-mill, the salt and pepper, and continue cooking for about 20 minutes. Sprinkle the mushrooms with the chopped parsley before serving cold.

Mixed Vegetable and Cheese Salad

Arlecchinata

▱ 01:00   00:00 🍲

American	Ingredients	Metric/Imperial
1	Head of lettuce	1
2	Cucumbers	2
	Salt	
1	Bunch of radishes	1
1	Small cauliflower	1
5 oz	Gouda cheese	150 g / 5 oz
1	Lemon	1
Scant ¼ cup	Olive oil	3 tbsp
½ tsp	French mustard	½ tsp
1 tbsp	Anchovy paste	1 tbsp

1. Prepare all the vegetables. Remove the oldest leaves from the lettuce, keeping the inner part, take off the leaves one by one and wash well.
2. Scrape the cucumbers well without removing their skin, wash and slice them (not too thick and not too thin), sprinkle with fine salt and drain off the juice by squeezing them between 2 tilting plates.
3. Wash the radishes well, remove the leaves and the bottom part, cut into slices. Divide the cauliflower into heads and soak in cold water. After 30 minutes drain and cut into florets.
4. Cut the cheese into small cubes. Prepare the seasoning in a bowl by putting in lemon juice, olive oil, mustard and a little anchovy paste. Blend well, using a fork.
5. On a serving dish first arrange the lettuce leaves, well dried, the cauliflower, then 1 slice of cucumber, well dried, and 1 of radish, so that the colors alternate. Put the cubes of cheese in the middle. Serve the seasoning separately.

Insalata Belzebù

Beelzebub's Salad

00:20   00:00

American	Ingredients	Metric/Imperial
1	Head of lettuce	1
3 cups	Bean sprouts	175 g / 6 oz
5 oz	Emmental cheese	150 g / 5 oz
4	Anchovies in oil	4
5 oz	Cooked ham	150 g / 5 oz
1 tbsp	Capers	1 tbsp
1	Sweet yellow pepper	1
1	Sweet red pepper	1
1	Sweet green pepper	1
10	Small mushrooms	10
1	Hard-cooked (boiled) egg	1
⅔ cup	Olive oil	150 ml / ¼ pint
	Salt and pepper	
¼ tsp	Paprika	¼ tsp
3 tbsp	Soy sauce	2 tbsp

1. Clean the lettuce and the bean sprouts by rinsing in cold water, drain, dry with absorbent kitchen towels and put in a salad bowl.
2. Add small pieces of emmental cheese, the anchovies in oil, the cooked ham cut into thin strips, capers, the sweet deseeded yellow, red and green peppers, cut into strips, a few sliced mushrooms and the sliced hard-cooked egg.
3. Season with a mixture of olive oil, a pinch of salt, pepper, paprika and soy sauce. Toss the ingredients well in the dressing and serve.

Lattughe e pomodori in salsa profumata

Lettuce and Tomatoes in Flavored Sauce

00:45   00:12
Chilling time 01:00

American	Ingredients	Metric/Imperial
2	Small heads of lettuce	2
4	Tomatoes	4
1 cup	Mayonnaise (see page 175)	225 ml / 8 fl oz
5 oz	Tuna fish in oil	150 g / 5 oz
1 oz	Small pickled onions	25 g / 1 oz
2	Hard-cooked (boiled) eggs	2
2	Basil leaves	2
8	Sprigs of parsley	8
7	Mint leaves	7
3 tbsp	Vegetable oil	2 tbsp
12	Black olives	12

1. Thoroughly clean the lettuce detaching the leaves one by one, pat dry.
2. Wash and dry the tomatoes, then slice and let them drain.
3. Prepare the sauce by putting in the blender the mayonnaise, then add the tuna fish crumbled, the small onions sliced, the hard-cooked eggs in little pieces, the basil, half the parsley, the mint and the oil. Switch on the blender and mix until you obtain a smooth and creamy sauce.
4. Arrange the lettuce leaves radiating from the centre on a serving dish, insert the slices of tomato between the leaves and pour the sauce on top.
5. Decorate with black olives and parsley. Keep in refrigerator for 1 hour before serving.

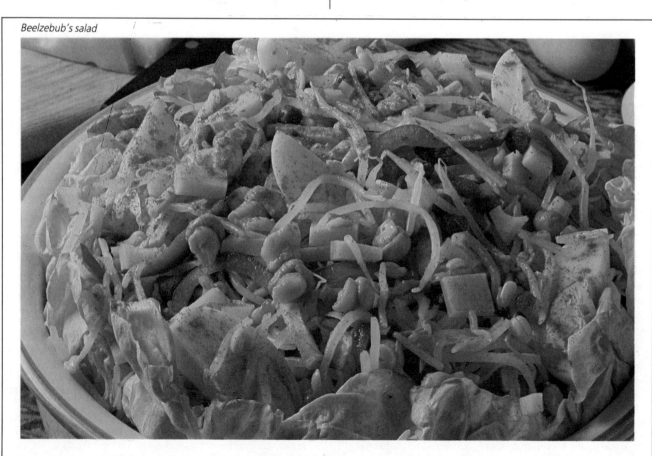

Beelzebub's salad

Orange salad

Orange Salad

Insalata di arance

⏱ 00:15   00:00 🍲

American	Ingredients	Metric/Imperial
4	Oranges	4
1	Garlic clove	1
	Salt	
1 tbsp	Olive oil	1 tbsp
1	Small onion (optional)	1

1. Using a very sharp small knife, remove the peel from the oranges and the white pith. Slice the orange as thinly as possible across the width.
2. Rub the sides of a glass salad bowl with a cut clove of garlic. Arrange the sliced oranges in the bowl. Season with salt, plenty of freshly-ground pepper, sprinkle with olive oil. Refrigerate for 30 minutes before serving.
3. Add the peeled onion, thinly sliced into rings, to the top of the orange if desired.

Zucchini [Courgette] Salad

Insalata di zucchine

⏱ 00:30   00:00 🍲

American	Ingredients	Metric/Imperial
4	Zucchini (courgettes)	4
½ cup	Vegetable oil	4 fl oz / 125 ml
	Salt and pepper	
1	Lemon	1
1 cup	Walnut kernels	100 g / 4 oz
½ cup	Pine kernels	50 g / 2 oz
1	Basil leaf	1

1. Thoroughly wash the zucchini, which must be fresh, then slice them very finely. Put them in a large bowl and season with plenty of oil, salt, pepper and the juice of a lemon. Leave to stand for 1 hour, turning from time to time.
2. Remove brown skin from walnut kernels. Chop walnuts and pine kernels carefully with a half-moon cutter. Chop basil and mix with nuts into zucchini.

Cruda e cotta
Raw and Cooked Salad

00:40   00:20

American	Ingredients	Metric/Imperial
¾ lb	Green beans	350 g / 12 oz
	Salt and pepper	
2	Potatoes	2
2	Small onions	2
2	Zucchini (courgettes)	2
2	Tomatoes	2
1	Cucumber	1
2	Egg yolks	2
⅔ cup	Vegetable oil	150 ml / ¼ pint
2 tsp	Light mustard	2 tsp
1 tbsp	Wine vinegar	1 tbsp

1. Remove the strings from the green beans and then cut into 2 in / 5 cm pieces and cook in a little salted boiling water for 7 minutes.
2. Boil the potatoes until tender but firm. Add the onions for the last 10 minutes. Drain and dice.
3. Blanch the washed zucchini in some boiling salted water for 4 minutes, drain. Cut into slices.
4. Place the beans, diced potatoes, sliced onion and zucchini in a bowl, mix well.
5. Slice the tomatoes and finely slice a cucumber. Mix the raw vegetables with the cooked ones.
6. In a small bowl, mix the egg yolks with the oil, added gradually, mix in the mustard, salt and pepper. Flavor with wine vinegar or lemon juice.
7. Dress the salad with this mixture and refrigerate for a while so that it can be served slightly chilled.

Carote alla piacentina
Piacenza-Style Carrots

00:20   00:10
Standing time 01:00

American	Ingredients	Metric/Imperial
¾ lb	New carrots	350 g / 12 oz
2	Lemons	2
	Salt and pepper	
2	Eggs	2
2 tsp	Chopped basil	2 tsp
1	Garlic clove	1
3 tbsp	Vegetable oil	2 tbsp

1. Scrape the carrots well and slice them very finely, then season at once with the juice of 2 lemons and some salt. Leave them to soak for 1 hour.
2. Hard-cook (boil) 2 eggs, cool under running cold water, shell and cut them into slices.
3. Chop the basil very finely and mix with a crushed garlic clove, add to this the oil, salt and pepper.
4. Season the carrots with the herb and oil dressing. Arrange the carrots in a dish garnished with the slices of egg and serve.

Cook's tip: this can be served as a first-course.

Insalata al prosciutto
Ham Salad

00:25   00:00

American	Ingredients	Metric/Imperial
¾ lb	Thick slice of cooked ham	350 g / 12 oz
4	Slices of pineapple, fresh or canned	4
1	Head of lettuce	1
3 tbsp	Brandy	2 tbsp
½ cup	Vegetable oil	125 ml / 4 fl oz
1 tbsp	Mustard	1 tbsp
2	Lemons	2
	Salt and pepper	
2	Bananas	2

1. Remove all of the fat from the ham and cut the meat into small dice.
2. If you use fresh fruit, peel and divide up the pineapple into cubes. Drain it well if using canned fruit and cube if necessary.
3. Clean the lettuce discarding any damaged leaves and wash under running water. Shake the lettuce in a colander and line the salad bowl with it.
4. Mix the brandy in a small bowl with the oil, mustard, half the lemon juice, salt and pepper. Beat slightly with a fork to blend the seasoning.
5. Pour the dressing over the cubes of ham and pineapple, mix well, arrange them on the lettuce leaves.
6. Cut the bananas into rings, cover with remaining lemon juice and arrange round the salad.

Asparagi imperiali
Imperial Asparagus

00:30   00:15

American	Ingredients	Metric/Imperial
2	Bundles of large asparagus	2
	Salt	
1	Lemon wedge	1
1	Truffle	1
4	Anchovies in brine, boned	4
1 ¼ cups	Mayonnaise	300 ml / ½ pint
2 tbsp	Tomato purée	1 ½ tbsp

1. Clean the asparagus well, scraping them one by one with a knife and cutting away the woodiest part. Cook in salted water with a lemon wedge, using the proper saucepan for asparagus, where they will be steamed without being reduced to a pulp. When cooked, take the asparagus out carefully and leave on one side to cool.
2. Arrange on an oval dish and sprinkle with thin slices of truffle. To do this properly and to obtain thin slices, use a truffle-slicer — a utensil that you will find in some kitchen shops, otherwise use a small sharp knife.
3. Decorate the dish with anchovy fillets, having trimmed and boned them.
4. Finally, cover the salad with well-seasoned mayonnaise mixed with tomato purée.

Ham salad

Asparagi di Bassano in salsa

Bassano Asparagus in Sauce

▱▷ 00:30   00:20 to 00:30 🥘

American	Ingredients	Metric/Imperial
1½ lb	Asparagus	700 g / 1½ lb
3	Eggs	3
1½	Lemons	1½
½ cup	Olive oil	125 ml / 4 fl oz
	Salt and pepper	
1 tbsp	Chopped parsley	1 tbsp

1. Prepare asparagus and boil in salted water until tender.
2. Hard-cook the eggs, cool under running cold water, shell and chop both yolks and whites finely.
3. Pour the oil into a bowl, add the lemon juice and beat vigorously; season with salt and pepper and mix in parsley.
4. Arrange the asparagus on a heated oval serving dish with the tips turned inwards, then pour over the oil and lemon sauce. Wait for it to be partly absorbed, then sprinkle with the chopped egg.

Asparagi alla legnanese

Legnano-Style Asparagus

▱▷ 00:20   00:15 🥘

American	Ingredients	Metric/Imperial
1½ lb	Asparagus	700 g / 1½ lb
	Salt	
3	Eggs	3
	Ground black pepper	
½ cup	Grated parmesan cheese	50 g / 2 oz
½ cup	Butter	100 g / 4 oz

1. Prepare the asparagus, tie into bundles and cook in boiling salted water.
2. Hard-cook the eggs, cool under running cold water and shell them. Sieve the yolks and chop the whites finely.
3. Heat a serving dish and when the asparagus are properly cooked, arrange them on the dish. Sprinkle with a little freshly ground black pepper and parmesan. Pour on the melted butter and on top arrange the egg yolks and whites in alternate rows. Serve immediately.

Bassano asparagus in sauce

Torta di asparagi
Asparagus Flan

	00:40		00:50

American	Ingredients	Metric/Imperial
1¼ cups	Béchamel sauce	300 ml / ½ pint
1 lb	Asparagus	450 g / 1 lb
½ lb	Shortcrust pastry	225 g / 8 oz
	Salt and pepper	
½ cup	Grated parmesan cheese	50 g / 2 oz

1. Make the béchamel sauce and cover with film to prevent a skin forming.
2. Discard the tough part of the asparagus and cook in boiling salted water until tender.
3. Preheat the oven to 400°F / 200°C / Gas Mark 6.
4. Roll out the pastry on a floured board and line an 8 in / 20 cm flan ring. Trim the top and prick the bottom with a fork. Rest in the refrigerator for 10 minutes. Prepare a piece of wax (greaseproof) paper to fit the flan and cover with baking beans.
5. Cook the flan case for 15 minutes, remove the baking beans and cook for a further 5 minutes.
6. Reduce oven heat to 325°F / 170°C / Gas Mark 3.
7. Remove from the oven, allow to cool slightly, add the chopped asparagus, season, and cover with the béchamel sauce. Sprinkle with cheese and cook in the oven for 20 minutes. Serve hot.

Carciofi di Tivoli
Tivoli Artichokes

	00:25		00:45

American	Ingredients	Metric/Imperial
8	Large artichokes	8
1	Lemon	1
½ lb	Mushrooms	225 g / 8 oz
10	Slices of lean bacon	10
½ cup	Vegetable oil	125 ml / 4 fl oz
3 tbsp	Chopped parsley	2 tbsp
4	Garlic cloves	4
	Salt and pepper	
¼ cup	Dry white wine	50 ml / 2 fl oz
½ cup	Stock	125 ml / 4 fl oz
	Sprigs of parsley	

1. Remove the prickles and the toughest leaves of the artichokes, wash very well both inside and out and spread out the leaves a little. Put in a pan with boiling water and lemon juice and parboil for 10-20 minutes depending on size.
2. Transfer them first into cold water, then upside down onto a plate to drain and dry.
3. Clean and wash the mushrooms. Cut into slices.
4. Chop up 2 slices of bacon, put in a frying pan with a little oil, bring to a medium heat and cook for 10 minutes with the mushrooms, parsley, crushed garlic, salt and pepper.
5. Carefully remove the choke from each artichoke and fill with the mushroom mixture. Cover with one of the remaining slices of bacon.

6. Preheat the oven to 425°F / 220°C / Gas Mark 7.
7. Tie up the artichokes with thick white thread and paint with oil, put them in an oiled ovenproof dish. Pour over the dry white wine and brown the artichokes in a hot oven for 10 minutes.
8. Lower the heat and sprinkle with the stock. Cook for a further 15 minutes then serve garnished with sprigs of parsley.

Sformato alla ligure
Ligurian Pudding

	00:30		00:40

American	Ingredients	Metric/Imperial
4	Artichoke hearts	4
2 cups	Béchamel sauce	450 ml / ¾ pint
2	Hard-cooked (boiled) eggs	2
½ lb	Shortcrust pastry	225 g / 8 oz
¼ cup	Grated parmesan cheese	25 g / 1 oz

1. Preheat the oven to 400°F / 200°C / Gas Mark 6.
2. Cook the artichokes, take off the leaves and remove chokes.
3. Make the béchamel sauce and season well.
4. Slice the artichoke hearts and eggs.
5. Line an 8 in / 20 cm flan dish with two-thirds of the pastry.
6. Arrange the artichokes and hard-cooked eggs in the dish.
7. Pour the béchamel sauce over the artichokes and eggs. Sprinkle with grated parmesan.
8. Roll the remaining pastry to fit the top, damp the edges with cold water and seal. Make 3 slits on the top. Put in the oven for 25 minutes. Serve hot.

Cestini con fondi di carciofo
Baskets of Artichoke Bottoms

	00:25		00:30

American	Ingredients	Metric/Imperial
4	Deep soft rolls	4
¼ cup	Butter	50 g / 2 oz
4	Artichoke hearts (fresh or frozen)	4
1¼ cups	Béchamel sauce	300 ml / ½ pint
2	Slices of emmental cheese	2
1	Egg	1
	Salt and pepper	
	Nutmeg	

1. Cut the tops of the rolls, hollow them out and brush the insides with melted butter.
2. Boil the artichoke hearts, then lightly fry in a frying pan with a little butter. Place an artichoke bottom in each roll.
3. Preheat the oven to 400°F / 200°C / Gas Mark 6.
4. Make some béchamel sauce and blend in the chopped emmental, egg yolk, salt, pepper and nutmeg. Finally, fold in the egg white, stiffly whipped and divide this mixture between the rolls.
5. Brush the outsides with melted butter and cook in a hot oven for about 15 minutes

Artichokes with garlic

Melanzane ripiene di riso
Eggplant (Aubergines) Stuffed with Rice

	00:25		00:20

American	Ingredients	Metric/Imperial
1 cup	Long grain rice	200 g / 7 oz
1	Stock cube	1
4	Eggplant (aubergines)	4
¼ lb	Raw ham	100 g / 4 oz
½ cup	Vegetable oil	125 ml / 4 fl oz
¼ lb	Fontina cheese	100 g / 4 oz

1. Cook the rice until 'al dente' in 2½ cups [600 ml / 1 pint] stock made from a cube.
2. Wash the eggplant, cut in half lengthways and blanch in salted boiling water for 5 minutes. Drain and place on an absorbent kitchen towel.
3. Preheat the oven to 400°F / 200°C / Gas Mark 6.
4. Scoop out the flesh, taking care not to damage the skin. Cut the ham into small pieces and combine with the chopped flesh of the eggplant. Add the rice to this mixture. Paint the eggplant halves with oil inside and out and fill the skins with mixture.
5. Cut the fontina into thin slices. Cover the eggplant with the cheese. Place in an ovenproof dish and put in the oven until the cheese has melted.

Cook's tip: this dish can be served either hot or cold.

Carciofi all'aglio
Artichokes with Garlic

	00:30		00:50

American	Ingredients	Metric/Imperial
8	Artichokes	8
1	Lemon	1
1	Garlic clove	1
⅔ cup	Vegetable oil	150 ml / ¼ pint
4	Anchovies in oil	4
⅓ cup	Black olives, pitted (stoned)	50 g / 2 oz
1 tsp	Capers	1 tsp
	Salt and pepper	
½ cup	Bread crumbs	50 g / 2 oz

1. Remove the toughest leaves from the artichokes, the prickles and the choke from inside. Cut into lengthwise pieces and cook in boiling water with a few drops of lemon. When the water comes back to the boil, cook for 10 minutes.
2. In another large pan, heat a clove of garlic in a little oil. Remove the garlic, add the drained anchovies, cut into small pieces, and stir until they have almost dissolved.
3. Add the drained artichokes and cook for 10 minutes.
4. Preheat the oven to 375°F / 190°C / Gas Mark 5.
5. Put the artichokes and anchovy sauce in an oiled ovenproof dish, add the olives, the chopped capers and sprinkle with salt and pepper and bread crumbs.
6. Pour over the oil in which the artichokes were cooked. Cook in the oven for about 20 minutes.

La parmigiana di melanzane
Eggplant (Aubergine) Pie

	02:00 Standing time 00:40		00:40

American	Ingredients	Metric/Imperial
4	Large round eggplant (aubergines)	4
2 lb	Tomatoes	1 kg / 2 lb
	Salt and pepper	
2 tsp	Basil	2 tsp
2	Eggs	2
¼ lb	Bologna sausage	100 g / 4 oz
½ lb	Mozzarella cheese	225 g / 8 oz
	Butter	
½ cup	Grated parmesan cheese	50 g / 2 oz

1. Preheat the oven to 350°F / 180°C / Gas Mark 4.
2. Wash and cut the eggplant in half lengthways. Season with salt and keep under a weight for 30 minutes in order to expel the bitter juices.
3. Rinse and dry well. Blanch in boiling water for 4 minutes.
4. Make the fresh tomato sauce by boiling the tomatoes for 1 minute. Remove the skins and mash in a bowl with seasoning and basil.
5. Hard-cook (boil) 2 eggs, cut the Bologna sausage into thin slices and slice the mozzarella cheese.
6. Butter an ovenproof dish and place a layer of eggplant, tomato sauce, slices of Bologna sausage, slices of hard-cooked egg, slices of mozzarella cheese. Continue making layers until all the ingredients are used, and, finally, finish with a sprinkling of grated parmesan. Put in the oven for 30 minutes. Serve hot.

Farnese-style asparagus

Asparagi alla farnesina
Farnese-Style Asparagus

	00:35		00:20

American	Ingredients	Metric/Imperial
2 lb	Asparagus	1 kg / 2 lb
½ lb	Fontina cheese	225 g / 8 oz
½ lb	Cooked ham	225 g / 8 oz
1 cup	Béchamel sauce	225 ml / 8 oz
½ cup	Butter	100 g / 4 oz
	Salt and pepper	
¼ tsp	Nutmeg	¼ tsp

1. Prepare the asparagus, then half-cook them in boiling water. Drain and allow to cool.
2. Wrap the green part of the asparagus with 1 slice of fontina and 1 of cooked ham, securing them with half a toothpick.
3. Preheat the oven to 400°F / 200°C / Gas Mark 6.
4. Lay all the asparagus in a buttered ovenproof dish, cover with béchamel sauce and dot with butter. Sprinkle with salt, pepper and nutmeg. Put in a hot oven for 20 minutes and serve immediately.

Pasticcio di asparagi
Asparagus Bake

	00:30		00:30

American	Ingredients	Metric/Imperial
2 lb	Asparagus	1 kg / 2 lb
	Salt and pepper	
2½ cups	Béchamel sauce	600 ml / 1 pint
¼ cup	Butter	50 g / 2 oz
½ cup	Grated parmesan cheese	50 g / 2 oz
¼ lb	Mozzarella cheese	100 g / 4 oz

1. Preheat the oven to 400°F / 200°C / Gas Mark 6.
2. Prepare the asparagus and cook in boiling salted water for about 10 minutes or until tender.
3. Meanwhile make the béchamel sauce and season well.
4. Drain the asparagus and dry in a clean cloth. Place in a buttered ovenproof dish, add a few knobs of butter, sprinkle with grated parmesan, slices of mozzarella and freshly ground pepper.
5. Pour the béchamel sauce over the asparagus. Put in a hot oven for about 15 minutes.

Zucchine alla mentuccia
Zucchini [Courgettes] with Pennyroyal

☐▷ 00:30   00:20 🍲

American	Ingredients	Metric/Imperial
1¼ lb	Small zucchini (courgettes)	600 g / 1¼ lb
	Flour as required	
½ cup	Sunflower oil	125 ml / 4 fl oz
	Salt	
Scant ¼ cup	Herb vinegar	3 tbsp
1	Small bunch of pennyroyal	1
1	Small onion	1
	Freshly ground pepper	

1. Peel the zucchini, wash and dry them, then cut them into strips, dip in flour and fry in very hot oil. Drain on a sheet of paper to absorb the excess grease and sprinkle with salt.
2. Pour the vinegar into an earthenware dish, add the small bunch of pennyroyal chopped finely, a small onion also chopped and a little pepper. Beat with a fork to blend well.
3. Arrange zucchini on a serving-dish and pour over sauce.

Frittelle di fagioli
Bean Pancakes

☐▷ 01:30   01:20 🍲
Soaking time 12:00

American	Ingredients	Metric/Imperial
1 lb	Dried haricot beans	450 g / 1 lb
2	Onions	2
12	Cloves	12
2 tbsp	Chopped parsley	1½ tbsp
Scant ¼ cup	Vegetable oil	3 tbsp
½ cup	Butter	100 g / 4 oz
¼ cup	Flour	25 g / 1 oz
½ cup	Milk	125 ml / 4 fl oz
1	Egg	1
	Salt and pepper	
½ cup	Bread crumbs	50 g / 2 oz

1. Soak the beans overnight in cold water.
2. Drain and put them in more water, bring to the boil, cover as tightly as possible and remove from the heat. Allow to stand for 1 hour: the beans will have become very swollen. Drain the water away, put in some fresh boiling water (do not salt), the onion studded with cloves, half the chopped parsley and 1 tablespoon of oil. Cook slowly for at least 1 hour until tender.
3. When the beans are cooked, drain and put them through a vegetable mill, blender or food processor.
4. Peel and chop the remaining onion finely and brown in a pot with a quarter of the butter.
5. Add half the flour, mix well, add the cold milk and stir in the mixture until it thickens.
6. Mix the bean purée, blend in the chopped parsley, the egg, the rest of the flour, salt and pepper.
7. Form into small flat cakes and coat in bread crumbs.
8. Heat the remaining butter and oil and fry the bean pancakes until golden brown.

Puré di fave
Bean Purée

☐▷ 00:15   01:00 🍲
Soaking time 12:00

American	Ingredients	Metric/Imperial
½ lb	Dried haricot beans	225 g / 8 oz
	Salt	
4 or 5	Sage leaves	4 or 5
¼ cup	Butter	50 g / 2 oz
4	Scallions (spring onions)	4

1. Put the beans to soak in cold water and leave overnight. Drain and put them in a saucepan, with cold water, salt and sage. Cook until soft.
2. Melt the butter in a frying pan and cook the chopped scallions (spring onions) over a very gentle heat. When they have become soft, mix butter and onions with the bean purée; sieve or blend. Adjust seasoning. This is an excellent side-dish for ragoût of oxtail.

Broccolini di Tropea
Whirlwind Broccoli

☐▷ 00:25   00:25 🍲

American	Ingredients	Metric/Imperial
2	Green broccoli	2
5	Anchovies in brine	5
1 cup	Black olives, pitted (stoned)	175 g / 6 oz
1	Onion	1
3 oz	Provolone cheese	75 g / 3 oz
	Butter	
¼ cup	Vegetable oil	50 ml / 2 fl oz
½ cup	Red wine	125 ml / 4 fl oz

1. Thoroughly clean the broccoli removing the damaged leaves and thick stalks, wash and blanch for 4 minutes in boiling salted water. Drain well.
2. Bone the anchovies. Divide the black olives into 4 and cut the onions and cheese into thin slices.
3. Preheat the oven to 350°F / 180°C / Gas Mark 4.
4. Arrange on the bottom of a buttered ovenproof dish the broccoli, a little sliced onion, a little cheese, a few small pieces of anchovy and olive and sprinkle with oil. Proceed in layers until all the ingredients are used up, moistening with a little oil and seasoning.
5. Pour over the red wine, a little more oil, cover with foil and put in the oven until tender.

Castagne e cavoletti
Chestnuts and Sprouts

☐▷ 01:00   00:45 🍲

American	Ingredients	Metric/Imperial
14 oz	Chestnuts	400 g / 14 oz
	Salt	
1	Bay leaf	1
1¾ lb	Brussels sprouts	800 g / 1¾ lb
⅓ cup	Butter	75 g / 3 oz

1. Put the chestnuts in salted cold water with a bay leaf, bring to the boil and simmer for 45 minutes. Drain, remove skins.
2. Wash and trim brussels sprouts and cook in a little boiling salted water for about 10 minutes until 'al dente'.
3. Melt the butter in a pan without browning, add the sprouts and chestnuts, shake over a low heat to mix and heat thoroughly before serving.

Cavoletti di Bruxelles gratinati
Brussels Sprouts au Gratin

00:15 00:30

American	Ingredients	Metric/Imperial
1 lb	Brussels sprouts	500 g / 1 lb
2 cups	Thin béchamel sauce	450 ml / ¾ pint
1 tbsp	Butter	15 g / ½ oz
	Salt and pepper	
7 oz	Emmental cheese	200 g / 7 oz

1. Trim the brussels sprouts, wash them and cook in a little boiling salted water.
2. Prepare a pouring béchamel sauce.
3. Preheat the oven to 425°F / 220°C / Gas Mark 7.
4. Butter an ovenproof dish and arrange the brussels sprouts in it in a single layer, very close together, salt and pepper them lightly and cover with béchamel. Sprinkle with the coarsely grated cheese and put in the oven for 10 minutes.
5. Heat the broiler (grill) for 5 minutes and finish the dish under the heat to form a golden crust. Serve hot.

Cook's tip: cooked cauliflowers, fennel, asparagus and Belgian endive can all be prepared in this way.

Cavolini di Bruxelles stufati
Stewed Brussels Sprouts

00:10 00:30

American	Ingredients	Metric/Imperial
2 lb	Brussels sprouts	1 kg / 2 lb
	Salt and pepper	
¼ cup	Butter	50 g / 2 oz
¼ lb	Cooked ham	100 g / 4 oz
½ cup	Coffee (single) cream	125 ml / 4 fl oz
1	Vegetable stock cube	1

1. Remove any damaged leaves from the brussels sprouts, trim the stalks. Wash well, then cook them in a saucepan containing a little boiling salted water for about 15 minutes, drain.
2. Melt the butter in a pan, add the sprouts and the cooked ham, cut into thin strips. Season well and allow to absorb the flavors, stirring from time to time.
3. In a small saucepan heat the cream and a crumbled stock cube, whisk until the cube has dissolved.
4. Pour over the brussels sprouts and leave to cook for a further 5-10 minutes over a low heat.
5. Serve hot sprinkled with freshly ground black pepper to accompany boiled or roast meats.

Verze ripiene alla Zia Tina
Aunt Tina's Stuffed Cabbage

00:30 00:40

American	Ingredients	Metric/Imperial
2	Small savoy cabbages	2
¼ cup	Butter	50 g / 2 oz
1 tbsp	Chopped parsley	1 tbsp
2	Garlic cloves	2
1 cup	Ground (minced) veal	225 g / 8 oz
½ lb	Liver	225 g / 8 oz
½ cup	Mushrooms	50 g / 2 oz
½ cup	Stock	125 ml / 4 fl oz
4	Canned tomatoes	4
1	Egg	1
1 oz	Cheese	25 g / 1 oz
1 cup	Béchamel sauce	225 ml / 8 fl oz

1. Discard the tough outer leaves and wash the savoy cabbages, and cook in boiling water for 7 minutes. Remove and drain upside down in a colander.
2. Put half the butter in a frying pan with some parsley and the crushed garlic. When it begins to brown, add the veal, the finely chopped liver and the washed and sliced mushrooms. Cook for 5 minutes adding a little stock and the sieved tomatoes.
3. Preheat the oven to 375°F / 190°C / Gas Mark 5.
4. Add an egg yolk, the cheese and the béchamel sauce to the meat. Mix well together and remove from the heat.
5. Open the cabbage leaves as wide as possible and fill with the meat mixture. Close up again.
6. Wrap the cabbage in buttered foil and place in an ovenproof dish. Cook for 20 minutes and serve from the folded-back foil.

Cavolfiore gratinato
Cauliflower au Gratin

00:05 00:30

American	Ingredients	Metric/Imperial
1	Cauliflower	1
1 tbsp	Butter	15 g / ½ oz
1 cup	Béchamel sauce	225 ml / 8 fl oz
	Salt and pepper	
3 tbsp	Grated parmesan cheese	2 tbsp

1. Preheat the oven to 375°F / 190°C / Gas Mark 5.
2. Cook the washed cauliflower in boiling salted water for about 10 minutes. Drain and, using a fork, divide into florets.
3. Butter an ovenproof dish and arrange the cauliflower in it.
4. Make the béchamel sauce and pour over the cauliflower, season well and sprinkle the surface with plenty of grated parmesan cheese.
5. Cook in the oven until it turns a pale golden color.

Cook's tip: for a rich cauliflower au gratin, add 2 egg yolks to the sauce. Whisk the whites until soft peaks stage and fold into the sauce.

Fennel pizza

Finocchi in pizza
Fennel 'Pizza'

◢ 00:25   00:35 🍲

American	Ingredients	Metric/Imperial
2 lb	Fennel bulbs	1 kg / 2 lb
	Salt and pepper	
¼ lb	Mozzarella cheese	100 g / 4 oz
2	Anchovies	2
⅔ cup	Black olives, pitted (stoned)	100 g / 4 oz
1 lb	Fresh tomatoes	500 g / 1 lb
1 tsp	Basil	1 tsp
1 tbsp	Oil	1 tbsp
¼ tsp	Oregano	¼ tsp

1. Cook the fennel 'al dente' in plenty of salted water. Drain well and dry. Slice evenly.
2. Preheat the oven to 400°F / 200°C / Gas Mark 6.
3. Cut the mozzarella into slices, trim the anchovies and chop into small pieces, cut the olives into halves.
4. Put the tomatoes in a pan with ⅔ cup [125 ml / ¼ pint] water, boil for 10 minutes, add salt and a little basil. Sieve to obtain the juice.
5. In an oiled baking pan, arrange a layer of cooked fennel, season well. Place the anchovies and the mozzarella on top. Cover with the purée from the tomatoes. Arrange the olives on the top, sprinkle with chopped oregano and basil and brush with oil.
6. Cook in the oven for 10-15 minutes. Serve immediately.

Finocchi della strega
Witch's Fennel

◢ 00:20   00:45 🍲

American	Ingredients	Metric/Imperial
4	Fennel bulbs	4
	Salt and pepper	
¼ cup	Butter	50 g / 2 oz
½ cup	Grated parmesan cheese	50 g / 2 oz
2½ cups	Béchamel sauce	600 ml / 1 pint
1 tsp	Hot paprika	1 tsp
4	Slices of cheese	4

1. Trim the fennel, cut into 4 and cook 'al dente' in plenty of salted water and drain.
2. Brown the fennel slices in a frying pan with half the melted butter for 4 minutes.
3. Sprinkle half the grated parmesan cheese over the fennel, stirring to mix well.
4. Preheat the oven to 350°F / 180°C / Gas Mark 4.
5. Make the béchamel sauce and add the paprika.
6. Butter an ovenproof dish and place the fennel in it. Put a slice of cheese on top of each piece, season well. Pour the béchamel sauce over, sprinkle with remaining parmesan and dot here and there with butter.
7. Put in the oven for about 30 minutes or until the cheese has formed a golden crust. Serve hot.

Polpette di lenticchie
Lentil Rissoles

◢ 00:20   01:30 🍲

American	Ingredients	Metric/Imperial
2 cups	Dried lentils	500 g / 1 lb
1 quart	Stock	1 litre / 1¾ pints
1	Onion	1
2 tbsp	Butter	25 g / 1 oz
1	Egg	1
3 tbsp	Chopped parsley	2 tbsp
	Salt and pepper	
	White flour	
	Oil for frying	

1. Pour boiling water on the lentils, allow to stand and remove any discolored lentils which come to the surface.
2. Put the lentils in a saucepan with the stock and bring to the boil, cover and leave to cook over a low heat for about 1 hour.
3. Peel and chop the onion, melt the butter in a pan and gently cook the onion until just colored.
4. Beat the egg and chop the parsley.
5. When the lentils are cooked, drain and blend or put through a food processor to make a purée. Add the purée to the onion, egg and parsley and season. Mix well until the mixture is smooth. This can also be done in the food processor. Leave for a few minutes in the refrigerator so that the mixture firms slightly.
6. Shape the rissoles from the mixture, flour lightly and leave to firm in the refrigerator or freezer while shaping the remainder.
7. Heat the oil in a large frying pan and cook the rissoles on both sides until golden, drain on absorbent kitchen towels. Serve with a charcuterie or broiled (grilled) meats or with a salad as a vegetarian dish.

Cook's tip: depending on type of lentils used you may have to add flour and bread crumbs to the mixture if it is not firm enough to shape.

Fagottini di lattuga
Sheaves of Lettuce

	00:45	00:40
	Frying time 00:05 for each batch of lettuce	

American	Ingredients	Metric/Imperial
16	Large lettuce leaves	16
1	Thick slice of Dutch cheese	1
Batter		
½ cup	Flour	50 g / 2 oz
	Salt	
1	Egg	1
1 tbsp	Vegetable oil	1 tbsp
Scant ¼ cup	Milk	3 tbsp
Sauce		
3 tbsp	Vegetable oil	2 tbsp
½	Onion	½
1	Celery stalk	1
1	Small carrot	1
1 lb	Peeled tomatoes	450 g / 1 lb
1	Bay leaf	1
½ tsp	Oregano	½ tsp
	Salt and pepper	
1	Stock cube	1
	Oil for frying	

1. Remove the largest undamaged leaves from the lettuces, wash and drain well. Cut the Dutch cheese into small cubes, divide amongst the lettuce leaves.
2. Fold the lettuce leaves into little parcels and secure with a toothpick.
3. Make some batter by sifting flour and salt into a bowl, beat in the egg, oil, and as much milk as necessary to make a thick batter. Cover and allow to stand for 10 minutes.
4. Prepare the sauce. Heat the oil in a pan, add the finely diced onion, celery and carrot, cook gently for 5 minutes.
5. Chop the peeled tomatoes, add to the vegetables with the bay leaf, oregano, salt and pepper. Add 2½ cups [600 ml / 1 pint] stock made with the cube. Simmer for 30 minutes.
6. Heat the oil in a deep frying pan.
7. Immerse the lettuce parcels in the batter, hold over the batter bowl to allow the excess to drain back into the bowl.
8. Cook 4 parcels in the heated oil, drain on absorbent kitchen towels. Continue with next batch. Serve hot with the sauce.

Funghi trifolati
Mushrooms with Garlic, Oil and Parsley

	00:10	00:15

American	Ingredients	Metric/Imperial
1	Garlic clove	1
3 tbsp	Butter	40 g / 1½ oz
3 tbsp	Vegetable oil	2 tbsp
1 lb	Mushrooms	500 g / 1 lb
	Salt and pepper	
1 tbsp	Chopped parsley	1 tbsp

1. Crush the garlic and fry it lightly in a frying pan with the butter and a little oil.
2. Wash the mushrooms and chop into pieces. Add them to the frying pan, flavor with salt and ground pepper and cook for 10 minutes over a brisk heat, stirring gently with a wooden spoon.
3. Just before turning off the heat sprinkle with the chopped parsley and serve on a heated serving dish.

Cook's tip: this is an ideal accompaniment to grilled meats.

Boleti ripieni
Stuffed Mushrooms

	00:30	00:30

American	Ingredients	Metric/Imperial
2 lb	Large mushrooms	1·kg / 2 lb
	Salt and pepper	
1	Large bunch of parsley	1
¼ cup	Vegetable oil	3 tbsp
¼ cup	Butter	50 g / 2 oz
4	Tomatoes	4
3 tbsp	Bread crumbs	2 tbsp

1. Wash and remove the stalks from the mushrooms. Chop the stalks. Wash the mushrooms and drain very thoroughly, place on a dish and sprinkle with salt.
2. Wash the parsley and chop.
3. Heat the oil and butter in a pan, add the parsley and cook for 2 minutes. Add the mushroom stalks and cook for a further 3 minutes.
4. Add the skinned and chopped tomatoes with 1 cup [225 ml / 8 fl oz] water. Season and simmer for 10 minutes.
5. Preheat the oven to 375°F / 190°C / Gas Mark 5.
6. Fill the caps with the mixture, sprinkle the bread crumbs on top and put in a buttered pan. Pour a little melted butter on top and cook for 15 minutes.

Funghi alla panna
Creamed Mushrooms

	00:10	00:35

American	Ingredients	Metric/Imperial
1¾ lb	Mushrooms	800 g / 1¾ lb
3 tbsp	Butter	40 g / 1½ oz
	Salt and pepper	
1	Garlic clove	1
1 cup	Coffee (single) cream	225 ml / 8 fl oz
1 tbsp	Chopped parsley	1 tbsp
	Triangles of toast	

1. Wash and dry the mushrooms with absorbent kitchen towels, trim the ends of the stalks, remove any bruised or damaged parts. Slice lengthwise.
2. Melt the butter in a thick pan, add the mushrooms, cook for a few minutes, until they become juicy, then season with salt, pepper and the crushed clove of garlic, continue cooking for a further 5 minutes.
3. Moisten the mushrooms with the cream and leave to simmer for about 10-15 minutes until the cream is absorbed. Serve, sprinkle with chopped parsley, surrounded by toast.

Sheaves of lettuce

Funghi ripieni al sapore di mare

Stuffed Mushrooms with a Tang of the Sea

00:45 00:30

American	Ingredients	Metric/Imperial
30	Large mussels	30
½ cup	Dry sherry or marsala	125 ml / 4 fl oz
8	Medium-sized mushrooms	8
1	Garlic clove	1
1 tbsp	Chopped parsley	1 tbsp
1 tbsp	Chopped shallot	1 tbsp
⅓ cup	Butter	65 g / 2½ oz
	Salt and pepper	
3 tbsp	Olive oil	2 tbsp
1 cup	Fresh bread crumbs	50 g / 2 oz

1. Thoroughly clean the mussels, wash them repeatedly under the cold running tap and put in a pan over the heat until they are all open (discard any which remain closed). Remove the mussels from the shells and keep them in a bowl, covered with sherry, for 1 hour.
2. Clean the mushrooms, detach the stalks from the caps. Chop the stalks and mix with the crushed garlic and the chopped parsley. Chop the shallot and cook this in 2 tablespoons [25 g / 1 oz] butter over a gentle heat with the mushroom stalks for 2 minutes. Add salt and pepper and keep warm.
3. Oil the mushroom caps and put them under the broiler (grill) for 5 minutes.
4. Preheat the oven to 425°F / 210°C / Gas Mark 7.
5. Divide the mixture between the caps, put 3 mussels on top, sprinkle with bread crumbs and pour melted butter over them. Cook the caps in a hot oven for 10 minutes and serve with lemon segments.

Sformato di pane

Savory Mushroom Bread Pudding

00:20 00:45

American	Ingredients	Metric/Imperial
¾ lb	Fresh mushrooms	350 g / 12 oz
3 tbsp	Butter	40 g / 1½ oz
1	Garlic clove	1
½ cup	Stock	125 ml / 4 fl oz
12	Slices of presliced bread	12
10	Slices of emmental or fontina cheese	10
2 oz	Raw ham	50 g / 2 oz
2	Eggs	2
2 cups	Milk	450 ml / ¾ pint
	Salt and pepper	

1. Preheat oven to 350°F / 180°C / Gas Mark 4.
2. Wash the mushrooms, slice and cook them in a pan with the butter and crushed garlic for about 10 minutes, add a little stock. Allow to cool.
3. Remove the crust from the slices of bread and put 6 in a large buttered ovenproof dish. Cover with the slices of cheese, arrange the mushrooms on top, the ham cut into strips and finish with the remaining slices of bread.
4. Beat the eggs in a bowl with the milk, salt and pepper, pour the liquid into the oven dish and allow to soak for 10 minutes, cover and keep cool.
5. Put the dish into a moderate oven for 30 to 35 minutes and serve hot.

Crostata di cipolle

Onion Tart

00:35 Resting time 00:20 00:40

American	Ingredients	Metric/Imperial
Pastry		
1½ cups	Flour	175 g / 6 oz
	Salt	
½ cup	Butter	100 g / 4 oz
Filling		
1 lb	Onions	450 g / 1 lb
⅓ cup	Butter	75 g / 3 oz
2	Egg yolks	2
1 tbsp	Flour	1 tbsp
⅔ cup	Coffee (single) cream	150 ml / ¼ pint
	Salt and pepper	

1. Prepare shortcrust pastry by sifting the flour and salt, add butter and a little water (see page 452). Knead the dough well with floured hands and allow to rest in the refrigerator for 20 minutes.
2. Peel the onions, wash and slice thinly.
3. Heat the butter in a pan and cook the onions over a low heat for 10 minutes.
4. Put the egg yolks in a bowl and mix without beating too much, add the flour and mix well. Thin the mixture by adding the cream a little at a time, making sure there are no lumps.
5. Remove the onions from the heat, blend the egg and cream mixture with them, season with salt and pepper and return to the heat for 4 minutes to thicken.
6. Preheat the oven to 400°F / 200°C / Gas Mark 6.
7. Roll out the short pastry on a floured board and line a pieshell (flan) ring, bottom and sides. Tip in the onion mixture and put into the oven for 25 minutes.

Cipolle alla sbirraglia

Spicy Stuffed Onions

00:30 00:35

American	Ingredients	Metric/Imperial
4	Good quality red-skinned onions of the same size	4
½ lb	Italian sausages	225 g / 8 oz
2 tbsp	Parsley	1½ tbsp
2	Garlic cloves	2
¼ cup	Grated parmesan cheese	25 g / 1 oz
2	Eggs	2
3 tbsp	Flour	2 tbsp
1 tsp	Curry powder	1 tsp
	Salt and pepper	

Spicy stuffed onions

1. Remove the first layer of skin from the onions and thoroughly clean the rest. Cut off the tops of the onions and put to one side. Hollow out with a sharp knife and remove all the inner flesh, leaving an outer shell with a thickness of about ¾ in / 2 cm.

2. Preheat the oven to 425°F / 220°C / Gas Mark 7.

3. Chop up the flesh of the onions, put in a bowl with the finely chopped sausage, the chopped parsley and crushed cloves of garlic. Add a little grated parmesan to the mixture, then 2 egg yolks and mix well.

4. Fill onions with this mixture, leaving a little space at the top.

5. Beat the egg whites to a froth. Sift the flour and curry powder together with salt and pepper and fold into the egg white with the remaining parmesan cheese. Season with salt and pepper.

6. Put this mixture into the top of the onions to complete the filling.

7. Place the onions on a heat-resistant tray or ovenproof dish. Pour a little water into the tray to prevent the onions burning while they are cooking.

8. Place in a hot oven for 35 minutes, then remove from the oven and serve hot.

Flan di spinaci

Spinach Savory

American	Ingredients	Metric/Imperial
1¼ lb	Spinach	600 g / 1¼ lb
2 tbsp	Butter	25 g / 1 oz
1	Garlic clove	1
2 cups	Béchamel sauce	450 ml / ¾ pint
	Salt and pepper	
2	Eggs	2

1. Wash and cook the spinach in a small amount of boiling salted water, drain and once it has cooled, squeeze the excess moisture out and put in a bowl with a little melted butter and a crushed clove of garlic.
2. Preheat the oven to 400°F / 200°C / Gas Mark 6.
3. Make the béchamel sauce, add to the spinach with salt and pepper.
4. Separate the eggs and add yolks to the spinach and mix. Whisk the egg whites and fold into the spinach mixture.
5. Tip the mixture into a deep buttered dish and cook in a bain-marie in the oven for about 20 minutes. Serve hot.

Cabiette

Nettle Gnocchi

American	Ingredients	Metric/Imperial
6 oz	Nettles	175 g / 6 oz
2 oz	Fontina cheese	50 g / 2 oz
2 lb	Potatoes	1 kg / 2 lb
2 cups	Rye flour	225 g / 8 oz
2	Eggs	2
1½ lb	Onions	700 g / 1½ lb
½ cup	Butter	100 g / 4 oz
	Salt and pepper	
½ cup	Rye bread crumbs	50 g / 2 oz

1. Wear an old pair of gloves to gather the nettles. Wash, squeeze and chop them finely, (the food processor is ideal for this).
2. Cut some fontina cheese into small pieces.
3. Peel, boil and mash the potatoes. Put the puréed potatoes in a bowl, add the nettles, the cheese, the sifted rye flour, mix together with the beaten eggs.
4. Cut the peeled onions into thin rings. Heat the butter in a pan and cook for 6 minutes over a gentle heat.
5. Form the potato mixture into small gnocchi (dumplings) and drop into boiling salted water. As soon as they have risen to the top of the pan, drain well.
6. Preheat the oven to 350°F / 180°C / Gas Mark 4.
7. Butter an ovenproof dish, place a layer of the potato dumplings on the bottom, then put some onions on top and sprinkle with melted butter. Continue adding another layer of gnocchi, seasoning well, until all the ingredients are used.
8. Sprinkle the final layer with bread crumbs. Put the dish in the oven for 45 minutes. Serve piping hot.

Stuffed mixed vegetables — eggplant, zucchini [courgettes], sweet pepper and onions

Crocchette di spinaci

Spinach Croquettes

00:45   00:05 each batch

American	Ingredients	Metric/Imperial
1 cup	Thick béchamel sauce (see p. 162)	225 ml / 8 fl oz
2 lb	Spinach or borage	1 kg / 2 lb
	Salt and pepper	
½ cup	Bread crumbs	50 g / 2 oz
	Oil for frying	

1. Prepare a very thick béchamel sauce. Cook on a low heat, stirring continuously until really thick, allow to cool.
2. Wash the spinach, cook in a little boiling salted water, drain well and squeeze out excess moisture. Chop roughly and add to the béchamel sauce and allow to cool.
3. Form into croquettes the size of golf balls, dip in bread crumbs.
4. Heat the oil in a deep fat pan until very hot and fry the croquettes. When they are golden brown, remove from the fat and drain off the excess oil with absorbent kitchen towels.

Rape allo zucchero
Turnips with Sugar

⏱ 00:15   00:15 🍲

American	Ingredients	Metric/Imperial
1 lb	Turnips	500 g / 1 lb
¼ cup	Butter	50 g / 2 oz
	Salt	
½ tsp	Sugar	½ tsp
1 tbsp	Flour	1 tbsp
2½ cups	Stock	600 ml / 1 pint

1. Peel and cut the turnips into slices, then into thin sticks of about 2 in / 5 cm long.
2. Melt a little butter in a pan, add the turnips, season them with salt and a pinch of sugar and sprinkle with flour, stir round for a few minutes.
3. Moisten with sufficient stock to cover the turnips and finish by cooking over a moderate heat.
4. When they are cooked, the sauce must have thickened enough to cover the turnips with a shiny film. Garnish with chopped parsley and serve with roast meat.

Misto ripieno
Stuffed Mixed Vegetables

⏱ 00:30   00:30 🍲

American	Ingredients	Metric/Imperial
2	Large zucchini (courgettes)	2
2	Eggplant (aubergines)	2
2	Sweet pepper	2
2	Onions	2
	Salt and pepper	
7 oz	Roast meat	200 g / 7 oz
¼ lb	Italian sausage	100 g / 4 oz
1 tbsp	Chopped parsley	1 tbsp
½ cup	Grated cheese	50 g / 2 oz
1	Egg	1
3 tbsp	Bread crumbs	2 tbsp
1 tbsp	Butter	15 g / ½ oz
3 tbsp	Vegetable oil	2 tbsp

1. Top and tail the zucchini and eggplant and cut in half. Peel onion, cut pepper in half and deseed. Blanch for 5 minutes in boiling salted water.
2. Drain and, using a tablespoon, extract the middle flesh, chop and put in 2 different bowls.
3. Chop up the roast meat and the sausage, add the chopped parsley, the grated cheese, egg, the bread crumbs, salt and pepper. Mix well and divide this mixture between the zucchini, eggplant, onion and pepper.
4. Preheat the oven to 400°F / 200°C / Gas Mark 6.
5. Mix the filling and season well. Stuff the two different vegetables with the respective filling.
6. Arrange the zucchini and eggplant in an ovenproof dish rubbed over with a little butter and oil. Seal with foil and cook for 30 minutes.

Verdure in salsa al Grand Marnier

Vegetables in Grand Marnier Sauce

	00:30		00:40

American	Ingredients	Metric/Imperial
½ lb	Green beans	225 g / 8 oz
3	Small new potatoes	3
	Salt and pepper	
4	Zucchini (courgettes)	4
1 lb	Fresh or frozen asparagus	450 g / 1 lb
Sauce		
3 tbsp	White vinegar	2 tbsp
	Salt and pepper	
3	Egg yolks	3
¾ cup	Butter	175 g / 6 oz
2	Oranges	2
2 tsp	Grand Marnier	2 tsp

1. Top and tail the beans, scrape the new potatoes. Wash the zucchini and cut into thick slices.

2. Cook the potatoes in cold salted water, bring to the boil and simmer briskly until tender but still firm.

3. Place the beans and zucchini in a little boiling salted water and cook for 5 minutes, drain well.

4. Cook the asparagus until tender but firm, according to type. (If using fresh see page 369).

5. Prepare the sauce by boiling together the vinegar, salt and pepper. Reduce by half. Add 1 tablespoon cold water. Blend in the 3 egg yolks and half the butter, cut into small pieces, mix well. Transfer the sauce to a bowl or double saucepan and cook over hot water. Do not let the sauce boil.

6. When the sauce begins to thicken, add the remaining butter a little at a time.

7. Remove from the heat, allow to cool down slightly, then add the juice of the oranges and the Grand Marnier.

8. Arrange the cooked vegetables on a heated platter, the potatoes may be sliced as liked, alternate the asparagus with the beans and zucchini.

9. Pour the sauce on top. For garnish a little grated orange rind may be sprinkled on top.

Misto di verdure al gratin

Mixed Vegetables au Gratin

	04:00		00:40

American	Ingredients	Metric/Imperial
1	Small cauliflower	1
	Salt and pepper	
¼ cup	Butter	50 g / 2 oz
2	Fennel bulbs	2
14 oz	Spinach	400 g / 14 oz
¼ tsp	Nutmeg	¼ tsp
½ cup	Grated cheese	50 g / 2 oz
1¼ cups	Béchamel sauce	300 ml / ½ pint

1. Remove the green leaves and part of the stalk from the cauliflower and cook in a little salted water for about 15 minutes, drain. Cut off the florets and toss very quickly in half the heated, browned butter.

2. Drain off the fat and arrange the cauliflower in a large ovenproof dish.

3. Remove the tough outer leaves from the fennel and cook in boiling salted water. Drain and divide into 4 pieces.

4. Add the fennel to the dish with the cauliflower.

5. Remove the stalks from the spinach and tear into small pieces. Cook in a little boiling salted water for 5 minutes. Drain well, put in the dish with the fennel and cauliflower.

6. Preheat the oven to 400°F / 200°C / Gas Mark 6.

7. Sprinkle the vegetables with salt, pepper, nutmeg and half the grated cheese and cover with béchamel sauce. Dot the surface with butter and sprinkle with remaining grated cheese. Cook in the oven for at least 20 minutes.

Budino di verdure

Vegetable Pudding

	00:50		01:25

American	Ingredients	Metric/Imperial
6 oz	Green beans	175 g / 6 oz
	Salt and pepper	
½ lb	Asparagus	225 g / 8 oz
2	Scorzonera (black salsify)	2
2	Potatoes	2
2	Carrots	2
1	Small cauliflower	1
3	Artichokes	3
½ cup	Butter	100 g / 4 oz
½ lb	Thin slices of cooked lean ham	225 g / 8 oz
2	Eggs	2
1 cup	Grated parmesan cheese	100 g / 4 oz

1. Choose some small, tender green beans, top and tail, wash and cook them whole in a little boiling salted water.

2. Remove and discard the white, woody part of the asparagus and steam them.

3. Scrape the scorzonera, wash, cut into pieces about the same size as the green beans and cook them in boiling salted water.

4. Cook the peeled, sliced potatoes and carrots 'al dente' like the other vegetables and drain them. Add to them the raw cauliflower, cut into florets.

5. Clean the artichokes, remove the tough outer leaves, the prickles and the choke, cut into pieces and add to the remaining vegetables.

6. Heat the butter, add all the vegetables and season with salt and pepper. Cook for 10 minutes.

7. Butter a 2 lb [1 kg / 2 lb] pudding mold and line the walls with slices of cooked ham. Fill with the mixed vegetables.

8. Beat the eggs well, add salt and pepper, the grated parmesan and pour all over the mixed vegetables, repeatedly banging the mold on the table so that the egg penetrates the spaces.

9. Put the mold into a bain-marie (or a baking pan filled with water to come halfway up the sides of the bowl) and cook for about 30 minutes. Turn out of the mold while it is still piping hot and serve immediately.

Cook's tip: unless young tender artichokes are available, it is probably better to use the canned variety.

Vegetable pudding

Cooking fresh vegetables

A helpful rule for cooking vegetables in water is that vegetables such as peas, beans and other greens which grow above the ground are put into boiling water. The root vegetables such as carrots, turnips and potatoes are best put into cold water and brought to the boil for even cooking.

If vegetables are cooked in a great deal of water much of the nutritive value is lost into the water. It is best, therefore, to cook vegetables in a covered pan in the minimum of water and use the cooking water to make soups and gravies. However, some vegetables such as tender young beans do need to be cooked in at least half a saucepan of water without a lid, for a short time, to prevent color loss. Vegetables which discolor such as artichokes, jerusalem artichokes, salsify, and cardoons, are best cooked with lemon juice added to the water.

Steaming

Cooking young tender vegetables in steam retains the nutrients and both the color and texture of fresh and frozen vegetables. Place the vegetables in a steamer over a pan of boiling water, so that the vegetables do not come into contact with the water. The steam will surround the vegetables but you will need to allow more time for cooking, usually about 10 minutes more than the time required to boil the vegetables.

Steaming saucepans are available which have an inside with holes to allow the steam to circulate. Alternatively, there are metal steaming baskets which stand on legs inside a saucepan.

It is possible to cook several types of vegetables together in a steamer providing they are wrapped in foil and are not packed tightly together. As water boils away in a steamer it is useful to have a kettle of boiling water ready to top up the water. Salt the vegetables, and not the water, lightly before cooking. More seasoning can be added at the table.

Using the microwave oven

This is an excellent method of cooking vegetables without loss of flavor or nutrients. Only a few spoons of water need to be sprinkled over the vegetables to retain moisture.

Pressure cooking

Although the principle of pressure cooking is the same for all cookers, the models vary and it is essential to follow the manufacturer's instructions for cooking vegetables. The pressure cooker retains the nutritive value of food and cooks more quickly, on average saving one-third of the total cooking time.

Puddings

Budino di cioccolata
Chocolate Pudding

◣▱ 00:35   01:00 ⬗

American	Ingredients	Metric/Imperial
¼ lb	Bitter chocolate	100 g / 4 oz
2 ½ cups	Milk	600 ml / 1 pint
⅔ cup	Sugar	150 g / 5 oz
¼ lb	Savoy biscuits	100 g / 4 oz
½ cup	Amaretto liqueur	125 ml / 4 fl oz
3	Eggs	3
1	Vanilla pod	1

1. Grate the chocolate and heat it in the milk in a double boiler over a low heat until it melts.
2. Raise the heat and when the mixture boils, add a little less than half the sugar and crumble in the savoy biscuits. Cook for 15 minutes, stirring continuously. Strain through a sieve into a bowl. Add the amaretto liqueur and leave to cool.
3. Preheat the oven to 325°F / 170°C / Gas Mark 3.
4. In a separate bowl, beat the eggs and flavor with the vanilla. Combine with the milk mixture.
5. Dissolve the remaining sugar in a few drops of water until pale golden, pour into a pudding basin.
6. Add the chocolate mixture and cook in the oven sitting on a pan of water for 1 hour. Serve hot or cold.

Torta di noci
Nut Pudding

◣▱ 00:30   01:20 ⬗

American	Ingredients	Metric/Imperial
4 cups	Walnuts	450 g / 1 lb
1 cup	Almonds	150 g / 5 oz
1 cup	Pine kernels	100 g / 4 oz
1 cup	Pistachio nuts	100 g / 4 oz
4 ¼ cups	Sugar	1 kg / 2 lb
1 cup	Sultanas	175 g / 6 oz
½ cup	Butter	100 g / 4 oz

1. Preheat the oven to 325°F / 170°C / Gas Mark 3.
2. Shell and grind the nuts in a blender. Put in a pan with the sugar and mix well. Heat and try to obtain a pale toffee consistency.
3. Butter a ring shaped mold well, quickly tip in the nuts, sultanas and any caramelized sugar left in the pan. Then bake for 1 hour.
4. Unmold onto a serving plate by putting the pan in boiling water for a few seconds before turning out. The consistency should be like soft toffee and it should be served at once.

Cook's tip: rum can be added to the mixture to give the pudding more flavor.

Chocolate pudding with sponge fingers and amaretti

Aspic di frutta
Fruit Jelly

00:25 Setting time 04:00 **00:10**

American	Ingredients	Metric/Imperial
6	Oranges	6
1	Lemon	1
10	Sugar lumps	10
14 oz can	Pineapple	420 g / 14 oz can
5 tsp	Gelatin	5 tsp
1½ lb	Fresh fruit in season: strawberries, apricots, peaches, grapes, plums etc.	700 g / 1½ lb

1. Cut the oranges and lemon in half and squeeze out the juice. Strain into a saucepan. Add sugar lumps and make up 2 cups [475 ml / ¾ pint] with pineapple juice (from the can) and water. Boil for a few minutes.
2. Dissolve the gelatin by sprinkling into a few tablespoons of boiling water, add this to the boiling liquid when the gelatin has dissolved completely.
3. Wash and chop the fruit, adding the canned pineapple. The jelly will have cooled a little by now.
4. Pour a little jelly into a mold and freeze for a few minutes. Stir the fruit into the remaining jelly and pour this into the mold. Refrigerate for a few hours.
5. Dip in warm water and turn out onto a plate.

Cook's tip: for a special occasion set the jelly in layers with carefully arranged slices of fruit of different colors on each layer of jelly. Allow each layer to almost set before adding the chopped fruit.

Macedonia nell'anguria
Fruit Salad in Watermelon

00:20 Chilling time 01:10 **00:00**

American	Ingredients	Metric/Imperial
1	Average size watermelon	1
8	Yellow and purple plums	8
2	Ripe peaches	2
1	Orange	1
1	Lemon	1
3 tbsp	Maraschino or cointreau	2 tbsp
1 tbsp	Confectioner's (icing) sugar	1 tbsp
½ lb	Raspberries	225 g / 8 oz

1. Cut the watermelon in half, scoop all the flesh into a bowl and patiently remove all the seeds. As the melon shell will be used as a container, even it out inside and wash it on the outside, drying well with absorbent kitchen towels.
2. Mix the melon flesh with the pitted (stoned) yellow and purple plums, the sliced peaches, orange and lemon juice, maraschino or cointreau and the sugar. Refrigerate for about 1 hour.
3. Carefully wash the raspberries and set aside. Turn the fruit salad into the melon shell, add the raspberries and return to the refrigerator for a few minutes to chill.
4. Serve within 30 minutes before the melon becomes watery, which would spoil the fruit salad.

Bavarese al caffè
Coffee Mousse

00:20 Chilling time 04:00 **00:30**

American	Ingredients	Metric/Imperial
1 cup	Strong black coffee	225 ml / 8 fl oz
5 tsp	Gelatin	5 tsp
1 cup	Milk	225 ml / 8 fl oz
⅔ cup	Sugar	150 g / 5 oz
1 cup	Whipping (double) cream	225 ml / 8 fl oz
2	Eggs, separated	2
1 tbsp	Cornstarch (cornflour)	1 tbsp
1 sachet	Vanilla sugar	1 sachet
2 or 3	Small glasses of brandy	2 or 3

1. Prepare some very strong coffee. Then sprinkle the gelatin on 3 tablespoons boiling water to dissolve.
2. Heat the milk. In a separate bowl pour the sugar, the egg yolks and cornstarch. Whisk thoroughly, adding the filtered coffee a little at a time. Continue whisking, add the boiling milk a little at a time to produce a creamy mixture.
3. Pour this into a double boiler, or place the bowl over a pan of boiling water on a medium heat. Reheat, and when it begins to thicken, add the vanilla sugar and allow to cool.
4. Add the brandy to the thoroughly dissolved gelatin and stir into the mixture. Strain into a bowl and stir several times.
5. Whisk the egg whites into soft peaks.
6. Whip the cream and fold gently into the mixture before it sets, then fold in the egg whites.
7. Pour into a mold, level it off and place a lightly buttered waxed (greaseproof) paper disc over the top. Refrigerate for 4 hours. To turn out, immerse in hot water for a few seconds.

Melone ripieno
Stuffed Melon

00:25 **00:00**

American	Ingredients	Metric/Imperial
1	Large ripe melon	1
1 lb	Strawberries	450 g / 1 lb
5 oz	Ricotta	150 g / 5 oz
2 tbsp	Confectioner's (icing) sugar	1½ tbsp
1	Egg yolk	1
1 tbsp	Liqueur	1 tbsp
1 cup	Whipping (double) cream	1

1. Cut the melon in half. Scoop out the flesh into a bowl, saving the empty melon shells.
2. Hull the strawberries, retain 8 for decoration, and soften them in water, drain and add to the chopped melon flesh. Combine with the ricotta and beat until the mixture is quite creamy. Blend in the confectioner's (icing) sugar, egg yolk and liqueur. This stage can all be done in a blender or food processor). Refrigerate for about 20 minutes.
3. Fill the melon halves with the mixture, whisk the cream and decorate the melon halves with whipped cream rosettes and whole strawberries. Refrigerate until ready to serve.

Zabaione
Zabaglione

Zabaglione is one of the most famous Italian puddings. It is very simple and quick to make.

00:05   **00:10 to 00:15**

American	Ingredients	Metric/Imperial
4	Fresh egg yolks	4
¼ cup	Fine granulated (castor) sugar	50 g / 2 oz
1 tsp	Cornflour (cornstarch)	1 tsp
¼ cup	Marsala	50 ml / 2 fl oz

1. Cream the yolks with the sugar and cornstarch (cornflour) (optional, but it prevents the yolks from curdling when being cooked) in a copper pan or bowl over a pan of hot water, making sure the bottom of the bowl does not touch the water. Whisk until pale and frothy and gradually whisk in the marsala.
2. Whisk over a moderate heat until the mixture is thick and creamy. Serve in

Cook's tip: preparation and cooking time will depend on whether an electric mixer or hand whisk is being used.

Mandarini a sorpresa
Tangerine Surprise

00:25   **00:00**

American	Ingredients	Metric/Imperial
8	Tangerines	8
1¼ cups	Fruit ice	300 ml / ½ pint
1 cup	Pistachio nuts	100 g / 4 oz

1. Cut the tops from 8 tangerines, seedless if possible. Save the tops.
2. Scoop out the flesh taking great care not to break the skin.
3. Sieve the flesh through a coarse sieve to remove any seeds or pith, mix with the fruit ice (any kind you like) and chopped pistachio nuts. Fill the tangerines with the mixture, cover them again with their tops and then freeze for 30 minutes. Serve with plain biscuits or sponge fingers.

Cook's tip: step 3 may be mixed in seconds in a food processor and give even distribution of ingredients.

Monte Bianco
Mont Blanc

00:30   **00:30**

American	Ingredients	Metric/Imperial
14 oz	Chestnuts	400 g / 14 oz
2 cups	Milk	450 ml / ¾ pint
¼ cup	Vanilla sugar	50 g / 2 oz
1 tbsp	Liqueur	1 tbsp
1 cup	Whipping (double) cream	225 ml / 8 fl oz
½ tsp	Vanilla essence	½ tsp
4	Marrons glacés	4
4	Candied violets	4

1. Shell the chestnuts and boil them for a few minutes to remove any inside skin. When they are quite clean, simmer in milk and sugar until perfectly tender.
2. Mash twice through a sieve, blender, food processor, or food mill to get a smooth cream. Allow to cool.
3. Flavor with 1 tablespoon liqueur (grand marnier is excellent with chestnuts).
4. Arrange the chestnut cream in a mound on a serving dish, whip the cream and add the vanilla flavoring, pipe or spread over the chestnut mound. Decorate with small pieces or marrons glacés and candied violets.

Gelato pasticciato
Mixed Ice Cream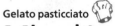

00:30   **00:00**
Freezing time 02:00
Serves 6

American	Ingredients	Metric/Imperial
2½ oz	Plain chocolate	65 g / 2½ oz
3 tbsp	Milk	2 tbsp
1 quart	Ice cream	1 litre / 1¾ pints
2 tbsp	Cherry syrup	1½ tbsp
3 tbsp	Red currant syrup	2 tbsp

1. Divide the ice cream into 3 parts in 3 bowls. Melt the chocolate with the milk, let it cool to avoid melting the ice cream and stir into the first bowl of ice cream. Turn into a mold and freeze.
2. Stir the cherry syrup into the second part, turn this on top of the first layer in the mold and return to the freezer.
3. Finally, stir the red currant syrup into the third part of the ice cream and turn on top of the other two. Freeze for 2 hours. Before serving, dip the mold into warm water quickly and turn out onto a serving dish.
4. The flavored ice cream can be decorated with cherries, whipped cream, candied fruit or melted chocolate.

Spiedini della Chiccolina
Fruit Kebabs

00:20   **00:00**

American	Ingredients	Metric/Imperial
2	Apples	2
3 tbsp	Lemon juice	2 tbsp
1¼ lb	Strawberries (preferably large)	600 g / 1¼ lb
¼ cup	Fine granulated (castor) sugar	50 g / 2 oz
3 tbsp	Vinegar	2 tbsp
8	Brandy cherries	8

1. Peel, core and cube the apples, cover with lemon juice.
2. Wash the strawberries and put into a bowl with the sugar and vinegar. Leave for 10 minutes. Besides giving an excellent juice which can be served separately, this method helps to preserve the true flavor and perfume of the strawberry.
3. On a small skewer thread a brandy cherry, a strawberry, a piece of apple, another strawberry, another piece of apple, finishing with a cherry.

Cook's tip: an excellent way to serve fresh fruit outdoors at barbecues and picnics.

Fruit kebabs

Cassata Siciliana
Sicilian Cassata

	01:00	00:03
	Chilling time 03:00	

American	Ingredients	Metric/Imperial
1 scant cup	Sugar	200 g / 7 oz
2 tsp	Vanilla sugar	2 tsp
¾ lb	Ricotta cheese	350 g / 12 oz
¾ lb	Mixed candied fruit	350 g / 12 oz
2 oz	Pistachio nuts	50 g / 2 oz
¼ lb	Bitter chocolate	100 g / 4 oz
¼ cup	Marsala wine	50 ml / 2 fl oz
1	Sweet tea loaf or brioche	1
1 lb	Apricot jam	450 g / 1 lb
1¾ cups	Confectioner's (icing) sugar	200 g / 7 oz
	Orange flower water	

1. Dissolve the sugar and the vanilla sugar in a little water over a very low heat, stirring continuously.
2. Rub the ricotta through a sieve and add to the syrup. Chop the candied fruit and add half to the mixture.
3. Blanch, peel and cut the pistachio nuts in half and add these to the other ingredients.
4. Grate the chocolate, mix in thoroughly and pour in the marsala.
5. Cut the bread into thin slices. Line a cake pan with wax (greaseproof) paper and line this with slices of bread, spread with a little sieved apricot jam to bind it.
6. Pour the ricotta mixture into the cake pan and level the surface. Cover with more slices of bread, spread with apricot jam. Refrigerate for 2 hours.
7. Prepare the apricot glaze by combining the remaining sieved apricot jam, the confectioner's (icing) sugar and a little orange flower water in a saucepan over a moderate heat. Remove the cassata from the refrigerator and turn it upside down on a serving dish, removing the wax (greaseproof) paper. Brush with the apricot glaze and decorate with the remaining candied fruit. Refrigerate for 1 hour before serving.

Budino di fragole
Strawberry Pudding

	01:00	00:15
	Chilling time 04:00	

American	Ingredients	Metric/Imperial
1 lb	Strawberries	450 g / 1 lb
½ cup	Brandy	125 ml / 4 fl oz
5 tsp	Gelatin	5 tsp
1 scant cup	Sugar	200 g / 7 oz
3	Egg whites	3
	Butter	

1. Clean the strawberries and arrange in a bowl. Pour over half the brandy and leave to marinate for 45 minutes.
2. Sprinkle the gelatin onto 3 tablespoons boiling water.
3. Pour the sugar into a saucepan and add about 2 cups [450 ml / ¾ pint] water. Place over a moderate heat to obtain a thick syrup. Do not allow the syrup to brown.
4. Remove from the heat and stir in the gelatin with the remaining brandy; continue stirring until the syrup has cooled.
5. Whisk the egg whites until stiff and fold into the syrup.

6. Butter a pudding basin and arrange a layer of strawberries on the bottom. Pour in half the mixture. If it is too runny, refrigerate until it is firmer. Make another layer of strawberries and pour on the remainder of the mixture. Refrigerate for about 4 hours.
7. To remove the pudding from the basin, immerse in hot water for a few seconds.

Torta di banane
Banana Tart

	00:20	00:30

American	Ingredients	Metric/Imperial
1 cup	All purpose (plain) flour	100 g / 4 oz
2 tsp	Baking powder	2 tsp
	Salt	
½ cup	Butter	100 g / 4 oz
½ cup	Sugar	100 g / 4 oz
2	Eggs	2
3 – 4	Bananas	3 – 4
1	Lemon	1
1 tsp	Sugar	1 tsp
½ cup	Chopped almonds	50 g / 2 oz

1. Preheat the oven to 350°F / 180°C / Gas Mark 4.
2. Sift the flour, baking powder and salt on to a plate.
3. In a bowl, cream the butter and sugar until light and fluffy. Add the lightly beaten eggs and little by little fold in the flour mixture. Stir until well mixed and smooth. Turn into a buttered and floured 8 in / 20 cm cake pan and spread evenly.
4. Peel the bananas, slice lengthwise and arrange on the cake. Sprinkle with lemon juice, 1 teaspoon of sugar and chopped almonds. Bake in a preheated oven for 30 minutes or until set. Allow to cool before serving.

Orange mousse
Orange Mousse

	00:30	00:20
	Serves 8	

American	Ingredients	Metric/Imperial
8	Eggs	8
1½ cups	Sugar	350 g / 12 oz
4	Large oranges	4
3 tbsp	Cornstarch (cornflour)	2 tbsp
5 tsp	Gelatin	5 tsp
1 cup	Whipping (double) cream	225 ml / 8 fl oz

1. Separate the eggs. In a bowl, cream the yolks with the sugar until light and fluffy over a pan of hot water. Add the strained juice of the oranges, grated rind of 2 oranges and the cornstarch (cornflour). Stir well.
2. Continue cooking over a low heat in a bain-marie whisking until the mixture thickens.
3. Sprinkle the gelatin over 2-3 tablespoons of boiling water, making sure it is dissolved. Whisk the cream until thick. Add gelatin to orange mixture.
4. Whisk the egg whites until fairly stiff and carefully fold into the mixture. Do the same with the whipped cream. Turn into 2 molds holding 4 portions, cover and freeze. Take out of the freezer 15 minutes before serving.

Macedonia di frutta secca e fresca

Fresh and Dried Fruit Salad

	00:30 Chilling time 01:00	00:00

American	Ingredients	Metric/Imperial
1½ lb	Mixed fresh fruit in season	700 g / 1½ lb
½ lb	Dried fruit (apricots, figs, dates)	225 g / 8 oz
3 tbsp	Sugar	2 tbsp
1 tbsp	Brandy	1 tbsp
½ cup	Dry white wine	125 ml / 4 fl oz
	Ice	
	Cream	

1. Wash the fresh fruit, cut into small cubes, place in a bowl.
2. Break the dried fruit into small pieces and mix with the fresh. Add the sugar, brandy, dry white wine and mix well. Refrigerate for 1 hour.
3. Before serving, set the fruit salad bowl into a larger bowl filled with crushed ice. Serve if liked with a jug of cream.

Babà au rhum

Rum Baba

	01:15 including rising time	00:20

American	Ingredients	Metric/Imperial
½ cup	Fine granulated (castor) sugar	100 g / 4 oz
½ cup	Milk	125 ml / 4 fl oz
¼ oz	Yeast or	7 g / ¼ oz
1 tsp	Dried yeast	1 tsp
1¼ cups	Flour	150 g / 5 oz
½ tsp	Salt	½ tsp
2	Eggs	2
¼ cup	Butter	50 g / 2 oz
	Oil	
½ cup	Whipped cream	125 ml / 4 fl oz
2 oz	Candied fruit	50 g / 2 oz

1. Dissolve 1 teaspoon sugar in the warmed (bloodheat) milk and activate yeast by crumbling into the mixture or, if using dried yeast, reconstituting according to package instructions.
2. Sieve slightly warmed flour into a bowl with ½ teaspoon salt. Add the milk and yeast, beat well to form a smooth batter. Allow to rise for about 30 minutes.
3. Beat in the eggs and softened butter by hand to form a thick batter.
4. Brush the baba mold or several small molds with oil and half fill with mixture. Cover with cling wrap and allow mixture to rise to the top of the molds.
5. Preheat the oven to 425°F / 220°C / Gas Mark 7.
6. Bake the mixture for 15-20 minutes, the baba should spring back when touched lightly. Turn out on to a wire tray and allow to cool.
7. Dissolve the sugar in ⅔ cup [150 ml / ¼ pint] water over a low heat, do not stir. When the sugar is dissolved, boil until the mixture thickens to a syrup. Add the rum.
8. Soak the baba in the rum syrup, fill with whipped cream and decorate with candied fruit.

Margherita cup

Coppa Margherita

Margherita Cup

	00:15 Chilling time 02:00	00:10

American	Ingredients	Metric/Imperial
¼ lb	Bitter chocolate	100 g / 4 oz
¼ cup	Cornstarch (cornflour)	25 g / 1 oz
2 cups	Milk	450 ml / ¾ pint
3 tbsp	Sugar	2 tbsp
1	Egg yolk	1
8	Savoy biscuits	8
3 tbsp	Cointreau	2 tbsp
½ cup	Whipped cream	125 ml / 4 fl oz
4	Cherries	4

1. Melt the broken pieces of chocolate in a bowl over a pan of water on a low heat.
2. Dissolve the cornstarch in the milk and add the sugar. Pour on to the melted chocolate and mix thoroughly. Raise the heat and boil until the mixture thickens.
3. Remove from the heat and add the egg yolk, stirring vigorously.
4. Soak the savoy biscuits in cointreau and place 2 in each cup. Pour in the chocolate cream and leave to cool in the refrigerator.
5. Before serving, decorate each cup with a swirl of whipped cream and a cherry. Serve at once.

Acini d'uva caramellati

Caramelized Grapes

00:25　　　　　　　00:15

American	Ingredients	Metric/Imperial
1½ lb	Grapes	700 g / 1½ lb
2 cups	Sugar	450 g / 1 lb
½ tsp	Cream of tartar	½ tsp
	Oil	

1. Cut the grapes from the bunch with a pair of pointed scissors, leaving a little stalk on each one. The grapes should be large, of good quality, and seedless with a firm skin.
2. Wash the grapes well and spread them out on a cloth to dry.
3. Combine the sugar with ½ cup [125 ml / 4 fl oz] of water and the cream of tartar in a saucepan and dissolve over a very low heat without stirring, then bring to the boil to obtain a thick syrup. Remove from the heat when the first tinge of color appears.
4. Immerse the grapes, one at a time. Stick each one on a toothpick, with the pointed end, piercing the grape. Lightly oil a plate to prevent the grapes from sticking and place the grapes on the plate to dry.

Caramelized grapes

Quick trifle

Zuppa inglese velocissima
Quick Trifle

	00:20	00:10
	Chilling time 02:00	

American	Ingredients	Metric/Imperial
½ lb	Dry crackers (biscuits) or sponge fingers	225 g / 8 oz
½ cup	Liqueur	125 ml / 4 fl oz
1 lb	Fresh mixed fruit	450 g / 1 lb
¼ lb	Walnuts or dried fruit	100 g / 4 oz
1 ¼ cups	Milk	300 ml / ½ pint
1 tbsp	Sugar	1 tbsp
1 tbsp	Cocoa	1 tbsp
2	Eggs	2
½ tsp	Vanilla essence	½ tsp
1 cup	Whipping cream	225 ml / 8 fl oz
	Chocolate flake	

1. Line a glass dish with a layer of crackers.
2. Sprinkle with some liqueur and cover with fruit mixed with a few chopped walnuts or any dried fruit. Add a second layer of crackers and fruit juice or liqueur.
3. Prepare the custard. Whisk together milk, sugar, cocoa and eggs and cook in a double boiler until slightly thick. Flavor with vanilla.
4. Pour the custard over the trifle and, when cool, cover the surface with whipped cream decorated with chocolate flake. Chill in the refrigerator for at least 2 hours.

Melone mixed
Fruit Salad in Melon Shells

	00:30	00:00

American	Ingredients	Metric/Imperial
1	Large sugar melon	1
¼ lb	Marrons glacés in pieces	100 g / 4 oz
5 oz	Candied citron	150 g / 5 oz
1 cup	Blanched, split almonds	100 g / 4 oz
3	Bananas	3
1	Lemon	1
1 tbsp	Sugar	1 tbsp
3 tbsp	Sweet liqueur	2 tbsp

1. Cut the melon in half, scoop out the flesh, remove the seeds and cut the flesh into small cubes.
2. Mix the melon in a bowl with the marron glacés, finely chopped candied citron, split almonds, sliced bananas (sprinkled with lemon juice to stop them turning brown), a little sugar and 1 tablespoon of any liqueur.
3. Sprinkle a little liqueur inside the 2 melon shells and refrigerate. Just before serving, turn the fruit salad into the melon shells and place them on a plate or in a wide bowl on a bed of crushed ice. Serve cold.

Macedonia colorata
Colored Fruit Salad

	00:30 Chilling time 01:00		00:00

American	Ingredients	Metric/Imperial
2 lb	Watermelon	1 kg / 2 lb
2 lb	Honeydew melon	1 kg / 2 lb
2	Peaches	2
½ lb	Raspberries	225 g / 8 oz
¼ cup	Almonds	40 g / 1½ oz
	Confectioner's (icing) sugar	
	Mint leaves	
1	Orange	1
1	Lemon	1

1. Halve a ripe, sweet watermelon and a honeydew melon. Remove seeds. Scoop out little balls of flesh into a large bowl.
2. Scald the peaches in hot water, skin and cube. Wash the raspberries under running water and combine with the peaches and melons. Cover the bowl and refrigerate for 45 minutes.
3. Drop the almonds into boiling water, skin and flake, add to the well chilled fruit salad. Sprinkle with sugar and garnish with mint leaves.
4. Pour over the juice of the orange and lemon and allow to chill for 15 minutes before serving.

Spuma di fragole
Strawberry Mousse

	00:30		00:00

American	Ingredients	Metric/Imperial
14 oz	Strawberries	400 g / 14 oz
3 tbsp	Confectioner's (icing) sugar	2 tbsp
1 tbsp	Orange liqueur	1 tbsp
1 cup	Whipping (double) cream	225 ml / 8 fl oz
2	Egg whites	2

1. Hull, wash and dry the strawberries. Reserve some for decoration and blend the rest with the sugar and the orange liqueur in a blender, then pour into a bowl.
2. Whip the cream and carefully fold most of it into the strawberry mixture, retain a little for decoration.
3. Whisk the egg whites until stiff and fold into the mixture carefully. Turn into a serving dish and serve with the cream.

Mattonella di frutta
Fruit Brick

This recipe is suitable for fruit which gives juice when mashed, such as strawberries, raspberries, grapes, bilberries, mulberries, oranges, peaches, morello cherries. Use fruit of one kind only.

	00:45 Chilling time 03:00		00:10

American	Ingredients	Metric/Imperial
1 quart	Fresh fruit to make fruit juice	1 litre / 1¾ pints
½ cup	Potato flour	8 tbsp
	Sugar to taste	
1	Orange	1
½ cup	Whipping (double) cream	125 ml / 4 fl oz

1. Prepare, wash and mash the fruit using a spoon, sieve, food mill, blender or food processor.
2. Strain the juice, measure the liquid and pour into a large pan. For each 1 quart [1 litre / 1¾ pints] add the measured potato flour.
3. Add sugar to taste depending on the sweetness of the fruit. Cut the orange rind, without pith, into thin strips and add to the pan. Bring slowly to the boil, stirring all the time.
4. Remove from the heat but continue stirring from time to time for a further 20 minutes. Pour into a rectangular loaf pan rinsed in cold water. Chill for 3 hours in the refrigerator.

Bavarese all'amaretto
Mousse with Macaroons

	00:45		00:15

American	Ingredients	Metric/Imperial
4	Egg yolks	4
2½ cups	Milk	600 ml / 1 pint
½ cup	Sugar	100 g / 4 oz
¼ cup	Flour	25 g / 1 oz
1	Vanilla pod	1
1	Lemon	1
25	Macaroons	25
⅓ cup	Candied fruit	50 g / 2 oz
¼ lb	Plain chocolate	100 g / 4 oz
½ cup	Brandy, rum or maraschino liqueur	125 ml / 4 fl oz
1 cup	Whipped cream	225 ml / 8 fl oz

1. Make a custard by whisking together the eggs, milk, sugar, flour, vanilla and rind of the lemon in a double boiler until thick.
2. Allow to cool. Add 5 crumbled macaroons and the chopped candied fruit.
3. Melt the plain chocolate in a bowl over hot water and mix into the custard.
4. Soak the macaroons in the liqueur diluted with 2 tablespoons water or fruit juice and line the base and sides of a serving dish with the macaroons.
5. Fold the lightly whipped cream into the custard, mixing very delicately. Pour into the dish and refrigerate.

Suprême de la Cote D'Azur
Apple Ring with Candied Fruit

	00:30		00:30

American	Ingredients	Metric/Imperial
2 lb	Apples	1 kg / 2 lb
1¾ cups	Sugar	400 g / 14 oz
2	Lemons	2
¼ lb	Candied fruit	100 g / 4 oz
2 tsp	Gelatin	2 tsp
1 cup	Whipped cream	225 ml / 8 fl oz
1 tbsp	Rum	1 tbsp

Strawberry mousse

1. Peel, core and slice the apples. Put sugar and about ¼ cup [50 ml / 2 fl oz] water in a saucepan. Boil until it turns into a thick syrup — but do not burn the sugar.

2. Grate the peel from the lemons and add to the pan with apples, lemon juice and half the candied fruits. Cook until the mixture is transparent and dry, stir in the gelatin which has been dissolved in 2 tablespoons boiling water.

3. Turn the apple mixture into a ring mold and leave in the refrigerator overnight.

4. Turn out and spread over the whipped cream flavored with rum. Decorate with candied fruits.

Cook's tip: for the best result this sweet should be made at least 24 hours before serving.

Frutta brinata
Frosted Fruit

	00:25	00:25

American	Ingredients	Metric/Imperial
½ lb	Seedless grapes	225 g / 8 oz
¼ lb	White currants	100 g / 4 oz
¼ lb	Red currants	100 g / 4 oz
2	Egg whites	2
1 cup	Fine granulated (castor) sugar	225 g / 8 oz

1. Preheat the oven to 350°F / 180°C / Gas Mark 4.
2. Using sharp scissors, cut the bunch of grapes into several small bunches. Put these and the currants in a colander and wash under running cold water. Spread out to dry on a cloth.
3. Whisk the egg whites until stiff. Dip the fruit in the egg whites and sprinkle with sugar. Arrange on a baking tray and cover with buttered wax (greaseproof) paper. Bake for a few minutes in a moderate oven until the frosting hardens. Serve cold, on a dish covered with a colored napkin to provide a bright contrast to the bunches of frosted fruit.

Frutta sciroppata
Fruit in Syrup

	00:30	00:03

American	Ingredients	Metric/Imperial
2 lb	Apples, pears, peaches, pineapple or Figs, cherries, plums, apricots	1 kg / 2 lb
2 cups	Water	450 ml / ¾ pint
1 ½ cups	Sugar	350 g / 12 oz
1	Small piece of lemon rind	1

1. The fruit used for this recipe should be in perfect condition and not very ripe. Peel the apples, pears, peaches, pineapple, etc. Or if using figs, cherries, plums and apricots, do not peel. Cut large fruit into chunks and small fruit in half, leaving figs whole.
2. Prepare the syrup by boiling water with the sugar and lemon rind for 2-3 minutes. Pour onto a serving bowl, allow to cool, then add prepared fruits.
3. Chill in the refrigerator, then serve with whipped cream.

Gelato di crema dell'Ivana
Ivana Cream Ice Cream

	00:35	00:07
	Freezing time 05:00	

American	Ingredients	Metric/Imperial
8	Eggs	8
½ lb	Sugar	225 g / 8 oz
1 quart	Milk	1 litre / 1¾ pints
1	Vanilla stick	1
1¼ cups	Whipped cream	300 ml / ½ pint
8	Cherries in liqueur	8

1. Whisk the egg yolks and sugar together thoroughly, using an electric whisk if possible.
2. Heat the milk and vanilla and remove from the heat as soon as it begins to boil. Remove the vanilla and gradually pour the milk into the egg mixture (as if pouring oil into mayonnaise), stirring vigorously all the time. Lastly fold in the stiffly whipped cream.
3. Pour the mixture into a rectangular mold and freeze, preferably freezing it as rapidly as possible. After 30 minutes, take it out of the freezer and whisk.
4. Pour into a cold round mold. Cover with cling wrap and freeze again at normal freezer temperature.
5. To serve, run the mold under warm water for a second and turn out on to a serving dish. Decorate with the cherries.

Gelato, melone e ribes
Ice Cream, Melon and Red Currants

	00:30	00:00
	Refrigeration time 01:00	

American	Ingredients	Metric/Imperial
2	Melons	2
½ cup	Porto or marsala wine	125 ml / 4 fl oz
½ lb	Red currants	225 g / 8 oz
2 cups	Strawberry ice cream	450 ml / ¾ pint

1. Using a ball utensil, scoop out the melons making lots of little balls. Put these in a bowl and pour over porto or sweet marsala and refrigerate for about 1 hour.
2. Carefully wash the red currants and remove the stalks. Put the currants on a plate.
3. Take the melon out of the refrigerator and scoop out small ice cream balls with the same scoop, mixing these with the melon. Decorate by scattering the red currants over the top. Serve immediately.

Sorbetto alle fragole
Strawberry Sorbet

	00:25	00:20
	Freezing time 04:00	

American	Ingredients	Metric/Imperial
Scant 2 cups	Sugar	400 g / 14 oz
1 ¼ cups	Water	300 ml / ½ pint
3 lb	Strawberries	1.4 kg / 3 lb
3 tbsp	Strega liqueur	1 tbsp

1. Put the sugar in the water in a thick based saucepan, mix round before putting on the heat. Allow to dissolve over a very low heat without stirring. Cook until a thick but colorless syrup is formed. Allow to cool.
2. Hull the strawberries and wash and allow to drain well. Sprinkle on the liqueur.
3. Mash the strawberries to a pulp in a blender or food processor.
4. Pour the strawberry pureé into the cold syrup and tip the whole mixture into a fairly shallow pan. Freeze for 2 hours and stir, freeze again for a further 2 hours.
5. Remove from the freezer at least 15 minutes before serving and spoon into individual glasses. Decorate with strawberries if available.

Strawberry sorbet

1. Add sugar to water in a thick-based saucepan and mix round before putting on the heat. Allow to dissolve over a low heat without stirring. Cook until a thick syrup is formed.

2. Hull the strawberries, wash and drain well. Mash the strawberries.

3. Mix the mashed strawberries with the syrup. Ladle the mixture into the container.

4. Scrape down the sorbet after the first freezing.

5. Whisk to break down the ice particles.

6. Return the whisked mixture to the container for the final freezing.

1

2

3

4

5

6

Plumcake

Plum Cake

◢ 00:45   00:45 🍲

American	Ingredients	Metric/Imperial
1 cup	Butter	225 g / 8 oz
1 cup	Fine granulated (castor) sugar	225 g / 8 oz
5	Eggs	5
¼ cup	Milk	50 ml / 2 fl oz
1	Lemon	1
2 cups	All purpose (plain) flour	225 g / 8 oz
1 tsp	Baking powder	1 tsp
⅓ cup	Sultanas	50 g / 2 oz
2 oz	Candied fruit	50 g / 2 oz
1 cup	Confectioner's (icing) sugar	100 g / 4 oz
1 tbsp	Kirsch	1 tbsp
	Morello cherries for decorating	

1. Preheat the oven to 350°F / 180°C / Gas Mark 4. Prepare an 8 in / 20 cm deep cake pan by rubbing well with a buttered paper.
2. Cream the butter and fine granulated sugar thoroughly. When thick and fluffy beat in 3 whole eggs followed by 2 yolks adding a little sifted flour between eggs. Then add milk and grated rind of lemon. Gradually add the sifted flour and baking powder, mixing well. Dip the sultanas and candied fruit in a little flour and fold into the mixture.
3. Turn into the cake pan and cook in the centre of the oven for at least 45 minutes.
4. While the cake is baking, prepare the icing. Mix the confectioner's sugar with 2 teaspoons water and 1 teaspoon kirsch, beat until smooth. When the cake is cooked, remove it from the oven, allow to cool and cover the top with the icing. Decorate with morello or glacé cherries.

Torta di ricotta

Ricotta Cake

◢ 00:35   00:45 🍲

American	Ingredients	Metric/Imperial
½ lb	Fresh ricotta	225 g / 8 oz
1 cup	Fine granulated (castor) sugar	225 g / 8 oz
2	Eggs, separated	2
2 cups	All purpose (plain) flour	225 g / 8 oz
	Salt	
1 tsp	Baking powder	1 tsp
1	Lemon	1
	Butter and flour for the baking pan	
	Confectioner's (icing) sugar	

1. Beat the ricotta and the sugar in a large bowl either with a wooden spoon or an electric mixer. After 10 minutes add the yolks one by one and continue beating.
2. Preheat the oven to 350°F / 180°C / Gas Mark 4.
3. Sift the flour into a bowl with the salt and baking powder. Mix well with the ricotta mixture and add the finely grated lemon peel.

4. Whisk the egg whites and carefully fold in. Turn into an 8 in / 20 cm buttered and floured baking pan, spread evenly and bake in a preheated moderate oven for 45 minutes. Insert a fine skewer to test whether it is sufficiently cooked. The skewer must come out clean. Turn on to a wire rack and allow to cool. Dust with confectioner's sugar and serve cold.

Pan di Spagna

Sponge Cake

◢ 00:20   00:30 🍲

American	Ingredients	Metric/Imperial
4	Eggs	4
2 cups	Confectioner's (icing) sugar	225 g / 8 oz
1	Lemon	1
1 cup	All purpose (plain) flour	100 g / 4 oz
	Butter	

1. Preheat the oven to 350°F / 180°C / Gas Mark 4.
2. Separate the eggs. Beat the yolks with the sugar in a bowl over a saucepan of warm water. Begin slowly, then with more energy, until the sugar is well incorporated and the mixture looks almost white.
3. Whisk the whites until quite stiff and fold carefully with a metal spoon into the mixture. Add grated lemon peel and sift in the flour. Mix well folding with a metal spoon and turn into a buttered and lightly floured 8 in / 20 cm baking pan.
4. Bake in a preheated oven for 30 minutes. The cake is cooked when it offers a certain resistance when pressed in the middle. A few minutes after taking it out of the oven, invert the pan onto a rack, remove and leave the cake until cool. This cake can be served with any filling.

Torrone d'Alba

Almond Slices

◢ 00:30   00:15 🍲

American	Ingredients	Metric/Imperial
6½ cups	Almonds	1 kg / 2 lb
1 scant cup	Sugar	200 g / 7 oz
2 lb	Honey	1 kg / 2 lb
2	Egg whites	2
	Sheets of rice paper	

1. Blanch the almonds and split (or use slivered almonds). Toast under a hot broiler (grill) for a few seconds.
2. Dissolve the sugar in ¼ cup [50 ml / 2 fl oz] water over a low heat, then bring to the boil.
3. Remove from the heat, add the honey and cook until a small quantity dropped on a cold surface top sets and readily cracks.
4. Whisk the egg whites until very stiff and gently fold into the syrup mixture. Add almonds to the mixture.
5. Pour the almond mixture into a flat pan lined with rice paper and cover with more rice paper.
6. Allow to cool, turn onto a plate, slice and serve.

Almond slices

Golden slices

Torta piemontese
Piedmontese Cake

◣ 01:00   01:00 ◖

American	Ingredients	Metric/Imperial
1¾ cups	Almonds	225 g / 8 oz
1 cup	Confectioner's (icing) sugar	100 g / 4 oz
6	Eggs	6
1 scant cup	Fine granulated (castor) sugar	200 g / 7 oz
⅔ cup	Cornmeal	75 g / 3 oz
⅓ cup	All purpose (plain) flour	40 g / 1½ oz
	Salt	
½ cup	Sultanas	65 g / 2½ oz
¼ cup	Butter	50 g / 2 oz
1 tbsp	Brandy	1 tbsp

1. Blanch and toast the almonds. Pound half with all the confectioner's (icing) sugar less 2 tablespoons [15 g / ½ oz] and grind the other half and put on one side. (This step can be done quickly in a blender or food processor.)
2. Preheat the oven to 400°F / 200°C / Gas Mark 6.
3. Break the eggs into a bowl, add the fine sugar, put on top of a pan of warm water on a low heat and beat until the mixture has warmed up.
4. Remove from the heat and continue beating until the mixture is light and creamy.
5. Sift the cornmeal, plain flour, potato flour and a pinch of salt into a bowl, sift again into the egg mixture folding in carefully. Add the ground almonds and soaked sultanas. Finally add the melted butter and the brandy.
6. Turn into a buttered baking pan and bake in a hot oven for about 1 hour. When the cake is ready, dust with remaining confectioner's sugar and sprinkle with ground almonds.

Chiacchiere
Golden Slices

◣   ◖

American	Ingredients	Metric/Imperial
2 cups	All purpose (plain) flour	225 g / 8 oz
¼ cup	Fine granulated (castor) sugar	50 g / 2 oz
½ tsp	Vanilla essence	½ tsp
2 tbsp	Butter	25 g / 1 oz
2	Eggs	2
1 tbsp	Marsala	1 tbsp
	Oil for frying	
3 tbsp	Confectioner's (icing) sugar	2 tbsp

1. Mix the sifted flour, sugar and vanilla in a bowl, make a well in the centre. Soften the butter and place with the eggs in the middle of the flour. Mix to a smooth dough adding a little marsala if it is too dry.
2. Roll out the dough on a floured board to a thin sheet and cut out rectangles. A serrated pastry wheel is useful for this. Make 3 cuts in the middle of each rectangle, but do not take them to the edges.
3. Half fill a thick pan with oil and heat. Put in the rectangles and cook until they are golden brown.
4. Spread on absorbent kitchen towels to absorb the excess fat, sprinkle with confectioner's (icing) sugar before serving.

Torta diplomatica
Diplomat's Cake

◣ 02:00   01:00 ◖

American	Ingredients	Metric/Imperial
⅓ cup	Butter	75 g / 3 oz
2 cups	Confectioner's (icing) sugar	225 g / 8 oz
	A few drops of vanilla essence	
1	Egg yolk	1
1 tbsp	Rum	1 tbsp
½ lb	Puff pastry	225 g / 8 oz
1	Sponge cake	1
½ cup	Maraschino	125 ml / 4 fl oz
1 lb	Apricot jam	450 g / 1 lb
½ cup	Chopped toasted hazelnuts	50 g / 2 oz

1. Preheat the oven to 425°F / 220°C / Gas Mark 7.
2. Cream together the softened butter, 1½ cups [175 g / 6 oz] sugar and the vanilla essence. Add the egg yolk and the rum, cream until smooth and light.
3. Cut the puff pastry into 2 equal pieces, roll out, prick with a fork and bake on 2 lightly buttered sheets. Allow to cool on a wire tray.
4. With a sharp knife, cut the sponge cake into 4 rounds. Lay a round of sponge cake on the first piece of puff pastry and trim to obtain a match. Repeat with the other piece of puff pastry.
5. Place a round of sponge cake on the serving dish and soak in maraschino. Cover with a third of the butter cream. Cover with a round of sponge cake soaked in maraschino. Spread on a layer of sieved apricot jam. Follow with a layer of puff pastry, more apricot jam, sponge cake, ending with the puff pastry.
6. Press down lightly with a spatula. Spread the remaining cream and crushed hazelnuts on the sides. Dust with confectioner's sugar and keep in a cool place.

Tortei veneti
Venetian Potato Cake

◣ 00:30   01:05 ◖

American	Ingredients	Metric/Imperial
1 lb	Potatoes	500 g / 1 lb
	Salt	
¼ cup	Butter	50 g / 2 oz
½ cup	Sugar	100 g / 4 oz
1¼ cups	All purpose (plain) flour	150 g / 5 oz
1	Egg	1
	Oil for frying	

1. Cook the unpeeled potatoes with a little salt. Drain, skin and mash, leave to cool.
2. Melt the butter and add to the purée. Stir in the sugar, sifted flour and egg, working all the ingredients well together.
3. Preheat the oven to 350°F / 180°C / Gas Mark 4.
4. Heat the oil until hot. Form the mixture into cakes and fry until golden on each side. When they are golden on one side, carefully turn them over with a palette knife without breaking them. Drain on kitchen towels. Place them 4 at a time on an oiled baking sheet, bake for 15 minutes and serve hot.

Maritozzi
Raisin Buns

01:15	00:15

American	Ingredients	Metric/Imperial
½ oz	Dry active yeast	15 g / ½ oz
1¾ cups	Flour	200 g / 7 oz
3 tbsp	Sugar	2 tbsp
⅓ cup	Sultanas	50 g / 2 oz
1 tbsp	Pine kernels	1 tbsp
	Salt	
2 oz	Candied orange peel	50 g / 2 oz
	Butter for baking sheet	

1. Combine the reconstituted yeast with a little flour and allow to stand until it has doubled in volume.
2. Knead in the remaining slightly warmed flour, the sugar, sultanas, pine kernels, salt and finely sliced candied orange peel. Add enough hand-hot water (100°F / 43°C) to form a soft dough.
3. Preheat the oven to 425°F / 210°C / Gas Mark 7.
4. Form small balls the size of an egg, place on a buttered and floured baking sheet, cover and leave in a dry place to rise.
5. Then flatten with the palm of the hand and bake in the oven. Serve at once when cooked.

Pampepato
Fruit and Honey Cake

00:25	00:45

American	Ingredients	Metric/Imperial
¼ lb	Honey	100 g / 4 oz
Generous ⅓ cup	Sugar	75 g / 3 oz
½ tsp	Bicarbonate of soda	½ tsp
1 tsp	Aniseed	1 tsp
1¼ cups	Flour	150 g / 5 oz
½ cup	Raisins soaked in water	75 g / 3 oz
½ cup	Blanched almonds	50 g / 2 oz
¼ cup	Shelled walnuts	25 g / 1 oz
¼ cup	Pine kernels	25 g / 1 oz
1 oz	Candied citron	25 g / 1 oz
2 oz	Flaked chocolate	50 g / 2 oz
½ tsp	Cinnamon	½ tsp
	Salt and pepper	
¼ tsp	Nutmeg	¼ tsp
	Butter and flour for the baking pan	

1. Preheat the oven to 350°F / 180°C / Gas Mark 4.
2. Dissolve most of the honey, sugar, bicarbonate and aniseed in a bowl, adding water 2-3 tablespoons at a time and stirring constantly.
3. Slowly sift in the flour. Work the mixture with a wooden spoon.
4. Dry the raisins and add to the mixture with the almonds, walnuts, pine kernels, citron, chocolate, cinnamon, pinch of salt, pepper and nutmeg. Blend well and turn into a buttered and floured loaf pan or 6 in / 15 cm round cake pan. Level the top and brush all over with remaining melted honey. Bake in the oven for 45 minutes until the cake is a dark, golden color. Allow to cool before serving.

Tarte mousseline
Gâteau Mousseline

00:45	00:30

American	Ingredients	Metric/Imperial
3	Eggs, separated	3
½ cup	Sugar	100 g / 4 oz
½ cup	Flour	50 g / 2 oz
1 tsp	Baking powder	1 tsp
1 tbsp	Butter	15 g / ½ oz
1 cup	Whipped cream	200 ml / 7 fl oz
	Confectioner's (icing) sugar	

1. Preheat the oven to 350°F / 180°C / Gas Mark 4.
2. Whisk the egg yolks and sugar in a bowl over hot water for a few minutes, then remove from the heat and beat until light and fluffy.
3. In a clean bowl with a dry whisk, mix the egg whites until the mixture stands in soft peaks.
4. Sift the flour with the baking powder and fold into the egg yolk mixture alternately with the egg whites. Fold carefully to mix ingredients without losing air.
5. Grease an 8 in / 20 cm cake pan with butter and flour lightly, tip in the cake mixture and bake for 30 minutes.
6. Allow to cool for 4 minutes in the pan, turn out onto a new tray and cool.
7. Cut the cake in half to make 2 rounds, sandwich together with the whipped cream and serve sprinkled with a thick layer of confectioner's sugar.

Torta Moka
Gâteau Moka

00:35	00:30 for the cake

American	Ingredients	Metric/Imperial
3	Egg yolks	3
½ cup	Sugar	100 g / 4 oz
1 cup	Milk	225 ml / 8 fl oz
1	Piece of vanilla pod	1
¼ cup	Strong coffee	50 ml / 2 fl oz
⅓ cup	Butter	75 g / 3 oz
1	Sponge cake	1
¾ cup	Chopped sweet blanched almonds	75 g / 3 oz
2 oz	Flaked chocolate	50 g / 2 oz

1. Thoroughly whisk the yolks and sugar until white and fluffy.
2. Boil the milk with the vanilla and slowly pour in the mixture, stirring all the time, add the coffee. Turn into a double saucepan and cook on a low heat, stirring until the cream is thick without boiling. Remove from the heat and keep stirring for a few more minutes. Soften and cream the butter and gradually add to the coffee cream. Allow to cool.
3. With a sharp knife cut the sponge cake horizontally in half, giving 2 rounds. Place one on a serving dish, spread part of the cream on top and sprinkle with almonds. Cover with the second round. With a spatula spread the rest of the cream on the top and sides. Sprinkle the cake with the flaked chocolate.

1

2

3

4

5

6

7

To make an all-in-one sponge cake

1. Sift ½ cup [100 g / 4 oz] all purpose (self-raising flour) together with one level teaspoon of baking powder, add one tablespoon of powdered coffee and one tablespoon of cocoa powder.

2. Add ½ cup [100 g / 4 oz] fine sugar with ½ cup [100 g / 4 oz] soft margarine.

3. Add 3 eggs and beat together for 2 minutes.

4. Pour the beaten mixture into a greased cake pan. Cook for 25 minutes at 350°F / 180°C / Gas Mark 4.

5. To make the coffee cream, use the quantities given in Gâteau Moka opposite. Whisk the egg yolks and sugar until white and fluffy. Boil the milk and vanilla and add the beaten yolks and sugar, cook on a low heat stirring until thick, add the coffee. Allow to cool slightly. Soften and cream the butter and add to the coffee cream.

6. Whip 1 cup [125 ml / 4 fl oz] thick cream and grate some chocolate for decoration. Sandwich the cake together with the cooled moka cream.

7. Pile whipped cream on top and decorate with grated chocolate.

Pasta di mandorle
Almond Paste

American	Ingredients	Metric/Imperial
2⅔ cups	Confectioner's (icing) sugar	350 g / 12 oz
2¼ cups	Ground almonds	350 g / 12 oz
2	Eggs	2
1 tsp	Lemon juice	1 tsp
3 tbsp	Cornstarch (cornflour)	2 tbsp

1. Sift the confectioner's sugar into a bowl, add the ground almonds. Make a well in the centre and add the lightly beaten eggs and a few drops of lemon juice.
2. Form into a stiff dough and lightly knead in a little extra confectioner's (icing) sugar mixed with cornstarch (cornflour).
3. Use for decorating rich fruit cakes or making sweets.

Cook's tip: for extra flavor work in vanilla, rum, brandy, coffee or chocolate with the lemon juice in step 1. Varying the amount according to taste.

Giochini di pasta di mandorle
Marzipan Shapes

American	Ingredients	Metric/Imperial
2 cups	Ground almonds	225 g / 8 oz
2 cups	Confectioner's (icing) sugar	225 g / 8 oz
3	Egg whites	3
1 tsp	Port	1 tsp

1. Preheat the oven to 400°F / 200°C / Gas Mark 6.
2. Tip the almonds into a bowl. Add the sugar and mix thoroughly. Add a drop of port and work the unbeaten egg

whites in the mixture a spoonful at a time, stirring well to form a firm paste.
3. Moisten the worktop surface and then spread the paste about ½ in / 1.25 cm thick. Shape as you like, making little animals, cars or stars etc. Cook the shapes in a hot oven on a buttered baking sheet for about 10 minutes.

Pan di Spagna alle lamponi
Sponge Cake with Raspberries

American	Ingredients	Metric/Imperial
¾ lb	Raspberries	350 g / 12 oz
½ cup	Confectioner's (icing) sugar	50 g / 2 oz
½ cup	Spumante, or dry white wine (or lemon juice)	125 ml / 4 fl oz
1	Sponge cake	1
1 cup	Zabaglione (see page 438)	225 ml / 8 fl oz
	Whipped cream	

1. Sprinkle the raspberries with sugar, pour over the wine or some lemon juice, mix well and leave to soak for about 1 hour.
2. With a sharp knife cut the sponge cake into three rounds. Place the first round on a serving plate and cover with half the raspberries and all of the juice. Pour over half of the zabaglione. Cover with the second round of sponge cake and repeat the operation. Cover with the last round. Decorate with rosettes of whipped cream and a few whole raspberries.

Salame finto di cioccolata
Chocolate Sausage

00:35   Chilling time 04:00   00:00

American	Ingredients	Metric/Imperial
½ lb	Sweet crackers (digestive biscuits)	225 g / 8 oz
1 tsp	Instant coffee	1 tsp
⅔ cup	Butter	150 g / 5 oz
1 tbsp	Liqueur	1 tbsp
⅓ cup	Sugar	65 g / 2½ oz
¼ lb	Sweet cocoa	100 g / 4 oz
2	Eggs, separated	2
10	Walnuts	10

1. Crumble the crackers (biscuits), pounding them in a blender or food processor or crumb in a plastic bag with a rolling pin.
2. Mix the crumbs with the instant coffee, dissolved in a little boiling water, the butter, liqueur, sugar and sweet cocoa. Add the egg yolks, the stiffly beaten egg whites, mix well and add more cocoa to make a firm mixture.
3. Shape into a sausage, wrap in foil and chill for 1 hour.
4. Chop the walnuts, cover a piece of paper with the nuts, unwrap the sausage and roll over the nuts so that they penetrate the sausage. Return to foil and chill for a further 3 hours.
5. Place on a serving plate and slice at the table.

Sponge cake with raspberries

Index

ACKNOWLEDGEMENTS

APRIFEL, AOC, Archivio IGDA, Badia a Coltibuono, Berdoy, Bird, Anthony Blake Photo Library, Bouillard, Michael Boys, BPCC/Aldus Archive, BRITISH CHICKEN INFORMATION SERVICE, Brock, Gary Chowitz/EWA, Connors, Consorzio del Formaggio Parmigiano Reggiano, Decros, Dirand, Patrick Eagar, Editoriale del Drago Milano, Elia, Elliott, Ferrand, FOOD & WINE FROM FRANCE, Fouili, Gain, Galbani (London) Ltd, Hamot, Hispard, Holsnyder, IGDA, IMAGE BANK, Italian Trade Centre, Jannes, Jozefson, Kay, Conny van Kasteel, KENWOOD, Korniloff, Lamaire, Leale, Leger, Leroy, Maison de Marie-Claire/Bouchet/Le Foll, Maison de Marie-Claire/ Dirand, Maison de Marie-Claire/Schoumacher/Duffas, Maltaverne, Masi Agricola S.p.A., Mayers, MOULINEX, O'Leary, ORBIS, Pascal, Pedersen, PHILIPS, Martin Rigdale, SCOOP, SEB, SOPEXA, TEFAL, Traeger, Jan Traylen, Tuff, VEDETTE, Williams